THE RULE OF MANHOOD

Through stories of lustful and incestuous rulers, of republican revolution and of unnatural crimes against family, seventeenth-century Englishmen imagined the problem of tyranny through the prism of classical history. This fuelled debates over the practices of their own kings, the necessity of revolution, and the character of English republican thought. *The Rule of Manhood* explores the dynamic and complex languages of tyranny and masculinity that arose through these classical stories and their imaginative appropriation. Discerning the neglected connection between concepts of power and masculinity in early Stuart England, Jamie A. Gianoutsos shows both how stories of ancient tyranny were deployed in the dialogue around monarchy and rule between 1603 and 1660 and the extent to which these shaped English classical republican thought. Drawing on extensive research in contemporary printed texts, Gianoutsos persuasively weaves together the histories of politics and manhood to make a bold claim: that the fundamental purpose of English republicanism was not liberty or virtue, but the realisation of manhood for its citizens.

JAMIE A. GIANOUTSOS is Associate Professor of History at Mount Saint Mary's University, Maryland. She has been a recipient of IHR Mellon Pre-Dissertation, Huntington Library, and Charles Singleton Center Fellowships, and has published articles in *History of Education* and *Renaissance Quarterly*.

CAMBRIDGE STUDIES IN EARLY MODERN BRITISH HISTORY

SERIES EDITORS

MICHAEL BRADDICK
Professor of History, University of Sheffield
ETHAN SHAGAN
Professor of History, University of California, Berkeley
ALEXANDRA SHEPARD
Professor of Gender History, University of Glasgow
ALEXANDRA WALSHAM
Professor of Modern History, University of Cambridge, and Fellow of Trinity College

This is a series of monographs and studies covering many aspects of the history of the British Isles between the late fifteenth century and the early eighteenth century. It includes the work of established scholars and pioneering work by a new generation of scholars. It includes both reviews and revisions of major topics and books which open up new historical terrain or which reveal startling new perspectives on familiar subjects. All the volumes set detailed research within broader perspectives, and the books are intended for the use of students as well as of their teachers.

For a list of titles in the series go to
www.cambridge.org/earlymodernbritishhistory

THE RULE OF MANHOOD

Tyranny, Gender, and Classical Republicanism in England, 1603–1660

JAMIE A. GIANOUTSOS

Mount Saint Mary's University

CAMBRIDGE
UNIVERSITY PRESS

University Printing House, Cambridge CB2 8BS, United Kingdom

One Liberty Plaza, 20th Floor, New York, NY 10006, USA

477 Williamstown Road, Port Melbourne, VIC 3207, Australia

314–321, 3rd Floor, Plot 3, Splendor Forum, Jasola District Centre, New Delhi – 110025, India

79 Anson Road, #06–04/06, Singapore 079906

Cambridge University Press is part of the University of Cambridge.

It furthers the University's mission by disseminating knowledge in the pursuit of education, learning, and research at the highest international levels of excellence.

www.cambridge.org
Information on this title: www.cambridge.org/9781108478830
DOI: 10.1017/9781108778916

© Jamie A. Gianoutsos 2021

This publication is in copyright. Subject to statutory exception and to the provisions of relevant collective licensing agreements, no reproduction of any part may take place without the written permission of Cambridge University Press.

First published 2021

A catalogue record for this publication is available from the British Library.

Library of Congress Cataloging-in-Publication Data
NAMES: Gianoutsos, Jamie A., 1984– author.
TITLE: The rule of manhood : tyranny, gender, and Classical Republicanism in England, 1603–1660 / Jamie A. Gianoutsos.
DESCRIPTION: First edition. | New York : Cambridge University Press, 2020. |
SERIES: Cambridge studies in early modern British history | Includes bibliographical references and index.
IDENTIFIERS: LCCN 2020022781 (print) | LCCN 2020022782 (ebook) | ISBN 9781108478830 (hardback) | ISBN 9781108746243 (paperback) | ISBN 9781108778916 (epub)
SUBJECTS: LCSH: Great Britain–Politics and government–17th century. | Masculinity–Political aspects–Great Britain–History. | Despotism–Great Britain–History–17th century. | Republicanism–Great Britain–History–17th century. | Political culture–Great Britain–History–17th century. | Great Britain–History–James I, 1603–1625. | Great Britain–History–Charles I, 1625–1649. | Great Britain–History–Commonwealth and Protectorate, 1649–1660.
CLASSIFICATION: LCC DA391 .G53 2020 (print) | LCC DA391 (ebook) | DDC 942.06–dc23
LC record available at https://lccn.loc.gov/2020022781
LC ebook record available at https://lccn.loc.gov/2020022782

ISBN 978-1-108-47883-0 Hardback

Cambridge University Press has no responsibility for the persistence or accuracy of URLs for external or third-party internet websites referred to in this publication and does not guarantee that any content on such websites is, or will remain, accurate or appropriate.

For Jessy

Contents

List of Figures	*page* ix
Acknowledgements	x
Introduction	1

PART I EMASCULATED KINGSHIP

1	Tyranny, Manhood, and the Study of History	21
2	A Chaste Virginia: Tyranny and the Corruption of Law in Jacobean England	66
3	'And thus did the wicked sonne murther his wicked mother': Nero and the Tyrannical Household in Late Jacobean England	108
4	Neronian Corruption in Caroline England	158

PART II THE MASCULINE REPUBLIC

	INTRODUCTION TO PART II	221
5	John Milton, Marriage, and the Realisation of Republican Manhood	231
6	'Begin now to know themselves men, & to breath after *liberty*': Marchamont Nedham and the Republican Empire	274

vii

viii *Contents*

7 'So much power and piety in one': Oliver Cromwell
and the Masculine Republic 310

Conclusion 353

Bibliography 370
Index 413

Figures

1 Anon., A Brief Cronology of Great Britain (London, 1656). *page* 354
2 Titlepage, John Speed, *The history of Great Britaine under the conquests of ye Romans, Saxons, Danes and Normans* (London, 1611).   356
3 Titlepage, John Stow and Edmund Howes, *The Annales, or, a generall chronicle of England...* (London, 1615).   359

Acknowledgements

In creating and completing this project, I am grateful for the generosity and support of a number of institutions and individuals. The Johns Hopkins University, Folger Shakespeare Library, Huntington Library, National Humanities Center, London Institute of Historical Research, Charles Singleton Center for the Study of Pre-modern Europe, and Mount Saint Mary's University all provided fellowship and research support. For permission to reprint excerpts from two prior essays, I am grateful to Palgrave Macmillan Publishers and the Renaissance Society of America, acting through the University of Chicago Press. I remain indebted to the Marshall Scholarship Commission for supporting my postgraduate education in the United Kingdom; my hope is that this work of scholarship continues to aid its mission.

This project began as a dissertation at the Johns Hopkins University, and I am particularly thankful for the supervision, significant generosity, and continued friendship of John Marshall. Other members of my dissertation committee, who provided essential comments and ideas for the development of this project, included J. G. A. Pocock, Mary E. Fissell, Sharon Achinstein, and Gabrielle Spiegel; I likewise appreciate the formation I received as a graduate student through seminars, courses, and conversations with Richard Kagan, David Bell, Michael Kwass, and Christopher Celenza. I benefitted enormously from the Hopkins community of students and scholars with whom I engaged at the European Seminar, Gender History Workshop, Monday Seminar, and the Hopkins Philological Society, and the encouragement and support of a number of peers and Hopkins alum, including Adam Bisno, Will Brown, David Cassazza, Jessica Clark, Nathan Daniels, Andrew Devereux, Carrie Euler, Jeremy Fradkin, Matthew Franco, Emma Hart, Katie Hemphill, Amanda Herbert, Catherine Hinchliff, Katie Hindmarch-Watson, Jessica Keene, Lauren MacDonald, Timothy Phin, Denis Robichaud, Carolyn Salomons,

Acknowledgements xi

Kenneth Shepard, Heather Stein, Jessica Walker, Molly Warsh, Neil Weijer, and Olivia Weisser.

The support of scholars outside of Hopkins has also been invaluable. I especially appreciate Quentin Skinner, Clare Jackson, Mark Goldie, Aysha Pollnitz, Nigel Smith, Peter Lake, Alex Shepard, Laura Gowing, Richard Whatmore, Thomas Cogswell, David Norbrook, Laura Lunger Knoppers, Heather Wolfe, Jeffrey Miller, Richard Whatmore, Rachel Weil, Amy Blakeway, Darcy Kern, and Marianna Stell for guidance, conversations, and constructive feedback. Suggestions from the Cambridge series editors were also very helpful as I brought the project to fruition. Several of my colleagues at Mount Saint Mary's University have been highly supportive, particularly fellow early modernist Gregory Murry, and I am especially appreciative of several current and former Mount students, including Elizabeth Boyle, Micaela Kowalski, Molly Gerwig, Caitlin Flay, John-Paul Heil, Chris Rippeon, and Daniel Majerowicz. For my early intellectual formation, I am indebted to Estelle Haan, Dwight Allman, and faculty in the Great Texts Program at Baylor University. Finally, the friendships I forged while pursuing postgraduate study at the Queen's University, Belfast and the University of Cambridge, especially with Leatitia Ransley Kennedy, Rei Kanemura, Elaine Farrell, Kate Kirk, Kathleen Claussen, and Siobhan Connolly, have been particularly meaningful.

I regularly take my work home, as I have been blessed with a partner who shares a love of learning, language, philosophy, and the intellectual past. Being married to a meta-ethicist, whose work has focused on the twentieth-century neo-Aristotelian tradition, has been extremely helpful for testing ideas and finding resources to understand the classical philosophical tradition over time. But, even more significantly, this book would not have been completed without my husband's daily eagerness to share the responsibilities of household and parenthood for our three young children – Samuel, Micah, and Claire. Thank you, Jessy.

Introduction

Desiring to deepen his understanding of the present world by turning to the past, between 1644 and 1652 the Cambridge student William Bright filled a small book with notes and commonplaces gleaned from political, historical, and religious writings. In 1648 he recorded political and military observations drawn from an anonymous pamphlet by 'D. P. Gent', listing five 'chiefe Causes of *th*e mutations of Monarchies': 'Wants of Issue', 'Ambition', 'Lust', 'Effeminacy', and 'Taxes'. The original pamphlet, entitled *Severall politique and militarie observations* (1648), had listed six causes of the mutations of monarchy, with the first being the 'crying sinnes of a Nation'.[1] Bright, however, only copied into his notebook those causes which could be illustrated by historical and contemporary rather than by divine example. Beside each of the causes, he included a short list of such *exempla*, including Julius Caesar and Richard III for 'Ambition'; Sextus Tarquin and Appius Claudius for 'Lust'; and Sardanapalus of Assyria for 'Effeminacy'.[2] Bright's notes illustrate well the entanglement of political, gendered, and historical thinking in seventeenth-century England. Statesmen in Stuart England widely held that the rise and fall of historic kingdoms, republics, and empires formed patterns from which the student of contemporary politics might learn, and this record testified that the 'lustful' or 'effeminate' ruler who committed sins of the bedroom or household might topple an empire just as surely as might unjust taxation or crises in hereditary succession. Indeed, both Bright's notes and the pamphlet from which they were drawn argued that the effeminacy or lust of a ruler could well be the very cause of unjust taxation or hereditary crisis.

---

[1] D. P., *Severall politique and militarie observations: upon the civill, and militarie governments; the birth, increase, and decay of monarchies, the carriage of princes, magistrates, commanders, and favourites.* London, 1648, 59. The Thomason copy includes the annotation, 'May 3d'.

[2] Cambridge University Library GBR/0012/MS Add.6160. p. 4.

2 Introduction

Bright's practice of copying historical notes was commonplace in seventeenth-century England, a society saturated with imagery and ideas drawn from the ancient and near past.[3] Schoolrooms, churches, libraries, playhouses, the court, and the palace, manuscripts and printed works were all sites of historical thinking in England. The subject of History, and the historically informed study of Latin, Greek, and Hebrew languages and texts, held pride of place in humanist grammar school and university curricula.[4] The political and legal structure of England was understood to have been founded upon conceptions of the ancient constitution and the common law, as well as constitutional structures, customs, and laws derived from the Roman legal tradition.[5] And the political imagination and culture of England, tied as it was to continental humanism, drew very heavily upon historical exempla.[6]

[3] In their study of history, readers frequently 'were encouraged to "harvest" and excerpt what they judged note-worthy'. See Freyja Cox Jensen, *Reading the Roman Republic in Early Modern England* (Leiden: Brill, 2012), 38; Peter Mack, *Elizabethan Rhetoric: Theory and Practice* (Cambridge: Cambridge University Press, 2004), esp. 135–75; Heidi Brayman Hackel, *Reading Material in Early Modern England* (Cambridge: Cambridge University Press, 2005), 137, 145–46. Harold Love has further argued that personal miscellanies, into which compilers entered texts of varying lengths from printed works or from short manuscripts, or 'separates', were often 'personal' in so far as the particular configuration of material depended upon the tastes and interests of the compiler and would not be repeated exactly, but that there was usually a strong family resemblance between manuscripts arising from particular institutions or sub-regions. Material copied into miscellanies would have ideological and timely reasons for their selection. See Love, *The Culture and Commerce of Texts: Scribal Publication in Seventeenth-Century England* (Amherst: University of Massachusetts Press, 1993).

[4] Mordechai Feingold, 'The Humanities', in N. Tyacke, ed. *The History of the University of Oxford, Volume IV: Seventeenth Century Oxford* (Oxford: Oxford University Press, 1997), 211–357, esp. 257–60; Jensen, *Reading the Roman Republic*, 25–37; Daniel Woolf, *The Idea of History in Early Stuart England: Erudition, Ideology, and the 'Light of Truth' from the Accession of James I to the Civil War* (Toronto: University of Toronto, 1990).

[5] J. G. A. Pocock, *The Ancient Constitution and the Feudal Law: A Study of English Historical Thought in the Seventeenth Century* (Cambridge: Cambridge University Press, 1957 and 1987); Andrew Lewis, '"What Marcellus Says Is against You": Roman Law and Common law', in *The Roman Law Tradition*, ed. A. D. E. Lewis and D. J. Ibbetson (Cambridge: Cambridge University Press, 1994), 199–208; R. H. Helmholz, 'The Roman Law of Guardianship in England, 1300–1600', *Tulane Law Review* 52.2 (1978): 223–57; D. J. Seipp, 'Roman Legal Categories in the Early Common Law', in *Legal Records and Historical Reality*, ed. T. G. Watkin (London and Ronceverte: Hambledon, 1989), 9–36.

[6] R. Malcolm Smuts, 'Court-Centred Politics and the Uses of Roman Historians, c. 1590–1630', in *Culture and Politics in Early Stuart England*, ed. Kevin Sharpe and Peter Lake (Basingstoke: Palgrave Macmillan, 1994), 21–43; Paulina Kewes, ed., *The Uses of History in Early Modern England* (San Marino, CA: Huntington Library Press, 2006); David Norbrook, *Writing the English Republic: Poetry, Rhetoric and Politics, 1627–1660* (Cambridge: Cambridge University Press, 1999); Lisa Jardine and Anthony Grafton, '"Studied for Action": How Gabriel Harvey Read his Livy', *Past and Present* 129 (Nov. 1990): 30–78.

Introduction 3

Within this intellectual milieu, the history of Rome held an especially significant place, as scholars such as Paulina Kewes and Malcolm Smuts have shown. Kings repeatedly represented themselves as Roman in print, portraits, performances, and public processions. By 1640, at least fifty-seven Roman history plays had been produced in England, of which forty survive, and printed English translations of classical accounts of Rome flourished, including by Livy, Sallust, Suetonius, Caesar, Tacitus, Lucan, Plutarch, Polybius, Seneca, Horace, and Cicero.[7] Alongside descriptions of scripture and of England's own past, interpretations of the history and historical exempla of Rome became a primary way that English subjects complimented, counselled, and criticised their monarchs – hailing or condemning King James, for example, as a new Augustus, a Julius Caesar, or a Nero.[8]

Attention to the history of history has borne great fruit in historical scholarship on seventeenth-century England, enriching our understanding of the political culture and of the intellectual origins of English republican thought. This book intends to deepen still further our understanding of the extent and character of historical thought in seventeenth-century England, and its significance in English political thinking, by attending to vibrant discourses of tyranny within early Stuart historical thought and the ways by which these conceptions of tyranny eroded support first for the Stuart monarchs and thereafter for Oliver Cromwell. Through closely analysing a series of Roman historical exempla and their public appropriation, the following chapters provide a detailed portrait of the multivalent images of tyranny which classical history afforded to English statesmen in this period. As Bright's notebook demonstrates, historical diagnoses of tyranny could lead the English student to analyse and to condemn a monarch's public and private performances – his political, moral, and familial activities. Simultaneously, this book seeks to remedy an unfortunate lacuna in the scholarship on history, political culture, and republicanism by focusing especially on ideas of gender, and particularly of manliness, which saturated both classical and early modern ideas of tyranny and of virtue, citizenship, governance, and statecraft.

---

[7] Other classical authors included Florus, Ammianus Marcellinus, Herodian, Josephus, Justinus, Appian, Dio, etc. See Jensen, *Reading the Roman Republic*, chapter 2; Daniel Woolf, *The Idea of History in Early Stuart England*, 172.

[8] For Augustus and Caesar, see Kewes, 'Julius Caesar in Jacobean England', *The Seventeenth Century* 17 (2002): 155–86; Smuts, 'Court-Centred Politics and the Uses of Roman Historians', 38–40. For Nero, see Chapters 3 and 4.

4 Introduction

The first half of this book argues that classical discourses of tyranny and of gender fuelled important contestations over conceptualisations of power, patriarchy, and masculinity in early Stuart England, and that the appropriation of classical stories helped to forge conflict in this period through affording statesmen languages with which to warn, to counsel, and also to criticise their monarchs as tyrannical and failed men. The second half of this book argues that English republican thought developed significantly as a solution to the perceived problem of emasculating tyranny experienced during the reigns of the early Stuarts. By attending to the centrality of tyranny and of gender in classical discourses of republicanism, and to important texts which supported and contested the rise of Cromwell through this classical lens, the book's final chapters argue that the fundamental purpose of English republicanism was the realisation of manhood for its citizens. Cromwell as lord protector represented the hopes of this republican discourse and its significant fragility as he was depicted as becoming a tyrant himself. Through these arguments, this book seeks to contribute to a number of historical debates simultaneously concerning the political thought and discourse of early Stuart and Interregnum England, conceptions of masculinity and patriarchy in the early and mid-seventeenth century, the cultural and intellectual origins of the English Revolution, and the character of English republican thought.

In the classical world as well as in the seventeenth century, articulations and conceptualisations of power were canvassed recurrently through formulations of gender. In ancient societies, gender was viewed as a fundamental structure of the 'natural' order of things and of people through the articulation of differences between and within the sexes. Manliness in the ancient world, tied particularly to conceptualisations of power, autonomy, and legitimacy, was a quintessentially public value performed, tested, won, or compromised in the context of public service or duties.[9] Moreover, classical definitions of moral goodness for the individual man and for the political actor or ruler were persistently coded through languages of masculinity, with the lack or failure of goodness being portrayed as emasculated, effeminate, or feminine.[10] Aristotle's political and ethical

[9] Lin Foxhall, *Studying Gender in Classical Antiquity* (Cambridge: Cambridge University Press, 2013), 1–23; Myles McDonnell, *Roman Manliness: Virtus and the Roman Republic* (Cambridge: Cambridge University Press, 2006), xiii.

[10] For example, the Greek term *malakia* had the double meaning of 'softness' or 'feminine', both signifying a lack of masculinity. See, e.g., Aristotle's discussion *On Virtues and Vices* in Aristotle, *Athenian Constitution. Eudemian Ethics. Virtues and Vices*, trans. H. Rackham, Loeb Classical Library 285 (Cambridge, MA: Harvard University Press, 1935), 496–99; Todd W. Reeser,

Introduction 5

writings, which all educated Englishmen imbibed in late grammar school and university education, provided exclusionary claims concerning the male human. Grounded in biological theories of the female as the privation of the male, Aristotle understood only men as capable of realising the human potential of self-governance by reason, and thereby, the potential to rule self and others.[11] Cicero, whose influence equalled or even exceeded that of Aristotle in this period, not only attended in great detail to the qualities of *virtus*, or manliness, as necessary for political authority but in his writings even masculinised the trait of *ratio* as that which must control (*coerceat, imperet*) the emotional and soft part of the soul which supposedly acted like a woman (*molle, muliebrieter*), in the same way that a master must control his slave, a commander his soldier, or a father his child. As Craig Williams describes Ciceronian thinking, 'We observe that all the images used [of *ratio*] are of men, not women, and all of them are in Roman terms men who by definition have authority and power over others: *dominus, imperator, parens.*'[12] The influence of these two classical writers on early seventeenth-century England cannot be overstated, as Aristotelian thought 'became so deeply ingrained in the European consciousness as to be accepted unquestioningly' and Cicero's writings formed the heart of grammar school education and of English characterisations of the active political life.[13]

In their conscious revival, appropriation, and reinterpretation of the classical world in the sixteenth and seventeenth centuries, English writers imported not only the histories, grammar, aesthetic tastes, and political and moral ideals of the ancients such as Aristotle and Cicero; they simultaneously imported ancient ideas concerning gender, which helped to shape early Stuart and then Cromwellian understandings of tyranny, power, and legitimacy. As we will see, these classical vocabularies intermingled in this period with the broad and complex vocabularies of masculinities expressed in honour and chivalric codes, religious belief

---

Moderating Masculinity in Early Modern Culture (Chapel Hill: North Carolina studies in the Roman Languages and Literatures, 2006), 66.

[11] Christine Garside-Allen, 'Can a Woman Be Good in the Same Way as a Man?', *Dialogue* 10 (1971), 534–44; Lynda Lange, 'Woman Is not a Rational Animal: On Aristotle's Biology of Reproduction', in *Discovering Reality*, ed. Sandra Harding and Merrill B. Hintikka (Dordrecht: Kluwer, 2003), 1–15.

[12] Craig A. Williams, *Roman Homosexuality: Ideologies of Masculinity in Classical Antiquity* (Oxford: Oxford University Press, 1999), 132–34.

[13] For Aristotle, see Charles B. Schmitt, 'Towards a Reassessment of Renaissance Aristotelianism', *History of Science* 11 (1973): 159–93, esp. 174. By the end of the sixteenth century in English schoolrooms, Cicero's writings became more commonly used for Latin study and double translation practice than Biblical scriptures. See Freyja Cox Jensen, *Reading the Roman Republic*, 28.

6　　　　　　　　　　　　　　Introduction

and practice, warfare and domestic governance, householding and patriarchy, fashion, national identity, and languages of Englishness, rights and freedoms.[14] Over thirty years ago, Joan Wallach Scott called for historians to explore the usefulness of gender as a category of historical analysis in realms such as politics, which had been a territory 'virtually uncharted' when she wrote in the 1980s.[15] While Scott sought to explain, if briefly, the significance of gender employed literally or analogically in political theory 'to justify or criticise the reign of monarchs and to express the relationship between ruler and ruled', three decades later these issues still have not been adequately addressed in British political and intellectual history, especially in studies of the period of male rulers.[16] Gender as a category of historical analysis has now been established firmly, including recognition that men as well as women were (and are) 'carriers' of gender; however, within scholarship on seventeenth-century Britain, most studies

[14] See, for example, Alexandra Shepard, *Meanings of Manhood in Early Modern England* (Oxford: Oxford University Press, 2003); Hilary Larkin, *The Making of Englishmen: Debates on National Identity, 1550–1650* (Leiden: Brill, 2014); Elizabeth A. Foyster, *Manhood in Early Modern England: Honour, Sex and Marriage* (London and New York: Longman, 1999); Margaret R. Sommerville, *Sex & Subjection: Attitudes to Women in Early Modern Society* (London and New York: Arnold, 1995); Anthony Fletcher, *Gender, Sex and Subordination in England, 1500–1800* (New Haven: Yale University Press, 1999); Brendan Kane, *The Politics and Culture of Honour in Britain and Ireland, 1541–1641* (Cambridge: Cambridge University Press, 2010); Cesare Cuttica, *Sir Robert Filmer (1588-1653) and the Patriotic Monarch: Patriarchalism in Seventeenth-Century Political Thought* (Manchester: Manchester University Press, 2012); Su Fang Ng, *Literature and the Politics of Family in Seventeenth-Century England* (Cambridge: Cambridge University Press, 2007); Simon Ditchfield and Helen Smith, eds., *Conversions: Gender and Religious Change in Early Modern Europe* (Manchester: Manchester University Press, 2017).

[15] Joan Wallach Scott, *Gender and the Politics of History*, revised edition (New York: Columbia University Press, 1999), 46.

[16] Much more has been done on issues of gender and power during the reign of Queen Elizabeth. See, for example, Carole Levin, *Heart and Stomach of a King: Elizabeth I and the Politics of Sex and Power* (Philadelphia: University of Pennsylvania Press, 1994); A. N. McLaren, *Political Culture in the Reign of Elizabeth I: Queen and Commonwealth, 1558–1585* (Cambridge: Cambridge University Press, 1999); *Dissing Elizabeth: Negative Representations of Gloriana*, ed. Julia M. Walker (Durham, NC: Duke University Press, 1998 and 2004).

　　Work that has been undertaken for the Stuart period includes Michael B. Young, *James VI and I and the History of Homosexuality* (Basingstoke: Macmillan, 2000); Susan Amussen and David Underdown, *Gender, Culture, and Politics in England, 1560–1640: Turning the World Upside Down* (London: Bloomsbury, 2017); Alastair Bellany, *The Politics of Court Scandal in Early Modern England: News Culture and the Overbury Affair, 1603–1660* (Cambridge: Cambridge University Press, 2002), esp. chapter 3. For the English civil wars and revolution, Anne Hughes has provided the most important analysis in *Gender and the English Revolution* (New York: Routledge, 2012); see also Hilda Smith, *All Men and Both Sexes: Gender, Politics, and the False Universal in England, 1640–1832* (Cambridge: Cambridge University Press, 2005). Literary contributions include Laura Lunger Knoppers, *Constructing Cromwell: Ceremony, Portrait, and Print, 1645–1661* (Cambridge: Cambridge University Press, 2000); Diane Purkiss, *Literature, Gender and Politics during the English Civil War* (Cambridge: Cambridge University Press, 2010).

Introduction 7

concerning conceptions of masculine governance, patriarchy, and male and female relations have focused on the level of the household, leaving still unexplored many of the vital relationships between traditional political theory, political culture, and ideas of masculinity.[17]

Scholars of political culture and intellectual historians have insufficiently engaged with the findings of gender historians. The outpouring of scholarship on classical republicanism and historical thought has identified the humanist study of the classical tradition as forming a central political vocabulary in seventeenth-century republicanism. Although debates persist concerning whether one classical tradition, or an amalgamation of traditions, most influenced English writers, the obvious intellectual debt to Greek, Roman, and Hebrew sources has been widely substantiated.[18] The field of republican scholarship, however, has largely failed to analyse the highly gendered nature of the classical tradition which influenced it, as well as the ways that classical understandings of manhood in particular were espoused and rejected by the Stuart kings and inherited by English republican writers. For example, Quentin Skinner's ground-breaking scholarship in the history of republicanism has rightly emphasised the

---

[17] John Tosh, 'What Should Historians Do with Masculinity? Reflections on Nineteenth-Century Britain', *History Workshop Journal* 38 (1994), 180.

[18] J. G. A. Pocock, *The Machiavellian Moment: Florentine Political Thought and the Atlantic Republican Tradition* (Princeton and London: Princeton University Press, 1975); Quentin Skinner, *The Foundations of Modern Political Thought, Volume 1: The Renaissance* (Cambridge: Cambridge University Press, 2002); Skinner, *Visions of Politics,* vol. II (Cambridge: Cambridge University Press, 2002); Markku Peltonen, *Classical Humanism and Republicanism in English Political Thought, 1570–1640* (Cambridge: Cambridge University Press, 1995); Jonathan Scott, *Commonwealth Principles: Republican Writing of the English Revolution* (Cambridge: Cambridge University Press, 2004); Norbrook, *Writing the English Republic: Poetry, Rhetoric and Politics, 1627–1660*; Eric Nelson, *The Greek Tradition in Republican Thought* (Cambridge: Cambridge University Press, 2004); Nelson, *The Hebrew Republic: Jewish Sources and the Transformation of European Political Thought* (Cambridge, MA: Harvard University Press, 2011); Andrew Hadfield, *Shakespeare and Republicanism* (Cambridge: Cambridge University Press, 2005).

The rewards for integrating gender history with political and intellectual history have been much more fully realised in studies of the French Revolution, which have identified issues of gender as a significant cultural contributor to the origins of the Revolution through political scandals, *mauvais discours* against the monarchy and aristocracy, and Enlightenment thought; and have demonstrated how the French Revolution generated feminist ideas, contested patriarchal ideals and structures, and affected relationships between men and men and women and men. See, for example, Sarah Maza, *Private Lives and Public Affairs: The Causes Célèbres in Pre-Revolution France* (Berkeley: University of California Press, 1993); Roger Chartier, *The Cultural Origins of the French Revolution*, trans. Lydia G. Cochrane (Durham, NC: Duke University Press, 1991); Hunt, *The Family Romance of the French Revolution*; Hunt, 'The Many Bodies of Marie Antoinette', in *The French Revolution: Recent Debates* (London: Routledge, 2006), 201–18; Olwen Hufton, *Women and the Limits of Citizenship* (Toronto: Toronto University Press, 1992). Of note for its exploration of these concepts in legal practice is Suzanne Desan, *The Family on Trial in Revolutionary France* (Berkeley: University of California Press, 2006).

8   Introduction

significance of liberty as non-domination in the Roman tradition, noting the fundamental division in Roman and other ancient societies as being between free and servile.[19] Yet while the Roman legal definition of liberty did rest upon non-domination, Roman articulations of the relationship between free and servile relied heavily upon gendered attributions of masculinity and effeminacy. Moreover, the characteristics of ideal manhood which were considered necessary for an individual to possess autonomy and to govern others included much more than freedom from subjection. A man's public reputation for *virtus*, or manliness, was central to his ability to wield power and was simultaneously fragile. Scholars of the classical world (and also of Stuart England) have argued that much of the invective concerning polarising dichotomies between *viri* and non-*viri*, between men and lesser males or non-males, functioned to divide men into legitimate and illegitimate players in the political realm; contestations over political authority and ability centred upon the demonstration of manly activity and ability within the private and public realm.[20] Thus the importance of non-domination as a legal distinction for Roman liberty cannot be disputed, but the practice of liberty within the Roman context rested upon a much broader notion of masculine autonomy than has usually been analysed. Attending to discourses of manliness greatly enriches and expands our understanding of the significance of the Roman heritage in English republican thought.

I.1   Origins of Revolution and Republicanism

The time period addressed by this study begins with the accession of James to the English throne in 1603 and ends with the writings of 'Good Old Cause' republicans just weeks before the restoration of the Stuart

---

[19] Skinner drew the definition of *civis* from Justinian and other writers as 'someone who is not under the dominion of anyone else [i.e. a slave], but is *sui iuris*, capable of acting in their own right'. See Skinner, 'Liberty and the English Civil War', in *Visions of Politics*, vol II., 313. For an excellent discussion of this view in the early seventeenth century, see 'John Milton and the politics of slavery', in *Vision of Politics*, vol. II, 286–307. See also *Liberty before Liberalism* (Cambridge: Cambridge University Press, 1998).

[20] See Richard Alston, 'Arms and the Man: Soldiers, Masculinity and Power in Republican and Imperial Rome', in *When Men Were Men: Masculinity, Power, and Identity in Classical Antiquity*, ed. Lin Foxhall and John Salmon (London and New York: Routledge, 1998), 205–224, esp. 207; J. Albert Harrill, 'Invective against Paul (2 Cor. 10:10), the Physiognomics of the Ancient Slave Body, and the Greco-Roman Rhetoric of Manhood', in *Antiquity and Humanity: Essays on Ancient Religion and Philosophy* (Tübingen: Mohr Siebeck, 2001): 189–213, esp. 201–5; Jennifer Larson, 'Paul's Masculinity', *Journal of Biblical Literature* 123.1 (Spring 2004): 85–97, esp. 86–87. For early Stuart England, see Foyster, *Manhood in Early Modern England*, 15–20.

Introduction

monarchy in 1660. Across the earlier part of this period, we find a growing divide in expressions of masculinity between those men considered fashionable in the Stuart court and those outside or critical of it, including divisions over whether virtuous manhood was enacted through negotiations of peace or through military ventures; in debates over elaborate or austere clothing and long or cropped hair; and in contestations over the worship of God in ornate and allegedly more effeminate and idolatrous ritual or in more austere fashion. In the midst of such debates, imaginative works began to pose questions about tyrants, including the point at which a king who trespassed gendered norms became unfit to rule. These cultural divisions would help to form the competing sides of the English civil wars.

Over the past four decades, 'revisionist' scholars have questioned whether the conflicts of the 1640s and the regicide of 1649 were the result of dynamic and long-standing legal, constitutional, and social divisions, as preceding liberal and Marxist histories had long asserted, or were instead contingent, essentially an aberration in English politics.[21] Revisionist accounts have emphasised the intellectual and social conservatism of early Stuart England, arguing for wide-scale consensus and a predominantly shared world-view of king, court, and subjects.[22] Simultaneously, leading scholars have questioned whether republicanism should be characterised as a response to civil war and regicide or a cause. As Blair Worden has maintained for the revisionist position: 'Regicide was not the fruit of republican theory. Most of its organisers were concerned to remove a

---

[21] Before revisionism, the English Revolution was understood as 'one of the decisive political episodes of modern times', and historians engaged in bitter debates over its religious, political, social, and economic causes. Marxists understood the revolution as bourgeois, helping to facilitate an emerging capitalist system, while 'Whigs' focused primarily on the constitutional principles established through Parliament, especially the House of Commons, as well as the activities and writings of Puritans. For significant 'revisionist' challenges to this view, see Kevin Sharpe, 'A Commonwealth of Meanings: Languages, Analogues, Ideas and Politics', in *Politics & Ideas in Early Stuart England* (London and New York: Pinter, 1989), 3–71; Conrad Russell, ed. *The Origins of the English Civil War* (Basingstoke: Macmillan, 1973); Russell, *Parliaments and English Politics 1621–1629* (Oxford: Oxford University Press, 1979); John Morrill, *The Revolt of the Provinces* (London: George Allen and Unwin, 1976); Sharpe, *The Personal Rule of Charles I* (London and New Haven: Yale University Press, 1992). For an overview of the historiographical landscape, see Richard Cust and Anne Hughes, eds., 'Introduction', *The English Civil War* (New York and London: Arnold, 1997), 1–30.

[22] See, for example, Sharpe, 'A Commonwealth of Meanings', 64–71. The real task, in Sharpe's view, was to explain how the civil war could have possibly erupted in Stuart England with its basis of political consensus and lack of fundamental ideological disagreements between king and parliament. Their main target was Lawrence Stone, *The Causes of the English Revolution, 1529–1642* (London: ARK, 1972).

Introduction

particular king, not kingship. They cut off King Charles' head and wondered what to do next.'[23]

Revisionist correctives have often been salutary, and have deepened our understanding of the 'politics of religion' and of the operation of political institutions on the national and local level, while elevating the provincial archive as a site of significant historical research.[24] At the same time, however, the privileging of manuscript and scribal sources within these studies has sometimes narrowed conceptions of the 'political' and even of political 'ideas' and has resulted in some neglect of wider cultural and intellectual contexts of the seventeenth century. 'Post-revisionist' accounts therefore have begun recently to address these contexts through emphasising the construction, circulation, and varied political meanings of images, events, scandals, and prejudices.[25] Due in significant measure to the revisionist position that the 1640s and 1650s were a deviation from the

---

[23] Blair Worden, 'Milton's republicanism and the tyranny of heaven', in *Machiavelli and Republicanism*, ed. Gisela Bock, Quentin Skinner, and Maurizio Viroli (Cambridge: Cambridge University Press, 1991), 225–46, esp. 226. In a similar vein, Pocock contended that republican doctrine in England developed as 'men came to face the fact that the historic constitution had collapsed'. English republicanism 'was a language, not a programme'. Pocock, 'Introduction', in *Political Works of James Harrington* (Cambridge: Cambridge University Press, 1977), 15.

[24] See, e.g., John Morrill, *Revolt in the Provinces: The People of England and the Tragedies of War, 1630–1648* (London: Routledge, 1976); Anthony Fletcher, *A County Community in Peace and War: Sussex, 1600–1660* (London: Longman, 1975); Ann Hughes, 'Militancy and Localism: Warwickshire Politics and Westminster Politics, 1643–1647', *Transactions of the Royal Historical Society*, 5th ser., 31 (1981): 51–68; Morrill, 'The Religious Context of the English Civil War', in *Transactions of the Royal Historical Society* 34 (1984): 155–78; Conrad Russell, 'Parliamentary History in Perspective, 1604–1629', *History* 61 (1976): 1–27.

[25] The narrowing of the political is especially true of works following Conrad Russell's studies of parliamentary history, focusing upon high politics to the neglect of the political and cultural perceptions which may have influenced the high political realm. Within revisionist scholarship, Kevin Sharpe's work greatly broadened this narrower view of the political, although Sharpe's work still tended to be concerned with self-representation and self-interest rather than ideas. Russell, *Parliaments and English Politics 1621–1629* (Oxford: Oxford University Press, 1979); Sharpe, *Criticism and Compliments: The Politics of Literature in the England of Charles I* (Cambridge: Cambridge University Press, 1987). For a perceptive reflection on these trends, see John Morrill, 'Revisionism's Wounded Legacies', *Huntington Library Quarterly* 78.4 (Winter 2015): 577–94.

For post-revisionist accounts, see Johann Sommerville, *Politics and Ideology in England, 1603–1640* (London: Longmans, 1986); L. J. Reeve, *Charles I and the Road to Personal Rule* (New York and Cambridge: Cambridge University Press, 1989); Richard Cust, *The Forced Loan and English Politics, 1626–1628* (Oxford: Oxford University Press, 1987); Anne Hughes, *The Causes of the English Civil War* (London: Macmillan, 1991); Thomas Cogswell, *The Blessed Revolution: English Politics and the Coming of War, 1621–1624* (Cambridge: Cambridge University Press, 1989); Alastair Bellany, *The Politics of Court Scandal in Early Modern England: News Culture and the Overbury Affair, 1603–1660* (Cambridge: Cambridge University Press, 2002); Hughes, *Gender and the English Revolution*; Andrew McRae, *Literature, Satire, and the Early Stuart State* (Cambridge: Cambridge University Press, 2004); Curtis Perry, *Literature and Favoritism in Early Modern England* (Cambridge: Cambridge University Press, 2006); Peter Lake, 'Anti-Popery: the Structure of a Prejudice', in *Conflict in Early Stuart England*, ed. Richard Cust and Anne Hughes (New York:

Introduction 11

mainstream consensus of English politics, the kinds of cultural and intellectual analyses applied by scholars such as Lynn Hunt and Roger Chartier to explain the genesis of the French Revolution have not been pursued much in the field of English history, but these 'post-revisionist' works are in some ways similar to that scholarship on the pre-Revolutionary French eighteenth century.[26] Attributing intellectual and cultural origins to the English Revolution is not the same as establishing causes, nor does it require one to view the 1640s as ideologically determined. Paralleling the approach of Chartier in studying the period before the French Revolution, it is important for historians to identify some of the conditions which made English republicanism and the English Revolution possible because they were culturally and politically conceivable.[27]

The following intellectual and cultural history thus joins hands with recent 'post-revisionist' works, and is indebted to the sensibility of scholars of the origins of the French Revolution, as it explores the emergence of important articulations of tyranny during the reigns of King James and King Charles. Critical writers in this period more often opposed the practices of a particular king than kingship itself, and many sought to counsel their king for the preservation and benefit of the monarchy and realm. Yet, historians must also attend to the ways that specific criticisms against monarchs could translate into arguments against hereditary monarchy more generally in this period. This study suggests that these discourses need to be understood as part of the cultural and intellectual origins of the English Revolution – as part of what made revolution possible because conceivable. This study maintains that ruptures in the political culture of England emerged, in part, from and through languages of tyranny and of gender derived from classical history.

Through classical stories of lustful and incestuous tyrants, of republican revolution, of unnatural crimes against family, Englishmen envisioned kings who were tyrants (*tyrannus ex parte exercitii*). Roman stories of wicked rulers and revolution were popular in seventeenth-century England not only due to their dramatic and exciting content but because they raised

---

Longman 1989), 72–106; Lake with Michael Questier, *Anti-Christ's Lewd Hat: Protestants, Papists and Players in Post-Reformation England* (New Haven & London: Yale University Press, 2002).

[26] For intellectual and cultural origins of the French Revolution, see, e.g., Chartier, *The Cultural Origins of the French Revolution*; Maza, *Private Lives and Public Affairs*; Robert Darnton, *The Literary Underground of the Old Regime* (Cambridge, MA: Harvard University Press, 1982); Keith Michael Baker, *Inventing the French Revolution: Essays on French Political Culture in the Eighteenth Century* (Cambridge: Cambridge University Press, 1990).

[27] Chartier, *The Cultural Origins of the French Revolution*, 2.

12   Introduction

significant and timely questions about the rise and fall of empires, the morality and immorality of rulers, the customs and *mores* of peoples, and the gendered expectations of men and women established in Rome – one of the most influential of all previous societies, and a society whose customs were expected to be reiterated by subsequent peoples and empires. These stories of Rome were frequently canvassed in literary, poetic, and dramatic writings, as well as in more traditional political sources such as parliamentary speeches and political treatises, and simultaneously they provided authoritative, imaginative, and safer media – in a society of censored speech – through which to study the problem of tyranny and its solutions. Moreover, stories of corruption and power in imperial Rome gained in significance and urgency in the seventeenth century as English kings represented themselves through imperial imagery and increasingly professed the ability to rule above the law and without parliament.[28]

Literary scholars have begun the fruitful work of analysing these types of imaginative sources for understanding republican and quasi-republican thought prior to the English civil wars.[29] But much more remains to be done. This study, especially in Part I, employs a number of literary materials to explore the ways that Roman stories and classical vocabularies infiltrated and shaped English political thought and culture prior to the civil wars. Through detailed analyses of Roman stories of tyranny and

---

[28] For imperial self-representations of the Stuart kings, see Sharpe, *Image Wars: Promoting Kings and Commonwealths in England, 1603–1660* (New Haven and London: Yale University Press, 2010), 58–88, 190–229. For declarations of rule, see *His Maiesties dclaration [sic] to all his louing Subiects, of the causes which moued him to dissolue the last Parliament* (London, 1628). See, also 'His Maiesties Declaration, Touching His Proceedings in the *Late Assemblie and Conuention* of Parliament', in *King James VI and I: Political Writings*, ed. Johann P. Sommerville (Cambridge: Cambridge University Press, 1994), 258–59. For discussions of the rise of influence in Tacitean histories due to these developments, see Alan T. Bradford, 'Stuart Absolutism and the "Utility" of Tacitus', *Huntington Library Quarterly* 46.2 (Spring 1983): 127–55; J. H. M. Salmon, 'Stoicism and Roman Example: Seneca and Tacitus in Jacobean England', *Journal of the History of Ideas* 50.2 (Apr.–Jun. 1989): 199–225.

[29] Of these accounts, David Norbrook's work has most effectively rescued pre-civil war republican figures from the shadows and demonstrated the energetic republican culture that thrived through literary writings, and especially poetry, derived from Lucan and other classical authors. See *Writing the English Republic*. See also Peltonen, *Classical Humanism and Republicanism*; Hadfield, 'Republicanism in Sixteenth- and Seventeenth-Century Britain', in *British Political Thought in History, Literature, and Theory, 1500–1800*, ed. David Armitage (Cambridge: Cambridge University Press, 2006): 111–28; Hadfield, *Shakespeare and Republicanism*. In response to these studies, Blair Worden has argued that identifying republicanism as a language corresponding to themes, ideas, and affiliations runs the risk of creating an over-inclusive understanding of republicanism, which may, for example, classify any discussion of 'virtue' as republicanism. See Worden, 'Republicanism, Regicide and Republic: The English Experience', in *Republicanism: A Shared European Heritage, Volume 1: Republicanism and Constitutionalism in Early Modern Europe*, ed. Martin van Gelderen and Quentin Skinner (Cambridge: Cambridge University Press, 2002), 307–27.

Introduction 13

revolution, these chapters underscore how these materials helped English statesmen conceptualise masculine governance and counsel, support, and critique their monarchs. Literary productions of the seventeenth century at times presented contemporary criticisms in only thinly veiled terms, while at other times they provided more abstract ruminations upon political themes and questions. Although some scholars have stressed the former, emphasising particular productions or libellous poems that included significant markers of contemporary concern, this book studies how an array of circulated material helped perform cultural and intellectual work in the seventeenth century, sometimes tied to specific complaints against individual monarchs, and sometimes presenting general or more theoretical languages of corruption, gender, and monarchy as works of political theory. These classical stories and vocabularies helped lay the groundwork for larger transformations in political culture and thought in England by providing significant historical models and examples of governance and of tyranny which Englishmen had been trained to read from early in their intellectual formation. Simultaneously, imaginative writing more effectively avoided the threat of censorship for printed materials in Stuart England. Although inconsistent and often haphazard, Stuart press controls and censorship often succeeded in keeping unauthorised discussions of contemporary politics and political debate out of print and suppressed ideas deemed threatening to the regime. These activities encouraged writers to veil their arguments and to seek indirection in their writing, a primary strategy of which involved the discussion of distant times and places.[30]

I.2 Methods and Structures

The Rule of Manhood adopts a two-part structure, with chapters organised chronologically but also thematically. Its early chapters consider how Englishmen appropriated particular stories of the Roman past to develop critical discourses about tyranny and political virtue and to fuel

---

[30] Cyndia Susan Clegg, *Press Censorship in Jacobean England* (Cambridge: Cambridge University Press, 2001); Clegg, *Press Censorship in Caroline England* (Cambridge: Cambridge University Press, 2008); Sheila Lambert, 'The Printers and the Government, 1604–1640', in *Aspects of Printing from 1600*, ed. Robin Myers and Michael Harris (Oxford: Oxford University Press, 1987); Debora K. Shuger, *Censorship and Cultural Sensibility: The Regulation of Language in Tudor-Stuart England* (Philadelphia: University of Pennsylvania Press, 2006); Annabel Patterson, *Censorship and Interpretation: The Conditions of Writing and Reading in Early Modern England* (Madison: University of Wisconsin Press, 1984).

contestations over definitions of masculine governance, patriarchy, and power; later chapters consider the effect of these Roman stories, and the gendered grammar of tyranny they provided, on English republican thought and English political culture during and following the civil wars and revolution.

Part I, entitled 'Emasculated Kingship', begins with a first chapter detailing the significance of classical history in Stuart England, and providing an overview of how conceptualisations of manly rule and tyranny were defined through political and gendered vocabularies within these classical sources. English boys learned, translated, and performed at grammar schools and universities these gendered, often Roman stories of warriors and tyrants and revolutions. Once grown, they encountered them on the theatrical stage and in costly as well as in cheap print; they recorded them in commonplace books and miscellanies; they used them in public debate; and they heard them referenced frequently from the pulpit. Within Roman stories circulated in this period, images of idealised manhood primarily focused upon three male roles, those of law-giver, warrior, and father, through which men exhibited their *virtus,* or manliness, in the governance of lesser men, women, children, and slaves. Within this classical context, Englishmen encountered numerous representations and treatises characterising tyranny broadly as a failure in masculinity, and more specifically as wicked activities resulting from the tyrant's lawlessness, disordered soul, or pursuit of private gain over public good. The exemplum of Junius Brutus is analysed as a first example of these concepts in the context of early Stuart England. This chapter is intended to provide an introduction to classical discourses of masculinity and tyranny and their appropriation in English political thought and culture before these themes will be deepened and developed throughout subsequent chapters.

The second, third, and fourth chapters provide detailed case studies focusing upon specific historical exempla in order to construct a portrait of how tyranny, envisioned as a failure in the masculine roles of father, law-giver, and warrior, was conceptualised in early Stuart England. Each chapter seeks not only to explore the highly gendered and complex discourses of tyranny which developed through these stories but also the ways that Roman history could be employed to advance timely criticisms against and counsel for King James and King Charles.

Chapter 2 considers how English appropriations of the Roman story of Appius Claudius and Virginia provided important discourses of tyranny and judicial corruption in Jacobean England. As recounted by Livy and Dionysius, Appius was a Roman decemvir whose unlawful pursuit of a

Introduction 15

chaste maiden, Virginia, eventually led to his government's overthrow through a republican revolution led by Virginia's father, Virginius. Through this story of lust, corruption, sacrifice, and revolution, the chapter paints an image of how Englishmen conceptualised tyranny as the perversion of a ruler's soul, especially due to the vice of lust, and as a failure in the masculine role of law-giver. In each account, Appius's vice was importantly contrasted with the virtues of Virginia and Virginius through idealised portrayals of their family. These stories articulated a significant vision of tyranny and good governance through a patriarchal model, while proposing the provocative claim that a citizen may be more virtuous and exemplary than his ruler. Finally, the chapter considers how this Roman story offered a powerful portrait of the tyrant as failed law-giver, a ruler so corrupted and emasculated by inordinate lust and passion that he would manipulate the common law and commit legal injustices to gratify his own vicious cravings. The chapter argues that this particular portrayal of tyranny was a timely one in Jacobean England, as scandals over the Chancery Court and the Overbury Affair brought King James's arguments for the royal prerogative and the monarch's position over the law into public question.

Chapters 3 and 4 build upon and expand this portrait of tyranny by studying a series of plays, libels, poems, treatises, and speeches concerning the infamous Emperor Nero. Chapter 3 first argues for the significance of Nero's history in the mid-1620s as a battleground for debates concerning monarchical absolutism and as a vehicle whereby James's pacific policies could be publicly defended and challenged. The particular stories of Nero which early Stuart writers adapted in the 1620s, however, further underscore the centrality of issues of gender and family for conceptions of tyranny, for writers focused especially on Nero's family relationships: his failure as a husband, how he was formed within his mother's womb, his incestuous sexual relationships, and his eventual murder of brother and mother. Much like portrayals of Appius, these writers characterised tyranny through a combination of classical conceptions of the failed man and law-giver, but stories of Neronian vice further emphasised gender inversion (the emasculation of male tyrants and the masculinisation of female tyrants), and how a tyrant's vicious activities undermined law, military valour, religion, family, order, and virtue in society. Oppositional writers especially championed Nero's history to cast King James's refusal to commit troops to the Bohemian Crisis as unmanly, cowardly, and irreligious. Simultaneously, Edmund Bolton's history of Nero, which was crafted to defend King James and monarchical absolutism, similarly

16 Introduction

adopted a gendered discourse of tyranny to characterise Nero's failures and to blame his most heinous crimes upon his mother, Julia Agrippina, who was portrayed as vicious and unruly. The chapter argues that Bolton's history, while defending monarchy, also exposed for its readers the danger of hereditary monarchy as bred through the womb of a tyrannical mother, and cast tyranny as a private vice with ruinous public consequences.

Focusing on how Neronian portraits of tyranny developed in the late 1620s and 1630s, the fourth chapter considers how critics covertly charged King Charles and his government with tyrannical activity throughout the years of the personal rule. Appropriations of Nero in this period continued to emphasise gendered themes of emasculation, portraying tyranny as the perversion of gender identity and order for individuals as well as society. Two significant new themes arose, however, in Neronian oppositional discourses in this period: uxoriousness and persecution. The first, uxoriousness, continued to define tyranny through household disorder but supported particular criticisms of King Charles's marriage to the Catholic Henrietta Maria. By the 1630s, Puritans challenging Laudian reforms further appropriated these gendered stories of Nero to condemn the King and Archbishop William Laud. William Prynne accused the King and Queen of publicly corrupting the moral foundation of society by blurring the distinction between male and female, virtue and vice, true religion and idolatry. Prynne, John Bastwick, and Henry Burton – who were publicly mutilated in 1637 after deeming the Church of England popish and idolatrous – declared themselves Christian martyrs under Nero, and employed classical languages of tyranny and masculinity to legitimise their activities to the English public.

Part II, 'The Masculine Republic', continues and deepens this story from the Stuart period into the period of the English Revolution, considering how classical and gendered discourses of tyranny within these earlier decades expanded and were transformed. These chapters argue that classical images of masculinity, based partly upon the ideals of the warrior, law-giver, and/or father, and partly upon the fear of tyranny and its emasculating effects, forged a central language of republican writings and culture. English republicans, convinced that the Stuart regime and civil wars had compromised the masculinity not only of its king but also of its subjects, held the restoration of the masculinity of English governors and citizens as the primary motivation and fundamental concern of their writings. For these reasons, English republican writers did not seek to destroy notions of paternal rule, nor did they seek to create a 'band of

Introduction 17

brothers', as Lynn Hunt has argued about the French Revolution.[31] Instead, in the wake of the regicide, they sought to create a 'band of fathers', of virtuous and manly fathers, warriors, and law-givers, who would rule England justly, and thereby provide a solution for the problems of emasculating tyranny. Within this context, Oliver Cromwell would be supported strongly initially as an appropriate military and masculine ruler; but by many whose hopes had been raised by the creation of a republic, he too would thereafter be condemned as having become a tyrant.

Chapter 5 studies these developments through the writings of John Milton, taking seriously Milton's claim that it was 'within his own household that [King Charles] began to be a bad king'.[32] The chapter first considers the ways that Milton's conceptions of masculinity and of tyranny became forged through the study of classical history and philosophy, and how Milton in his early career participated in the political culture traced in Part I of this study. It then turns to Milton's writings of the 1640s and early 1650s to understand how these classical discourses transformed in his oppositional writings against Charles and Henrietta Maria, and at the same time, how these shaped Milton's discussions of manly liberty and participatory government in his early prose writings, especially the divorce tracts. In the divorce tracts, Milton argued that good marriage, and the masculine-controlled household resulting from good marriage, were necessary components of the virtuous republic. This component of Milton's republican thought has not been emphasised sufficiently in current scholarship. Finally, the chapter considers how Milton, within his republican writings of the 1650s, built his mature conceptualisations of liberty and of the free commonwealth upon the realisation of manhood classically understood.

Like Milton, his close associate Marchamont Nedham understood republicanism as creating a free state in which males could become fully realised as men, but Nedham's writings demonstrate the significant impact of masculinist republican rhetoric upon languages of conquest and empire in the 1650s. Chapter 6 provides a close study of the political writings of Nedham, wherein we find celebrations of republican government as manly due not only to the exercise of reason and self-governance, but especially due to the regular exercise of arms and the 'propagation' of liberty to other

---

[31] Lynn Hunt, *The Family Romance of the French Revolution* (Berkeley: University of California Press, 1992).

[32] John Milton, *Defensio pro Populo Anglicano* (1651), *Complete Prose Works of John Milton*, 10 volumes, gen. ed. Don M. Wolfe (New Haven: Yale University Press, 1953–82), IV.2.52–21.

countries. As newswriter and propagandist working within the the office of John Thurloe, head of British Intelligence, Nedham witnessed and encouraged the conquest of the Irish and Scots, and wielded republican languages of masculine governance to support the imperial aspirations of the English republic beyond the confines of the three kingdoms, including in the conquest of Jamaica. The chapter argues that Nedham's writings on republican conquest reflected his own hopes for a thoroughly masculine commonwealth capable of subduing or liberating those under the servile yoke of tyranny at home and abroad. Despite the significant differences between Milton and Nedham's mature republican writings, both thinkers demonstrate the centrality of classical understandings of tyranny and of masculinity in English republican thought.

The final chapter considers the effect of gendered discourses of tyranny on the languages of debate and dissent during the Interregnum by analysing public representations of Oliver Cromwell. The chapter explores the extensive ways that writers defended Cromwell as the best answer to Stuart tyranny and as the most virtuous, republican citizen through adopting classical conceptualisations of tyranny, masculinity, and good governance. As a father, military leader, and religious man, and as one enforcing 'morality' laws such as the Adultery Act, Cromwell appeared to fulfil idealised standards of manhood in myriad ways, and even to surpass the examples of grave republican and militaristic leaders of the classical Roman past. Cromwell, it was argued, restored manliness to Englishmen through encouraging virtuous and pious living and courage displayed in arms. Yet, while Cromwell's supporters adopted classical discourses to defend the Lord Protector, deeming him a Junius Brutus, Julius Caesar, or Augustus, Royalists and Presbyterians denounced Cromwell in part by adopting historical and oppositional discourses of tyranny, thereby translating these vocabularies from the Stuart period into criteria by which Cromwell would be justified or judged. These critics appropriated stories of Nero and other classical tyrants to castigate Cromwell as a dangerous, usurping ruler and failed man. In the end, Cromwell's rule as lord protector would disappoint deeply the masculinist hopes and rhetoric of English republican thinkers.

PART I

Emasculated Kingship

CHAPTER I

Tyranny, Manhood, and the Study of History

IMP. IACOBVS MAX.
CÆSAR AVG. P. P.
PACE POPVLO BRITANNICO
TERRA MARIQVE PARTA
IANVM CLVSIT. S. C.[1]

In his magnificent entrance to London on the Ides of March 1603/4, King James was hailed and celebrated as a new Caesar Augustus, ushering in 'those golden times ... returned againe', as Ben Jonson described through the words of Vergil, 'wherein *Peace* was with vs so aduannced, *Rest* receaued, *Libertie* restored, *Safetie* assured, and all *Blessednesse* appearing in euery of these vertues her perticular Triumphe ouer her opposite euill'.[2] Amongst the classical arches and scenes erected for the King's entertainment and celebration, processors dramatically enacted the Vergilian prophecy of a peaceful empire by closing the gate of a reconstructed Temple of Janus upon which the words were inscribed: 'James the greatest emperor, Caesar Augustus the Father of his Country, as peace has been brought forth for the British people on land and sea, a decree of the Senate has closed the gate'. By resurrecting 'these dead rites' on English soil, Jonson fashioned James's great procession as a triumphal entry of peace rather than of war and his new king as possessing 'strong and potent vertues' beyond those of Mars.[3] These intricate devices, comprising speeches,

---

[1] Ben Jonson, *His Part of King James his Royall and Magnificent Entertainment through his Honorable Cittie of London, Thurseday the 15. of March 1603* (London, 1604), sig. D1v. Jonson designed the first and last devices of the entertainment.
[2] Ibid., sig. C2v.
[3] Ibid., sig. Dv–D2r. See Stephen Orgel, *James I and the Politics of Literature: Jonson, Shakespeare, Donne, and Their Contemporaries* (Baltimore: Johns Hopkins University Press, 1983), 28–54; Lawrence Manley, 'Scripts for the Pageant: The Ceremonies of London', in *Literature and Culture in Early Modern London* (Cambridge and New York: Cambridge University Press, 1995), 212–93; David M. Bergeron, *English Civic Pageantry, 1558–1642*, rev. ed. (Tempe: Arizona Center for Medieval and Renaissance Studies, 2003).

Emasculated Kingship

interludes, costumes, pageantry, and architectural staging, were designed to serve as public legitimisations of a new sovereign upon his accession, establishing his nobility, virtue, power, and authority. Simultaneously, these devices, crafted through historical and mythical exempla, presented idealised political expectations for the King and Stuart family, qualities that the sovereign should possess and practise publicly and privately.

James's accession was an important but not wholly unusual day; the Stuart kings frequently promoted identification between themselves and the classical past. Far more than his predecessors and immediate successors, King James acted as his own spokesman in print and in speech, wherein he often employed historical exempla to characterise his own reign and to make arguments concerning political policies and the rights of kings more generally; at the same time, James gave patronage to works that represented him as one of several historical figures identified with reigns of peace and prosperity, such as Caesar Augustus, King David, and King Solomon.[4] He was the first English monarch to portray himself on his coinage as a Roman Emperor.[5] Although King Charles was more reluctant than his father to represent himself through his own spoken and written word, he similarly identified with the Roman emperors and publicly fashioned himself as *imperator* through public pageantry, images, and portraiture.[6] Anthony Van Dyck's half-length portrait of King Charles in armour holding a baton modelled Titian's portrait of the Emperor Otho from the *Twelve Caesars* royal collection. *Charles with Monsieur de St Antoine* (1633) represented the King as gracefully guiding a white horse through a triumphal Roman arch beside a shield decorated with the arms of his empire. Positioned at the end of the St. James gallery displaying the *Twelve Caesars* and Giulio Roman's equestrian portraits of the emperors, this image portrayed Charles as the successor of an ancient lineage of rule.[7] These images gained a wider public through print and commemorative

---

[4] E.g., *A Meditation Vpon the 27. 28. 29. Verses of the XXVIII. Chapter of Saint Matthew. Or A Paterne for a Kings Inavgvration. Written by the Kings Maiestie.* (London, 1619); Henry Petowe, *Englands Caesar* (London, 1603), sigs. B1r–v and C1r–v; Robert Pricket, A *souldiers vvish vnto His Soveraigne Lord King Iames* (London, 1603), sigs. B2v and B4r. See Jonathan Goldberg, *James I and the Politics of Literature* (Baltimore: Johns Hopkins University Press, 1983), 33–50; Kevin Sharpe, *Image Wars: Promoting Kings and Commonwealths in England, 1603–1660* (New Haven and London: Yale University Press, 2010), 11–57, 79–88.

[5] Linda Levy Peck, 'The Mental World of the Jacobean Court: An Introduction', in *The Mental World of the Jacobean Court* (Cambridge: Cambridge University Press, 1991), 1–20, esp. 5.

[6] See Chapter 4.

[7] Karen Hearn, ed. *Van Dyck & Britain* (London: Tate, 2009), 74; Susan J. Barnes, Nora De Poorter, Oliver Millar, and Horst Vey, *Van Dyck: A Complete Catalogue of the Paintings* (New Haven and London: Yale University Press, 2004), 463–64; Sharpe, *Image Wars*, 201–2.

medals, which sported equestrian portraits of Charles as well as comparisons between the King and mythical Roman gods such as Mars and Mercury.[8] Classical models of kingship such as these significantly shaped the understanding and construction of images of good governance and of tyranny in the seventeenth century. They were also highly gendered, importing notions of *imperium* through representations of *virtus*, or manliness, often imagined through tropes of martial prowess and conquest.

In order to understand these classical models and the place of historical *exempla* in English political culture, this chapter first provides a brief overview of humanist understandings of classical history and its place within English schooling and political speech. The later sections then begin to canvass a central argument of this study: that conceptions of gender and especially masculinity were central to these popular histories and stories of the Roman past, and that these classical conceptions of masculinity shaped seventeenth-century understandings of politics and gender. Scholars of the classical period have produced fruitful studies on the significant, multivalent codes of manliness, or *virtus*, which developed throughout the Roman republican and imperial eras; yet, the appropriation of classical writings and their gendered meanings in the early modern period has not been fully recognised or explored, especially within English understandings of politics and political thought.[9] The Roman past offered both idealised portrayals of manhood and important portrayals of its failure for Stuart audiences. Classical Latin distinctions between *vir* (man) and *homo* (lesser male) were recognised and explicitly discussed in seventeenth-century England. And idioms of tyranny based upon masculine failure formed significant languages of monarchical counsel and criticism in Stuart England. To exemplify these connections, the chapter concludes by providing a brief case study of the exempla of Junius Brutus and of Tarquin, focusing on how English writers imported and appropriated Roman models of manhood and condemnations of tyranny through their deployment of classical histories.

---

[8] Sharpe, *Image Wars*, 215–23.

[9] The best studies for the late Tudor and early Stuart periods have hailed from literary scholars. See, for example, Rebecca Bushnell, *Tragedies of Tyrants: Political Thought and Theater in the English Renaissance* (Ithaca, NY: Cornell University Press, 1990); Mark Breitenberg, *Anxious Masculinity in Early Modern England* (Cambridge: Cambridge University Press, 1996); Bruce R. Smith, *Shakespeare and Masculinity* (Oxford: Oxford University Press, 2000); Robin Headlam Wells, *Shakespeare on Masculinity* (Cambridge: Cambridge University Press, 2004).

24 Emasculated Kingship

1.1 History and Humanist Pedagogy

The classics served as the foundation of seventeenth-century English pedagogy and civic education, and as a cornerstone of ethical education alongside the Christian tradition. Writers and texts from the classical tradition were thought to distil wisdom, to guide behaviour, and to provide timeless knowledge about human character and political structures. For this reason, as one recent historian has noted, students 'developed an emotional commitment to antiquity and its repository of useful knowledge', which they often continued to pursue in private study even beyond the university.[10] Formal instruction from an early age relied heavily upon the Latin classics to teach the humanist subjects of grammar, rhetoric, poetry, history, and philosophy. The teaching of Roman authors in the English grammar school curriculum, which at a minimum included Cicero, Caesar, Sallust, and very often Livy, along with Terence, Vergil, Ovid, and Horace, ensured deep familiarity with Roman history for all educated Englishmen, and all school children were drilled in Latin grammar beginning at the age of seven.[11] Within the later grammar school levels and the university, Greek texts such as Aristotle's *Politics* and *Ethics* and Homer's epics similarly formed the backbone of political and moral learning. At this age, many began the study of the Greek language, although the popularity of advanced study in Greek for most statesmen began to wane during the seventeenth century. We find at least some statesmen warning their sons in the 1650s that 'the attaining of Latin is most of use, the Greek but loss of time'.[12]

Tudor and Stuart Englishmen made grand claims concerning the craft of history and its role in producing political knowledge. In the first English translation of Tacitus's *Annals* (1598), Richard Greneway characterised history as 'the treasure of times past, and as well a guide, as image of mans present estate, a true and liuely pattern of things to come, and as some terme it, the work-mistresse of experience, which is the mother of

---

[10] Mordechai Feingold, 'The Humanities', in N. Tyacke, ed. *The History of the University of Oxford, Volume IV: Seventeenth Century Oxford* (Oxford: Oxford University Press, 1997), 229.

[11] Other classical authors included Florus, Ammianus Marcellinus, Herodian, Josephus, Justinus, Appian, Dio, etc. Freyja Cox Jensen, *Reading the Roman Republic in Early Modern England* (Leiden: Brill, 2012), 27–28; Daniel Woolf, *The Idea of History in Early Stuart England: Erudition, Ideology, and the 'Light of Truth' from the Accession of James I to the Civil War* (Toronto: University of Toronto, 1990), 172; Peter Mack, *Elizabethan Rhetoric: Theory and Practice* (Cambridge: Cambridge University Press, 2004), 13–15; Warren Chernaik, *The Myth of Rome in Shakespeare and His Contemporaries* (Cambridge: Cambridge University Press, 2011), 7–8.

[12] Qtd in Feingold, 'The Humanities', 260.

Tyranny, Manhood, and the Study of History

prudence'.[13] Greneway's introductory remarks clearly summarised what contemporary Englishmen understood as the two principal benefits of studying history. Due to history's cyclical patterns, and the belief that human nature remained the same over time, the study of history was understood to reveal lessons applicable to past, present, and future. The seventeenth-century scholar or statesman who carefully studied history believed he could acquire invaluable political information and experiential knowledge, a guide to contemporary political action, and a key to predict the future. As one seventeenth-century treatise described, 'Onely the persons and Actors of the Historie doe succeede new every age; and the names being changed, the stories are now told as it were of our selves.'[14] This advice permeated conduct manuals and advice letters. As Henry Oxinden advised his son, 'If you bee desirous to know what shall bee, reade & obserue histories, & consider what hath bene, for all things in the world att all times haue their uerie encounter with the times of old, there being no new thing under the Sun.'[15] Simultaneously, through its exempla, or its depictions of a specific action, event, or person which represented a state of affairs, virtue, vice, or character, history was thought to aid in the acquisition of prudence, whereby one could learn to distinguish good and virtuous activity from the shameful and vicious. By presenting the experiences of others, history was 'philosophy teaching by examples'.[16]

Englishmen had drawn these ideas about the function of history from classical authors such as Polybius and Livy and from humanist Italian thinkers who had developed the theory over the preceding two centuries.[17]

---

[13] *The Annales of Cornelius Tacitus. The Description of Germanie,* trans. Richard Grenewey (London, 1598), dedicatory epistle to Robert Devereux, second earl of Essex.

[14] [I. R.], *Organon reipvblicae* (London, 1605), sig. c4r. Qtd and trans. in Markku Peltonen, *Classical Humanism and Republicanism in English Political Thought, 1570–1640* (Cambridge: Cambridge University Press, 1995), 168–69.

[15] British Library, Add. MS 28001, 117v.

[16] George H. Nadel, 'Philosophy of History before Historicism', *History and Theory* 3.3 (1964): 291–315, esp. 295–98. For a discussion of the shift in the use of *exempla* over the seventeenth century, see Daniel Woolf, 'From Hystories to the Historical: Five Transitions in Thinking about the Past, 1500–1700', in *The Uses of History in Early Modern England,* ed. Paulina Kewes (San Marino, CA: Huntington Library, 2006), 31–68.

[17] 'For that there is no way more easie to reforme and better Men, then the Knowledge of things past ... Knowledge of Histories is a true Discipline and Exercise for the Conduct and managing of the Affaires of a Common-wealth, and ... she onely is the Mistris, and meanes to beare the Variety and inconstancy of Fortune patiently, by reason of the example of another mans aduersities ...'. Polybius, *The History of Polybius the Megalopolitan. The fiue first bookes entire,* trans. Edward Grimeston (London, 1633), 1. See also Livy's introduction in *The Romane historie vvritten by T. Livius of Padua. Also, the Breviaries of L. Florus: with a chronologie to the whole historie: and the*

26 Emasculated Kingship

In *Discourses on Livy* (c. 1513–1519), for example, Niccolò Machiavelli adopted Polybius's explanation of constitutional change as a historically repeating pattern: monarchy and tyranny to aristocracy and oligarchy to democracy and ochlocracy and back again.[18] Bernardo in Francesco Guicciardini's *Dialogue on the Government of Florence* (c. 1521–25) similarly summarised the lessons of reading history:

> For having read so many histories of various nations in ancient and modern times ... it won't be difficult for you to judge what the future will be. For the world is so constituted that everything which exists at present has existed before, under different names, in different times and different places ... [S]omeone with a sharp eye, who knows how to compare and contrast one event with another ... knows how to calculate and measure quite a lot of the future.[19]

In England, we find numerous arguments for the study of history by kings and statesmen alike. King James, in his conduct manual of kingship dedicated to Prince Henry, encouraged his son to be 'well versed' in 'authentick histories and Chronicles' whereby 'yee shall learne experience by Theoricke, applying the bypast things to the present estate, *quia nihil nouum sub sole*' (for there is no new thing under the sun). 'And likewise', he continued, 'by the knowledge of histories, yee shall knowe how to behaue your selfe to all Embasadours and strangers; being able to discourse with them vpon the state of their owne countrey'.[20]

History also bolstered the Renaissance pursuit of civic humanism for statesmen, and especially conceptions of the *vita activa*, or active political

---

Topographie of Rome in old time, trans. Philemon Holland (London, 1600), 2. Nadel, 'Philosophy of History before Historicism', 295 and 305.

History was one of the principal pursuits of the *studia humanitatis*, along with grammar, rhetoric, moral philosophy, and poetry. See Paul Oskar Kristeller, 'Humanism', in *The Cambridge History of Renaissance Philosophy*, ed. C. B. Schmitt, Quentin Skinner, Eckhard Kessler, and Jill Kraye (Cambridge: Cambridge University Press, 1988), 111–38, esp. 113–14; Donald R. Kelley, 'Philosophy and Humanistic Disciplines: The Theory of History', in *Cambridge History of Renaissance Philosophy*, 746–62, esp. 749–50 and 753. For the reach of humanism in England, see Peltonen, *Classical Humanism and Republicanism*; Quentin Skinner, *The Foundations of Modern Political Thought, Volume 1: The Renaissance* (Cambridge: Cambridge University Press, 2002), 193–212.

[18] See J. G. A. Pocock, *The Machiavellian Moment: Florentine Political Thought and the Atlantic Republican Tradition* (Princeton and London: Princeton University Press, 1975), 77–80; Kelley, 'The Theory of History', 753.

[19] Francesco Guicciardini, *Dialogue on the Government of Florence*, ed. Alison Brown (Cambridge: Cambridge University Press, 1994), 16.

[20] *King James VI and I: Political Writings*, ed. Johann P. Sommerville (Cambridge: Cambridge University Press, 1994), 46. Reference to Ecclesiastes 1:9. See Aysha Pollnitz, *Princely Education in Early Modern Britain* (Cambridge: Cambridge University Press, 2015), 344–53.

Tyranny, Manhood, and the Study of History

life pursued for the sake of the commonwealth.[21] English statesmen argued that real political wisdom would be gained from studying the words, deeds, and character of past men, the rise and fall of empires, and the causes and effects of their activities. This wisdom derived from history would aid statesmen in fulfilling their duties to the common good, including the crafting and upholding of good laws and the offering of wise counsel and persuasive orations. In this way, the disciplines of history and ethics frequently aligned with that of rhetoric, whereby men learned judicial or forensic speech attached to the court of law, deliberative or persuasive speech attached to politics, and demonstrative speech devoted to praise or blame.[22]

The infusion and appropriation of classical history, its stories, figures, and exempla, was widespread in seventeenth-century England, often appearing not only in the representation of kings and court culture but also in political speeches in parliament, in letters, and in printed books. Statesmen, scholars, and gentlemen often relied upon historical exempla, which they collected in commonplace books and notebooks from grammar school, university, or private study, to add authority or illustrations in their writing, to aid in the invention or the criticism of arguments, to demonstrate their own learning, and/or to instruct others.[23] References to classical history inundate writings and speeches from the period, and shaped the very structure and design of writings and speeches, such that it would be impossible to identify a statesman or scholar in this period who did not employ historical references or imagery himself. The following chapters focus upon writings or recorded speeches that dwelt upon particular historical exempla in lengthy detail or to great effect.

Alongside these formal political realms, history and its lessons shaped sermons, poetry, drama, imagery, and performances in early Stuart England's wider cultural and political imagination. Stories of Rome had wide appeal, showing up frequently in costly as well as cheap print, in the theatre, in manuscript and oral culture, in visual culture, and in public performances. In addition to classical orations and declamations, grammar school and university students frequently performed classical comedies and tragedies, and created their own academic performances based upon these models. Such exercises were devised to give participants and spectators

---

[21] Peltonen, *Classical Humanism and Republicanism*, 147–48; Pollnitz, *Princely Education*, 5–6.

[22] Brian Vickers, 'Rhetoric and Poetics', in *The Cambridge History of Renaissance Philosophy*, ed. C. B. Schmitt, Quentin Skinner, Eckhard Kessler, and Jill Kraye (Cambridge: Cambridge University Press, 1988), 713–45, esp. 715–17.

[23] Mack, *Elizabethan Rhetoric*, 74–75.

28 Emasculated Kingship

hands-on experience with Latin and Greek, and with ancient history and mythology.[24] But classical poetic and theatrical material was similarly accessible to those not receiving formal education. By 1640, at least fifty-seven Roman history plays had been produced on the public stage in England, and several of these were re-played often in Jacobean theatres.[25] Performances of *Julius Caesar*, for example, were so popular and commonplace that other contemporary dramas frequently included satirical allusions to the play due to the assumed thorough-going knowledge of the play on the part of their audiences. This was even before the first printed version of *Julius Caesar* in 1623.[26]

These history plays and other imaginative historical writings provided a valuable way to directly and indirectly comment on political events and figures, while simultaneously avoiding the threat of censorship. Throughout the Jacobean period, the English government sought to suppress free enquiry and what was considered 'dangerous' or 'libellous' speech by writers, playwrights, printers, and readers through imprisonment, interrogation, fines, public shaming, and even mutilation. Although some scholars have questioned how extensive or comprehensive the machinery of censorship was in Stuart England – for censorship was not evenly nor systematically enforced – literary historians have found that the *fear* of censorship significantly shaped the writing practices of English authors, especially when printing material. Writers often adopted poetic as well as historical writing due to the standard principle in English defamation law called '*mitior sensus*', or literally, the 'milder sense', which stated that if someone said or wrote a phrase that had two common meanings, one more offensive and one less offensive, the court would accept the less offensive. By situating offensive speech within a story of a distant place and time, or using indirection when criticising contemporaries, writers could avoid arrest, imprisonment, trial, and punishment.[27] Historical stories and

---

[24] Jonathan Walker, 'Introduction', in *Early Modern Academic Drama*, Paul D. Streufert and Walker, eds. (New York: Routledge, 2016), 2–5.

[25] Daniel Woolf, *The Idea of History in Early Stuart England: Erudition, Ideology, and the 'Light of Truth' from the Accession of James I to the Civil War* (Toronto: University of Toronto, 1990), 172; Paulina Kewes, 'Julius Caesar in Jacobean England', *The Seventeenth Century* 17 (2002): 155–56.

[26] John Ripley, *Julius Caesar on Stage in England and America, 1599–1973* (Cambridge: Cambridge University Press, 1980), 13–14.

[27] See Debora Shuger, *Censorship and Cultural Sensibility: The Regulation of Language in Tudor-Stuart England* (Philadelphia: University of Pennsylvania Press, 2006), 183. For censorship and manuscript culture, see Noah Millstone, *Manuscript Circulation and the Invention of Politics in Early Stuart England* (Cambridge: Cambridge University Press, 2016). See also Andrew McRae, *Literature, Satire, and the Early Stuart State*; Antony Milton, 'Licensing, Censorship, and Religious

Tyranny, Manhood, and the Study of History

imaginative literature thereby became a primary vehicle of British culture and expression in the seventeenth century for criticising the monarch or discussing sensitive political and religious issues. And because the Stuart monarchs often presented themselves through classical imagery and pageantry, hostile or critical speech crafted through historical themes and examples would have been understandable and effective for seventeenth-century audiences.

In the 1650s, commentators placed such great stock on the influence of the classics upon English statesmen that they blamed their study for the tumultuous and rebellious wars of the decade prior. Thomas Hobbes most famously betrayed this conviction in *Leviathan*:

> It is an easy thing, for men to be deceived, by the specious name of Libertie; ... And when the same errour is confirmed by the authority of men in reputation for their writings in this subject, it is no wonder if it produce sedition, an change of Government. In these westerne parts of the world, we are made to receive our opinions concerning the Institution, and Rights of Common-wealths, from *Aristotle*, *Cicero*, and other men, Greeks and Romanes, ... And by reading of these Greek, and Latine Authors, men from their childhood have gotten a habit (under a false shew of Liberty,) of favouring tumults, and of licentious controlling the actions of their Soveraigns; and again of controlling those controllers, with the effusion of so much blood; as I think I may truly say, there was never any thing so deerly bought, as these Western parts have bought the learning of the Greek and Latine tongues.[28]

Writing to his friend Benjamin Worsley, William Rand concurred with Hobbes's assessment: 'I am of the opinion & have long bin with Mr Hobbs that the reading of such bookes as Livy's History has bin a great rub in the way of the advancement of the Interest of his Leviathanlike Monarchs.'[29] The reading and study of history could be a dangerous activity, leading to views critical of monarchy or even to republican views.

Orthodoxy in Early Stuart England', *Historical Journal* 41 (1998): 625–51. For reader reception of print and authority during the English Revolution, see Jason Peacey, *Print and Public Politics in the English Revolution* (Cambridge: Cambridge University Press, 2013), 116–22. For the revisionist argument against perceptions of a 'single abusive authoritarian system' of censorship, see Cyndia Susan Clegg, *Press Censorship in Jacobean England* (New York: Cambridge, 2001).

[28] Thomas Hobbes, *Leviathan*, ed. Richard Tuck (Cambridge: Cambridge University Press, 1996), 149–50.

[29] Rand to Worsley, 11 Aug. 1651, Hartlib Papers (Sheffield) 62/21/2A. Qutd in Skinner, 'Classical liberty, Renaissance Translation and the English Civil War', in *Visions of Politics*, vol. 2 (Cambridge: Cambridge University Press, 2002), 308–43, esp. 308.

1.2 Masculine Identities in Rome and England

'To base school learning so solidly upon the language and moral principles of Roman writers was to encourage early modern men to think along Roman lines; Roman ideas inherited in early education were an ever-present background against which any thinking about society and politics in adult life would take place.'[30] Few would dispute Freyja Cox Jensen's remarks about the centrality of Roman thought and education for English political life and culture in the seventeenth century, yet not enough has been done to consider how thinking along Roman lines shaped not only political action and moral thought in seventeenth-century England but also fundamental conceptualisations of masculinity, of what in this period it meant to be the ideal aristocratic man. Every chapter in Part I seeks to demonstrate the significance of Roman historical exempla for constructions of masculine identity and of kingship, and for the criticism of tyranny in seventeenth-century England.

Within Roman stories frequently referenced and circulated in this period, images of idealised manhood primarily focused upon three male roles: warrior, law-giver, and father. Upon the battlefield, the ideal man proved his physical courage, cunning, and leadership over other men; in the senate house or court, he crafted and upheld just laws and served the interests of the common good above his own personal desires; and within his household, he commanded respect, demanded obedience, orderliness, and chastity from his wife, children, and servants, and ensured their protection.

Roman conceptions of the ideal man, especially of the warrior, often fit well with the chivalric and baronial ideals that historians have already identified as important to noblemen of the early seventeenth century and, decades later, to those supporting the Long Parliament and subsequent parliamentary cause of the 1640s. The king served as the head of the community of honour and the fount of honour; his military role was fundamental to his authority and his image.[31] Throughout the seventeenth

---

[30] Jensen, *Reading the Roman Republic*, 29–30.

[31] In 1621, James had defended the court of chivalry as 'being immediately derived from us, who are the fountaine of all honoure'. Qtd in Mervyn James, *Society, Politics and Culture: Studies in Early Modern England* (Cambridge: Cambridge University Press, 1986), 380. Military and heraldic treatises from the period frequently touted that 'the power and authority to bestow honour resteth only with the prince'. See William Segar, *Honor Military, and Civill* (London, 1602), 113; James Cleland, *Propaideia, or the Institution of a Young Noble Man* (Oxford, 1607), 4; Francis Markham, *The Booke of Honour; or, Five Decads of Epistles of Honour* (London, 1625), 11.

Tyranny, Manhood, and the Study of History

century, conceptions of 'true honour and nobility' served as far more than vague synonyms for moral worth and talent, even as particular medieval codes of honour related to lineage and competitive assertive violence became contested. 'Honour' entailed a particular catalogue of male virtues including physical courage, constancy, and liberality, which could be indexed to the medieval chivalric as well as the classical past.[32] Thus pamphlets of honour and warfare, such as William Segar's *Honor Military, and Civill* (1602), emphasised that princes be prepared for peace and war by conjoining 'good Lawes vnto Armes: th'one command, th'other to execute', both for the defensive protection of their subjects and the glory and growth of their regimes. Preparation for arms required physical skill and self-discipline as well as study, including being 'well studied in histories', for one must learn military lessons from one's ancestors, ancient and medieval. Moreover, Segar argued, those who 'so desireth to knowe the originall name and dignitie of Knighthood' must be informed about the classical practices of the 'Romanes, among whom Martiall discipline was first esteemed, and titles guien to men for valorus merit'.[33]

Each of these roles of warrior, law-giver, and father required self-mastery, characterised by rationality and temperance. Similarly, in each of these roles, the ideal man exhibited the virtue of justice, through which the principles of society and its common bonds were thought to be maintained. Cicero's discussion of justice in *De Officiis* provides a good foundational definition of this virtue for the early modern period, as this work was daily presented to European schoolchildren alongside the Bible and formed the cornerstone of Renaissance conceptions of the *vita activa*.[34] Cicero declared justice to be the 'crowning glory of the virtues' and that by which 'men are called good men'. The duties of justice were manifold, both within the commonwealth and in regards to one's enemies in war, but Cicero defined these duties very broadly as keeping men from harming one another unless provoked by wrong, and leading men to use

---

[32] Anna Bryson, *From Courtesy to Civility: Changing Codes of Conduct in Early Modern England* (Oxford: Clarendon Press, 1998), 235–37; William Hunt, 'Civic Chivalry and the English Civil War', in *The Transmission of Culture in Early Modern Europe*, ed. Anthony Grafton and Ann Blair (Philadelphia: University of Pennsylvania Press, 1990), 204–37, esp. 208; James, *Society, Politics and Culture*; Brendan Kane, *The Politics and Culture of Honour in Britain and Ireland, 1541–1641* (Cambridge: Cambridge University Press, 2010).

[33] Segar, *Honor Military, and Civill*, 1, 45, 51

[34] Richard Tuck, 'Humanism and Political Thought', in *The Impact of Humanism on Western Europe during the Renaissance*, ed. A Goodman and Angus Mackay (London and New York: Routledge, 1990), 43–65, esp. 43; Quentin Skinner, *Reason and Rhetoric in the Philosophy of Hobbes* (Cambridge: Cambridge University Press, 1996), 76–83.

32   Emasculated Kingship

common possessions for the common good, private possessions as their own.[35] The virtue of justice thereby related significantly to self-mastery, which enabled one to fulfill one's obligations to the community. In Book III of *De Officiis*, Cicero extended his definition of justice into a universally binding law, whereby a man ought never to use violence or theft against any other human for his personal advantage. This extension of justice included protection even of the humblest and those of poorest fortune, such as slaves who 'must be required to work' and yet 'must be given their due'.[36] The reiteration and application of this view appeared frequently in humanist writings from the last sixteenth through seventeenth century. The town clerk of Tewkesbury, John Barston, for example, explained Cicero's understanding of justice in *The Safegarde of Societie* (1576) as a hallmark of the virtuous magistrate: '[I]nsomuch as all men depend on him [the magistrate] for iustuce, and all haue referred the vttermost of all to him alone,' Barston argued, the magistrate 'must forget his priuate being, so long as his office lasteth, and should more esteeme public vtilitie than his own lucre.'[37] As will be discussed in greater detail later, the failure to practise justice became frequently cited as a characteristic of tyranny.

The roles of warrior, law-giver, and father thereby required autonomy, dominance, and the exercise of the virtues; not just any male could fulfil these conditions. In Rome as well as early Stuart England, manhood required the age of full adulthood and usually marriage or the acquisition of a household under one's control. Similarly, full Roman manhood required aristocratic status, while in England, conduct writers very often related patriarchal standards of masculinity to the ideals of gentility, civility, and aristocratic culture.[38] Classical Latin texts usually referred to

---

[35] Marcus Tullius Cicero, *On Duties*, trans. Walter Miller, Loeb Classical Library 30 (Cambridge, MA: Harvard University Press, 1913), 21–23.

[36] Cicero, *On Duties*, 45, 207–209. See Martha C. Nussbaum, 'Duties of Justice, Duties of Material Aid: Cicero's Problematic Legacy', *Journal of Political Philosophy* 8.2 (Jun. 2000): 10–17; Dean Hammer, *Roman Political Thought: From Cicero to Augustine* (Cambridge: Cambridge UP, 2014), 39–43.

[37] John Barston, *The safegarde of societie: describing the institution of lawes and policies, to preserue euery felowship of people by degrees of ciuill gouernements* (London, 1576), fo. 82v.

[38] For Rome, see J. Albert Harrill, 'Invective against Paul (2 Cor. 10:10), the Physiognomics of the Ancient Slave Body, and the Greco-Roman Rhetoric of Manhood', in *Antiquity and Humanity: Essays on Ancient Religion and Philosophy* (Tübingen: Mohr Siebeck, 2001): 189–213, esp. 191; Jennifer Larson, 'Paul's Masculinity', *Journal of Biblical Literature* 123.1 (Spring 2004): 85–97, esp. 91; Myles McDonnell, *Roman Manliness: Virtus and the Roman Republic* (Cambridge: Cambridge University Press, 2006), 177–80. For England, see Todd W. Reeser, *Moderating Masculinity in Early Modern Culture* (Chapel Hill: North Carolina Studies in the Roman Languages and Literatures, 2006), 88–101; Alexandra Shepard, Meanings of Manhood in Early Modern England (Oxford: Oxford University Press, 2003), 34–38 and 87–89; Blair Worden, *The*

Tyranny, Manhood, and the Study of History 33

such an aristocratic male as *vir*, a designation which formed the root of the word for manliness or virtue, *virtus*. Unlike a *homo*, which was the generic or sometimes hostile word used for a person in ancient Rome, the word *vir* often entailed a mature man of the upper class who wielded legitimate power as a *paterfamilias*, the oldest living male of a *familia*.[39] The opposition between *vir* and non-*vir* (between 'real man' and woman, boy, slave, effeminate, or beast) revolved largely around the issue of whether one was a free man exercising power and authority over oneself and others, or whether one was subject to someone else's power and authority.[40] A man's public reputation for *virtus* was central to his ability to wield power and was also highly fragile. As scholars have demonstrated, in classical Rome (and also in Stuart England) spoken and written invectives frequently labelled others as legitimate or illegimite political actors based upon polarising characterisations of men as *viri* possessing masculine traits or as non-*viri* failing in masculinity.

The Roman concepts of *vir* and *virtus*, including their grammatical distinctions and their social meanings, were recognised and appropriated in seventeenth-century England. Adam Littleton's celebrated *Lingua Latinae Liber Didionarius Quadripartitus* (1678) not only distinguished *vir* from 'child', 'woman', 'slave', and 'brute', but provided a number of English to Latin translations which underscored *vir* as signifying mature

---

Sound of Virtue: Philip Sidney's Arcadia *and Elizabethan Politics* (New Haven, CT: Yale University Press, 1996), 23–37.

[39] Although a Roman son could only become a *paterfamilias* on the death of his father, the Republic's institutions allowed young Roman men to transition from being sons under bondage in the private sphere of the *familia* to being *viri* of equal status to the *paterfamilias* in the public sphere through military service. Roman youth were thought to move from their childhood (*pueritia*) to adulthood (*inventa*) at the age of seventeen, which corresponds to the age at which young men normally began military service. The right of passage marking this transition included the removal of childhood garments (the *toga praetexta* and the *bulla*) to don the garment of manhood, *toga virilis*. Myles McDonnell explains that during the republican period, 'this rite of passage occurred when the *paterfamilias* deemed the youth mature enough to fight in the army'. See *Roman Manliness*, 177–80. As Richard Alston argues, however, the term *vir* became more problematic in its application to career soldiers in the last centuries of the Republic due to their decline in social status. By the first century, several writers penned hostile commentary against soldiers, deeming them non-*viri* whose power threatened society. See 'Arms and the Man: Soldiers, Masculinity and Power in Republican and Imperial Rome', in *When Men Were Men: Masculinity, Power, and Identity in Classical Antiquity*, ed. Lin Foxhall and John Salmon (London and New York: Routledge, 1998), 205–24, esp. 207.

[40] Erik Gunderson, 'Discovering the Body in Roman Oratory', in *Parchments of Gender: Deciphering the Bodies of Antiquity*, ed. Maria Wyke (Oxford: Oxford University Press, 1998), 169–90, esp. 170; Larson, 'Paul's Masculinity', 93.

34   Emasculated Kingship

manhood.[41] Littleton's definition of *virtus* underscored the broad, semantic range of the term, defining it as 'Vertue, force, power, strength, … courage, bravery, gallantry', as well as 'value, worth, authority; merit, desert'.[42]

In printed works we find writers frequently explicating the meaning of *vir* and *virtus* in similar ways. As a political treatise drawing heavily upon classical sources, the English edition of Pierre La Primaudaye's *French Academie* (1618), for example, described the fifth estate of man, or adulthood, through the language of *vir*: 'Of the name of this age, I meane of this Latine word *Vir*, did vertue first take her name, which in Latine is *Virtus*: because this word *Vir*, signifieth him that is in the age of virilitie, or mans estate, as if you would say, apt to be a minister and practitioner of virtue'. During this 'age of virilitie', according to the treatise, a man should possess all 'honestie and vertue', including 'prudence, temperance, fortitude and iustice … '.[43] Another work which emphasised the ancient connection between conceptions of manhood and martial prowess was William Gouge's sermon on *The Dignitie of Chivalry* (1626). Gouge, a puritan rector known to draw large crowds in London, had already written at length about household order and the proper roles of men as husbands and fathers in his treatise, *Of Domesticall Duties* (1622). Preaching on II Chronicles 8:9 before the Artillery Company of London, Gouge described the Israelites deemed 'Men of Warre' as 'No Slaues, no Captiues, no Aliens, no Forrainers, but Fre [*sic*] men, Free-borne, Natiue Subiects, Naturall Citizens.'[44] According to Gouge, these men were 'distinguished from the vulgar, common sort of men' in the very language that the Hebrews, Greeks, and Latins used to describe them: The Greeks distinguished between ἄνθρωπος and ἄνηρ, much as 'the Latines betwixt *Vir* and *Homo*', with *vir* signifying 'of virtue & prowess'. Gouge then lamented that, unlike these languages of old, English was so 'penurious' that 'it wanteth fit words to expresse this difference'.[45]

---

[41] Adam Littleton, *Linguae Latinae Liber Didionarius Quadripartitus* (London, 1678), sigs. T3r and CCCCC2v. Compare, for example, 'To play the man. *Viriliter ago, virum se præstare*' to 'A man or woman. *Homo*'.

[42] Ibid., sig. CCCCC2v.

[43] Pierre La Primaudaye, *The French academie Fully discoursed and finished in foure bookes.* (London, 1618), 234.

[44] II Chronicles 8:9, 'But of the children of Israel did Solomon make no servants for his work; but they were men of war, and chief of his captains, and captains of his chariots and horsemen' (King James Version).

[45] William Gouge, *The dignitie of chivalry; Set forth in a Sermon preached before the Artillery Company of London, 13. Iune 1626* (London, 1626), 4–6.

Tyranny, Manhood, and the Study of History   35

As Gouge's sermon attests, seventeenth-century Englishmen not only recognised the historic and linguistic distinctions associated with *vir* but translated and incorporated its significance into contemporary discourses concerning masculinity and Christianity. One particularly fruitful example can be found in a printed sermon from 1651 by the Cambridge professor of divinity and popular London preacher Richard Holdsworth. In his explication of James 1:12, 'Blessed is the man that endureth temptation ... ', Holdsworth focused on the meaning of 'man' in the classical and Christian heritage, emphasising that the word 'is not ἄνθρωπος but ἄνηρ, it is not *Beatus homo*, but *Beatus vir* ... *Homo* is a word of *nature*, *Vir* is a *word* that betokeneth *vertue* ... '. The word *vir*, Holdsworth explained, normally had three significations related to '*Sex, Age, Dignity*'. In this particular verse of Scripture, he argued, the focus primarily was on 'Dignity' and the relationship between *vir* and *virtus*, a relationship which he described by citing classical and ecclesiastical authors:

> Whatsoever comes neere, and toucheth upon *vertue*, is *Masculine*, and *Xenophon* gives the reason of it, because sayth he, by *nature* both the *body* and the *mind* of *man*, are so framed, as to be better enabled to *indure* labour, and *paine*, and travell and *torment*, then the *weaker* Sex. Then if we look to *Ecclesiasticall* Writers, it is frequent in the Fathers. Take that of *Lactantius* for all, he observes that *Vir* and *Virtus* come both from the same. Therefore it is observed in the three *Learned* Languages, that the same word signifieth *Valour* and *Manhood*, and *Fortitude*, the same word signifies to be a *Man*, and to be *Valiant*. Then if we come to the witnesse of the *Scripture*, there is frequent use of the word to call a *valiant, stout, godly, zealous* man, indefinitely by the name of a *man, Jer.* 5.1. when God bids them run up and downe the Streets of *Jerusalem. See if you can find a man*. It is not meant simply, if you can find *Hominem*, but *Virum*, a man, a *godly* man, one that *executeth judgement*, and *righteousnesse*, there was a multitude of *hominum*, abundance of *men*, but there was a great *paucity virorum*, of *vertuous* men.[46]

Importantly, this passage highlights both how Scriptural writers Christianised Roman conceptions of masculinity and how Englishmen followed their example. The word *vir* not only denoted 'man' to the exclusion of other groups based on age or sex but also the qualities or excellences of that man, which would include Christian as well as pagan virtues.[47] Notably,

---

[46] Richard Holdsworth, *The Valley of Vision, or A clear sight of sundry sacred Truths. Delivered in Twenty-one Sermons* (London, 1651), 189–90. My citation reflects corrected pagination.

[47] Holdsworth was careful to argue in this particular passage of Scripture, however, that the term *vir* here signified virtue without the exclusion of children or women, for if one looks to the example of martyrs, 'God did put *Spirit*, and vertue, and *courage*, into the mouths and hearts of *Babes*, and *Sucklings* ... ; they have a *Masculine*, and manly spirit given them to *indure* suffering'. Likewise

Emasculated Kingship

most of these examples also defined *virtus* both as a particular excellence (martial prowess) and as a broad ethical term signifying a number of excellences necessary for ideal manliness (i.e. justice, temperance, wisdom).

The definition of *vir* and its attachment to the concept of *virtus* formed a significant part of the classical vocabulary and reading of seventeenth-century educated culture. Constructions of manliness, thus conceived, relied upon the notion of men exerting autonomy, authority, and moral excellence in numerous arenas of life, but questions of how such manliness should be practised, where, and by whom generated great cultural and social contestation in the classical world and in the seventeenth century. Classical humanist thought of the Stuart period especially reflects these questions and the influence of ancient political constructions of manhood upon English political thought and activity. Numerous writers articulated the necessity of living within a political realm in which *virtus* could be exercised through public service.

In *De Officiis*, Cicero taught the 'whole glory of virtue is in activity'; while numerous professions must pursue study due to their occupation with the search for truth, 'to be drawn by study away from the active life is contrary to moral duty'.[48] Moreover, Cicero maintained that the virtuous man must pursue this activity in service to the common, rather than private, good.[49] This emphasis upon the *vita activa*, or *negotium*, the life of action through public service as particularly masculine, became restated a significant number of times in political writings and speeches in the late Elizabethan through the Stuart period, as Markku Peltonen and others have demonstrated.[50] Peltonen highlighted the thought of Thomas Scott in the early 1620s, for example, who emphasised that the English commonwealth must be cured and eradicated from its corruption through reversing its values, esteeming frugality over luxury, and allowing members of the body politic to engage in the *vita activa*, for '*virtus in actione consistit*', Scott contended, and virtuous action is the chief quality of true nobility.[51] Such activity lay in the pursuit of martial valour on the

---

women such as Agatho and Apollonia were granted '*Heroick* spirits' to endure tribulation. For our purposes, however, these cases seem to be exceptions that prove the rule. See Holdsworth, *The Valley of Vision*, 192.

[48] '... *cuius studio a rebus gerendis abduci contra officium est. Virtutis enim laus omnis in actione consistit*', Cicero, *On Duties*, 20–21.

[49] Ibid., 156.

[50] Markku Peltonen, *Classical Humanism and Republicanism*, 18–22; Richard Cust, 'The 'Public Man' in Late Tudor and Early Stuart England', in *The Politics of the Public Sphere in Early Modern England* (Manchester: Manchester University Press 2012), 116–43, esp. 118.

[51] Ibid., 243–47.

Tyranny, Manhood, and the Study of History   37

battlefield, in the political arena of parliament or as councillor to the king, and in the complex network of political association and discussions found in Stuart England in group gatherings, such as through the 'Mermaid Club' or 'Sireniacs' from the Inns of Court.[52] Such action often involved the *ars rhetorica*, by which statesmen would attempt to foster their involvement in the 'commonweal' through persuasion and counsel.[53] As Francis Bacon described, the 'ancient times' held 'both the incorporation and inseparable conjunction of counsel with kings, and the wise and politic use of counsel by kings'.[54]

Advocates of royal absolutism in the seventeenth century, however, defended a political order in which the subject's active role appeared greatly circumscribed. Obedience became the chief moral virtue touted in absolutist defences of monarchy throughout the period. James's *Trew Law of Free Monarchies* (1598) described the performance of obedience as an essential and natural duty of subjects, and labelled the displacement of kings or the seizing of their powers as an abhorrent, sinful, and unnatural act, an inversion of 'the order of all Law and reason', whereby 'the commanded may be made to command their commander, the iudged to iudge their Iudge, and they that are gouerned, to gouerne their time about their Lord and gouernour'.[55] With obedience, works such as William Willymat's *A loyal svbiects looking-glasse* (1604) placed 'fear' as a second desirable quality of the subject, for the 'dutie' of fear ensured subjects would 'haue an eye vnto the good and safetie of higher powers and magistrats,... euen like as the good and dutifull child is afraide to offend or incur the displeasure of his good, kind, louing, and naturall parents, or as the good and louing wife is afraid to misbehaue her selfe either by saying or doing any thing that her louing and kind husband may iustly take offence at'.[56] Accounts emphasising deferential obedience provided few discussions of meaningful active service to the commonwealth for statesmen who served in local or public office, apart from the few elite allowed

---

[52] Ibid., 248–54, 258–59; Michelle O'Callaghan, "Talking Politics': Tyranny, Parliament, and Christopher Brooke's the Ghost of Richard the Third (1614)', *The Historical Journal* 41.1 (Mar. 1998): 97–120, esp. 101–3.

[53] David Colclough, *Freedom of Speech in Early Stuart England* (Cambridge: Cambridge University Press, 2005), 39–40. For the classical inheritance of rhetoric from Cicero and Quintilian, see Skinner, *Reason and Rhetoric*, 66–74.

[54] *Bacon's Essays*, ed. F. G. Selby (London and New York: Macmillan, 1892), 52. See John Guy, 'The Rhetoric of Counsel in Early Modern England', in *Tudor Political Culture*, ed. Dale Hoak (Cambridge: Cambridge University Press, 1995), 292–310.

[55] *King James VI and I: Political Writings*, 76.

[56] William Willymat, *A loyal subiects looking-glasse, or a good subiects direction* (London, 1604), 24.

38 Emasculated Kingship

into the King's bedchamber or Privy Council. Rhetoric mystifying kingship often promoted claims of the supremacy of bishops and kings over parliaments and the denial of the authority of parliament to counsel the king on matters of policy.[57]

Moreover, such accounts portrayed English statesmen in positions of significant dependence upon and deference towards the monarch, a view which contrasted with Roman conceptualisations of autonomy and became exacerbated by the mystification and exercise of monarchical prerogative over the following decades. James's *Declaration* (1622), for example, published shortly after he dissolved parliament for discussing foreign policy and the Spanish Match, asserted that the House must not 'meddle with matters of gouernment, or mysteries of State' concerning the traditional realms of war and foreign policy, and that parliamentary speech in general 'deriued from the grace and permission of Our Ancestours and Vs'.[58] A vogue for Tacitean and Senecan depictions of court corruption in the Stuart period represented how many contemporaries understood the corruption and dangers of the absolutist developing state.[59] Within the Stuart court, like the Roman Principate, it was argued that active and virtuous statesman would become an image of bygone times in an imperial court filled with flatterers and unscrupulous statesmen seeking personal glory through princely favours. Thomas Gainsford's exposition in *Obseruations of State, and Millitary affaires for the most parte collected owt of Cornelius Tacitus* (c. 1612), which circulated in manuscript, well represents the pessimistic view of human nature and court politics articulated within this framework, wherein humans appear mainly ignoble and motivated by ambition and avarice. 'Of the corruption of times: of the conditions of men; nothing was euer established, but what pleased the humors of *Princes*', Gainsford maintained. Princes rule by 'Polleticks of State' which seek to legitimise even oppressive laws through 'adulteratt excuses of cowstome, establishment of peace, preuention of innouation, contempt of regall awthority, despertion of good orders, neglect of superiors, and discouery of turbulent spiritts'.[60] In such a climate, 'To perswade a Prince,

---

[57] See, e.g., O'Callaghan, 'Talking Politics', 109–10.

[58] *King James VI and I: Political Writings*, 261.

[59] See, e.g., Alan T. Bradford, 'Stuart Absolutism and the "Utility" of Tacitus', in *Huntington Library Quarterly* 46.2 (Spring 1983): 127–55; J. H. M. Salmon, 'Seneca and Tacitus in Jacobean England', in *The Mental World of the Jacobean Court*, ed. Linda Levy Peck (Cambridge: Cambridge University Press, 1991), 169–88; Mary F. Tenney, 'Tacitus in the Politics of Early Stuart England', *The Classical Journal* 37.3 (Dec. 1941): 151–63.

[60] Thomas Gainsford, *Obseruations of State, and millitary affaires for the most parte collected owt of Cornelius Tacitus* (1612), 10. Huntington Library EL 6857. I am indebted to the Duke and

Tyranny, Manhood, and the Study of History

what is meet, is a point of some difficullty: To flatter any Prince needeth small endeuor.'[61] The response often provided by these neo-Stoic writers frequently promoted deference and withdrawal from public life. As Gainsford summarised, 'The safest way to liue vnder Tyrants is to doe nothing, becawse of nothing no man is to yeeld an accownt.'[62]

As Thomas Cogswell and Alastair Bellany have indicated, this vocabulary of permission and deference contrasted with the ideas and practices of political engagement in the period. This included MPs, for example, who were driven by ideas as much as by interest and motivated in many ways by the eager sharing and growing consumption of 'news' in the 1620s and beyond.[63] The more that the Stuart monarchs appeared to threaten the ability of statesmen to play an active role in the political life of England, through activities including the dissolution of parliaments and the pursuance of peace, the easier it became for men to view themselves as robbed in the exercise of *virtus*, of masculine pursuits for the benefit of the public good.

1.3 Classical Tyranny and the Failed Man

Declarations of the *vita activa*, often based upon classicised images of masculine activity on the battlefield, in the senate house, and in the household, afforded images of *virtus* connected to moral excellences within these realms. Similarly, images of the failed man and the failed ruler in Roman texts and their English appropriations revolved around these arenas of manliness and formed a significant vocabulary of counsel, censure, and criticism. In its narrowest definition, the Roman tyrant received this derogatory title either through the usurpation of power or by unjust and wicked practice. The former, *tyrannus ex defectu tituli*, would rise to power through force or the use of terror; the latter, *tyrannus ex parte exercitii*, was one initially right in power who committed tyrannical and unjust actions. In classical texts, both types of tyrants were often imagined and maligned as failed men. Tyrants by usurpation caused harm to others for personal

---

Duchess of Sutherland for their generosity in allowing me to view this manuscript at their estate in Merton, St. Boswell's, Roxburghshire. For reason of state, see Maurizio Viroli, *From Politics to Reason of State* (Cambridge: Cambridge University Press, 1992).

[61] Gainsford, *Obseruations*, p. 23.   [62] Ibid., p. 34.

[63] Thomas Cogswell, *The Blessed Revolution: English Politics and the Coming of War, 1621–1624* (Cambridge: Cambridge University Press, 1989), esp. 318–21. The tie between news and political engagement is also shown in Alastair Bellany, *The Politics of Court Scandal in Early Modern England: News Culture and the Overbury Affair, 1603–1660* (Cambridge: Cambridge University Press, 2002), 74–135.

40   Emasculated Kingship

gain, thereby transgressing the laws of justice. Simultaneously, the force of arms these tyrants employed to achieve conquest or to incite terror was often linked to personal moral failings such as rashness, cruelty, and intemperate anger. Tyrants by wicked activity could similarly possess these same moral failings, but they could also possess their opposites – the tyrant who acted in a wicked manner might exhibit cowardice rather than rashness, for example, or the lack of firmness and righteous anger necessary to order one's inferiors and chastise wrongdoers. The primary examples of tyranny explored below and in the following chapters adopted this range of language and usually included rulers who fit the definition of tyranny in both realms; indeed, by the thirteenth century, the word 'tyrant' in the English language already signified both types of unjust ruler.[64] However, the early Stuart appropriations of classical stories explored in this book more often highlighted the moral failings of a tyrant than his unlawful rise to power.

Classical and Renaissance discourses of tyranny and its distinctions often adopted antithetical rhetoric which opposed the figure of the king to that of the tyrant and, simultaneously, either to characterisations of the ideal, masculine man or to the failed, emasculated man. This antithetical rhetoric emphasised the opposing qualities and defects of kings and tyrants, and was usually based upon especially Greek understandings of tyranny as a perversion of monarchy, which Roman and English writers later adopted. For Xenophon, an early Greek authority on tyranny, the central distinction between the king and tyrant was the rule of law. In a brief dialogue he constructed between Pericles and Alcibiades, two prominent citizens of Athens, Xenophon emphasised that kings rule according to laws that have been created through the persuasion of citizens. Xenophon characterised force, however, as the opposite of persuasion and the negation of law; the tyrant 'constrains the weaker to do whatever he chooses, not by persuasion but by force'.[65]

Plato's *Republic* presented the fullest psychological and moral analysis of the tyrannical man, focusing upon the order or disorder of the tripartite

---

[64] See *Oxford English Dictionary*, 'tyrant, n. 1. One who seizes upon the sovereign power in a state without legal right; an absolute ruler; a usurper . . . 3. A king or ruler who exercises his power in an oppressive, unjust, or cruel manner; a despot. 4. a. Any one who exercises power or authority oppressively, despotically, or cruelly; one who treats those under his control tyrannically. 4. b. By extension: Any one who acts in a cruel, violent, or wicked manner; a ruffian, desperado; a villain. Hence as a term of reproach.'

[65] Xenophon, *Memorabilia. Oeconomicus. Symposium. Apology*, trans. E. C. Marchant, O. J. Todd, revised by Jeffrey Henderson, Loeb Classical Library 168 (Cambridge, MA: Harvard University Press, 2013), I.40–45, pp. 38–41.

Tyranny, Manhood, and the Study of History

soul, and particularly, whether the ruler was himself governed by his reason or his appetites.[66] In Book IX, Socrates explained that the tyrannical man, like the drunken, lustful, or insane man, is ruled utterly by the appetitive or lowest order of the soul, causing his 'beastly and savage part' to not 'hold back from any terrible murder or from any kind of food or act. But, rather, erotic love lives like a tyrant within him, in complete anarchy and lawlessness as his sole ruler, and drives him, as if he were a city, to dare anything that will provide sustenance for itself and the unruly mob around it.'[67] This bars the tyrant from freedom as well as true friendship, as he lives internally enslaved and emasculated by fears and erotic desires of all kinds which he cannot satisfy, and externally is 'always a master to one man or a slave to another' in pursuit of these passions. Socrates further maintained that, already 'envious, untrustworthy, unjust, friendless, impious, host and nurse to every kind of vice' as a private man, the tyrant's 'ruling makes him even more so'. This makes the polity under a tyrant most wretched.[68]

Whereas Xenophon identified tyrants according to their rule by force instead of law, and Plato according to the disordering of the ruler's soul, Aristotle held the fundamental distinction between a king and a tyrant to be whether a man ruled in his people's interest or his own.[69] Aristotle's initial description of tyranny was very brief, but later in the *Politics*, he did provide a somewhat fuller description of how tyrannical states are usually preserved. The tyrant stirs up war and keeps his people impoverished, Aristotle explained, in order that they might be too busy and too in need of a leader to oppose him; moreover, the tyrant is distrustful of friends, loves the flatterer, and hates the proud or free-spirited person. And under a tyranny, one will find 'dominance of women in the homes ... and lack of discipline among the slaves', both marks of disorder and the loss of manly rule in the state.[70]

Each of these particular Greek visions of classical tyranny – the tyrant who rules by force in a lawless manner, the tyrant who is governed by his own appetites, or the tyrant who seeks private over public gain – denotes the tyrant as failing fundamentally in his masculinity, and each of these definitions can be found in Roman as well as much later English accounts of tyranny. English statesmen accessed these political concepts through

---

[66] For a helpful analysis of these distinctions, see Bushnell, *Tragedies of Tyrants*, 7–36, 48.

[67] *Republic*, trans. G. M. A. Grube, revised by C. D. C. Reeve, in *Plato: Complete Works*, ed. John M. Cooper (Indianapolis and Cambridge: Hackett, 1997), IX.571d–575a, pp. 1180–83.

[68] Ibid., 576a, 579a–580a, p. 1184 and 1187–88.

[69] Aristotle, *Politics*, trans. H. Rackham, Loeb Classical Library 264 (Cambridge, MA: Harvard University Press, 1932), IV.VIII.1295a10–15, pp. 324–27.

[70] Ibid., V.IX.1313b20–1314a5, pp. 460–63.

42 Emasculated Kingship

Greek as well as Roman texts, for very often, popular Roman writers such as Livy, Sallust, or Cicero presented a combination of these failed or immoral qualities as part of their descriptions and condemnations of tyranny. Examinations of Livy's and Sallust's histories are presented in detail in what follows. It is important first to consider briefly Cicero's account of tyranny, as his dialogues and political writings were foundational for seventeenth-century Englishmen and those particularly committed to a vision of classical republican thought.

In his attacks on the violence and greed of the late Roman Republic and pronouncements on the assassination of Caesar, Cicero described tyranny as a pseudo-state, derived from the degeneration of just constitutional forms due to man's frailty and, in particular, his ambition for power.[71] The best ruled state, as the interlocutor Scipio describes in *De Re Publica*, is that ruled by the virtuous: 'For then the man who rules others is not himself a slave to any passion, but has already acquired for himself all those qualities to which he is training and summoning his fellows. Such a man imposes no laws upon the people that he does not obey himself, but puts his own life before his fellow-citizens as their law.'[72] In the pseudo-state of tyranny, however, the unjust ruler seeks private gain rather than the common good. It mattered not when it came to defining tyranny if the state was ruled by the one, few, or many, for tyrants within any of these constitutional forms would seek private ends, and they would gain or maintain their power through instilling fear by the use of force; Cicero characterised tyrannical rulers as living in perpetual fear of assassination, conspiracy, and revolt due to their subjects' hatred.[73] Cicero's examples of the tyranny of single rulers included Tarquin the Proud and Julius Caesar; the tyranny of the few included the Decemvirs under Appius Claudius, and Cicero's discussion of the tyranny of the many provided few historical examples but relied heavily upon Plato's analysis of the tyrannical mob in the *Republic*.[74] Within this account, thereby, we find a mixing of insights similar to Xenophon, Aristotle, and Plato.[75]

---

[71] Cicero, *On Duties*, 27.

[72] Cicero, *On the Republic. On the Laws*, trans. Clinton W. Keyes, Loeb Classical Library 213 (Cambridge, MA: Harvard University Press, 1928), I.XXXIV.52–53, p. 79.

[73] Cicero, *On Duties*, II.23–25, pp. 190–93; Neal Wood, *Cicero's Social and Political Thought* (Berkeley: University of California Press, 1991), 155–57.

[74] Cicero, *On the Republic*, I.44, I. 58, II. 46, II.62, III.44, pp. 69–71, 87, 155–56, 174–75, 220–21. For an analysis of these historical examples, see Tarquin the Proud, Section I.5; Julius Caesar, Section 7.1; Appius Claudius, Chapter 2.

[75] Although, as Mary Nyquist has emphasised, because the experience of Roman slavery and languages of antityrannicism were shaped in a highly militaristic context of conquest, they differ in significant ways from Athenian antityrannical discourses. See *Arbritrary Rule: Slavery, Tyranny, and the Power of Life and Death* (Chicago: University of Chicago Press, 2013), esp. 49–54. Cicero was most likely

Tyranny, Manhood, and the Study of History 43

Referring to Tarquin the Proud, the last Roman king overthrown by Junius Brutus following the rape of Lucretia, Cicero explained how the monarchical form of government could easily degenerate into tyranny:

> For as soon as this king turned to a mastery less just than before, he instantly became a tyrant; no creature more vile or horrible than a tyrant, or more hateful to gods and men, can be imagined; for, though he bears a human form, yet he surpasses the most monstrous of the wild beasts in the cruelty of his nature. For how could the name of human being rightly be given to a creature who desires no community of justice, no partnership in human life with his fellow-citizens – aye, even with any part of the human race?[76]

Within this passage, Cicero emphasised the damaging effects and vileness of tyranny for the community and the tyrant himself. We have already seen that Cicero held justice to be the 'crowning glory of the virtues', that by which 'men are called good men', and a universally binding law. Cicero's definition of justice as keeping men from harming one another unless provoked by wrong, and leading men to use common possessions for the common good, private possessions as their own, related directly to his definition of tyranny, for the tyrant was one who broke these rules of justice. This failure in the virtue of justice thereby threatened the community and the tyrant's relationship to his fellow men – the very fabric of a cooperative society. Simultaneously, Cicero described the tyrant as forfeiting not only human community but his own humanity, and the dual languages of manhood and bestiality in the above quotation should be noted. Although appearing a man, the tyrant has surpassed wild beasts in his cruelty, according to Cicero, descending not only from the standards of ideal men (*virorum*) but even from the status of human person (*hominis*).[77]

As we will see, classical texts and their seventeenth-century appropriations often portrayed the tyrant as not only failing in manliness but as 'degenerating' like other failed men into a state of bestiality, slavishness, effeminacy, and/or petulance. One often finds an elision of these concepts in Roman writings, especially in political discourses and invectives. In a discussion of manly bravery and the endurance of pain in Cicero's *Tusculan Disputations*, for example, the ideals of true manhood are said to include the mastery of oneself and manly conduct such as endurance,

---

acquainted with the positions of these writers through the traditions of the schools. As a youth, he went to Greece to study rhetoric and philosophy with Diodotus, the Peripatetics, and the Academics.

[76] Cicero, *On the Republic*, II.XXVI.48, pp. 158–59.   [77] See also Nyquist, *Arbitrary Rule*, 50.

44   Emasculated Kingship

courage, and greatness of soul, which 'not only brings the soul under submission, but actually serves somehow to mitigate pain as well'.[78] The disputation continues by describing those who cannot endure pain as unmanly, servile, and womanish. The 'principal precaution to be observed in the matter of pain', the speaker claims, 'is to do nothing in a despondent, cowardly, slothful, servile or womanish spirit, and before all to resist and spurn those Philoctetean outcries ... What is more disgraceful for a man [*viro*] than womanish weeping?'[79] Those who failed in the performance of manliness were rhetorically reduced into one or several of the broader categories of non-male, including slave, woman, child, or beast.

Emperors or dictatorial rulers who degenerated into one of these non-male categories not only undermined their own masculinity but simultaneously emasculated those in their realm, according to classical historians. To survive in the tyrannical regime, most statesmen had to abandon true counsel and adopt flattery, self-debasement, and cowardice, reflecting the literal meaning of the Latin term for flattery (*adulatio*) as the fawning or cringing of a dog.[80] For example, Tacitus's *Annals* – which enjoyed wide popularity in seventeenth-century Europe[81] – recorded how statesmen became so degraded and brutal during the reign of the tyrannical Emperor Tiberius that senators competed to 'move the most repulsive and extravagant resolutions', while even the great personages of the state 'had to shield their magnificence by their servility'.[82] 'The tradition runs', Tacitus continues, 'that Tiberius, on leaving the curia, had a habit of ejaculating in Greek, "These men! – how ready they are for slavery!" Even he, it was manifest, objecting though he did to public liberty, was growing weary of

---

[78] '*Ostendi autem quod esset imperandi genus, atque haec cogitatio, quid patientia, quid fortitudine, quid magnitudine animi dignissimum sit, non solum animum comprimit, sed ipsum etiam dolorem nescio quo pacto mitiorem facit*'. Cicero, *Tusculan Disputations*, trans. J. E. King, Loeb Classical Library 141 (Cambridge, MA: Harvard University Press, 1927), II.53, pp. 208–9.

[79] '*Sed hoc quidem in dolore maxime est providendum, ne quid abiecte, ne quid timide, ne quid ignave, ne quid serviliter mulibriterve faciamus, in primisque refutetur ac reiiciatur Philocteteus ille clamor ... Quid est enim fletu muliebri viro turpius?*' Ibid., II.55 and 58, pp. 209–13.

[80] Harrill, 'Invective against Paul', 205–206.

[81] Peter Burke, 'A Survey of the Popularity of Ancient Historians, 1450–1700', *History and Theory* 5.2 (1966): 135–52, esp. 136; Burke, 'Tacitism, Scepticism, and Reason of State', in *The Cambridge History of Political Thought 1450–1750*, ed. J. H. Burns and Mark Goldie (Cambridge: Cambridge University Press, 1991), 479–98.

[82] '*Ceterum tempora illa adeo infecta et adulatione sordida fuere ut non modo primores civitatis, quibus claritudo sua obsequiis protegenda erat, sed omnes consulares, magna pars eorum qui praetura functi multique etiam pedarii senatores certatim exsurgerent foedaque et nimia censerent*'. Tacitus, *Histories: Books 4–5. Annals: Books 1–3*, trans. Clifford H. Moore, John Jackson, Loeb Classical Library 249 (Cambridge, MA: Harvard University Press, 1931), 624–27.

Tyranny, Manhood, and the Study of History   45

such grovelling patience in his slaves.'[83] Plutarch, whose works were very widely read indeed in Elizabethan and Stuart England, similarly characterised flatterers as opponents of virtue and the 'bastard members of human life, subsisting at the beck and nod of the wealthy; free-born by freak of fortune, but slaves by choice'.[84] These historians and others provided numerous stories documenting how those who refused to flatter and who sought to maintain their nobility were left to choose between a life of silent retreat or persecution.[85] When living in the tyrannical regime, even good men had to forfeit ennobling political and martial activities necessary for the performance of masculinity.

1.4 Contestations of Manhood

While articulations and conceptualisations of power were thus canvassed recurrently through formulations of gender in the classical world and Stuart England, no single monolithic or ideal standard of manliness existed in either context. Gender historians have demonstrated across a variety of historical regions and periods that normative standards of gender were frequently contested, and their very creation generally arose from combative rather than cooperative processes.[86] Particularly within the classical tradition, and especially between Greek and Roman sources, we find distinctions and disagreements between conceptions of the ideal man as the warrior, for example, and conceptions of the ideal man as the orator and law-giver or, even more broadly, the ideal man as the morally excellent person. As Myles McDonnell's work has shown, Roman conceptions of *virtus*, or manliness, more often prized the warrior above the orator; indeed, prior to the first century in republican Rome, *virtus* only denoted martial courage. The qualities often paired with this term included those praising martial reputation, such as *gloria*, *honos*, and *fama*, or those connected to physical and active labour, including *industria* (purposeful activity), *labor* (toil), *diligentia* (attentiveness), and the adjective *strenuus* (vigorous).[87] The Greek

---

[83] '*Memoriae proditur Tiberium, quoties curia egrederetur, Graecis verbis in hunc modum eloqui solitum: 'O homines ad servitutem paratos!' Scilicet etiam illum qui libertatem publicam nollet tam proiectae servientium patientiae taedebat*'. Ibid., 626–27.

[84] Plutarch, *Moralia, Volume I*, trans. Frank Cole Babbitt, Loeb Classical Library 197 (Cambridge, MA: Harvard University Press, 1927), 63.

[85] See, for example, the story of Cordus in Tacitus, *Annals: Books 4–6, 11–12*, trans. John Jackson, Loeb Classical Library 312 (Cambridge, MA: Harvard University Press, 1937), 59–63.

[86] Joan Wallach Scott, *Gender and the Politics of History*, revised edition (New York: Columbia University Press, 1999), 43.

[87] McDonnell, *Roman Manliness*, 130. Note that these qualities were not usually classified as *virtutes*.

46   Emasculated Kingship

conception of masculinity, however, enjoyed a broader semantic range, tied principally to the concept of ἀρετή [areté], or character excellence, of which martial courage, often expressed as ἀνδρεία [andreia], represented only one aspect. By the fifth century BC, even the concept of ἀνδρεία [andreia] transformed from being defined solely 'as an observable act of facing death on the battlefield' to a collective political conception in Platonic and Aristotelian thought as the pursuit of excellence and the avoidance of public shame indexed to the human emotion of fear.[88] Whereas the Greek term ἀρετή [areté] had a long history of encompassing the intellectual and moral virtues in Greek literature and culture, the Latin term *virtus* did not denote a conception of ethical and political excellence beyond martial prowess until, at the earliest, the late Roman Republic in the first century BC; most often, the republican author who employed the term *virtus* in defence of this broader conception was Cicero. Notably, though, even Cicero highly praised courage as truly masculine, and physical courage or martial prowess remained after Cicero's death the primary definition of *virtus* and the central element of manliness in Rome, including throughout the late Republican period and into the Empire.[89]

The influence of writers such as Cicero and Aristotle on Tudor and Stuart thought more generally, and their importance in humanist grammar school and university curricula, ensured that writers and classical republican thinkers had a rich array of varied sources for conceptualising male citizenship, kingship, and tyranny on a classical and gendered model.[90] Those preferring Greek philosophical texts such as Aristotle and Plato

[88] Karen Bassi, 'The Semantics of Manliness in Ancient Greece', in *Andreia: Studies in Manliness and Courage in Classical Antiquity*, ed. Ralph M. Rosen and Ineke Sluiter (Leiden: Brill, 2003), 25–58, esp. 26, 50–56.

[89] For example, Cicero's *Tusculan Disputations*: 'perhaps, though all right-minded states are called virtue, the term is not appropriate to all virtues, but all have got the name from the single virtue which was found to outshine the rest, for it is from the word for "man" that the word virtue is derived; but man's peculiar virtue is fortitude, of which there are two main functions, namely scorn of death and scorn of pain'. Cicero, *Tusculan Disputations*, 195. See Bassi, 'The Semantics of Manliness', 130–34; McDonnell, 'Roman Men and Greek Virtue', in *Andreia: Studies in Manliness*, 235–61, esp. 235–36.

[90] Since the end of the thirteenth century, an almost complete corpus of Aristotle's writings in Latin had been available, and historians such as Jill Kraye and Paul Oskar Kristeller have persuasively shown the humanists' deep interest especially in Aristotle's ethical writings, including the *Nicomachean Ethics*, *Politics*, and *Economics*. Kristeller argued that, due to a widespread study of Aristotle, 'practically every writer of the period was acquainted with the main doctrines of Aristotelian ethics and was inclined to adopt them or at least to discuss them'. See Paul Oskar Kristeller, 'Humanism and Moral Philosophy', in *Renaissance Humanism: Foundations, Forms and Legacy*, vol. 3, ed. Albert Rabil, Jr. (Philadelphia: University of Pennsylvania Press, 1988), 271–309, esp. 278; Jill Kraye, 'Philologists and Philosophers', in *Cambridge Companion to Renaissance Humanism* (Cambridge: Cambridge University Press, 1996), 142–60, esp. 143; James McConica,

Tyranny, Manhood, and the Study of History 47

more often espoused notions of classical masculinity based upon a broad conception of moral excellence and oratorical skill, while those favouring Roman authors such as Livy or Sallust were more likely to emphasise martial prowess as a necessary quality of manhood. What has been generally overlooked by scholars of seventeenth-century England is the way that these varied and even competing classical definitions of masculinity helped to shape a growing divide in early Stuart England between those participating in Jacobean and Caroline court culture and those challenging or rejecting it. Many historians have recognised the pronounced differences in the presentation of masculine identity in the 1640s between 'cavaliers' and 'roundheads', while failing to ask how these competing identities developed culturally and politically in the decades preceding civil war. Historians who have investigated Stuart court culture, although warning against calcified narratives of a 'court' and 'country' split in pre-civil war England, have illuminated significant elements of a cultural and religious divide between the court, with its more cosmopolitan and Baroque religious attitudes, and provincial England with its greater population of vocal adherents to the Reformed tradition.[91] This book posits that the adoption of classical languages and historical exempla, often focused on the warrior, law-giver, and father, further advanced this cultural divide through competing conceptions of masculine identity and practice beginning early in the Stuart period.

The greatest divide following the accession of James to the English throne concerned the conception of the ideal man or ruler as warrior. The martial prowess of a swordsman on the battlefield had traditionally afforded admission to the community of honour and gentility in England, but under James an increasing number of 'new men' who received knighthoods and the privileges of honour were not men of war.[92] One libel from the period, which counselled farmers to lay down their ploughs and purchase knighthoods, reflected on the loss of honour associated with James's policy:

'Humanism and Aristotle in Tudor Oxford', *The English Historical Review* 94.371 (Apr. 1979): 291–317, esp. 291–93, 303, 314.

[91] See Richard Cust and Ann Hughes, eds., *Conflict in Early Stuart England* (New York: Longman, 1989), 13–14; Dwight D. Brautigam, 'The Court and the Country Revisited', in *Court, Country, and Culture: Essays on Early Modern British History in Honor of Perez Zagorin*, ed. Bonnelyn Young Kunze and Brautigam (Rochester: University of Rochester Press, 1992), 55–64; Malcolm Smuts, *Court Culture and the Origins of a Royalist Tradition in Early Stuart England* (Philadelphia: University of Pennsylvania Press, 1987).

[92] James, *Society, Politics and Culture*, 375.

48   Emasculated Kingship

> Knighthood in old Time was counted an Honour,
> Which the best Spiritts did not disdayne:
> But now it is us'd in soe base a manner,
> That it's noe Creditt, but rather a Staine.[93]

Even within the royal family, there were competing narratives concerning the status of military bravery in conceptions of masculinity and honour, as James the *Rex Pacificus* challenged the classical and chivalric glorification of warfare and his eldest son, Prince Henry, revived the English chivalric tradition.[94] James preferred to present himself as a peacemaker; Henry's representations frequently featured equestrian and military poses, with the prince bedecked in Roman armour.[95] As one writer boldly claimed, though James ruled through peace, he had trained his son in that 'wit for to make warre'.[96] These cultural divisions did reflect true differences of policy between these members of the royal household and between the Jacobean elite. James's early settlement of peace with Spain and his continued reluctance to enter Continental conflicts in support of a united Protestant agenda against the forces of Catholicism and 'Anti-Christ', especially following the Bohemian Revolt, fuelled frustration, anger, and disappointment amongst hotter Protestants.[97] Whereas militant Protestants clamoured to enter war, several members of the pro-Spanish party formed an anti-chivalric subculture, complete with mock-chivalric 'orders' of knights and gentry who met in alehouses to stage burlesques of the chivalric orders of knighthood; they declared mock oaths, sported ribbons and badges, pledged false allegiances, and adopted hyperbolic titles and names. These groups not only ridiculed the culture of knighthood but held a robustly anti-puritan character and politics, celebrating the names, for example, of those who fought on the side of the Spanish Hapsburgs.[98]

---

[93] BL Add. MS 5832, fol. 206r–v. See 'Early Stuart Libels: An Edition of Poetry from Manuscript Sources', ed. Alastair Bellany and Andrew McRae, *Early Modern Literary Studies Text Series* I (2005), [http://purl.oclc.org/emls/texts/libels/].

[94] Roy Strong, *Henry Prince of Wales and England's Lost Renaissance* (New York: Pimlico, 1986); Richard Badenhausen, 'Disarming the Infant Warrior: Prince Henry, King James, and the Chivalric Revival', *Papers on Language and Literature* 31 (1995): 20–37.

[95] Jerry Wayne Williamson, *The Myth of the Conqueror: Prince Henry Stuart, a Study in Seventeenth Century Personation* (New York: AMS Press, 1978), 22–23, 27–29, 67–69; Sharpe, *Image Wars*, 81–82. See, e.g., the cover image of Prince Henry's armour from 1607, depicting the life of Alexander the Great.

[96] William Alexander of Menstrie, *A Paraenesis to the Prince* (London, 1604), sig. C3v.

[97] Thomas Cogswell, 'Phaeton's Chariot: The Parliament-men and the Continental Crisis of 1621', in J. F. Merritt, ed., *The Political World of Thomas Wentworth, Earl of Strafford, 1621–1641* (Cambridge: Cambridge University Press, 1996), 24–46, esp. 41–42.

[98] J. S. A. Adamson, 'Chivalry and Political Culture', in *Culture and Politics in Early Stuart England*, ed. Kevin Sharpe and Peter Lake (Stanford: Stanford University Press, 1993), 161–98, esp. 166–67.

Tyranny, Manhood, and the Study of History   49

Although Charles prior to his reign joined the 'patriot coalition', and in the early years of rule (unsuccessfully) sought the entry of England and Scotland into the Continental conflict, his 'personal rule' which followed similarly relied upon an image of triumphal kingship as the securing of harmony and peace.[99] The death of Buckingham and first pregnancy of Henrietta Maria made the King 'very forward to have a peace' with France by 1629; the Peace of Madrid similarly became a necessity, as the final dissolution of parliament marked an empty Exchequer, massive debt, and no further subsidies.[100] Charles sought to dissociate himself from the legend of the Elizabethan chivalric 'golden age', especially as the Caroline expeditions at the Isle de Rhé and at La Rochelle failed remarkably in relation to Elizabeth's triumphs at Cadiz and against the Spanish Armada.[101] Whereas the tournament had been the principal and most costly display of court grandeur under Elizabeth and James, the practice ended with Charles's accession: 'Knights ... yielded place to masquers' as the fundamental representation of monarchy.[102] Charles did seek to reform and restore the honours system, especially to repair James's selling of honours and creation of new knights and an order of baronets, although significant difficulties in erasing the destructive consequences of these practices and of reining in the divisions between heralds and civilians, as Richard Cust has shown, greatly curtailed this programme.[103] Cust has sought further to argue against scholars emphasising adjustments to the Order of the Garter, contending that the King remained wedded to its militaristic ideals.[104] Those wishing to serve in battle, however, had to do so in foreign contexts not formally associated with the English king or court. To Charles I, the dignity of chivalry 'lay primarily in the religious bonds of loyalty between the sovereign and his knights: a sacralised loyalty within his order of chivalry that was to serve, in microcosm, as the highest example of the loyal service which was every subject's obligation'.[105] Those criticising the Stuarts on the grounds of militarism argued that the pursuance of peace even in the face of religious continental war, the debasement of honours through widespread practices of venal office-holding, and the celebration of cultural forms such as masques rather than tournaments,

---

[99] See, e.g., Aurelian Townshend, *Albions Triumph, Personated in a maske at court. By the Kings Maiestie and his lords. The Sunday after Twelfe Night. 1631* (London, 1631), 6 and 10.

[100] Sharpe, *The Personal Rule of Charles I* (New Haven: Yale University Press, 1992), 65–66.

[101] Adamson, 'Chivalry and Political Culture', 169.   [102] Ibid., 165 and 170.

[103] Richard Cust, *Charles I and the Aristocracy, 1625–1642* (Cambridge: Cambridge University Press, 2013), 140–71, esp. 169–71.

[104] Ibid., 131–39.   [105] Adamson, 'Chivalry and political culture', 175.

50   Emasculated Kingship

stripped English noblemen of their ability to practise martial valour and feminised the English commonwealth. Moreover, the King's refusal to engage in warfare marked his own failure to fulfil his monarchical duties, and Christian duties, insofar as he warred for the sake of true religion. As we will see, the restoration of English militarism and masculine courage became a principal argument in the 1650s for the support of Oliver Cromwell and of the republican form of government.

At the same time, alternative visions of masculinity throughout the early to mid-seventeenth century included significant debates about the role of elite men in political governance, especially around activities of parliament, legislation, and monarchical counsel. The growth of the self-image of the counsellor across the sixteenth and early seventeenth century, and the increasing purchase of civic humanism and of articulations of the virtuous citizen's active political life, relied significantly upon notions of classical political activity and manhood imported through Greek and Roman texts. Richard Braithwaite's *History surveyed in a brief epitomy, or, A nursery for gentry* (1638), for example, extolled the eminence of Athenian and Roman orators who, although often from obscure beginnings, 'by their inward abilities they became a glory to their Countrey', and especially glorious when, 'in their Opposition to the greatest Enemies of State, they stood constant for the liberty of their Countrey . . . '. In these times, 'Corruption was a stranger to the hand or heart of a Counsellour', Brathwaite continued. The orator 'would not be seene in a Cause that would not beare weight; Nor interesse himselfe in ought that might not conduce to the benefit of the State'.[106] Despite these celebrations of classical oratory and the role of counsel, '[f]inding a convincing equivalent to the assembly or forum, though', as David Colclough has argued, 'was more than most English writers could (or dared to) manage, and many of the greatest anxieties surrounding rhetoric and free speech in this period centre on its proper place'.[107] Especially under a monarchical regime, the ability of statesmen to serve the public good through oratory was greatly limited. Most writers sought to outline the role of speech through counsel to the king, delivered through the truly noble man or parliament man. *Imperium* and *consilium* became imagined as symbiotic ideals sustained through counsel, and virtuous counsellors as providing the best safeguards against corruption and tyranny. Moreover, writers presented images of classical

---

[106] Richard Brathwaite, *A suruey of history: or, a nursery for gentry Contrived and comprised in an intermixt discourse upon historicall and poeticall relations* (London, 1638), 260–62.

[107] Colclough, *Freedom of Speech in Early Stuart England*, 40.

Tyranny, Manhood, and the Study of History 51

tyrants such as Tarquin the Proud as tyrannical, in part, for refusing counsel and receiving flattery.[108]

Under a divine-right system of rule, however, counsel remained only a moral suggestion for the monarch. Authority was the monarch's alone under God; the king could never be obliged to take the counsel of law or parliament, nor, prior to the 1640s, even to call parliament at frequent intervals.[109] James and Charles consistently insisted that princes 'are not bound to giue accompt of their actions but to God alone', nor to receive the opinion of those beneath them in grave matters of policy.[110] In the Jacobean period, these languages shifted even further away from counsel and towards statecraft, which appeared to make the king particularly vulnerable to 'bewitching' and insulating counsel.[111] Anxiety concerning the curtailment of political participation through the realm of persuasion, parliament, and wise counsel increasingly became expressed through the image of the evil counsellor whispering flattery and lies into the monarch's ear for the sake of self-advancement.[112]

Importantly, the least amount of disagreement between alternative visions of masculine identity in the early seventeenth century can be found in the views of fatherhood. Significant debates arose during and following the 1650s concerning the supposed patriarchal origins of government through the figure of Adam, and even earlier concerning the use of the familial analogy to justify monarchical absolutism, especially in relation to a seemingly unlimited or arbitrary use of power without the ability to resist. Indeed, James used the familial analogy to full effect in the *Trew Law of Free Monarchies* to argue that subjects, as children, never had the right to commit patricide against their father, the king.[113] It does not appear that those crafting supportive or oppositional literature of the Stuart kings disagreed on the general importance of a paternal ordering of

---

[108] See Guy, 'The Rhetoric of Counsel', 292–94; O'Callaghan, 'Talkin Politics', 111–12; Peltonen, *Classical Humanism and Republicanism*, 45, 214, 284.

[109] Pocock, *Machiavellian Moment*, 353.

[110] *His Maiesties dclaration [sic] to all his louing Subiects, of the causes which moued him to dissolue the last Parliament* (London, 1628). See e.g., 'His Maiesties Declaration, Touching his proceedings in the late Assemblie and Conuention of Parliament', in *King James VI and I: Political Writings*, 258–59.

[111] Pocock, *Machiavellian Moment*, 353–54; Salmon, 'Seneca and Tacitus in Jacobean England', 169–88;

[112] Alastair Bellany and Thomas Cogswell, *The Murder of King James I* (New Haven: Yale University Press, 2015); Curtis Perry, 'Theatre of Counsel: Royal Vulnerability', in *The Making of Jacobean Culture: James I and the Renegotiation of Elizabethan Literary Practice* (Cambridge: Cambridge University Press, 1997), 83–114; Guy, 'The Rhetoric of Counsel', 292–99; Cust, 'The 'Public Man' in Late Tudor and Early Stuart England', 127–31.

[113] *King James VI and I: Political Writings*, 77–78.

52 Emasculated Kingship

commonwealth through households, however.[114] On this model, the father was meant to be ruler of his family, and his household meant to function as a miniature commonwealth. This is not to claim that manhood and patriarchy were equated within this period, nor that the meanings of patriarchy and its practice were not complex, muddled, or debated.[115] But it is significant that even those criticising King James or King Charles for failing as men in acts of martial courage, for example, or for refusing to receive the counsel of orators, still shared traditional views of structures of authority resting upon a vision of male heads of households. One of the central representations of both James and Charles was that of the husband and father, a *paterfamilias* blessed by God with multiple children following the rule of three childless Tudor monarchs.[116] In *Basilicon Doron*, James had warned his son 'neuer' to allow his wife 'to meddle with the Politicke gouernment of the Commonweale, but holde her at the Oeconomicke rule of the house: and yet all to be subiect to your direction'.[117]

Oppositional writings within the Stuart period often argued not against the importance and necessity of paternal dominance within families, but against the Stuart kings as making absolutist claims based on paternal power and as failing to fulfil this central masculine role; moreover, oppositional writings often expressed criticisms against the court or favourites as setting an example of moral impiety or sexual depravity which undermined marriage and legitimate paternity. Later republican authors following the English Revolution did decry rule by a private family and the familial analogy for its justification of absolute kingship (the analogy that kings were to subjects as fathers to children); however, republicans in general did not ultimately reject a governmental model of paternity in favour of a fraternity model.[118] They sought to replace rule by one patriarch with rule by a collection of fathers, or *patres*, who would rule their private households justly while publicly serving the common interests of the commonwealth. Fathers formed a 'natural aristocracy' of responsible elders, such as in the Roman senate; their positions within government

---

[114] Cesare Cuttica, *Sir Robert Filmer, (1588–1653) and the Patriotic Monarch: Patriarchalism in Seventeenth-Century Political Thought* (Manchester: Manchester University Press, 2012); *Idem.*, 'The English Regicide and Patriarchalism: Representing Commonwealth Ideology and Practice in the Early 1650s', *Renaissance and Reformation* 36.2 (Spring 2013): 131–64, esp. 133.

[115] See Shepard, *Meanings of Manhood.*   [116] See Sharpe, *Image Wars*, 76–79, 258–66.

[117] *King James VI and I: Political Writings*, 42.

[118] This is in contrast to the French Revolution where images of paternity were frequently replaced with those of fraternity. See Lynn Hunt, *The Family Romance of the French Revolution* (Berkeley: University of California Press, 1992).

Tyranny, Manhood, and the Study of History 53

rested upon their superior virtues and wisdom gained, in part, through the management of household.[119]

1.5 Tarquin and Brutus

Thus far, this chapter has sought to demonstrate the centrality of historical study in the political culture of seventeenth-century England, and the vast array of classical sources available to Englishmen to conceptualise masculinity. It has suggested that these idealised images of manhood primarily focused upon three male roles, the warrior, the law-giver, and the father, and that within the classical tradition as well as the early modern world, substantial differences arose about conceptualisations of masculinity within these realms. Tyranny, a term defined initially according to a ruler's status as a usurper and/or as a wicked ruler, was understood in the classical tradition to be a degeneration of kingship based upon the ruler's lawlessness and use of force, his disordered soul, and/or his seeking of private gain over public good. Across these accounts, classical writers very often expressed and understood tyranny as a failure of masculinity, and the tyrant as the opposite of the ideal man. Whereas the ideal father ruled his household with justice, or the warrior fought with courage and prudence, the tyrant acted unjustly or as a coward within these realms, and was thereby often imagined as emasculated and degenerated, as being womanish, childish, slavish, or bestial. At the same time, it was understood that a ruler's masculine deficiencies would emasculate his male subjects by greatly hampering their performance of masculine roles in politics or on the battlefield or by literally stripping them of their rights and liberties through unlawful legislation, imprisonment, or persecution.

In what remains, this chapter will present a brief case study of these classicised languages of manhood and tyranny from the late Tudor and early Jacobean period, with the aim of illustratively drawing together the themes presented above. It will focus on the historical exemplum of Junius Brutus, the early hero credited with establishing the republican form of government in Rome after expelling Tarquin the Proud, the last king of Rome.

The story of Junius Brutus and the rape of Lucretia, which served as the founding myth of the Roman republic, was widely known in Elizabethan

---

[119] Gaby Mahlberg, 'Patriarchalism and Monarchical Republicans', in *Monarchism and Absolutism in Early Modern Europe*, ed. Cesare Cuttica and Glenn Burgess (London: Pickering & Chatto, 2012), 47–60, esp. 54–55.

54   Emasculated Kingship

and Jacobean England, both from its original classical sources such as
Livy's *Ab Urbe Condita* (or *Early History of Rome*)[120], which boys who
attended grammar school would have read, studied, and translated, and
from popular, vernacular and visual sources in print and onstage. As Livy
tells it, Lucius Tarquin, who was called Tarquin the Proud [*Lucius Tarquinius Superbus*], had usurped his father-in-law's throne after being
spurred on by his proud and wicked wife, Tullia. Tarquin earned the
name Proud for a number of brutal policies that characterised his arbitrary,
tyrannical rule: He murdered the former king then forbade his burial,
slaughtered all of the previous king's supporters, surrounded himself with
an armed guard, judged capital crimes by himself, exiled his enemies and
seized their property, diminished the number of senators and refused to
listen to their counsel. During the siege of Ardea, Tarquin's son, Sextus,
witnessed a debate amongst his commanders over who had the best wife.
The debate grew heated, until Collatinus claimed that he could demonstrate the superiority of his wife Lucretia in a matter of hours. The men
accepted the bet, and rode into Rome in the night to compare the
behaviour of their wives. In Rome, all of the commanders found their
wives feasting and cavorting with other nobles, except for Collatinus,
whose wife, Lucretia, was sitting chastely amongst her ladies-in-waiting
knitting by lamp light. At seeing Lucretia's beauty and chastity, Sextus
Tarquin, the king's son, became fired with lust for her, and a few days later
returned to Collatinus's house alone to have his way with her. After
Lucretia offered him hospitality for the night, Sextus sneaked into her
bedchamber, and despite her pleas and protestations, brutally raped
her after threatening her with death and public shame.

   Following the rapist's departure, Lucretia sent a letter to her husband
and his noble friends summoning them to the house. Once the men
arrived, she revealed what had befallen her, made them swear they would
seek revenge, then stabbed herself in the heart. Junius Brutus, who until
this time had acted a fool in order to protect himself in Tarquin's
tyrannical regime, pulled the bloody dagger from Lucretia's wound and
vowed to drive out the entire, wicked Tarquin family. 'By this blood, most
chaste until a prince wronged it', Brutus declared, 'I swear, and I take you,
gods, to witness, that I will pursue Lucius Tarquinius Superbus and his
wicked wife and all his children with sword, with fire, aye with whatsoever

---

[120] Also found in Dio Cassius, *Roman History, Volume I: Books 1–11*, trans. Earnest Cary, Herbert
    B. Foster, Loeb Classical Library 32 (Cambridge, MA: Harvard University Press, 1914), Book II,
    p. 77–91.

Tyranny, Manhood, and the Study of History

violence I may; and that I will suffer neither them nor any other to be king in Rome!'[121] Turning their grief to anger, the men paraded Lucretia's broken body into the streets of Rome to stir on their comrades to revolution, and after casting out the Tarquin family, Brutus instituted rule by consuls and the senate, thus establishing the Roman republic. As one of the first consuls, Brutus continued to prove his unshaken loyalty to the republic through a number of actions, most famously his decision to enforce capital punishment against his own sons who had joined a conspiracy to return the Tarquins to power. As he watched his sons stripped nude, beaten with rods, then decapitated, Livy explained that 'all men gazed at the expression on the father's [Brutus's] face, where they might clearly read a father's anguish, as he administered the nation's retribution'.[122]

In seventeenth-century England, Junius Brutus was an exemplary figure of masculinity, celebrated for his constancy in virtue, his guarding of female chastity, and his championing of impartial justice. His great significance in England is most apparent in the 1650s, as panegyrists likened Oliver Cromwell to Brutus for establishing a new republic void of the threat of vicious rape and protective of female honour and chastity.[123] Payne Fisher, for one, declared in 1654 that Brutus would have rejoiced to live under Cromwell, for he established a sober commonwealth, avoiding the vices of gluttony and luxury, while upholding the order of civil and moral society.[124] It is fitting that the exemplum of Junius Brutus became prominent in the decade of the 1650s, as Englishmen sought to understand and justify the regicide and the eventual rise of Cromwell as lord Protector. Yet, imaginative appropriations of Brutus's story and the founding of the Roman republic reached their height in England fifty years prior with a series of publications exploring the rape of Lucretia and Brutus's revolution, including Shakespeare's narrative poem, *Lucrece* (printed in 1594) and Thomas Heywood's tragedy, *The Rape of Lucrece* (1608).

---

[121] '"*Per hunc*", inquit, "*castissimum ante regiam iniuriam sanguinem iuro, vosque, di, testes facio me L. Taquinium Superbum cum scelerata coniuge et omni liberorum stirpe ferro, igni, quacumque denique vi possim, exsecuturum nec illos nec alium quemquam regnare Romae passurum*"'. Livy, *History of Rome, Volume I: Books 1–2*, trans. B. O. Foster, Loeb Classical Library 114 (Cambridge, MA: Harvard University Press, 1919), 204–5.

[122] ' . . . *cum inter omne tempus pater voltusque et os eius spectaculo esset eminente animo patrio inter publicae poenae ministerium*'. Ibid., 232–33.

[123] Payne Fisher, *Inauguratio Olivariana, sive Pro Præfectura Serenissimi Principis Angliæ, Scotiæ, & Hiberniæ, Dom. Protectoris Olivari: Carmen Votivum* (London, 1654), 43–44. See Section 7.1.

[124] 'ubi sobria quisque / Adspersis salibus, nulla formidine, miscet. / Ebrietas ubi non, Gula vel circumflua luxu / Fœdatam, norunt vitiis temerare, salutem'. Livy, *History of Rome*, 44.

56   Emasculated Kingship

The importance of Lucretia's story in Elizabethan and early Jacobean England, and the question of what her story reveals about views of female chastity, subjectivity, and reputation in this period, have received considerable treatment by literary scholars and historians, not least because it was Shakespeare who crafted one of these works.[125] Beyond questions of feminine honour, agency, and its limitations, scholars have also closely examined the political implications of Lucretia's rape and the place of republican Rome in Elizabethan England, even to the extent of arguing that 'the installation of the Republic which is the consequence of [Lucretia's] act affirms a model of state politics based on consent'.[126] However, the significance of Junius Brutus as a figure of exemplary masculinity in Stuart England and Tarquin as a negative exemplum of tyranny and failed masculinity has been much more neglected.[127]

In Tudor and Stuart England, Junius Brutus was most often discussed in books or literary writings concerned with classical history, or in moral treatises which relied upon historical exempla to bolster their arguments. In these latter kinds of writings, Brutus was most often cited as a positive exemplum of impartial justice, a virtue frequently espoused as a tenet of ideal masculinity and good governance. Joseph Hall in his *Two Guides of a Good Life* (1604), for example, employed Brutus's story to exemplify the 'perfect vse of Iustice', which makes 'no difference of men eyther in reguard of wealthe, kindred, friendship, pouerty or dignitie'. As consul of Rome, thereby, Brutus 'caused his owne sonnes to be beheaded, for an offence which they hadde committed'.[128] Similarly, Sir William Leighton in his extended poem, *Vertve Trivmphant* (1603), hailed Junius Brutus's judgment against his own sons as a 'rare example and of great effect, / How iustice should with fauour none respect'.[129] For these writers, Brutus's willingness to enact justice against his own sons highlighted his grave respect for the laws of the republic and pursuit of the public over private

---

[125] See, for example, Lynn Enterline, '"Poor Instruments" and Unspeakable Events in *The Rape of Lucrece*', in *The Rhetoric of the Body from Ovid to Shakespeare* (Cambridge: Cambridge University Press, 2000), 152–97; Catherine Belsey, 'Tarquin Dispossessed: Expropriation and Consent in *The Rape of Lucrece*', *Shakespeare Quarterly* 52.3 (2001): 315–35; Coppélia Kahn, 'The Rape in Shakespeare's Lucrece', *Shakespeare Studies* 9 (1976): 45–72; Jan H. Blits, 'Redeeming Lost Honor: Shakespeare's Rape of Lucrece', *Review of Politics* 71.3 (Summer 2009): 411–27.

[126] Belsey, 'Tarquin Dispossessed', 335; Andrew Hadfield, 'Beginning of Republic: *Venus and Lucrece*', in *Shakespeare and Republicanism* (Cambridge: Cambridge University Press, 2005).

[127] The exception to this is Breitenberg's *Anxious Masculinity*, discussed later in the chapter.

[128] Joseph Hall, *Two Guides to a good Life. The Genealogy of Vertue and The Anathomy of Sinne. Liuely displaying the worth of the one, and the vanity of the other* (London, 1604), sig. K1r.

[129] Sir William Leighton, *Vertve Trivmphant, or A Lively Description of the Fovre Vertves Cardinall: Dedicated to the Kings Maiestie* (London, 1603), n. p., stanza 200.

Tyranny, Manhood, and the Study of History

good; simultaneously, it highlighted Brutus's double role as father of the republic and father of his household – which, in this case, unfortunately led to tragic conflict.

Even in these brief examples of Brutus's representation in moral treatises, we find important reflections upon masculinity and governance – with Brutus as a governor of the commonwealth and of household, and Brutus as an enactor of justice. At the same time, the story of Lucretia compellingly emphasised how contradictory and fragile these concepts of honour and virtue were as the basis of male identity. The public reputation of Lucretia's husband Collatinus, for example, rested not upon his own behaviour but the destruction of chastity carried out by another.[130] Yet Junius Brutus's actions in restoring order after the violation of Lucretia's chastity bolstered his masculine authority, and the later punishment of his own sons for treason could be thought to demonstrate Brutus's ability to control and discipline himself and his inferiors for the sake of good governance.

While descriptions of Brutus's virtue in relation to the punishing of his sons were largely positive, discussions of the Roman as the liberator who banished the wicked Tarquins were numerous and more controversial. Was Brutus's expulsion of the Tarquins justified, English commentators questioned, and what were his motivations? Unsurprisingly, several Tudor and Stuart authors condemned Rome's first republican revolution for its undermining of the God-ordained office of kingship.[131] In 1601, William Fulbecke characterised Brutus's expulsion of the kings as 'fatall to the estate of the Romane Common-weale'. In banishing the Tarquins, the Romans had 'changed gold for brasse, and loathing one king suffered manie tyrants, scourging their follie with their fall, and curing a festred sore with a poisoned plaister'.[132] Writers condemning this Roman revolution often maligned Brutus's character directly. In a 1604 *Treatise of Vnion of the Two Realmes of England and Scotland*, for example, John Hayward characterised Brutus as having 'expelled the gouernment of the

---

[130] Breitenberg, 'Publishing Chastity: Shakespeare's 'The Rape of Lucrece', in *Anxious Masculinity in Early Modern England*, 97–127.

[131] In 1531, Thomas Elyot's *Boke named the Governour* argued that 'one soueraygne gouernour ought to be in a publyke weal' in part by arguing that acts of Brutus and Collatinus in establishing a republic left Rome 'vtterly desolate' due to strife and civil war until the triumphant reign of Augustus. Sir Thomas Elyot, *The boke named the Governour* (London, 1531), sig. 11v.

[132] William Fulbecke, *An abridgement, or rather, A bridge of Roman histories to passe the neerest way from Titvs Livivs to Cornelivs Tacitvs* (London, 1608), 170–71; Fulbecke, *An historicall collection of the continuall factions, tumults, and massacres of the Romans and Italians during the space of one hundred and twentie yeares next before the peaceable empire of Augustus Caesar* (London, 1601), 1–2.

Kings out of *Rome*, being stirred thereto, as well vpon hatred as desire to be chiefe, two respects which lead men easily into desperat aduenture'.[133] Rather than one in control of his passions and dedicated to the common good, Brutus here became represented as a man overtaken by hatred and ambition, the seeds of Roman discord thereby sown by the vicious motivations of a lesser man.

These contradictory views of Brutus as just legislator and unjust revolutionary shed light on why Shakespeare and Heywood's lengthy treatments of Brutus's story, which focus on Brutus's activities prior to and during the revolution, most significantly shaped positive views of Brutus in the seventeenth century. In his extended poem, *Lucrece*, Shakespeare first discussed Brutus in the opening prose 'Argument', where he briefly recounted the historical story. According to the 'Argument', Tarquin was a tyrant infamous for his usurpation of the throne and his cruel political actions 'contrary to the Roman laws and customs'. The 'Argument' explained that after Tarquin's son, Sextus, viciously raped Lucretia, Brutus and his comrades swore a vow of revenge, and Brutus 'acquainted the people with the doer and manner of the vile deed, with a bitter invective against the tyranny of the king'. Brutus's words 'so moved' the people, that 'with one consent and a general acclamation, the Tarquins were all exiled, and the state government changed from kings to consuls'.[134] Here already, Shakespeare identified Brutus as the agent and natural leader of revolutionary change, as the one who transformed private revenge into public justice.

Within the poem, Shakespeare did not mention Brutus by name until the final stanzas at the moment of Lucretia's suicide, when Brutus removes the knife from her breast: 'And from the purple fountain Brutus drew / The murd'rous knife, and as it left the place, / Her blood in poor revenge held it in chase;'.[135] Just prior to this action, Lucretia called upon the men accompanying Collatinus to the 'swift pursuit' of vengeance as a 'meritorious' pursuit for 'knights'. Although each man promises her such revenge, directly following Lucretia's suicide her husband Collatinus and father Lucretius completely lose their rational composure, falling upon Lucretia's

---

[133] Sir John Hayward, *A treatise of vnion of the two realmes of England and Scotland* (London, 1604), 32.

[134] Shakespeare, 'The Rape of Lucrece', in *Shakespeare's Poems (Arden)*, ed. Katherine Duncan-Jones and H. R. Woudhuysen (London: Thomson Learning, 2007), 235–36. Hereafter identified by line numbers.

[135] Ibid., L1734–1736.

Tyranny, Manhood, and the Study of History 59

body weeping and bitterly arguing with each other about who 'should weep most, for daughter or for wife'.[136] As Breitenberg has argued, this disagreement between father and husband re-incorporated Lucretia's 'transcendent' suicide back down into the system of anxious masculine honour and male possessiveness that this poem had previously explored.[137] It is Brutus who interrupts this scene of unrestrained emotion with a show of dispassionate reason and duty. He pulls the bloody dagger from her heart and dons the attire of 'state and pride'. In emboldened speech, Brutus criticises Lucretius and Collatinus for their 'dew of lamentations', and he even questions Lucretia's act of suicide as unproductive – 'Thy wretched wife mistook the matter so, / To slay herself, that should have slain her foe'. Drawing the men together in an oath, and thereby recalling their masculine honour and vigour, Brutus kisses the fatal, bloody knife and vows revenge for Lucretia's 'chaste blood so unjustly stained' and for 'all our country rights in Rome maintained'.[138]

In this vibrant portrait, Shakespeare represented Brutus as a man wholly ruled by reason and duty. His response is one of restraint – both in his refusal to mourn Lucretia's body with tears and in his decision to banish the Tarquin family rather than kill the perpetrators. In calling his comrades to an oath of revenge both for Lucretia and for Roman rights, Brutus appeals to their honour, and the men become united around a common cause of restoring just, patriarchal governance in household and country. Indeed, the patriarchal family was the core of Roman life and governance, but such a family could not exist, it was believed, without rational, virtuous, and duty-bound male governors commanding their own passions and controlling the passions of others. In the final lines of the poem, we learn that Brutus succeeded in aligning the concerns of household order with societal justice, as 'The Romans plausibly did give consent / To Tarquins' everlasting banishment'.[139]

Unlike Shakespeare's poem, Thomas Heywood's play *The Rape of Lucrece* represented in detail the tyrannical rise of Tarquin to the throne, as well as the revolutionary activities of several Roman men following Lucretia's rape, thereby providing a more multivalent representation of masculine political codes as well as failed masculinity. This play was very popular in Stuart England, being first performed at the Red Bull playhouse

---

[136] Ibid., L1791–1792. [137] Breitenberg, *Anxious Masculinity*, 114.
[138] Shakespeare, 'The Rape of Lucrece', L1807–1855. [139] Ibid., L1854–1855.

60 Emasculated Kingship

sometime between 1606 and 1608 and subsequently performed before Prince Henry in 1612 and the Duke of Buckingham in 1628. It also enjoyed at least five print editions. Importantly, the play opened with a representation of masculine failure in the character of Tarquin. The opening lines are spoken by Tullia, Tarquin's impertinent wife, who commands her husband to join her in a private conference then reprimands him for not yet disposing of her father and claiming the Roman throne. With Tarquin uxoriously controlled by his wife, and thereby compromised in his masculinity as head of household, this opening scene significantly connected the disorder within Tarquin's household with the plot he will enact to overthrow Rome's rightful governor, King Servius.

With the government of Rome, and Rome's principal household, thus disordered, Heywood's play represented Tarquin's tyranny as causing the emasculation of Rome's principal men. As the character Horatius notes in the play, 'Tarquins abilitie will in the weale, / Beget a weake vnable impotence: / His strength, make Rome and our dominions weake, / His soaring high make vs to flag our winges, . . . '.[140] When Tarquin refuses to listen to the counsel of Rome's great men, provide them with positions of authority, and enter war for the increase of Rome's dominion – when he refuses to allow them the roles of warrior and orator – the noblemen of Rome are left with few exploits except those of idleness, luxury, and perversity. Moreover, they are encouraged in these very pursuits by the negative and vicious example of their own ruler. Thus we find the character Scevola reason with his fellow courtiers, ' . . . since the Court is harsh, / And lookes askaunce on souldiers, lets be merry, / Court Ladies, sing, drinke, dance, and euery man / Get him a mistris'.[141] The scene continues with a series of songs which emphasise repeatedly the emasculation of Rome's statesmen, for their survival consists in trading war and service for the public weal with the vain pursuits of women and merrymaking, and with flattering the new king and competing for his attention. Even those statesmen who seek to resist the tyrant must participate in this culture, putting on 'new humors / . . .for safety'; they must arm themselves 'Against the pride of *Tarquin*, from whose danger, / None great in loue, in counsell or opinion / Can be kept safe'.[142]

Having established this context, Heywood's audience would have viewed the play's later scenes of household disorder in Rome as logical conclusions of a disordered realm. It would have been unsurprising for a

---

[140] Heywood, *The Rape of Lucrece: A True Roman Tragedie* (London, 1608), sig. B4v.
[141] Thomas Heywood, *Rape of Lucrece*, sig. C2r.   [142] Ibid., sig. C2v.

Tyranny, Manhood, and the Study of History 61

seventeenth-century audience that the noblemen who placed a wager on who had the best wife would discover their women merrymaking in lewd pursuits while their husbands were away, for without virtuous, fully masculine husbands to discipline them, women would similarly fall into error. And Sextus Tarquin's rape of Lucretia, while tragic and abominable, would have seemed fitting in its logical continuation of the cycle of usurpation and loss of manly control already represented onstage. Simultaneously, though, Lucretia's chastity and wifely obedience in the midst of this defiled Roman state would have seemed ever more admirable.

Against this backdrop, the characterisation of Brutus within this play is striking. In several early scenes of the play, the audience is introduced to Brutus as a nobleman playing the fool to protect himself and, ostensibly, to await the occasion when he might free Rome from the Tarquin family. In the short run, Brutus's feigned status as a madman frees him to speak truth to power in a court where good counsel has been suppressed, such as when Brutus in supposedly a madman's fit upbraids Tarquin for treasonously disposing of the late king and for allowing his wife to commit patricide.[143] Significantly, as the play progresses, Brutus is the one nobleman who remains behind and takes charge of the army while the other men ride into Rome to spy upon the behaviour of their wives; Brutus's restrained actions keep his own wife and household shielded from Tarquin's corrupt gaze.[144]

The most significant moment that defines Brutus's masculinity, however, is at the same moment we encountered in Shakespeare's poem: when Brutus commands his fellow noblemen to swear an oath avenging Lucretia. In Heywood's play, Brutus declares:

> As you are Romans, and esteeme your fame
> More then your liues, all humorous toyes set off,
> Of madding, singing, smilings, and what else,
> Receiue your natiue vallours, be your selues,
> And ioyne with Brutus in the iust reuenge
> Of this chaste rauisht Lady, sweare.[145]

Brutus commands his peers to restore their honour by laying aside foolish pursuits and donning the valorous life of action. Unlike Shakespeare's poem, however, which emphasised reason as the male attribute necessary

---

[143] For example, when Brutus is cast away from the senate house just before Tarquin's coup because there 'is no roome for fooles', Brutus retorts, 'Youle haue an emptie parliament then'. Heywood, *Rape of Lucrece*, sig. D2r–v.
[144] Ibid., sig. F1r. [145] Ibid., sig. H3r.

62 Emasculated Kingship

to restore order, Heywood's Brutus emphasises the need for men to practise strength through military feats. Heywood concludes the play with a series of scenes (drawn from other episodes of Roman history) which demonstrate this new found masculine vigour in arms, including Horatius valiantly holding off Tarquin's army at the bridge and Scevola burning off his own hand after failing to assassinate Porsenna. In a very significant departure from the original historical account, Heywood portrays Brutus and his men as slaying Tarquin and Tullia on the battlefield, directly followed by Brutus and Sextus dying in hand-to-hand combat as Brutus cries, 'much honour shall I winne / To reuenge Lucrece, and chastise thy sin'.[146]

As these brief analyses highlight, Shakespeare and Heywood appropriated not only the stories of Rome but also classical, gendered images of masculine rule and misrule. While their productions helped form the cultural discourse around masculine codes of behaviour in this period, they also provided a significant platform for challenging and potentially criticising masculine standards and their failure in the royal court and monarchy. We see this particularly well in Heywood's play with its large number of topical references to James I and Stuart England. Beyond establishing a broad affinity between Rome and England through frequent, anachronistic references, the play characterises the tyrant Tarquin as pursuing the very activities and policies for which James was criticised in the opening years of his reign. The pastimes of singing, dancing, and play-acting in which Rome's emasculated men engage reflected James's own proclivities in court life, and the Clown in Heywood's play reflects explicitly on 'newes at Court, ... that a small legge and a silke stockin are in fashion for your Lord',[147] which reflected letters and libels describing the King and his court's culture. An epistle from the Earl of Suffolk to Sir John Harington in 1611, for example, advised the courtier on fashionable new clothes to purchase, for the 'King is nicely heedfull of such points, and dwelleth on good looks and handsome accoutrements'. Suffolk's letter also famously described James's admiration for his new favourite, Robert Carr, and the favourite's well-dressed, 'straight-limbed, well-favourede, strong-shoulderd, and smooth-faced' appearance.[148]

There was also much reporting in letters about the King's court entertainments and parties, oft described as disorderly and full of courtiers

---

[146] Ibid., sig. K1r.   [147] Ibid., sig. C2v.

[148] John Nichols, *The Progresses, Processions and Magnificent Festivities of King James the First, His Royal Consort, Family, and Court*, vol. II (London: J. B. Nichols, 1828), 412–14.

Tyranny, Manhood, and the Study of History 63

behaving badly. Sir John Harington's description of the visit of Christian IV of Denmark in 1606 detailed court ladies who 'roll about in intoxication' and masque actors forgetting lines and falling over dignitaries due to drunkenness. With 'the gunpowder fright ... got out of all our heads', Harington explained, ' ... we are going on, hereabouts, as if the devil was contriving every man shoud blow up himself, by wild riot, excess, and devastation of time and temperance'.[149] It has been argued that Harington's letter is likely exaggerated, yet his does not stray very far from other descriptions of James's court which continued to emphasise disorderly conduct, drunkenness, vanity, and corruption.[150] This period witnessed a sharp rise in the volume of news and gossip circulating in manuscript and print about court affairs and scandals, such that Heywood's audience members very likely would have seen the portrayal of Tarquin's court as recognisably Jacobean.[151]

Furthermore, within the play Heywood significantly departed from Livy's historical record to portray Tarquin as refusing to engage in military conquests, and instead seek marriage alliances and foreign peace treaties as strategies for subduing one's neighbours. As Tarquin explains, ' ... whom we could not conquer by constraint / Them ha we sought to winne by courtesie'. Thus he marries his daughter to the neighbouring Latin king, Tusculan, in order to make 'his peoples ours'.[152] As a later chapter will consider, the proposed marriage between Charles and the Spanish Infanta in the 1620s would bring James the most strident criticism for seeking marriage alliance over war, but even in the earlier context of this play, James pursued a number of controversial policies in the pursuance of peace, foreign allies, and the union of neighbours. His ministers negotiated peace with Spain in 1604, and in the years following the King often entertained foreign suitors for his daughter, Elizabeth. Upon arriving in England, James most significantly pursued the controversial policy of union between England and Scotland, calling upon his subjects to consider themselves 'one people, brethren and of one body'. As Leah Marcus has

---

[149] 'Sir John Harington to Mr. Secretary Barlow, [from London], 1606,' in *Nugæ Antiquæ*, vol. I, ed. Henry Harington (London: Vernor and Hood, 1804), 348–52.

[150] Maurice Lee, Jr., *Great Britain's Solomon: James VI and I in His Three Kingdoms* (Urbana and Chicago: University of Illinois, 1990), 130–32. Lee, for example, cites Dudley Carleton's account of the Twelfth Night festivities in 1605, which included actors painted in black, tables overturned, and a woman losing her honesty at the top of the terrace.

[151] R. Malcom Smuts, *Court Culture and the Origins of a Royalist Tradition in Early Stuart England* (Philadelphia: University of Pennsylvania, 1987), 73–82; Bellany, *Politics of Court Scandal*, esp. 136–80.

[152] Heywood, *Rape of Lucrece*, sig. D1r.

64 Emasculated Kingship

emphasised, James sought to wed nations and peoples as well as the individuals within his court, often with the goal of bridging political and religious divides: 'From *Hymenaei* in 1606 to the masques for the palsgrave Frederick and the king's daughter, Elizabeth, in 1613, nearly every court marriage important enough to be celebrated with a wedding masque at all was celebrated as a particular instance of the king's wider project for united England and Scotland.'[153] One of the wedding masques opened with a prefatory poem asking, 'Who can wonder then / If he, that marries king-domes, marries men?'[154] Like Tarquin in Heywood's play, James's favoured policy was to win allies by 'courtesie' rather than arms.

Finally, Heywood included within the play the very lines that James made famous in his political writings and speeches. Tullia, the wicked wife of Tarquin, declares: 'Kings are as Gods, and diuine scepters beare, / The Gods command for mortall tribute feare'.[155] The refrain that 'Kings are as Gods' was a frequent one throughout James's published writings and speeches. In his 1605 speech delivered to parliament, which subsequently enjoyed three printings, James claimed that 'Kings are in the word of GOD it selfe called Gods, as being his Lieutenants and Vice-gerents on earth, and so adorned and furnished with some sparkles of the Diuini-tie'.[156] Even more striking are the opening lines from the sonnet-styled 'Argument' of James's *The Basilicon Doron*, printed in the 1599 and 1603 editions:

> God giues not Kings the stile of *Gods* in vaine,
> For on his Throne his Scepter doe they swey:
> And as their subiects ought them to obey,
> So Kings should feare and serue their God againe:[157]

---

[153] Leah S. Marcus, *Puzzling Shakespeare: Local Reading and its Discontents* (Berkeley: University of California Press, 1988), 122; Malcolm Smuts, 'The Making of *Rex Pacificus*: James VI and I and the Problem of Peace in an Age of Religious War', in *Royal Subjects: Essays on the Writings of James VI and I*, ed. Daniel Fischlin and Mark Fortier (Detroit: Wayne State University Press, 2002), 371–88, esp. 377.

[154] Ibid.   [155] Heywood, *Rape of Lucrece*, sig. D1r.

[156] 'A Speach in the Parliament Hovse as Neere the Very Words as Covld be Gathered at the Instant [9 Nov. 1605]', in *King James VI and I: Political Writings*, 147. Moreover, by 1608 James had already encountered opposition to his views concerning the royal prerogative and had sought to override legal restrictions through legal appeal in the King's Bench and Exchequer – an issue we will consider more fully in the next chapter. One example is the famous and widely debated Case of the Post-Nati, or Calvin's Case, raised in 1606 and settled in 1608, addressing the naturalisation of Scotsmen in England and their ownership of English property. When Parliament failed to settle the issue, James took recourse in the King's Bench; eventually the case was decided by the Exchequer. See William Ferguson, *Scotland's Relations with England: A Survey to 1707* (Edinburgh: Saltire Society, 1994), 104–5

[157] *King James VI and I: Political Writings*, 1.

Tyranny, Manhood, and the Study of History 65

Tullia's speech reflected very nearly the key words and themes of James's sonnet, including the words 'Gods', 'scepters', and 'feare'. In a significant departure, however, Heywood's crafting of Tullia's speech omitted the monarch's righteous fear of God, and instead referenced the fear only of subjects for their monarch. This alteration further emphasised the absolute *imperium* being claimed by Tarquin. Moreover, throughout his actions and speeches, Tarquin within the play underscores that he rules without counsel and without consent. Responding to Tullia, Tarquin declares, 'thou art our Oracle, and saue from thee / We will admit no counsell'; together, through the exercise of the royal 'prerogatiue', Tarquin and Tullia would arraign, judge, or execute 'without counsell' any who threatened the state.[158]

These portrayals of Brutus and Tarquin, thereby, included significant reflections upon manliness, *virtus*, and its restraint and failure in the society ruled by tyranny. Tarquin, emasculated by his wife and overruled by his passions, demonstrated the degeneration of kingship through his lawlessness and use of force, his disordered soul, and his seeking of private gain over public good. His son's brutal rape of Lucretia enacted the ruination of state and household through tyrannical disorder. Tarquin's rule not only proved his own emasculation, but that of his subjects as well, who being denied the just work of statesmen and warriors for the public good wasted their days in debilitating and effeminate luxury, flattery, and vice. Against this backdrop, Brutus's *virtus* became the more significant, as he alone resisted such corruption and fulfilled his roles as father, warrior, and just lawgiver, one who placed public duty over private gain. The highly popular story of Brutus provides one example of the ways classical conceptions of masculinity shaped English political thinking in this period. As we will see in the following chapters, a series of other Roman stories provided a significant language whereby kingship and its failures were examined and debated in the early Stuart period.

[158] Heywood, *Rape of Lucrece*, sigs. C4v–D1r.

CHAPTER 2

A Chaste Virginia
Tyranny and the Corruption of Law in Jacobean England

> *Behold before thee where Virginia's plac't,*
> Her white breast with a griefly wound defac't.
> The bloudie knife doth witnesse the sad stroke,
> Which freed her body from lusts servile yoke:
> Whose modest innocence so farre extends,
> Her fathers act she in her death commends.
> —Thomas Heywood, *A Curtaine Lecture* (1637)[1]

In the third chapter of his *Curtaine Lecture* (1637), intended as 'Encouragement to young Virgins and Damosells to behave themselves well in their single estate, that they might become eminent Wives and Matrons', Thomas Heywood praised 'that brave Roman knight' and great 'Archchampion of virginitie', Virginius, for killing his chaste daughter Virginia rather than allowing her body to be 'vitiated and dishonoured' at the hands of the corrupt and lustful judge, Appius Claudius.[2] As a *Curtaine Lecture,* intended to satirise how wives 'carp' at their husbands in bed, Heywood presented the state of marriage as honourable and to be desired as long as unruly wives could be tamed.[3] To exhort women to such good behaviour, Heywood employed historical exempla, 'calling to remembrance the famous and notable acts of illustrious persons', that women may through 'observation and imitation' become 'inflamed' to 'aspire unto that celsitude honour and renowne to which they arrived before us'.[4] In this context,

---

[1] Thomas Heywood, *A Curtaine Lecture* (London, 1637), 71–72.   [2] Ibid., 70–71.
[3] LaRue Love Sloan, '"I'll watch him tame, and talk him out of patience": The Curtain Lecture and Shakespeare's *Othello*', in *Oral Traditions and Gender in Early Modern Literary Texts*, ed. Mary Ellen Lamb and Karen Bamford (Burlington, VT: Ashgate Publishing, 2008), 85–100, esp. 87–91; Frances E. Dolan, 'Texts and Contexts', in *The Taming of the Shrew* by William Shakespeare, ed. Dolan (Boston: Bedford Books of St. Martin's Press, 1996), 325; Anthony Fletcher, *Gender, Sex and Subordination in England, 1500–1800* (New Haven: Yale University Press, 1999), 119–20.
[4] Heywood, *A Curtaine Lecture*, 14.

Tyranny and the Corruption of Law in Jacobean England 67

Virginia, a chaste Roman woman who through 'modest innocence' subjected herself to death rather than defilement, became a central exemplum of virginity, obedience, and patriarchal submission. Her story provided a remarkable opportunity for the Stuart public to explore imaginatively the ruthlessness of tyranny, conceived through a classical depiction of intended rape, lawlessness, and emasculation, and to assess personal, political, and even revolutionary solutions.

To understand the various meanings and applications of Virginia's exemplum in the Tudor and Stuart period, it is helpful to rehearse briefly her story as provided by the classical sources available to early modern readers, including Livy and Dionysius of Halicarnassus, and to a lesser extent Valerius and Silius Italicus, as well as the medieval sources in the *Roman de la Rose*, John Gower's *Confessio Amantis*, and Geoffrey's Chaucer's *Canterbury Tales*. The classical histories recounted that in the fifth century BC, the Romans abolished government by tribunes and consuls and established a legal council of ten men called the Decemvirate, whom they tasked with creating the Twelve Tables. This first written codification of Roman law, intended to curtail the arbitrary and unjust practice of power, had long been desired and agitated for by the plebeian class. The Decemvirate was designed to be an elective body serving one-year terms, yet a corrupted Decemvir named Appius Claudius successfully manipulated the election of the second Decemvirate and packed the council with his own faction, crafting an absolute power without elective limits and placing himself as chief Decemvir. Alongside his lustful appetite for power, Appius became enamoured with the chaste maiden Virginia, and when she refused his impious advances, he ordered one of his clients, Marcus Claudius, to seize her in the marketplace and to swear that she was not a free citizen, but the daughter of his slave and thereby his possession. Amidst public outcry for justice over Virginia's capture, Claudius dragged her before the tribunal on a day that Appius alone sat administering the law. Through two legal episodes, Appius, 'intoxicated' with his 'unbridled lust', denied Virginia her freedom and claimed her as his household's property. Her desperate father Virginius, a virtuous military commander, pleaded that he might at least bid farewell to his only daughter, and as he brought her aside, he spied a butcher's shop from which he grabbed a knife and proclaimed, 'My sweete daughter, no other meanes have I but this only to set thee free.' Virginius then stabbed his daughter in the heart, and exclaimed that he had sent her forth 'free and virtuous', for if she had lived, she 'could not have enjoyed these two blessings because of the

68   Emasculated Kingship

tyrant'.[5] Virginia's trial and death led to the abolition of the Decemvirate
government by military revolution, as the incensed Roman people realised
that they too had become bondservants to Appius; as Virginius, who led
the revolution, declared, 'once the law which secured their liberty was
violated, there was nothing to prevent their own wives and daughters also
from suffering the same treatment'.[6]

Livy's and Dionysius's historical accounts of this story focused primarily
on the political ramifications of tyrannical government by the Decemvirate; Machiavelli adopted these concerns in his *Discourses on Livy*
(c. 1513–19) by emphasising the absolute authority of the Decemvirate
and its corruption through Appius's ambition and cunning.[7] Medieval
sources more often focused upon Virginia's virtuous conduct and death,
creating a moralising tale that promoted virtue and chastity for young
women and rulers alike. In the particular case of the *Roman de la Rose*, the
tale's main purpose was to illustrate that injustice can exist in the courts of
justice.[8] As we will see, all of these views influenced the later English
treatment of this multi-faceted story.

Virginia's story provided sixteenth- and seventeenth-century writers
with a moral and political lesson for maiden and statesman, subject and
governor alike, for while Virginia personally represented virginity and
obedience, her martyrdom served as the dramatic climax of a story with
great political significance. English accounts of Virginia's story differed
depending on their use of source texts and their foci, yet all shared an
important and potentially revolutionary analysis of tyranny and governmental corruption, in which Virginius was shown to rule his household
more virtuously than Appius ruled Rome. For Englishmen, this story
powerfully depicted how an absolute ruler, the very *Pater patriae*, could
become tyrannical and violent towards his subjects or 'children'. It imagined tyranny as the perversion of the ruler's soul and passions, which

---

[5] *The Romane Historie Written by T. Livivs of Padva. Also, the Breviaries of L. Florus: with a Chronologie
to the whole Histories: and the Topographie of Rome in old time. Translated out of Latine into English, by
Philemon Holland, Doctor in Physicke* (London, 1600), 120; Dionysius of Halicarnassus, *Roman
Antiquities, Volume VII: Books 11–20*, trans. Earnest Cary, Loeb Classical Library 388 (Cambridge,
MA: Harvard University Press, 1950), XI.37, 123.

[6] Dionysius, *Roman Antiquities*, XI.35, 117.

[7] See *Machiavels Discovrses. upon the first Decade of T. Livius*, trans. E[dward]. D[acres]. (London,
1636), Bks. I.XXXV and XL, 146–48 and 165–75. Although this was the first published English
edition of Machiavelli's *Discourses*, the work circulated widely in Italian in Elizabethan and Jacobean
England and also in various manuscript translations, three of which survive. See Felix Raab, *The
English Face of Machiavelli* (London: Routledge and Kegan Paul, 1964), 52–53.

[8] Lee C. Ramsay, 'The Sentence of It Sooth: Chaucer's "Physician's Tale"', *The Chaucer Review* 6.3
(Winter 1972): 185–97, esp. 190–93.

Tyranny and the Corruption of Law in Jacobean England 69

would lead him to trespass and manipulate the laws and institutions of the commonwealth for personal gain at the expense of the public. The implications of this story were significant in Jacobean England, for the patriarchal relationship of the King to his people, and the King's status as a judge above and not subject to the law, were central concepts in King James's efforts to justify and to sacralise absolute monarchy.[9] Even when English writers did not include the revolutionary ending of Virginia's story in their appropriations, an audience who had read its Livy in university and grammar school would have known the full historical account: that the disordering of Rome's commonwealth and the corruption of Rome's laws by Appius not only caused Virginia's personal tragedy but became the impetus for successful republican revolution.

This chapter explores the significance of Appius and Virginia's story especially in Jacobean England, considering in detail the potential political messages conveyed to the public through its performances and printed retellings. After first examining the themes of virtue and household order central to an Elizabethan performance of Appius and Virginia, the chapter considers the significance of two Jacobean appropriations of the story, arguing that these works offered powerful, gendered portraits of classical tyranny which cautioned Englishmen that rule by an absolute judge could lead to the disordering of society, the corruption of law, and the abolition of subjects' liberties. Moreover, these accounts significantly contrasted the highly personal and gendered criticism of Appius's tyranny with idealised portraits of the virtues and family relationships of Virginius and Virginia, articulating a vision of good rule through a paternal model and suggesting that a ruler's subjects may be more virtuous than their ruler. Although scholars have almost completely neglected the importance of the story of Appius and Virginia in early Stuart England, this story exemplifies how historical exempla aided English statesmen in the creation of significant gendered vocabularies of tyranny, vocabularies which problematised the claims of divine kingship advanced by James and others in this period. As

---

[9] I define 'absolutism' following the 'common usage' definition Glenn Burgess provided, which defines the king as possessing '*general* freedom – as opposed to specific and limited freedoms – from human law'. Alongside this view, an absolutist would claim subjects have the duty of unlimited obedience. Burgess, *Absolute Monarchy and the Stuart Constitution* (New Haven and London: Yale, 1996), 211. For an example of King James's discussions of absolute and sacred power, see *The Trew Law of Free Monarchies* in *King James VI and I: Political Writings*, ed. Johann P. Sommerville (Cambridge: Cambridge University Press, 1994), 62–84, in which James argued that subjects must obey their monarch in all his commands and never resist, even when a monarch becomes tyrannical (78–84). A 'good king will frame all his actions to be according to the Law', James further argued, 'yet is hee not bound thereto but of his good will, and for good example-giuing to his subiects' (75).

70   Emasculated Kingship

we will see, the language of tyranny and law which developed through
this story would shape the character of English republican thought in
later decades and combine productively with portraits of other Roman
tyrants.

   In the unfolding of Rome's lengthy history described by Livy and other
classical writers, Appius and Virginia's story was very often compared to the
better-known tale of the rape of Lucretia, in which the rape and subsequent
suicide of the chaste maiden, Lucretia, by the ruling king's son, Sextus
Tarquin, resulted in Junius Brutus's abolition of the Roman kingship and
the institution of republican government by consuls.[10] Virginia was
regarded as a second Lucretia, and Appius as a second Tarquin, for both
stories included a virtuous woman who suffered sexual violence by a lustful
tyrant, resulting in revolution and the establishment of republican government. Simultaneously, these plots demonstrated how Rome's constitution
passed from a form of absolute power through monarchy or oligarchy, to its
degenerate form as a tyranny, and finally into a republic, and they both
elaborately portrayed tyranny as male sexual violence against a female
citizen. Livy introduced Virginia's story by highlighting these very similarities, claiming that the 'heinous deede' against Virginia 'began of wanton
lust, and had as foule and shamefull an end, as that, which upon the carnall
abusing and bloudie death of *Lucretia*, cast the Tarquines out of the cittie,
and deprived them of their regall dignitie'.[11] Seventeenth-century writers
very frequently cited these considerable similarities, but they also treated
Lucretia's and Virginia's stories as distinct due to perceived differences in
virtue between these women and due to the specific aspect of tyranny
diagnosed. The question of Lucretia's virtue had a significant bearing on the
republican implications of her wider revolutionary story, and seventeenth-
century writers, following Augustine and others, actively debated if Lucretia's suicide implicated her as guilty of lust and even seduction.[12] According
to this view, if Lucretia were not chaste, then not only her suicide but also
Brutus's abolition of kingship and establishment of a republican government in Rome could be challenged and condemned. For Virginia's story,
however, Tudor and Stuart writers emphasised and even celebrated that

---

[10] See Section 1.5.   [11] Livy, *Romane Historie*, 116–17.
[12] In *The City of God* (Book I.19), Augustine questioned why Lucrece committed suicide if she indeed
   were innocent of fault. For a consideration of the early modern dilemma of Lucrece's corruption by
   Tarquin, see Laura G. Bromley, 'Lucrece's Re-Creation', *Shakespeare Quarterly* 34.2 (Summer
   1983): 200–11; Warren Chernaik, *The Myth of Rome in Shakespeare and his Contemporaries*
   (Cambridge: Cambridge University Press 2011); Sasha Roberts, *Reading Shakespeare's Poems in
   Early Modern England* (London: Palgrave Macmillan, 2003).

Virginia's virginal body remained sexually unbroken – and thus sexually pure – due to her death at her father's hands.

While Virginia's exemplum thereby escaped the horrifying scrutiny of Lucretia's sexual purity, admiration for Virginia was no less disturbing by modern standards, and analysing the logic of this distinction between Lucretia and Virginia provides us with further evidence as to how Elizabethan and Jacobean writers perceived and promoted women's virtues. As we will see, writers discussing Virginia's exemplum advocated that truly virtuous women should possess physical and mental virginity and chastity, and they further commemorated Virginia's possession of other virtues, especially obedience to patriarchal authority, submissiveness, silence, and restraint.[13] To them, Virginia's death not only physically ensured the preservation of her virginity but it further demonstrated her full submission to the authority of her father. Although the stories of Lucretia and Virginia both concluded with the political spectacle of the broken female body, Virginia's wound received in the preservation of virginity was thought to confirm her purity and the justice of her cause, while simultaneously promoting a patriarchal ordering of society in which daughters submit to their fathers, and by extension, wives submit to the male authority of their husbands.

2.1 An Elizabethan Virgin

For Jacobean writers, the story of Appius and Virginia presented a significant drama of judicial corruption, emasculating tyranny, and republican revolution. Centred upon the contrasting figures of Appius and Virginius – the one a corrupted tyrant enslaved by his cruel lusts and passions, the other a virtuous warrior and father, a liberator of Rome – seventeenth-century portrayals of this tale offered a significant study of political manliness, *virtus*, its fragility and corruption. In earlier appropriations, however, the story of Appius and Virginia afforded a moralising tale focused more centrally upon femininity rather than masculinity, and on the promotion of particularly female virtues including obedience, submission, virginity, and chastity in celebration of England's own virgin queen,

---

[13] Chastity and virginity have been listed as separate virtues due to an important distinction in their definitions. Virginity refers to 'abstinence from, or avoidance of all sexual relations', while chastity can refer to 'purity from *unlawful* sexual intercourse' (OED, my emphasis). An unmarried woman, therefore, could possess the virtues of virginity and chastity; a married woman could only possess chastity. Heywood in the *Curtaine Lecture* and R. B. in *A New Tragicall Comedie of Apius and Virginia* both employ this distinction, as they encourage chastity for married women and virginity for unmarried maids.

72   Emasculated Kingship

Elizabeth.[14] The most thorough and vivid portrayal of this in sixteenth-century England was a court play by R. B. entitled, *A New Tragicall Comedie of Apius and Virginia, Wherein is liuely expressed a rare example of the vertue of Chastitie, by Virginias constancy, in wishing rather to be slaine in her own fathers handes, then to be deflowred of the wicked Iudge Apius* (1575). The play, which presented Virginia as worthy of imitation for young maidens, may have been written by Richard Bower, master of the choristers of the Chapel Royal, and performed at Queen Elizabeth's court as early as 1563.[15] *A New Tragicall Comedie of Apius and Virginia* reflected prescriptive literature, sermons, and popular pamphlets of the sixteenth century, which understood the family as the basis for social and political order and advocated particular roles in marriage, the household, and sexual morality through gendered and patriarchal terms.[16] The genre of the work further promoted the virtuous imitation of Virginia by borrowing from the late medieval morality play tradition in two ways: it included a set of allegorical *dramatis personae*, and it presented Virginia's 'tragicall' death as resulting in the wicked finding punishment and the righteous attaining eternal reward.[17]

---

[14] See William Painter, *The Palace of Pleasure beautified, adorned, and well furnished, with pleasaunt histories and excellent nouelles, selected out of diuers good and commendable authors* (London, 1566), fol. 13a–19b; Matteo Bandello, *Certaine tragicall discourses written out of Frenche and Latin, by Geffraie Fenton* . . . (London, 1567), epistle dedicatory and fol. 25b; Alexander Siluayn, *The orator handling a hundred seuerall discourses, in forme of declamations . . . Englished by L. P.* (London, 1596), 254–56. Lodowick Lloyd, however, discussed Appius and Virginia as another example of Rome changing from a monarchy to a republic. See *The Consent of time disciphering the errors of the Grecians in their Olympiads . . . and of the vanities of the Gentiles in fables of antiquities . . . Wherein is also set downe the beginning, continuance, succession and ouerthrowes of kings, kingdomes, states, and gouernments* (London, 1590), 500; and *The pilgrimage of princes* (London, 1573?), fol. 79b.

[15] R.B., *A new Tragicall Comedie of Apius and Virginia, Wherein is liuely expressed a rare example of the vertue of Chastitie, by Virginias constancy, in wishing rather to be slayne in her own fathers handes, then to be deflowred of the wicked Iudge Apius* (London, 1575). For authorship see Frank Humphrey Ristine, *English Tragicomedy: Its Origin and History* (New York: Columbia University Press, 1910), 62–63; for dating see Robert Dodsley and John Payne Collier, *A Select Collection of Old Plays in Twelve Volumes*, vol. 12 (London: Septimus Prowett, 1827), 339.

[16] Susan Dwyer Amussen, *An Ordered Society: Gender and Class in Early Modern England* (Oxford: Blackwell, 1988), 1–2, 34–66; Kathleen M. Davies, 'Continuity and Change in Literary Advice on Marriage', in *Marriage and Society: Studies in the Social History of Marriage*, ed. R. B. Outwaite (London: Europa, 1981), 58–78; Laura Gowing, *Domestic Dangers: Women, Words, and Sex in Early Modern London* (Oxford: Clarendon, 1996), 1–8, 24–29, 79–110; Lawrence Stone, *Family, Sex and Marriage in England, 1500–1800* (London: Harper & Row, 1977), esp. 151–218. For studies related to the European continent more broadly, see Lyndal Roper, *The Holy Household: Women and Morals in Reformation Augsburg* (Oxford: Clarendon, 1989), 56–88; Natalie Zemon Davis, 'Women on Top', in *Society and Culture in Early Modern France: Eight Essays* (Stanford: Stanford University Press, 1975), 124–51.

[17] Ristine, *English Tragicomedy*, 63. W. Roy MacKenzie instead classified it as a historical play with Morality features. See *The English Moralities from the Point of View of Allegory* (New York: Haskell, 1970), 10–11.

A New Tragicall Comedie of Apius and Virginia presented Virginia as a fully virtuous woman, 'a virgin pure, an imp of heavenly race, / Both sober, meek, and modest too, and virtuous in like case'.[18] Importantly, the dramatist presented these qualities as an outcome and a necessary component of an ordered, godly household, in which Virginia's obedience to parental authority, and her mother's submission to her father Virginius, produced love, kindness, and cooperation. In order to represent Virginia's household in this manner, R. B. intentionally departed from his classical sources by including Virginia's 'Mater' as a character, even though Virginia's mother was said to have died while her daughter was yet an infant.[19] The opening scene entails a lengthy celebration of the ordered household in which Virginius, Mater, and Virginia express their 'happy state' in fulfilling their particular roles. Virginius, the 'king' and 'kaiser', is described by his wife as 'so loving, / Granting and giving to all thing behoving,/ Joying in me and in the fruit of my womb', as Virginia extols her mother for attending upon husband and child as a faithful 'nurse' and 'comfort', and thereby being a 'gem' and 'jewel' to her husband.[20] In her first speech onstage Virginia demonstrates her obedience to this parental structure by listening to her mother's advice and vowing that, although she dearly cherishes 'Diana's gift' of virginity, she will not be 'obstinate' but will willingly yield to wedlock '[w]hen you command, and not before'.[21] These sentiments culminate in a song celebrating mutual cooperation by all three family members.[22]

This embellished scene depicting familial bliss echoed sixteenth-century prescriptive literature and sermons which commanded 'euery one abyde in the callying wherin he is called' by fulfilling their duties and responsibilities in the ordered household, resulting in a peaceable and loving family, and a peaceable realm.[23] Indeed, each verse of the song promotes this relationship between godly household and commonwealth through several historical exempla, such as the tale of King Nisus whose realm was defeated due to his daughter's treasonous lust for the invading Minos.[24] Throughout

---

[18] *An Edition of R. B.'s* Appius and Virginia, ed. Judith Hedley (NY & London: Garland, 1988), 5. Citations hereafter will be from this edition.
[19] Dionysius, *Roman Antiquities*, IX.30, 101.   [20] R. B., *Apius and Virginia*, 8–9.   [21] Ibid., 7.
[22] Ibid., 10.
[23] [Compiled from William Tyndale, Heinrich Bullinger, Miles Coverdale, and John Bale], *The Christen rule or state of all the worlde from the hyghest to the lowest: and how euery man shulde lyue to please God in hys callynge. Item, the Christian state of matrimony and how man and wife shuld kepe house together with loue. Item, the maner oe* [sic] *saynge grace after the holy scripture* (London?, 1548?), 2a–b, 5a–23b.
[24] R. B., *Apius and Virginia*, 10.

74 Emasculated Kingship

this opening scene, the dramatist framed Virginia's chastity as the outcome of a godly and harmonious household, and in turn, depicted the godly household as the foundation of corporate morality and a peaceable commonwealth. This exultation of virginity and good governance would have had further resonance when performed in Elizabeth's court.[25]

Through the conventions of a morality play, *Apius and Virginius* provided a contrasting portrait of the disordered household and realm as governed by the allegorical character Haphazard. In a second song, the play comically presented the married yet unruly servants Mansipulus and Mansipula, who follow Haphazard and ground their happiness in vicious behaviour and chance. Even though brawling and railing against each other onstage, the two in this disordered relationship work together to 'prank' their masters.[26] Because the audience might dismiss their portrayal due to the common trope of low-class immorality, Haphazard insists within the play that *any* man may happen to follow him and act so ignobly, whether he be gentleman, courtier, captain, ploughman, merchant, or beggar.[27] Indeed, according to Haphazard, any family ruled by chance would disrupt the political, social, and gender hierarchy by creating a world turned upside down, where 'wives wear the codpiece, and maidens coy strange. / ... So maids would be masters, by the guise of this country'.[28] This model of the disordered household and commonwealth, whose members follow chance and mischief rather than virtue, is thus characterised by dissonance, violence, the deterioration of gendered roles and emasculation of husbands, and finally, disharmony in the political realm.

---

[25] For discussions of the significance of virginity to Queen Elizabeth's reign, see Carole Levin, *'The Heart and Stomach of a King': Elizabeth I and the Politics of Sex and Power* (Philadelphia: University of Pennsylvania Press, 1994); Sarah L. Duncan, 'The Two Virgin Queens', in *Elizabeth I and the 'Sovereign Arts': Essays in Literature, History and Culture*, ed. Donald Stump, Shenk, and Levin (Tempe, AR: Arizona Center for Medieval and Renaissance Studies, 2011); Frances Yates, *Astraea: The Imperial Theme in the Sixteenth Century* (London: Routledge and Kegan Paul, 1975); Elkin Calhoun Wilson, *England's Eliza* (Cambridge, MA: Harvard University Press, 1939); Robin Headlam Wells, *Spenser's Faerie Queen and the Cult of Elizabeth* (Totowa, NJ: Barnes and Noble, 1983); Roy Strong, *Cult of Elizabeth: Elizabethan Portraiture and Pageantry* (Wallop, Hampshire: Thames and Hudson, 1977).

[26] R. B., *Apius and Virginia*, 17. It is unclear if 'Mansipulus' and 'Mansipula' are intended to pun on the Latin noun, 'Manipulus', which means 'a handful, bundle'.

[27] For the association of class with moral worth, see Amussen, *Ordered Society*, 3.

[28] R. B., *Apius and Virginia*, 19. See Zemon Davis, 'Women on Top', 124–51; Christopher Hill, 'The Many-Headed Monster in Late Tudor and Early Stuart Political Thinking', in *From the Renaissance to the Counter-Reformation, Essays in Honour of Garrett Mattingly*, ed. C. H. Carter (NY: Random House, 1966), 296–324.

Tyranny and the Corruption of Law in Jacobean England 75

Appius enters the stage directly after these idealised portraits of the ordered and disordered family, and his opening speech reveals that, despite his princely position, he has become ruled by his lower passions.[29] Appius explicitly laments his desperate sexual desire to possess Virginia – to have 'her tender skin to bathe where I do wash' and 'her soft sweet lips to touch my naked flesh' – but due to the gods' refusal to grant him this request, his soul and his realm have become subject to lust and to fortune:

> The sorrowed face of Fortune's force my pinching pain doth move:
> I, settled ruler of my realm, enforcèd am to love.
> Judge Appius I, the princeliest judge that reigneth under sun,
> And have been so esteemèd long, but now my force is done:
> I rule no more, but rulèd am; I do not judge but am judged;
> By beauty of Virginia my wisdom all is trudged.[30]

Due to this all-encompassing desire which has already taken possession of Appius, he agrees to 'be ruled' by Haphazard for the chance to 'deflower' Virginia with violence. He embraces this malevolent role, announcing that he will become like 'Tarquin' who 'Lucrece fair by force did once oppress!'[31]

Although Appius would qualify as *tyrannus ex defectu tituli*, due to his usurpation of Roman rule, R. B.'s account presented him primarily as *tyrannus ex parte exercitii*, one who committed wicked tyrannical actions. Indeed, his play portrayed a psychological depiction of corruption which echoed numerous classical depictions of tyranny. 'A real tyrant is really a slave', Socrates maintained in the *Republic*, due to his maddening, insatiable desires, and especially the desires of erotic love; the evil the tyrannical man heaps upon himself greatly multiplies as he 'tries to rule others when he can't even control himself'.[32] Similarly, Book II of Cicero's *Tusculan Disputations* followed a long Greek tradition of describing the soul according to a tri-partite division between the rational, spirited, and appetitive.[33] Whereas the man of absolute wisdom, according to Cicero, 'will govern the lower part of his nature in the same way as a righteous parent governs sons of good character', the tyrant becomes so enflamed with his lower

---

[29] The author conflates Appius's position as a judge and monarch, which made this play more applicable to the English case and which further emphasised Appius's absolute power in Rome.

[30] R. B., *Apius and Virginia*, 19–20.   [31] Ibid., 28.

[32] *Republic*, trans. G. M. A. Grube, revised by C. D. C. Reeve, in *Plato: Complete Works*, ed. John M. Cooper (Indianapolis and Cambridge: Hackett, 1997), IX.577d–e, p. 1185 and IX.579c–e, p. 1187.

[33] In England, Cicero's *Tusculan Disputations* were printed in English in 1561 and in Latin in 1591, 1599, 1615, 1628, 1636

Emasculated Kingship

passions that he lives as an imprisoned and enslaved man, trembling in fear of losing his power and desires.[34]

In *Apius and Virginia*, Appius's tyrannical and disordered passions cause him to pursue and succeed in an unjust judicial suit against Virginia, and Virginius is presented the ultimatum of handing over his daughter to the filthy ruler or perishing. Virginius desires his own death 'Rather than see my daughter deflowered / Or else in ill sort so vilely devoured', but Virginia argues that it is she who must die:

> Thou knowest, oh my father, if I be once spotted,
> My name and my kindred then forth will be blotted,
> And if thou, my father, should die for my cause,
> The world would account me as guilty in cause.[35]

The disturbing logic of this plea highlights the severity of this drama's moral claims about female virginity and submission. Despite being the victim of Appius's corrupted violence, Virginia places the burden of family honour upon herself. Virginius affirms his daughter's reasoning, claiming that even if he died Virginia would still be seized by Appius, causing her family shame: 'And better it is to die with good fame, / Then longer to live to reap us but shame'.[36] According to the stage directions, Virginia then willingly kneels for her execution. Between cries of consent by her and woeful apologies by Virginius, the father strikes off his daughter's head, as she exclaims, 'Now, father, work thy will on me, that life I may enjoy.'[37]

This scene departed from the classical story of Virginia, in which Virginius was described as seizing a knife from a butcher's stall and stabbing his daughter in the heart without ever seeking her consent. Instead, R. B. followed the medieval depiction of Virginia's death as a consensual and voluntary martyrdom in preservation of her virginity,[38] a tale which well exemplified the medieval celebration of virginity as a denial of self and mortification of the flesh differing little from martyrdom. As Desiderius Erasmus described:

> A true virgyn doth differre very lyttell from a martyr. A martir suffreth the executioner to mangle his fleshe: a virgin dayly dothe with good wyll mortifie her fleshe ... And therefore whan a virgin is delyvred to the

---

[34] Cicero, *Tusculan Disputations*, trans. J. E. King, Loeb Classical Library 141 (Cambridge, MA: Harvard University Press, 1927), 205; 259; 483–87.

[35] R. B., *Apius and Virginia*, 39–40.   [36] Ibid., 40.   [37] Ibid., 41–42.

[38] For a discussion of the medieval tradition, see Ramsay, 'Chaucer's Physician's Tale', 192; Judith Hedly, 'Literary Introduction', *R. B.'s Apius and Virginia*, 50–51.

Tyranny and the Corruption of Law in Jacobean England   77

executioner, she dothe not begynne her martyrdome, but makethe an ende of that that she beganne longe before.[39]

In the play, Virginia's decision to be executed is presented as an extension of her virtuous life, but unlike the tradition of Christian martyrdom in which the virgin bride eagerly awaits eternal life with Christ, her heavenly spouse, Virginia's is a classicised martyrdom with a reward of earthly renown, for which Dame Fame and Memory ensure her lasting remembrance.[40] The 'tragicall comedie' presented Virginia as such an immortal example of virginity and female submission.[41]

The play concluded with final judgement upon Appius for his wickedness, and the exoneration of Virginius for infanticide, even as he stands onstage holding Virginia's severed head. Justice and Reward arrive and condemn the ruler for his behaviour: 'O gorgon judge, what lawless life hast thou, most wicked, led? / Thy soaking sin hath sunk thy soul, thy virtues all are fled'.[42] Following Chaucer and other medieval authors, this version of Appius and Virginia omitted Virginius's military revolution as its conclusion, but it did not omit a significant display of inversion. Appius, a high but wicked ruler, has disordered his commonwealth, while Virginius, a low but virtuous householder, has rightly ordered his family. In this play, it is not Virginius but Justice herself who rebalances the scales by casting down the vicious tyrant. The moralised tale thus drawn to a close, R. B.'s epilogue summarised his exemplum as follows:

> And by this poet's feigning here example do you take
> Of Virginia's life of chastity, of duty to thy make;
> Of love to wife, of love to spouse, of love to husband dear,
> Of bringing up of tender youth; all these are noted here.[43]

Chastity, submission, and order: this was the message that Virginia's exemplum advanced to its sixteenth-century audience. In its focus on personal, familial, social, and political duty, however, *A New Tragicall Comedie of Apius and Virginia* not only promoted the patriarchal ordering

---

[39] Qtd in Karen Bamford, *Sexual Violence on the Jacobean Stage* (New York: St. Martin's Press, 2000), 25.

[40] R. B., *Apius and Virginia*, 51. For a discussion of Christian martyrdom and the Reformation, see Bamford, 'The Legend of the Saints', in *Sexual Violence*, 25–32.

[41] R. B., *Apius and Virginia*, 3–4. In the prologue, R. B. extended these claims of virginity to married women by exhorting them to chastity and to submission to their husbands, as we see modelled in the character Mater.

[42] Ibid., 46. Here 'gorgon' is thought to mean 'petrifying, terrible'. See OED, 'gorgon, n. (and adj.)'.

[43] R. B., *Apius and Virginia*, 52.

78   Emasculated Kingship

of society; it raised the provocative claim that a ruler would be cast down
by Justice if he failed to uphold this order by ruling with without virtue.

2.2 Tyranny and the Corruption of Law

Although abandoning the personification of Justice in their retellings of
Appius and Virginia, Stuart appropriations of this Roman story focused
explicitly on tyrannical injustice, especially the threat of immoral governors
who caused great harm by ruling above the law and by compromising legal
protections for citizens and subjects. This was a salient subject in the early
seventeenth century, as Stuart debates concerning the relationship between
monarchical prerogative and the English common law tradition began as
early as James's English coronation ceremony when the King had his oath
translated into the English language for the first time. Amidst declarations
of political obligation, James's coronation oath rendered the contentious
line '*quas vulgus elegerit*' as 'the laws the people have' rather than 'the laws
the people shall or have chosen'.[44] Moreover, the King's promise to
uphold the 'Laws and Customs' of England and its clergy included an
enhancement of 'agreeing to the Prerogative of the Kings thereof'.[45] In
these lines, James's initial oath to the English people emphasised his own
authority over the law and his sacral monarchy, statements which offered a
foretaste of debates that would develop over the two decades of his English
reign. Controversies concerning this very language would arise again in the
1640s about whether Charles I and Archbishop William Laud had
amended the oath to favour monarchical power over the English common
law tradition.[46] Jacobean retellings of Roman history provided one significant avenue to explore these disputed issues. Although a historical exemplum of virginity and submission, the wider drama of judicial corruption,

[44] Linda Levy Peck, ed. *The Mental World of the Jacobean Court* (Cambridge: Cambridge University
Press, 1991), 6; David Cressy, *Charles I & the People of England* (Oxford: Oxford University Press,
2015), 79; Burgess, *Absolute Monarchy and the Stuart Constitution*, 145, esp. n. 78; Leopold
G. Wickham Legg, ed., *English Coronation Records* (Westminster: Archibald Constable, 1901),
xxviii–xxxi; C. Wordsworth, ed., *The Manner of the Coronation of King Charles I* (London: Harrison
and Sons, 1892), 22. The tradition of the Coronation Oath of 1308, from which James created his
translation, emphasised the King's obligation both to past and future law, a more comprehensive
interpretation than that translated by James or pursued by William Prynne and Robert Brady in the
1640s debates. As Robert Hoyt argued, 'The king is bound not only with respect to the past,
reckoning from the date of his coronation, but also with respect to laws and customs which *shall
have been* "elected" at any given date in the future.' Robert S. Hoyt, 'The Coronation Oath of
1308', in *English Historical Review* 71.280 (Jul. 1956): 353–83, esp. 369.
[45] Legg, *English Coronation Records*, xxxi; Wordsworth, *Manner of the Coronation*, 19.
[46] Charles's coronation, however, followed his father's earlier adjustments.

Tyranny and the Corruption of Law in Jacobean England   79

tyranny, and republican revolution in Appius and Virginia became the focus of Stuart writers appropriating this story. As we will see, they employed this history to demonstrate how the absolute rule of a tyrant might threaten law, justice, order, and the liberties of subjects.

The two fullest accounts of Appius and Virginia in the Jacobean period included an anonymous extended poem and satire entitled, *That Which Seemes Best is Worst. Exprest in a Paraphrastical Transcript of Ivvenals tenth Satyre. Together with the tragicall narration of Virginias death interserted* (1617),[47] and a play by John Webster and probably Thomas Heywood entitled, *Appius and Virginia. A Tragedy* (1654). Most scholars seem to agree that Webster and Heywood co-authored this play, but its dating and performance have continued to raise substantial controversy over the past century. Most contemporary scholars place the work as written sometime between 1608 and 1626, with some preferring a date from the 1620s due to perceived allusions to the Duke of Buckingham in the play; others subscribe to an earlier date based on Robert Anton's *Philosophers Satyrs* (1616) which mentioned 'Virgineae's rape' as performed onstage. Those who argue for an earlier date also cite similarities between this play and other early Jacobean plays such as Heywood's *The Rape of Lucrece a true Roman Tragedie* (1608), considered in Chapter 1.[48] My aim in this chapter is not to resolve this long-standing debate, but to focus on the significant arguments that both *Appius and Virginia* and *That Which Seemes Best is Worst* provided for their Jacobean audiences. Although, as we will see, important differences exist between these works, both presented important criticisms of royal corruption, supplied timely definitions of tyranny as injustice, and suggested how statesmen and subjects could respond to corruption and protect those laws which uphold their liberties.

Throughout James's reign, the jurisdiction, interpretation, and authority of the common law was a particularly salient issue of political discussion through which statesmen debated the source of their lawful rights and

---

[47] I have only discovered one surviving copy worldwide: British Library [C.39.a.4], although another copy may be located at the Bayerische Staatsbibliothek (Bavarian State Library), in Munich, Germany.

[48] Peter Culhane, 'The Date of Heywood and Webster's *Appius and Virginia*', *Notes & Queries* 51.3 (Sept. 2004): 300–1; D. Gunby, et al. (eds), *Works of John Webster* (Cambridge: Cambridge University Press, 2003), II, 443–46; Gunby and H. Lees-Jeffries, 'George Villiers, Duke of Buckingham and the Dating of Webster and Heywood's *Appius and Virginia*', *Notes & Queries* 49.3 (2002): 324–27; Michael Payne Steppat, 'John Webster's *Appius and Virginia*', *American Notes and Queries* 20, issue 7/8 (1982): 101; Rupert Brooke, 'The Authorship of the Later *Appius and Virginia*', *Modern Language Review* 8.4 (1913): 433–53, and greatly expanded in Brooke, *John Webster and the Elizabethan Drama* (New York: John Lane, 1916), 165–210.

80 Emasculated Kingship

liberties and the law's ability to define and limit the king's prerogatives. From the disputes concerning the union of England and Scotland in 1604 and 1607, to the debate over impositions in 1610, the 1616 legal strife between Edward Coke and Lord Ellesmere over the Court of Chancery, and the impasse in 1621 over the Commons' freedom of speech in foreign policy, the Jacobean period witnessed lawyers and the king drawing upon the common law tradition to defend rival versions of the ancient constitution; of whether England was a 'constitutional monarchy governed by the common law', a law that stood above kings and parliaments distributing monarchical prerogatives and the liberties of subjects, or was a 'constitutional monarchy created by kings' in which monarchs limited their own powers by creating laws and the institutions of governance.[49] One important issue within these competing visions was whether the *Rex est Judex*, the *Lex loquens*, and the supplier of law. Beyond formal parliamentary and legal debates, the common law had immense cultural and intellectual authority, and in order to legitimate its sovereignty, signs and symbols of the ancient constitution were consciously developed from classical and continental sources, especially in the Inns of Court.[50] Within this locus of legal culture, thought, and politics, the story of Appius and Virginia would have provided a significant portrayal of how the liberties of subjects might be challenged and abolished through the jurisdiction of an absolute judge who sat above the law. Although Appius derived his power as a Decemvir, which was a form of government foreign to seventeenth-century England, *That Which Seemes Best is Worst* and *Appius and Virginia* represented Appius as a monarchical figure or as a judge, thereby crafting this Roman story as an applicable case for English legal debate.

In 1617, the newly printed *That Which Seemes Best Is Worst* provided a loose translation of Juvenal's 'Tenth Satire' through rhyming couplets. This poem was the first printed edition of Juvenal in the English language,

---

[49] Paul Christianson, 'Royal and Parliamentary Voices on the Ancient Constitution, c. 1604–1621', in *The Mental World of the Jacobean Court*, ed. Linda Levy Peck (Cambridge: Cambridge University Press, 1991), 71–95, esp. 72; Corinne C. Weston, 'England: Ancient Constitution and Common Law', in *The Cambridge History of Political Thought, 1450–1700* (Cambridge: Cambridge University Press, 1991), 374–411, esp. 374–76; J. G. A. Pocock, 'The Common-law Mind: Custom and the Immemorial', in *The Ancient Constitution and the Feudal Law: A Study of English Historical Thought in the Seventeenth Century* (Cambridge: Cambridge University Press, 1987), 30–55.

[50] Paul Raffield, *Images and Cultures of Law in Early Modern England: Justice and Political Power, 1558–1660* (Cambridge: Cambridge University Press, 2004), 1–3. Lawyers and the Inns of Court community exercised great influence in both the political and cultural realm of law, serving in high offices and Parliament, drafting legal statutes, and developing these symbols of law. See J. P. Sommerville, *Politics and Ideology in England, 1603–1640* (London and New York: Longman, 1986), 86–87.

Tyranny and the Corruption of Law in Jacobean England 81

and its author, 'W.B.', remains a mystery, although several nineteenth-century scholars suggested the poet William Basse or the actor William Barkstead.[51] Since the nineteenth century, no scholar has seriously studied this work.[52] The poem is 49 pages long (1,348 lines), 30 pages of which follow Juvenal's satire quite closely, and 19 pages of which depart from Juvenal in order to narrate the tragedy of Appius and Virginia in great detail. Although a seemingly odd placement for this story, Juvenal's original Latin 'Tenth Satire' provided an interesting commentary on Appius's story, for it argued that the folly of humans is praying for what, if granted, would only result in their own harm and ruin. After considering wealth, political power, military glory, long life, and beauty as the objects of human prayer, Juvenal finished his satire by arguing that humans should rightly pray for a 'healthy mind in a healthy body' (*mens sana in corpore sano*), a 'valiant heart which has banished the fear of death', and endurance for every kind of hardship.[53] He concluded that such a virtuous life would lead to tranquillity. For its Jacobean audience, Juvenal's 'Tenth Satire' offered a reflection upon the ruinous consequences of ambition, pride, and immoral living.

Whereas R. B.'s *Tragicall Comedie of Apius and Virginia* appropriated the Appius and Virginia narrative through a morality play, Juvenal's satiric voice was that of the *vir iratus*, the angry or indignant man whose inflammatory denunciations betrayed resentment and a sense of personal injustice. Those Renaissance writers who were favourable to Juvenal emphasised his 'moral sublimity which was thought to justify his acerbity'. Although the subject of the 'Tenth Satire' was potentially tragic, with Juvenal dismissing every human aspiration as futile, he adopted the detached and bitterly comic view of a Democritus, or laughing philosopher, and his ethical philosophy more closely adhered to a Stoic rather than relativistic stance.[54] Although seventeenth-century critics following Isaac Causabon began regarding Horace as the true model of satire, the

---

[51] See Edward F. Rimbault, 'William Basse and His Poems', *Notes & Queries* 17 (Feb. 23, 1850): 265–66; William Thomas Lowndes and Henry G. Bohn, *The Bibliographer's Manual of English Literature*, vol. II (London: Bell & Daddy, 1871), 1249; A. B. G., 'Barksted, William (fl. 1611)', in *Dictionary of National Biography*, vol. III, ed. Sir Leslie Stephen (London: Smith, Elder, 1885), 217–18.

[52] The only contemporary reference I have found is by Andrew McRae, who mentions the poem's discussion of Sejanus. See *Literature, Satire, and the Early Stuart State* (Cambridge: Cambridge University Press, 2004), 123.

[53] Juvenal, *The Satires*, trans. Niall Rudd (Oxford: Clarendon Press, 1991), 98.

[54] Raman Selden, *English Verse Satire 1590–1765* (London: George Allen & Unwin, 1978), 29, 30–34, 42.

82 Emasculated Kingship

verse satire of the Jacobean period still fused Elizabethan models of the Complaint genre, a primarily moral and corrective homily, with cynical Juvenalian invective.[55] The result was a satire cutting in its bitter condemnation of societal vices and simultaneously moralising and Christianised in its message. Within this model, *That Which Seemes Best* presented Appius and Virginia as a moralised tale, but one which offered a probing and sharp critique of political and social corruption.

As Andrew McRae has demonstrated, satire also provided a significant form of political speech and culture in Jacobean England, even shaping the very contours of political debate in an age of censorship and the suppression of radical political discussion.[56] Whereas McRae's work has highlighted the significance of such political speech in the wider public sphere of Stuart England, Juvenal's 'Tenth Satire' influenced even the formal debates of parliament. In 1614, Sir Edwin Sandys employed Juvenal's 'Tenth Satire' in an important speech arguing that all kings, elective or successive, 'settle their states by consent of their people' and could be legitimately removed. He concluded his speech with Juvenal's incendiary remark:

> Ad generum Cereris sine caede et vulnere pauci
> Descenderunt reges, et sicca morte tyranni.
>
> [Few kings go down to Ceres' son-in-law (Pluto) without slaughter and carnage, few tyrants avoid a bloodless death.][57]

Describing the close of the so-called Addled Parliament, Sir John Holles reported that, due to his speech 'on elective and successive kings, and his rehearsing two verses in Juvenal *Ad generum Cereris sine caede*', Sandys was summoned before the Privy Council and his speech 'questioned' for

---

[55] Ibid., 47–50, 72. Selden and McRae cite the Bishops' Ban of 1599 as bringing an abrupt end to late Elizabethan developments in vigorous formal satire. See Selden, *English Verse Satire*, 51 and 72; McRae, *Literature, Satire, and the Early Stuart State*, 5–6.

[56] McRea, 'Introduction', *Literature, Satire and the Early Stuart State*, 1–19. McRae followed a more fluid definition of satire for this period than Selden and other literary critics, adopting Edward Rosenheim, Jr.'s definition of satire as an 'attack by means of a manifest fiction upon discernible historical particulars' (8–9). As *That Which Seemes Best Is Worst* provided a translation of a Juvenalian satire, a more formal definition of satire has proved helpful for my analysis, but I do not object to analysing other less formal libels and pamphlets as also properly 'satiric' in this period as McRae has done.

[57] *Juvenal and Persius*, ed. and trans. Susanna Morton Braund, Loeb Classical Library Edition (Ann Arbor, MI: Edwards, 2004), 375. Maija Jansson, ed., *Proceedings in Parliament, 1614 (House of Commons)* (Philadelphia: American Philosophical Society, 1988), 316; N. E. McClure, ed., *The Letters of John Chamberlain*, 2 vols. (Philadelphia, 1939): 1.533. Chamberlain substituted 'sanguine' for 'vulnere'.

Tyranny and the Corruption of Law in Jacobean England   83

seditious implications.[58] In theory, genre, and practice, Juvenal's 'Tenth Satire' thus afforded Jacobean statesmen a caustic, moralising, and potentially subversive vehicle for public discourse.

Juvenal's satire, as a whole, considered how all aspirations, other than that of virtue, lead to ruin, but the particular and lengthy exploration of Appius and Virginia's story in *That Which Seemes Best* emphasised how a commonwealth and its subjects are ruined by corrupted governors who seek the fulfilment of their own lustful, violent, and unjust appetites. Significantly, the seventeenth-century satire focused considerably on masculinity and its corruption rather than feminity, and on the character of Appius instead of Virginia's virtues. As the poem remarked, 'Graue Appius' was the 'chiefe of the *Decemuiri*', living 'in glitter and authoritie' and holding the judicial power in Rome so that 'He punisheth and pardons as him list'. Due to Appius's age and authority, the satire claimed he should have been a man 'wise and stay'd', but instead 'many a fault in silence yet is hisht: To feare and flatter he doth encline, / Which is the ruine of all discipline'; for Virginia, Appius had become enflamed with savage lust.[59]

The poem's portrait of Appius as a corrupt judge emphasised how his appetites made him effeminate and ineffective. His inability to have Virginia 'so kils his heart', the poem explained, that Appius walks alone 'with deiected eyne' as he 'growes flag and waxeth leane', wasting his days in 'wanton courting', 'meditating', 'plotting', 'sighing', 'looking wild', and even 'weeping' about how he might have her.[60] The anonymous satirist adopted the mocking tone of Juvenal in characterising Appius's actions and postures as weak and unmanly:

> A silent tongue he hath, but speaking eyes,
> Yet who saies *Appius* loues *Virginia*, lies
> Fie *Appius*! fie for shame! ne're be so weake,
> What! be fraid vnto a girle to speake? . . .
> Then *Appius* speake thy mind, and be a man.[61]

Although the most powerful man in Rome, Appius's passions render him pathetic, speechless, and incapable of *virtus*.

---

[58] Sir John Holles, *Historical Manuscripts Commission, Manuscripts of His Grace the Duke of Rutland* (London: HM Stationery Office, 1888), 9:138.

[59] W.B., *That Which Seemes Best is Worst. Exprest in a Paraphrastical Trascript of Ivvenals tenth Satyre. Together with the Tragicall Narration of Virginias death inserted* (London, 1617), 21, 23–24 (my pagination, to be continued hereafter).

[60] Ibid., 22.   [61] Ibid., 23.

84   Emasculated Kingship

In this portrait of Appius, *That Which Seemes Best* emphasised the direct connection between Appius's faults and the commonwealth's disorder. Noting that his behaviour brought 'disorder, pride, and luxurie, / Discord, and in the end anarchy', the poem argued that Appius's example caused the Roman youth to themselves become 'effeminate', 'dissolute', and rebellious through 'scorn[ing] the magistrate', for

> If *Appius* loue how can the younger fry
> But liue and wallow in foule luxurie?
> Why? doth not *Appius* thus (say they) and thus,
> And shall it not be lawfull then for vs?
> If *Appius* his *Virginia* must haue,
> Some liberty, as well as he wee'le craue.[62]

This warning concluded with the moral that people would follow the faults of their superiors, which makes their 'ill example hurt a great deale more' than others. Disorder extended from Appius through Rome's citizens and even beyond her walls, according to the satirist, allowing Rome's enemies, the Sabines, to make military incursions on Rome's borders.[63] This portrait of Appius thereby underscored his uncontrolled and effeminate passions, which caused him and his commonwealth to become emasculated through corruption, disordered through rebellious living, and vulnerable to their enemies.

Importantly, *That Which Seemes Best* detailed Appius's tyrannical activity as that of a judge distorting and trespassing upon the public laws of Rome – laws which Appius himself had crafted in the Twelve Tables. As Dionysius established, Appius's desire to have Virginia was itself illegal on many counts, for Virginia was betrothed to Icilius, Appius was already lawfully wedded, and under the Twelve Tables, his patrician status meant that he could not take a wife from a plebeian family.[64] According to the poem, despite these obstacles Appius's 'loue' for Virginia hatched 'fearelesse lust' and eventually became 'fury', which led him to attempt a plot which further violated Roman law.[65] After sending Virginia's father away to war, Appius laid a secret trap to have his client, Claudius, challenge Virginia's legal status as a free citizen, although he knew Virginia had been born free. Arranging for Claudius to drag Virginia to court when he alone

---

[62] Ibid., 24.   [63] Ibid.

[64] Dionysius, *Roman Antiquities*, IX.28, 95. The author of *That Which Seemes Best* seems to have relied heavily upon Dionysius's account as well as Livy's, especially for the speeches and dramatic action around the court, but the material concerning Appius's and Virginia's behaviour more likely stemmed from the medieval tradition or R. B.'s *A New Tragicall Comedie*.

[65] *That Which Seemes Best*, 26–27.

Tyranny and the Corruption of Law in Jacobean England   85

sat in judgment, Appius violated the Twelve Tables in the first session by ruling that Virginia would be housed with Claudius until her father returned for the trial; according to the law, Virginia should have retained her status of freedom and been allowed to remain at large until found guilty by trial.[66] As the poem relayed, Appius eventually reversed this ruling out of fear that Virginia's impassioned fiancé Icilius would successfully stir the crowd to sedition, but even then, through hidden treachery, Appius sought to prevent a just trial by ordering his military commanders to deny Virginius leave from his military camp and hence keep him from appearing at the trial and standing witness.[67] Appius's letter arrived too late, however, and just after he took his 'seate of Iustice' the next day, Virginius entered the forum with his daughter.[68] The poem stressed that throughout this trial the mournful and just pleas rendered by Virginius, Icilius, and the crowd did nothing but enrage Appius, and it portrayed Appius as unable to rule with impartiality. The incensed judge, described as 'cruell' and 'wicked', 'moue'd with no remorse' due to 'lusts rage', and 'swolne with lust and wroth', eventually decreed the woman to be Claudius's slave, and thus a slave of his own household.[69]

This scene in *That Which Seemes Best* persuasively demonstrated the frailty of law in protecting citizens from tyranny, as it provided a dramatic and moving portrait of a tyrannical judge as one who, through lust, corruption, and eventually fury, commits unlawful violence against his subjects and forcefully disrupts the rightful social order. It powerfully illustrated that absolute legal power would enable such a tyrant to distort public law with partiality and enslave even citizens. The satirical poem further elaborated the violence of this injustice by depicting judicial tyranny as sexual violence against the innocent, with Virginia represented as a martyr who, in Christological terms, stood silently through her unjust trial as a 'lambe' brought 'to the butchering'.[70] Virginius repeatedly described his blameless child as one made a 'slaue' through 'lust' and 'violence', although she had been raised to 'be a wife', and not 'a whore'.[71]

Finally, the poem articulated how such a violation of one innocent subject would result in violence against all subjects, destroying the distinctions, protections, and proper relationships of an ordered and civilised society. As Virginius argued:

---

[66] Ibid., 29; Livy, *Romane Historie*, 117; Dionysius, XI.30, p. 101–3.
[67] *That Which Seemes Best*, 29–31.   [68] Ibid., 32.   [69] Ibid., 33–34.   [70] Ibid., 32.
[71] Ibid., 33–35.

86 Emasculated Kingship

> What? shall we liue like beasts promiscuously,
> Without distinction in foule luxurie?
> O age and sexe shall no regard be had?
> Shall each man by his beastly lust be lad?
> If these (the people here) shall this permit,
> Others I know which will not suffer it.[72]

In a significant departure from Livy and Dionysius, the author of *That Which Seemes Best* depicted Virginia as actively consenting to death at the hands of her father, for after Virginius implores her if she would rather be a slave or be 'set free' by death, she clings to her father's 'bosome . . . , / As if, she said, good father, let me die, / Rather then liue with *Claudius* as his slaue'.[73]

The connection between the violated female body and the violated city or body politic brought to ruin was one previously central to Shakespeare's 'Lucrece', when Lucrece had compared her plight to the fall of Troy: 'As Priam [Sinon] did cherish, / So did I Tarquin, so my Troy did perish'.[74] According to *That Which Seemes Best*, after Virginia's death her body became an image of injustice, being 'laid . . . out to all the people's sight' as a spectacle to demonstrate the violent result of 'rape and lust'.[75] Her body the image of a pillaged city, Virginia's memorial became the symbol of a disordered and enslaved society. The poem emphasised this image of judicial tyranny yet again when returning to Juvenal's satire after completing the narration of Virginia's story. In the immediately succeeding section of the poem, the author turned to the story of Nero castrating the boy Sporus in order to take him as a bride, raising the broad warning: 'Neuer was tyrant yet, that ere would geld, / That boy in whom he beauties want beheld'.[76]

Through this vivid depiction of injustice, *That Which Seemes Best* reflected a range of classical definitions of tyranny focused on rule by force rather than law, and rule by one with a disordered soul. Xenophon had argued that the tyrant 'constrains the weaker to do whatever he chooses, not by persuasion but by force'.[77] Cicero's depiction of tyranny in *De Re Publica*, in which he cited Appius Claudius and the Decemvirate as an

---

[72] Ibid., 34.   [73] Ibid., 37.

[74] Shakespeare, 'Lucrece', lines 1545–46; Mercedes Maroto Camino, *The Stage Am I? Raping Lucrece in Early Modern England* (New York: E. Mellen, 1995), 40.

[75] *That Which Seemes Best*, 39.   [76] Ibid., 41.

[77] Xenophon, *Memorabilia. Oeconomicus. Symposium. Apology*, trans. E. C. Marchant, O. J. Todd, revised by Jeffrey Henderson, Loeb Classical Library 168 (Cambridge, MA: Harvard University Press, 2013), I.40–45, pp. 38–41.

Tyranny and the Corruption of Law in Jacobean England   87

example, portrayed the tyrant as pursuing corrupted and private gains over the common good and seeking to gain or maintain power through instilling fear and the use of force.[78] In his particular example of the decemvirs, Cicero characterised Appius's government as indulging 'in licence in all their governmental acts, and in cruelty and greed toward the people'. He continued by acknowledging that the 'story of Decimus Virginius is of course well known, being recorded in many of the greatest works of our literature: how, after killing his virgin daughter with his own hand in the Forum on account of the mad lust of one of these decemvirs, he fled weeping to the army . . . '[79] *That Which Seemes Best*, unlike its Elizabethan predecessor, more carefully highlighted Appius's position as a judge and his corruption of the law for his own 'mad lust'. In 1617, such an emphasis reflected contemporary political debates concerning justice and law, including King James's handling of two important legal disputes: the Overbury Murder Scandal and the debate between Coke and Ellesmere over the Court of the Chancery.

As Alastair Bellany has documented well, the Overbury Murder Trials of 1615–16 involved an exceptional scandal that brought significant questions of court morality, corruption, and justice before the Jacobean public. The trials emerged after Robert Carr, the earl of Somerset and James's beloved favourite, the countess of Somerset, and a motley band of accomplices were arrested for allegedly murdering the courtier Thomas Overbury by means of a poisonous enema while he was imprisoned in the Tower of London. During these trials the public was bombarded with portrayals of the King as a wise, impartial, and righteous judge and the agent of God's justice; the sins of the Overbury murderers were diagnosed as the product of a royal court in moral disarray. Painting James as the judicial avenger of injustice or as a victim, contemporary representations of the scandal initially dissociated the King from the Overbury murderers. However, when James failed to fulfil these portrayals by refusing to convict and execute his favourite, the earl of Somerset, and the countess of Somerset for their part in the murder, many felt 'true justice' had not been served.[80]

Simultaneously in 1616, the chief justice of the King's Bench, Sir Edward Coke, who had angered James through his heavy involvement investigating the Overbury Scandal,[81] attempted on the bench to rescue

---

[78] Cicero, *De Re Publica, De Legibus*, trans. Clinton Walker Keyes, Loeb Classical Library 213 (Cambridge, MA: Harvard University Press, 1970), 69–71, 87, 174–75.

[79] Ibid., 175.

[80] Alastair Bellany, *The Politics of Court Scandal in Early Modern England* (Cambridge: Cambridge University Press, 2002), 179, 214, 243–45.

[81] Ibid., 209–10.

88   Emasculated Kingship

the common law from what he understood to be unlawful prerogative rule: The Lord Chancellor, Thomas Egerton Ellesmere, was employing injunctions in the Court of Chancery to set aside judgments made by common-law courts. The Court of Chancery had jurisdiction over matters of equity and was tasked to dispense an 'extraordinary justice remedying the defects of the common law on the grounds of conscience and natural justice', thus serving as the 'Keeper of the King's Conscience'.[82] Chief Justice Coke understood the Court of Chancery as the supreme 'prerogative court'. He argued that it should not interfere with the common law, but that its activity should only entail watching over other courts to ensure they did not exceed their powers of law.[83] Coke had previously argued through his *Reports* (1600–15) that 'the King hath no prerogative but that which the law of the land allows him', and he had actively opposed what he understood as James's increasing usurpation of judicial independence, of the legislative powers of parliament, and of the common law through proclamations and other means. As Coke noted in his *Reports*: 'On Nov. 2, 1608, the King had said that he was the supreme judge, inferior judges his shadows and ministers ... and the King may, if he please, sit and judge in Westminster Hall in any Court there, and call their Judgments in question. The King beinge the author of the Lawe is the interpreter of the Law.' Coke rebutted James's claim of being supreme judge by arguing that 'true it was that God had endowed his Majesty with excellent science and great endowments of nature, but his Majesty was not learned in the laws of his realm of England ... *quod Rex non debet esse sub homine sed sub Deo et lege, quia lex facit regem* [that the king should not be under men but under God and the law, for the law makes the king]'.[84]

Just as the king, in Coke's view, was subordinate to the common law, so too were the church courts, Chancery, and civil (or Roman) law courts. In 1616, Coke challenged the Chancellor by encouraging two con artists named Glanville and Allen, who had been acquitted in common law courts and then found guilty in the Court of Chancery, to bring charges of *praemunire* against the Chancery. That same year, when Ellesmere fell ill, Coke overruled Ellesmere's judgment in the *Earl of Oxford's Case*, for which he had contradicted the common law by ruling through the 'Law of

---

[82] Philip H. Pettit, *Equity and the Law of Trusts*, 11th ed., (Oxford: Oxford University Press, 2009), 4–5; Sir Duncan Mackenzie Kerly, *An Historical Sketch of the Equitable Jurisdiction of the Court of Chancery* (Cambridge: Cambridge University Press, 1890), 89.

[83] John Hamilton Baker, 'The Common Lawyers and the Chancery: 1616', in *The Legal Profession and the Common Law: Historical Essays* (London: Hambledon, 1986), esp. 206–8.

[84] See Raffield, *Images and Cultures of Law*, 72–73.

Tyranny and the Corruption of Law in Jacobean England   89

God'. Ellesmere appealed to the King for both cases, who commanded his Attorney General, Francis Bacon, to settle the matter. When Bacon ruled in Ellesmere's favour, James decreed:

> Now, foreasmuch as mercy and justice be the true supports of our Royal Throne; and it properly belongeth to our princely office to take care and provide that our subjects have equal and indifferent justice ministered to them; and that when their case deserveth to be relieved in course of equity by suit in our Court of Chancery, they should not be abandoned and exposed to perish under the rigor and extremity of our laws.[85]

James's decree established that 'mercy and justice' flowed from the throne, and that it was the king's duty to ensure the administration of 'equal and indifferent justice'. In his 'Speach in the Starre-Chamber' on 20 June 1616, James had articulated that 'Kings are properly Iudges, and Iudgement properly belongs to them from God'; thus they retained their judicial power, and had the authority to 'keepe euery Court within his owne bounds', even in settled monarchies where kings employed subordinate magistrates as their legal deputies.[86] Although this speech was perceived as more moderate than the judges had expected, Timothy Tourneur, a barrister at Gray's Inn, recorded an outraged reaction to the affair, arguing that the Chancellors

> insinuate with the King that his prerogative is transcendant to the common law. And thus in a short time they will enthral the common law (which yields all due prerogative), and by consequence the liberty of the subjects of England will be taken away, and no law practised on them but prerogative, which will be such that no one will know the extent thereof. And thus the government in a little time will lie in the hands of a small number of favourites who will flatter the King to obtain their private ends, and notwithstanding the King shall be ever indigent. And if these breeding mischiefs are not redressed by Parliament the body will in short die in all the parts. But some say that no Parliament will be held again in England, *et tunc valeat antiqua libertas Anglie.*[87]

By November 1616, Coke was dismissed from his position as chief justice, and in 1617, Sir Francis Bacon ascended to the Chancery upon Ellesmere's death. From the perspective of legal history, Bacon was able to settle the judicial terms of this conflict peaceably; however, as Tourneur

---

[85] King's decree 14 Jul. 1616; Kerly, *Historical Sketch*, 112–15.

[86] *James VI and I: Political Writings*, 205 and 213. In referring specifically to the Chancery dispute, James further declared, 'I meane not, the Chancerie should exceed his limite; but on the other part, the King onely is to correct it, and none else' (215).

[87] BL M.S. Add. 35957, f. 55v, translated by Baker, *Legal Profession and Common Law*, 222.

90 Emasculated Kingship

demonstrates, contemporaries understood this debate and James's decree as having great and lasting political significance, in which the rights of Englishmen might be threatened by the overthrow of common law through prerogative rule.

Coke's legal disputes ignited political discourse concerning the king's relationship to the law; the Overbury Scandal, in response to which James disappointed the Jacobean public by failing to act as the divine avenger of injustice, similarly fuelled public debate over the relationship between impartial and righteous justice and the divine legitimacy of the crown. As James himself explained in his 1616 speech, 'Good ruiers cannot flow but from good springs; if the fountaine be impure, so must the riuers be.'[88] A number of poems, libels, and pamphlets between 1615 and 1616 explored this relationship between the king's justice and his legitimacy, such as Thomas Scot's poem, 'Regalis Iustitia Iacobi', which had the King deliver this speech:

> The crowne for Iustice sake,
> Heav'n plac'd vpon our head; which none can shake
> Or touch, till with vniustice we make way,
> And (for respect) that strict rule disobay.
> God is our guard of proofe, that we may be
> A guard to you vnpartial, iust, and free.[89]

A legitimate and divine king must be a just and impartial judge; he cannot be overthrown unless he rules with injustice.

In this context, *That Which Seemes Best* offered a poignant portrait of a system in which justice *had* been poisoned by an absolute judge, who through lust, immorality, and partiality had consciously violated the freedom of Roman citizens and destroyed the just and lawful order. Because Appius stood above Roman law, he successfully manipulated it to enforce his unjust passions upon the Roman people. By providing this dramatic and scathing portrait of legal corruption, *That Which Seemes Best* offered a startling condemnation of judicial tyranny, highlighting the significant dangers of political doctrines which placed rulers above the law rather than subject to it.

The solution to such tyranny offered in *That Which Seemes Best* appears to follow what Richard Tuck, J. H. M. Salmon, and others have identified as a major thread of argumentation under the Jacobean court, called

---

[88] *James VI and I: Political Writings*, 205 and 208.
[89] Thomas Scot, *Philomythie or Philomythologie, wherin Outlandish Birds, Beasts, and Fishes are taught to Speake true English plainely* (London, 1616), sig. K4r. See Bellany, *Politics of Court Scandal*, 235.

Tyranny and the Corruption of Law in Jacobean England   91

Senecan or Tacitean stoicism, 'new humanism', or neostoicism, which promoted the quiet life of detachment from the passions. The virtuous statesmen, in this account, should withdraw from corrupt government and seek contemplation and prudence.[90] Juvenal's 'Tenth Satire' sought to demonstrate that the pursuit of wealth, political power, military glory, long life, and beauty would result in ruin and misery. Following the lengthy insertion of the Virginia story, *That Which Seems Best* included Juvenal's conclusion, arguing that humans should seek either death or the virtuous and quiet life of withdrawal for their happiness in a world of corruption.[91] The pamphlet had represented the woman Virginia as one fully emulating these ideals, for she valiantly endured suffering and death rather than living unchastely and in bondage.

At the same time, Virginia's story, as presented in this pamphlet, highlighted a number of significant and unresolved difficulties. Through 85 lines of poetry, Virginius and Virginia weep into each other's bosoms, kiss each other, and gaze into each other's eyes, as Virginius weighs with grief whether he can withstand seeing his only child enslaved and defiled by 'these lustfull beasts [that] shall spill her', or whether he himself can spill her blood and thus set her free.[92] With his final cry, 'You shamelesse letchers, shall she sate your lust? / I'le kill her first; O doe not! But I must', Virginius stabs his daughter then turns 'to the iudgement seate' proclaiming:

> Thus, *Appius*! for thy sake *Virginia* dies:
> Vpon thy head her blood I consecrate,
> She shall not be a slaue thy lust to sate:
> Before she should be prostitute to thee,
> This haue I done, thus haue I set her free.[93]

Through thus emphasising the tragedy of Virginia's death and the guilt of the wicked Appius, *That Which Seemes Best* may have intended to leave its readers questioning if Virginia's sacrifice was enough – the lust of Appius had not been sated; had justice been satisfied? Indeed, the poem posed this question by reporting that the Roman citizens, upon seeing this display, debated whether to commend or to blame Virginius for his action, although they all agreed that Appius and his favourite Claudius were ultimately culpable due to their 'rape and lust'. The tyrant's passions had

---

[90] Richard Tuck, *Philosophy and Government, 1572–1651* (Cambridge: Cambridge University Press, 1993), 6–7, 51–52, 55, 93; J. H. M. Salmon, *Renaissance and Revolt: Essays in the Intellectual and Social History of Early Modern France* (Cambridge: Cambridge University Press, 2003), 27, 45, 65.
[91] *That Which Seemes Best*, 48–49.   [92] Ibid., 36–38.   [93] Ibid., 38–39.

92   Emasculated Kingship

been thwarted, but in this narrative, the unjust and tyrannical legal structures which had led to Virginia's demise remained in place.

2.3   Virginius's Revolution

John Webster and Thomas Heywood's important tragedy, *Appius and Virginia*, provided the most classicised portrayal of this exemplum in Stuart England, and while its exact dating remains a point of contention to scholars, it is clear that the play's message would have been politically salient and potentially subversive at the time. Indeed, in 1628, when the House of Commons actively voiced its concerns about King Charles's exercise of prerogative powers over the common law and liberties of English subjects, House representatives cited the exemplum of Appius to express and legitimate their grievances against the King. In the spring of 1628, the House debated how Charles's levying of taxes through the Forced Loan and his imprisonment by 'special command' of those who refused to pay violated the rights of English subjects under the common law. According to one of the central House opposition leaders, Sir Robert Phelips, the commissionary lieutenants who exercised the king's power in the counties 'do deprive us of all liberty'. 'There's now a decemvir in every county', he declared, 'and amongst that Decemvir there's some Claudius Appius that seek their own revenges'.[94] Sir Thomas Wentworth similarly identified the King's enacting of the Forced Loan, his imprisonment of subjects, and his compulsory billeting of soldiers as an act of Roman tyranny, arguing that lieutenants who enforced this law 'are *decemviri*, or Marcus Claudians, which for their own ends and lusts will draw the country into any inconvenience'.[95] By June of 1628, the House of Commons had become so concerned about the crown's exercise of prerogative powers that they presented the Petition of Right as a formal grievance against Charles. The Petition upheld four fundamental English liberties – freedom from arbitrary arrest and imprisonment, from arbitrary or non-parliamentary taxation, from the billeting of troops, and from the imposition of martial law – stating that the subjects 'have inherited this freedom' from the 'good laws and statutes of this realm'.[96]

---

[94] Robert C. Johnson and Maija Jansson Cole, eds. *Commons Debates 1628: Volume II: 17 March–19 April 1628* (New Haven and London: Yale University Press, 1977), 62.
[95] Ibid., 73.
[96] Conrad Russell, *Crisis of Parliaments: English History 1509–1660* (Oxford: Oxford University Press, 1971), 306–7; Mark Kishlansky, *A Monarchy Transformed: Britain 1603–1714* (London: Allen Lane, Penguin Press, 1996), 110–12.

Tyranny and the Corruption of Law in Jacobean England 93

In the years preceding these famous legal disputes, historical exempla such as Appius and Virginia had already fuelled English political thought about the relationship of the king to the common law; during the Interregnum, this exemplum would provide a positive exploration of military revolution as the solution to monarchical tyranny. The potentially corrosive effects of these stories on conceptions of monarchical authority deserve our study. Webster and Heywood's *Appius and Virginia* is a clear example of this, for it is driven by themes, ideas, and 'moral seriousness', which, due to its lack of complex plot or rich characterisation, make it a tragedy somewhat disappointing to literary scholars but highly intriguing for historians of political thought. Accordingly, this chapter's analysis of *Appius and Virginia* will attend to its substantial political messages.

Appius and Virginia has an 'almost classical simplicity of construction', with its five acts betraying an unbending focus on the conflict between the two central male characters, Appius and Virginius, in the private and public spheres of Rome.[97] The tragedy directly examined tyranny and good governance by contrasting Appius's public rule with Virginius's private rule of his household and military camp, establishing a contrasting dichotomy between public disorder and private order much like that found in its Elizabethan predecessor, *A New Tragicall Comedie of Apius and Virginia*. The play entreated its seventeenth-century audience to compare and judge the virtues and political capacities of each patriarch – Appius and Virginius – and to study the revolutionary consequences of tyrannical rule which corrodes the patriarchal ordering of society. Whereas the Elizabethan *Apius and Virginia* relied upon Justice and Reward to restore the world turned upside down, and *That Which Seemes Best* caustically diagnosed tyranny without advancing a clear revolutionary solution, Webster and Heywood's *Appius and Virginia* powerfully depicted how a fully virtuous man, Virginius, enacted the duties of father, warrior, and orator to set Rome free from violent bondage and misrule. This tragedy was the first to portray, and even justify, Virginius's revolution as a necessary and rightful response to Appius's tyranny.

Literary scholars have largely overlooked how anti-monarchical this play was, not only in its representation of a successful political revolution but also in its employment of monarchical symbolism. Arguments have been made concerning the drama's possible references to Buckingham or to specific political crises in the early 1620s, but *Appius and Virginia* presented a harsh critique of a corrupted ruler, which would have been recognised both in the Jacobean period and perhaps even more in this play's eventual publication in 1654,

---

[97] F. L. Lucas, *The Complete Works of John Webster*, vol. III (London: Chatto & Windus, 1928), 146.

94 Emasculated Kingship

1655, and 1659.[98] Indeed, the very fact that this drama was not printed until after the beheading of Charles I is itself suggestive. Although the play begins with Appius being elected to government, its language quickly shifts to represent Appius as a royal monarch. Within the play, Appius adopts the language of monarchy immediately after assuming his position, employing the 'royal we', describing himself as possessing 'princely' virtues, and being flattered by Clodius as creating 'divine policy'.[99] In his final scene, Appius's remark that 'judges are term'd / the Gods on earth', conspicuously echoed King James's much repeated claim, 'The State of MONARCHIE is the supremest thing vpon earth: For Kings are not onely GODS Lieutenants vpon earth, and sit vpon GODS throne, but euen by GOD himselfe they are called GODS'.[100] Appius's position as a judge would not have made his statement less effective, for James in his 1616 speech had explained that, because Kings 'themselves are called Gods' and 'sit in the Throne of God', they are also 'properly Iudges'.[101]

The most striking association of Appius with monarchy is Webster and Heywood's comparison of Appius to an oak tree, a metaphor which in 1654 would have clearly identified Appius's reign with the royalist cause and his fall with that felled tree, Charles I.[102] Robert Herrick, for example, in his poem 'All Things Decay and Die' (1648) clearly associated the corrupted oak tree with monarchy and its fall:

> That Timber tall, which three-score *lusters* stood
> The proud *Dictator* of the State-like wood:
> I meane (the Soveraigne of all Plants) the Oke
> Droops, dies, and falls without the cleavers stroke.[103]

---

[98] Macdonald P. Jackson, 'Textual Introduction', *Works of John Webster*, 494.

[99] See John Webster [and Thomas Heywood], *Appius and Virginia. A Tragedy* (London, 1654), 7, 8, 22, and 37. Here I am following the spelling of 'Claudius' found in the 1654 printed edition.

[100] 'A Speach to the Lords and Commons of the Parliament at White-Hall, on Wednesday the XXI. of March. Anno 1609', in *James VI and I: Political Writings*, 181. James made this same declaration in *Basilicon Doron*, his 1605 speech to Parliament, the *Trew Law of Free Monarchies*, his 1616 speech in the Star Chamber, and his declaration about the proceedings of Parliament in 1622. See, *James VI and I: Political Writings*, 1, 24, 45, 64, 147, 204–5, 250.

[101] Ibid., 204–5.

[102] Charles II later hid in an oak tree to survive capture from a Roundhead army following the Battle of Worcester in 1651. Charles Larson, 'Fairfax's Wood: Marvell and Seventeenth-Century Trees', *Durham University Journal* 80 (1987): 27–35; Joanna Picciotto, *Labors of Innocence in Early Modern England* (Cambridge, MA: Harvard University Press, 2010), 58; Nigel Smith, *Literature and Revolution in England, 1640–1660* (New Haven and London: Yale, 1994), 8; Smith, ed. *The Poems of Andrew Marvell* (Harlow: Pearson, 2007), n. 233; John Rogers, *The Matter of Revolution: Science, Poetry, and Politics in the Age of Milton* (Ithaca: Cornell University Press, 1996), 57–60.

[103] *Hesperides, or, The works both humane & divine of Robert Herrick, Esq.* (London, 1648), 22. Other significant writers who employed this metaphor include Marchamont Nedham, James Howell, Abraham Cowley, and Richard Lovelace.

As Herrick and other poets such as Andrew Marvell described, the oak tree could topple from its own internal corruption.[104] The play portrayed Appius in these very terms. In the first act, Appius claims that he possesses the fortitude of a grown tree, despite how unsettled he is due to his unfulfilled lust for Virginia: 'I am not a twig / that every gust can shake, but 'tis a tempest / that must be able to use violence / on my grown branches'.[105] Throughout the tragedy, however, Appius's gnawing lust corrupts him and leads him to vicious plots, which eventually cause his own fall. Icilius, after witnessing Appius and Clodius brilliantly manoeuvre the courtroom to charge Virginia as a slave, forcefully predicts Appius's fall from power in this way:

> Must we be slaves both to a tyrants will,
> and confounding ignorance at once?
> Where are we, in a mist, or is this hell?
> I have seen as great as the proud Judge have fell:
> the bending Willow yielding to each wind,
> shall keep his rooting firme, when the proud Oak
> braving the storme, presuming on his root,
> shall have his body rent from head to foote.[106]

In the final act, as Icilius and Virginius lead their revolutionary troops into Rome to overthrow Appius, Icilius exclaims, 'March on, and let proud *Appius* in our view / like a tree rotted, fall that way he grew'.[107] Appius's fall was presented as a result of his own corruption and not the forced machinations of soldiers. It is significant, however, that the revolution on display at the end of *Appius and Virginia* was an orderly, military revolution, led by a virtuous captain who would assume power as a consul after Appius's defeat. Such a portrayal would have surely resonated with supporters of Oliver Cromwell in 1654. These further monarchical images throughout *Appius and Virginia* suggest that this play may have been altered from its original Jacobean version to fit an Interregnum audience.

Appius and Virginia explored Roman republican thought and the problem of tyranny through many themes, including liberty, virtue, and patriarchal order, but its most extensive focus was on the concept of justice and the tyrant's corruption of law. With the words 'justice', 'just', 'judge',

---

[104] In *Upon Appleton House*, Marvell, in what is considered by scholars to be an oblique reference to the regicide, described how the 'hewel', or 'woodpecker', felled the mighty oak because the tree had already been internally corroded by a worm. See stanzas LXVIII–LXX.
[105] Webster [and Heywood], *Appius and Virginia*, 6.   [106] Ibid., 36.   [107] Ibid., 57.

96 Emasculated Kingship

and 'judgment' appearing 67 times throughout the play,[108] and the play's concluding tribute to those 'Two fair, but Ladies most infortunate, / ...Lucretia and Virginia, both renown'd / for chastity', who 'have in their ruins rais'd declining Rome', Appius and Virginia fused together a portrait of Virginia's exemplary chastity, Appius's judicial tyranny, and the restoration of justice through republican revolution.

In its opening, Appius and Virginia provided a definition of justice while representing Appius as a dissembler, falling far short of this criterion. The definition arises when Appius, who has been offered a position as Decemvir, cunningly feigns his acceptance as an act of virtuous duty. Appius proclaims of himself:

> henceforth Ile know you
> but only by your vertue: brother or father
> in dishonest suite shall be to me
> as is the branded slave. Justice should have
> no kindred, friends, nor foes, nor hate, nor love,
> as free from passion as the gods above.
> I was your friend and kinsman, now your Judge,
> and whilst I hold the scales, a downy feather
> shall as soone turne them as a masse of Pearle
> or Diamonds.[109]

Although related in a speech of deviance, Appius's definition of justice is labelled 'excellent' by his interlocutors and would have resonated with Jacobean images of kingly justice. As James advised in Basilicon Doron (1598), the prince should not fear 'vproares for doing of iustice ... prouiding alwaies, that ye doe it onely for loue to Iustice, and not for satisfying any particular passions of yours, vnder colour therof', for an unjust judge is guilty before God.[110] In his later 'Speach in the Starre-Chamber' (1616), James emphasised how 'vnpartiall' he himself had been 'in declaring of Law', only tempering acts of justice with 'clemencie: for no Iustice can be without mercie'.[111] The contemporary emblem book The Mirrour of Maiestie (1618) similarly represented the judging king as a lion crowned with the rod of divine wisdom who balances the scales of justice to provide punishment and prosperity. Standing poised above the 'thronging clamours' of his people, the king as judge is 'addrest to giue a constant

---

[108] With the play being 61 pages in print, this means that on average one of these words appears at least once per page. The actors performing this play in the Restoration likewise recognised this emphasis, renaming the play The Roman Virgin or Unjust Judge, as later printed in 1679.

[109] Webster [and Heywood], Appius and Virginia, 4.   [110] Ibid., 22.   [111] Ibid., 209.

Tyranny and the Corruption of Law in Jacobean England   97

weight / To formall shewes, of *Vertue*, or *Deceit*. / Thus arm'd with *Pow'r* to punnish or protect, / When I haue weigh'd each scruple and defect'.[112] The emblem emphasised that the king through impartial arbitration weighed his suitors according to their 'Merit', which allowed him to give 'to whom 'tis due'.

Those sworn in to serve as judges similarly received counsel to listen thoroughly before rendering judgments and to weigh decisions with impartiality. Lord Chancellor Ellesmere, in his swearing in of Sir Henry Montague as Lord Chief Justice of the Kings Bench, advised that Montague practise the two necessary qualities of '*Patience* and *Justice*': 'First to heare the counsell of Clients with patience though Counsell were Tedious, and sometymes impertinent and extravangant by which he should well vnderstand the Cause at length, And Then to determine rightly; Otherwyse the Client should many tymes suffer for the fault & indiscretion of the Counsell which is iniustice.'[113] Montague's inauguration followed the King's removal of Coke in 1616. Similarly, Sir Richard Gosvenor advised that those in the 'publick deportment' of justice of the peace must exhibit impartiality in fulfilling their oaths of office:

> When you are in execution of your office let noe private interests possess any roome in you. Walk upprightly in your place haveinge a judiciouse ey to the cawse without respect of persons. Remember your oath and worke not your owne ends by your publicke callinge: for eviry good magestrate should have his thoughts soe strongly possessed with zeale of the common good that he should have noe leasure to intertaine thoughts of private ends.[114]

While diverse, these portrayals consistently reflected Stuart characterisations of justice as one of the four cardinal virtues, in which justice, as a character trait or disposition, allowed its possessor to perform just actions with integrity, rectitude, and impartiality.[115] According to Aristotle, justice (δικαιοσύνη) was the highest of all the virtues and the 'perfect virtue', for he who possessed it practised virtue not only towards himself but also in

---

[112] H. G., *The Mirrour of Maiestie: or, the Badges of Honour Conceitedly Emblazoned: with Emblems Annexed, Poetically Unfolded* (London, 1618), 3. The latin motto surrounding the image, 'Nvllvm Bonvm Inremvneratvm', translates to 'No good merit unrewarded'.

[113] 'An abreviate of the Lord Chancellors speach to Sr Henry Mountague, when he was received Lord Chiefe Justice of the Kings Bench', British Library, Add. MS 34217, fo. 6v.

[114] *The Papers of Sir Richard Grosvenor, 1st Bart (1585–1645)*, ed. R. P. Cust, Lancashire and Cheshire Record Society CXXXIV (1996), 36–38.

[115] Aristotle, *Nicomachean Ethics*, trans. H. Rackham, Loeb Classical Library 73 (Cambridge, MA: Harvard University Press, 1926), V.1129a.7–9, p. 253; *OED*, 'justice, n.', def. I.1.

98 Emasculated Kingship

his relations with his fellow men, and as we have seen, Cicero relatedly defined justice as the protection even of the most vulnerable.[116]

The third scene of *Appius and Virginia* forcefully demonstrated that Appius lacked this virtue of justice and that he judged with partiality for the sake of his own vicious passions. The scene commences in a private setting, with Appius entering the stage in a 'melancholly' manner due to his unfulfilled and growing desire for Virginia. He adopts the metaphor of civil war to describe how his melancholy has been produced, for his unrequited passion viciously battles against his other faculties leaving his soul in disarray: 'there's discord in my blood, / my powers are all in combat, I have nothing / left but sedition in me'.[117] Echoing Plato's *Republic*, Appius appears to be on the brink of becoming the fully tyrannical man, whose appetitive cravings overcome his reasoning and win this inward civil war until he acts with utter lawlessness,[118] and indeed, by the end of this scene, Webster and Heywood portrayed Appius as acting with such a singular, tyrannical purpose. What settles Appius's interior conflict is a plot advanced by his favourite, Clodius, in which Appius would ensure his possession of Virginia by impoverishing her family and thereby making her susceptible to his expensive gifts and advances. Appius would do so by withholding financial support from Virginius and his Roman army. From this private setting in which Appius's disordered soul and wicked motivations are poignantly revealed, *Appius and Virginia* then moves to a dramatic public display in the courtroom where Virginius requests financial support for the Roman armies, and Appius unjustly refuses him. This plot was an invention on Webster and Heywood's part, and by thus departing from the classical and medieval accounts of this story they could portray Appius as repeatedly abusing his power and authority in pursuit of vicious lust.

This first courtroom scene was highly significant, for not only did it effectively demonstrate why Appius ruled unjustly, but it further depicted how Appius employed and manipulated the language and prerogatives of monarchy to do so. Before even entering the courtroom, Appius adopts the trappings of kingship by using the 'royal we' in his speech.[119] Once

---

[116] Ibid., V.1129b.25–35, p. 259; δικαιοσύνη (*dikaiosynē*) also means righteousness; see also V.1129b.17–26, p. 259. For Cicero, see Chapter 1.

[117] Webster [and Heywood], *Appius and Virginia*, 6.   [118] *Republic*, IX.571–573b, p. 1180–81.

[119] Throughout this scene, Appius may at times be using 'we' to refer to the other leaders present on the bench; however, he also clearly adopts this language speaking only of himself, such as his reply when summoned to the bench, 'We will attend' and his insistence, 'Ours is a willing presence to the trouble / of all State cares'. He also adopts the 'royal we' when privately chastising Icilius, 'As

Tyranny and the Corruption of Law in Jacobean England 99

assuming the bench, he rebukes Virginius for daring to counsel him and for attempting to impose limits on his power. This exchange underscored how tyrants might refuse virtuous statesmen of their duties to participate in governance and political speech. After claiming complete authority over the military camp, Appius characterises any support to the soldiers as a gift rather than political obligation:

> *Virginius*, we would have you thus possess'd,
> we sit not here to be prescib'd [*sic*] and taught,
> nor to have any suter give us limit,
> whose power admits no curb. Next know, *Virginius*,
> the Camp's our servant, and must be dispos'd,
> controul'd and us'd by us, that have the strength
> to knit it or dissolve it. When we please
> out of our Princely grace and clemency
> to look upon your wants, it may be then
> we shall redress them ... [120]

Appius here claims to rule from his own pleasure and prerogative, and he cunningly justifies this response by invoking the ideas of 'Princely grace and clemency'. In the Senecan model of kingship, made famous by sixteenth-century humanists such as Desiderius Erasmus and George Buchanan, it was argued that good kings should be self-governed by virtue and reason and should be known particularly for their clemency.[121] James, who had been taught a strict model of Senecan kingship from his tutor Buchanan, retained the view that clemency was a particular princely virtue, advising his son in *Basilicon Doron* that a good king must 'mixe Iustice with Mercie'. In his defence of the Chancery Court in 1616 and his position that 'Kings are properly Iudges', James declared that kingly justice 'may bee moderated in point of clemencie: for no Iustice can be without mercie', and he connected this view to the Chancery conflict by claiming

---

for the Maid *Virginia*, wee are far / even in least thought from her'. *Appius and Virginia*, 7 and 22. For further arguments regarding how Appius adopts the 'royal we', see Gunby and Lees-Jeffries, 'George Villiers, Duke of Buckingham', 235.

[120] Webster [and Heywood], *Appius and Virginia*, 8.

[121] Seneca, *Moral Essays, Volume I: De Providentia. De Constantia. De Ira. De Clementia*, trans. John W. Basore, Loeb Classical Library 214 (Cambridge, MA: Harvard University Press, 1928), 397–99 and 409–11; Desiderius Erasmus, *Education of a Christian Prince*, ed. Lisa Jardine (Cambridge: Cambridge University Press, 1997), 13, 63, 135; Aysha Pollnitz, *Princely Education in Early Modern Britain* (Cambridge: Cambridge University Press, 2015), 85; Peter Stacey has elegantly outlined the significance of clemency in Seneca's model of kingship, although his pro-absolutist interpretation of Seneca's philosophy in early modern England departs significantly from other scholars. See *Roman Monarchy and the Renaissance Prince* (Cambridge: Cambridge University Press, 2007), 30–41.

that the Chancery Court exceeded other courts because it dispensed the 'Kings Conscience' by 'mixing Mercie with Iustice'.[122] A king's ability to exercise clemency was thereby understood as a supra-legal right of the monarch intended to temper the rigidity, and possible cruelty, of the impartial rule of law. In Webster and Heywood's play, however, Appius publicly fashions himself as a Senecan prince acting through mercy and justice for the protection of his subjects, but in reality he manipulates this supra-legal privilege in order to fulfil personal, violent, and unjust desires. Appius's continual manipulation of law and prerogative throughout *Appius and Virginia* fulfilled Tourneur's worries after the Chancery conflict in 1616: that rule by prerogative, rather than law, would produce monarchical power without limit and the abolition of the liberty of subjects.[123]

Whereas Appius was portrayed as manipulating monarchical authority to implement unjust acts, Webster and Heywood represented Virginius as truly embodying the qualities of a good republican and a virtuous king. When speaking passionately in the courtroom on behalf of the Roman military camps plagued by famine and bereft of supplies, Virginius demonstrated that, unlike Appius, his entire concern was for the public good of his commonwealth. He warns that failing to pay the soldiers would result in enslavement, as the 'forrain fires' of Rome's enemies would 'climb o're these buildings', and 'sword and slaughter / chase the gown'd Senate through the streets of Rome'.[124] When refused support, Virginius declares in an aside that these unmanly and luxurious governors would be unable to protect Roman liberty from such catastrophe, for 'They lay their heads / on their soft pillowes, pore upon their bags, / grow fat with laziness and resty ease', while not sparing a drachma for the soldiers who 'stand betwixt them and disaster'.[125]

Virginius's speeches reflected a theme central to classical republican thought: that good laws and good arms were essential for the republic to remain free and to flourish.[126] Livy's history powerfully depicted how the Roman people became a 'free state' without the bondage of kings, making the 'authoritie and rule of law, more powerfull and mightie than that of men'.[127] Livy demonstrated that, after banishing the Tarquins, the Romans retained or recovered their freedom and expanded their glory by military conquest. Similarly, Sallust, who was arguably the most popular

[122] *James VI and I: Political Writings*, 22–23, 43, 204–5, 209, 214.   [123] See Section 2.2.
[124] Webster [and Heywood], *Appius and Virginia*, 8–9.   [125] Ibid., 10.
[126] Markku Peltonen, *Classical Humanism and Republicanism in English Political Thought, 1570–1640* (Cambridge: Cambridge University Press, 1995), 41.
[127] Livy, *Romane Historie*, 44.

Tyranny and the Corruption of Law in Jacobean England 101

classical historian in early modern Europe, had equated republican liberty and greatness, arguing that a commonwealth not repressed by kings could use its talents to attain glory.[128] Throughout the sixteenth and seventeenth century, English writers of military treatises often remarked, as Thomas Procter did, that 'Never was theare a great & famous estate, wherearein armes and lawes, civill governement, and martiall prowesse florished not together.'[129] English statesmen had available Machiavelli's *Arte of Warre* in English beginning in 1560, and by the 1650s, as David Armitage has demonstrated, English republicans actively drew upon Sallust and Machiavelli to understand the military successes of the Rump Parliament as products of republican government.[130] As we will see, Marchamont Nedham touted that these martial victories demonstrated how a liberated people would become peculiarly courageous.[131] 'When Rome lived in the fullness of liberty,' Algernon Sidney later maintained, 'the scope of the law was to preserve every particular man in the enjoyment of his liberty and property ... The Roman virtue was the effect of their good laws and discipline.'[132] In *Appius and Virginia*, Virginius through his public role as military captain sought to ensure Rome's freedom in a way consistent with his republican heritage, while Appius, as a luxurious ruler, threatened this very liberty and the martial valour of his realm.

Virginius, however, was represented by Webster and Heywood not only as a good republican soldier but also as one endowed with the qualities of a virtuous statesman, including liberality and clemency. The dramatists displayed his liberality immediately after Appius refused to support the soldiers, for Virginius vows that he will sell all his possessions, 'even to my

---

[128] Sallust, *The War with Catiline. The War with Jugurtha*, ed. John T. Ramsey, trans. J. C. Rolfe, Loeb Classical Library 116 (Cambridge, MA: Harvard University Press, 2013), 31–35; See Freyja Cox Jensen, *Reading the Roman Republic in Early Modern England* (Leiden: Koninklijke Brill NV, 2012), 26–29, 60–66, 77–82. P. Burke, 'A Survey of the Popularity of Ancient Historians, 1450–1700', in *History and Theory* 2 (1966): 135–52; Quentin Skinner, *Liberty before Liberalism* (Cambridge: Cambridge University Press, 1998), 61–5; David Armitage, 'Empire and Liberty: A Republican Dilemma', in *Republicanism: A Shared European Heritage, volume 2: The Values of Republicanism in Early Modern Europe*, ed. Martin van Gelderen and Skinner (Cambridge: Cambridge University Press, 2002), 29–46, esp. 30.

[129] Qtd in Peltonen, *Classical Humanism*, 41.

[130] Sydney Anglo, 'Machiavelli as a Military Authority. Some Early Sources', in *Florence and Italy: Renaissance Studies in Honour of Nicolai Rubinstein*, ed. Peter Denley and Caroline Elam (London: Committee for Medieval Studies, 1988): 321–34, esp. 325–26; David Armitage, 'John Milton: Poet Against Empire', in *Milton and Republicanism*, ed. Armitage, Armand Himy, Quentin Skinner (Cambridge: Cambridge University Press, 1995), 206–25, esp. 209.

[131] See Sections 6.3 and 6.4.

[132] Algernon Sidney, *Court Maxims*, ed. Hans W. Blom, Eco Haitsma Mulier, and Ronald Janse (Cambridge: Cambridge University Press, 1996), 136–37. See Armitage, 'Empire and Liberty: A Republican Dilemma', 37–38.

skin', to fund them himself; yet, fearful that his troops will become mutinous against Rome and threaten her safety if they know of Appius's injustice, Virginius conceals his personal generosity and claims that Appius himself sent the provisions.[133] We can assume that Webster and Heywood very intentionally portrayed Virginius in this fashion, for these initial scenes in the courtroom and camp departed entirely from classical and medieval sources of this history. Liberality, like clemency, was understood as another significant virtue of princes according to the Senecan model, with Erasmus notably arguing that 'kindliness and generosity are the special glory of princes', and that the 'skillful and vigilant' prince would endeavour to help everyone through liberality.[134] According to the hierarchy of benefits that Seneca established, Virginius's liberality would have been considered of the highest order because he gave a 'necessarie' benefit 'without which wee cannot liue'; 'necessarie' benefits included such acts as delivering people 'out of the enemies handes', or saving them from 'a tyrants wrath and proscription'.[135] Virginius, by feeding his starving troops, protected not only their lives but also the lives of all Roman subjects defended by the army.

Webster and Heywood further elaborated Virginius's kingly qualities by depicting him as possessing the virtue of clemency. Finding his men on his return to the camp on the brink of mutiny due to their suffering, Virginius firmly rebukes his soldiers in a display of 'just anger', causing the soldiers, who hold great respect for their captain, to repent and beg for mercy. When his soldiers exclaim 'wee'l starve first, / wee'le hange first, by the gods, doe any thing / ere wee'le forsake you', Virginius mixes mercy with justice, and pardons his troops.[136] These depictions of Virginius as a virtuous ruler would not have been lost on the Jacobean audience, for Webster and Heywood made explicit Virginius's kingly resemblance by having the Roman general, Minutius, draw a comparison between kings and captains after witnessing Virginius's clemency: 'every Captain', he explains, 'beares in his private government that forme, / which Kings should ore their Subjects, and to them / should be the like obedient'.[137]

Virginius was thus presented as a true *vir* possessing *virtus*, especially in the three roles of warrior, orator, and father. He serves as a foil to Appius in his republican fortitude, virtuous concern for the public welfare, and manly conduct. Webster and Heywood made a further distinction

---

[133] Webster [and Heywood], *Appius and Virginia*, 18.
[134] Erasmus, *Education of a Christian Prince*, 77.
[135] Webster [and Heywood], *Appius and Virginia*, 7–8, 11.   [136] Ibid., 16–17.   [137] Ibid., 17.

Tyranny and the Corruption of Law in Jacobean England 103

between the military captain and the judge through scenes displaying their private lives. Whereas Appius's first private scene revealed him as disordered in his soul and seeking the advice of the deviant Clodius, Virginius's household was represented as orderly and virtuous. Webster and Heywood's *Appius and Virginia* lacked the song of patriarchal order found in R. B.'s *Apius and Virginia*, but the dramatists nevertheless represented Virginia as showing due subservience to her father's authority. In the play, she 'most humbly / prostrates her filial Duty' upon his arrival and declares her submission to his charge to marry Icilius by vowing, 'I am my fathers daughter, and by him / I must be swaid in all things'.[138] Unlike R. B.'s *Apius and Virginia* and *That Which Seemes Best*, however, throughout this tragedy Virginia's role is circumscribed and her emotional presence limited, which allowed Webster and Heywood to emphasise Virginius's qualities as a patriarch instead. The playwrights concluded this scene by depicting Virginius's activities in ordering his obedient household as a mirror to his just commanding of the military camp: He arranges the marriage contract between Icilius and Virginia, then immediately rides off to tend to that 'universal businesse . . . / that toucheth a whole people', the ordering of his troops.[139]

Appius and Virginia thereby offered two important and contrasting portraits: a virtuous military commander, who seeks to protect and maintain the common good, law, and rightly ordered household, and a luxurious ruler overrun by lust, who forfeits the preservation of his commonwealth for private passion. This highly critical and subversive comparison, performed in Stuart playhouses, was a timely one, for as the next chapters will show, both James and Charles were sharply criticised for their seeming lack of military prowess and poor household management. Moreover, as *Appius and Virginia* was printed three times during the Protectorate, with its initial date of 1654 corresponding with the rise of Oliver Cromwell as lord protector, the portrait of a successful, virtuous, and revolutionary military commander defeating a cowardly and corrupt ruler offered a compelling parallel for Cromwell's supporters.[140]

Throughout the tragedy, Webster and Heywood repeatedly stressed that the source of Appius's judicial tyranny lay in his private lust, a symptom of his perverse soul, and that his unjust use of prerogative powers threatened the very liberty of Rome and its citizens. Like R. B.'s *Apius and Virginia* and *That Which Seemes Best*, the dramatists clearly connected Appius's disordered passions with the disordering of Roman society; however, they

---

[138] Ibid., 10–11. [139] Ibid., 11. [140] See Section 7.1.

104 Emasculated Kingship

adopted a portrayal of social disorder that better reflected Roman law and
the classical, republican accounts of Livy and Dionysius. The law of Rome
expressed through the *Codex* of Justinian admitted a 'fundamental division
within the law of persons' wherein 'all men and women are either free or
are slaves', with slavery being 'an institution of the *ius gentium* by which
someone is, contrary to nature, subject to the dominion of someone else',
and freedom meaning one is '*sui iuris*', or not under another's dominion
and thereby free to act in their own power.[141] The dramatic conflict
presented in *Appius and Virginia* focused less on the threat to Virginia's
chastity as on the threat to her status, and the status of all Roman citizens,
as *sui iuris*. In the tragedy, Appius's first plot endangered the status of
Rome as a free state by impoverishing the military, thereby placing Rome
at risk for being conquered and enslaved by its enemies; his second plot,
which closely followed Livy and Dionysius's accounts, threatened the
particular enslavement of Virginia, and, according to Virginius, the status
of all free people in Rome:

> Thou hast a daughter, thou hast a wife too,
> so most of you have Souldiers. Why might not this
> have hapned you? Which of you all, deer friends,
> but now, even now, may have your wives deflowred,
> your daughters slav'd, and made a Lictors prey?
> Think them not safe in *Rome*, for mine lived there.[142]

Virginia's trial exhibited how Appius's power to rule according to his will
and pleasure placed every Roman citizen at risk of enslavement. For the
Stuart audience, Webster and Heywood placed onstage the precise ways
that Appius and Clodius manipulated the Roman legal system to obtain
this result: They falsely charged Virginia as a bondservant and Virginius
with treason, broke Roman law by trying to detain Virginia before her
trial, hired a 'Quick-silver' tongued orator, produced forged documents
and false witnesses for evidence, and rashly dismissed Virginius's witness
before hearing her testimony, all the while feigning impartiality and a
concern for justice.

While Webster and Heywood produced a more classicised production
of this history, they also implicated Appius as a wicked *pater patriae*, who
employed the language of fatherhood while seeking to strip a rightful
father of his child. When Numitorius, Virginia's uncle, begs for Appius

---

[141] Qtd in Skinner, 'John Milton and the Politics of Slavery', in *Visions of Politics*, vol. II (Cambridge:
Cambridge University Press, 2002), 289.
[142] Webster [and Heywood], *Appius and Virginia*, 51.

Tyranny and the Corruption of Law in Jacobean England 105

to stay the trial until Virginius could return from the camp, Appius argues that the father's presence is not necessary, for 'Who stands for father of the Innocent, / if not the Judg?' And just as Appius feigns the virtues of a prince while unjustly denying aid to the troops, he adopts the language of a virtuous householder when trying to argue, against Roman law, that Virginia should remain in his custody before the trial: 'I'l take the honoured Lady / into my guardianship, and by my life, / I'l use her in all kindness as my wife'.[143] At the same time, Webster and Heywood importantly portrayed much of Appius and Clodius's case as resting upon a suspicion of female virtue, especially of the female members of Virginius's household. The hired orator claims that Virginia's mother was 'deceitful', and tricked her husband by 'fain[ing] the passions / of a great bellyed woman'.[144] As the audience knows, this depiction of Virginia's mother is entirely false, but when Virginia's nurse protests and seeks to bear witness to the birthing – a testimony which, according to early modern standards, only she and a handful of other women could produce – Appius casts her out as a liar. Within the tragedy, thereby, Virginia's chastity and obedience, as well as her household being rightly ordered by Virginius, became the essential safeguards of social order and liberty against Appius's tyranny.

The play further emphasised the great political significance of female virtue through Virginia's death. Like other writers, Webster and Heywood departed from Livy and Dionysius by having Virginia request her own death, but their portrayal characterised her sacrifice as motivated by a desire to preserve civil liberty. Before the trial commences, she tells Virginius:

> O my dear Lord and father, once you gave me
> a noble freedom, do not see it lost
> without a forfeit; take the life you gave me
> and sacrifice it rather to the gods
> then to a villains Lust. Happy the Wretch
> who born in bondage lives and dies a slave,
> and sees no lustful projects bent upon her,
> and neither knowes the life nor death of honor.[145]

Virginia's virtue is predicated upon her chastity, but her liberty rests upon her birth as the lawful daughter of a free citizen; thereby, Appius's 'lustful project' threatens not only her chaste status but also her legal freedom. The tragedy's emphasis upon liberty is indeed significant, and moves beyond

[143] Ibid., 34–35.   [144] Ibid., 42.   [145] Ibid., 40.

106 Emasculated Kingship

the martyrdom account of the Elizabethan *Apius and Virginia*; however, even in Webster and Heywood's play, Virginia's liberty remains prescribed within the narrow confines of society ordered by gender, rank, status, and age. Within the play, it is clear that rule by consuls would not overturn but restore and even strengthen the patriarchal order. Exultation of Virginia's liberty thereby went hand-in-hand with the exultation of her prescribed role as chaste, obedient, and submissive daughter and spouse. The flattening of Virginia's character throughout the tragedy further offered her as an idealised *exemplum* of Roman freedom for women in the patriarchal order, whose 'rights' are preserved not through active political participation but through submission, protection, and sacrifice.

Webster and Heywood's *Appius and Virginia* provided the only full portrayal of Virginius's republican revolution in Tudor and Stuart literature. Significantly, it is not the revolution of the headless mob, but of an ordered military that brings justice to Rome and thereby restores Rome's freedom.[146] As Icilius declares in the final scene: '*Rome* thou at length art free, / restored unto thine ancient liberty'.[147] Virginia's death in this tragedy, thereby, is swift and silent, lacking the emotional appeal of earlier texts, for Webster and Heywood portrayed her death not as a private martyrdom for the cause of chastity, but as a public sacrifice made for the 'common cause' of Rome. Afterwards Virginius does initially lament how he 'plaid the Parricide', describing how his 'rude hands ript her, and her innocent blood / flow'd above my elbowes', yet, as Icilius succinctly charges, Virginius through this act has proven himself 'a noble *Roman*, / but an unnatural Father', deciding that his daughter should rather 'die with honour, then to live / in servitude'.[148] Thus, as he leads the military into Rome to overthrow the Decemvirate, Virginius sets aside his anguish and declares, 'Be't my pride / that I have bred a daughter whose chast blood / was spilt for you, and for *Romes* lasting good'.[149] Due to Virginia's public sacrifice, Virginius, Icilius, and their armies unite and bring Appius and Clodius to justice. With the Decemvirate thus abolished, the Roman people name Virginius and Icilius as consuls, restoring that form of government 'which bold *Iunius Brutus* first / begun in *Tarquins* fall'.[150]

Appius and Virginia thereby offered a significant, if limited, declaration of Roman liberty as the solution to monarchical tyranny, and this idea challenged Stuart proclamations concerning the divine right and prerogative powers of kings. The tragedy argued that statesmen such as military

---

[146] Gunby, 'Critical Introduction', 465.   [147] Webster [and Heywood], *Appius and Virginia*, 61.
[148] Ibid., 50 and 55.   [149] Ibid., 51. See Gunby, 'Critical Introduction', 456–7.   [150] Ibid., 61.

Tyranny and the Corruption of Law in Jacobean England 107

captains could prove themselves better judges and rulers than kings. Quentin Skinner, amongst others, has already demonstrated how arguments supporting Roman liberty were essential to early critics of the Stuart monarchy and to defenders of the English Revolution.[151] Appius and Virginia's story demonstrates some of the intellectual resources that historical exempla provided for thinking about common law and monarchical prerogative well before the Petition of Right. What is more, the circulation of this story through plays and satire suggests that these ideas enjoyed a wider public than parliamentary debates and political treatises, and even shaped these debates on which intellectual historians have tended to focus. Although this chapter has revealed substantial differences between Elizabethan and Jacobean productions of the Appius and Virginia story, all of these authors identified tyranny as the corruption of a ruler's soul, expressed through vicious passions and the compromising of his masculinity. To pursue his insatiable passions, a tyrant such as Appius would corrupt the public law or institutions for personal, brutish gain. Simultaneously, each of these works represented political freedom and good governance as protected through an ordered, patriarchal society. According to these portrayals, the world would be turned right-side up when male virtue lawfully ruled in protection of liberty and female chastity.

---

[151] See 'John Milton and the Politics of Slavery', and 'Classical Liberty, Renaissance Translation and the English Civil War', in *Visions of Politics* II, 286–307 and 308–43; Armitage, 'Empire and Liberty'.

CHAPTER 3

'And thus did the wicked sonne murther his wicked mother'
Nero and the Tyrannical Household in Late Jacobean England

> Domitius *Nero*, one of the ancient Roman
> Emperours, who killed his mother *Agrippina*,
> his wife *Octavia*, the Poet *Lucan*, and *Seneca*
> his master.[1]

In May of 1626, Sir John Eliot notoriously summarised the charges of the House of Commons against the royal favourite George Villiers, the duke of Buckingham, by providing a lengthy and detailed comparison between Buckingham and Tacitus's Sejanus.[2] According to the classical historian Tacitus, Lucius Aelius Sejanus was an ambitious soldier who held a corrupting influence over the Emperor Tiberius, leading a benign and even good ruler to degenerate into a savage, lewd, and cruel tyrant. Drawing upon this popular history, Eliot declared that Sejanus and the contemporary Sejanus, Buckingham, were men of boldness, flattery, slander, corrupt preferment, and pride, thoroughly unworthy of honour.[3]

Some sections of Chapters 3 and 4 have been reproduced from the following article: Jamie Gianoutsos, 'Criticizing Kings: Gender, Classical History, and Subversive Writing in Seventeenth-Century England', *Renaissance Quarterly* 70.4 (Winter 2017): 1366–96. Copyright: © 2017 Renaissance Society of America.

[1] Quote in title from Pedro Mexía, *The imperiall historie: or The liues of the emperours, from Iulius Caesar, the first founder of the Roman monarchy, vnto this present yeere containing their liues and actions, with the rising and declining of that empire; the originall, and successe, of all those barbarous nations that haue inuaded it, and ruined it by peece-meele … translated into English by W.T.: and now corrected, amplified and continued to these times by Edvvard Grimeston Sergeant at Armes* (London, 1623), 66. Definition of Nero from Edward Phillips, *The new world of English words, or, A general dictionary containing the interpretations of such hard words as are derived from other languages* (London, 1658), sig. Dd3r.

[2] See Curtis Perry, *Literature and Favoritism in Early Modern England* (Cambridge: Cambridge University Press, 2006), 229–75, 229.

[3] In particular, he was accused of holding too many offices; of aiding French Catholics by delivering English ships to the French for use against the Huguenots; of selling honours and offices for personal profit; of procuring titles and favours for kinsmen; and of poisoning James I. See Roger Lockyer, 'Villiers, George, first duke of Buckingham (1592–1628)', in *Oxford Dictionary of National Biography* (Oxford University Press: 2004), online edn, May 2011, www.oxforddnb.com/view/article/28293.

108

'And thus did the wicked sonne murther his wicked mother' 109

The charge of favoritism through the historical exemplum of Sejanus carried the further accusation of sexual immorality. According to Tacitus, before Sejanus had 'won the heart of Tiberius', he 'had sold his person to Apicius, a rich debauchee'; the historian Suetonius similarly described Tiberius's debauchery in great detail.[4] Eliot did not explicitly extend his historical parallel to include Caesar Tiberius and the English king, Charles I, but the implied comparison between Tiberius and Charles was not lost on contemporaries, nor on Charles himself, who was said to have remarked: 'If the Duke is Sejanus, I must be Tiberius.'[5] Furious that parliament would condemn his favourite, and understanding these charges as an attack also upon himself, his monarchical rights and privileges, Charles dissolved parliament before the lords could finish their impeachment proceedings and ordered that Sir Dudley Diggs and Sir John Elliot, who had delivered the prologue and epilogue of the impeachment, be committed to the Tower.

Although dramatic, this episode in political history should not be considered an anomaly, but rather as one indication of the power and prevalence of historical exempla, especially of the Roman Principate, in shaping the language and understanding of politics in Stuart England. The first two chapters concentrated on the importance of the history of the Roman republic in defining and shaping conceptions of manliness or *virtus*, tyranny, and good governance in England; however, as we move into the 1620s, a period characterised by royalist, parliamentary, and constitutional debates over the prerogatives of kingship, we find the history of the Roman Principate to be especially significant. Drawing upon popular classical authors including Tacitus, Suetonius, Dio Cassius, Pliny

---

[4] Tacitus's history of Tiberius is found in Books I–VI of *The Annals*, although significant portions of Book V have been lost. Moses Hadas, ed. *The Complete Works of Tacitus*, trans. Alfred John Church and William Jackson Brodribb (New York: Modern Library, 1942), 144–227, esp. 144–5, 168–9, 178, 183, 189–90; Gaius Suetonius Tranquillus, *The Twelve Caesars*, trans. Robert Graves (Aylesbury: Penguin, 1979), 135–36; Michael B. Young, *James VI and I and the History of Homosexuality* (Basingstoke: Macmillan, 2000), 58–60.

[5] Samuel Rawson Gardiner, *History of England from the Accession of James I to the Outbreak of the Civil War, 1603–1642*, 10 vols. (London: Longmans, Green, & Co., 1884), VI: 107–8. An anonymous paper delivered to the King further argued: 'That this great opposition against the Duke, was stirred up and maintained by such as seek the destruction of this free Monarchy. Because they find it is not yet ripe to attempt against the King himself, they endeavour it through the sides of the Duke.' Moreover, the paper warned, 'since the time of Henry the Sixth, these Parliamentary discoursings might never be suffered, as being but certain symptoms of subsequent Rebellions, Civil Wars, and the dethroning our King.' John Rushworth, *Historical Collections Of Private Passages of State, Weighty Matters in Law, Remarkable Proceedings in Five Parliaments: Beginning The Sixteenth Year of King James, Anno 1618. And Ending the Fifth Year of King Charles, Anno 1629. Digested in Order of Time* (London: Browne, 1721), I.356.

110 Emasculated Kingship

the Elder, Seneca, and Lucan, writers in the 1620s and 1630s often discussed the examples of Tiberius, Caligula, and Claudius, but it was the Emperor Nero who earned the title 'worst tyrant in history'.[6] Between 1615 and 1640, Nero was cited as an example of tyranny at least 3,440 times in over 670 printed works, with the tyrant receiving sustained treatment in a plethora of plays, sermons, treatises, histories, pamphlets, and poetical and political works, especially in the 1620s.[7] From copies of sermons, libels, ballads, and commonplace books, it appears that Nero's story was very commonly referenced and would have been recognised broadly. In particular, writers detailed Nero's heinous violent and sexual crimes, such as torturing Christians, burning Rome, murdering family members, and committing acts of rape, sodomy, incest, and bestiality, in order to demonstrate the atrocity of tyranny and to debate whether limits existed for obeying monarchical power.

The history of Nero was placed centre stage in debates concerning monarchical absolutism, tyranny, and obedience not only because he was deemed the worst tyrant in history but because his reign provided the context for the thirteenth chapter of Romans, a central passage of scripture that seemed to justify unlimited obedience even to the worst of tyrants:

> Let every soul be subject unto the higher powers. For there is no power but of God: the powers that be are ordained of God. Whosoever therefore resisteth the power, resisteth the ordinance of God: and they that resist shall receive to themselves damnation. For rulers are not a terror to good works, but to the evil. Wilt thou then not be afraid of the power? do that which is good, and thou shalt have praise of the same: For he is the minister of God to thee for good. But if thou do that which is evil, be afraid; for he beareth

---

[6] As Marchamont Nedham would later declare, 'And who was *Emporour* at that time but *Nero?* no ordinary Tyrant, but the most notorious cruell Tyrant in the world: so that in all times since his name hath been made use of, by all Nations, as an ordinary Appellation for the worst of *Tyrants'*. *The Case of the Common-Wealth of England, Stated: or, the Equity, Vtility, and Necessity, of a Submission to the present GOVERNMENT* (London, 1650), 107.

[7] Estimate based on an *Early English Books Online* keyword search, May 2018; Specific examples include Anon., *The Tragedy of Nero* (London, 1624); Thomas May, *The Tragedy of Julia Agrippina* (acted 1628); Edmund Bolton, *Nero Caesar, or Monarchie Depraved* (London, 1624); George Chapman, *A iustification of a strange action of Nero* (London, 1629); Tacitus, *Annales* (London, 1622); Thomas Lodge, *The workes of Lucius Annaeus Seneca* (London, 1620); *L. & M. Annaei Senecae tragoediae: post omnes omnium editiones recensionesque editae denuò & notis Tho. Farnabii illustratae* (London, 1624); Mexía, *Imperiall Historie*; Sir Richard Barckley, *The felicitie of man, or, his summum bonum* (London, 1631); Samuel Garey, *Great Brittans little calendar: or, Triple diarie, in remembrances of three daies Diuided into three treatises...* (London, 1618); John Higgins, *The Falles of vnfortunate princes being a true chronicle historie of the vntimely death of such vnfortunate princes ...* (London, 1619); Thomas Nash, *Quaternio or A fourefold vvay to a happie life set forth in a dialogue between a countryman and a citizen, a divine and a lawyer* (London, 1633); John Taylor, *All the vvorkes of Iohn Taylor the water-poet Beeing sixty and three in number* (London, 1630); Timothy Rogers, *The Roman-Catharist: or the Papist is a Puritane* (1621).

'And thus did the wicked sonne murther his wicked mother' 111

not the sword in vain: for he is the minister of God, a revenger to execute wrath upon him that doeth evil. Wherefore ye must needs be subject, not only for wrath, but also for conscience sake.[8]

By deeming the ruler a rightful minister of God upon the earth, the apostle Paul appeared to equate resistance to a monarch with resistance to God's laws and thus extended the punishment for rebellion beyond the present life to damnation in the afterlife. The connection between this Biblical passage and Nero was frequently emphasised by Stuart writers, for Paul composed his exhortation while living as a subject under Nero and willingly accepted persecution and martyrdom under Nero for the cause of Christ. For those defending absolutism in Jacobean England and thereby understanding the king as possessing 'general freedom – as opposed to specific and limited freedoms – from human law' and subjects as owing unlimited obedience, Paul's exhortation to obedience in Romans 13 very significantly represented divine as well as political law.[9] As Anglican clergymen Richard Bernard and Richard Alleine explained in 1616, those who resist God's anointed king and ministers 'are truely Θεομάχοι, fighters against God himselfe'. Christians are called to 'be subiect therefore to the power ordained of God, and not to resist the same, Rom. 13. 1. 2'.[10]

Defenders of monarchical absolutism continued to rely upon Nero's example to make their arguments throughout Charles's reign, and his story remained important during the civil wars. On 5 May 1639, for example, following the Scottish Rebellion and Covenant, the bishop of Durham Thomas Morton preached a sermon on Romans 13:1 before King Charles. His sermon declared that God required subjection even to the cruellest tyrants and persecutors of faith, including

> Emperour *Nero*, who was the *highest Power* in the world at this time. He, after the fift yeare of his Empire, became so bloody a *Tyrant*, even to his owne heathenish people, that they branded him with the blacke marke of a *Monster*. And he was so vile and violent an Opposer of Christian Religion, that his Raigne hath beene registred ever since by Christians to have beene their *First fierie persecution*. . . All this notwithstanding, *S. Paul* requireth *Subjection* to this, and to all Other never so Tyrannous Governours.[11]

---

[8] Romans 13:1–5, King James Version (KJV).

[9] I define *absolutism* following the 'common usage' definition in Glenn Burgess, *Absolute Monarchy and the Stuart Constitution* (New Haven and London: Yale, 1996), 211.

[10] B[ernard], R[ichard], and R. A., *Davids mvsick: or Psalmes of that royall prophet, once the sweete singer of that Israel: vunfolded logically* (London, 1616), 58–59.

[11] Thomas Morton, *A sermon preached before the Kings most excellent Majestie, in the cathedrall church of Durham Upon Sunday, being the fifth day of May. 1639. By the Right Reverend Father in God, Thomas Lord Bishop of Duresme. Published by his Majesties speciall command* (London, 1639), 19–20. In the

Emasculated Kingship

These arguments defended the rights of monarchy even if a king became as vicious or more vicious than Nero, for as Morton claimed, tyranny was 'permitted' by God and therefore required obedience.[12] Simultaneously, though, if Charles and his father James qualified as rulers 'never so Tyrannous' as Nero – and surely they did, supporters argued – then who could claim that resistance against the English king was ever justified? In this way, royalists believed the very comparison between Nero and an English ruler might serve to deflate criticisms of contemporary monarchy.

At the same time, Nero's exemplum proved dangerous for arguments in support of monarchy, for the tyrant's history was filled with shocking stories of perversity and heinous violence. The brief summary of Nero in *The Lives of all the Roman Emperors* (1636), for example, listed a great number of examples of his 'insolency and cruelty': killing Seneca, stealing from the temple, causing 'his owne Mother *Agrippina* to be slaine, and her body to be ript open, that he might see the place wherein he lay', slaying '*Poppae* his wife with a spurne or kicke', practising magic, laughing as he set the city on fire, and persecuting and killing 'an infinite number of Christians', until he 'stabbed himselfe to the joy of the whole World' in the fourteenth year of his reign, at the age of 32.[13] To be asked to obey such a monstrous ruler proved difficult, and the emperor's history demonstrated how such tyrannical activity would indeed lead to rebellion. Nero was threatened by a revolt of the ancient Britons under Boudica, Piso's conspiracy, and, finally, the revolt of Galba under Julius Vindex, which led the Senate to declare the emperor an enemy of the people and order Nero's execution. To deem one's monarch a Nero, thereby, was to level a significant charge of corruption – political, sexual, and religious – against one's king and to insinuate that he might suffer an untimely and violent end.[14]

Scholars have previously examined how questions of resistance in seventeenth-century England relied upon the history of the Roman Principate; what have been largely overlooked, however, are the significant ways that Nero's story was appropriated in the 1620s to debate ideas of

---

mid-1630s, Charles himself was being deemed a Nero for persecuting 'true' believers. See Section 4.6.

[12] Ibid., 23.

[13] R. B., *The Lives of all the Roman Emperors, being exactly Collected, from Iulius Cæsar, unto the now reigning Ferdinand the second. With their Births, Governments, remarkable Actions, & Deaths* (London, 1636), 14–16.

[14] Indeed, this was one of the primary charges levelled against William Prynne in his trial concerning *Histrio-mastix* (1633). See Section 4.5.

'*And thus did the wicked sonne murther his wicked mother*' 113

patriarchalism as well as obedience and to define tyranny through gendered language as the failure to govern household as well as commonwealth.[15] Classical portrayals of Nero and their Stuart appropriations described and castigated Nero as a thoroughly failed and emasculated man. Despite Nero's myriad transgressions, writers very often detailed the tyrant's most heinous crimes as murdering mother, brother, and wife, and thereby trespassing his natural duty and obligation as family member and head of household.[16] As we will see in this chapter and the next, the seemingly perverse and perhaps incestuous relationship between Nero and his mother, Julia Agrippina, fascinated Stuart writers, in part because it suggested that monarchical vice could be bred through the royal family line. Nero's transgressions against family mapped onto and threatened ideas of patriarchalism in seventeenth-century England, which understood the king as the father of his people and thus as owing paternal care and necessary discipline to his children the subjects, and the subjects as owing reverence and obedience in return. As scholars have documented, seventeenth-century political writers went beyond the metaphor of family to locate political authority in a history of patriarchy, tracing the origins of political government to the authority of Adam. Political obligation, then, was said to have developed out of the natural human relationships of familial obligation and paternal authority.[17]

King James frequently touted his patriarchal authority, for through it he could delineate and justify a broad range of kingly duties and activities and also condemn any justification of resistance by the people. He evoked the idea of the father-king in his two most important political treatises: *Basilicon Doron* (1598, revised 1603) and *The Trew Law of Free Monarchies*. In *Basilicon Doron*, James promoted the notion of the king as father on two levels: literally, as a 'naturall Father' of a family, he crafted the book

---

[15] Historical accounts of early Stuart Neronian histories have instead focused almost solely on the resistance of Boudica and Julius Vindex, the lives of Seneca and Lucan, and the persecution of Christians within Nero's reign. See Alan T. Bradford, 'Stuart Absolutism and the 'Utility' of Tacitus', *Huntington Library Quarterly* 46.2 (Spring 1983): 127–55; Burgess, *Absolute Monarchy*, 61–62; Daniel Woolf, *The Idea of History in Early Stuart England* (Toronto, Buffalo, London: University of Toronto Press, 1990), 193–97.

[16] For example, Edward Phillip's brief explanation of Nero stated the following: 'Domitius *Nero*, one of the ancient Roman Emperours, who killed his mother *Agrippina*, his wife *Octavia*, the Poet *Lucan*, and *Seneca* his master'. See, *The new world of English words*, sig. Dd3r.

[17] J. P. Sommerville, 'Absolutism and Royalism', in *The Cambridge History of Political Thought, 1450–1700*, ed. J. H. Burns (New York and Cambridge: Cambridge University Press, 1991), 347–73, esp. 355, 358–59; Gordon J. Schochet, *Patriarchalism in Political Thought* (New York: Basic Books, 1975), 55; Rachel Weil, *Political Passions: Gender, the Family and Political Argument in England, 1680–1714* (Manchester: Manchester University Press, 1999), 22–25.

as practical advice for his son and heir, Henry; politically, as a *'communis parens'*, or common father to his people, James outlined the duties and attributes of a good king, charging Henry to continue in the practices of 'naturall father and kindly Master' towards his subjects just as his father and father's father had.[18] While *Basilicon Doron* offered practical advice on the duties of kings, *The Trew Law* offered a political justification of James's divine right principles and an extensive allegorical explanation of the king as father. As a father is bound 'to care for the nourishing, education, and vertuous gouernment of his children', to bestow 'toile and paine' for their 'profite and weale', to protect them from dangers, to correct them with 'father chastisement seasoned with pitie', and to take his 'chiefe ioy' in his children's welfare, so should the king become 'a naturall Father to all his Lieges'.[19]

Moreover James stressed his authority and power as a father in his speeches before parliament as well as his writings. In 1610, he summarised the *Patriam potestatem* as *'Potestatem vitae & necis'*, the power of life and death 'ouer their children or familie'.[20] A witness to the King's speech before parliament in 1623 recorded James's adaptation of the familial metaphor to emphasise his duties in matrimonial terms:

> That a good Kinge sholde be lyke a husbande to his wief; And as Christe is sayde to be the head of the Churche: so agood Kinge sytting on his throne and vnited to his Kingdome is lyke vnto Christ espoused to his Churche. And it sholde be the husbands parte to cherishe and to comforte his wief and sholde reconcyle hymself vnto her. And so it is my desire to cherishe youe my people.[21]

Beyond the king's obligation to his people, this familial relationship, especially when described through the father–child dichotomy, entailed unlimited obedience from the subjects, according to James: 'consider, I pray you, what duetie his children owe to him, & whether vpon any pretext whatsoeuer, it wil not be thought monstrous and vnnaturall to his sons, to rise vp against him, to control him at their appetite, and when they thinke good to sley him, or cut him off . . . ?'[22] The relationship between kings and subjects, fathers and children, then, was one of mutual obligation, but not of contract. A king failing in his duties must still be

---

[18] *King James VI and I: Political Writings*, ed. Johann P. Sommerville (Cambridge: Cambridge University Press, 1994), 2, 36, 20.
[19] Ibid., 65–66.   [20] Ibid., 182.
[21] 'His Maiesties speeche in the parliament house: 19 die February 1623', British Library, Add. MS 61683, fo. 42r.
[22] *King James VI and I: Political Writings*, 77.

'*And thus did the wicked sonne murther his wicked mother*' 115

honoured, respected, and obeyed by his subjects, according to James, for rebelling subjects committed political patricide.

As we will see in this chapter and the next, writers discussing Nero simultaneously focused on Nero's failure as political governor and as family man, including his duties as son, husband, and father. Attending to these discussions, which scholars have overwhelmingly neglected, this chapter explores how King James in the final years of his reign was explicitly associated with the Emperor Nero, and how gendered portrayals of Nero were used to challenge and to defend James's political policies, kingly authority, and masculinity. The chapter will argue that Nero's history, much like the histories of Tarquin and Appius, provided an imaginative and gendered definition of tyranny as disorder and inversion: the disorder of the monarch's person, his household and country, and in relation, the inversion of his prescribed gender and gendered roles. This representation of tyranny necessarily employed gendered language, for the question of the tyrant's ability to follow the laws of nature, rule himself, and govern his household and country was a question of the tyrant's *virtus*, or manliness, and his possession of what were then held to be the 'manly' virtues of reason, constancy, courage, and justice.

The opening sections of this chapter explore criticisms of James during the Bohemian and Spanish Match crises, specifically focusing on the anonymous *Tragedy of Nero* (1624) and an anonymous libel. These incendiary writings characterised the King as emasculated, cowardly, Catholic, and corrupt, thereby unfit to protect 'true religion' in the face of European war. More broadly, these texts imagined tyranny as a failure in public policy and also household relations and sordid morality, especially uxoriousness, cuckoldry, and sodomy. Nero's story demonstrated how deviant passions and patriarchal failure would undermine true religion, the liberty and manliness of male subjects, and the lawful order of society. Conversely, the final section considers Edmund Bolton's *Nero Caesar, or Monarchie Depraued* (1624). Despite its creation for the defence of monarchy, Bolton's mammoth history likewise adopted highly gendered characterisations of tyranny and the royal household, defending monarchical absolutism by placing the blame for Nero's crimes on vicious female transgressors. As we will see, while seeking to diminish Nero's culpability for his lustful passions and parricidal murders, Bolton's arguments simultaneously, and unintentionally, revealed the dangers of hereditary monarchy as they emphasised how a vicious tyrant could be the product of a wicked woman's womb. These texts when considered together underscore how debates concerning tyranny, hereditary monarchy, and obedience

116   Emasculated Kingship

often centred upon discussions of family relations, gender, and the failure of kings and queens to perform their marital and parental duties.

3.1 Continental War and Masculine Failure

In 1618, James, the *rex pacificus*, witnessed the eruption of the Bohemian Revolt and what would become the Thirty Years' War in Europe, as Bohemian nobles successfully overthrew Ferdinand II, the appointed Catholic king of Bohemia, and elected the Protestant Frederick V of the Rhineland-Palatinate, who was married to James's daughter, Elizabeth. Frederick's acceptance of the kingship defied the Holy Roman emperor, and war ensued when Ferdinand and the Spaniards gathered forces to reclaim the estate and title. In 1620, Ferdinand smashed Frederick's troops at the Battle of White Mountain, and by 1622 the Habsburgs controlled Bohemia and much of the Palatinate. James's initial response to the crisis was diplomatic, for not only did he have a history of successfully negotiating peace with opposing religious forces on the Continent but he further doubted the authority of a monarch by election rather than inheritance, and thereby could only uneasily support the claim of his son-in-law.[23] James set his sights on negotiations with Spain by sending ambassadors, making the English presence felt through a series of small naval manoeuvres, and attempting to contract a marriage alliance between the Spanish infanta Maria Ana and his son Charles.[24] However, this international policy of balancing confessional divides for pacific ends exasperated many Protestants who believed God was calling the English to protect the true church through war. Although calling for a parliament in 1621 to provide him financial means for military defence, James by 1624 had still not taken military action.

James's desired rapprochement with the powerful Catholic Habsburgs confused and angered many English supporters of the Protestant cause.[25] 'Hotter' Protestants understood the Continental struggle as part of Protestant apocalyptic history in which the true church opposed the forces of

---

[23] W. B. Patterson, 'Outbreak of the Thirty Years' War', in *King James VI and I and the Reunion of Christendom* (Cambridge: Cambridge University Press, 1997), 291–338; Rei Kanemura, *The Idea of Sovereignty in English Historical Writing, 1599–1627* (PhD Thesis, University of Cambridge, 2012); Robert Zaller, '"Interest of State": James I and the Palatinate', *Albion* 6, No. 2 (Summer, 1974): 144–75, esp. 144–46.

[24] Zaller, 'Interest of State', 147–48.

[25] For general parliamentary confusion at James's war strategy, see Thomas Cogswell, 'Phaeton's Chariot: The Parliament-men and the Continental Crisis of 1621', in J. F. Merritt, ed., *The Political World of Thomas Wentworth, Earl of Strafford, 1621–1641* (Cambridge: Cambridge University Press, 1996), 24–46, esp. 41–42.

'And thus did the wicked sonne murther his wicked mother' 117

Antichrist. Through pamphlets, polemical tracts, sermons, and corantos, or weekly news books, these supporters voiced their discontent with the royal pacific policy and urged a militant, interventionist alternative. The outpouring of libellous public criticisms against James and his foreign policy became so pronounced in the early 1620s that the King twice passed proclamations banning censorious speech.[26] The target of these proclamations included a significant number of libels and pamphlets that criticised the King's inactivity in the war as a failing of masculinity, characterised English society as awash in gender disorder, and denounced the seeming transformation of men and women into emasculated or hermaphroditic monsters. *Hic mvlier: or, The man-woman* (1620) held masculine women responsible for this perceived gender trouble, while an anonymous reply, *Hæc vir: or The womanish-man* (1620), placed the blame for gender disorder on the failings of men: 'For this you haue demolish'd the noble schooles of Hors-manship ... hung vp your Armes to rust, glued vp those swords in their scabberds that would shake all Christendome with the brandish and entertained into your mindes such softnes, dulnesse, and effeminate nicenesse, that it would euen make *Heraclitus* himselfe laugh'.[27] For virtue and order to be restored to the commonwealth, men must behave as men. The tract concluded: 'Be men in shape, men in shew, men in words, men in actions, men in counsell, men in example: then will we loue and serue you; then will wee heare and obey you.'[28] Although these pamphlets responded particularly to the Bohemian Crisis, the topos of 'effeminate peace' was pervasive in Renaissance literature, from Richard of York decrying peace as 'effeminate' in Shakespeare's *1 Henry VI* to Byron's condemnation of Henry's peace in Chapman's *Tragedie of Byron*.[29]

---

[26] Proclamations passed in 1620 and 1621. James F. Larkin and Paul L. Hughes, eds., *Stuart Royal Proclamations, vol I: Royal Proclamations of James I, 1603–1625* (Oxford: Clarendon, 1973), 495–96 and 519–20.

[27] See Anon., *Hæc-vir; or The womanish-man: being an answere to a late booke intituled Hic-mulier. Exprest in a briefe dialogue betweene Hæc-vir the womanish-man, and Hic-mulier the man-woman* (London, 1620), C2ʳ. The reply may have been written by the same author.

[28] Ibid., C3ᵛ.

[29] William Shakespeare, *The First Part of Henry the Sixth*, in *The Oxford Shakespeare: The Complete Works*, ed. Stanley Wells, Gary Taylor, John Jowett, and William Montgomery, 2nd ed. (Oxford: Clarendon, 2005), 153 (5.6.107). As Byron says, 'The world is quite inuerted: vertue throwne / At Vices feete: and sensuall peace confounds / Valure, and cowardise': George Chapman, *The conspiracie, and tragedie of Charles Duke of Byron, Marshall of France. Acted lately in two playes, at the Black-Friers* (London, 1608), K1r (1.2.14–16). These sentiments likewise find expression by Clermont in Chapman's *The Revenge of Bussy D'Ambois. A Tragedie* (London, 1613), B1v (1.1.41–47). Chapman's use of this trope can also be seen in Section 4.2.

118 Emasculated Kingship

Other tracts emphasised English warfare as the one and necessary solution. Published in Utrecht and anonymised, the *Votivae Angliae* (1624), for example, sought 'to perswade his Majestie to drawe his Royall Sword, for the restoring of the Pallatynat, and Electorat', to the 'Glorie of God, and the defence and protection of his afflicted Spouse the Church'. The pamphlet argued that war was 'as necessarie as just', and urged the King that 'it must bee your Sword, not your Tongue, not your Treaties, not your Letters, not your Ambassadours... For all other meanes are fledd ... , and this of Warre is onlie left you to effect it, which will not fayle, nor cannot deceive you in the performance therof'.[30] These pamphlets often sought to rouse suspicion and hostility towards Spain and the Catholic religion for the sake of war, such as the second part of the *Vox Populi* (1624) which represented the Spaniards, especially the 'Machiavellian' Spanish Ambassador Gondomar, as plotting to overthrow the Protestant religion in England. According to the pamphlet, the Spanish desired peace with England, the 'sleepie Lyon', for fear of certain defeat by her military should she awake.[31] Similarly, pamphlets such as the first part of the *Vox Populi* (1624) criticised the intended Spanish Match, blaming the 'begging and beggarly Courtyers' and 'Romish Catholiques' for desiring the match, the former that 'they might haue to furnish their wants' and the latter 'who hoped hereby at least for a moderation of fynes and lawes, perhaps a tolleraaion [sic], and perhaps a total restauration of their religion in England'.[32]

Proponents of Spanish peace, however, understood the House of Habsburg as representing monarchical legitimacy, stability, and social order in the face of anti-monarchical fervour, rebellion, and extreme religion. This faction, mainly comprising the powerful and largely Catholic

---

[30] [John Reynolds], *VOTIVAE ANGLIAE: OR THE DESIRES AND VVISHES OF ENGLAND. Contayned in a Patheticall Discourse, presented to the KING on New-yeares Day last. Wherein are vnfolded and represented, manie strong Reasons, and true and solide Motives, to perswade his Majestie to drawe his Royall Sword, for the restoring of the Pallatynat, and Electorat, to his Sonne in Lawe Prince FREDERICKE, to his onlie Daughter the Ladie ELIZABETH, and theyr Princelie Issue. AGAINST THE TREACHEROVS VSVRPATION, and formidable Ambition and Power of the Emperour, the King of Spayne, and the Duke of Bavaria, whoe unjustlie Possesse and detayne the same. Together with some Aphorismes returned (with a Large interest) to the Pope in Answer of his.sig.* (Utrecht: 1624), sig. c1r–v.

[31] T. S. [Thomas Scot], *The second part of Vox populi, or Gondomar appearing in the likenes of Matchiauell in a Spanish parliament wherein are discouered his treacherous & subtile practises to the ruine as well of England, as the Netherlandes faithfully transtated [sic] out of the Spanish coppie by a well-willer to England and Holland* (Goricum: 1624), 41–42, 50.

[32] Anon. [Thomas Scot], *Vox Populi, or Newes from Spayne, translated according to the Spanish coppie. Which may serve to forwarn both England and the Vnited Provinces how farre to trust to Spanish pretences* ([London]: 1620), sig. B2r.

'And thus did the wicked sonne murther his wicked mother' 119

Howard family, opposed the persecution of Catholics and supported an Anglo-Spanish alliance, rather than an Anglo-French alliance or bellicose intervention.[33] To this group, James's early actions did not disappoint. As England had fostered a closer relationship with Spain in the years preceding the crisis, discussing and negotiating the revolt with the Spanish and their allies seemed natural and potentially productive to the King.[34] James fashioned himself in the midst of ensuing continental war as the mediator of peace, offering to resolve the conflict diplomatically rather than militarily. Even after a Spanish army invaded the Lower Palatinate in the autumn of 1620, James and the pro-Spanish party could maintain that the 'emperor was perfectly justified in what he had done', for Frederick had risen in rebellion. In *His Maiesties Declaration* (1622), James argued, 'We would neuer haue constantly denyed Our Sonne in law, both the title and assistance in that point, if Wee had beene well perswaded of the iustice of his quarrel.' Frederick's 'vniust vsurpation', the King maintained, 'hath giuen the Pope, and all that partie, too faire a ground, and opened them too wide a gate for the curbing and oppressing of many thousands of Our religion, in diuers parts of Christendome'.[35] In these years, King James became so motivated to avoid the entanglements of war, and he fostered such good rapport with the Spanish Ambassador Gondomar, that he purposely sabotaged the belligerent Parliament of 1621 in order to avoid military intervention.[36]

Between 1619 and 1625, James's image as a pacific, wise, and authoritative prince in the midst of political crisis was fashioned through a series of courtly entertainments for the royal court and visiting Spanish ambassadors. These productions sought to instil obedience and respect for James's non-interventionist policies, casting zealots, warmongers, and newsmongers as the anti-masquers whose defeat or reform was necessary to achieve order, harmony, and godly control in the realm.[37] In the

---

[33] C. H. Carter, 'Gondomar: Ambassador to James I', *The Historical Journal* 7.2 (1964): 189–208, esp. 193–94; Simon Adams, 'Foreign Policy and the Parliaments of 1621 and 1624', in *Faction and Parliament: Essays on Early Stuart History*, ed. Kevin Sharpe (Oxford: Oxford University Press, 1978), 139–71, esp. 141. See also Adams, 'Spain or the Netherlands? The dilemmas of early Stuart foreign policy', in Howard Tomlinson, ed., *Before the Civil War: Essays on Early Stuart Politics and Government* (London: Macmillan, 1983), 79–101.

[34] Patterson, *King James VI and I*, 297–98; Carter 'Gondomar: Ambassador to James I', 205–8.

[35] *Political Writings of James VI and I*, 258.

[36] Brennan C. Pursell, 'James I, Gondomar, and the Dissolution of the Parliament of 1621', *History* 85.279 (Jul 2000): 428–45.

[37] See Martin Butler, *The Stuart Court Masque and Political Culture* (Cambridge: Cambridge UP, 2008), 239–75; Stephen Orgel, *The Illusion of Power: Political Theater in the English Renaissance* (Berkeley and LA: University of California Press, 1975), 70–77.

120   Emasculated Kingship

1621 portrait of James by Daniel Mytens, the King was portrayed as sitting
prominently on a throne wearing a sheathed sword and the full robes of
the Most Noble Order of the Garter. While these conspicuous symbols of
chivalry, military prowess, monarchical authority, and masculinity lay in
the fore, a tapestry draped behind the throne displayed the Tudor Rose
with the motto *BEATI PACIFICI*, 'Blessed are the Peace-makers'.

Scholars have shown how the debate between pro- and anti-Spanish
factions in the 1620s ensued through speeches, sermons, pamphlets,
corantos, and libels, but what has been neglected is how contemporaries
enmeshed in this conflict understood historical exempla, especially concerning Nero, as a significant source for understanding monarchical
authority, its responsibilities and limitations. As we will see, Edmund
Bolton, who supported the pro- Spanish faction, crafted his history, *Nero
Caesar, or Monarchie Depraued,* as a justification of strong monarchical
government. For the ultra-Protestant position, in contrast, anonymous
writers turned to Nero's history to question and to censure the moral
character and authority of the monarch and his policies. By choosing
creative and anonymous discourses relying upon these stories, writers
could level highly critical and effective charges against the King which
would resonate with the English public, even while under the threat of
state censorship and discipline following James's proclamations in
1620 and 1621 against the 'licentious passage of lavish discourse, and bold
Censure in matters of State'.[38] Like other libellous works, the anonymous
Tragedy of Nero (1624) defied this proclamation by providing a timely
criticism of James's pacific policies and dramatically emphasising the wider
devastation wrought by unconstrained tyranny and court corruption.

3.2   The Tragedy of Nero

On 15 May 1624, *The Tragedy of Nero* was allowed to be printed, but little
other information survives about its production or performance.[39] The
stark title page labelled the work 'Newly Written', perhaps to emphasise its
relevance to contemporary politics or perhaps to distinguish it from the
earlier *Tragedy of Claudius Tiberius Nero* (1607).[40] It is unclear if the play
was acted in the 1620s, although a surviving manuscript copy and an

---

[38] Larkin and Hughes, eds., *Stuart Royal Proclamations*, 495–96 and 519–20.
[39] Joseph Quincy Adams, ed. *The Dramatic Records of Sir Henry Herbert: Master of the Revels,
1623–1673* (New Haven: Yale University Press, 1917), 28.
[40] A. H. Bullen, ed. 'Introduction to the *Tragedy of Nero*', in *A Collection of Old English Plays*, vol. 1
(London: Wyman & Sons, 1882), 3–10, esp. 10.

'*And thus did the wicked sonne murther his wicked mother*'   121

allusion to *The Tragedy of Nero* identified in John Fletcher and Philip Massinger's *Little French Lawyer* (written c. 1619–23, printed 1647) suggest that it was familiar enough to have been acted or at least widely circulated, whether in the public playhouse or the semi-private estates and spaces of noble and educated men. It was also popular enough to be cited in Samuel Butler's commonplace book, reprinted in 1633, and was later acted with minor adjustments in 1676.[41]

Although anonymous, the title page of *The Tragedy of Nero* does offer the names of the printers John Norton and Augustine Mathewes. Mathewes (with Michael Sparkes) was later brought before the Star Chamber for producing William Prynne's *The Chvrch of England's Old Antithesis to New Arminianisme* (1629), which was considered 'offensive' and printed without 'license or warrant'.[42] In his defence for producing this book and others, Sparkes made an extraordinary speech objecting to the binding authority of the Star Chamber decree for regulating printing as directly violating the liberty of subjects, including their persons and goods, as outlined in the Magna Carta, Petition of Right, and other statutes, and he defended Prynne's book as a just and necessary defence of the Church of England against the Arminians.[43] Although Mathewes printed a large number of works throughout his career, it seems significant that in the 1630s he offended the Star Chamber again by printing Milton's *Comus, a Mask Presented at Ludlow Castle* in defiance of the *Decree of Starre-Chamber, Concerning Printing* of 1637, which allowed only approved presses to remain in operation.[44] In the 1620s, Augustine Mathewes also served as Thomas May's printer, most importantly printing the 1627 English edition of Lucan's *Pharsalia*, which was dedicated to a network of statesmen who had refused to pay the forced loan.[45] Due to this connection between Mathewes and May, it has been suggested that the *Tragedy of Nero* was written by the young May, whose *Tragedy of Julia Agrippina* we will consider

---

[41] British Library, MS Egerton 1994, fos. 245–67. See Gerald Eades Bentley, '*The Tragedy of Nero (Piso's Conspiracy)* (>1623?)', in *The Jacobean and Caroline Stage: Plays and Playwrights*, vol. V (Oxford: Clarendon Press, 1956), 1379–82. The manuscript holds a number of plays including at least two in Thomas Heywood's own hand.

[42] W. H. Hart, *Index expurgatorius Anglicanus: or, a Descriptive Catalogue of the Principal Books Printed or Published in England, which have been suppressed, or burnt by the Common Hangman, or Censured, or for which the Authors, Printers, or Publishers have been Prosecuted* (London: John Russell Smith, 1872), 72.

[43] Ibid., 72–73.

[44] Ian Gadd, 'Stationers', in *The Milton Encyclopedia*, ed. Thomas M. Corns (New Haven: Yale University Press, 2012), 348–52, 349.

[45] See Section 4.4. Augustine Mathewes also printed Thomas May's *The Heire. A Comedie* (London, 1633) and *Virgil's Georgicks Englished* (London, 1628).

122 Emasculated Kingship

in detail in the next chapter; what seems more certain from its publication history, and especially from its content, however, is that the tragedy was produced by someone sympathetic to the Protestant cause and perhaps critical of the policies undertaken in James's reign.[46]

The tragedy, which is set in Rome during the late years of Nero's reign, opens with a strident censure of cowardly foreign policy, court immorality, and ineffective governance. Nero, absent from his court in the first scene, appears onstage in the second scene following reports that he has completed a triumphal procession through the streets of Rome, not for a military 'conquest', as was traditional of victorious Roman generals and Caesars, but for 'hauing Greece in her owne arts ouerthrowne; / In Singing, Dauncing, Horserase, Stage-playing'.[47] Nero boasts in this bloodless 'victory' over Greece, claiming he has conquered by his 'cunning, not his force', and thereby obtained 'Not spoyles with blood bedew'd, / Or the vnhappie obsequies of Death'.[48] As reported by common Roman citizens, this triumph is of comic proportions. Nero has won 'Eighteene hundred and eight Crownes' through his 'singing' and 'stage-playing', and he adorns himself as an Apollo or Hercules, presumably for completing such extraordinary labours.

Within this early scene, the playwright invited his audience to draw connections between Nero and their own King James, whose court and courtiers preferred sporting and courtly delights to engaging in warfare. The libel, 'Fortunes wheele. or Rota fortunæ in gyro', written at the end of James's reign, reflected this view in its discussion of the attempted workings of false gods to dismember the English state. While the true God prevented such a false one, Baalam, from succeeding in the early Gunpowder Plot, Balaam succeeded afterward through learning the 'alluringe lessons . . . / of pride, luste, avarice, & wretched hate'. The libel concluded by arguing that 'presentlie the kinge affects his peace / proposinge nothinge but delights increase'. Courtiers pretend to give the King honour, 'though out of private endes'. The court 'swarmes . . . with youthfull gallants brave', who seek the 'kinges love' instead of engaging their bravery in true battle.[49]

---

[46] F. G. Fleay further argued, 'The fact that *Nero*, T., 1624, was transferred with May's *Heir* and his *Lucan* translation, S. R. 1633, Oct. 24, by T. Jones to Matthews makes me suspect that it also was by May. These two plays alone out of six mentioned in this entry had been originally licensed independently of the Stationers by the Master of the Revels.' *Biographical Chronicle of English Drama, 1559–1642* (London: Reeves and Turner, 1891), II.83–84.

[47] Anon., *The Tragedy of Nero* (London, 1624), sig. A4v.   [48] Ibid., sig. B1r.

[49] 'Fortunes wheele. or Rota fortunæ in gyro', Alastair Bellany and Andrew McRae, eds. 'Early Stuart Libels: An Edition of Poetry from Manuscript Sources', *Early Modern Literary Studies Text Series I* (2005), http://purl.oclc.org/emls/texts/libels/.

'*And thus did the wicked sonne murther his wicked mother*' 123

Within the *Tragedy of Nero*, the citizens enraptured by Nero's triumphs name him 'the true *Augustus*', with one citizen claiming that Augustus's triumph 'was not like to this' in glory. In seventeenth-century England, Augustus was the central exemplum of the prince of peace or *rex pacificus*, a ruler who ushered in prosperity and letters to Rome, whose power was proclaimed not by war but by learned 'words and deeds', and whose 'sober and mindful' reflections allowed him to reign by reason not passion.[50] Written encomia and processions honouring James very commonly praised him as an Augustus due to his scholarly pursuits, his peaceful succession to the throne and his international pacific policies, and indeed by late in his reign, James showed his preference for Augustus as his kingly parallel in the *Meditation* (1619).[51] James's coronation medallion named him 'IAC : I : BRIT : CAE : AVG : HAE CAESARVM CAE. D. D'. (James I, Caesar Augustus of Britain, Caesar the heir of the Caesars); his coronation banners proclaimed him 'Augustus Novus'.[52] Through these parallels, the *Tragedy of Nero* identified the parading tyrant with James, while simultaneously mocking James's identification as peacemaker. The avoidance of war, coupled with lavish entertainments and spending, merely mimicked the triumphs of peace wrought by military victory.

Through this association of James and Nero, the *Tragedy* deemed the King's refusal to enter war for the Protestant Cause as effeminate and cowardly. Tacitus and Dio Cassius in their histories had characterised Nero's activities to win fame and to court the common masses by singing and acting as disgraceful, humiliating, and unbefitting to his station, but *The Tragedy of Nero*, while acknowledging this censure, more specifically attacked Nero's dalliances as a sign of his deficient military valour, courage, and manliness. Queen Poppaea, for one, powerfully presents this criticism

---

[50] Jonathan Goldberg, *James I and the Politics of Literature: Jonson, Shakespeare, Donne, and Their Contemporaries* (Stanford: Stanford University Press, 1989), 47 and 50; Todd Wayne Butler, *Imagination and Politics in Seventeenth-Century England* (Burlington, VT: Ashgate, 2008), 51. For an example of an extended list of Caesar Augustus's qualities, see Pedro Mexía, *Imperiall Historie* (London, 1623), 37.

[51] Paulina Kewes, 'Julius Caesar in Jacobean England', *The Seventeenth Century* 17 (2002): 155–86, esp. 179; Goldberg, *James I and Politics of Literature*, 27; James, *A MEDITATION Vpon the 27. 28. 29. Verses of the XXVII. Chapter of Saint Matthew. or A PATERNE FOR A KINGS INAVGVRATION*, in *James VI and I: Political Writings*, 235. For an early comparison with Augustus, see the second dedicatory sonnet in *The Essayes of a Prentise, in the Divine Art of Poesie* (Edinburgh ('Cvm Privilegio Regall'), 1584).

[52] I am grateful to Mary (Molly) Gerwig for notifying me of this medallion. See Barbara Parker, *Plato's Republic and Shakespeare's Rome: A Political Study of the Roman Works* (Cranbury, NJ: Rosemont, 2004), 105; Walter S. H. Lim, *The Arts of Empire: The Poetics of Colonialism from Raleigh to Milton* (Newark, DE: University of Delaware Press, 1998), 220–21.

124 Emasculated Kingship

in a sarcastic speech to Nero praising his 'witt . . . that choose such safe / Honors, safe spoyles, wonn without dust or blood'. When Nero asks, 'What mocke ye me *Poppea*?' she replies cunningly:

> Nay, in good Faith my Lord, I speake in earnest,
> I hate that headie, and aduenturous crew,
> That goe to loose their owne, to purchase, but
> The breath of others, and the common voyce,
> Them that will loose there hearing for a sound;
> That by death onely, seeke to get a liuing,
> Make skarrs their beautie, and count losse of Limmes
> The commendation of a proper man,
> And so, goe halting to immortalitie:
> Such fooles I loue worse then they doe their liues.[53]

By the end of the scene, Nero seems to interpret Poppaea's speech as condemning the courage of soldiers and their hard won immortal fame; a seventeenth-century audience, however, would recognise the acclaimed virtues of courage and constancy that were thought to constitute manliness. Later in the tragedy, Lucan and the other grave men of Piso's conspiracy scoff at Nero's men 'arm'd / With Luts [*sic*], and Harpes, and Pipes, and Fiddle-cases: / Souldyers to th' shadow traynd, and not the field'.[54] Like images in the earlier *Rape of Lucrece*, these men have become emasculated through their ruler preventing them from the true manly practices of warfare.[55] Whereas the conspirators liken themselves to Cassius and Brutus in their valour, and indeed appear to be manly, grave, and courageous soldiers acquainted with true battle and death, Nero's triumphal procession only exemplifies his cowardice and vanity, which the character Lucan summarises in the play as 'the shame, and Womanhood of *Nero*'.[56]

Moreover, *The Tragedy of Nero* portrayed the tyrant's court as a bed of immorality, deviance, and disorder, and thereby echoed charges of court corruption levelled against King James's costly consumption, perceived decadence, and love of the theatre. Negative portrayals of James often described the King as 'very liberal'; as Sir Anthony Weldon, in his bitter invective against James, would later claim, 'he had rather spend 100,000£ on Embassies, to keep or procure peace with dishonour, then 10,000£ on an Army that would have forced peace with honour'.[57] Although Elizabeth

---

[53] *Tragedy of Nero*, sig. B1v–2r.   [54] Ibid., sig. B3r.   [55] See Section 1.5.
[56] Ibid., sig. C4r–v. By the end of the *Tragedy of Nero*, however, we see several conspirators act cowardly after the discovery of their plot.
[57] Sir Anthony Weldon, *The Court and Character of King James* (London, 1650), 57.

'And thus did the wicked sonne murther his wicked mother' 125

had left England in good financial health, and James did not spend on wars, he accrued significant debts even early in his reign by bestowing gifts and favours, hosting lavish festivities, increasing his entourage of attendants such as ushers, grooms, and gentlemen of the privy chamber, and adorning himself in expensive attire.[58] Whereas wardrobe costs for Elizabeth in her final four years averaged £9,500, James's expenditure in the first five years averaged £36,000 per annum. Elizabeth's ordinary expenditure had rested at £300,000 per annum; James was very soon spending half a million pounds annually. According to Exchequer accounts, his spending alone on 'fees and annuities' paid to courtiers reached £47,783 in 1605; 'diverse causes and rewards' amounted to £35,239 in the same year. Throughout his reign, the King's festivities were numerous and opulent, characterised by detractors at least as 'persistent prodigality' – 'gambling and feasting and lavish weddings became the commonplaces of court life'.[59]

Contemporary critics often associated the expenses of Stuart court extravagance with debauchery and sexual impropriety. As one libel declared upon the death of James's Lord Treasurer Thomas Sackville, Lord Buckhurst, 1st earl of Dorset in 1608:

> Heere lye's a Lord that Wenching thought no sinne
> and bought his flesh by selling of our skinne
> His name was Sackvile & so Void of Pitty
> as hee did rob the Country with the Citty.[60]

Perpetuators of cheap print and oral culture in Jacobean England transformed what were intended to be legitimate expressions of the dignity of courtiers and the King through fashion, finery, and festival into sartorial transgressions. They portrayed the King and court's luxury as extravagant, and associated their practices with illicit sexuality, popery, effeminacy, and disorder.[61]

---

[58] For the highly demanding and ritualised system of court patronage in Stuart England, see Linda Levy Peck, '"For a King not to be bountiful were a fault": Perspectives on Court Patronage in Early Stuart England', *Journal of British Studies* 25.1 (1986): 31–61.

[59] One significant reason for the jump in cost between Elizabeth and James was his large family, which required wardrobe and separate households; however, James clearly exacerbated these costs. For example, he increased the Gentlemen of the Privy Chamber for his own use from 18 to 42 between 1603 and 1624, and also added 200 gentlemen extraordinary to the Court. See S. J. Houston, *James I*, 2nd ed. (London and New York: Longman, 1995), 14–21; Maurice Lee, Jr., *Great Britain's Solomon: James VI and I and His Three Kingdoms* (Urbana: Illinois University Press, 1990), 148–49; Roger Lockyer, *James VI and I* (London and New York: Longman, 1998), 85, 96–97.

[60] British Library MS Harley 3991, fo.126v.

[61] Alastair Bellany, *The Politics of Court Scandal in Early Modern England: News Culture and the Overbury Affair, 1603–1660* (Cambridge: Cambridge University Press 2002), 153–62.

126   Emasculated Kingship

Significantly, *The Tragedy of Nero* opens at the royal court, while Nero is still absent due to his 'triumphal parade'. Nero's wife Poppaea struts 'royally attended ... ouer the Stage, in State', as a group of courtiers comment upon her proud majesty and debate whether they, like so many others, should bed Poppaea or seek a common 'wench' instead. When the courtier Antonius notes that although Poppaea is a 'Great Queene' she has not 'chastitie', the scornful courtier Petronius replies:

> Chastitie, foole! a word not knowne in Courts:
> Well may it lodge in meane and countrey homes,
> Where pouertie, and labour keepes them downe,
> Short sleepes, and hands made hard with *Thuscan* Woll.
> But neuer comes to great mens Pallaces,
> Where ease, and riches, stirring thoughts beget,
> Prouoking meates, and surfet wines Inflame:
> Where all there setting forth's but to be wooed,
> And wooed they would not be, but to be wonne.
> Will one man serue *Poppaea*? Nay, thou shalt
> Make her, as soone, contented with an eye.[62]

Chastity thrives in the meagre country home of the simple shepherd; throughout the play the audience finds the sins and moral failings of this court to be pervasive – indeed, 'Night sports' are 'done in open day'.[63] The tragedy demonstrates how these 'sports' have wrecked the stability and order of the royal household and government, especially as Nero is frequently cuckolded due to his queen's insatiable desire for sex. In ballads as well as public shaming rituals in Stuart England, cuckolds were abused in their communities for failing to control their households, satisfy their wives, and serve their patriarchal duty, for a wife's adulterous exploits were believed to stem not only from promiscuity but also from rebellion.[64] This view is illustrated in a number of ballads and cheap print, such as the later ballad, *Cuckold's Haven, Or, The marry'd man's miserie* (1638): 'My wife hath learn'd to kisse, / and thinkes'tis not amisse: / Shee oftentimes doth me deride, / And tels me I am hornify'd. / What euer I doe say, / shee will haue her owne way; / Shee scorneth to obey'.[65]

---

[62] *Tragedy of Nero*, sig. A3v.   [63] Ibid., sig. B4v.

[64] See David Underdown, 'The Taming of the Scold: the Enforcement of Patriarchal Authority in Early Modern England', in *Order and Disorder in Early Modern England*, ed. Anthony Fletcher and John Stevenson (Cambridge: Cambridge University Press, 1985), 116–36, esp. 127; Joy Wiltenburg, *Disorderly Women and Female Power in the Street Literature of Early Modern England and Germany* (Charlottesville: University Press of Virginia, 1992), 152–56; Laura Gowing, *Domestic Dangers: Women, Words, and Sex in Early Modern London* (Oxford: Oxford University Press, 1999), 95–96.

[65] Qtd in Wiltenburg, *Disorderly Women*, 153.

'*And thus did the wicked sonne murther his wicked mother*'   127

Cuckoldry, irreligion, and political rebellion were intertwining and very often associated in the Jacobean period, with household disorder tied to political tyranny or anarchy. During Charles's courtship with the Spanish Infanta Maria in 1623, a riotous song described sexual rebellion and cuckoldry as one of the many dangerous consequences of the English being bought off by a Spanish dowry. After the 'Potents of Spaine' will load Charles's wagon with Spanish gold, the song exclaimed, the women of the City 'shall swive / Exchange time in the morne', while 'each Cuckold shall blowe / And Guilt the tippe of his horne'.[66] In the *Tragedy of Nero*, Poppaea's explicit affair with Nimphidius signals her rebellion as well as her lover's rebellion. In a soliloquy Nimphidius explains that he has an 'aspiring thirst / to *Neroes* Crowne' and envisions Poppaea's bed as 'a step vnto his Throne'.[67] The *Tragedy of Nero* thereby intertwined Nero's ineptitude in foreign policy with his failure as a patriarch, indicating that Nero's tyranny stemmed from his failure to govern household, court morality, and kingdom, not just from his more infamous vicious and cruel activities.

By the climax of the play, Nero has grown incensed by a handful of courtiers who dared frown, laugh, sleep, look 'sourely on', or failed to applaud Nero's performance of *Orestes*.[68] Characters within the *Tragedy* emphasise that Nero performs Orestes's murder of his mother Clytemnestra from experience, for Nero had already defiled his own household by committing matricide against Julia Agrippina.[69] Due to the perceived offenses of these individuals in his audience, Nero boldly declares that he will not take revenge by 'singling out them, one by one to death', but instead 'Behold the world enwrapt in funerall flame', for a 'Princes anger must lay desolate / Citties, Kingdomes consume, Roote vp mankind'.[70] By the next scene, frenzied Roman citizens run centre stage crying, 'Fire, fire, helpe, we burne', and Antonius describes the ever-increasing flames as overtaking fields and husbandmen, neighbourhoods and households, and even 'litle sonnes with trembling hands'.[71] In the midst of this devastation, the anonymous author of the tragedy calls for 'Soft Musique' to play as Nero enters 'aboue alone with a Timbrell'. Singing of Troy in her flames, he bathes in the visual carnage of his destroyed city, delighting especially in the 'sceane' of a mother cradling her burnt child and a young man

---

[66] Beinecke Library MS Osborn b.197, pp. 110–11. See 'Early Stuart Libels'.
[67] *Tragedy of Nero*, sigs. A3r, A4r and B2r.   [68] Ibid., sig. D4v.
[69] For example, Poppaea remarks, 'Did he not wish againe his mother liuing? / Her death would adde great life vnto his part'. Ibid., sig. D3v.
[70] Ibid., sig. D4v.   [71] Ibid., sig. E2r.

128   Emasculated Kingship

caressing the body of his burnt father. As Philip Robinson has demonstrated, London was popularly understood and very often deemed a 'New Troy' in the seventeenth century, especially in the annual mayoral shows. Retellings of the myth were complex, and often highlighted anxieties that London as a Troia Nova might herself face annihilation due to her host of sins, although her glory may also outshine that of Rome, the other city descendant of Troy.[72] *The Tragedy of Nero* offered the horrific image of a 'New Troy', Rome, destroyed at the hands of a sinful ruler, and the city rudely memorialised by the very man responsible for its ruin.

Simultaneously, the author of the *Tragedy of Nero* seems to have drawn upon the 'black legend' of Spanish cruelty and tyranny, with this gruesome scene reflecting the Dutch propaganda that, since the sixteenth century, had portrayed the Spanish Inquisition as enacting horrific violence and burnings of Protestant families, including babies and the aged. For example, a detailed image of the 'Council of Blood' from *Warachtige Beschrijvinghe ... vande meer dan onmenschelijke end Barbarische Tyrannije* (1621) luridly depicted an overwhelming scene of torture and destruction of Protestants by burning at the stake, the gallows, the rack, the wheel, and water torture.[73] *The Tragedy of Nero* portrayed the tyrant, while surrounded by a similarly astonishing site of destruction, as revelling in his grotesque entertainment, beckoning the mother and young man to 'play on ... /With cryes, and pitie; with your blood'. The scene concludes, however, with a foreshadowing of Nero's own destruction, as the man and woman plead heaven that he 'that all this blood hath shed' may die friendless and unburied at 'the wish, and hate of all'.[74] The tragedy's climax thus emphatically argued that siding with (Spanish and Catholic) tyranny was siding with the brutal murder of innocents, an act which God would justly punish.

This climactic scene brilliantly illustrates the pathos of the *Tragedy of Nero*, and the particular ability of drama to evoke a passionate criticism of monarchy that pamphlets, libels, and histories could not. Even if read and not performed, the tragedy allowed its audience to experience the brutality

---

[72] This is partially due to the founding myth of King Brutus. Philip Robinson, 'Multiple Meanings of Troy in Early Modern London's Mayoral Show', *Seventeenth Century* 26.2 (Oct. 2011): 221–39, esp. 228–9.

[73] John Marshall, *John Locke, Toleration and Early Enlightenment Culture: Religious Intolerance and Arguments for Religious Toleration in Early Modern and 'Early Enlightenment' Europe* (Cambridge: Cambridge University Press, 2006), 62–63; Simon Schama, *The Embarrassment of Riches: An Interpretation of Dutch Culture in the Golden Age* (Berkeley and Los Angeles: University of California Press, 1988), 82–93. For portrayals of the Inquisition in England, see Edward Peters, *Inquisition* (Berkeley and Los Angeles: University of California Press, 1989), 150–54.

[74] *Tragedy of Nero*, sig. E3v.

'And thus did the wicked sonne murther his wicked mother' 129

of tyranny, for as Sir Philip Sidney argued in *The Defence of Poesy* (1595), tragedy 'openeth the greatest woundes, and sheweth forth the ulcers that are covered with Tissue'.[75] By puncturing the scars of infected government, tragedy could illustrate the hidden corruption of tyrannical courts, and it could move its viewers to fear, to sorrow, and even to virtuous action. The audience feels moved by the suffering of Roman citizens. Nero's death in the final scene, in contrast, inspires little pity or fear. Learning he has been sentenced to a tortuous death by the Senate, Nero begs two Roman citizens, 'Will you by dying, teach me to beare death / With courage?'[76] These citizens, who have voluntarily committed to aid Nero in dying a less painful death than that decreed, are disgusted by their emperor's cowardice, and after Nero bids farewell to his theatres and popular applause, he ineloquently '*fals on his sword*' out of his fear of a more painful and frightening end.[77] His country and himself thrown into rebellion and chaos, Nero dies pathetically onstage while seeking the courage of lower men.

In these ways, the *Tragedy of Nero* provided a virulent attack on James, his court, and on the King's pacific and seemingly pro-Catholic policies. James's determination to conquer by diplomacy was likened to Nero's conquest by minstrelsy; alliances with Spanish and Catholic powers were questioned through grotesque images of the burning of innocents. Moreover, the tragedy displayed Nero's tyranny through his disordered household, especially his inability to control and to satisfy his own desires and the desires of Poppaea. Beginning in the royal household in which Nero is importantly absent, each act of the play uncovers the effects of household mismanagement and a disordered soul upon the management of commonwealth; Nero watches from his private apartments as his city burns before him.

Although censuring monarchy, however, the *Tragedy* did not support active resistance or regime change. Piso's conspirators voice the ideals of an active, courageous, and virtuous citizenry, but as Lucan explains, they seek not 'libertie':

> We are contented with the galling yoke,
> If they will only leaue vs necks to beare it;
> We seeke no longer freedome, we seeke life
> At least, not to be murdred, let vs die
> On Enemies swords ... [78]

Contented with the institution of monarchy, the conspirators seek an emperor who will protect his subjects and fulfil his duties, who will raise

---

[75] Sir Philip Sidney, *The Defence of Poesie* (London, 1595), sig. E4v.   [76] *Tragedy of Nero*, sig. I2v.
[77] Ibid., sig. I2v–3r.   [78] Ibid., sig. C4v.

130 Emasculated Kingship

armies of swords and not lutes. In the end, the *Tragedy* does follow historical accounts of Nero which claimed that the Senate sentenced Nero to death for his crimes against Rome; lest the audience mistake whose authority ultimately decreed Nero's demise, however, the *Tragedy* concluded with a Roman subject declaring: 'Thus great bad men aboue them finde a rod: / People depart, and say there is a God'. In these ways, *The Tragedy of Nero* did not question the *institution* of monarchy, but it importantly presented the portrait of a tyrant as emasculated cuckold, coward, and persecutor, whose deficient character and household mismanagement resulted in his country's destruction and his own downfall.

3.3 A Neronian Libel

The Tragedy of Nero was not the only piece of literature which challenged James and his government through the exemplum of Nero in the early 1620s, nor the only one which located tyranny in the royal household. In the same moment, a significant libel circulated which explicitly compared James to Nero and warned that the English king could even surpass the Roman emperor in tyrannical infamy.[79] In 1651, an anonymous pamphlet entitled *The None-Such Charles His Character: Extracted Out of divers Originall Transactions, Dispatches and the Notes of severall Publick Ministers, and Councellours of State as wel at home as abroad* printed this libel as part of a salacious attack upon the late King Charles. The pamphlet, which was probably crafted by the one-time cultural and political agent of Buckingham Sir Balthazar Gerbier, emphasised that Charles's downfall had chiefly been a family affair.[80] It celebrated that God had enacted his just wrath upon the 'crying sinnes' of 'King *James's* Family', and advised 'all men to take heed how they side with that bloody House, least they be found to be the opposers of Gods purposes'.[81] In its section concerning the sins of James, the pamphlet charged the late king with 'hipocrisie and

---

[79] For the culture of libels, and their presentation of radical scepticism about discourses of authority, see Andrew McRae, *Literature, Satire and the Early Stuart State* (Cambridge: Cambridge University Press, 2004).

[80] [Sir Balthazar Gerbier], *The None-Such Charles his Character: Extracted, Out of divers Originall Transactions, Dispatches and the Notes of severall Publick Ministers, and Councellours of State as wel at home as abroad* (London, 1650), 2–3; Maria Keblusek, 'Introduction: Double Agents in Early Modern Europe', in *Double Agents: Cultural and Political Brokerage in Early Modern Europe*, ed. Keblusek and Badeloch Vera Noldus (Leiden: Koninklijke Brill NV, 2011), 1–3; Jeremy Wood, 'Gerbier, Sir Balthazar (1592–1663/1667)', in *Oxford Dictionary of National Biography* (Oxford University Press: 2004), online edn, Jan. 2008 [www.oxforddnb.com/view/article/10562].

[81] [Gerbier], *None-Such Charles*, 2–3.

'And thus did the wicked sonne murther his wicked mother'   131

impiety', claiming that he had refused to reform the ecclesiastical government of Bishops and deceived his subjects by acting as a 'Juggler'. His civil crimes and religious sins were so acute, according to the pamphlet, that the following libel was left on James's cupboard for him to discover:

> Aula profana, religione vana,
> Spreta uxore Ganyraedis amore,
> Lege sublata, prerogativa inflata,
> Tolle libertatem, incede civitatem,
> Ducas spadonem et Superasti Neronem

> [The palace has been desecrated, religion is vain,
> (Your) wife has been spurned for the love of Ganymede,
> Law has been destroyed, and prerogative expanded,
> Abolish liberty, march on the commonwealth,
> Marry a eunuch and you have trumped Nero][82]

Just as the *Tragedy of Nero* associated Nero's depraved household with his ungodly, vicious, and persecuting rule, the libel connected James's perverse love of Ganymede over the pious love of wife with the desecration of court, religion, law, and the unlawful practice of political authority. Supposedly found tucked away within a cupboard in James's household, the libel described the political intimacy and sexual corruption of royal favoritism, and thereby highlighted the fear that James was personally compromised and that his favourite wielded a powerful and dangerous influence.[83]

Ganymede, a widespread term for 'catamite' or 'sodomy' in Stuart England, was the beautiful Trojan boy in classical mythology with whom Jupiter fell passionately in love and stole away to Mount Olympus, where he made the boy his lover and the cup-bearer of the gods.[84] Within this

---

[82] *Riders dictionarie* (1626) defines '*prærogativa,-ae*' as 'a preheminence, authoritie, and rule aboue other'. See sig. zzz3r.
   At least one printed and three manuscript copies of this libel survive: Balthazar Gerbier, *The None-such Charles his Character* (London, 1651), 17; British Library MS Add. 78423, fo. 60v; University of Minnesota Library MS 690235 f, 181; Bodleian MS don b. 8, p. 183. C. R. Harris claimed that this libel was written in the hand of Sir John Peyton. As Harris provided no evidence for this assertion, I am unclear how Peyton, who served as lieutenant of the Tower of London or the governor of Jersey for most of his life, would have had such access to James's lodgings. His son's access is likewise questionable. See Harris, 'The Court and Character of James I', *Notes & Queries*, 3rd series, vol. V, (Jan.-Jun. 1864): 451–53, 53.
[83] See Perry, *Literature and Favoritism*, 131–37.
[84] Gordon Williams, ed. 'Ganymede', in *A Dictionary of Sexual Language and Imagery in Shakespearean and Stuart Literature*, vol. II (London: Athlone, 1994), 577–79; Young, *James VI and I*, 53–54; Alan Bray, *Homosexuality in Renaissance England* (London: Gay Men's Press, 1982), 13 and 65; James M. Saslow, *Ganymede in the Renaissance* (New Haven: Yale University Press, 1986), 1–3; Bruce R. Smith, *Homosexual Desire in Shakespeare's England* (Chicago: Chicago University Press, 1991).

Emasculated Kingship

story, Ganymede played the sexual role of the younger, passive partner who submitted to an older and more powerful male.[85] As several historians have persuasively demonstrated, not only do innumerable examples of this motif exist in English literature of the period, but several poems and libels explicitly refer to James's favourite, Buckingham, as Ganymede.[86] Buckingham first served James as his cup-bearer, and their intimate relationship echoed the age and social disparity of Ganymede and Jupiter. Since English conventions of male friendship required friends to have comparable social status and to be bound for non-mercenary reasons, James and Buckingham's great social disparity, and James's lavish showering of gifts, favours, and titles upon the Duke, provoked great suspicion and censure.[87]

As Curtis Perry, Alastair Bellany, and Andrew McRae have convincingly illustrated, by envisioning the problem of royal favourites in erotic terms, libels and other imaginative literature in Stuart England made it possible to criticise not only royal favourites but the monarch himself. Charges of erotic favoritism underscored that it was the King's depraved and unregulated passions which made him susceptible to being controlled by his corrupted associates.[88] The author of the *None-such Charles* emphasised as much throughout his pamphlet, arguing that although the royal court had included 'a number of Courtly silk-wormes', the royal family's 'crying sinnes' required 'a more serious inspection' than the mere 'various vicissitudes of men'; the King's own decisions and policies, driven by his desires, compromised right religion and good governance.[89] The libel associated the King's corrupted passions, expressed through sodomy, with the desecration of true religion, the unlawful extension of royal authority, and the compromise of the native liberties of subjects, for a king unruly in his desires would not refrain from trespassing the laws of nature and of God or of making an idol of worldly passions. Of these connections, homosexuality and '*religione vana*', or Catholicism, were most often associated in seventeenth-century English culture, with sodomy understood as a

---

[85] Young, *James VI and I*, 53.
[86] Bellany, *Politics of Court Scandal*, 254–61; Young, *James VI and I*, 54; Smith, *Homosexual Desire*, 202–3; Curtis Perry, 'The Politics of Access and Representations of the Sodomite King in Early Modern England', *Renaissance Quarterly* 53.4 (2000): 1075–77.
[87] Bray, 'Homosexuality and the Signs of Male Friendship in Elizabethan England', *History Workshop* 29 (Spring 1990): 1–19, esp. 11–12. Buckingham wrote to James in response to his generosity, 'you have filled a consuming purse, given me fair houses [and] more land than I am worthy of. . .filled my coffers so full with patents of honour, that my shoulders cannot bear more'. Qtd. in Young, *James VI and I*, 32.
[88] Perry, *Literature and Favoritism*, 135–36; Bellany, *Politics of Court Scandal*, 255–61; McRae, *Literature, Satire, and the Early Stuart State*, 80.
[89] [Gerbier], *None-such Charles*, 2–3.

'And thus did the wicked sonne murther his wicked mother'   133

typically popish sin due not only to familiar charges of buggery within monasteries but also because it 'involved the abuse of natural faculties and impulses for unnatural ends', and thereby symbolised 'idolatrous' Catholic practices.[90] A king debased in his passions and religion posed the greatest threat to society, for his seemingly unrestrained and perverted desires might lead him to compromise the law – that safeguard of subjects' liberties – and liberty itself.

These particular accusations against James help us date the origins of this otherwise anonymous libel. Bellany has shown that libels explicitly charging the King and favourite with sodomitical activity tended to cluster chronologically around the Bohemian Crisis and Spanish Match from 1618–23, which places its original production in the same years as the *Tragedy of Nero*.[91] The libel's accusation of *religione vana* similarly suggests this period in James's reign due to his concessions to recusants and desire to negotiate peace with Catholic powers through diplomacy and the Spanish Match. Three manuscript copies of this libel survive, one of which confirms this dating through the added title, written lengthwise, '*Deprædator Belgicus*', or the 'Dutch Pillager'.[92] The title referenced hostile criticisms of James for refusing to commit troops for the Protestant Cause, and thereby allowing his Christian brethren to lose life and goods to Catholic forces. This copy of the libel similarly included the charge of homosexual immorality and the related destruction of palace, law, and liberty, but very significantly replaced '*Prerogativa*' with '*Tyrannide*' and implicated the nobility and clergy in the commonwealth's demise:

> Aulâ profanâ
> Religione simulata
> Nobilitate spurâ
> Clericatu Apostata
> Spreta Uxore
> Ganimedis amore
> Lege decollata
> Tyrannide inflata
> Abduxisti libertatem
> Incendisti nationem
>   Ducas Spadonem
> et superasti Neronem

[90] Peter Lake, 'Anti-Popery: the Structure of a Prejudice', in *Conflict in Early Stuart England*, ed. Richard Cust and Anne Hughes (New York: Longman 1989), 72–106, esp. 75; Bellany, *Politics of Court Scandal*, 257–58.

[91] Bellany, *Politics of Court Scandal*, 255.   [92] University of Minnesota Library, MS 690235 f, 181.

134 Emasculated Kingship

> [The palace has been desecrated
> Religion pretended
> Nobility dirtied
> Apostate for clergy
> (Your) wife has been spurned
> for the love of Ganymede
> Law has been beheaded
> Tyranny inflated
> You have removed liberty
> You have set fire to the nation
>   Marry a eunuch
> and you have trumped Nero][93]

Here the sins, tyranny, and lawlessness of nobility, religion, royal family, and king are tied directly to the destruction of liberty and country, and this destruction extended beyond the shores of England to the Christian allies abroad plundered at the hands of Catholic oppressors.

Other versions of the libel, however, more narrowly located political injustice in the royal family and household, characterising tyranny as a family made violent and disordered. In the 1650s, while in exile in France, the royalist Sir Samuel Tuke recorded a significant version of the libel in his miscellany alongside extensive notes on Roman history, Donne's poems, Montagne's essays, Descartes' *Meditations* and *Principes de la Philosophie*, and Hobbes' *Leviathan*:

> Matris Capite truncato
> Nato venenato
> Spreta uxore, Ganimedis amore
> Ducas spadonem,
> Superasti Neronem
>
> [The mother beheaded
> The son poisoned
> The wife spurned, for the love of Ganymede
> Marry a eunuch,
> You have trumped Nero][94]

From his earlier notes on Roman history in the miscellany, it is clear that Tuke knew Nero's story very well. He recorded how Nero poisoned his older brother, Britannicus, who was the rightful heir to the Roman throne, and how Nero also commanded Anicetus to kill his mother, Julia Agrippina, a woman considered ambitious and depraved who had

---

[93] Ibid. [94] British Library MS Add. 78423, fo. 60v.

'And thus did the wicked sonne murther his wicked mother'   135

'prostituted her body to her son'.[95] The libel mapped this history directly onto the Stuart royal family, comparing the untimely death of James's son, Henry, with the murder of Britannicus, and James's Catholic mother, Mary Queen of Scots, with Julia Agrippina. Tuke's copy of the libel, thereby, identified James's sodomitical activity as part of a family portrait of infamy, much as his historical notes had described Nero's family.

Such a comparison between Prince Henry and Britannicus offered a staunchly Protestant rebuke of the royal family. Prince Henry, by the time of his premature death in 1612, had been the darling of the militantly anti-Catholic faction at court. His personal practice of religion, fervent commitment to rooting out Catholic recusants, and generous patronage to the godly captivated a reformed war party frustrated by James's pacific policies.[96] As one popular song expressed:

> Henry the 8. pulld down abbeys and cells
> But Henry the 9. shall pull down Bishops and bells.[97]

His sudden death in 1612 crushed these expectations, resulting in widespread speculation that he had been poisoned in a popish plot. By comparing James to Nero, who had poisoned his older brother Britannicus, the libel implicitly charged James and James's family with the death of Henry, or at least associated the King's household with suspected Catholic perpetrators.

Another version of the libel, recorded by the antiquary and courtier Sir William Haward, so closely associated Nero's family history with James's that it not only associated James with the poisoning of Henry but accused the King himself of perpetrating the murder of his mother, Mary Stuart:

> Religione vanâ; Aulâ prophanâ;
> Lege sublatâ; pręrogatiuâ inflatâ;
> Spretâ Uxore Catamitę amore;
> Matre percussâ pertua jussa;
> Proprio Nato veneno sublato;

---

[95] Ibid., fos. 407–9, 420, 423. Britannicus and Nero could only succeed to the helm of the Roman Empire because their mother married her uncle, Emperor Claudius, and had his former mistress beheaded. On the significance of poison and court scandal, see Alastair Bellany and Thomas Cogswell, *The Murder of King James I* (New Haven: Yale, 2015), 165.

[96] James M. Sutton, 'Henry Frederick, prince of Wales (1594–1612)', in *Oxford Dictionary of National Biography* (Oxford: Oxford University Press, 2004), online edn, Jan. 2008 [www .oxforddnb.com/view/article/12961]; Roy C. Strong, *Henry, Prince of Wales, and England's Lost Renaissance* (New York: Thames and Hudson, 1986).

[97] C. A. Patrides, '"The Greatest of the Kingly Race": the Death of Henry Stuart', *The Historian* 47 (1985): 402–8, esp. 404.

136 Emasculated Kingship

Currum ascende, urbem incende,
Ducas Spadonem, & superasti Neronem.

[Religion is vain; the palace has been desecrated;
Law has been destroyed; prerogative inflated
Your wife has been spurned for the love of a Catamite;
Your mother struck by your command;
Your own son suffered poison;
Ascend your chariot, burn the city,
Marry a eunuch, & you have trumped Nero.][98]

The analogy that these copies of the libel presented between James's mother, Mary Queen of Scots, and Nero's mother, Julia Agrippina, incriminated King James. Mary Queen of Scots had been deemed sexually depraved, rebellious, and dangerous by reformed Scotsmen and godly Englishmen due to her Catholic religion and personal conduct. James's paternity was questioned after Queen Mary's estranged husband, Henry Stewart, Lord Darnley, refused to attend James's Catholic baptism in December 1566. The Queen's marriage in 1567 to James Hepburn, earl of Bothwell, the suspected murderer of her husband Darnley, led to her overthrow by a confederacy of lords rebelling in the name of James VI.[99] After living under house arrest for twenty years, Mary was infamously tried and beheaded for plotting the assassination of Queen Elizabeth. Alongside questions of her treason, the perceived ability of women even to occupy such positions of power in Tudor and Stuart society was complex and often problematic, due to women's supposed natural inferiority and obligated obedience.[100] As the *Second Tome of the Homilies* (1563) summarised, 'For the woman is a weake creature, not endued with like strength and constancie of mynde, therefore they be the sooner disquieted, and they be the more prone to all weake affections and dispositions of mynde, more then men be, and lyghter they be, and more vayne in theyr fantasies and opinions.'[101] A threat to social order and stability, women were expected to

---

[98] Bodleian Library, MS. Don b. 8, p. 183.

[99] Michael Lynch, 'Queen Mary's Triumph: The Baptismal Celebrations at Stirling in December 1566', *Scottish Historical Review* 69 (1990): 1–12.

[100] Margaret R. Sommerville, *Sex & Subjection: Attitudes to Women in Early Modern Society* (London: Arnold, 1995): 8–16.

[101] 'An Homilie of the State of Matrimonie', in *The Seconde Tome of Homilies, of such matters as were promysed and intituled in the former part of homilies, set out by the authoritie of the Queenes Maiestie. And to be read in euery paryshe Church agreablye* (London, 1563), 255r. Alexandra Shepard has argued, however, that prescriptions of female weakness might have been somewhat exaggerated in early modern literature which stressed the need of women to be subordinate to their husband's authority. See *Meanings of Manhood in Early Modern England* (Oxford: Oxford University Press, 2006), 72.

'And thus did the wicked sonne murther his wicked mother' 137

'perfourme subiection', as the *Homily* put it, to be modest, submissive to the authority of fathers and husbands, and sexually chaste. The connection between women's transgressions and their perceived rebellion to the patriarchal society is evinced in the fact that women who killed their husbands were charged with the crime of petty treason rather than murder.[102] Queen Elizabeth had sought to legitimise her rule through multi-faceted representations, fashioning her rule as ordained by God and herself as exceptionally virtuous, chaste, and equipped with the superior qualities of kings.[103] Perceived as compromised in her sexual purity and religion, Mary Queen of Scots's ability to legitimise her political activity became more difficult over the course of her Scottish reign.

Even though a Scottish confederacy had separated Mary Queen of Scots from her son James in his infancy, writers criticising James and the Stuart household still questioned if Mary had indelibly corrupted her son through her very womb. It was widely believed in seventeenth-century England that a mother's cravings, longings, actions, or thoughts could, intentionally and unintentionally, alter, shape, and mark the disposition and physical attributes of her child in the womb, giving vicious women an enormous power over the character of their children.[104] 'We know by experience that women transmit marks of their fancies to the bodies of the children they carry in their womb', Montaigne, for one, described in his *Essays*.[105]

In a significant note just following the libel, Tuke recorded in his miscellany that Queen Mary's turpitude had indeed become imprinted onto James's character while he grew within her womb. He recorded how she, 'beeing great with childe of Kg James was present when her fauorite dauid reizo a musitien, an Italian was murdred by the erles of her husband'. According to Tuke's notes, the 'naked sword, was soe neere her bellie', and she 'shewing much frighted', that James in his *adult* life 'wuld not indure a naked sword'.[106]

---

[102] It was treason because 'there is subjection due from the wife to the husband, but not *e converso*'. See Garthine Walker, *Crime, Gender and Social Order in Early Modern England* (Cambridge: Cambridge University Press, 2003), 138.

[103] Sommerville, *Sex & Subjection*, 51–60; See also Carole Levin, *Heart and Stomach of a King: Elizabeth I and the Politics of Sex and Power* (Philadelphia: University of Pennsylvania Press, 1994); A. N. McLaren, *Political Culture in the Reign of Elizabeth I: Queen and Commonwealth, 1558–1585* (Cambridge: Cambridge University Press, 1999).

[104] Mary Fissell, Vernacular Bodies: *The Politics of Reproduction in Early Modern England* (Oxford: Oxford University Press, 2004), 65–66; Marie-Hélène Huet, *Monstrous Imagination* (London and Cambridge, MA: Harvard University Press, 1993), 16–27, 33–34; Katharine Park, *Secrets of Women: Gender, Generation, and the Origins of Human Dissection* (New York: Zone Books, 2006), 144–45; Lorraine Daston and Katharine Park, *Wonders and the Order of Nature: 1150–1750* (New York: Zone Books, 2001), 189.

[105] Qtd in Huet, *Monstrous Imagination*, 13.   [106] British Library MS Add. 78423, fo. 60v.

138   Emasculated Kingship

The fear of the naked sword had been imprinted upon James in the womb at the moment his mother's favourite had been murdered in front of her eyes. This moment in Mary's life, when she had been very pregnant with James, was often portrayed with great drama in Scottish histories. William Camden's description of this scene, for example, emphasised the significant effect it had upon Queen Mary, describing not only the naked sword drawn before her eyes, but claiming that one soldier had set 'a Pistoll at her breast; so that shee was in danger of abortion'.[107] In his miscellany, Tuke went on to confirm, following the printed account of Sir Kenelm Digby, that James had been so inflicted by his mother's imagination that when the King knighted Digby, 'hee had like to haue putt the sword in [the knight's] eyes' due to his fear of the weapon.[108]

This account supported the suspicion that James had been tainted by his depraved, Catholic mother, much as the wicked Nero had been moulded by the sexually and rebelliously corrupt Julia Agrippina. Such a charge especially implicated James's masculinity. If James 'wuld not indure a naked sword' out of fright, he would be incapable of performing the violence and acts of courage necessary to enforce monarchical imperatives, to wage war, and to judge and honour those men who proved themselves meritorious in battle.[109] This view echoed others who criticised James's pacifism as a consequence of his seemingly natural propensity for fear and cowardice. In his bitter invective against King James, for example, Sir Anthony Weldon argued that while 'the World did beleeve the Kings inclination [for peace] was out of a religious ground, that he might not revenge, yet it was no other but a cowardly disposition that dust not adventure'.[110] Others 'suspect[ed]

[107] William Camden, *The historie of the life and death of Mary Stuart Queene of Scotland* (London, 1624), 33.

[108] British Library MS Add. 78423, fo. 60v. Digby's printed account is as follows: 'I reccounted unto her also the strange antipathy which the late King *Iames* had to a naked sword, whereof the cause was ascribed, in regard some *Schotch* Lords had entered once violently into the bed-chamber of the Queen his mother, while she was with child of him . . . Hence it came that her son King *Iames* had such an aversion all his life time to a naked sword, that he could not see one without a great emotion of the spirits, although otherwise couragious enough, yet he could not over-master his passions in this particular. I remember when he dubbed me Knight, in the ceremony of putting the point of a naked sword upon my shoulder, he could not endure to look upon it, but turned his face another way, insomuch, that in lieu of touching my shoulder, he had almost thrust the point into my eyes, had not the Duke of *Buckingham* guided his hand aright.' See Sir Kenelm Digby, *A Late Discourse Made in a Solemne Assembly of Nobles and Learned Men at Montpellier in France, Touching the Cure of Wounds by the Powder of Sympathy, with Instructions how to make the said Powder; whereby many other Secrets of Nature are unfolded*, trans. from French into English by R. White, Gent. (London, 1658), 104–5.

[109] Shepard, 'The Violence of Manhood', in *Meanings of Manhood*, 127–51.

[110] Sir Anthony Weldon, *The court and character of King James whereunto is now added The court of King Charles: continued unto the beginning of these unhappy times: with some observations upon him*

'And thus did the wicked sonne murther his wicked mother' 139

that his peaceable disposition hath not proceeded so much out of his Christian pietie and justice, as out of meere impotencie, and basenesse of mind'.[111] Accounts of James's life described the act of war as 'being contrary to his very *Nature*', and his viewing of military exercises as exciting fear in him.[112] Moreover, early in his reign, critics lampooned his seemingly excessive and indiscriminate meriting of knighthoods to men who had never proven their valour, such as the well over nine hundred knights he created in 1603.[113] Tuke's miscellany, which included the Neronian libel as well as notes about Mary's imprinting upon James in the womb, construed the monarch as too effeminate and cowardly to fulfil his necessary duties as a king, to exercise patriarchal authority, to command the respect of his nobles and soldiers, and to lead English troops to defend the Protestant Cause.

Descriptions of Mary Stuart's enduring influence upon James carried a further significance in the context of the Bohemian Crisis, for Frederick's rise to the throne through election prompted a heated debate in England and the Continent about the legitimacy and relative merit of elected monarchy. In the *Trew Law of Free Monarchies*, James had staunchly opposed elective kingship and, within Biblical precedent, characterised Saul's kingship as 'founded by God himselfe', not the people's election.[114] After 1618, the anti-Spanish faction in England interpreted Frederick's election positively as the work of God. As Archbishop George Abbot argued:

> That God had set up this Prince, his Majesty's Son-in-law, as a Mark of Honour throughout all Christendom, to propagate the Gospel, and to protect the oppressed. That for his own part, he dares not but give advice to follow, where God leads...That by peace and peace, the Kings of the Earth, that gave their power to the Beast, shall leave the Whore, and make her desolate. That he was satisfied in Conscience, that the *Bohemians* had just cause to reject that proud and bloody Man, who had taken a course to

---

instead of a character / collected and perfected by Sir A. W. (London, 1651), 148–49. The original was written in the years following Weldon's dismissal in 1617, and circulated in manuscript until this printing.

[111] George Calvert, Lord Baltimore, *The answer to Tom-Tell-Troth the practise of princes and the lamentations of the kirke / written by the Lord Baltismore, late secretary of state* (London, 1642), 2.

[112] Arthur Wilson, *The history of Great Britain being the life and reign of King James the First, relating to what passed from his first access to the crown, till his death* (London, 1653), 285.

[113] Lockyer, *James VI and I*, 203. David Hume estimated that the King had bestowed knighthoods on no less than 237 persons within the first six weeks of his reign as King of England. *The History of Great Britain, Under the House of Stuart* (London: Millar, 1759), 3.

[114] *King James VI and I: Political Writings*, 67 and 70. Peter Lake, 'The King (the Queen) and the Jesuit: James Stuart's *True Law of Free Monarchies* in context/s', in *Transactions of the Royal Historical Society*, vol. 14 (Cambridge: Cambridge University Press, 2004), 243–61, esp. 257.

140   Emasculated Kingship

> make that Kingdom not elective, in taking it by the Donation of another.[115]

Abbot defended Frederick's election as an act of God against the forces of Catholicism and anti-Christ, which had swept the Continent through Habsburg strength. His argument further justified election as the constitutional precedent of Bohemia, thereby casting Ferdinand's taking of the Kingdom by 'Donation' as the true usurpation.

King James, however, in an interpretation of events greatly at odds with Abbot, 'was not pleased that his Son should snatch a Crown out of the fire'. He sought to defend monarchy by inheritance, for in his experience, arguments for elective kingship went hand-in-hand with legitimisations of resistance and even the deposition of lawful, hereditary monarchs. James justified his refusal to enter war immediately on Frederick's behalf by arguing that Frederick's acceptance of the Bohemian crown 'had no reference to the Cause of Religion but only by reason of his right of Election (as he called it.). And we should be sorry that that aspersion should come upon our Religion, as to make it a good pretext for dethroning of Kings, and usurping their Crowns; And we would be loath that our People here should be taught that strange Doctrine.'[116] These debates highlight the timeliness and further significance of a libel comparing James with Nero. By characterising tyranny as bred and nurtured within the royal family, the libel exposed hereditary monarchy as potentially more vicious, dangerous, and anarchic than elective monarchy. Whereas God might raise up a virtuous prince through election to free his people, hereditary monarchs appeared to be in the grip of tainted succession through the wombs of vicious mothers.

3.4 Nero and the Defence of Monarchy

Thus far, this chapter has considered examples of how critics adopted the history of Nero to condemn King James, his personal failings, his policies, his family, and his court, especially in the final years of James's reign when he refused to enter continental war and when he became the increasing target of criticisms for his close relationship with his favourite,

---

[115] John Rushworth, *Historical Collections Of Private Passages of State, Weighty Matters in Law, Remarkable Proceedings in Five Parliaments: Beginning The Sixteenth Year of King James, Anno 1618. And Ending the Fifth Year of King Charles, Anno 1629. Digested in Order of Time* (London: Browne, 1721), I.12.

[116] Rushworth, *Historical Collections*, I.49.

'And thus did the wicked sonne murther his wicked mother' 141

Buckingham. As emphasised in the chapter's introduction, however, Nero's history was significant in seventeenth-century debates concerning kingship not only due to the heinousness of his story but also because defenders of absolutism employed Paul's epistle to the Romans, penned under the reign of Nero, to argue for unlimited obedience. This last section will turn to an extraordinary pro-monarchical history of Nero to demonstrate its argumentative character and to consider the perils of adopting Nero's story in the 1620s.

Edmund Bolton's *Nero Caesar, or Monarchie Depraued* (1624) was the longest history of Nero in seventeenth-century England, and Bolton sought to provide a well-researched examination of the emperor by drawing together the 'choysest pieces which lay dispersed throughout in best antiquities, among Historians, Philosophers, Orators, Poets, Coigns, Inscriptions, and all sorts of such monuments'.[117] Throughout the history, it is evident that Bolton principally drew his information from Tacitus, Dio Cassius, Suetonius, Josephus, and Seneca.[118] Bolton took his historical craft seriously. The first English translator of the Roman historian, Florus, and the author of the essay, *Hypercritica, or, A Rule of Judgement, for Writing or Reading our Histories* (written c. 1618–21), Bolton argued that history was 'an act of high wisdom, and not of eloquence only', and hence the 'Art, & Style' of histories without 'truthe ... come into the nature of crimes by imposture'.[119] Due to these commitments, Bolton, with the support of Buckingham, sought to establish an 'Academ Roial' or 'College of Honor', which would hold 'lectures & exercises of heroick matter & of the antiquities of Great Britain' outside of the university, for the gentry and nobility, and he spent his career seeking the patronage of great courtly men.[120] Bolton was well acquainted with the famed

---

[117] Edmund Bolton, *NERO CÆSAR, or Monarchie depraued. An Historicall worke. Dedicated, with leaue, to the DVKE of BVCKINGHAM, Lord Admirall, by the translator of Lvcivs Florvs* (London, 1627), sig. A3r–v.

[118] See Tacitus, *The Annals*, bks. XI–XVI; Suetonius, 'Nero Claudius Cæsar', in *Lives of the Twelve Caesars*; Dio Cassius, *Epitome of Roman History*, bks. XLI–XLIII; Flavius Josephus, *The Jewish War*, bk. II; Seneca, *Tragedy of Octavia*.

[119] *Hypercritica; or A Rvle of Ivdgment, For writing, or reading our Histories*, copied by Anthony Hall, Oxford Bodleian Library, MS Wood F.9, fo. 1.

[120] 'Bolton to Buckingham', Harleian MS 6103 (1619), qtd in Ethel M. Portal, 'The Academ Roial of King James I', *Proceedings of the British Academy* (1915–16): 189–208, 192. Bolton listed eighty-four elite individuals, including well-known poets, scholars, and many of his Catholic friends, to fill the tripartite structure of the academy. Although Buckingham greatly supported this cause, the society never came to fruition due to James's death in 1625. See *State Papers* 16/12 f. 152, Dec. 30 1625; Porter, 'Academ Roial', 197. Bolton also sought patronage from Robert Cecil, earl of Salisbury, Sir Julius Caesar, and the earl of Northampton. See British Library, MS Add. 12497, fo. 235r–236r; *State Papers* 16/12 f. 148; *State Papers* 16/524; British Library, MS Lansdowne Vol/

142   Emasculated Kingship

historians of his time, and his writing betrayed a thorough involvement in
the historiographical debates of the period and a deep-held interest in the
way non-literary evidence, such as monuments and coins, could be useful
sources for reconstructing 'true' history.[121] Methodologically, Bolton
admirably committed himself to writing a critical and well-researched
history in *Nero Caesar*, investigating Neronian legends and dismissing
those stories which lacked proper evidence.[122] However, his historical
method and commitment to writing factually did not prevent him from
writing politically, especially as he wished to support strong monarchy and
the pro-Spanish faction in the midst of the Bohemian Crisis.

Bolton was a practising Catholic in a country hostile to religious
difference generally and Roman Catholicism particularly. Raised in a
Catholic household and taking the middle name of Mary, Bolton presumably masked his religious affiliation in order to attend university at Trinity
College, Cambridge, in 1589. After Cambridge, Bolton moved to the
Inner Temple, and in about 1606 married the Catholic Margaret Porter,
the sister of Endymion Porter, a courtier and future servant to the royal
favourite, Buckingham, and to King Charles. It was through Cambridge,
the Inner Temple, and his brother-in-law Porter that Bolton built an
influential, if at times limited, network in Stuart England.[123] Bolton
enjoyed the peaceful practice of his religion during James's reign, but after
James's death, Charles pursued a more vigorous policy of religious
persecution. In 1628, Bolton was deemed a recusant, and, unable to pay
his fines, he was imprisoned at Fleet Prison and then Marshalsea, probably
until his death sometime after 1634.[124]

Bolton's most significant patron was Buckingham.[125] He dedicated his
translation of Florus's *Epitome* to Buckingham in 1618, and through this

---

90, fo.180; D. R. Woolf, 'Bolton, Edmund Mary (b. 1574/5, d. in or after 1634)', *Oxford Dictionary of National Biography* (Oxford University Press: 2004) online edn. Jan. 2008 [www .oxforddnb.com/view/article/2800].

[121] These included William Camden, John Selden, Sir Robert Cotton, Henry Howard, earl of Northampton, and the London historian John Speed. In his early career, Bolton published two poems in defence of Ben Jonson's classicism. See Thomas Blackburn, 'Edmund Bolton, Critic, Antiquary, and Historian: A Biographical and Critical Study with an Edition of *Hypercritica*' (Ph. D. thesis, Stanford University, 1963), 24.

[122] For instance, Bolton relayed the 'manie doubts' he had about the story of Agrippina successfully swimming to shore after Nero attempted to murder her by drowning, and he relied upon his common sense to fill the story's gaps. See Edmund Bolton, *Nero Caesar, or Monarchie Depraved* (London, 1624), 36–37.

[123] Woolf, 'Bolton, Edmund'.   [124] Woolf, *Idea of History*, 191.

[125] Bolton most likely made his connection to Buckingham through his brother-in-law, Endymion Porter, who may not have appreciated Bolton's constant badgering for patronage. This seems clear from a letter Bolton wrote to Porter in 1630, in which he noted that his brother-in-law had '[torn]

'And thus did the wicked sonne murther his wicked mother' 143

relationship, Bolton spent time with the King himself, '[giving] entertainment to his Maj*estie*' on Buckingham's behalf in 1624.[126] Bolton was well suited for the company of Buckingham and James, for he was an avid defender of monarchy present and past. In the early 1620s he composed his *Nero Caesar* as a pro-monarchical history, and by a decade later had completed another piece entitled, *AVERRVNCI or The Skowrers [Scours]. Ponderous and new considerations vpon the first six books of the Annals of CORNELIVS TACITVS concerning TIBERIVS CÆSAR* (c. 1629–34). Claiming to cleanse or 'skowrer' the reputation of the Emperor Tiberius, often considered a tyrant in Stuart England, Bolton intended to bring to light 'those truths in poinct of iudgement vpon persons, facts, and circumstances, which [Tacitus] hath darkned, and wronged by his ouer earlie sowing seeds of terrible aversion against that Emperour'.[127] Bolton sought to defend Tiberius by marshalling evidence from other historians and by analysing critically Tacitus's history. He argued that Tiberius's first sixteen years were marked by respect for the Senate and an able administration of the provinces, and, even after the Sejanus affair, Tiberius sought the restoration of law and order.[128] With Buckingham accused of being a Sejanus in the impeachment trial of 1626, it was no accident that Bolton chose this historical story. As Patricia Osmond summarised, 'If Bolton could not refute the widespread notion of *similitudo temporum* and the habit of analogical thinking ... , if he could not persuade his readers that Stuart England was very different from the Rome of Tiberius, he would have to convince them that Tiberius was not the deceitful and bloody tyrant depicted in Tacitus's *Annals*.'[129]

Nero Caesar, which Bolton wrote at the end of James's reign, should be understood as a thoroughly royalist piece. Within the opening pages of the 1627 edition, Bolton included a series of epistles dedicated to James and Buckingham in order to situate his history as a work receiving the King's approbation and even his editorial comment. He claimed in the first two epistles that he had presented a manuscript copy of his history to the King in 1622 with the hope of receiving James's authorisation. As Bolton explained, 'I durst not in duty suffer a line to passe out of my hands,

---

into pieces the enclosed scroll' he had sent. National Archives *State Papers* 16/170 f. 23, Jul. 2, 1630.

[126] Porter, 'Academ Roial', 194.

[127] Qtd. Patricia J. Osmond, 'Edmund Bolton's Vindication of Tiberius Caesar: A "Lost" Manuscript Comes to Light', *International Journal of the Classical Tradition* 11.3 (Winter 2005): 329–43, esp. 331.

[128] Ibid., 332.   [129] Ibid., 333.

which had not first passed your Maiesties most authorising doome.'[130] Bolton then announced the success of his endeavour in the third epistle, declaring to Buckingham, 'Royal approbation of the [history] (with the greatest improbation of Nero) hath made it so honorablie capable of best acceptance, as it may well be called his Maiesties.'[131] Bolton could not have levelled such a claim about the King's involvement had it been untrue, and, according to the timeline provided by the epistles, we can assume that James personally edited the history between the manuscript's presentation in 1622 and its publication in 1624, significantly during the height of the Spanish Match Crisis. Indeed, Bolton's brother-in-law, Porter, served as Buckingham's Master of the Horse and accompanied Buckingham and Prince Charles on their fateful mission to Madrid in 1623 to woo the Spanish Infanta. Bolton himself supported Spanish peace, and like his later history of Tiberius, he conceived of *Nero Caesar* as providing timely historical information for contemporary politics, especially in support of monarchical power and legitimacy against the resistance arguments of anti-monarchical writers.[132]

Bolton represented the content of his work as supporting the position of Stuart absolutism articulated by King James. In justifying his decision to present his history of Nero to the King, Bolton argued that the exemplum of Nero was particularly suited to teach a 'pretious secret' about monarchy:

> Nor was there cause to trouble your sacred Maiestie with any but only *Nero*. For he is the man whom your most Princely detestation of his manners noted out vnto mee, with the proper word of his merits, *Villaine*. Yet hee notwithstanding (for the great aduantage of truth) will teach this pretious secret; *No Prince is so bad as not to make monarckie seeme the best forme of gouernment.*[133]

Here, and throughout *Nero Caesar*, Bolton presented his argument in favour of monarchical government as resting upon a depiction of Nero as the most unfavourable, detestable tyrant, for Bolton desired to demonstrate how government even by the most despicable ruler was better than non-monarchical government. This argument would require Bolton to perform a precarious juggling act, condemning Nero on the one hand while lauding monarchical government on the other, and distancing his own King James from the abominable character of Nero while at the same

---

[130] Bolton, *Nero Caesar*, sig. A3r.   [131] Ibid., sig. A4r.

[132] Rei Kanemura, 'Roman Imperialism and Ancient British Liberty in the 1620s', in *The Idea of Sovereignty in English Historical Writing, 1599–1627* (PhD Thesis, University of Cambridge, 2012).

[133] Ibid., sig. A3v.

'*And thus did the wicked sonne murther his wicked mother*' 145

time upholding James's political views about monarchical absolutism. Bolton's history clearly reflected James's position in *The Trew Law of Free Monarchies*, in which the King had argued that the 'looseness' of rebellion would result in greater peril and disorder than tyranny, for 'it is certaine that a king can neuer be so monstrously vicious, but hee will generally fauour iustice, and maintaine some order, except in the particulars, wherein his inordinate lustes and passions cary him away'.[134]

Very significantly, to enact such a statement in his historical writing Bolton described his methodology as consciously separating the private life of Nero from the public life of Nero's realm, and his purpose was to portray Rome as orderly even when ruled by a disorderly tyrant – a view which fundamentally rejected the classical concept that the soul of the ruler mirrored that of the city.[135] Unlike the Tacitean historians, or 'popular Authors' as Bolton called them, who 'so busied themselues to lay open the priuate liues of Princes in their vitious, or scandalous qualities (which often times doe not concerne the people in any point so much as not to haue them laid open)' with the result that 'the nationall and publick Historie is almost thereby vtterly lost', Bolton claimed to fashion an 'Imperiall Historie', gleaned from the 'choysest pieces' of historical evidence and providing a 'summe' of 'facts'.[136] Bolton believed his Imperial history would prove James's arguments concerning monarchy. He summarised as much in *Nero Caesar* in his conclusion about Nero's first five years: 'That sacred monarckie could preserue the people of ROME from finall ruine, notvvithstanding all the prophanations, blasphemies, & scandals of tyranous excesses, vvherevvith NERO defiled & defamed it, is the vvonder vvhich no other forme of gouernement could performe.'[137]

In theory and motivation, Bolton undoubtedly desired to provide his historical account as an Imperial history that bolstered James's political activities and writings, avoided the dangers of Tacitean histories, and promoted obedience to monarchy, that 'sacred' form of government, and he claimed he would do so even through the detestable Nero. In practice, however, Bolton's *Nero Caesar* betrayed the significant difficulty of this task. While generally seeking to separate Nero's private scandals from the public governance of Rome, especially in the seventy pages discussing

---

[134] *King James VI and I: Political Writings*, 79.
[135] Although most famously outlined in Plato's *Republic*, writers such as Cicero followed this line of argumentation as well. See Section 1.3.
[136] Bolton, *Nero Caesar*, sig. A3r. For Bolton's place in the anti-Tacitean reaction, see Bradford, 'Stuart Absolutism and the "Utility" of Tacitus', 127–55.
[137] Bolton, *Nero Caesar*, 69.

146   Emasculated Kingship

Nero's first five years (when the ruler supposedly governed well), Bolton focused almost exclusively on the personal life of Nero rather than the Imperial or public history of Rome.

Moreover, although Bolton deemed Nero a detestable 'Villaine' in his dedication, he sought to defend and ameliorate Nero's vices by adopting a particular gendered portrayal of Nero's early life and household with a focus on Nero's mother, Julia Agrippina, and their deviant relationship. Through seeking to limit Nero's culpability for tyrannical injustice by denouncing female transgression and influence, however, Bolton's history highlighted the dangers of hereditary monarchy, how male rulers could be birthed through the wombs of vicious women such as Julia Agrippina and Poppaea, Nero's later wife.[138] In the context of discussions about Mary Queen of Scots, castigating Nero's degenerate mother and ancestors was a particularly dangerous endeavour. Scholars writing about *Nero Caesar* have focused almost exclusively on Bolton's portrayal of the revolts against Nero, and their debates have centred on the nature of Bolton's absolutist doctrine, his view of unlimited obedience, and his historical method.[139] No scholarly account to date has studied Bolton's important representation of Nero's family, the murder of Julia Agrippina, or the explicitly gendered language he employed in his history.

Bolton provided a vitriolic and unforgiving portrait of Nero's mother, Julia Agrippina, in *Nero Caesar*, representing her transgressions as naturally reviling and politically rebellious. Reflecting the anxiety expressed by his contemporaries towards female power and treasonous speech, Bolton deemed Agrippina violent, ambitious, sexually lewd, murderous, and at fault for bringing Nero to the throne by usurping the rightful succession of Nero's stepbrother, Britannicus: 'The principall agent in that iniurie of disenherison, was violent AGRIPPINA, her incentiue ambition, her instrument that lordly freedman PALLAS; the meanes, incest, adulterie, paricidial poison, and murther.'[140] By charging Agrippina with disrupting the royal succession, Bolton immediately disqualified her, despite her royal pedigree, from rightfully assuming royal authority, and the particular crimes Bolton listed as Agrippina's undoubtedly labelled her as an extreme form of rebellious and dangerous woman. In English society, incest and

---

[138] Several scholars have noted how Bolton sought to limit Nero's culpability in later sections of *Nero Caesar*. See Woolf, *Idea of History*, 194; Bradford, 'Stuart Absolutism', 142; Burgess, *Absolute Monarchy*, 61–62.

[139] See Burgess, *Absolute Monarchy*, 61–62; Bradford, 'Stuart Absolutism'; Woolf, *Idea of History*, 190–99.

[140] Bolton, *Nero Caesar*, 2.

'And thus did the wicked sonne murther his wicked mother'   147

adultery offended sexual and patriarchal laws by undermining what was understood as the natural order of family and household, and the perceived motives for adulterous escapades were lasciviousness as well as rebellion.[141] Widows were deemed to be lustier and more unruly than maidens or married women, which made them targets for accusations of 'witch-craft'.[142] Bolton explicitly charged Agrippina, a dangerous widow, as committing sexual crimes with a rebellious motivation, arguing that she 'meerely for prowd ends did most alluringly offer her body to the lustfull embraces of him [Nero] who scarcely twenty yeares before was bred therein'.[143] Bolton further described Agrippina's means of murder as poison, a form of 'treason' associated with the 'utter subversion and dissolution of human society', and especially associated with rebellious women whose cowardice and weakness required them to murder in secret.[144] Thus, on Bolton's account, Agrippina's unruliness and 'contemn[ation of] all the lawes of god, & man' was a result of her 'desire' for 'Domination',[145] and, as such a woman, Agrippina stood as a threat to the royal household and the royal governance of Rome.

Bolton further characterised Agrippina as a bad mother, deeming her more like an 'infernal furie than a matron, who with such waste of all conscience, and of all common honestie, affected supreme command'.[146] Early in his history, Bolton tied Nero's tyranny to his very birth from the womb of Agrippina. He explained that Nero 'came into the world an agrippa, or borne with his feete forward ... and turnd the world vpside downe before he went out of it'. Bolton's interpretation of this event claimed its authority from Pliny the Elder's *Natural History*: 'But that præposterous natiuitie foreboded nothing, in Plinies conceipt (who notes that all aggripæ were vnfortunate) but the parties disaster'.[147] Pliny, when detailing the extent to which agrippae were unfortunate, had described Nero as 'pernicious to the whole earth' and the 'very enemy to all mankind'. Pliny followed his discussion of agrippae by a brief chapter on 'Births cut out of the wombe', in which he claimed that 'more fortunate are they a great deale whose birth costeth their mothers life, parting from

---

[141] Wiltenburg, *Disorderly Women*, 104.
[142] Lyndal Roper, *Witch Craze* (New Haven: Yale University Press, 2006), 160–78.
[143] Bolton, *Nero Caesar*, 23.   [144] Bellany, *Politics of Court Scandal*, 144–45.
[145] Bolton, *Nero Caesar*, 5.   [146] Ibid., 23.
[147] Ibid., 2–3. Bolton seems to be almost punning the word 'præposterous', which could mean 'inverted in position or order' or 'monstrous; foolish, perverse'. See OED, 'preposterous, adj'. Pliny the Elder, *The historie of the vvorld Commonly called, the naturall historie of C. Plinius Secundus. Translated into English by Philemon Holland Doctor of Physicke. The first tome* (London, 1601), VII.8, 'Of Agrippae'.

148 Emasculated Kingship

them by means of incision', including Scipio Africanus, Julius Caesar, and Manlius.[148] Nero, through his inverted birth from the living and non-sacrificial body of Agrippina, marked his and his family's disastrous misfortune and the end of the Julio-Claudian ancestral line, while Caesar's caesarean birth had established this line of emperors.

In Bolton's telling, this 'omen' of disaster came true principally through the activity of Agrippina. As he explained, the Chaldeans prophesied that the newly born Nero would seal the eventual death of Agrippina: 'When the Chaldæans pronounced, according to their art, that hee should reigne, but murther his mother; shee submitted herselfe to that destinie, and in the furie of her pride fatallie said alowd, and let him kill me so as that proues true.'[149] Deeming Agrippina's 'Acceptance' of this prophecy as 'dangerous', Bolton characterised Agrippina's consent to death not as sacrificial, selfless, and maternal, but as frenzied and proud. As we will see later on, in the moment of assassination Bolton portrayed Agrippina as consenting to death by offering her womb to be stabbed, thus bringing the Chaldean prophecy to brutal fulfilment.

Bolton's emphasis on Agrippina as the root cause of Nero's tyranny and crime of matricide is even evinced in Bolton's inclusion of a chapter on 'Nero's behaviour, and words in priuate, vpon the view of Agriprina's corse'. This chapter detailed how Nero supposedly fawned with morbid fascination over his mother's corpse, 'praising this part, and dispraysing that', viewing her body and handling her limbs and wounds. 'There goes a rumour also', Bolton related, 'that he saw her body opened, to behold the place of his conception', and after examining her, 'impenitently said, that *Hee did not suppose hee had had so faire a mother.*'[150] Nero's infatuation with Agrippina disclosed not only an incestuous sexual desire for her but a desire to understand his own formation by viewing 'the place of his conception', where Agrippina had imprinted her nature upon him. Bolton remarked in *Nero Caesar* that Agrippina indeed was 'the roote of such an of-spring' as Nero, due to 'her nature being bloudy, fierie, and busie'.[151] Within her womb lay the original source of Nero's tyranny.[152]

---

[148] *Historie of the vvorld*, VII.9, 'Births cut out of the wombe'.   [149] Bolton, *Nero Caesar*, 3.

[150] Ibid., 43–44. Bolton at first sounds sceptical that Nero beheld Agrippina's womb, claiming that 'there is no authenticke testimony that I can find; nor other ground of coniecture (if that may be a ground) then a meere supposition, that shee was embowell'd before her burning'. However, as the chapter continues, he concedes that 'authors do not probably wrong him in these most infamous reports concerning his behauiour ouer his murtherd mother', and argues that the character of Nero as a murderer was such that it should not be doubted. See *Nero Caesar*, 43–46.

[151] Bolton, *Nero Caesar*, 55.

[152] For a fascinating discussion of Nero's dissection of Agrippina, see Park, *Secrets of Women*, 150–58, 234–49.

'And thus did the wicked sonne murther his wicked mother' 149

Bolton further emphasised Nero's viciousness as bred and birthed through his mother by neglecting to include the details of Nero's paternal inheritance. *Nero Caesar* noted only briefly a second birthing prophecy recorded by Dio Cassius or Suetonius, in which Nero's father Domitius Ænobarbus 'vnpremeditately answerd his congratulating friends, that nothing could possiblie come of Agrippina, and him, but cursed stuffe, ordaind to vndo the world, or words to such effect'.[153] Suetonius's history, however, had emphasised that Nero's great-great-great-grandfather, and every successive male householder, exhibited vicious inclinations, including the desire for fame and propensity to anger, cowardice, lust, hypocrisy, arrogance, extravagance, cruelty, violence, dishonesty, treason, adultery, and incest.[154] For Suetonius, it was relevant 'to say something about a number of members of the family, since this will suggest that Nero's vices were inherited from each of them, while at the same time degenerating from their virtues'.[155] *Nero Caesar* does not discuss this paternal inheritance and also neglects discussing Nero's adoptive father, the Emperor Claudius, an uxorious cuckold, according to Tacitus, who was enslaved by his passion for women and pushed into the 'most heinous crimes' of tyranny by their wiles.[156] As Bolton relied extensively upon Tacitus and Suetonius in writing *Nero Caesar*, these omissions appear intentional and suggest that Bolton sought to exonerate the male, patriarchal line of monarchical succession from the taint of tyrannical corruption. For Bolton, it seems to have been the imperial mother, the unstable, rebellious woman of the household, who noxiously contaminated the imperial seed.

In Bolton's account, Agrippina not only bred Nero's disaster through her womb but she also failed in nurturing him as a child. She 'auerted his affections from the studie of all philosophie' and instead allowed him to pursue those vain excitements he naturally desired, including 'that which might enable him to winn crownes of leaues, or garlands, for singing, fidling, piping, acting on stages, and the like ignobler trials'.[157] Agrippina, herself a 'gracelesse woman', lacked a knowledge of philosophy, Bolton argued, and hence she failed to understand 'how much more glorious it is, to affect honest things rather than great, or to compasse great things honestly'.[158] According to Bolton, Seneca was also 'part in the blame'

---

[153] Cassius Dio, *Epitome*, LXI.2; Suetonius, *The Twelve Caesars*, 216. Bolton, *Nero Caesar*, 3.
[154] Suetonius, *The Twelve Caesars*, 213–15.   [155] Ibid., 214.
[156] *Complete Works of Tacitus*, 227, 242–49.   [157] Bolton, *Nero Caesar*, 4.
[158] Bolton argued that Seneca 'kept [Nero] from solid eloquence proper to the antient orators, to hold him the longer in admiration of himselfe, Who taught him how to answear readely, who much more profitably might haue taught him how to thinck deeply', Bolton, *Nero Caesar*, 4–5.

150   Emasculated Kingship

for Nero's deficient education, and between Agrippina and Seneca's failings, Nero was left with a 'nature most vnboundedly affecting immortality of fame'.[159]

Bolton thus crafted a vivid portrait of Agrippina as an aggressive, rebellious woman and unfit mother, driven to seductive and treasonous behaviour for the sake of domination and corrupting Nero through her maternal body and activity; his representation of Nero, however, drew a stark contrast. According to Bolton, Agrippina deliberately and cruelly plotted for her own domination and power, while Nero lived an extended adolescence, dallying in vain and vulgar pursuits to please his curiosity and his growing appetite for popularity and bodily pleasure. Bolton characterised some of Nero's pursuits, such as fiddling and seeking fame, as 'not dishonest' although 'vtterly vnseemely in a prince'; yet he argued that Nero also took pleasure in pursuits 'not honest in any man', including 'wilde maskings, and riotous wanton women'.[160] Although already a married man and a prince, Nero chased women as if he were single and lowborn, Bolton explained: 'No pleasures are more agreeable to health in youth, and heighth in fortune, then femall society, though many bee more warrantable: but that fond prince who sayls by such vncertaine starres, hazards his estate, and doth more then hazard his glory.'[161] Bolton here, and throughout his history, deemed Nero a man pursuing alluring adolescent temptations.

Writers in seventeenth-century England commonly drew distinctions between men in their 'youth' and in their 'manhood', with the age of youth understood as a period of instability and extremes, marked by spiritedness and a seemingly unlimited capacity for vice. *The Office of Christian Parents* (1616), for example, argued that young men between the ages of 14 and 28 would be 'easily drawne to libertie, pleasure, and licentiousnes ... which if they take deepe rooting in this age, they will hardly or never be remooved ... and the poore young man laid open to the snares of the devill, to be holden at his pleasure with the tight chaine of his raging concupiscence'.[162] For Bolton, Nero seemed to be such a youth who lacked the constant vigilance of parental supervision necessary to tame his 'inordinate affections', and thus his character became rooted in lascivious behaviour. Bolton explained that even the 'honest and safe delight of marriage', which should have ushered Nero into his years of civilised manhood, became corrupted as Nero pursued mistresses such as the

---

[159] Ibid., 4.   [160] Ibid., 12.   [161] Ibid., 22.
[162] Qtd in Shepard, *Meanings of Manhood*, 23–24.

'*And thus did the wicked sonne murther his wicked mother*' 151

bondwoman, Acte, and the beautiful noblewoman, Poppaea.[163] Bolton depicted Nero as growing in sexual depravity, being at one time 'on the point of yeilding to his mothers prophane allurements, had not SENECA found meanes to terrifie him fro*m* it', and describing a rumour that Nero 'saw [his mother's] body opened, to behold the place of his conception' after murdering her, but Bolton more often defended Nero's sexual depravity as that of the extremes of an unformed young man.[164] Departing from the libels which accused James of taking a Ganymede, Bolton denied Suetonius and Tacitus's claims that Nero took a male concubine, Sporus, or 'suffered by his tituliarie husband', Pythagoras,[165] instead siding with Josephus who labeled these stories 'impudent vntruthes or (to vse his own rough roundnesse) lyes'.[166] Nero, then, on Bolton's account, fit the trope of an adolescent man conquered by unbridled passions, rather than a sodomite.

The first picture Bolton provided of Agrippina and Nero, then, was one that emphasised Agrippina's characteristics as a bad mother and unruly woman, driven by rebelliousness and lust for domination, and that identified Nero as a youth clearly born of Agrippina's vices. Although Nero engaged in improper dalliances and lusting for women, Bolton's portrayal of Nero as an adolescent shifted the blame for these nascent vices to his supervisors, especially his mother but also his counsellors. Bolton similarly emphasised that Nero was *privately* vicious, lustful of women not of power, and through this claim sought to deny that Nero held any desire to usurp the laws or constitution of Rome. This argument allowed Bolton to uphold James's view that the commonwealth, even when ruled by the worst tyrant, would remain generally ordered and just.

Significantly, Bolton carefully employed these images of adolescence to exonerate Nero of even his most heinous crimes, including the parricidal murders of his stepbrother, mother, and wife. In the tenth chapter of *Nero Caesar*, 'The Poisning of Britannicus', Bolton strategically blamed Agrippina as the 'impulse' behind Nero's parricide, even though it was undoubtedly Nero who enacted the poisoning.[167] Britannicus was the first son of

[163] Shepard, *Meanings of Manhood*, 74; Bolton, *Nero Caesar*, 21. [164] Bolton, *Nero Caesar*, 43–44.
[165] Suetonius calls him Doryphorus.
[166] Bolton, *Nero Caesar*, 69. Bolton does later concede that Nero, while grieving Poppaea's death, 'sought to conuert pretie SPORVS, a delicate youth, into a girle, because he nearly resembled [Poppaea]', but even in this passage he does not claim Nero took Sporus sexually. See Ibid., 250.
[167] In this chapter, Bolton is almost reluctant to admit that Nero committed the crime: 'Within the first tweluemoneth of his gouernment he spotted, and defloured the maiden candor of his fortunes by poisning BRITANNICVS ... This fact, considered in it selfe, though it directly violated the maine foundations of the world laid deepe by god in naturall pietie, yet some other appellation

Emasculated Kingship

Emperor Claudius and the rightful heir to the Roman throne, and although the Senate, through the persuasion of Seneca, had supported Nero over his older stepbrother, the accession remained insecure as long as Britannicus lived. Nero's murder of Britannicus could easily have been deemed an act motivated by ambition and the desire to destroy a rival, as Dio Cassius described it; Suetonius had argued that Nero poisoned Britannicus because he feared 'that [Britannicus] might sometime win a higher place than himself in the people's regard because of the memory of his father'.[168] Bolton, however, stressed that Nero murdered Britannicus because Agrippina, 'being crost by SENECA, and BVRRHVS, she durst threaten to set vp [Britannicus] as the righter heir, and thereby dubbed him the obiect of feare, and danger'.[169] In this rendering, Nero did not murder his brother as part of a careful plot to ensure domination; rather, he committed crimes such as poisoning Brittanicus because he was directly threatened by his mother. To further emphasise that Nero's murder lacked a motivation for power, Bolton described how the poisoning delighted Nero's curiosity, as he 'curiously beheld the poison confected, & boild to a speeding height'.[170] Through this portrayal, Bolton could continue to identify Agrippina as the 'principall agent of that iniurie of disenherison' and guilty of the crime of poison, as he had argued in the first chapter, while de-emphasising Nero's role in the usurpation.

Bolton similarly depicted Nero's murder of his mother as not principally motivated by designs for power:

> The chief impulsiues wherefore which moued the sonne to hate and persecute to death the author of his life, and empire (concubinarie loue growne farre more potent in him than filiall pietie) were securely to bring about his marriage with POPPÆA SABINA ... and then (as the lesser care) to assure to himselfe the ROMAN scepter, which he feared left AGRIP-PINA in her furie and offense would seeke to wrest away. A Lady, not vnlikely to effect it, considering her spirit, friends, and blood.[171]

As this passage suggests, Nero's mistress Poppaea received harsh treatment in Bolton's history as well, even bearing part of the blame for Nero's

---

would have beene inuented for auoiding the proper of paricide (as I haue said before) had not the carriage of his part in it, and the horrour of the circumstances made it wholly his own.' *Nero Caesar*, 12–13. However, in chapter VIII, he uses the example of Nero poisoning Britannicus to try to persuade his audience that Nero was capable of treating his mother so unjustly. Even in this chapter, though, the poisoning is still not described as a crime motivated by politics or ambition. See Ibid., 45–46.

[168] See Dio Cassius, *Epitome of Roman History*, Bk. LXI; Suetonius, *Twelve Caesars*, 231.

[169] Bolton, *Nero Caesar*, 13.   [170] Ibid.   [171] Ibid., 24–25.

'And thus did the wicked sonne murther his wicked mother'   153

matricide. Bolton colourfully depicted Nero's mistress and later wife as 'noble by birth, but by beauty more', whose incomparable beauty and 'art' created a snare to 'bewitch' Nero.[172] Beholden to vain pursuits, Poppaea engaged in 'polishing mysteries', according to Bolton, bathing herself in the milk of 'five hundred asses' for the care of her skin. Bolton believed the mistress proved 'what a painted dunghill dishonest beauty is', as she seduced Nero through 'amorous enchantments', driving 'all regard to naturall duties quite away'.[173] Such a depiction of a vain, 'painted' woman as a deceitful dissimulator fit well into the series of treatises produced during the Overbury Murder Scandal (1615–16).[174] As Thomas Tuke declared in his treatise, *A discourse against painting and tincturing of women Wherein the abominable sinnes of murther and poysoning, pride and ambition, adultery and witchcraft are set foorth and discovered* (1616), '[T]he condition of the mind is discerned in the state and behauior of the body. Without doubt then a deceitfull and effeminate face, is the ensigne of a deceitfull and effiminate heart'.[175] That Nero could be prone to the enchantments of Poppaea is unsurprising in Bolton's account, for Bolton deemed Nero so taken by lust and adolescent cowardice that when Poppaea 'plide him vpon the weake side with terrifying suggestions', he could not help but comply.[176] Bolton, then, held Poppaea partially responsible for Nero's matricide, and continued his hostile portrayal of women connected to royal power.

As Agrippina threatened Nero's authority, opposed his marriage to Poppaea, and set a vicious example for Nero in her mothering and her failure to educate and nurture him in virtue, Bolton even depicted Agrippina's murder as deserved and as necessary for Nero to free himself from unwarranted domination. As Bolton argued, Agrippina 'was a mother . . . whom it was no shame for a sonne to kill, that sonne being NERO; and she her selfe affirmed at her death no lesse'.[177] 'An infernall furie', one with 'such waste of all conscience, and of all common honestie', who 'affected supreme command', Agrippina's behaviour required just retribution, Bolton argued, and thus he maintained that 'If one wickedness therefore might authorise another, none could condemne [Nero] as impious, for killing that woman.'[178] Bolton further argued that Agrippina's murder served as an 'example of celestiall iustice, which euened all scores with

---

[172] Ibid., 244.   [173] Ibid., 247, 25.   [174] Bellany, *Politics of Court Scandal*, 176.
[175] Here Tuke claims to be quoting Saint Ambrose. Thomas Tuke, *A Discourse against painting and tincturing of women* (London, 1616), 17.
[176] Bolton, *Nero Caesar*, 25.   [177] Ibid., 23.   [178] Ibid.

154   Emasculated Kingship

wickednesse, and left no tally vnstrucken'.[179] James had contended in his *Trew Law of Free Monarchies* that a wicked king 'is sent by God for a curse to his people, and a plague for their sins', and that God would work justice through the acts even of 'the king of *Babel*' or 'Nero' until God saw fit to punish the tyrant himself.[180] Following this reasoning, Bolton labelled Nero's parricidal murders as serving God's justice. He made this claim explicitly not only about Agrippina's death but also the later murder of the then pregnant and sickly Poppaea, who having incensed Nero by 'pertly pratling', 'reproaching' and 'taunting' him for being away too long, received from him 'a kicke of his heele on her belly', from which 'abortion followed, and shee her selfe died of the cruell blow'.[181] Although a horrific scene, Bolton depicted it as an act of divine justice previously forewarned: 'The vengeance therefore forewarned to her, and euer to be expected of her likes, was thus paid throughly home. My heart in the meane time is at good peace within it selfe to behold the honour of heauenly iustice thus fully clear'd and settled.'[182]

Bolton believed that Agrippina's 'vnwomanly vices merited shee should perish' in a 'tormented' and 'exemplary' fashion,[183] and he portrayed her death accordingly. As a woman charged with enacting sexually depraved and incestuous acts to pursue an unnatural ambition for domination, and a woman who birthed, formed, and nurtured the unfortunate Nero, Agrippina's murder, in Bolton's account, was represented as a highly sexualised act in which the previously dominating Agrippina herself became sexually and violently defeated. Nero, enraged by a series of failed attempts to murder Agrippina, sent to his mother's palace three assassins, Anicetus, Herculeus, and Oloaritus. As Bolton described it, '[f]inding the gates of the palace shut', Anicetus and his men broke down the doors and forcibly entered, refusing to stop until 'rush[ing] vp to the very dores of [Agrippina's] priuate lodgings, which the ROMANS (for the maiestie of such a person) reputed sacred, and inuiolable'.[184] Having penetrated her geographical space, the assassins covertly entered Agrippina's dim room, lit by only one small candle, and proceeded to surround her in a 'gastly dumbe show' of silence.[185] Bolton claimed they next 'cast themselues about her' as she lay on her bed, and, as he conceived it, Herculeus with a short club marshalled himself at the bed's head, and the other two at the sides. As

---

[179] Ibid., 24.   [180] *King James VI and I: Political Writings*, 79 and 83.
[181] Bolton, *Nero Caesar*, 248.   [182] Ibid.
[183] Ibid., 35. This statement comes in the context of Bolton explaining why Agrippina did not die from the earlier assassination attempt of the trick galley.
[184] Ibid., 40.   [185] Ibid., 41.

'And thus did the wicked sonne murther his wicked mother'   155

Oloaritus unsheathed his sword, Agrippina 'laide her bare belly open, and challenged him to strike that, as deseruing it, for hauing brought forth monster Nero'.[186] The men hesitated, 'troubled with the horror of such a voyce, and action', Bolton claimed, but when Agrippina began to raise herself up, Herculeus clubbed her over the head, and the others stabbed her many times, her 'deaths wound' being 'in her brest'.[187]

Bolton compiled this account of Agrippina's murder principally from Tacitus, as well as Seneca, Dio, and Suetonius, but he added several details in order to represent the scene as a sexual assault, such as the exact positions of the murderers around Agrippina's bed. He also deliberately chose which classical sources to trust and which to overlook. Every classical author had declared that Agrippina commanded her murderers to strike her womb, but only Seneca in his *Tragedy of Octavia* depicted the mortal wound as being in her breast, and Bolton significantly departed from Tacitus and his other favoured sources in order to include this important detail.[188] The breast had two principal meanings in seventeenth-century England, both of which aptly described what Bolton considered to be Agrippina's primary faults and those deserving of retributive justice. On the one hand, the breast, as the organ of feeding and nurturing babies and young children, referred particularly to motherhood. Sixteenth and seventeenth-century medical treatises understood the womb as intimately connected with other major organs in the body, including the breasts; they identified breast milk as whitened blood, the same blood released in menstruation and used to feed the foetus in the womb after it converted into female seed.[189] Good mothers fed and nurtured their children through their breasts, and thus were likened to pelicans that sacrificially pecked the blood from their own breasts to feed their young ones.[190] In *Nero Caesar*, however, Bolton identified Agrippina as a bad mother who formed and shaped Nero's tyrannical passions even within her own body.

The second meaning of the breast provided a particular indictment against Agrippina. As related by the *Oxford English Dictionary*, the breast figuratively meant the 'seat of the affections and emotions; the repository of consciousness, designs, and secrets; the heart; *hence*, the affections,

---

[186] Ibid., 42.   [187] Ibid.

[188] For a discussion of Julia Agrippina's command to strike her womb, see Section 4.4.

[189] Marylynn Salmon, 'The Cultural Significance of Breastfeeding and Infant Care in Early Modern England and America', *Journal of Social History* 28.2 (Winter, 1994): 247–69, 251; Laura Gowing, *Common Bodies: Women, Touch and Power in Seventeenth Century England* (New Haven: Yale University Press, 2003), 22.

[190] Fissell, *Vernacular Bodies*, 83–84.

156   Emasculated Kingship

private thoughts and feelings' of an individual. As Robert Burton, like many of his contemporaries, claimed, the heart was 'the seat and fountaine of life, of heat, of spirits, of pulse and respiration, the Sunne of our Body, the King and sole commander of it: The seat and Organe of all passions and affections'.[191] Agrippina's heart was the physical location of her lust, incest, deceit, and inordinate hunger for power. These passions, in Bolton's account, corrupted Agrippina as a woman and as a mother, and hence her breast became the symbol of her maternal and moral failure.

In this scene, Bolton depicted Agrippina as disciplined through male, penetrative violence, graphically describing her murder through the language of rape: The assassins violate her 'priuate lodgings' in the dark, surround her as she lay in a vulnerable, supine position upon her bed, and then penetrate her with their knives multiple times. Agrippina, as she already had in the Chaldean prophecy, submits to the sexual violence by laying bare her belly and calling for its penetration – an activity fitting with her sexual character as described by Bolton. Although Agrippina's agency in this command is importantly denied, making the murder discipline for what were considered her devious desires, Agrippina is not presented as a victim of this rape/murder. In Bolton's account, she received just discipline, a deserved and fitting punishment.

In *Nero Caesar*, Agrippina's death does not transform Nero's vicious tyranny. Bolton explained that Nero still was he 'in whom alone all the corruptions which had beene engendred in ROME, from the birth of ROME till his owne dayes, seem'd drawne together into one apostem, or bile'.[192] However, through his matricide, Nero gained control of his household and country, for he successfully 'got loose from all the modest tyes of his breeding' and 'turn'd absolute' as a ruler.[193] Nero continued to pursue his private lusts throughout the course of his reign, but Bolton argued that this had little public effect, nor did what Nero commit 'vniust [ly] for his own satisfaction . . . vpon what grounds soeuer' much worry the senate and the people 'so long as it went well with themselves'.[194] Indeed, Bolton argued that even with Nero as absolute ruler, the public 'ioynts, and compactures of the empires fabricke' remained 'so supple, and solid', that Rome itself could be preserved.[195] It seems Bolton believed that male tyranny could be contained within the privacy of the palace, while female tyranny undermined the very fabric of monarchy and society. Female

---

[191] Qutd in Michael Carl Schoenfeldt, *Bodies and Selves in Early Modern England* (Cambridge: Cambridge University Press, 1999), 24.
[192] Bolton, *Nero Caesar*, 70.   [193] Ibid., 56.   [194] Ibid., 57.   [195] Ibid., 69.

'And thus did the wicked sonne murther his wicked mother' 157

tyranny required punishment and censure, whereas male tyranny could only be punished by God, and thereby required unlimited obedience: 'And though wicked deeds should not bee done at all, yet when they were don by him whom they could not punnish, euen good men were glad to make the best of that which neither could be recalled nor holpen. A patriots, and a wisemans office.'[196]

In these ways, Bolton's *Nero Caesar* offered a complex portrayal of monarchical tyranny intended to justify the absolutist doctrines of King James. His account proposed a strict, gendered ordering of society, which promoted the exemplary punishment of female transgressors while exonerating male aggression. By characterising Nero's failures through the trope of male adolescence, Bolton even sought to domesticate several of Nero's most monstrous and notorious crimes. However, the historical account of *Nero Caesar* unintentionally provided a poignant portrayal of the potential danger of hereditary monarchy through depicting the transgressions of Nero's family in sordid detail. By portraying tyranny as bred within the female womb, nurtured within the royal household, and encouraged through the enchantments of seducing women, Bolton invited his readers to reflect upon the breeding of their own king through the womb of Mary Stuart; his later edition of *Nero Caesar* in 1627 would have further invited reflection on the influence of the new Catholic queen, Henrietta Maria, on King Charles and the future royal children produced by their match. Whereas Bolton sought to separate private vice from public consequences, the *Tragedy of Nero* and the Nero libel demonstrate how the burgeoning vocabulary of tyranny in these years, conceived in classical and gendered terms, drew an explicit connection between the tyrant's corrupted soul and 'private crimes' and the wider ruination of family, religion, liberty, and commonwealth. This vocabulary would continue to develop through Caroline appropriations of Nero's history, becoming a powerful tool of criticism before the English civil wars.

---

[196] Ibid., 57.

CHAPTER 4

Neronian Corruption in Caroline England

In 1629, the celebrated poet, playwright, and translator George Chapman (1559/60–1634) wrote a pamphlet allegedly justifying the burial of a single strand of hair. In *A iustification of a strange action of Nero; in burying with a solemne funerall, one of the cast hayres of his mistresse Poppæa. Also a iust reproofe of a Romane smell-feast, being the fifth satyre of Ivvenall*, Chapman satirically described a scene in which the 'mighty Emperor' Nero solemnly marched in mourning clothes, followed by a train of 'all the state of the Empire either present or presented'.[1] With such a show of funeral pomp, all assembled to witness the procession expected the sombre hearse, decorated with honours at the end of the procession, to house Nero's mother, Julia Agrippina, or his wife, Octavia, both of whom were murdered through the emperor's tyranny. The hearse that passed, however, contained a single 'poor hayre broken loose' from the head of Nero's beloved mistress, Poppaea. Such a scene, Chapman remarked, 'may perhaps breed a wonder in those that know not the cause, and laughter in those that know it'; as for Nero, the cast hair of his favourite mistress deserved political honour and public expense.[2]

As perceptible distrust between parliament and king over church reform, foreign policy, and constitutional structures escalated into King Charles's final dissolution of parliament, such a satire of tyranny was far from light-hearted or irrelevant. For the English public, Nero's name had become synonymous with tyranny; his wicked exemplum was invoked

---

I am grateful to Palgrave Macmillan for permission to reprint excerpts from the following book chapter: Jamie Gianoutsos, 'Loyalty to a Nero? Publicising Puritan Persecution in the 1630s', published in *Loyalty to the Monarchs of Late Medieval and Early Modern Britain, c. 1400–1688*, edited by Matthew Ward and Matthew Hefferan, 2020, Palgrave Macmillan, reproduced with permission of Palgrave Macmillan.

[1] George Chapman, *A iustification of a strange action of Nero; in burying with a solemne funerall, one of the cast hayres of his mistresse Poppaea. Also a iust reproofe of a Romane smell-feast, being the fifth satyre of Iuuenall. Translated by George Chapman* (London, 1629), 1–2.

[2] Ibid.

158

Neronian Corruption in Caroline England 159

very frequently in treatises and cheap print, sermons and speeches, libels and bawdy songs, for burning Rome, persecuting Christians, murdering his family, exulting deviant sexuality, and being fatefully overthrown. As the previous chapter demonstrated, late in James's reign Nero's exemplum had become a battleground for debates concerning unlimited obedience and the morality of the royal household. Anonymous writers had employed stories of Nero to craft a significant gendered language of criticism, portraying the King as enslaved to perverse passions, popish, and effeminate, and his household and court as debauched, effeminate, and corrupt. Even royalist treatments of Nero, such as Edmund Bolton's *Nero Caesar* (1624, 1627), which characterised the emperor's tyranny as resulting from the wicked influence of royal mother and mistress, could not fully exonerate Nero.

As Chapman's satire demonstrates, these Neronian images eventually transferred from James to his son Charles, with certain important changes. Images of Nero employed to malign Charles's government, household, or court in the 1620s often focused on Charles's marriage to the Catholic and foreign Henrietta Maria and his early reliance upon Buckingham. In the early 1630s, those angered by the personal rule and its court culture continued to adopt classical imagery of tyranny as a disordered household and court corruption. With increased public opposition to Archbishop William Laud and the persecution of puritans, however, images of Christian martyrdom under Nero became more prominent in the final years of personal rule.

Despite arguments that little dissent was voiced against King Charles or his government, especially during the years of personal rule, the domain of political discourse in early Stuart England and the vocalisation of dissent was indeed much wider in this period, 'and sometimes nastier', as David Cressy has argued, than historians have often recognised.[3] The dangerous and treasonous words spoken by ordinary people which Cressy has studied included negative gendered characterisations of Charles as an unfit man. Hugh Pyne notoriously likened Charles to 'a child with an apple', both infantilising Charles and accusing him of having significant weakness of will, much like a child 'doth esteem an apple more than his father's

---

[3] Kevin Sharpe, 'A Commonwealth of Meanings: Languages, Analogues, Ideas and Politics', in *Politics & Ideas in Early Stuart England* (London and New York: Pinter, 1989), 3–71; Sharpe, *The Personal Rule of Charles I* (New Haven: Yale University Press, 1992); David Cressy, *Dangerous Talk: Scandalous, Seditious, and Treasonable Speech in Pre-Modern England* (Oxford: Oxford University Press, 2010), 133.

160 Emasculated Kingship

inheritance'.[4] In the same years, ordinary subjects made pronouncements against Charles's family lineage, similar in many ways to those presented in the Neronian libel against James.[5] William Wraxall disparaged the royal family, describing how Charles's grandfather had been 'hanged on a pear tree', his grandmother 'beheaded', his elder brother possibly poisoned, and his sister 'driven out of her country'. From this Wraxall concluded, 'There is a curse laid upon him or the kingdom.'[6] Wraxall's commentary did not include the even more frequent accusation that King James himself had been poisoned by his favourite, Buckingham.[7]

Discussions of tyrannical government through classical history similarly indicate dissatisfaction with the Stuart king and those he placed in authority. In Charles's reign, images of classical tyrants such as Nero continued to gain cultural significance not only due to the continued use of Paul's argument in Romans to justify absolute monarchy, as we saw in the previous chapter, but similarly due to the King's public representation as a Roman emperor. Although Charles, in comparison with his father, was reluctant to justify and represent his authority through speeches and the written word, the King was a significant patron of the visual and dramatic arts, and 'his aesthetic interests were always allied to his dynastic ambitions and beliefs'.[8] As early as 1627, Charles purchased the Gonzaga art collection from Mantua, including Titian's *Twelve Caesars*, as well as Andrea Mantegna's nine-painting series, *Triumphs of Caesar*, which depicted Julius Caesar in triumphal procession from the Gallic Wars. Charles seems to have admired these collections greatly, as in late 1631 when Dorchester was said to have found the King calmly arranging his busts of the Roman emperors in chronological order while his court and council were abuzz with news of the German crisis.[9]

Charles not only collected such art; he publicly fashioned himself as *imperator* through his portraiture. Anthony Van Dyck's *Charles with Monsieur de St Antoine* (1633) represented the King as gracefully guiding

---

[4] Cressy, *Dangerous Talk*, 116. As discussed in the prior chapter, writers in seventeenth-century England commonly drew distinctions between men in their 'youth' and in their 'manhood', with the age of youth understood as a period of instability and extremes, marked by spiritedness and a seemingly unlimited capacity for vice. See Alexandra Shepard, *Meanings of Manhood in Early Modern England* (Oxford: Oxford University Press, 2003), 47–69.

[5] See Section 3.3.   [6] Cressy, *Dangerous Talk*, 140.

[7] Alastair Bellany and Thomas Cogswell, *The Murder of King James I* (New Haven: Yale University Press, 2015).

[8] Kevin Sharpe, *Image Wars: Promoting Kings and Commonwealths in England, 1603–1660* (New Haven and London: Yale University Press, 2010), 190. See also Richard Ollard, *The Image of the King: Charles I and Charles II* (London: Phoenix Press, 2000), 37–39.

[9] L. J. Reeve, *Charles I and the Road to Personal Rule* (New York and Cambridge: Cambridge University Press, 2003), 178; *State Papers* 81/37 fos. 167r–168r.

Neronian Corruption in Caroline England　　161

a white horse through a triumphal Roman arch beside a shield decorated with the arms of his empire. Placed at the end of the St. James gallery, alongside Titian's *Twelve Caesars* and Giulio Roman's equestrian portraits of the emperors, Charles's masterful control of his horse became a visual metaphor for his command of 'empire', and his succession from this ancient lineage of rule.[10] Van Dyck's later half-length portrait of the King in armour holding a baton modelled Titian's portrait of the Emperor Otho from the *Twelve Caesars* royal collection, while the famous equestrian portrait *Charles I on Horseback* (c. 1635–6?) implicitly compared the King to Marcus Aurelius.[11] Modelled upon Titian's image of *The Emperor Charles V at Mühlberg*, Van Dyck's *Charles I on Horseback* most probably represented, following contemporary courtesy literature, Charles's mastery of the horse as symbolic of his mastery of wild nature and of the passions, and thereby, his fitness and self-discipline necessary for virtuous rule.[12]

Simultaneously, Charles represented himself as emperor in his royal masques. In *Albion's Triumph* (performed 1631), he played the part of Romano-British Emperor Albanactus and donned a costume, designed by Inigo Jones, reminiscent of the virtuous Trajan and godly Constantine.[13] Riding in a chariot from his 'sumptuous Pallace' through a '*Romane Atrium*, with high Collombs of white Marble', Charles's triumph in the masque was declared 'Mighty, as the Man deisgn'd / To weare those Bayes; Heroicke, as his mind; / Iust, as his actions; Glorious, as his Reigne'.[14] Although ruling a country at peace, Charles 'dayly Conquers a world of Vices', the masque proclaimed: 'Ambition is a Lyon; Cruelty, a Beare; Avarice, a Wolfe. Yet He subdues them all. To be short, no Vyce is so small, to scape him: Nor so great, but he overcomes it: And in that fashion he Triumphes overall the Kings, and Queenes that went before him'.[15]

---

[10] Karen Hearn, ed. *Van Dyck & Britain* (London: Tate, 2009), 74; Susan J. Barnes, Nora De Poorter, Oliver Millar, and Horst Vey, *Van Dyck: A Complete Catalogue of the Paintings* (New Haven and London: Yale University Press, 2004), 463–64; Sharpe, *Image Wars*, 201–2; Richard Cust, *Charles I: A Political Life* (New York: Routledge, 2007), 159.

[11] Jeremy Wood, 'Van Dyck's "Cabinet de Titien": The Contents and Dispersal of His Collection', *The Burlington Magazine* 132.1052 (Oct. 1990): 680–95, esp. 680; Roy Strong, *Van Dyck, Charles I on Horseback* (London: Allen Lane, 1972), 45–57; Sharpe, *Image Wars*, 198–203. The equestrian portrait was also likely modelled on Titian's image of *The Emperor Charles V at Mühlberg*. See Hearn, *Van Dyck & Britain*, 18.

[12] Hearn, *Van Dyck & Britain*, 18; Barnes, et. al., *Van Dyck*, 468–69.

[13] John Peacock, 'The Image of Charles I as a Roman emperor', in *The 1630s: Interdisciplinary Essays on Culture and Politics in the Caroline Era*, ed. Ian Atherton and Julie Sanders (Manchester and New York: Manchester University Press, 2006), 50–73, esp. 59.

[14] Aurelian Townshend, *Albions Triumph, Personated in a maske at court. By the Kings Maiestie and his lords. The Sunday after Twelfe Night. 1631* (London, 1631), 6.

[15] Ibid., 10.

162 Emasculated Kingship

Alongside these imperial and dynastic themes, Charles's masques and portraiture emphasised the centrality and symbolism of marriage as a representation of his reign. Early in the 1630s, Charles commissioned Daniel Mytens to create a double portrait of himself and Henrietta Maria, which portrayed Charles and his bride holding a laurel wreath, symbolic of victory and an attribute of Apollo and Daphne.[16] The 'great peece of our royal self, consort and children' painted by Van Dyck in 1632 emphasised patriarchal and dynastic communion in the royal household against the backdrop of sovereignty and rule, including the imperial crown, sceptre, orb, and the vista of Westminster Hall and the Parliament House.[17] Within the painting, the Queen looks to her husband lovingly and submissively, the image of household harmony.

Printing and circulating sensational tales of tyrannical emperors, such as Nero, provided a challenge to these royal representations in broad and specific ways, and formed important counterpoints to royalist thought in Stuart England. Whereas the masques and portraiture of King Charles represented marital harmony, self-restraint, and virtuous rule, Neronian imagery portrayed the royal household as uxorious and untamed, the royal court as corrupted and effeminate, and the practice of true religion as perverted and persecuted. Against this backdrop of imagery portraying Stuart good rule and masculine triumph, discussions of Nero afforded Englishmen a significant vocabulary, drawn from the classical world, of dangerous tyranny and failed masculinity.

4.1 George Chapman and Classical Masculinity

George Chapman's greatly understudied satirical writings of the 1620s provide ample opportunity to consider the adaptation and continuation of subversive language between the reigns of King James and King Charles. Whether describing an effeminate ruler, lounging in regal apartments as Christian soldiers suffer, or portraying an emperor so enslaved by his mistress that he throws a state funeral for a cast-off piece of her hair, Chapman's writings adopted classical stories and reflections upon tyranny by characterising the tyrant as a failed man. Chapman's background and

---

[16] Sharpe, *Image Wars*, 194.

[17] *Charles I and Henrietta Maria with their two eldest children, Prince Charles and Princess Mary* by Anthony van Dyck, 1632. See Hearn, *Van Dyck & Britain*, 68; Barnes, *Van Dyck*, 459–60; Sharpe, *Image Wars*, 207.

Neronian Corruption in Caroline England 163

his many reflections upon classical learning and classicised conceptions of masculinity and power help explain his late satirical works.

Chapman first found success as a writer in the 1590s with a series of poems in the metaphysical style; simultaneously, he wielded his pen for the playhouses with a number of comedies in the late Elizabethan period and several celebrated tragedies following the Jacobean succession. Prior to the start of his writing career, he fought the Spaniards in the Low Countries, and upon his return received literary patronage from the circle of Sir Walter Raleigh, until winning the patronage of Robert Devereux, the Second Earl of Essex, in 1598.[18] Chapman's early military activities and political alliances underscore his support for bellicose intervention for Continental Protestants and for a court culture that valued chivalric honour. His works in the 1590s praised the cult of the virgin Queen Elizabeth, connecting the significance of individual self-restraint to the corporate mastery of the body politic and empire: 'a *pax imperii* both inward and outward'.[19]

After King James's rise to the throne in 1603 and successful negotiation of peace with Spain, Chapman allied himself with the court of Prince Henry and other Protestant imperial nationalists who opposed James's fashions and policies and memorialised Elizabethan chivalry and its heroes, Essex and Sir Philip Sidney. Gilles Bertheau has contended that Chapman's writings in these years, including idealised portrayals of Queen Elizabeth in *Bussy D'Ambois* (1604) and *The conspiracie, and tragedie of Charles Duke of Byron* (1607–8), as well as his *An epicede or funerall song: on the most disastrous death, of the high-borne prince of men, Henry Prince of Wales* (1612), offered early veiled criticisms of monarchical absolutism and the new king.[20] Chapman's *Conspiracie, and tragedie of . . . Byron* similarly suggested parallels between Byron's rebellion in France and Essex's in England; a scene depicting the French queen and the king's mistress in a row led to the imprisonment of some of the actors.[21] In 1605, Chapman

---

[18] Willem Schrickx, 'George Chapman in Middelburg in 1586', *Notes and Queries* 283:2 (1993): 165; Paul Franssen, 'George Chapman's Learned Drama', in *The Cambridge Companion to Shakespeare and Contemporary Dramatists*, ed. Tom Hoenselaars (Cambridge: Cambridge University Press, 2012), 134.

[19] Gordon Braden, 'George Chapman', in *Elizabethan Dramatists*, ed. Fredson Bowers, *Dictionary of Literary Biography* 62 (Detroit: Gale Research, 1987), 4.

[20] Gilles Bertheau, 'Jacques I au miroir de la Tragedie Chapmanienne', *Bulletin de la Société d'Etudes Anglo-Americaines des XVII et XVIII Siècles* 62 (2006): 193–207. See also Bertheau, 'George Chapman's French Tragedies, or, Machiavelli beyond the Mirror', in *Representing France and the French in Early Modern English Drama*, ed. Jean-Christophe Mayer (Newark: University of Delaware Press, 2008), 110–24.

[21] Franssen, 'George Chapman's Learned Drama', 136.

164   Emasculated Kingship

himself was imprisoned alongside Ben Jonson for co-writing *Eastward Ho*, a comedy staged without licence that ridiculed James for selling knight-hoods, mocked the Scottish accent, and made jeering reference to the Virginia expeditions.[22] Rumours circulated that Jonson and Chapman would suffer their ears and noses cut – a punishment for crimes deemed rebellious or seditious – but both were released after two months most likely due to the intercession of the Earl of Suffolk.[23]

Saturated with learned classical allusions, Chapman's writings sought to attract an elite and educated audience.[24] As will be seen, his reliance upon the classical past also afforded him an important lens through which to criticise the Stuart kings and court. In a dedicatory epistle in 1595, Chapman claimed that he crafted his poetry not for 'the prophane multi-tude I hate', but for 'serching spirits, whom learning hath made noble, and nobilitie sacred'.[25] His early translations of Homer described the 'Reader' as an intelligent, educated, and virtuous person; his *Achilles shield* (1598) addressed the audience as 'vnderstander' rather than 'Reader'.[26] And as Paul Franssen has pointed out, even Chapman's comedies for public theatres were often based on classical sources, contained Latin proverbs, alluded to classical mythology, and included stage directions in Latin.[27]

From these early writings, courtly associations, and activities, it is clear that Chapman admired men who exhibited self-discipline and self-sufficiency as truly masculine, truly Christian, and truly noble. Being a man of considerable learning, Chapman's conception of masculinity was shaped by his understanding of Stoic philosophy, found in Seneca and Epictetus; by his study of classical, exemplary figures; and by his religious beliefs. In *Euthymiæ raptus; or The teares of peace: with interlocutions* (1609), for example, Chapman emphasised the significance of learning

---

[22] See, for example, George Chapman, Ben Jonson, and John Marston, *Eastward Ho*, ed. R. W. Van Fossen (Manchester: Manchester University Press, 1999), 156–57 (4.1.197–201): '*1 Gent.*: I ken the man weel, he's one of my thirty-pound knights. / *2 Gent.*: No, no, this is he that stole his knighthood o'the grand day for four pound, giving to a page all the money in's purse, I wot well'. The third collaborator, John Marston, escaped imprisonment.

[23] For the punishment of mutilating noses or ears in England, see Garthine Walker, *Crime Gender and Social Order in Early Modern England* (Cambridge: Cambridge University Press 2008), 91–93.

[24] The most in-depth study of Chapman's classical and Renaissance influences can be found in Franck L. Schoell, *Etudes Sur L'humanisme Continental En Angleterre À La Fin De La Renaissance* (Paris: Honoré Champion, 1926).

[25] Chapman, *Ovid's banqvet of sence. A coronet for his mistresse philosophy; and his amorous zodiack* (London, 1595), dedicatory epistle to Matthew Roydon.

[26] Bertheau, 'Prince Henry as Chapman's "Absolute Man"', in *Prince Henry Revived: Image and Exemplarity in Early Modern England*, ed. Timothy Wilks (London: Paul Holberton, 2007), 134–45, esp. 136.

[27] Franssen, 'George Chapman's Learned Drama', 134.

Neronian Corruption in Caroline England 165

for its ethical implications, as true knowledge would help men achieve harmony within the human soul through the 'gouernance' of one's 'sensuall parts':

> But this is Learning; To haue skill to throwe
> Reignes on your bodies powres, that nothing knowe;
> And fill the soules powers, so with act, and art,
> That she can curbe the bodies angrie part;
> All perturbations; all affects that stray
> From their one obiect; which is to obay
> Her Soueraigne Empire.[28]

Set as a dialogue, Chapman's personification of Peace contrasted the man of true learning with three types of failed men who are 'foes ... / To Learning and her loue', as well as foes to themselves and to Peace: '*Actiue, Passiue,* and *Intellectiue* men'. Active men through ambition soar Icarus-like into the hands of death; passive men, 'So call'd of onely passing time in vaine', stuff their 'manlesse breasts' with others' ends, never seeking their own *teloi*; and intellective men 'study hard / Not to get knowledge, but for meere reward'.[29] The solution Chapman proposed for these failed men was an ethical life, for which they would 'turne to making strong, their rule of Passion' and rest their eyes on God.

Throughout his career, Chapman frequently defined ideal masculinity as ethical resolve and virtuous heroism. His writings often promoted a Stoic philosophy that extolled manly heroes or explored the conflict between virtuous statesmen and corrupted governments. Gordon Braden has characterised Chapman's writings as 'the most concerted effort in English to create an image of "Senecal man" as an ethical norm', and this can be seen in writings such as Chapman's Roman tragedy *Caesar and Pompey* (1631).[30] This tragedy celebrated Cato, contrasting his self-control and virtue with the ambitious and Machiavellian Caesar and the ambitious, although more sympathetic, Pompey.[31] In the opening scene, Cato

---

[28] Chapman, *Euthymiæ raptus; Or The teares of peace: with interlocutions* (London, 1609), C3^r.

[29] Ibid., C1^v–C2^r.

[30] Braden, 'George Chapman', 4. Although printed in 1631, the tragedy was probably written prior to 1607, as there appears to be an allusion to the play in *Northward Ho* (1607). For further information on dating, see Mark Thornton Burnett, 'Chapman, George (1559/60–1634)', in *Oxford Dictionary of National Biography* (Oxford: Oxford University Press, 2004), online edn, May 2006 [www.oxforddnb.com/view/article/5118].

[31] The 'Argument' claims that Pompey resorts to war 'more for feare of *Ceasars* violence to the State, than mov'd with any affectation of his own greatnesse', and he deepens in virtue and constancy after suffering defeat against Caesar. Chapman, *The Warre of Pompey and Caesar, Out of whose euents is euicted this Poposition. Only a iust man is a freeman* (London, 1631), A4^v.

labelled Caesar 'tyranous' and a threat to Rome, surrounded by 'such a flocke of Puttocks' drawn to his 'ill-disposed Purse' as well as 'Impostors, Flatterers, Fauorites, and Bawdes, / Buffons, Intelligencers, selects wits; / Close Murtherers, Montibanckes, and decaied Theeues'.[32] In contrast, Cato's suicide near the end of the play is described as a 'thing manly, / and merely heauenly' for the sake of 'iust mens liberties'; his final speeches include praise for his son-in-law, Marcus Brutus, whom the audience knows will later defend Rome's liberty by assassinating Caesar.[33] Before falling upon his sword, Cato advises his children that the virtuous man must remain constant and 'thriue in honor', even in corrupt times 'howsoeuer ill'. In this way, Chapman promoted the theme, 'Iust men are only free, the rest are slaves'.[34]

Early on, Chapman applied his ethical views of virtuous manhood to political sovereignty, especially through his publications dedicated to the young Prince Henry. In his dedication to the 'High / Borne Prince of / Men', Chapman argued that princes may not find 'perfect happinesse' through birth or wealth or any 'outward State'; the Prince truly 'blest' is he that 'gouernes inward',

> and beholdeth theare,
> All his affections stand about him bare;
> That by his power can send to Towre, and death,
> All traitrous passions; marshalling, beneath
> His justice, his meere will; and in his minde
> Houlds such a scepter, as can keepe confinde
> His whole lifes actions in the royall bounds
> Of Vertue and Religion; and their grounds
> Takes-in, to sowe his honors, his delights,
> And compleat empire.[35]

Here Chapman identified the true prince as the man possessing complete empire over the self through the execution of the passions; for this prince, justice, virtue, and religion reign supreme. In these ways, Chapman's views of masculinity aligned with those often espoused by his contemporaries, emphasising the performance of manhood as central to the order and discipline of society. For the sake of themselves and the commonwealth, it was argued that men needed to develop two key male attributes, reason and strength, and they needed to exercise these capacities in the control

---

[32] Ibid., B1^{r-v}.   [33] Ibid., I2^r, I4^r.   [34] Ibid., I4^r, K1^r.

[35] Chapman, *Homer prince of poets: translated according to the Greeke, in twelue bookes of his Iliads* (London, 1609), dedication to Prince Henry.

Neronian Corruption in Caroline England   167

and discipline of themselves as well as their inferiors.[36] Because masculinity required performance, manhood itself was always insecure even when temporarily achieved. Thus, the espousal of idealised standards of normative masculinity, and the application of these standards to kingship, laid the monarchy open to very significant scrutiny and criticism.

As Gilles Bertheau has demonstrated, Chapman's exultation of the masculine qualities of the truly noble prince further reflected his concept of the 'absolute man'. Drawing upon Chapman's dedications and Jacobean tragedies, Bertheau established that the absolute man was, in part, shaped through Greek mythology; Chapman described him as a Homeric hero who possesses not only the strength of Hercules but the *virtù* of Achilles and the wisdom of Ulysses.[37] Chapman's fullest definition of the absolute man, however, can be found in a passage from *The conspiracie, and tragedie of Charles Duke of Byron*, which praised Queen Elizabeth in masculine terms:

> Ther's a Queene
> Where nature keepes her state, and state her Court,
> *Wisdome* her studie, *Conntinence* her fort,
> Where *Magnanimity, Humanitie*:
> Firmnesse in counsaile and integritie:
> Grace to her porest subiects: Maiestie
> To awe the greatest, haue respects diuine,
> And in her each part, all the vertues shine.[38]

This passage not only defined the absolute man as possessing all princely virtues but simultaneously presented the ironic argument that a woman, Elizabeth, had exhibited far more masculine qualities than her male successor, King James. Chapman extended his praise of the absolute man to Prince Henry for possessing such 'unmatched' virtues; as Jean Jacquot and Bertheau have noted, the poet often exalted the son at the expense of his father. Significantly, Chapman also employed this image to praise the

---

[36] As Elizabeth Foyster and Alexandra Shepard have emphasised, *reason* in this account connoted the virtue of temperance or self-control as well as wisdom. It was thought that a man must be able to govern himself with reason before he could govern 'weaker vessels' as a father, husband, or master. Masculine strength indicated not only physical force but courage or fortitude as exemplified in sporting activities and the battlefield. Elizabeth A. Foyster, *Manhood in Early Modern England: Honour, Sex and Marriage* (London and New York: Longman, 1999), 28–48; Shepard, *Meanings of Manhood*, 21–46. See also Mark Breintenberg, *Anxious Masculinity in Early Modern England* (Cambridge: Cambridge University Press, 1996), 69–96.

[37] Bertheau, 'Prince Henry as Chapman's "Absolute Man"', 140.

[38] Chapman, *The conspiracie, and tragedie of Charles Duke of Byron, Marshall of France. Acted lately in two playes, at the Black-Friers* (London, 1608), F2^{r-v}; Bertheau, 'Prince Henry as Chapman's "Absolute Man"', 141.

168 Emasculated Kingship

'matchless Earl of Essex', who had already suffered the scaffold for his Elizabethan revolt.[39] Chapman's conception of masculinity thereby promoted the high ideal of self-control and the virtuous life for individual men as well as monarchs. In the decades following the death of Prince Henry, Chapman continued to apply this standard of masculinity to King James as well as King Charles, and found both monarchs wanting.

4.2 James As a Venus? Chapman and the Protestant Cause

With James's refusal following the Bohemian Crisis to enter England into continental religious warfare, Chapman, like a number of vocal, if anonymous, dissenters in the early 1620s, sought to persuade King James to pursue bellicose intervention both for the sake of 'true' Christians at home and abroad and for the preservation of masculine honour amongst England's own subjects and soldiers. The cacophony of libellous pamphlets reached such a pitch in these years that James twice issued proclamations banning censorious speech.[40] Anonymous author(s) of the pamphlets *Hic mvlier: or, The man-woman* (1620) and *Hæc vir: or The womanish-man* (1620), for example, discussed England's gender trouble in its refusal to enter war. *Tom Tell Troath* (1622) and Thomas Scott's *Vox Populi* (1620) mocked James specifically for his seemingly cowardly and sluggish pursuits of scholarship, while branding the King's arguments for peace as weak and effeminate. Similar to Chapman's idealised portrayals of Elizabeth, these tracts expressed a yearning for the 'old days' when England's manhood had been preserved through military ventures under 'that deceased English *Virago*', Queen Elizabeth.[41] The anonymous tracts also echoed *Hic mvlier* and *Hæc-vir* in arguing that a call to arms was England's only solution to the crisis of religion on the Continent and the crisis of masculinity at home.

In the wake of these pamphlets, Chapman published an encomium for the English general, Horace Vere, which implored the King to support the Protestant cause and especially Vere's English troops on the Continent

---

[39] The quotations are from Bertheau, 'Prince Henry as Chapman's "Absolute Man"', 141–42; see also Jean Jacquot, *George Chapman (1559–1634), sa vie, sa poésie, son théâtre, sa pensée* (Paris: Société D'éditions 'Les Belles Lettres', 1951), 47.

[40] Proclamations passed in 1620 and 1621. James F. Larkin and Paul L. Hughes, eds., *Stuart Royal Proclamations, vol I: Royal Proclamations of James I, 1603–1625* (Oxford: Clarendon, 1973), 495–96 and 519–20. For further discussion of these tracts, see Section 3.1.

[41] Michael B. Young, *James VI and I and the History of Homosexuality* (Basingstoke: Macmillan, 2000), 85–101, esp. 91; Carole Levin, *Heart and Stomach of a King: Elizabeth I and the Politics of Sex and Power*, 2nd edition (Philadelphia: University of Pennsylvania, 2013), 121–48.

Neronian Corruption in Caroline England

who were suffering a debilitating siege by Imperialist and Spanish forces. Entitled *Pro Vere, Avtvmni Lachrymæ. Inscribed to the immortal memorie of the most pious and incomparable souldier, Sir Horatio Vere, Knight: besieged, and distrest in Mainhem* (1622), Chapman's poem celebrated the military general as 'This Thunderbolt of Warre', whose defence of Christendom underscored his august faith, heroism, and virtuous character.[42] Hitherto overlooked by scholars, Chapman's poem adopted gendered and historical language to voice significant opposition to King James. Throughout the poem, Chapman warned that Vere's demise at the hands of Catholic forces would mean the defeat not only of a great man and of the Continental Protestants he defended but also of England. Thus, England must intervene with great military force:

> But (being There
> Circled with Danger) Danger to vs All;
> As Round, as Wrackfull, and Reciprocall.
> Must all our Hopes in Warre then: Safeties All;
> In Thee (O Vere) confound their Spring and Fall?
> And thy Spirit (Fetcht off, Not to be confinde
> In lesse Bounds, then the broad wings of the Winde)
> In a Dutch Cytadell, dye pinn'd, and pin'de?
> O England, Let not thy old constant Tye
> To Vertue, and thy English Valour lye
> Ballanc't (like Fortunes faithlesse Leuitie)
> Twixt two light wings: Nor leaue Eternall Vere
> In this vndue plight. But much rather beare
> Armes in his Rescue.[43]

In this passage and throughout the poem, Chapman played upon the words 'Vere' and 'spring' to emphasise the general's youthful vigour and bravery, as well as the great hope that England should place in him; in the opening lines, he even hailed Vere as the 'full Spring of Man', adopting the same phrase that he had used to eulogise Prince Henry.[44]

This portrait of a besieged yet heroic general provided the potent argument that the King must exercise armed force rather than diplomacy in defence of the 'true' Christian faith. His cry for England to 'Muster

---

[42] George Chapman, *Pro Vere, Avtvmni Lachrymæ. Inscribed to the Immortal Memorie of the most Pious and Incomparable Souldier, Sir Horatio Vere, Knight: Besieged, and distrest in Mainhem* (London, 1622), A4ᵛ–B1ʳ. Entered into Stationers' Register on 8 Nov. 1622, corresponding with the imminent fall of Mannheim to Tilly's forces.

[43] Ibid., B2ʳ⁻ᵛ.

[44] Ibid., A4ʳ; Chapman, 1612, D2ᵛ. See Phyllis Brooks Bartlett, ed. *The Poems of George Chapman* (New York: MLA, 1941), 466.

170 Emasculated Kingship

then / ... all thy Armed Men, / ... and plough vp all the Seas of *Gall'* aligned productively with ultra-Protestant tracts of the period, such as *Votivæ Angliæ* (1624), which sought 'to perswade his Majestie to drawe his Royall Sword, for the restoring of the Pallatynat, and Electorat', to the 'Glorie of God, and the defence and protection of his afflicted Spouse the Church'. The *Votivæ Angliæ* urged the King that 'it must bee your Sword, not your Tongue, not your Treaties, not your Letters, not your Ambassadours .... For all other meanes are fledd ... and this of Warre is onlie left you to effect it, which will not fayle, nor cannot deceive you in the performance therof'.[45] The wave of ultra-Protestant pamphlets and weekly news corantos released from the early 1620s onwards often adopted the language of anti-popery described by Peter Lake, which involved encouraging English military involvement by rousing suspicion and hostility towards Spain as a popish and aggressively foreign threat.[46] Chapman's *Pro Vere*, however, exhorted the King to pursue a bellicose policy not for fear of Spanish treachery but out of a fundamental concern that England would lose its 'old constant Tye / To Vertue' and 'English Valour'. At stake, Chapman argued, was the masculinity and virtue of England's king and subjects.

Chapman emphasised the centrality of gender in his poem by adopting contrasting images of the soft and luxurious life of peace, imagined as feminine or effeminate, and the hard and demanding task of war, which he characterised as truly masculine. In the central lines of the poem, Chapman poignantly referenced book 2 of Aristotle's *Politics*, in which Aristotle argued that 'libertie which was giuen vnto women, is hurtfull and incommodious, both for the purpose of their Commonweale, and also for the happie estate therof'. In this section, Aristotle had warned that the failure

---

[45] [John Reynolds], *Votivae Angliae: Or the Desires and VVishes Of England. Contayned in a Patheticall Discourse, presented to the King on New-yeares Day last* ... (Utrecht, 1624), C1^{r-v}. See Thomas Cogswell, *The Blessed Revolution: English Politics and the Coming of War, 1621–1624* (Cambridge: Cambridge University Press, 1989), 288–90.

[46] Peter Lake, 'Anti-Popery: the Structure of a Prejudice', in *Conflict in Early Stuart England*, ed. Richard Cust and Anne Hughes (New York: Longman 1989), 72–106; Lake, 'Constitutional Consensus and Puritan Opposition in the 1620s: Thomas Scott and the Spanish Match', *Historical Journal* 25.4 (1982): 805–25. For example, the second part of the *Vox Populi* (1624), which represented the Spaniards, especially the 'Machiavellian' Spanish Ambassador Gondomar, as plotting to overthrow the Protestant religion in England. According to the pamphlet, the Spanish desired peace with England, the 'sleepie Lyon', for fear of certain defeat by her military should she awake. See [Thomas Scott], *The second part of Vox popvli, or Gondomar appearing in the likenes of Matchiauell in a Spanish parliament wherein are discouered his treacherous & subtile Practises to the ruine as well of England, as the Netherlandes. Faithfully transtated [sic] out of the Spanish coppie by a well-willer to England and Holland* (Goricum, 1624), 41–42, 50.

Neronian Corruption in Caroline England

of lawgivers to order and discipline women, permitting them 'to liue in all licentiousnesse and dissolute intemperancie', would 'cause an undecencie and indecorum in the Commonweale' and further 'engender auarice and couetousnesse'. To demonstrate his claim, Aristotle had turned to the example of Sparta, in which women had been given such command over themselves that their commanders were essentially 'commanded by women', with the 'most part of their [men's] affairs ordered by the direction of women'.[47] Aristotle contended that Lycurgus could only seek to establish his constitution over the Spartans by reining in the liberty of women for the sake of the military state – disciplining Venus for the sake of Mars.[48]

Chapman drew upon this argument in *Pro Vere*, maintaining that England for a 'long time' had 'serued (the Paphian Queene)', Venus, and that the English King and subjects should now 'resemble her' by laying aside the feminine vices to create a masculine militarised state:

> When (all asham'd of her still-giglet Spleen)
> She [Venus] cast away her Glasses, and her Fannes,
> And Habites of th'Effeminate *Persians*,
> Her *Ceston*, and her paintings, and in grace
> Of great Lycurgus, tooke to her Embrace,
> Cask, Launce, and Shield . . .
> . . . .
> . . . Be (I say) like her,
> In what is chaste, and vertuous, as well
> As what is loose, and wanton; and repell
> This Plague of Famine, from thy fullest Man.[49]

In this striking image, borrowed from Plutarch's *De fortuna Romanorum*, Chapman offered Venus as both a censure and a model for James.[50] Chapman contended that James, like Venus, had donned the trappings of vanity, Asiatic luxury, and effeminate peace, a description that reflected contemporary criticisms of the King for ostentatious expenditures, cloth-

---

[47] Aristotle, *Aristotles politiqves, or Discovrses of government. Translated ovt of Greeke into French, with expositions taken out of the best authours . . . concerning the beginning, proceeding, and excellencie of ciuile gouernment.* Trans. Loys Le Roy (London, 1598), 110.

[48] Ibid., 110, 113. This edition of Aristotle's *Politics* from the sixteenth century was translated and interspersed with significant commentary on Aristotle's text by Loys Le Roy. I have restricted my analysis to Aristotle's text only.

[49] Chapman, *Pro Vere*, B3ʳ.

[50] Schoell, *Etudes Sur L'humanisme Continental En Angleterre*, 221–22, 239; Bartlett, *The Poems of George Chapman*, 466.

172   Emasculated Kingship

ing, and playful pursuits at court.[51] Simultaneously, Chapman's poem urged James to model Venus's transformation from a goddess of pleasure to one of war in the aid of Lycurgus, a transformation that would require James to abandon effeminate pursuits and pursue manly acts of war for the sake of Vere, here described as 'thy fullest man'. Chapman's comparison of James to Venus provided a significant contrast to his earlier commendations of Elizabeth as a queen exhibiting the virtues of the 'absolute man'. Whereas Elizabeth was a female monarch whose virtues resembled those of a classical god or hero, the ostensibly male James acted like a female goddess who still needed to be transformed. Although contemporaries in these years often accused James of failed masculinity through charges of sodomitical behaviour with the favoured Duke of Buckingham, as Alastair Bellany and Andrew McRae have demonstrated, Chapman's attack imagined James as effeminate due to his seemingly vain and womanish practices.[52]

Following this description of Venus, Chapman highlighted the austere conditions that Vere and his soldiers endured on the Continent. Whereas Englishmen pursuing peace were envisioned with effeminate 'Glasses' and 'Fannes', Chapman boasted that Vere and his men 'liue in Forts and Tents, / And not in soft Sardanapalian Sties / Of Swinish Ease, and Goatish Veneries'. Their camp served as an exemplary model of masculine valour, so 'Diuinely rare' in their virtue that 'No Earthy Powre' should dare to hazard their ruin by neglect.[53] Within these lines, Chapman enhanced his warning that England's old virtue and valour, and even 'The World it selfe, and all Posteritie', may be lost with Vere's defeat: 'For worthy men the breeders are of Worth, / And Heauens broode in them (cast as Offall forth) / Will quite discourage Heauen to yeeld vs more'.[54] Here Chapman seems to have been employing *breed* in two ways, describing Vere and his soldiers' ability to instruct other men in virtue through their example, as well as their virility, which would literally produce the next generation of honourable men.[55] In sum, Chapman

---

[51] See Chapter 3. See S. J. Houston, *James I*, 2nd ed. (London and New York: Longman, 1995), 14–21; Maurice Lee, Jr., *Great Britain's Solomon: James VI and I and His Three Kingdoms* (Urbana: Illinois University Press, 1990), 148–49; Roger Lockyer, *James VI and I* (London and New York: Longman, 1998), 85, 96–97. For the demanding and ritualised system of court patronage in Stuart England, see Linda Levy Peck, '"For a King not to be bountiful were a fault": Perspectives on Court Patronage in Early Stuart England', *Journal of British Studies* 25.1 (1986): 31–61.
[52] Alastair Bellany, *The Politics of Court Scandal in Early Modern England: News Culture and the Overbury Affair, 1603–1660* (Cambridge: Cambridge University Press, 2002), 254–61; Andrew McRae, *Literature, Satire, and the Early Stuart State* (Cambridge: Cambridge University Press, 2004), 75–82.
[53] Chapman, *Pro Vere*, B4^{r-v}.   [54] Ibid., B4^v.
[55] See *Oxford English Dictionary*, s.v. 'breeder', *n.*1.a. 'That which breeds or produces offspring', and *n.*3. 'One who brings up; a trainer, instructor'.

Neronian Corruption in Caroline England 173

envisioned masculine honour as passing down through the nature and nurture of 'good breeding'. The loss of men such as Vere and his troops would thereby lead to the demise of English valour for future generations.

In these ways, Chapman framed an argument for war in highly gendered terms, painting the path of peace as effeminate and dangerous to the virtue, safety, order, and future of the commonwealth. Drawing upon the classical philosophy and historical exempla of Aristotle and Plutarch, Chapman argued that virtuous men must rule, lest the commonwealth degenerate into the cowardly and supposedly womanish pursuits of vanity, luxury, and greed. Chapman envisioned effeminacy, then, as the practices of Stuart fashions and court life, and thereby wielded a gendered language of dissent that would have combined effectively with contemporary portrayals of the King as compromised by sodomitical and popish favourites. Simultaneously, Chapman regarded General Vere and his soldiers as modelling the activities of ideal men, courageously hazarding their lives through battle and famine for true religion and the commonwealth.

Chapman concluded *Pro Vere* by petitioning the 'kind and Pious' King James to lend rescue to the troops abroad, but his poem raised significant doubts that the English King would or could fulfil this call. Indeed, Chapman's scepticism can be found upon the very title page of *Pro Vere* in the opening epigram, drawn from Persius's fourth satire against men in power who lack self-control and self-knowledge: '————— ————————— da verba & decipe neruos' ('lie and deceive your nerves'). Renaissance commentators interpreted Persius's satires as launching visceral, if clandestine, attacks against the emperor Nero.[56] Persius's fourth satire, from which Chapman drew his quotation, vehemently criticised the tyrant's moral failings and his inability to rule, identifying the tyrant's wickedness as lust, cruelty, vanity, luxury, drunkenness, and effeminacy. The unjust ruler was a man whose summum bonum was 'to have always lived with a delicious dish', the satire contended, and it compared tyrants with old women who waste their time seeking delicacies

---

[56] Isaac Casaubon made this argument in the prolegomena of his 1605 edition of Persius. John Dryden later emphasised this claim in the argument of the prologue to his translation of Persius: 'The Design of the Authour was to conceal his Name and Quality. He liv'd in the dangerous Times of the Tyrant *Nero*; and aims particularly at him, in most of his Satyrs.' Kirk Combe has argued that Dryden's translations of Persius themselves took aim at William III. See Kirk Combe, 'Clandestine Protest against William III in Dryden's Translations of Juvenal and Persius', *Modern Philology* 87 (1989): 36–50; John Dryden, trans. and ed., *The satires of Decimus Junius Juvenalis. Translated into English verse. By Mr. Dryden and several other eminent hands. Together with the satires of Aulus Persius Flaccus. Made English by Mr. Dryden* ... (London, 1693), 2.

174 Emasculated Kingship

and a 'body smooth and delicate' by 'vile arts'.[57] Chapman's brief epigram referenced a particular passage from the fourth satire in which Persius described how gladiators, upon receiving blows in the arena, would cover their wounds with golden girdles or belts in order to deceive themselves and their spectators about their true injuries; similarly, rulers, by appearing to be resplendent in honour and wealth, cover their deep flaws and wickedness from the people: 'Deep within your groin you have concealed a wound; but your belt, with its broad gold, covers it: as you wish, lie and deceive your nerves, if you can.'[58] Chapman's epigram implied that King James similarly sought to conceal his failings through rich display and spectacle, a charge that would have perhaps resonated in 1622 not only due to the King's courtly expenses, as mentioned previously, but also his costly construction of the Banqueting House from 1619 to 1622, the very years that Protestants were calling for war.[59] James's only recourse, Chapman argued, was to cast off the habits of Venus and don the armour of Mars.

4.3 A Funeral for a Hair: Neronian Criticisms of Charles

In contrast to his father, Charles I enjoyed a brief period of immense popularity from late 1623 to early 1625, a popularity fuelled by his desired reform of the policies of peace and the practices of the Jacobean court. Charles and Buckingham had vigorously aligned with the 'Patriot

---

[57] *Juvenal and Persius*, ed. and trans. Susanna Morton Braund, Loeb Classical Library Edition (Ann Arbor, MI: Edwards, 2004), 88, 90 (Persius's fourth satire, lines 17–19, 35–36): 'quae tibi summa boni est? uncta vixisse patella / semper et adsiduo curata cuticula sole? / expecta, haut aliud respondeat haec anus'. 'penemque aracanaque lumbi / runcantem populo marcentis pandere bulbos'.

[58] Ibid., 50 (lines 44–45): 'Ilia subter, / caecum vulnus habes, sed lato balteus auro / prætegit. ut mavis, da verba et decipe nervos, / si potes'. I translate the phrase 'dare verba' following Ovid's Latin, but maintain 'nervos' more literally based in part upon Dryden's translation in 1693 and Causabon's discussion of this passage in 1647. In a textual note, Dryden explained that he understood the line to be a sexual innuendo: 'That is, thou can'st not deceive thy Obscene part, which is weak, or Impotent, tho thou mak'st Ostentation of thy Performances with Women.' In his commentary on Persius, Casaubon identified this metaphor as drawn from Horace *Epist.* 2.2.97: 'caedimur, et totidem plagis consumimus hostem'. See Dryden, *The satires of Juvenalis*, 52; Isaac Casaubon, *Auli Persi Flacci Satirarum Liber. Isaacus Casaubonus recensuit, & Commentario Libro illustravit* (London, 1647), 313–54, esp. 347.

[59] One libel from the early 1620s, for example, charged that courtiers lined their pockets from corrupt and scandalous practices, while Parliament had to foot the bill for the King's luxurious expenditures on the new Banqueting House: 'When the Banquetting howse is finished quite / then Jones Sir Inigo we will call / & Poetts Ben brave maskes shall write / & a Parliament shall pay for all'. 'When Charles, hath got the Spanish Gearle', Oxford Bodleian Library MS Ashmole 38, fos. 229[r–v] in 'Early Stuart Libels'.

Neronian Corruption in Caroline England 175

coalition' in Parliament, backing bellicose policies as Charles's positive reputation soared in the months following the failed Spanish Match. Returning from Spain in October 1623, Charles was greeted by widespread festivals and celebrations, including at least 335 bonfires between Whitehall and Temple Bar alone, as one witness counted, and enthusiastic (as well as inebriated) subjects shouting acclamations like 'madde men' along his route. Since 'the peoples harts did burn to see him', Charles 'leaned his body out of the coach, with his hatt in the hand and gave thancks to them all for their loves'. Several responded 'God save your Highnes', while others rejoiced 'we have him … we have our prince again'.[60]

Such enthusiasm waned quickly in Charles's reign. Reflecting back on early 1625, Sir John Eliot described the optimistic mood in nostalgic terms: 'King James being dead and with him the fearful security and degenerate vices of a long corrupted peace in hope and expectation laid aside, with the new King a new spirit of life and comfort possessed all men.'[61] As new king, Charles had been eager to lend assistance to his brother-in-law, the Elector Frederick, and to engage England in the European struggle against Spain and the Hapsburgs. Optimism amongst MPs for these new policies deteriorated quickly through what became a disastrous session of parliament in 1625, in which the King misjudged that the simple notification of his wishes, without the management of Parliament, would command obedience.[62] Whereas the King demanded the prioritisation of supply for war, with domestic matters being delayed through prorogation until autumn, the Commons held the redress of grievances and matters of religion, especially the toleration of recusants negotiated for the French marriage proposal, as more pressing.[63] The

---

[60] Qtd in Thomas Cogswell, 'England and the Spanish Match', in *Conflict in Early Stuart England: Studies in Religion and Politics 1603–1642*, ed. Richard Cust and Ann Hughes (London: Routledge, 2014), 107–33, esp. 108.

[61] Maija Jansson and William B. Bidwell, *'Negotium Posterorum'*, in *Proceedings in Parliament 1625* (Rochester: University of Rochester Press, 1987), 491–92. In describing James's reign and the new hope of Charles, Eliot further described, ' … when it was thought what infelicities had been suffered, infelicities abroad, infelicities at home, in the consumption of the honor, consumption of the treasures of the kingdom, the martial powers neglected, the reputation of their wisdom in contempt, Mars and Apollo both forsaking them in that inextricable labyrinth of those treaties whereby religion was corrupted, justice perverted, and all this through facility and confidence, or a too much love of peace. The change which was not presumed in these by the new change of persons wrought a new change of hearts – all men's affections were transferred from doubt and jealousy into hope, and all their fears and sorrows did resolve themselves to joy.'

[62] Christopher Thompson, 'Court Politics and Parliamentary Conflict in 1625', in *Conflict in Early Stuart England*, 168–92, esp. 172 and 188.

[63] Ibid., 172–74.

176 Emasculated Kingship

resummons of Parliament to Oxford in 1625, in the midst of plague, turned disastrous and was dissolved after just two weeks. Despite Parliament's later success pushing Charles to enforce the anti-Catholic penal laws, fears concerning religion, including a growing 'Arminian' faction in the Church, heightened with Richard Montague's anti-Calvinist publications and Buckingham's attempt to resolve the theological rift at the York House conference.[64] Charles's subsequent parliamentary interactions from 1626–28 revealed his growing reluctance to bargain or grant concessions except in the most pressing of circumstances.[65]

The political climate grew in contention as the 1626 Parliament powerfully attacked the King's favourite, the duke of Buckingham, for what they understood to be his corrupting and Sejanus-like influence upon the monarch.[66] With a foreign crisis looming after the defeat of Christian of Denmark at the Battle of Lutter, the King's refusal to resummon Parliament created a stalemate which made arbitrary taxation virtually inevitable.[67] The King's adoption of the Forced Loan in 1626 led to one of the largest demonstrations of civil disobedience in England before the civil wars. First, the judges and several peers refused to uphold the loan's legality; then fifteen or sixteen peers and seventy-six persons, even when faced with imprisonment, resisted collecting the loan. The conflict came to a head in the *Five Knights Case* of 1627, in which the Court upheld the King's ability to imprison anyone by 'special command'. These events, combined with fears of the growing influence and power of Arminians over king and church, led the House of Commons in 1628 to present formal grievances against the King in the Petition of Right. The Petition upheld four fundamental English liberties: freedom from arbitrary arrest and imprisonment, from arbitrary or non-parliamentary taxation, from the billeting of troops, and from the imposition of martial law.[68]

Early in its 1629 session, these issues were far from resolved. The House of Commons had to investigate the printing of the Petition of Right, as the

---

[64] Michael Questier, *Catholicism and Community in Early Modern England* (Cambridge: Cambridge University Press, 2006), 428–31; Barbara Donagan, 'The York House Conference Revisited: Laymen, Calvinists and Arminians', *Historical Research* 64:155 (1991).

[65] Thompson, 'Court Politics and Parliamentary Conflict', 187; Richard Cust, 'Charles I, the Privy Council, and the Forced Loan', *Journal of British Studies* 24 (1985): 208–35.

[66] See Chapter 3.

[67] Reeve, *Charles I and the Road to Personal Rule*, 11–13; Conrad Russell, *Crisis of Parliaments: English History 1509–1660* (Oxford: Oxford University Press, 1971), 300–6; Cust, 'Charles I, the Privy Council, and the Forced Loan', 209–11.

[68] Russell, *Crisis of Parliaments*, 306–7; Mark Kishlansky, *A Monarchy Transformed: Britain 1603–1714* (London: Allen Lane, Penguin Press, 1996), 110–12.

Neronian Corruption in Caroline England 177

King had suppressed the initial printing and substituted a second edition that presented a case for the Crown. This activity, alongside significant debates over tonnage and poundage and the seizure of merchants' goods, reinforced the fear that the monarch continued to exercise arbitrary power over subjects' liberties as he had in the earlier Forced Loan conflict and resulting *Five Knights Case*.[69] Contemporaries understood the dissolution of parliament in March of 1629 as a significant event, signalling the failure of both church reform and pro-war policy, and the King's alignment with an insular set of advisors, Catholic, crypto-Catholic, and Laudian. Rule without parliament and its financial support required Charles to seek peace, even as many of his subjects continued to regard the Thirty Years' War as a necessary military engagement for 'true' Protestants and men.[70]

In 1629, the year that began Charles's personal rule, Chapman returned to rhetoric both classicised and gendered to criticise his monarch.[71] Within this new publication, however, the politics of the household rather than that of war became the primary emphasis. Chapman's dedicatory epistle betrayed his disillusionment with the political moment. Writing to Richard Hubert, Chapman lamented that 'Greate workes get little regard', while 'little and light are most affected with height'. It was 'now the fashion to iustifie Strange Actions', he contended, and although this activity was 'vtterly against mine owne fashion', he would follow the 'vulgar' by justifying a strange action of Nero's: the burying of a single strand of his mistress Poppaea's hair.[72] Chapman's *Iustification* should be understood as a paradoxical encomium, a popular and distinct genre of Renaissance writing that often masked serious political and cultural criticism through the absurd celebration of 'unworthy, unexpected, or trifling objects'.[73] As Erasmus, whose *Praise of Folly* is the most famous example of the genre, explained, 'literary jests may have serious implications, and . . . a reader with a keen nose may get more from a skillful trifle than from a solemn and stately argument'.[74] Paradoxical encomia further offered writers the chance to exercise their wit in the creation of wholly original conceits and arguments. In the *Iustification*, Chapman drew upon

---

[69] Reeve, *Charles I and the Road to Personal Rule*, 91–93.
[70] Russell, *Crisis of Parliaments*, 309–13; Reeve, *Charles I and the Road to Personal Rule*, 89–90.
[71] It is difficult to pinpoint in which month Chapman published this piece in 1629, as no record of it exists in the Stationers' Register.
[72] Chapman, *A iustification of a strange action of Nero*, A2^{r-v}.
[73] Henry Knight Miller, 'The Paradoxical Encomium with Special Reference to Its Vogue in England, 1600–1800', *Modern Philology* 53.3 (Feb. 1956): 145–78, esp. 145.
[74] Quoted in ibid., 145–47.

historical accounts of Nero to invent a highly original, satirical piece that labelled uxorious and effeminate practices as tyrannical and destructive to the realm, and that, indirectly, derided King Charles and his court for participating in such practices.

As described previously, Chapman's *Iustification* opened with the description of a 'solemne Pageant' by the Emperor Nero, who wears a 'mourning habit'. After him process 'all the state of the Empire either present or presented', including 'Peeres' of the realm, and a hearse bearing a 'poore hayre broken loose' from the head of Nero's mistress, Poppaea.[75] From this initial description, the *Iustification* emphasised the dual meaning of its language. On the one hand, it presented Nero as truly mourning the loss of Poppaea's strand of hair and as earnestly believing such a trifle deserved honour. On the other hand, it signalled that many within Nero's realm viewed this ceremony with derision, and that the reader should as well. Some 'laugh in their sleeues' at the procession, Chapman explained, and the Peers process 'with drie eyes', presumably due to their recognition of the emperor's delusions.[76] The very use of the word *pageant* denoted the binary wordplay of the satire's prose. While *pageants* were generally defined as stately spectacles or processions, in 1608 Chapman had coined a new figurative meaning of the term as an empty, delusional, or specious display or tribute.[77] Chapman's *Iustification* thereby indicated the contemptibility of this funeral and the 'troope of fooles' gathered for it, but the speaker adopted the persona of a funeral orator (ostensibly) resolved to justify Nero's action against condemnation and 'detracting tongues'. He would present a speech to the emperor that 'shall make it appeare to all vpright eares, that it is an action most worthy your wisedome (my gracious Soveraigne) and that this silly, this base, this contemptible hayre on this Herse supported, receiues no thought of honour, but what it well deserueth'.[78]

Why would hair be the subject of Chapman's encomium and the honoured object of Nero's procession? The explicit answer Chapman provided was Nero's failure to heed the philosophical teachings of Seneca.[79] '*Etiam capillus unus habet umbram suam* [even one hair has a

---

[75] Chapman, *A iustification of a strange action of Nero*, 1. [76] Ibid., 1–2.

[77] Chapman first coined this meaning in *The conspiracie, and tragedie of Charles Duke of Byron* (1608), H[v]: 'Without which loue, and trust; honor is shame; A very Pageant, and a propertie'. See *Oxford English Dictionary*, s.v. 'pageant', 1.

[78] Chapman, *A iustification of a strange action of Nero*, 3.

[79] Seventeenth-century histories, plays, and poems commonly reflected upon Nero's failure to learn philosophy from his tutor Seneca.

Neronian Corruption in Caroline England

shadow], was the saying of your master *Seneca*', the orator explained, 'and may not your Highnesse goe one step further, and say, *Etiam capillus unus habet urnam suam* [even one hair has an urn]?'[80] Within this clever joke Chapman crystallised Nero's transgressive blindness and self-deception. Rather than realising through philosophical contemplation that even his smallest action would leave a mark on the world around him, Nero sought to worship the trivial and thereby caused devastating harm.

To more fully understand the significance of the subject of hair for Chapman's audience, however, scholars must consider more broadly the development of considerable cultural divisions in Stuart England between elite courtiers who boasted Continental styles and Italian manners and the godly who objected to such 'civility' and viewed court styles as vainglorious and blasphemous.[81] The Puritan vogue for cropped hair would peak in the 1640s with the outbreak of the Civil War, but as early as the turn of the seventeenth century, godly writers had questioned and condemned long hair on men and excessive hairstyles in general as promoting vanity and pride, undermining masculinity, and blurring gender distinctions.[82] The lovelock or *cadanette*, for which gentlemen fashioned a long curl from the nape of the neck over the shoulder and often decorated with a bow or jewel, appeared especially effeminate and offensive. These writers turned to several Biblical proofs for this view, such as the Old Testament story of the rebellious Absalom, who suffered defeat in the Battle of Ephraim after being caught in a tree by his hair; they also drew upon the apostle Paul, who maintained in 1 Corinthians, 'Doth not even nature itself teach you, that, if a man have long hair, it is a shame unto him? But if a woman have long hair, it is a glory to her: for her hair is given her for a covering.'[83] The author of *Absolom his fall, or The ruin of Roysters, Wherein euery Christian may in a mirrour behold, the vile and abominable abuse of curled long haire* (1590), for example, relied heavily upon both Biblical sources, denouncing the pride and ambition of the age and arguing that men who dressed as women, or wore their hair in a long, feminine style, were an 'abhomination to the Lord' by altering the 'order of nature'.[84]

---

[80] Chapman, *A iustification of a strange action of Nero*, 3.

[81] For understandings of court civility, see Anna Bryson, *From Courtesy to Civility: Changing Codes of Conduct in Early Modern England* (Oxford: Clarendon Press, 1998).

[82] Will Fisher, *Materializing Gender in Early Modern English Literature and Culture* (Cambridge: Cambridge University Press, 2006), 130–31; Hilary Larkin, *The Making of Englishmen: Debates on National Identity, 1550–1650* (Leiden: Brill, 2014), 117–22.

[83] 1 Corinthians 11:14–15 (KJV).

[84] *A godly and profitable treatise, intituled Absolom his fall, or the ruin of Roysters, Wherein euery Christian may in a mirrour behold the vile and abominable abuse of curled long hair* ... (London, 1590), 9.

180   Emasculated Kingship

In 1628, William Prynne published a fiery censure of such fashions in *The vnlouelinesse, of lovelockes. Or, A svmmarie discovrse proouing: the wearing, and nourishing of a locke, or loue-locke, to be altogether vnseemely, and vnlawfull vnto Christians. In which there are likewise some passages collected out of fathers, councells, and sundry authors, and historians, against face-painting; the wearing of supposititious, poudred, frizled, or extraordinary long haire; the inordinate affectation of corporall beautie: and womens mannish, vnnaturall, impudent, and vnchristian cutting of their haire; the epidemicall vanities, and vices of our age.* In typical Prynne fashion, this treatise's lengthy title encapsulated an extensive list of 'epidemicall vanities and vices', whose adoption in Prynne's view had led to '*these Degenerous, Vnnaturall, and Vnmanly times*', in which women '*are Hermophradited, and transformed into men*', and men are 'wholy degenerated and metamorphosed into women'.[85] Prynne understood vain fashion as posing an exceptionally dangerous threat to the gendered order of society, and even more, to the very character of the English nation and their eternal salvation. Such fashions were especially to be found at court, where the gentry 'hold a Counsell about euery Haire', he claimed, for 'Would they not rather haue the Common-wealth disturbed, then their Haire disordered?'[86] The lovelock was indeed the fashion of King Charles himself, who sported it in a number of Van Dyke paintings. Moreover, moralising authors such as Prynne censured 'face-painting' and hair-tincturing women for their seeming vanity, self-absorption, wastefulness, and deception, and even more, as refusing to submit passively to the rightful social order by redefining their own value through counterfeiting.[87]

Within this context, it seems clear that Chapman's *Iustification* presented a significant and timely criticism of the vanities and sinfulness of the King and court that would not have been lost on his contemporaries. His text indicated that Poppaea's hair had indeed been crafted by an unnatural process, as its colour and substance would be 'impossible for nature in her whole shop to patterne it'.[88] Laying in its hearse, the hair no longer suffered the 'cruell combe', 'curling bodkins', or being 'tied vp each night

---

[85] William Prynne, *The Vnlouelinesse, of Love-Lockes. or, A Svmmarie Discovrse proouing: The wearing, and nourishing of a Locke, or Loue-Locke, to be altogether vnseemely, and vnlawfull vnto Christians* (London, 1628), A3ʳ ('To the Christian Reader'). Here Prynne is describing an actual metamorphosis between the sexes. See Fisher, *Materializing Gender*, 134–35.

[86] Prynne, 'To the Christian Reader'.

[87] Francis E. Dolan, 'Taking the Pencil out of God's Hand: Art, Nature, and the Face-Painting Debate in Early Modern England', *Publications of the Modern Language Association of America* 108.2 (Mar., 1993): 224–39, esp. 229–30.

[88] Chapman, *A iustification of a strange action of Nero*, 7.

Neronian Corruption in Caroline England 181

in knots' by Poppaea seeking to style it.[89] That Nero obsequiously mourned such a piece of hair indicated his delusional and dangerous passion for his mistress, his corrupted nature, and his emasculation; what was more, it was believed that a practice so decadent and effeminate would disrupt the rightful order of societal and gendered hierarchies across the realm.

This connection between hair, passion, and court corruption was further supported through one of Chapman's historical sources, Pliny the Elder's *Natural History*. Pliny described that among Nero's other 'fooleries and gauds wherein he shewed what a monster he was in his life', the emperor became so enamored with his mistress's hair that he created a 'sonnet in praise of the haire ... , which he compared to Amber'.[90] Nero's enthusiasm for his mistress's amber hair encouraged the vanity and decadence of his court, according to Pliny, as the 'daintie dames and fine ladies have begun to set their mind upon this colour, and have placed it in the third rank of rich tincture'.[91] In the *Iustification*, Chapman played upon this description of Poppaea's hair colour by arguing that it not only enflamed Nero's passion and provoked courtly vanity but further betrayed Poppaea's moral character. 'As red hayre on a man is a signe of trechery', he explained, 'what tis in a woman, let the sweet musique of rime inspire vs.'[92] Presumably, as it rhymed with 'trechery', a woman's red hair was a sign of lechery. Poppaea's amber hair, thereby, denoted her habitual lustful indulgence, and Nero's worship of this hair implicated his own sordid activities and desires.

Chapman's *Iustification* further provided a portrait of tyranny by emphasising the obscenity and destructiveness of the tyrant's disordered passions and disordered household. As the encomium explained, Poppaea's hair was so very exceptional that it moved 'into softnesse' even the 'Adamantine heart' of Nero, who 'neuer was knowne to shrinke at the butchering of his owne mother *Agrippina*; and could without any touch of remorse, heare (if not behold) the murther of his most deare wife *Octavia* after her diuorce'.[93] In this passage Chapman stressed the horror of Nero's crimes against family by adopting the word 'butchering' and then

[89] Ibid., 9.
[90] *The Historie of the World. Commonly called, The Natvrall Historie of C. Plinivs Secvndvs. Translated into English by Philemon Holland* (London, 1601), 608–9.
[91] Ibid.
[92] Chapman, *A iustification of a strange action of Nero*, 6. Chapman here may have been thinking of Judas Iscariot, who traditionally was depicted as having red hair.
[93] Ibid., 7.

'murther'. Chapman similarly highlighted the irony of Nero's deep affection for the cast-off hair, stating that any subject viewing the grand burial procession would assume the hearse to be Nero's 'deare Mother *Agrippina*' or his 'beloued wife *Octauia*', until realising it was for 'her whom you preferre to them both, your diuine *Poppaea*'.[94] Nero's sinful passion for Poppaea, then, destructively inverted the rightful place of mother and wife; his and Poppaea's unlicensed sexuality corrupted the natural social order. To fulfil this inversion, Chapman adopted the language of enslavement to summarise the emperor's position: This single strand of hair, 'so subtill and slender as it can scarce be seene, much lesse felt', was indeed 'so strong as it is able to binde *Hercules* hand and foot'.[95] Through another classical allusion, Chapman signalled that the inversion of a royal family could similarly lead to the destruction of a kingdom, as was the case with Nisus, who was betrayed by his own daughter, Scylla, due to a lustful passion she had developed for Minos. When Minos attacked Megara, Scylla betrayed and destroyed her father and homeland by plucking the purple hair from his head upon which his life depended.[96]

Finally, Chapman's *Iustification* emphasised that Nero's personal enslavement and failure to exert patriarchal control had direct consequences for the behaviour of his court. In language that reflected the opening scenes of *The Tragedy of Nero* (1624),[97] Chapman's satire argued the noble indulged openly in lewd acts, while the lower-class exacted a price for their sins: 'And how many yong gallants doe I know my selfe, euery hayre of whose chin, is worth a thousand crowns; and others (but simple fornicators) that haue neuer a hayre on their crownes, but is worth a Kings ransome?'[98] Throughout the *Iustification*, thereby, Chapman connected the monarch's personal character, household governance, and court morality. 'All the state of the Empire either present or presented' marched alongside Nero and his mistress's hearse bearing a single strand of hair; his destructive, moral failings infected and threatened the entire commonwealth.

A *Iustification* emphasised how uxoriousness and effeminacy could corrupt monarchical power, charges that would only grow in significance during and after the 1620s. Indeed, following the assassination of the King's favourite, Buckingham, in 1628, Charles's affection for his Catholic queen grew perceptibly. Courtiers noted that Charles 'wholly made over al

---

[94] Ibid., 2. [95] Chapman, *A iustification of a strange action of Nero*, 8.
[96] Ibid., Bartlett, *The Poems of George Chapman*, 467. [97] See Section 3.2.
[98] Chapman, *A iustification of a strange action of Nero*, 8.

Neronian Corruption in Caroline England

his affections to his wife', and by the early 1630s, Henrietta Maria boasted an intimate family life with a husband who adored her.[99] Her political influence further swelled after 1628 as a number of Buckingham's former clients transferred their services and allegiances to the Queen, including Henry Rich, George Goring, and Henry Jermyn. Those who had been distrustful of Buckingham's influence upon Charles found further alarm in Henrietta Maria as a replacement. As Michelle White has summarised, the Queen offended many English subjects through her foreignness, 'whorish' behaviour of dancing and acting in court masques, and her ardent Catholicism expressed overtly through religious services and public pilgrimages, such as her pilgrimage in 1626 through Hyde Park to the Tyburn gallows, the site of many executed Catholic martyrs.[100] Historians have noted that uxoriousness became a significant criticism of Charles's reign in the 1640s, with opponents viewing the Queen's foreign and Catholic influence as compromising the King's masculine rule and religion.[101] What has been overlooked, however, is how writers such as Chapman voiced such opposition more subtly in the preceding decades. Through *Pro Vere* and *A iustification of a strange action of Nero*, Chapman already warned that the masculinity of the English sovereign and England's state of virtue had been cast aside for the dangerous worship of an alluring strand of hair.

4.4 Revisiting Julia Agrippina: Court Corruption, and Female, Household Tyranny

Despite important differences between the policies and courtly styles of James and Charles, stories of Nero conjured vast images of court corruption and deviance in the Stuart period, whether appropriated and penned during the reign of James or his son. As Linda Levy Peck argued almost three decades ago, the 'language of corruption provided a powerful mode of criticism and challenge to the court and the king in a society shaped by

---

[99] Thomas Cary to James, Earl of Carlisle, 21 Dec. 1628: Public Record Office, SP 16/123, fol. 3ᵛ. Quoted in Michelle Anne White, *Henrietta Maria and the English Civil Wars* (Burlington: Ashgate, 2006), 14–15.

[100] White, *Henrietta Maria*, 24–29.

[101] As one anonymous author contended in 1644, the King 'should have been a *Sun*, shining by example and maintaining the *Light* of the *Gospel*', but he was 'totally eclipsed by [the Queen's] Counsell, who under the Royall Curtaines, perswaded him to advance the Plots of the Catholikes, under the colour of maintaining the *Protestant Religion*'. Anon., *The great eclipse of the sun, or, Charles his waine over-clouded, by the evill influences of the moon, the malignancie of ill-aspected planets, and the constellations of retrograde and irregular starres* ([London], 1644), 3–4. See White, *Henrietta Maria*, 141–49; Dolan, *Whores of Babylon: Catholicism, Gender, and Seventeenth-Century Print Culture* (Ithaca and London: Cornell University Press, 1999), 95–156.

184 Emasculated Kingship

order and consensus. Corruption became a political issue capable of helping to undermine governmental legitimacy', especially when tied to other critical issues.[102] More recent studies of the Stuart period have highlighted the influence of numerous discourses of court corruption concerning political scandals, conspiracies, and myths which circulated through 'news', libellous, and satirical writings.[103] Alastair Bellany and Thomas Cogswell's exploration of *The Murder of James I*, and particularly the significant political culture which formed through accusations that Buckingham poisoned his king, has highlighted how libellous and seditious writings concerning favouritism and court corruption fuelled the turbulent politics of Stuart England and betray the underlying ideological and political forces which became unsettled in this period.[104] Earlier studies by Curtis Perry and Andrew McRae similarly emphasised how literary productions of the period helped 'perform a kind of cultural work usually thought of only as the job of political theorists' in developing ideas and questions concerning the relationship between monarch and subject and hostility towards the emergence of personal monarchy.[105]

Literary productions of the seventeenth century at times presented clear, contemporary criticisms only thinly veiled, while at other times provided more abstract reflections upon political themes and questions. Historians have often preferred the former, and have even cast aspersions upon those who seek to find substantive meaning in literary productions that did not provide unmistakable equivalences between contemporary political statesmen and situations and those presented in print or onstage.[106] Cultural appropriations of Nero offer an example of both types of writings at work. Imaginative writings which performed particular criticisms of people, policies, or iconography in the early Stuart period provide historians with examples of political dissent and subversive language critical for understanding the development of politics and political culture. *The Emperor's*

---

[102] Peck, '"For a King not to be bountiful were a fault"', 11.

[103] See Bellany, *Politics of Court Scandal*; Bellany, 'Railing Rhymes Revisited: Libels, Scandals, and Early Stuart Politics', *History Compass* 5:4 (2007): 1136–79; Cressy, *Dangerous Talk*; Cust and Hughes, eds., *Conflict in Early Stuart England*; Thomas Cogswell, 'Underground Verse and the Transformation of Early Stuart Political Culture', in Susan Amussen and Mark Kishlansky, eds., *Political Culture and Cultural Politics in Early Modern England* (Manchester: Manchester University Press, 1995).

[104] *Murder of King James I.*

[105] Curtis Perry, *Literature and Favoritism in Early Modern England* (Cambridge: Cambridge University Press, 2006), 3–4. See Andrew McRae, *Literature, Satire and the Early Stuart State*, 10–11.

[106] See, e.g., Malcolm Smuts, *Court Culture and the Origins of a Royalist Tradition in Early Stuart England* (Philadelphia: University of Pennsylvania Press, 1987), 81–82.

Favourite, for example, a play likely produced by John Newdigate in the late 1620s or early 1630s, employed the story of Crispinus, one favourite of the Emperor Nero, to provide significant contemporary criticisms of Buckingham.[107] To do so, the play interwove Nero's history as drawn from Tacitus, Juvenal, and Suetonius with fictional storylines and anachronistic references. Crispinus, like Buckingham, rises suddenly in Nero's court from an obscure social background, promotes his relatives and secures them titles and advantageous marriages, and trades in monopolies and sexual activities.[108] His eventual assassination similarly echoes Buckingham's, as do his military misadventures. These parallels encouraged Newdigate's audience to see Nero as Charles', Bellany and Cogswell have argued, and within the play, Nero articulated significant theories of arbitrary rule, including his right to treat subjects as slaves:

> Kings must direct their sub*ject*s, they obey
> In duty & in silent execution
> The meanest man in *Rome* com*m*ands his slaue
> And giues no reason why, o*ur* priuiledge
> Sure goes as farr as his.[109]

In a later passage, Nero described the throne as 'more vnbounded then the cottage', for a Prince 'hath all things below him but him self / The same law is restrictuve to the sub*ject* / That guies the prince a spacious scope & freedome'.[110]

Plays such as the *The Emperor's Favourite* significantly underscore not only the ways that Stuart statesmen read Roman history for understanding contemporary events but also the ways that contemporaries understood such histories as offering a malleable framework for producing critical political comment in an age of censorship.[111] Other textual productions, however, detailed more generally the threat of emasculating corruption and tyranny. These played a significant role in shaping the culture of

---

[107] Siobhan Keenan, 'Staging Roman History, Stuart Politics, and the Duke of Buckingham: The Example of *The Emperor's Favourite*', *Early Theatre* 14 (2002): 63–103; Keenan, ed. *The Emperor's Favourite* (Manchester: Manchester University Press, 2010), xxxiv–xxxv; Bellany and Cogswell, *Murder of King James I*, 377–79.

[108] Keenan, 'Staging Roman History', 69–70; Bellany and Cogswell, *Murder of King James I*, 377.

[109] *Emperor's Favourite*, 6; Bellany and Cogswell, *Murder of King James I*, 378.

[110] *Emperor's Favourite*, 14. These lines concerning slavery and freedom above the law are emphasised in the play through being repeated by Corbulus, who is in disbelief that the emperor could hold such views. See Ibid., 15.

[111] Annabel Patterson, '"Roman-Cast Similitude": Ben Jonson and the English Use of Roman History', P. A. Ramsey, ed., *Rome in the Renaissance: The City and the Myth* (Binghamton: Center for Medieval and Early Renaissance Studies, 1982), 381–94, esp. 382.

186   Emasculated Kingship

thought and the development of language necessary for imagining new political models and English republican thought in the mid-seventeenth century. As with Edmund Bolton's *Nero Caesar* explored in detail in the previous chapter, Stuart historical writings which sought to offer faithful accounts of classical history, rather than appropriated or altered accounts, often included political arguments concerning power, authority, and obedience. Thomas May's *Tragedy of Julia Agrippina* (1628) was one such production in the Caroline period. Through its depiction of the rise, fall, and assassination of Nero's mother, the play significantly advanced gendered portrayals of tyranny and depicted the consequences of feminine usurpation in royal households.

Thomas May is not often characterised as a 'republican' until late in his life, when his *Discourse Concerning the Success of Former Parliaments* (1642) argued that the very institution of monarchy threatened a commonwealth's liberty. After training at Sidney Sussex College, Cambridge, and Gray's Inn, the poet, dramatist, and historian sought patronage from King Charles in the 1630s and hoped to follow in Ben Jonson's footsteps as poet laureate. With the outbreak of civil war, and Sir William Davenant's rise to the post of poet laureate, May became a public propagandist and secretary for Parliament, completing his *History of the Parliament of England which Began November the Third, 1640* in 1647, eventually siding with the Independents and receiving a state funeral and memorial in Westminster Abbey upon his death in 1650.[112] Despite his activity within Charles's court, scholars should not overlook or understate the importance of May's early career, when he produced a number of classical translations and dramas that already criticised monarchical government and its corruption in the heated political climate of the late 1620s. In 1627, May significantly created an English translation of Lucan's *Pharsalia, or De Bello Civili*, a Roman epic poem about the civil wars between Julius Caesar and Pompey the Great in the final years of the Roman republic.

As a work that caustically illustrated the devastations wrought by imperial corruption and civil discord, Lucan's *Pharsalia* was a central poem of the republican imagination of Stuart England.[113] In the dedicatory epistle to William Cavendish, earl of Devonshire, May emphasised that

---

[112] David Norbrook, 'May, Thomas (b. in or after 1596, d. 1650)', *Oxford Dictionary of National Biography* (Oxford: Oxford University Press, 2004), online edn. Jan. 2008 [www.oxforddnb.com/view/article/18423].

[113] For an excellent treatment of the significance of Lucan's poetry for the republican imagination in England, see Norbrook, 'Lucan and the poetry of civil war', in *Writing the English Republic: Poetry, Rhetoric and Politics, 1627–1660* (Cambridge: Cambridge University Press, 1999), 23–62.

Neronian Corruption in Caroline England 187

English statesmen should consider Lucan's poem carefully as a 'true *History*' unadulterated by '*Poetical rapture*',[114] for he interpreted the *Pharsalia* as revealing that moment in Roman history when Rome fell from her great height of republican virtue into the monarchical corruption of the Caesars:

> The blood of [Rome's] valiant citizens, and the conquests, and triumphs of so many ages had raised her now to that vnhappy height, in which shee could neither retaine her fredome without great troubles nor fall into a *Monarchy* but most heauy and distastfull. In one the greatnes of priuate citizens excluded moderation, in the other the vast strength and forces of the Prince gaue him too absolute and vndetermined a power. The vices of *Rome* did at this time (saith learned Heinsius) not only grow vp to their power but ouerthrow it. *Luxury & Pride* the wicked daughters of so noble a Mother as the *Roman Vertue*, began to consume that which brought them forth. These were the seeds of that faction, which rent the State, and brought in violently a change of government.[115]

When contrasted with royalist portrayals of imperial Rome in this period, such as Bolton's *Nero Caesar* which aimed to teach the 'pretious secret' that '*No Prince is so bad as not to make monarckie seeme the best forme of gouernment*',[116] May's dedicatory epistle seems strikingly anti-monarchical. May here described the Roman transition from republican to monarchical government as a transition from freedom to slavery, a slavery which took root in the corruption of Rome's virtue and blossomed into absolute monarchical power. Later in the seventeenth century, John Aubrey remarked that May's 'translation of *Lucans* excellent Poeme made him in love with the Republique'.[117]

As David Norbrook has argued, May's translation of Lucan articulated staunch republican values during the political crises of 1627, betraying his support for the Protestant cause on the Continent against Catholic forces believed to be the work of Antichrist and tyrannical monarchy, while promoting the parliamentary cause in England against a king enlarging

---

[114] 'To ... William, Earle of Deuonshiere, &c'., in *Lvcan's Pharsalia: or The Civill Warres of Rome, between Pompey the great, and Ivlivs Cæsar. The whole ten Bookes Englished by Thomas May, Esquire* (London, 1627), sig. a2v.

[115] Ibid., sig. a3r–4r.

[116] Edmund Bolton, *NERO CÆSAR, or Monarchie depraued. An Historicall worke. Dedicated, with leaue, to the DVKE of BVCKINGHAM, Lord Admirall, by the translator of Lvcivs Florvs* (London, 1627), sig. A3v.

[117] Oxford Bodleian Library MS Aubrey 8, fo.. 27r; John Aubrey, *Brief Lives*, vol II, ed. Andrew Clark (London: Oxford, 1898), 56.

188 Emasculated Kingship

his prerogative power through the Forced Loan.[118] Within his translation of Lucan, May showcased his support and encouraged their continued fight by dedicating each chapter to 'patriots' who had fought for the Protestant cause abroad or defied King Charles at home by refusing to pay the Forced Loan, including the earl of Lincoln who was in political trouble for circulating a pamphlet which accused Charles of seeking to 'suppresse Parliaments'.[119] In the translation, May compared Lincoln to Pompey, the earl of Pembroke to Cato and Brutus, and he claimed that the earl of Warwick resembled Cato, whose 'strength orecome what taske so ere / His cruell Mistresse Vertue could command' and thus won 'more honour far / Then any Laurell'd Roman Conquerer.'[120] General Horace Vere was honored at the beginning of the seventh book for protecting 'Belgia liberty' in the Thirty Years War.[121] And May commended the third earl of Essex for his military campaign in the Rhineland with the dedication of the fourth book of the *Pharsalia*, which recorded the 'truth and faithfull loue. Showne ... / By valiant Souldiers to a valiant Chiefe', and the death of the 'bold Vulteius', 'Scorning to yeeld to Cæsar's enemies'.[122] These acclamations celebrated the unbending virtue and military valour of Roman heroes, and encouraged English patriots to remain steadfast in their own courageous fight against tyranny. Most likely due to the political nature of these dedications, many of them were hastily cut out, even to the damage of pages containing Lucan's verse, before being distributed in 1627.[123]

May wrote his *Tragedy of Julia Agrippina* just one year after translating Lucan's *Pharsalia*, but most historians and literary scholars have neglected this important drama and have also failed to recognise the vital connection between both works.[124] Although Lucan's extended poem focused on the civil wars of the late Roman republic, Lucan himself was the nephew of Seneca and had suffered under Nero, and his *Pharsalia*, a poem about imperial corruption, condemned and mocked Nero. May highlighted as much in the 'Life of Lucan', which he included in the opening pages of his *Pharsalia* translation. The brief life explained that the young Lucan had grown 'into great fauour' with Nero until the 'iealous tyrant' suppressed his works.[125] In response, Lucan joined Piso's Conspiracy against Nero,

---

[118] Norbrook, *Writing the English Republic*, 43.   [119] Ibid., 43–45.
[120] *Lvcan's Pharsalia*, sig. Q2r.
[121] George Chapman also valorised Vere's nobility while criticising the King for military inaction in the poem, *Pro Vere*. See Section 4.2.
[122] *Lvcan's Pharsalia*, sig. F2r.   [123] Norbrook, *Writing the English Republic*, 47–8.
[124] One exception is Perry, *Literature and Favoritism*, 258–65.
[125] May, 'Life of Lucan', *Lucan's Pharsalia*, sig. b1r.

Neronian Corruption in Caroline England 189

which eventually proved unsuccessful, and he ended his life committing suicide, as Seneca had done. May memorialised Lucan's stoic suicide on the very frontispiece of his *Pharsalia* translation, presenting an idealised image of Lucan as his blood poured from his muscular body, under which he included two lines of Martial's epigram to Lucan: 'Heu Nero crudelis, nullaq*ue* inuisior umbra, / Debuit hoc saltem non licuisse tibi' [O cruel Nero, never more loathed than now / Even you should not have been allowed such a crime].[126] In a famous passage of the *Pharsalia*, Lucan mocked Nero as having so much divine *gravitas* that, after his apotheosis in heaven, he would have to sit in the centre of the celestial sphere lest his massive weight bring the whole place crashing down.[127]

By writing a tragedy about Nero's tyrannical vices in 1628, May followed Lucan's example of condemning imperial corruption through a poetic treatment of Roman history. May's tragedy, with its focus on the conflict between the young Nero and his mother, provided a significant portrait of tyranny by revealing the unnatural and perverted consequences of despotic power. It imagined the tyrant as an individual made grotesque or monstrous in his gender and gendered relationships: Nero in the play is emasculated and dominated by his mother; his mother is masculinised through power and ambition.

In the opening of the *Tragedy of Julia Agrippina*, May presented Imperial Rome as a haven for vicious and cruel corruption, and the imperial palace as a location of demonic rather than divine purpose, as Megaera the fury ascends from below the stage and delivers a prologue and herself from hell:

> Thus to the *Romane* Palace, as our home
> And proper mansion, is *Megæra* come
> No stranger to these walls: not more in Hell
> Then here, doe mischiefs, and we Furies dwell
> Let the unenvy'd Gods henceforth possesse
> Poore Peasants hearts, and rule in Cottages;
> Let Vertue lurke among the rurall Swaines,
> Whilst Vice in *Romes* Imperiall Palace reignes,
> And rules those breasts, whom all the world obeys.[128]

---

[126] *Lucan's Pharsalia*, title-page.
[127] Ibid., sig. A2r–v; Norbrook, *Writing the English Republic*, 26–27.
[128] Thomas May, *The Tragedy of Julia Agrippina, Empresse of Rome* (London, 1639), 5 (prologue 3–11). Pagination and signature in the original is unreliable, so I have adopted the pagination, as well as the act and line numbers parenthetically, from the following facsimile edition: May, *Julia Agrippina*, ed. F. Ernst Schmid (Louvain: Uystpruyst, 1914).

190 Emasculated Kingship

Within this opening speech and throughout the first act, characters emphasised that 'not the Senate, / But *Caesars* chamber did command the world, / And rule the fate of men', so that the central location of authority in Roman government rested within this corrupted Imperial palace and family.[129] In order to '*preserve* that interest, and keep high / Our hold in this commanding family', Megaera summons the 'cruel ghost' Caligula, the former emperor of Rome and Nero's uncle, to aid her cause in banishing 'Piety', 'Justice', 'Conscience', and the sacred ties of 'Nature' and 'Religious Lawes' and in incensing the royal family to commit a series of parricides: Agrippina killing her husband, Claudius, and Nero killing both his stepbrother, Britannicus, and his mother, Agrippina.[130] Because May drew this opening from Seneca's *Thyestes*, in which Megaera summons Caligula to consider the crimes of the Imperial family, his prologue well emphasised the long-standing pattern of repeated corruption found in royal households.[131] His tragedy illustrates the fulfilment of these crimes in Nero's first five years of rule through a careful study of the tyranny of Nero and Agrippina. The first two acts portray Agrippina effectively orchestrating Nero's rise to power. In the third act, Nero is made Caesar due to Agrippina's success, but by the end of the fourth act he resents her power and influence, causing him to attempt to murder her through cowardly plots in the fifth act, until the final scene when his assassins stab her through the womb. The dramatic narrative juxtaposes the fall of Agrippina with the rise of Nero, and through this story of both female and male tyranny, May demonstrated how tyrannical power disrupted the natural, gendered inclinations of rulers and contaminated the order and proper relationship of family and patriarchy.

Because both writers relied upon many of the same classical texts for their sources, May's portrayal of Agrippina echoed Bolton's earlier *Nero Caesar* in several regards.[132] However, May characterised Agrippina as a specifically Machiavellian figure, enacting deceitful plots for power while describing herself as fighting fortune's wheel. At the height of her power, Agrippina proclaims in a boasting speech:

---

[129] Ibid., 5 (prologue 19–20)

[130] '...let the wife / With impious rage destray her husbands life, / The brother kill the brother, and the Sonne / Rip up his parents bowels.' ... Ibid., 7 (prologue 65–68).

[131] Perry, *Literature and Favoritism*, 259.

[132] See Section 3.4. According to F. Ernst Schmid, May's sources included Tacitus's *Annales*, Joannes Xiphilinus' epitome of Dio Cassius' *Roman History*, and scattered material from Suetonius, Petronius Arbiter, Sallust, Pliny, and Vergil. See Schmid, 'Introduction', *Julia Agrippina*, 10–79; Gerald Eades Bentley, *Jacobean and Caroline Stage: Plays and Playwrights*, vol. IV (Oxford: Clarendon Press, 1956), 837–38.

Neronian Corruption in Caroline England

> This is the day that sets a glorious Crown
> On all my great designes this day declares
> My power, and makes the trembling world to know
> That Agrippina only can bestow
> The Roman Empire, and command the wheel
> Of suffring Fortune, holding in her hand
> The fate of nation.[133]

To achieve this, Agrippina modelled her behaviour partly on the exempla of Julius Caesar and Lucius Sylla [Sulla], writing commentaries on Latin history while plotting to usurp Roman power. Three counsellors, Seneca, Vitellius, and Pollio, fall to flattering her Latin commentary, agreeing her style is 'full and Princely', 'Stately and absolute, beyond what ere / These eyes have seene', and owing 'Nothing at all to Fortune'.[134] Even the renowned Seneca succumbs to flattering and fails to correct or counsel Agrippina, although in several asides he laments her shocking behaviour:

> Oh strange male spirit!
> Can there be found no other parallell
> But *Julius Caesar* to a womans minde? . . .
> The soules of *Sylla* and of *Caesar* both
> I thinke have enter'd her.[135]

In this opening and throughout, Agrippina shockingly seeks to adopt the role of an ambitious, masculine, glory-seeking prince, while the court around her, by contrast, is obsequiously effeminate, refusing to discipline the monstrous woman before them.[136] To fight fortune and pursue her aims, Agrippina employs 'reason of state' politics, and is successful because of the corrupted state of Imperial Rome.

May's depiction of Agrippina as a Machiavellian employing 'reason of state' politics reflected a transition in political thinking in seventeenth-century England. The humanist conception of politics commonly articulated in sixteenth and early seventeenth-century England had understood politics as the art of ruling a commonwealth with reason, justice, and virtue for the sake of the common good. Cicero's *De Officiis* had served as the handbook for this tradition, and with its adoption as a fundamental

---

[133] May, *Tragedy of Julia Agrippina*, 54 (3.374–380).   [134] Ibid., 18–19 (1.327–30 and 363–64).
[135] Ibid., 19–20 (1.381–383).
[136] In my portrayal of this relationship between favourites and prince, I disagree with Perry that the favourites in *Julia Agrippina* dominate the play's action and structure. Agrippina and Nero have a far greater presence in the play, with Agrippina dominating the first half and Nero the second. However, like Perry, the conclusions I draw from this play underscore May as challenging imperial absolutism. See Perry, *Literature and Favoritism*, 258–65.

192   Emasculated Kingship

text of grammar school and university education, English statesmen inherited a political tradition that lauded civic discipline and sought to constrain political governments and statesmen to virtuous, legal, and ethical behaviour. As Cicero himself stated in *De Officiis*, 'The occasion cannot arise when it would be to the state's interest to have the wise man do anything immoral.'[137] As Maurizio Viroli and Richard Tuck have shown, however, this humanist understanding of politics became challenged in England in the 1590s by a political philosophy of 'reason of state', and by a 'new humanism'.[138] Reason of state, which developed in Italy in the early sixteenth century, emphasised that the goal of politics was the preservation of power at any cost, and that a population had to be manipulated and disciplined for the sake of the state's security; the new humanism, which turned from Ciceronian thought to scepticism and stoicism, identified political survival and self-preservation as the statesman's goal in politics. To remain virtuous, the statesman must withdraw to the *vita contemplativa* rather than engage in the world of flattery, deceit, lies, and vicious behavior characteristic of the politics of power preservation. English statesmen developed these views chiefly by reading the neo-Stoic writings of Justus Lipsius, Senecan philosophy, and Tacitean histories. By the Stuart period a flutter of pamphlets and speeches expressed the worry that James's and Charles's courts had become lairs of scandal, corruption, evil counsel, flattery, and Machiavellian politics, from which the virtuous necessarily withdrew.

Within *The Tragedy of Julia Agrippina*, May lamented this shift in English political thought through a dramatic portrayal of the banishment of Ciceronian virtue politics by the Machiavellian Agrippina, who boasts:

> had I rul'd
> Rome and her Senate then, as now I doe,
> Not all th' Orations that e're *Cicero*
> Made in the Senate, should have sav'd one haire
> Of an offendour, or condemn'd a Mouse.[139]

To Agrippina's brash announcement Seneca only comments limply, 'I am amaz'd: but let her have her way', and after quietly begging the ghost of Cicero for pardon, he resigns himself that "'tis now / Too late to give

---

[137] Cicero, *De Officiis*, bk. I.159.
[138] Richard Tuck, *Philosophy and Government, 1572–1651* (Cambridge: Cambridge University Press, 1993); Maurizio Viroli, *From Politics to Reason of State: The Acquisition and Transformation of the Language of Politics 1250–1600* (Cambridge: Cambridge University Press, 1992).
[139] May, *Tragedy of Julia Agrippina*, 21 (1.438–42).

Neronian Corruption in Caroline England   193

[Agrippina] counsell'.[140] Agrippina then enacts a series of cruel and calculating reason-of-state policies: having her rival Paulinae Lollia beheaded, assassinating the Emperor Claudius, stacking the Senate with bribed statesmen, and reordering the army for her cause. The viciousness of her policies is brought centre stage as a tribune carries the severed head of Paulinae Lollia before her assassin, Agrippina, and the audience. Although at first mocking the bloody, dismembered body before her, Agrippina explains that her 'nature could have pardon'd' Lollia, her rival, but 'Reason of state forbade it, which then told mee / Great ruines have been wrought by foolish pity'.[141]

As a female usurping power, Agrippina performs many of her initial heinous designs through seduction and sexual crimes, feeding upon the corruption and licentiousness of Emperor Claudius and his court.[142] Within the play, May presented Claudius as lustful, cowardly, and sexually depraved, and thereby easily enslaved by the seduction of flatterers and beautiful women. After beheading her rival, Agrippina is visited onstage by the uxorious Emperor who fawns over his new 'sweet' wife and grants her control not only of himself but of Roman policy. Agrippina informs her submissive husband that she has been 'Weighing the troubles of a Princely state, / And all the dangers that still threaten it'; although a woman who presumably has no experience in military affairs, she successfully recommends that Claudius replace the captains of his Praetorian Guard with Burrhus, a commander that the audience learns has sided with Agrippina's designs.[143] Throughout her speeches, Agrippina plays upon the lustful and cowardly passions of Claudius. 'Shee strikes upon the fittest string; / No passion reignes in him so much as feare', Pallas remarks during the scene, and by the end of Agrippina's speech Claudius agrees to the proposition since his 'sweet Agrippina / ... wilt have it so'.[144]

These scenes emphasised Agrippina's 'unnatural' domination over Claudius, who was represented as excessively submissive, uxorious, and even cuckolded by his new wife after she takes Pallas as her lover. Seventeenth-

---

[140] Ibid., 21 and 23 (1.446–449 and 492–93).   [141] Ibid., 22–23 (1.489–90).

[142] In a significant departure from typical portrayals of Agrippina, however, May never portrayed Agrippina as committing incest, nor do the characters within the play ever hint at her doing so. Suetonius, Pliny the Elder, Tacitus, and Seneca all accused Agrippina of incestuous relationships beyond that of her relationship with Emperor Claudius. As Claudius was Agrippina's uncle, their relationship was defined as incestuous according to Roman law, but from seventeenth-century English standards, such a match would not be understood as incestuous, or especially less so than a sexual relationship between siblings or mother and son.

[143] May, *Tragedy of Julia Agrippina*, 24–25 (1.528–29).

[144] Ibid., 24–25 (1.533–34 and 592–93).

194   Emasculated Kingship

century Englishmen understood uxoriousness as a failure of husbands to assert their natural and rightful control over their wives, and cuckoldry was characterised in a similar fashion, as ballads and public shaming rituals abused cuckolded husbands for failing to rule their households and serve their patriarchal duty. In each case, husbands were condemned for falling short of masculine expectations, and the related virtues of discretion, order, respectability, and control.[145] May's tragedy brilliantly demonstrated the political consequences of a failed patriarch and ruler, as Claudius's submission to Agrippina's machinations directly resulted in the making of state and military policy. Following these scenes, Agrippina pursues her rebellious activity to what Stuart audiences would have considered its logical end: She murders Claudius, and thus commits treason against husband and king.[146] Thus dangerously unruly until achieving dominance, Agrippina triumphantly declares that her new found widowhood has granted her more power than even her royal position: 'There is no power, no state at all, but what / Is undependent, absolute and free./ . . . I was an Empresse but ne're reign'd till now'.[147] Claudius's tyranny made him effeminate, enslaved, and a failed patriarch; Agrippina's tyranny made her cruel, politically cunning, sexually rebellious, and independent. In these ways, May presented tyranny as the reversal of gender and gendered roles: the female Agrippina enacting domination as if she were a man, and the male Claudius performing submission as if he were a woman.

May's portrayal of Nero's tyranny followed suit. In the *Tragedy* the young Emperor has an inordinately lustful and acquisitive nature, which causes his sexual and political relationships to become controlling and dangerous. Similar to earlier portrayals of Appius Claudius as a lustful and thereby corrupted ruler,[148] the *Tragedy* equated lust with tyranny; within the play Nero's passions lead him to pursue indiscriminately all pleasures whether they be bodily or political, sexual or power-seeking. The structure of the play emphasised the private and public consequences of

---

[145] Shepard, *Meanings of Manhood*, 25–26; David Underdown, 'The Taming of the Scold: the Enforcement of Patriarchal Authority in Early Modern England', in *Order and Disorder in Early Modern England*, ed. Anthony Fletcher and John Stevenson (Cambridge: Cambridge University Press, 1985), 116–36, esp. 127; Joy Wiltenburg, *Disorderly Women and Female Power in the Street Literature of Early Modern England and Germany* (Charlottesville: University Press of Virginia, 1992), 152–56; Laura Gowing, *Domestic Dangers: Women, Words, and Sex in Early Modern London* (Oxford: Oxford University Press, 1999), 95–96.

[146] From 1351 to 1828, the wilful murder of a husband by his wife constituted 'petty treason', because 'there is subjection due from the wife to the husband, but not *e converso*'. Walker, *Crime, Gender and the Social Order*, 138.

[147] May, *Tragedy of Julia Agrippina*, 64 (4.305–6 and 312).   [148] See Chapter 2.

Neronian Corruption in Caroline England

such lust/tyranny. In the subplot, Nero chases Acte and Poppaea with insatiable desire until sexually obtaining them, while in the main plot, he greedily seizes upon state power until becoming absolute ruler; by the fifth act of the tragedy, Nero acquires both absolute power and Poppaea. Through an important speech of Narcissus, a virtuous statesman forced to retire from the corrupt court, May explicitly connected Nero's sexual and political conduct, while simultaneously attributing this tyrannical activity to his nature, not adolescence:

> Those that are neere,
> And inward with his nature, doe suspect
> In [Nero] all seedes of vice and tyranny,
> Though smoother'd for a time, at least, not hurtfull
> While he refraines from medling with the state
> That his night rambling revels, drinking feasts,
> And cruell sports that he's delighted in,
> Are vices of his nature, not his youth.[149]

In these ways, May's depiction of Nero embodied Plato's description of the tyrannical soul in the *Republic*, especially as Socrates argued that within every person a 'dangerous, wild, and lawless form of desire' existed, which would not shrink from any beastly or savage behaviour, even 'trying to have sex with a mother, as it supposes, or with anyone else at all, whether man, god, or beast', or committing 'any foul murder' or any other shameless act. The tyrant, like an insane, drunken, or deranged man, becomes ruled by this insatiable desire, and is thereby led into every destructive activity.[150] Through his portrayal of Nero as possessing an utterly corrupted nature which leads him into cruel sports and cruel governance, May illustrated the paradox of tyrannical absolutism which Plato had observed, that the tyrant 'tries to rule others when he can't even control himself . . . In truth, then, and whatever some people may think, a real tyrant is really a slave, compelled to engage in the worst kind of fawning, slavery, and pandering to the worst kind of people'.[151] Within the play, Nero's achievement of absolute power over Rome coincides with his complete enslavement to his passions and the wicked people surrounding him. To achieve this position of power, Nero in a significant soliloquy at the end of the fourth act, with 'his lookes . . . wilde / And full of rage',

---

[149] May, *Tragedy of Julia Agrippina*, 57 (4.50–57).
[150] *Republic*, trans. by G. M. A. Grube, revised by C. D. C. Reeve, in *Plato: Complete Works*, ed. John M. Cooper (Indianapolis and Cambridge: Hackett, 1997), IX.571c–573c, pp. 1180–81.
[151] *Republic*, IX.579c–e, pp. 1187.

196 Emasculated Kingship

declares that he has no choice but to commit the unnatural crimes of parricide in order to secure his own power and manhood:

> My feares have been too slow, and twas high time
> That *Agrippinaes* thundring threats had wak'd
> My sleeping mischeefes; which shall now no more
> Study disguises, but appeare in bold
> And open acts with *Caesars* stampe upon um,
> Feirelesse of vulgar whispering jealousyes.
> Upon thy death, *Brittanicus*, a price
> No lesse then *Romes* imperiall wreath is set.
> The deede, when done, will priviledge it selfe,
> And make the power of *Nero* strong enough
> To warrant his misdeede, who dare revenge
> Or blame th'offerce that frees mee from a rivall?
> But I shall leave a worse, and nearer farre
> Behind, my mother *Agrippina* lives;
> Shee lives my rivall, nay my partner still,
> Nay more then that my Queene and Governesse.
> I am no Prince, no man, nothing at all
> While Agrippina lives ... [152]

Directly following this speech, the audience finds that Nero has not committed bold acts of murder as he claims, but has rather succumbed to the 'womanly' plots of poison and witchcraft by hiring the witch, Locusta, to murder Britannicus. Learning that Locusta's poisonous craft has failed, Nero launches into a rage and brutally beats Locusta onstage while berating her as 'hagge ... Witch. / Feind, fury, divell'.[153] Nero similarly hides like a coward behind the treachery of an assassin, Anicetus, to complete his matricide during the final act. Learning that his secret plot to drown Agrippina has failed, the tyrant screams, 'Oh, I am lost and dead ... / ... What shall I doo?', and he begs his mistress, Poppaea, and assassin, 'Advise mee, ... But yet advise mee nothing but [Agrippina's] death, / No other course is safe. *Nero* must dy / If Agrippina live'.[154] In his fear, Nero uxoriously follows Poppaea's advice, deciding Anicetus should finish her off. This is Nero's last appearance onstage.

May named his play *The Tragedy of Julia Agrippina*, and it is indeed the fall of Agrippina that concludes his drama. Unlike his portrayal of the tyrant Nero, who plots in irrational frenzy at the advice of his mistress, May depicted the tyrant Agrippina as sitting alone in 'solitude' and

---

[152] May, *Tragedy of Julia Agrippina*, 82–83 (4.961–978).   [153] Ibid., 83 (4.993–94).
[154] Ibid., 97 (5.479 and 484–87).

Neronian Corruption in Caroline England 197

'Ill-boding silence', contemplating her fate, bidding farewell to the world's 'fading glories' and remembering those she has wronged.[155] As Anicetus and the other assassins burst into her room, Agrippina turns to rational speech as her defence, bidding them 'heare mee but speake' and attempting to persuade her murderers that their crime will only bring them ruin. Anicetus remains unconvinced by Agrippina's rhetoric, and he pronounces the chilling lines, 'Can they bee innocent, / That disobey their Prince his will?' With Nero's will thus declared, Agrippina resigns herself to her fate and delivers the final lines of the play:

> Then strike this wombe
> This tragicall, and ever cursed wombe,
> That to the ruine of mankinde brought forth
> That monster Nero, here, here take revenge
> Here Justice bids you strike. Let these sad wounds
> Serve to appease the hatred of the earth
> 'Gainst Agrippina for dire Nero's birth.[156]

There was not a classical writer who denied that Agrippina demanded the assassins strike her womb; none claimed, however, that she got her wish. May in this final scene departed from a long tradition of classical scholarship by depicting Agrippina onstage as not only crying for a stab in her womb, but dying from its blow. The location of this wound was central for May's depiction of tyranny as the disruption of gender. Agrippina's womb represented her own femininity, and thus her limitation as a masculine actor; it also represented that which created 'that monster Nero', and thus engendered the 'ruine of mankind' and of Agrippina herself. By commanding the destruction of her womb, Agrippina resembled an infanticidal mother who would pervert the ideals of maternal nurture through the unnatural and savage shedding of blood; in this case, however, it is the womb itself and not the womb's product that receives the blow.[157]

Although shocking, Agrippina's final act appears congruous with her character throughout the play. May never portrayed Agrippina as possessing the natural tenderness of a mother, nor does he physically locate her within the space of the home except for the final scene. His Agrippina acts in public, political, and masculine spaces, and even in her death she exhibits, and is granted, agency. By calling for the destruction of her

---

[155] See ibid., 99–100 (5.537–77).   [156] Ibid., 100–1 (5.599–600 and 611–17).

[157] See Mary Fissell, *Vernacular Bodies: The Politics of Reproduction in Early Modern England* (Oxford: Oxford University Press, 2004), 74–78.

198 Emasculated Kingship

womb, Agrippina demands that her gender inversion be made complete, and with it any semblance of future pregnancy or motherhood.

The destruction of the womb at the same time labelled Nero as a monstrous birth, which in this period could be understood as an omen of God's judgement for heretical or sinful living, the product of a lascivious woman's womb, or the result of a pregnant woman's *vis imaginativa* or contemplation of images.[158] Throughout the tragedy, the first two explanations seem most plausible, and May employed scenes of the court and Agrippina's immoral behaviour to represent the royal household and its members as corrupted, as compared to the virtue lurking in the cottages of rural swain. The destruction of her womb marked the completion of Agrippina's masculinity and her own ruin, but the prevalence of the monster, Nero, hauntingly remained. With the banishment of Ciceronian civic virtue, with Nero's rise to absolute power, and with his subjugation to passions and mistress, the cycle of tyranny would continue: a tyranny which perverted the very gender of the ruler and the gendered order of family and society. For some commentators in the next decade, such gender inversion would be enacted on the royal stage.

4.5 Nero and the Love of Stage Plays

In February 1634, the prolific puritan pamphleteer and lawyer William Prynne was charged and found guilty in the Star Chamber of writing a seditious book, *Histrio-mastix* (1633), which attacked stage-plays, masques, dancing, and festivals as 'sinfull, heathenish, lewde, ungodly spectacles, and most pernicious corruptions', and denounced the King and Queen for allowing, sponsoring, and participating in such activities. According to his accusers, Prynne's *Histrio-mastix* preached rebellion, as he 'indeavoured to infuse an opinnyon into the people that ytt is lawfull to laye violent hands vppon Princes that are either actors, favourers, or spectatores of stage playes'.[159] Attorney General William Noy defended these charges by citing numerous examples (easily found) in the thousand-

---

[158] For monstrous births as judgement, see John Marshall, *John Locke, Toleration and Early Enlightenment Culture* (Cambridge: Cambridge University Press, 2006), 268–70, 297–302; Aaron W. Kitch, 'Printing Bastards: Monstrous Birth Broadsides in Early Modern England', in *Printing and Parenting in Early Modern England* (London: Ashgate, 2005), 221–36; for monstrous births and the mother's imagination, see Marie-Hélène Huet, *Monstrous Imagination* (London and Cambridge, MA: Harvard University Press, 1993), 15–27.

[159] Prynne, *Histrio-mastix, the Players Scovrge, or, Actors Tragædie* (London, 1633), title page; Samuel Rawson Gardiner, ed. *Documents relating to the Proceedings against William Prynne, in 1634 and 1637* (London: Nichols, 1877), 1–2.

Neronian Corruption in Caroline England 199

page *Histrio-mastix*, and he characterised Prynne's writing as deeply inflammatory, even when indirect. Noy maintained that Prynne often refused to write by 'precepts', which 'would be to[o] playnne' for his purpose, preferring instead to censure the monarch by adopting 'examples and other implicite meanes', including 'sheweinge the lyfe and death of princes that loved stage playes'. Prominent among these historical examples was Nero, the 'playerlyke, citharedicall lyfe of this vitious emperour, which made him soe execrable to some noble Romanes, that to vindicate the honnor of the Romane empire, which was thus basely prostituted, they conspired his distrucion'.[160] In the end, Prynne's book was deemed to be such a 'huge, scandalous, infamous, and seditious lybell against the Kinge and Queene', that he was sentenced to perpetual imprisonment and a five-thousand pound fine, stripped of his legal practice and university degrees, expelled from Lincoln's Inn, publicly humiliated in the pillory, his ears mutilated at Westminster and Cheapside, and his books burned by the hangman in front of his eyes – the last being an innovative punishment in Caroline England.[161] The charge of sedition for a printed book was itself an innovation. In 1578, judges had ruled that 'sedition cannot be committed by words, but by publick and violent action'.[162] With the case of Prynne, one could be charged with sedition for words, even when those words heavily referenced the historical past.

Annabel Patterson has well described the irony of Prynne's book: 'That drama could have any didactic or analytical function was endlessly denied; yet Prynne himself made copious use of the dramatists' sources of indirection: old stories, other men's words.'[163] Prynne's *Histrio-mastix* not only borrowed the imaginative and historically centred allusions of dramatists, poets, and historians; his work simultaneously employed the critical language of opposition against corruption and tyranny in Charles's government that these previous writers had developed. Some scholarly accounts have downplayed the oppositional character of Prynne's *Histrio-mastix*,

---

[160] Gardiner, *Proceedings against Prynne*, 12–13. By 'citharedicall', Prynne is referring to Nero's citharising, or passion for playing the harp. See *OED* 'citharize, v'. and 'cither, n'.

[161] Gardiner, *Proceedings against Prynne*, 20–21.

[162] Cyndia Susan Clegg, *Press Censorship in Caroline England* (New York: Cambridge, 2001), 120; Christine Noelle Reese, *Controlling Print? Burton, Bastwick and Prynne and the Politics of Memory* (PhD Thesis, Pennsylvania State University, 2007), 35.

[163] Annabel M. Patterson, *Censorship and Interpretation: The Conditions of Writing and Reading in Early Modern England* (Madison: University of Wisconsin Press, 1984), 114. What David Cressy has likewise highlighted was the remarkable theatricality of Prynne's public performances and publications. See 'The Portraiture of Prynne's Pictures: Performance on the Public Stage', in *Travesties and Transgression in Tudor and Stuart England* (New York: Oxford University Press, 2000), 213–33

arguing that he 'had not attacked the crown, even if he had been rude about amusements patronised by it', or that he 'had *merely* spoken in rude and intemperate language of amusements patronised by the King'. Others, ignoring the vast contemporary responses to Prynne, have claimed that his case received 'little public attention or sympathy'.[164] What these statements overlook is how very significant Prynne's gendered and exemplary language was in an early Stuart context where the King's 'amusement' could be understood as directly compromising his masculinity, religion, and ability to rule, just as it had compromised Nero. They also tend to overlook how very central and well-known Prynne's case became in Caroline England, due in many ways to Prynne's own self-representation as being a victim of the King and the Church's overweening power and persecution of the godly. Prynne's work, as Mark Kishlansky has demonstrated, was fundamentally a work of sedition against King Charles.[165] A significant but often overlooked aspect of this sedition were the gendered criticisms that Prynne levelled against Charles and his government through the use of historical examples. This section will analyse how *Histrio-mastix*, like other texts before it, developed a gendered construction of monarchy and the historical past which criticised the masculinity, and thereby effectiveness, of King Charles, and the gendered and sexual order of Charles's household and court. Through his arguments, Prynne did not seek to abolish monarchy as such in England, but he called for the reformation of Charles, as well as Henrietta and their cavalier court, lest the kingdom of England fall to ruin and divine punishment.

Prynne's *Histrio-mastix* condemned the 'sinfull, wicked, unchristian pastimes, vanities, cultures, and disguises' of the ungodly. Although the theatre was the primary target of his treatise, Prynne also argued passionately against numerous other activities, games, and fashions as being 'wicked, sinfull, unchristian' in their own right and 'concomitants or fruites of Stage-playes'. These 'vanities' included:

---

[164] [My emphasis]. William Lamont, 'Prynne, William (1600–1669)', *Oxford Dictionary of National Biography* (Oxford: Oxford University Press, 2004), online edn, May 2011 [www.oxforddnb.com/view/article/22854]; Lamont, *Marginal Prynne* (London: Routledge & Kegan Paul, 1963), 33; Kevin Sharpe, *The Personal Rule of Charles I* (New Haven: Yale University Press, 1992), 676 and 680.

[165] Mark Kishlansky, 'A Whipper Whipped: The Sedition of William Prynne', *The Historical Journal* 56.3 (2013): 603–27. For the wider political and cultural significance of Prynne's trial, see McRae, 'Stigmatizing Prynne: Puritanism & Politics, 1630s', in *Literature, Satire, and the Early Stuart State*, 188–207; Cressy, 'The Portraiture of Prynne's Pictures', 213–33; Bellany, 'Libels in Action: Ritual, Subversion, and the English Literary Underground, 1603–42' in *The Politics of the Excluded, c. 1500–1850*, ed. Tim Harris (Basingstoke: Palgrave Macmillan, 2001), 99–124.

Neronian Corruption in Caroline England

effeminate mixt Dancing, Dicing, Stage-playes, lascivious Pictures, wanton Fashions, Face-painting, Health-drinking, Long haire, Love-lockes, Periwigs, womens curling, pouldring and cutting of their haire, Bone-fires, New-yeares-gifts, May-games, amorous Pastoralls, lascivious effeminate Musicke, excessive laughter, luxuriovs disorderly Christmas-keeping, Mummeries, with sundry such like vanities which the world now dotes on.[166]

The practices here described were not merely amusements patronised by the King; they were condoned, culturally associated with, and exercised by the King and his court. Indeed, the royal court's fashions, entertainments, and displays of magnificence, consumption, and cultural patronage were central to the King's performance of power and international diplomacy, and to the court's function as an honourable and profitable opportunity and marriage market for aristocratic families.[167] On the elaborate sets of Whitehall Palace, and in the gardens and great halls of aristocratic households, the King, Queen, and courtiers staged luxurious and deliberately wasteful entertainments, meant to emphasise their grandeur and status. Even those not invited to dance and act in these performances or to witness their spectacles could read about the decadent sets, costumes, and designs in printed accounts or experience them through repeat performances on the public stage.[168]

Criticisms of the indecent 'wanton Fashions' of the King's court, including face-painting and elaborate long hair, were longstanding, and they were especially circulated in the wake of political scandals such as the Overbury Affair and Buckingham's assassination. A number of letters, pamphlets, treatises, and libels denounced the 'painted pride, lust, malice, powdered hair, yellow bands, and all the rest of the wardrobe of Court-vanities', as one letter described it.[169] Thomas Tuke's *Discovrse against Painting and Tincturing of Women* (1616), packed with Biblical and patristic allusions similar to *Histrio-mastix*, denounced face-painting as vain, duplicitous, and idolatrous, as a cause of '*Murther* and *Poysoning*: *Pride* and *Ambition*: *Adultery* and *Witchcraft*', and as being 'the roote' of

---

[166] Prynne, *Histrio-mastix*, 'To the Christian Reader'.

[167] Caroline Hibbard, 'Henrietta Maria in the 1630s: perspectives on the role of consort queens in *Ancien Régime* courts', in *The 1630s: Interdisciplinary Essays on Culture and Politics in the Caroline Era*, ed. Ian Atherton and Julie Sanders (Manchester: Manchester University Press, 2006), 92–110, esp. 102; Sharpe, *Image Wars*, 93–99; Sharpe, *Personal Rule*, 131–208.

[168] Lauren Shohet, *Reading Masques: The English Masque and Public Culture in the Seventeenth Century* (Oxford: Oxford UP, 2010), 63-66 and 81-124.

[169] Letter from John Castle to James Miller, British Library MS Cotton Titus B.vii, fol. 476. Qtd in David Lindley, *Trials of Frances Howard: Fact and Fiction at the Court of King James* (London: Routledge, 1993), 179.

'*Disobedience to the Ministery of the Word*'.[170] By 'adultering her face' with 'vile drugs', Tuke argued, the painted woman 'Closely allures the adulterers imbrace'.[171] Tuke's treatise directly connected such 'wanton fashion' with the royal court, including an image of a court lady dressed in ostentatious style on the title page. Prynne's attack upon amusements thereby assaulted practices at the heart of monarchical and aristocratic representation and culture.

Histrio-mastix further targeted Stuart policies concerning observance of the Sabbath, challenging King James's ruling that many sports and games may be appropriately exercised on Sundays. '[D]auncing, either men or women, Archerie for men, leaping, vaulting ... May-Games, Whiston Ales, and Morris-dances, and the setting vp of Maypoles' had all been justified in James's *Book of Sports* (1618), which rebuked 'Puritanes' for prohibiting recreations on the Sabbath and holy days which the King deemed 'lawfull' and 'honest'.[172] Throughout the late 1620s, Sunday Sabbatarians, who tended to be Puritans but also included Anglicans, argued that Christians should observe a strict Sabbath and thereby honour the fourth commandment and the practices of the primitive Christian church.[173] As Prynne sat imprisoned in the Tower for *Histrio-mastix*, Charles republished his father's book, intending to remind his subjects of the 'princely wisdom' of allowing 'lawfull Sports' and presumably also intending to refute Prynne.[174]

Beyond these explicit assaults upon Charles's government, Prynne himself most emphasised that his accusers had charged him with deliberately attacking Queen Henrietta Maria for her participation in these courtly activities, especially as she rehearsed Walter Montague's masque *The Shepherd's Pastoral* (1633) for a performance just six weeks after the printing of *Histrio-mastix* had commenced. Although Prynne had spent more than seven years constructing his large book, and thereby defended himself as not commenting upon current affairs, it was argued that he had expanded the index to *Histrio-mastix* during the Queen's rehearsals.[175]

---

[170] Thomas Tuke, *A Discovrse against Painting and Tincturing of Women* (London, 1616), titlepage and 2.

[171] Here Tuke was drawing upon a description of Jezebel from Josuah Sylvester's translation of Du Bartas. See, *Discovrse against Painting*, B2v.

[172] James VI and I, *The Kings Maiesties Declaration to His Subiects, Concerning lawfull Sports to be vsed* (London, 1618), 2 and 7.

[173] See, for example, Theophilus Brabourne, *A Discourse vpon the Sabbath* (London?, 1628), 2–3.

[174] *The Kings Maiesties Declaration to His Subiects, Concerning lawfull Sports to bee vsed* (London, 1633), 2.

[175] Prynne claimed in his preface 'To the Christian Reader' that the book took him seven years to compose, and he later argued it during his trial. However, Prynne would have probably had access to his index during the work's printing, and the particular index entry in question was on one of the very last pages of the text.

Neronian Corruption in Caroline England 203

The index entry that carried special offence in relation to the Queen was 'Women-Actors, notorious whores', which cited a law of Justinian banning female actors and several Biblical examples from the Apostle Paul before concluding: 'And dare then any Christian women be so more then whorishly impudent, as to act, to speake publikely on a Stage, (perchance in mans apparell, and cut haire, here proved sinfull and abominable) in the presence of sundry men and women? ... O let such presidents of impudency, of impiety be never heard of or suffred among Christians.'[176] Although some scholars have written this off as merely a 'careless entry' on Prynne's part,[177] this entry was very characteristic of *Histrio-mastix* as a whole and labelled the practices of the royal court and queen as indecent, irreligious, and a threat to the gendered order of society. In seventeenth-century England, 'whore' was an extremely common term of abuse which signified all unchaste sexual behaviour, including purchased sexuality and unpurchased promiscuity, adultery, and fornication outside of wedlock. Because women's lust was understood as peculiarly high due to the humoral composition of their bodies and their supposedly less-developed rational capabilities, their subordination to men and the stamping out of whoredom was deemed necessary for the spiritual and political order of society.[178] Female actors were similarly 'notorious', in Prynne's view, because they performed before men and mixed audiences; as Prynne underscored, Saint Paul had admonished women from speaking publicly in the church, teaching, or 'usurp[ing] authority over the man'.[179] Prynne's rhetoric thereby emphasised that women actors threatened to undermine the gendered order of the realm, allowing women to assume an unnatural role in the social hierarchy over the command of men – 'ouerruling nature and their Husbands both at once'.[180] In this position, women actors could engender sinful sexual appetites and irreligious behaviour in the men they dominated.

Prynne's admonishment that women-actors may wear 'mans apparell, and cut haire' further betrayed his anxiety that sinful fashions and pastimes blurred gendered distinctions, even to the point of metamorphosing men

---

[176] *Histrio-mastix*, index, 'Women-Actors'. This index entry was cited explicitly at the trial. See Gardiner, *Proceedings against Prynne*, 10–11.

[177] Leo E. Solt, *Church and State in Early Modern England, 1509–1640* (Oxford: Oxford University Press, 1990), 186.

[178] Margaret R. Sommerville, *Sex & Subjection: Attitudes to Women in Early Modern Society* (London and New York: Arnold, 1995), 8–18; Lake with Questier, *Anti-Christ's Lewd Hat*, 67–68; Gowing, *Domestic Dangers*, 59–110.

[179] Prynne, *Histrio-mastix*, index, 'Women-Actors'. He cited I Corinthians 14:34 and I Timothy 2:12.

[180] Prynne, *Histrio-mastix*, 205.

204 Emasculated Kingship

and women into the alternative gender. Prynne had argued in his earlier *The Vnloueliness of Loue-Locks* (1628) that 'our Mannish Impudent, and inconstant Female sexe, are Hermophradited, and transformed into men', while 'so diuers of our Masculine, and more noble race, are wholy degenerated and metamorphosed into women' when women adopted cut hair and men long hair.[181] Throughout this work, Prynne did not argue that these men and women merely look like the other gender, but that they actually undergo a physical transformation.[182] Prynne continued this logic in *Histrio-mastix*, arguing that male players were 'metamorphosed into women' by adopting female hair, gestures, and speech.[183] In his discussions of women transforming into men, Prynne often emphasised an association between the Roman Catholic religion, gender alteration, and patriarchal disorder. He cited with disdain the 'solemne Ceremony at the admission of all their Nonnes [nuns] into their unholy orders, to poll their heads, and cut their haire, in token that they are now immediately espoused unto Christ, and so are freed from all subiection to men, or to their husbands, (as I presume those English women think they are, who cut their haire)'. An example of this was Pope Joan, who gained power by 'transforming her selfe into the habit and tonsure of a man'.[184] Englishwomen who crop their hair similarly intend 'to turne men outright and weare the Breeches, or to become Popish Nonnes', Prynne explained.[185] What was at stake in these portrayals was a disruption of the gendered hierarchy. Targeting female actors and Roman Catholics, *Histrio-mastix* unmistakably criticised Queen Henrietta Maria.

In these chapters, we have seen through a large number of texts that the historical exemplum of Nero was especially significant for the seditious denigration of monarchy; this claim is verified by Prynne's trial, as Attorney General Noy accused Prynne of committing a crime against the King's person by comparing the King to such a 'vitious emperor'.[186] Noy argued

---

[181] Prynne, *The Vnloueliness of Loue Locks*, 'To the Christian Reader'.
[182] For a further discussion of this, see Fisher, *Materializing Gender*, 133–35.
[183] Prynne, *Histrio-mastix*, 171.   [184] Ibid., 185.   [185] Ibid., 185, 201–2.
[186] Kishlansky, 'A whipper whipped', 618–19. Prynne also specifically apologised for comparing the King to Nero in *Mr William Prynn his defence of stage-plays, or A retractation of a former book of his called Histrio-mastix* (London, 1649), 5–6: ' ... it is no disparagement for any man to alter his judgement upon better information, besides it was done long ago, and when the King (whose vertues I did not then so perfectly understand) governed without any controul, which was the time that I took the better to shew my conscience and courage, to oppose that power which was the highest, but had I truly known the King, I must confesse with sorrow, I should not have compared him to *Nero* the most wicked of the Roman Emperors (as I did in that book) for loving of Stage-playes; nor have given the Queen those bitter and cruell words of whore and strumpet, for playing a part in Mr *Montagues* Pastorall.'

Neronian Corruption in Caroline England

that Prynne in the 'Epistle Dedicatory' had made the King worse than Nero by describing how many more playhouses Charles had opened in London than Nero in Rome. Later, Prynne had compared Charles to Nero as a person of 'rancke and quallitye', whose voluntary acting in or attending plays led to his downfall; what was most disturbing about this second example, in Noy's view, was Prynne's argument that Nero's 'playerlyk, citharedicall lyfe ... made him so execrable to some noble Romanes, that to vindicate the honnor of the Roman empire, which was thus basely prostituted, they conspired his distrucion'.[187] Prynne's crimes thereby rested both in the direct comparison he was accused of drawing between Nero and Charles, and in the very treasonous suggestion that Charles's activities could lead to regicide, as Nero's activities had led to his own death. The prosecution clearly understood Prynne's turn to history as motivated by rebellious intent and as aiding this rebellion, for as the Solicitor General explained, 'Yf [Prynne] had possitively named his Maiestie in theis places, his meanynge would have been to[o] playnne, therefore he names other princes, and leaves the application to the reader'.[188] That Prynne was charged and severely punished for, among other things, comparing the 'best of men to the worst of tyrantes' illustrates how very seriously Charles and his government understood negative historical exempla, especially of tyrants and tyrannicide, as a threat to the King's sacred image and authority.

Noy's charge that Prynne treasonously encouraged regicide was very significant, but historians should not overlook that the Attorney General also highlighted the connection Prynne drew between Nero's love of entertainments and the Roman nobility's claim that such activity 'basely prostituted' the Roman Empire. Like the many Tudor and Stuart authors before him who connected Nero's vices and effeminacy with the ruin of Rome, Prynne's treatment of Nero focused primarily on how the Emperor's 'private' vices led to 'public' corruption and disorder. One of many examples can be found in Prynne's discussion of how plays lead to the 'generall depravation' of the 'mindes' and 'manners' of actors and audiences. Tacitus and other authors

> inveigh much against that Monster Nero, ... and other dissolute Roman Emperours; for acting, countenancing and frequenting Playes; and harbouring Stage-players, which did not only exhaust their treasures, and impoverish their subiects, but even corrupt their discipline, and strangely vitiate and deprave not onely their owne, but the very peoples mindes and

---

[187] Gardiner, *Proceedings against Prynne*, 11–13.   [188] Ibid., 10.

Emasculated Kingship

manners, by drawing them on to all licentious dissolutenesse, and excess of vice, to the very utter subversion of their States, as these Authors ioyntly testifie, whose walls could not secure them when as their vertues, their manners were gone quite to ruine.[189]

Within this passage, Prynne highlighted that Nero's passion for amusements fiscally undermined the realm and morally corrupted the thoughts and actions of the Roman people. The first charge would have been very significant in Stuart England, where King James's notorious love of fine clothing and entertainments, and Charles's expensive literary and artistic patronage, court masques, and art collecting had been blamed (and indeed were partially responsible) for the fiscal conflicts of the 1620s, unjust taxation such as the Forced Loan, seemingly decadent court culture, and pursuance of peace even in the face of Continental war. One Stuart libel, for example, charged that courtiers lined their pockets from corrupt and scandalous practices, while parliament had to foot the bill for the King's luxurious expenditures on the newly renovated Banqueting House:

> When the Banquetting howse is finished quite
> then Jones Sir Inigo we will call
> & Poetts Ben brave maskes shall write
> & a Parliament shall pay for all.[190]

Much like the King's patronage of Jones and Jonson, Nero put himself up to 'miserable expenses' by 'prostituting' his 'grace and favour unto Players' and sponsoring their entertainments, according to Prynne.[191] In *Histrio-mastix*, Prynne further connected such lavish spending and corruption with the loss of martial prowess, arguing that empires that wasted their wealth on spectacles undermined their ability to secure the realm against foreign invasion. Greece, for example, had 'left no mony in their Exchequer to rigge their Ships, to set forth their Navy, or to defend their Country: in so much that their enemies laying hold on this their penury, prevailed much against them'.[192] Prynne's sentiment resonated with another libel from the 1630s, which commanded England to 'Come arme they self . . . / Put on thin iron coate' and shed those 'silken robes of peace / Which made our enymyes / And our passions cease'.[193]

---

[189] Prynne, *Histrio-mastix*, 451–52.

[190] 'When Charles, hath got the Spanish Gearle', Oxford Bodleian Library MS Ashmole 38, fos. 229r–v. See 'Early Stuart Libels: an edition of poetry from manuscript sources', ed. Alastair Bellany and Andrew McRae, *Early Modern Literary Studies Text Series* I (2005), [http://purl.oclc.org/emls/texts/libels/].

[191] Prynne, *Histrio-mastix*, 318. [192] Ibid., 312. For the discussion of Nero doing such, see 318.

[193] British Library MS Sloane 1792, fos. 74v–75v. See 'Early Stuart Libels', [http://purl.oclc.org/emls/texts/libels/].

Neronian Corruption in Caroline England 207

Prynne went far beyond describing the monetary drain of luxury, however; within the above passage and throughout *Histrio-mastix*, he emphasised the moral depravity of decadent entertainments through explicitly gendered language. As we saw with women-actors, Prynne urged his readers to forswear acting, dancing, and theatrical entertainments lest they pervert gender, the social hierarchy, and nature itself. Through his historical exempla, Prynne especially exhorted monarchs to forbid stage-plays within their realm, both because monarchs carried the power to outlaw such activities and because stage-plays would corrupt monarchs themselves to the detriment of the entire realm. Indeed, 'Roman Emperours who delighted most in Stage-playes', Prynne warned, 'were the most deboist, luxurious, dissolute, ebrious, of all others.' The emperors' insatiable passions for amusements betrayed their souls as out of order, their intemperate appetites as enslaving their reason. Rather than exercising the control and sobriety expected of grown men and householders, they enjoyed excess associated with loose women or adolescents, and thereby, would be unable to discipline their social inferiors.[194] Prynne further emphasised that Nero not only delighted in amusements, and hence suffered a corrupted moral character, but he was 'so much besotted with Stage-playes, as sometimes to play the Actor, to his eternall infamy'.[195] These exhortations would have been very offensive to King Charles and even accusatory, as the King enjoyed theatrical entertainments and publicly acted and danced in several masques throughout the 1630s.

The 'pernicious effects' of stage-plays numbered at least twenty, Prynne argued, including wastefulness, sexual perversion, dissimulation, excessive indulgence, violence, effeminacy, irreligion, idolatry, and as a result, divine punishment and damnation.[196] Although 'effeminacy' received its own chapter in *Histrio-mastix*, almost every one of these vices was understood as a characteristic of failed masculinity in seventeenth-century England, where the ideal man was thought to be rational and in control of his passions.[197] Nero's history served as a significant example of the danger of theatre for a monarch's masculinity, and thereby effectiveness as a ruler. His 'grosse intemperance', Prynne argued, including excessive drunkenness and luxury, acting on the stage, wearing of women's clothing and adopting of women's gestures, had 'effeminated' Nero's body; as a result,

---

[194] See Shepard, 'The Violence of Manhood', in *Meanings of Manhood*, 127–51; Foyster, *Manhood in Early Modern England*, 39–48.
[195] Prynne, *Histrio-mastix*, 511 and 460.
[196] Prynne explored each of these through twenty 'scenas' in 'Actus 6'.
[197] Foyster, *Manhood in Early Modern England*, 39–48; Shepard, *Meanings of Manhood*, 21–38, 46.

208 Emasculated Kingship

the tyrant indulged in 'lewd' and 'whorish' practices, even 'sodomiticall ones' inspired by his 'invirility'.[198] Being thus corrupted in body and practice, Nero corrupted the entire 'Roman Nation', Prynne concluded, 'and drew them on to all kinde of vice of luxury and lewdnesse'.[199] Simultaneously, his kingdom suffered divine punishment through plagues, pestilences, and civil discord.[200] Prynne's *Histrio-mastix* thereby connected the love of stage-plays with tyranny, as 'tyrannicall dispositions' drove emperors to stage-plays, and as stage-plays caused the tyrannical ruin of kingdoms.[201]

Prynne's characterisation of tyranny resonated with previous treatments of Nero in the 1620s and 1630s, while hardly masking his condemnation of the contemporary practices of Stuart court and King. Significantly, at the end of Prynne's trial when the attorney general listed the three worst instances of sedition contained within *Histrio-mastix,* two related to Roman stories already studied in this book: the comparison of Charles I with Nero and the praise for Roman assassins of monarchs.[202] Although *Histrio-mastix* was perhaps more forceful in explicating the relationship between the monarch's 'private' sinful indulgence, the corruption of his gender, and the resulting ruin of the kingdom, it was not wholly exceptional in its views, as these past chapters have demonstrated.

4.6 'Neronian' Trials

Accusations of tyranny could become especially significant when individuals suffered religious persecution, and the performance of persecution in spaces such as the courtroom and scaffold, and in manuscript and print, provided significant platforms for religious dissidents to woo popular audiences to their cause. During the reforms of Archbishop William Laud in the 1630s, protesting Protestants such as William Prynne, John Bastwick, and Henry Burton effectively utilised these spaces of persecution to challenge the English Church and crown by comparing their persecutors to Nero and their own deaths to the ordeal of the Apostle Paul – perhaps the most adored biblical figure for Protestants apart from Christ himself. Although Charles's government sought to stigmatise heretical sedition through punishment, the prosecuted wielded languages of martyrdom, entombment and heroic suffering to present themselves as victims of

---

[198] See Prynne, *Histrio-mastix*, 200, 206, 208–9, 213, 511, 514.   [199] Ibid., 451.
[200] Ibid., 562.   [201] Ibid., 517.   [202] Kishlansky, 'A whipper whipped', 622.

Neronian Corruption in Caroline England 209

tyranny, and found numerous supporters who interpreted their ordeal accordingly.

The activities of William Prynne, John Bastwick, and Henry Burton, although not initially coordinated, together presented the most thorough and vociferous challenge to the Caroline Church and policies of Archbishop William Laud during the 1630s; their puritan sermons, pamphlets, and treatises deemed Anglican bishops, high liturgical ceremonialism, and Arminian tendencies as popish, absolutist, idolatrous – the very corruption of Antichrist. In 1637, all three were tried together under the prerogative court of Star Chamber and convicted of seditious libel for their writings. These included Bastwick's *Apologeticus ad Praesules Anglicanos* (1636) and *The Letany of John Bastwick* (1637), Burton's Gunpowder Treason sermons entitled, *For God, and the King* (1636), his *Apologie of an Appeale* (1636), and *A Divine Tragedie Lately Acted* (1636) against Sabbath-breakers, and Prynne's *News from Ipswich* (1636), penned while already confined in the Tower for *Histrio-mastix*.[203] Their punishment for seditious libel included imprisonment, degradation, pillorying, mutilation, and exorbitant fines of £5,000 each. On 27 August 1637, the Privy Council (members of which had sat with the chief justices in the Star Chamber trial), ordered the libellers reassigned to remote islands rather than imprisoned on domestic sites – Prynne to Jersey, Burton to Guernsey, and Bastwick to the Isles of Scilly. This was a truly innovative punishment intended to prevent further 'contagion' by these heretics and to ensure their inability to pursue legal recourse, including the writ of habeas corpus.[204]

Sympathetic accounts of the public drama of Prynne, Bastwick, and Burton emphasised their steadfastness in the face of suffering and their imitation of Christ through 'martyrdom'. One account described Burton, upon viewing the three pillories on the scaffold, as remarking, 'Me thinks ... I see mount Calvary; there are 3 Crosses, one for Christ, & the other for 2 theeues; & if Christ was numbred amongst theeues, shall Christians thinke much to be numbred among rogues? Such wee are condemned to be: surely if I am a rogue, I am Christs rogue, & noe mans else.'[205] On the scaffold, all three 'martyrs' spoke directly to the audience witnessing their mutilation. Bastwick declared the day his collar day – or day of chivalric honour – in the king's palace. Prynne protested his

---

[203] David Cressy, 'Puritan Martyrs in Island Prisons', *Journal of British Studies* 57 (2018): 736–54, esp. 739–40.
[204] Cressy, 'Puritan Martyrs in Island Prisons', 739–40.   [205] Ox. Bod. MS Tanner 299, f. 140r.

210   Emasculated Kingship

innocence, as Burton declared it the 'happiest pulpit he had ever preached in'. Two hours later, the hangman began the cutting of ears. The crowd was said to roar and weep and grieve with the chopping of Burton's ears, as if 'every one of them had at the same instant lost an ear'. Bastwick provided the knife for the hangman, that his ears may be chopped 'quickly and very close'. Prynne received the most gruesome treatment, being branded on both cheeks then having his ears hewed so 'scurvily' that he bled out greatly and fainted in the pillory.[206]

The public stage of martyrdom was titillating and moralising. It was also a highly contested space. Edward Rossingham's account explained that 'the humours of the people [witnessing the punishment] were various, some wept, some laughed, and some were very reservd'.[207] A Dorset draper named Dennis Bond described the three on the scaffold as 'wonderfully patient' – they 'carried themselves so meekly and resolutely that all beholders except some ruffians ... shed many tears'.[208] Fellow Puritans deemed the punishment a martyrdom and 'glorious wedding day', and the minister Miles Burkitt preached that 'though the faithful were molested, persecuted and cropped, yet they would continue faithful still'.[209] Others, however, read the events very differently, deeming the three 'delinquents' justly punished. High conformists witnessing and discussing their treatment expressed that the sentences against Prynne, Bastwick, and Burton were too light, and that they wished 'the pillory had been changed into a gallows'. The Catholic Sir Kenelm Digby famously scoffed at the 'venerations' practised by those 'puritans' witnessing the mutilation, who 'keep the bloody sponges and handkerchiefs that did the hangman service in the cutting off their ears'.[210] Other ministers preached and warned that those who showed compassion to these rogues would themselves incur damnation.

Scholars have rightly recognised the punishment, imprisonment, and later triumphal re-entry of these three banished 'martyrs' as significant moments – both culturally and politically – in the lead-up to the first English civil war.[211] What has not been emphasised adequately is how

---

[206] Ibid., 140r–143r; Gardiner, *Proceedings against Prynne*, 86–87.   [207] Ibid., 87.
[208] Historical Manuscripts Commission, *Report on the Manuscripts of Lord De l'Isle, Preserved at Penshurst Place*, vol. vi (1966), 96. Qtd in Cressy, *Travesties and Transgressions*, 224.
[209] Qtd in Cressy, *Travesties and Transgressions*, 226.
[210] Thomas Longueville, *The Life of Sir Kenelm Digby* (London and New York: Longmans, 1896), 240.
[211] See Cogswell, 'Underground Verse', 277–78; Cressy, *Travesties and Transgressions*, 225–26; McRae, *Literature, Satire, and the Early Stuart State*, 189–90.

Neronian Corruption in Caroline England 211

Bastwick and Burton, alongside Prynne, appropriated stories of the Neronian persecution of Christians to represent themselves as true martyrs and to castigate the English prelacy and also government as tyrannical. In these final Neronian examples, the focus lay not with failed militaristic policies, household governance, gender inversion, or court corruption but with the exercise of 'false religion' and persecution, especially through unjust power placed in the ecclesiastical and legal structures of England.

On 23 October 1634, John Bastwick, a member of the College of Physicians, stood before the ecclesiastical Court of High Commission. Bastwick would be charged with an extensive list of transgressions, including his authorship and distribution of *Elenchus religionis papisticæ* [*A Refutation of the Religion of the Papists*], which had seen numerous editions since 1624, and his maintaining of 'schismatical and heretical opinions', including speaking 'against kneeling at the receiving of holy communion' and 'against bowing at the name of Jesus', and arguing 'that the institution of bishops was not *de jure*, and that there is no difference between a bishop and a presbyter or ordinary minister, and that bishops are no lords'.[212] On 9 October, Bastwick had refused to take the oath to answer charges against him, and, after being ordered to pay a bond of £300, was committed to the Gatehouse. As he stood before the Court again two weeks later, his answers 'were adjudged scandalous, and he was admonished to answer *plenè, planè, et directè*, upon the pain of 100*l.* fine, with intimation that if he stand out, the court will impose greater fines'. Refusing to enter bond for his reappearance, Bastwick baulked at the court and declared that 'he stood before them as Paul stood before Nero'.[213]

Bastwick's description of himself as the Apostle Paul imprisoned under Nero was a significant one in Stuart England. As we saw in Chapter 3, Paul penned his exhortation in the thirteenth chapter of Romans for Christians to obey the higher secular powers as he himself suffered imprisonment under Nero and would later suffer martyrdom. John Foxe's *Actes and Monuments*, which discussed Paul's beheading under Nero as one of the 'fyrst persecutions of the primitiue church', reflected upon the apostle's great transformation from being himself a persecutor of Christians to one later persecuted by Nero for his 'labours in promoting the gospel of

---

[212] *Acts of the Court of High Commission, During the Month of February 1634–5*, SP 16/261 f. 159. For his own account, see John Bastwick, M. D. *Praxeis ton episkopon sive apologeticus ad praesules Anglicanos criminum ecclesiasticorum in curia celsae commissionis ...* (Leiden? 1636), 5–6.

[213] *Acts of the Court of High Commission during the Month of October 1634*, SP 16/261 f.76.

Emasculated Kingship

Christ'.[214] The *Actes and Monuments* celebrated Paul's longsuffering; although no man had stood with Paul in his first imprisonment, 'the Lorde stoode with [him]', Foxe recounted, 'and did comfort [him], that the preaching of his word might procede by [him], and that all the Gentiles myght heare and be taught'. Paul was thus, after his first imprisonment, 'deliuered [by God] out of the Lyons mouth'.[215] Once Paul finished this work for the Gospel, however, he willingly accepted his second imprisonment under Nero, and was later beheaded.

During and following their Star Chamber trial, Bastwick, Burton, and Prynne frequently employed the historical exemplum of the Apostle Paul's persecution under Nero to characterise their suffering as highly unjust according to religious and legal precepts, and to threaten the Privy Councillors and Lords overseeing their trial that this injustice would be publicised to the far reaches of Christendom. Prior to the Star Chamber hearing in 1637, Prynne had already castigated Laudian bishops as surpassing Nero and 'the very Divell himselfe' in their unlawful persecution of true Christians. 'And whereas *Paul* though imprisoned under that most bloody Divell and Tirant *Nero* in Pagan Rome, had so much liberty, *as to dwell two yeares space together in his owne hired house, and receive all that came in unto him: Preaching the Kingdome of God,*' Prynne contended, 'Yet these Lord Prelates to shew themselves more cruelly barbarous and Tyrannicall then either the Divell or *Nero*, have anciently, and yet daily doe shut up diverse of Gods Ministers and people close prisonners ... ', refusing them the company of friends and the ability to preach sometimes for years.[216]

During the 1637 Star Chamber trial, however, it was John Bastwick who initially and repeatedly employed this imagery to criticise his legal treatment. Arguing that the Lords would be unlawful according to the 'law of nature, & the law of nations, & the law of God' to censure him without reading his book and written answers, Bastwick proclaimed that even 'the governour, that St Paul was carried before, did first heare his cause' before censuring him.[217] Moreover, in reference to a decree already gone forth about the chopping of his ears, Bastwick exclaimed, 'I may say, as the Apostle saith, will ye whip a Romane vncondemned?' Most significantly, after describing the precedent of a former case where, unlike his trial, the

---

[214] John Foxe, *The Unabridged Acts and Monuments Online* or *TAMO* (1570 edition) (HRI Online Publications, Sheffield, 2011). Available from: www.johnfoxe.org [Accessed: 20/1/2018], book 1, p. 68.
[215] Ibid.   [216] Prynne, *A looking-glasse for all lordly prelates* (?, 1636), 6.
[217] Bod. Ox. Tanner MS 299, f. 137v.

Neronian Corruption in Caroline England 213

Lords had extended a great deal of 'paines' and 'pateince' to hear answers and depositions, Bastwick threatened:

> But if that will not prevaile with your honours to peruse my boke, & my answers, which heere I tender in the words of a soldier, a scholler, a gentleman, & a physition I will cloath them in Roman buffe, & haue them dispersed through out the Christian world, that future generations may see the innocence of my cause, & your proceedings in it. This I will doe, if I dy for it, when I haue done.[218]

Bastwick's declaration of publicising and clothing his trial 'in Roman buffe' for all of Christendom to see would prove to be a threat carried out by him as well as Burton and Prynne. Indeed, a different scribal copy of the Star Chamber trial recorded this warning twice and claimed that Prynne, rather than Bastwick, had asked that the Lords 'lay aside your Censure for this day, & inquire into my cause, heare my answeare read; which if you refuse to doe, I heare professe, I will cloath it in Roman Buffe, & send itt abroad unto the uiew of all the world, to cleare mine innocencie, and see your great iniustice in this cause'. In the speech directly following, the account described Prynne as again announcing that he would 'cloath them (as I said before) in Roman Buffe, & disperse them throughout the Christian world, that future generations may see the Innocency of this cause, & your Honours uniust proceedings in itt; all which I will doe though itt cost mee my life'.[219] The printed account of their Star Chamber trial and censure included this warning twice and attributed the speeches to Bastwick.[220] And, likewise, it appeared in print again when Bastwick penned his *An Answer ... To the exceptions made against his Letany by a Learned Gentleman* (1637) while imprisoned and awaiting sentencing. In this epistolary pamphlet, which relied heavily upon the writings and examples of Paul to challenge the Laudian reforms and to label the sacramental practices of the Church of England as Catholic corruptions of the true faith, Bastwick declared his treatment by the High Commission and Star Chamber to be highly unjust, and he vowed to translate all the court documents and speeches from his ordeal into Latin in order to publicise this injustice to the far-reaching community of true Christians. 'And I doubt not', Bastwick concluded, 'but to make it the

---

[218] Ibid., ff. 138v–139r.   [219] BL MS. Add. 28011, f. 38r.

[220] Anon., *A Brief relation of certain speciall and most materiall passages, and speeches in the Starre-Chamber, occasioned and delivered Iune the 14th. 1637 ... truely and faithfully gathered from their owne mouthes by one present at the sayd censure* ([Amsterdam], 1637), 10 and 12. Reprinted in 1638 in Leiden.

214   Emasculated Kingship

famousest story that euer was agitated in any Court of iudicature, since Paul appeared before Nero ... I am onely sory I haue no more eares, nor liues to lose for the honour of God, my King and Religion'.[221]

Bastwick's reiterations that his ordeal be read through a Roman lens reflected earlier arguments in print by himself and by Burton that their legal treatment superseded that of Paul's for tyranny because they were required to take the *ex officio* oath. The *ex officio* oath, a seventeenth-century legal invention, forced the accused to swear before God to truthfully answer all questions even before knowing the nature of the accusations against them. It left witnesses with the 'cruel trilemma' of '(1) refusing to take the oath, which constituted contempt and subjected the person to torture; (2) taking the oath and telling the truth about their religious beliefs, which, if heretical, were punishable by death; or (3) taking the oath and lying, which was also punishable by death' or which could constitute a mortal sin for the accused.[222] Both Burton and Bastwick challenged the legality of these requirements in print by appealing to the example of Paul under Roman law. In *An apology of an appeal* (1636), Burton condemned the 'illegality' of the proceedings against him by describing how the Apostle Paul, 'when he was most unjustly accused (as I am now) by *Ananias* the high Priest with the Elders' of sedition, was taken before 'Faelix the Governour a temporal Magistrate, knowing well, that Sedition was not an *Ecclesiasticall*, but a Civill offence, of which Paul there purged himselfe, without being put to any *Ex officio Oath*, putting them to prove the crime objected by witnesses'.[223] *The answer of John Bastwick* (1637) likewise argued that the *ex officio* oath was against the 'Law of Nature, the Law of Nations, the Law of God, and the Law of the Land', as seen when 'Paul was brought before Felix, hee taketh not an oath of him to accuse himselfe, but sayth, when thy accusers come I will heare thee'.[224] In 1641, Prynne would also reflect upon the legal practices of Star Chamber and the Court of High Commission as tyrannical even in comparison to the practices of pagan judges, including Pilate's trial of Jesus and the Roman heathens who tried Paul.[225]

---

[221] Ibid., D4r.

[222] Leonard Williams Levy, *Origins of the Fifth Amendment: The Right against Self-Incrimination* (New York: Oxford University Press, 1968), 1–2.

[223] Burton, *An apology of an appeale* (1636), 13–14.

[224] Bastwick, *The answer of John Bastvvick, Doctor of Phisicke, to the information of Sir Iohn Bancks Knight, Atturney universall* ... ([Leiden], 1637), 28.

[225] Prynne, *A new discovery of the prelates tyranny in their late prosecutions of Mr. William Pryn* ... , *Dr. Iohn Bastwick, ... an Mr. Henry Burton* ... (London, 1641), 25–27 and 30–32.

As promised before Star Chamber, Bastwick, Burton, and Prynne did fulfil the warning that their ordeal would be widely publicised through this lens. The realisation of this promise by Bastwick himself, however, became initially hampered by his island imprisonment, which entailed the most severe isolation of the three martyrs. In St. Mary's Castle in the Isles of Scilly, Bastwick 'was kept close prisoner two years and four months and for seven days and nights, never came into any bed, but lay in a dungeon, and endured unsufferable misery from inhumane jailors', denied all books, writing, visitors, and conversation with the gaolers.[226] As David Cressy notes, even following his release, Bastwick's polemical writings did not tend to dwell on the particulars of his imprisonment.[227] Yet in his reflections in 1645 on his treatment by the Caroline regime in *Independency not Gods ordinance*, Bastwick did provide some detail concerning his treatment through the lens of Paul's suffering. Having received the 'ruin of me, my wife, and many small children ... through the power and exorbitant authority of the Prelates', Bastwick recorded, he had supplicated King Charles, 'who was the *Caesar* to whom onely I could then appeal' to hear his humble petition. Bastwick requested that the King employ his prerogative to allow Bastwick to depart the kingdom with his family. King Charles refused Bastwick's plea, which led the physician to lament that '*Paul* found more favour from a Heathen Roman *Caesar*, then I had from a Christian King, a defender of the faith'. Having no further legal recourse, Bastwick was sent into exiled isolation, where he 'lived a living death and a dying life'.[228] From his 'sad experience', Bastwick learned that he could only hope in and maintain 'the prerogative royall of the King of Saints, & King of Kings, the Lord Jesus Christ' rather than hope in any earthly Caesar.[229]

When Bastwick's exile curtailed his publicity of mistreatment in 'Roman buffe', Burton took up the torch. In *A Narration of the Life of Mr. Henry Burton*, written in 1643 following his release from offshore incarceration on Guernsey, Burton offered twenty-seven reasons why his persecution not only rivalled the Apostle Paul's under Nero but even surpassed it. Although he considered himself 'but a dwarfe' to Paul in spiritual matters, Burton argued that he had suffered in the same manner

---

[226] HL/PO/JO/101/202, Parliamentary Archives, qtd. in Cressy, 'Puritan Martyrs in Island Prisons', 750.

[227] Cressy, 'Puritan Martyrs in Island Prisons', 750–51.

[228] John Bastwick, *Independency not Gods ordinance: or A treatise concerning church-government, occasioned by the distractions of these times*. (London, 1645), 3–4.

[229] Ibid., 5.

216 Emasculated Kingship

and degree as the apostle throughout his career, and yet received no help from governmental authorities, in contrast to Paul in his initial imprisonment under Nero. As Burton explained, '*Paul* was rescued from the hands of the cruell Jewes, High Priests, and Pharises, by his appealing to *Caesar*, a heathen Emperour, who protected him from their violence: but I, by appealing from the cruell Prelates, was not rescued from their bloody hands'.[230] Here Burton not only castigated the ecclesiastical authorities as worse than Pharisees, but effectively charged King Charles for failing in his duty to rescue Christians from cruel and unjust persecution. Burton went even further than this, however, declaring that his punishment from the Star Chamber ruling indeed further exceeded Paul's suffering under the tyrant Nero:

> *Paul* (if the story be true) suffered death, by being beheaded, with the sword, under *Nero* at *Rome:* And I suffered that on the pilary in *England,* my native Country, which was more painefull, and no lesse, if not more disgracefull, then such a death. For my head hung two full hours on the pilary, as if it had been separate from my body; and there were my two eares disgracefully and butcherly cut off with the hangmans knife, whereby my blood was abundantly shed, even to the expiring of the soule; all which was, both for the present, and afterwards in the time of healing, much more painfull, then the chopping off of the head with one stroke.[231]

According to Burton, his mutilation greatly exceeded Paul's suffering. Furthermore, Charles's government had surpassed Nero's tyranny by refusing to allow Burton to meet with friends, use pen, ink, and paper while imprisoned, or bring witnesses to testify on his behalf before the Star Chamber. Bastwick and Burton's reflections demonstrate how the condemnation of churchmen and high courts could translate into condemnations of the failures of the English king to protect and promote the true Gospel in England.

In 1640, after three years of imprisonment following their public mutilation, the Long Parliament invited the 'three martyrs' to return triumphantly to London. They re-entered through a celebratory pilgrimage, with their way 'so full of Coaches, Horses, and people to congratulate their returne, that they were forced to make stoppes, and could not ride scarce one mile an houre'.[232] Prynne and other witnesses recorded that

---

[230] *A Narration of the Life of Henry Burton* (London, 1634), 35.   [231] Ibid., 35–36.

[232] Prynne, *A new discovery of the prelates tyranny, in their late prosecutions of Mr William Pryn, an eminent Lawyer; Dr. Iohn Bastwick, a learned physitian; and Mr. Henry Burton, a reverent divine* (London, 1641), 114.

Neronian Corruption in Caroline England 217

these exuberant crowds honoured them with bonfires and bells, rosemary and bays, with the godly praising the Lord for their return. 'Oh blessed be the Lord for this day', the puritan Robert Woodford joyfully composed, 'for this day those holy living martyrs Mr. Burton and Mr. Prynne came to town, and the Lord's providence brought me out of the Temple to see them. My heart rejoiceth in the Lord for this day; it is even like the return of the captivity from Babylon.' Even those not sharing in the euphoric refrains reported, as did Thomas Hobbes, that the men arrived 'as if they had been let down from heaven'.[233] According to several witnesses, there had never been a show like this in London nor one with such an impressive multitude: one report estimated it attended by one hundred to three hundred coaches, one thousand to four thousand horse, as well as 'a world of foot'.[234] Following this triumphal entry, the House of Commons heard Prynne's testimony and in April 1640 declared the Star Chamber sentence against Prynne to be 'unjust' and 'illegal, and given without any just Cause or Ground'; by June, the Commons approved a bill regulating the Privy Council and abolishing Star Chamber altogether.[235]

The public suffering and triumph of Prynne, Bastwick, and Burton dramatised how the Caroline government and its instruments, including Star Chamber and ecclesiastical prelates, had enacted vicious persecution resembling even that great tyrant, Nero. Through ruminations upon religious and classical history – upon the most righteous Apostle Paul and the most tyrannical Emperor Nero – the godly could and did preach for the cleansing of the Laudian church, the reformation of unjust legal systems, and the needed purification of the English monarch. While these men repeatedly represented and understood their protests as targeting Laudian 'innovations' and defending the royal prerogative, their employment of Pauline precedent and Neronian language levelled a much wider charge of tyranny against the English courts and eventually the monarch himself; for, continued reflections by Burton and Bastwick upon their mistreatment, 'cloathed in Roman buffe', included significant descriptions

---

[233] Qtd in Cressy, *Travesties and Transgressions*, 230–31; Hobbes qtd in Ethyn Williams Kirby, *William Prynne: A Study in Puritanism* (Cambridge, MA: Harvard University Press, 1931), 53.

[234] Cressy, *Travesties and Transgressions*, 230–31.

[235] Bastwick's ruling was likewise reversed on 25 Feb. 1640, and Burton's on 24 Mar. that year. For Prynne, see 'House of Commons Journal Volume 2: 20 April 1641', *Journal of the House of Commons: volume 2: 1640–1643*, British History Online, [www.british-history.ac.uk/report.aspx? compid=9825&strquery=star chamber].

218 Emasculated Kingship

of the failure of King Charles, their 'Caesar', to defend them from religious persecution.[236]

Prynne, Bastwick, and Burton had openly characterised the Caroline Church and their king's failure to protect them as Neronian, and they were not alone in so doing; in 1639, the year before their triumph, Thomas May had similarly warned the public of Neronian tyranny through the printing of his previously acted *Tragedy of Julia Agrippina*. What Nero's stories provided for these writers was a powerful and imaginative portrait of tyranny, which led to the destruction of family, court, church, and kingdom. An emasculated monarch, they argued, disordered political society and perverted religious belief and practice, thereby leaving subjects corrupted in a fallen world. In later years, puritan writers employed the story of Nero to decry the corruption of church and legal processes in England, which left subjects to be persecuted for the 'true religion'. Neronian history contested and deconstructed the image of sacred monarchy in dangerous, significant, and very public ways. Its repeated invocation should be considered as one cultural and intellectual influence on the origins of the civil wars which would soon erupt in Britain.

---

[236] Archbishop Laud had insisted during their ordeal that their quarrel with the bishops also implicated the King: '['T]is not we only, that is, the Bishops, that are struct at, but through our sides, Your Majesty, Your Honour, Your Safety, Your Religion, is impeached'. William Laud, *A Speech develiered in the Starr-Chamber* (London, 1637), sig. A4r. See Alistair Bellany, 'The Embarrassment of Libels: Perceptions and Representations of Verse Libelling in Early Stuart England', in *The Politics of the Public Sphere in Early Modern England* (Manchester: Manchester University Press 2012), 144–67, esp. 148.

PART II

The Masculine Republic

Introduction to Part II

The first half of this book has argued that the Roman past provided significant models of manliness and of masculine failure for early Stuart Englishmen. Classical histories, political treatises, and imaginative writings frequently portrayed idealised images of masculinity through stories of men excellent in the activities of war and of governance in the commonwealth and household, and they simultaneously underscored masculine failure and tyranny as the inadequate or vicious performance of men in these realms.

As we saw in Part I, these classical languages of tyranny and codes of masculinity were malleable; their appropriation and application helped Englishmen analyse and generate criticisms of contemporary monarchy in a number of contexts and textual productions across the Stuart period. They afforded statesmen, courtiers, poets, and thinkers a rich, shared language to craft overlapping and competing visions of masculinity, and to level significant charges against the Stuart kings as failed practitioners of *virtus*. According to classical exempla and treatises, tyranny [*tyrannus ex parte exercitii*] could take a number of forms, including the tyrant who rules by force in a lawless manner, the tyrant who is governed by his lower appetites, or the tyrant who seeks private over public gain. Several of the classical tyrants frequently canvassed in early Stuart England, including Tarquin, Appius Claudius, and Nero, were portrayed as exhibiting all three types of failure, and as degenerating thereby into a bestial, slavish, effeminate, and/or petulant condition. Through these classical models and through their own experiences of Stuart rule, English statesmen believed tyranny undermined the manliness of subjects, robbing them of political and/or militaristic activity and reducing them to flattery and self-debasement. Roman exempla, including Junius Brutus who opposed Tarquin and Virginius who overthrew Appius, presented violent revolution and the creation of republican rule as plausible solutions to ending the

222 The Masculine Republic

emasculating defilement of tyranny and restoring *virtus* to the commonwealth.

A period of extraordinary 'gender trouble' in England, the English civil wars became an ideal environment for the continuation and expansion of classical languages of masculinity and tyranny. As Cavaliers and Round-heads went to war, they denounced their rivals as failed, inadequate, effeminate men, and women engaged in unprecedented political and religious activity.[1] Contestations of power and of gender played out on the battlefield and in a developing 'public sphere', which included the explosion of printing and petitioning, the consumption of domestic news, and the expansion of spaces for intellectual debate, in part due to the collapse of censorship.[2] Oppositional groups widely debated masculine standards of rule and openly trumpeted their disdain to the public through the milieu of news, pamphlets, treatises, and literature.

Due to the expansion of printing and of literary *genres* in this significant period, writers opposing the Stuart regime no longer needed to adopt classical history to present veiled criticisms of the monarch or court. Yet more than ever, statesmen turned to classical history alongside Scripture and other sources of authority to understand their momentous political moment, to guide and advise their actions, and to justify and publicly defend themselves in a country divided and war torn. Political theorists and pamphleteers relied heavily upon classical models as they provided almost the only models for non-monarchical governance in seventeenth-century England.[3] As we will see, alongside Biblical and juridical

[1] As a description of the 1640s, the phrase 'gender trouble' is drawn from Mary Fissell's *Vernacular Bodies: The Politics of Reproduction in Early Modern England* (Oxford: Oxford University Press, 2004), 90. See also Ann Hughes, *Gender and the English Revolution* (New York: Routledge 2012); Diane Purkiss, *Literature, Gender and Politics during the English Civil War* (Cambridge: Cambridge University Press, 2010); Teresa Feroli, *Political Speaking Justified: Women Prophets and the English Revolution* (Newark: University of Delaware Press, 2006); Amanda Jane Whiting, *Women and Petitioning in the Seventeenth-century English Revolution: Deference, Difference, and Dissent*, Late Medieval and Early Modern Studies 25 (Turnhout: Brepols, 2015); Katherine Romack, *Women and the Poetics of Dissent in the English Revolution* (London: Taylor & Francis, 2016).

[2] Peter Lake and Steve Pincus, 'Introduction: Rethinking the public sphere in early modern England', in *The Politics of the Public Sphere in Early Modern England* (Manchester: Manchester University Press 2012), 1–30; Jason Peacey, *Print and Public Politics in the English Revolution* (Cambridge: Cambridge University Press, 2013); David Zaret, 'Petitions', in *Origins of Democratic Culture: Printing, Petitions, and the Public Sphere in Early Modern England* (Princeton, NJ: Princeton University Press, 2000), 217–65; Joad Raymond, *The Invention of the Newspaper: English Newsbooks 1641–1649* (Oxford: Clarendon, 1996).

[3] English republicans tended to favour the model of Rome over Venice (as Machiavelli described the dichotomy), and the idea of a large republic over that of a small republic. This made the contemporary examples of Venice, the Netherlands, and Geneva less desirable models, as did, in the case of the Netherlands, the Dutch support of Charles I. See Jonathan Scott, 'Empire', in

The Masculine Republic

frameworks, languages drawn from classical stories served as an important currency for debating, contesting, legitimising, defaming, and supporting political actors openly and directly. Classicised models of manhood and tyranny also became more commonplace in cheap print, including broadsides.[4] In the 1640s and 1650s there was therefore an expansion of the appropriation of classical history, including the number and types of writers who employed it.

Part II seeks primarily to defend and explicate two arguments. The first is that classical republican thought in England developed in part as a solution to the perceived problem of emasculating tyranny experienced under the Stuart regime. This argument aligns well with previous studies which have sought to demonstrate the centrality of classical humanism and humanist literary culture for the early development of English republican thought in seventeenth-century England.[5] David Norbrook, for instance, has demonstrated the energetic republican culture that thrived through literary writings, and especially poetry, derived from Lucan and other classical authors, across the seventeenth century.[6] Arguing for the presence of republican or quasi-republican political thought decades prior to civil war often requires the identification of republicanism as a language corresponding to particular themes, ideas, and affiliations, including theories of citizenship, public virtue, true nobility, and a belief in institutions to circumscribe the authority of a central power. Blair Worden has warned

---

Commonwealth Principles: Republican Writing of the English Revolution (Cambridge: Cambridge University Press, 2004), 210–32; Idem., 'Classical Republicanism in Seventeenth-Century England and the Netherlands', in *Republicanism: A Shared European Heritage, volume I*, ed. Martin van Gelderen and Skinner (Cambridge: Cambridge University Press, 2002), 61–84, esp. 70–71; David Armitage, 'John Milton: Poet against Empire', in *Milton and Republicanism* (Cambridge: Cambridge University Press, 1995), 206–25.

[4] See, e.g., Anon., *The Invincible Weapon, or Truths triumph over Errors* (London? 1647), which depicts a host of Roman Emperors drowning in the sea, or Anon., *A Brief Cronology of Great Britain* (London, 1656), which includes a section of '*Brief observations upon the untimely ends of the Roman Emperours*'.

[5] Markku Peltonen, for example, sought to demonstrate how 'a theory of citizenship, public virtue, and true nobility based essentially on the classical humanist and republican traditions, was taken up, studied and fully endorsed throughout the period'. See Peltonen, *Classical Humanism and Republicanism in English Political Thought, 1570–1640* (Cambridge: Cambridge University Press, 1995), 12. See also Andrew Hadfield, 'Republicanism in Sixteenth- and Seventeenth-Century Britain', in *British Political Thought in History, Literature, and Theory, 1500–1800*, ed. David Armitage (Cambridge: Cambridge University Press, 2006), 111–28; Patrick Collinson, *Elizabethans* (London: Bloomsbury, 2003), 1–58; Hadfield, *Shakespeare and Republicanism* (Cambridge: Cambridge University Press, 2005).

[6] David Norbrook, *Writing the English Republic: Poetry, Rhetoric and Politics, 1627–1660* (Cambridge: Cambridge University Press, 1999).

224   The Masculine Republic

that such a position runs the risk of creating an over-inclusive understanding of the concept, which may, for example, classify any discussion of 'virtue' as republicanism.[7]

The claim of this book – that classical republican thought in England developed in response to classicised understandings of perceived Stuart tyranny – largely agrees with the positions of Norbrook, Markku Peltonen, and others that a significant classical heritage began shaping the development of republican thought in the early seventeenth century. By seeking to connect the growth of republican thought to the development of a perceived crisis of monarchical tyranny as masculine failure, however, the book does recognise the development of republican thought and languages as uneven, complex, and often limited prior to the civil wars. Part I sought to demonstrate that classicised and gendered portrayals of tyranny in the early seventeenth century very often included reflections upon virtuous government, citizenship, and the rule of law drawn from classical republican texts and histories. It appears from these texts that languages of republicanism became operative, especially for the criticism of monarchy, prior to the English civil wars, and that these languages helped make the English Revolution possible because it was culturally and politically conceivable.[8]

The second, and most central, argument of Part II is a bold one: that the fundamental purpose of classical republicanism was to realise manhood – to allow men (of a certain status) to develop fully as rational, free, and virtuous individuals. This argument is clearly related to the first, but it seeks to provide a more foundational claim for the history of political thought, and one that would potentially shape our understanding of classical republican thought beyond the borders of England. Classical republics sought to afford the aristocratic man (or *vir*, as opposed to a lesser male, boy, woman, or slave) the authority to rule over himself and others, and to exercise his duties for the public good through multiple arenas – the household, the senate house, the battlefield. English republicans sought to emulate this model for the restoration and preservation of English manliness. As in the classical world, where Roman conceptions of

---

[7] Blair Worden, 'Republicanism, Regicide and Republic: The English Experience', in *Republicanism: A Shared European Heritage, Volume 1: Republicanism and Constitutionalism in Early Modern Europe*, ed. Martin van Gelderen and Quentin Skinner (Cambridge: Cambridge University Press, 2002), 307–27.

[8] I have drawn this formulation of revolution as possible because conceivable from Roger Chartier, *The Cultural Origins of the French Revolution*, trans. Lydia G. Cochrane (Durham, NC: Duke University Press, 1991), 2 and 169–70.

virtus most often favoured martial acts of bravery as truly masculine while Greek conceptions more often discussed a broader category of moral excellences,[9] the focus of English republican theorists on which virtue or activity most fundamentally defined *virtus* within the republic could betray some important differences. We will see these variations on display in the chapters that follow.

Historical scholarship over the past half-century has debated whether political liberty in the republican tradition should be defined positively as active political participation in the political process of self-determination, with civic virtue and citizen activity being intrinsic components of republicanism; or, whether republican political liberty should best be characterised negatively as freedom and independence from arbitrary or uncontrolled power. In the former model, articulated by J. G. A. Pocock and other historians concerned with languages of civic humanism, republican virtues (i.e. courage, temperance, prudence, patriotism, and service to the common good) result from political participation and republican institutions and also support these arrangements. Pocock's magisterial work *The Machiavellian Moment* formulated classical republicanism as a political and ethical vocabulary, drawn principally from Aristotle and Polybius, which considered how citizens could seek to become realised as flourishing humans through the active practice of virtue in a political community. Advocates of the *vivere civile* – or the 'way of life

---

[9] As Myles McDonnell's work has shown, Roman conceptions of *virtus*, or manliness, more often prized the warrior above the orator; prior to the first century in republican Rome, *virtus* only denoted martial courage. The qualities often paired with this term included those praising martial reputation, or those connected to physical and active labour. In contrast, the Greek conception of manliness enjoyed a broader semantic range, tied principally to the concept of ἀρετή [*aretê*], or character excellence, of which martial courage, often expressed as ἀνδρεία [*andreia*], represented only one aspect. By the fifth century, even the concept of ἀνδρεία [*andreia*] transformed from being defined solely 'as an observable act of facing death on the battlefield' to a collective political conception in Platonic and Aristotelian thought as the pursuit of excellence and the avoidance of public shame indexed to the human emotion of fear. Whereas the Greek term ἀρετή [*aretê*] had a long history of encompassing the intellectual and moral virtues in Greek literature and culture, the Latin term *virtus* did not denote a conception of ethical and political excellence beyond martial prowess until, at the earliest, the late Roman Republic in the first century BC; and most often, the republican author who employed the term *virtus* in defence of this broader conception was Cicero. Notably, though, even Cicero highly praised courage as truly masculine, and after Cicero's death, physical courage or martial prowess remained the primary definition of *virtus* and the central element of manliness in Rome, including throughout the late Republican period and into the Empire. See Myles McDonnell, *Roman Manliness: Virtus and the Roman Republic* (Cambridge: Cambridge University Press, 2006), 130; McDonnell, 'Roman Men and Greek Virtue', in *Andreia: Studies in Manliness and Courage in Classical Antiquity*, ed. Ralph M. Rosen and Ineke Sluiter (Leiden: Brill, 2003), 235–61, esp. 235–36; Karen Bassi, 'The Semantics of Manliness in Ancient Greece', in *Andreia: Studies in Manliness and Courage*, 25–58, esp. 26, 50–56.

226   The Masculine Republic

given over to civic concerns and the (ultimately political) activity of citizenship' – committed themselves to the development of political communities that supported and encouraged citizens to exercise their virtue through active participation in communal governance (the *vita activa*).[10] Political liberty on this model entails the *freedom to* engage in civil society and realise one's human potential.

In contrast, the latter model of republicanism rejects a perfectionist political philosophy, arguing that civic virtue and political participation are instrumental to preserving political liberty, understood as non-domination, rather than intrinsic to it. Quentin Skinner's extensive scholarship has emphasised the significance of liberty rather than virtue in the republican tradition, and the neo-Roman inheritance that afforded early modern theorists a negative conception of liberty as non-domination; positing the *civis* or free subject as 'someone who is not under the dominion of anyone else [i.e. a slave], but is *sui iuris*, capable of acting in their own right'.[11] Skinner articulated a 'third concept of liberty', not as 'absence of interference' but 'absence of dependence'. In this third concept, 'freedom is restricted not only by actual interference or the threat of it, but also by the mere knowledge that we are living in dependence on the goodwill of others ... Knowing that we are free to do or forbear only because someone else has chosen not to stop us is what reduces us to servitude'.[12] On this model, political liberty entails *freedom from*

---

[10] J. G. A. Pocock, *The Machiavellian Moment: Florentine Political Thought and the Atlantic Republican Tradition* (Princeton, NJ: Princeton University Press, 1975), 56–57. A similar view of republicanism as positive liberty was articulated by Hannah Arendt in 1968: 'If, then, we understand the political in the sense of the polis, its end or *raison d'être* would be to establish and keep in existence a space where freedom as virtuosity can appear.' See 'What Is Freedom?' in *Between Past and Future: Eight Exercises in Political Thought* (New York: Penguin (reprint) 2006), 153. For a more recent articulation of republicanism as positive liberty in alignment with Pocock, see Blair Worden, *Republicanism, Liberty, and Commercial Society, 1649–1776*, ed. David Wootton (Stanford: Stanford University Press, 1994), chapters 1–4.

[11] Quentin Skinner, 'Classical liberty, Renaissance translation, and the English civil war', in *Visions of Politics: Renaissance Virtues*, vol. II (Cambridge: Cambridge University Press, 2002), 308–43, esp. 313. For an excellent discussion of this view in the early seventeenth century, see 'John Milton and the Politics of Slavery', in *Visions of Politics*, vol. II, 286–307. See also Skinner, *Liberty before Liberalism* (Cambridge: Cambridge University Press, 1998).

[12] Skinner, 'A Third Concept of Liberty', in *Proceedings of the British Academy* 117 (2002): 237–68, esp. 247–48. Philip Pettit has sought to develop this conception of republican negative liberty into a contemporary political doctrine. See *Republicanism: A Theory of Freedom and Government* (Oxford: Clarendon Press, 1997). See also Maurizio Viroli, *Republicanism*, trans. Antony Shugaar (New York: Hill and Wang, 2002). For historical interpretations of republicanism which fit this model, see Viroli, *Machiavelli* (Oxford: Oxford University Press, 1998); Martin Dzelzainis, 'Milton's Classical Republicanism', in *Milton and Republicanism*, ed. David Armitage, Armand Himy, and Quentin Skinner (Cambridge: Cambridge University Press, 1995); and Dzelzainis,

The Masculine Republic

domination, and civic virtue and political participation are understood as instrumental (rather than intrinsic) to serving political liberty, as they aid in securing and preserving independence from arbitrary rule.

The tension between these accounts of liberty depends very much upon one's understanding of the classical republican heritage as either Greek, Roman, or a Greco-Roman syncretism. Earlier scholarly accounts of the republican tradition that favoured positive liberty often viewed 'classical' republicanism through a Greco-Roman conflation, focusing primarily upon arguments for the exercise of political virtue and the constitutional form of the mixed regime as drawn from Aristotle, Cicero, and Polybius. Pocock treated ancient Roman political thought as closely following Greek political conceptions of citizenship, and sixteenth and seventeenth-century republicans as deriving these principles directly and indirectly through the Greco-Roman tradition from Aristotle through Boethius. Scholars have challenged this Greco-Roman amalgam within the republican tradition in a number of ways. Skinner's model of negative political liberty as non-domination has drawn upon a distinctive Roman tradition from Justinian, Cicero, Sallust, Livy, and Tacitus. Other scholars have emphasised the ideological underpinnings of Greek and Roman political thought as deeply antagonistic, especially in regard to their views of justice.[13]

Whether conceiving of republican political liberty as positive or negative, or as Greek or Roman, republicanism historically has carried great restrictions on citizenship, often tied to gender, age, freed status, and property. Conceptions of the good life in ancient political texts often rested upon a notion of elite, patriarchal, and militaristic masculinity. The debate concerning whether civic virtue and political participation is an intrinsic or instrumental component of republican liberty, thereby, is very significant, for it raises the question as to whether sexism, elitism, patriarchalism, and militarism are necessary, inherent, or logical consequences of republican thought, or whether they were merely contingent historical prejudices that can (and should) be shed in contemporary republican theory.[14] Put differently: are these undesirable and even

---

'Republicanism', in *A Companion to Milton*, ed. Thomas Corns (Oxford: Blackwell, 2001), 294–308.

[13] See Eric Nelson, *The Greek Tradition in Republican Thought*, Eric Nelson, *The Greek Tradition in Republican Thought* (Cambridge: Cambridge University Press, 2004), 13–15.

[14] Frank Lovett, 'Republicanism', in The Stanford Encyclopedia of Philosophy (Spring 2017 Edition), ed. Edward N. Zalta, URL https://plato.stanford.edu/archives/spr2017/entries/republicanism/. See also Maurice Goldsmith, 'Republican Liberty Considered', *History of Political Thought* 21.3 (Mar. 2000): 543–59.

228 The Masculine Republic

dangerous prejudices essential to republican thought, or accidental to historical time and place?

Historians and political theorists have usually focused upon these debates concerning political liberty and civic virtue within the republican tradition while neglecting the discourses of gender and masculinity inherent to the historical development of republican thought. Although gender has been a 'persistent and recurrent way of enabling the signification of power in the West',[15] it has remained largely unstudied in accounts of the republican tradition. Scholars have, of course, often noted the traditional exclusion of women from active republican citizenship, whether in Greece, Rome, England, France, or early America, and they have studied the distinctions made in these later societies between 'active' male citizens and 'passive' female ones,[16] but they have often not paid heed to the masculine discourses of power central to republican thought. The tendency has either been to treat conceptions of 'manhood' as 'personhood', and thereby to ignore the exclusionary foundation of republicanism, or to argue that such sexist historical prejudices can be overcome by contemporaries through a suitably universalised articulation of republicanism.

As an historical study of the development of classical republican thought, this book has sought to demonstrate the centrality of debates concerning manhood in oppositional politics and languages of tyranny in seventeenth-century England. Rather than obscure gendered languages of power, its aim has been to highlight how deeply gendered and exclusionary the language of politics in England was in this period, and how very significant the classical heritage was to English conceptualisations of masculinity, masculine power, and tyranny. Part II argues that English classical republicanism in the 1650s cannot be understood fully unless historians recover the achievement of manliness as a fundamental driver of its theories and a central tenet of its formulation, for the fundamental purpose of classical republicanism just was the realisation of manhood for its citizens.

---

[15] Joan Wallach Scott, *Gender and the Politics of History*, revised edition (New York: Columbia University Press, 1999), 46.

[16] See, e.g., Joan B. Landes, *Women and the Public Sphere in the Age of the French Revolution* (Ithaca and London: Cornell University Press, 1988); Lynn Hunt, 'Male Virtue and Republican Motherhood', in *The French Revolution and the Creation of Modern Political Culture*, ed. Keith Michael Baker (Bingley: Emerald, 1994), 195–210; Linda K. Kerber, *Women of the Republic: Intellect & Ideology in Revolutionary America* (Chapel Hill: University of North Carolina Press, 1980).

The Masculine Republic

Attending to gender in English republican thought, and within the classical tradition that shaped it, provides a context for understanding the relationship between positive and negative conceptions of liberty within the republican tradition. While manhood, by definition, required non-domination in the classical world, proving one's masculinity in both ancient and early modern society required the performance of authority and virtue within the private, household realm and the political realm. Recovering the centrality of gender in the republican tradition, thereby, points the historian towards a conception of republican liberty as positive liberty. It has been persuasively argued that the republican and free male citizen could not be under the domination of another, but the citizen's realisation of manhood further required that he exert authority not only over himself and his lower passions but also over those then deemed to be lesser individuals – young, female, servile – through active participation in governance and the practice of virtue.

The following chapters seek to provide evidence for these two arguments through the writings of noted republican authors, most principally John Milton and Marchamont Nedham, and through lesser-explored writers and texts that sought to question or to fashion Oliver Cromwell as a potential republican solution to the problem of Stuart tyranny. These chapters consider how classicised languages of masculine power and tyranny expanded and transformed within the political culture of Britain more broadly, and in English republican culture specifically, during the 1640s and 1650s. As writers sought to create a commonwealth which would restore the masculinity of English citizens and government, they turned to the classical republican tradition and its aim of realising manliness, or *virtus*, in its active male citizens. Attaining *virtus* and a stable republic was a highly difficult endeavour, for both were fragile and easily corrupted. English republican writers, like their forbears, debated whether manhood and the republic should best be pursued and achieved through political activity within balanced, republican institutions or through grander promises of conquest and empire. In the end, however, these writers would face significant disappointment in the English republican project, as Cromwell and his protectorate would not fulfil the rule of manhood so eagerly longed for in England.

CHAPTER 5

John Milton, Marriage, and the Realisation of Republican Manhood

> The base degree to which I now am fall'n,
> These rags, this grinding, is not yet so base
> As was my former servitude, ignoble,
> Unmanly, ignominious, infamous,
> True slavery, and that blindness worse then this,
> That saw not how degeneratly I serv'd.[1]

When John Milton's Samson bemoans his fate in *Samson Agonistes* (c. 1671), he cries against his marriage with Dalila – his enslavement to an idolatrous woman – as even more degrading than the physical chains which bind him as a slave. 'True slavery', he claims, was that which he had suffered through 'degenerat' and 'misyoked' marriage to a heathen; his passivity and inability to escape such bondage, due to his untamed lust, had proven him incapable of exercising the manly attributes of rationality, temperance, and civic virtue necessary to remain free. Indeed, in *Samson Agonistes*, Milton's Samson regains a Stoic posture only through accepting his physical chains and seeking sacrificial death as a just ransom for his own masculine and moral failings.

Milton's tragic adaptation of the Biblical story of Samson and Dalila from the book of Judges significantly altered the original story to emphasise the gendered and political bondage of bad marriage.[2] Written over a decade after the Restoration, it reflected a long career of promoting masculinity and good marriage as significant cornerstones of liberty and virtue. Despite the many fruitful studies which have investigated Milton's conceptualisations of gender, sexuality, and marriage, influential studies of Milton's republican thought have often neglected the significant gendered

---

[1] *Samson Agonistes*, II.414–19.
[2] Rosanna Cox, 'Milton, Marriage, and the Politics of Gender', in *John Milton: Life, Writing, and Reputation*, ed. Paul Hammond and Blair Worden (Oxford: Oxford University Press, 2010), 125–45, esp. 141–42.

231

232 The Masculine Republic

languages and concepts which Milton employed at the heart of his most famous political writings.[3] Milton's conceptions of liberty, and his adverse descriptions of crouching bondage or tyrannical enslavement, adopted a classical vocabulary itself steeped in particular masculinist ideals.

Through a case study of Milton, this chapter offers an initial argument concerning the character of English classical republicanism proposed in this book: first, that classical republican thought in England developed as a solution to the perceived problem of emasculating tyranny experienced under the Stuart regime; and second, that English classical republicanism in the 1650s cannot be understood fully unless historians recover the achievement of manliness as a fundamental driver of its theories and a central tenet of its formulation. For Milton, as well as for other English authors steeped in the classical tradition, the fundamental purpose of classical republicanism just was the restoration and realisation of manhood for its citizens.

5.1 Milton and Manhood

John Milton developed his understanding of gender and of masculinity from scriptural and classicised sources. Much has been written concerning Milton's view of the relation between the sexes by focusing upon his representation of the paradisal couple in *Paradise Lost*. In Book IV of the epic poem, Milton introduces Adam and Eve through a description of Satan gazing upon them in the garden. The archfiend discovers the original man and woman in the bower united in 'naked Majestie' in the 'image of their glorious Maker', compatible and harmonious, and yet distinct in physiology and psychology, forming a seemingly natural hierarchy:

> Two of far nobler shape erect and tall,
> Godlike erect, with native Honour clad
> In naked Majestie seemd Lords of all,

[3] See, e.g., the collection of essays in *Milton and Gender*, ed. Catherine Gimelli Martin (Cambridge: Cambridge University Press, 2004); Sharon Achinstein, '"A Law in This Matter to Himself": Contextualizing Milton's Divorce Tracts', in *The Oxford Handbook of Milton*, ed. Nicholas McDowell and Nigel Smith (Oxford: Oxford University Press, 2011), 174–85; Diane Purkiss, 'Whose Liberty? The Rhetoric of Milton's Divorce Tracts', in *The Oxford Handbook of Milton*; Mary Nyquist, 'The Genesis of Gendered Subjectivity in the Divorce Tracts and *Paradise Lost*', in *Re-membering Milton: Essays on the Texts and Traditions*, ed. Nyquist and Margaret W. Ferguson (New York: Methuen, 1987), 99–127; Su Fang Ng, *Literature and the Politics of the Family* (Cambridge: Cambridge University Press, 2007); Joseph Wittreich, *Feminist Milton* (Ithaca, NY: Cornell University Press, 1988); James Grantham Turner, *One Flesh: Paradisal Marriage and Sexual Relations in the Age of Milton* (Oxford: Clarendon, 1987); Julia M. Walker, ed. *Milton and the Idea of Woman* (Urbana-Champagne: University of Illinois Press, 1988).

Milton, Marriage, & Realisation of Republican Manhood   233

> And worthie seemd, for in thir looks Divine
> The image of thir glorious Maker shon,
> Truth, wisdome, Sanctitude severe and pure,
> Severe, but in true filial freedom plac't;
> Whence true autoritie in men; though both
> Not equal, as thir sex not equal seemd;
> For contemplation hee and valour formd,
> For softness shee and sweet attractive Grace,
> Hee for God only, shee for God in him:
> His fair large Front and Eye sublime declar'd
> Absolute rule; and Hyacinthin Locks
> Round from his parted forelock manly hung
> Clustring, but not beneath his shoulders broad:
> Shee as a vail down to the slender waste
> Her unadorned golden tresses wore
> Dissheveld, but in wanton ringlets wav'd
> As the Vine curls her tendrils, which impli'd
> Subjection, but requir'd with gentle sway,
> And by her yielded, by him best receivd,
> Yielded with coy submission, modest pride,
> And sweet reluctant amorous delay (IV 288–311).

In this famous passage – controversial even in the seventeenth century – Milton drew upon Ovidian and Homeric tropes to depict Eve and womankind, with her physical frailty and untamed sexual passion, as naturally yielding to the superior 'contemplation' and 'valour' of Adam and mankind.[4] This reading of Genesis within *Paradise Lost*, as well as in Milton's earlier divorce tracts, places Eve as secondary to Adam in creation, and as an offering to fulfil Adam's 'rational burning', or need for fellowship. Adam here is a 'masculine, autonomous, articulate' individual; Eve is gift and helpmate to him.[5]

Adam's outward state – 'His fair large Front and Eye sublime', 'forelock manly hung', and 'shoulders broad' – reflect his internal rationality, valour, and fitness for 'Absolute rule'. These characteristics provide a significant contrast with Eve's 'slender waste', 'unadorned golden tresses' worn 'Dissheveld' and in 'wanton ringlets', feminine qualities which represented the potential sexual disorder of women. Moreover, the portrayal of Adam as

---

[4] For its echo of the classical tradition, see John Guillory, 'Milton, Narcissism, Gender: On the Genealogy of Male Self-Esteem', in *Critical Essays on John Milton*, ed. Christopher Kendrick (New York: GK Hall, 1995), 165–93. Most contentious for the earliest editors was Milton's description of Adam as created 'for God only, shee for God in him', a line which seemingly denied Eve direct access to her maker. See Cox, 'Milton, Marriage, and the Politics of Gender', 128.

[5] Nyquist, 'The Genesis of Gendered Subjectivity', 112–15.

234 The Masculine Republic

virile, free, and upright provided a contrast with male creatures in abject bondage, who due to their own moral failings or unfree state perpetually bow and cringe in abject postures much like the fallen angels of *Paradise Lost*.[6]

In this portrayal, Adam may have been created upright and free, but Milton in *Paradise Lost* and throughout his writings emphasised that men only remain as such through virtuous self-management and rationality. His reflections upon free will in *Paradise Lost*, for example, include a speech by God the Father explaining that he created Adam 'just and right, / Sufficient to have stood, though free to fall'. This passage describes not only human will but also reason as 'choice'; although humans have been formed 'free', they may also 'enthrall themselves' through vicious or irrational choices.[7] Milton summarised this position years earlier in *Areopagitica* (1644):

> Many there be that complain of divin Providence for suffering *Adam* to transgresse, foolish tongues! when God gave him reason, he gave him freedom to choose, for reason is but choosing; he had bin else a meer artificiall *Adam*, such as *Adam* as he is in the motions. We our selves esteem not of that obedience, or love, or gift, which is of force: God therefore left him free, set before him a provoking object, ever almost in his eyes: herein consisted his merit, herein the right of his reward, the praise of his abstinence. Wherefore did he creat passions within us, pleasures round about us, but that these rightly temper'd are the very ingredients of vertu?[8]

For Milton in both of these writings, virtuous manhood entailed rational choice and temperance in the face of temptation; a man's outward state of liberty became tethered to his inward state of virtue. The opposite of liberty would be licence, a movement of the soul motivated by the passions rather than reason.

While *Paradise Lost* initially presented Adam and defined his nascent masculine qualities through the binary of Eve and femininity, Milton mainly exercised his pen throughout his career defining masculinity not against femininity but against depictions of corrupted and failed forms of masculinity, often employing oppositional languages: mature manhood as opposed to boyhood; free manhood as opposed to the enslaved; rational

---

[6] David Lowenstein, 'The Radical Religious Politics of *Paradise Lost*', in *A New Companion to Milton*, ed. Thomas N. Corns (Chichester: Wiley Blackwell, 2016), 376–90, esp. 378.

[7] For the entire speech, see *Paradise Lost* III.95–128

[8] *Complete Prose Works of John Milton*. 10 volumes, gen. ed. Don M. Wolfe (New Haven: Yale University Press, 1953–82), II.527. Hereafter *CPW*.

Milton, Marriage, & Realisation of Republican Manhood 235

and temperate manhood as opposed to the bestial.[9] Within these dichotomies, Milton's writings frequently presented an elision of the concepts of the enslaved and the bestial, whether referring to an immoral and irrational state of depravity which enslaves men to their passions and makes them beasts, or referring to a political state of tyranny in which men lose their liberty and become as beasts of burden. In *Of Reformation* (1641), for example, Milton likened the activities of church prelates to ancient tyrants like Cyrus who enslaved their peoples through stoking their excessive passions and lower desires:

> Well knows every wise Nation that their Liberty consists in manly and honest labours, in sobriety and rigorous honour to the Marriage Bed, which in both Sexes should be bred up from chast hopes to loyall Enjoyments; and when the people slacken and fall to loosenes, and riot, then doe they as much as if they laid downe their necks for some wily Tyrant to get up and ride. Thus learnt *Cyrus* to tame the *Lydians*, whom by Armes he could not, whilst they kept themselves from Luxury; with one easy Proclamation to set up *Stews*, dancing, feasting, & dicing he made them soone his slaves. I know not what drift the *Prelats* had, whose Brokers they were to prepare, and supple us either for a Forreigne Invasion or Domestick oppression; but this I am sure they took the ready way to despoile us both of *manhood* and *grace* at once, ... [10]

These overlapping languages of slavish and bestial corruption reflected classical discourses, which frequently characterised the 'natural slave' as inferior in mental and moral qualities, and as a kind of 'thing' (κτῆμα) to be owned like a beast of burden.[11] Moreover, the warning that the vice of luxury in particular could corrupt individual men and enslave a free commonwealth was repeated frequently across the classical texts which populated grammar school and university curricula, from Suetonius and Tacitus's descriptions of the corrupted and corrupting Caesars, to Livy's warning of the decline of the Roman empire due to Asiatic luxury, to Sallust's account of the besetting Roman vices of avarice and ambition.[12]

---

[9] See Gina Hausknecht, 'The Gender of Civic Virtue', in *Milton and Gender*, 19–33, esp. 22–23.

[10] *CPW*, I.588.

[11] Although Roman legal statutes represented slavery as a legal rather than natural institution, Roman as well as Greek art very often type-casted slaves as beasts of burden in their comportment and rational capabilities. See J. Albert Harrill, 'Invective against Paul (2 Cor. 10:10), the Physiognomics of the Ancient Slave Body, and the Greco-Roman Rhetoric of Manhood', in *Antiquity and Humanity: Essays on Ancient Religion and Philosophy*, ed. Adela Yarbro Collins and Margaret M. Mitchell (Tübingen: Mohr Siebeck, 2001), 189–213, esp. 192–93.

[12] Suetonius, *Lives of the Caesars, Volume II*, trans. J. C. Rolfe, Loeb Classical Library 38 (Cambridge, MA: Harvard University Press, 1914), esp. 240–55. There are many such passages in Tacitus. See, e.g., Tacitus, *Histories: Books 4–5. Annals: Books 1–3,* trans. Clifford H. Moore and John Jackson,

236 The Masculine Republic

In Greek philosophy, Plato and Aristotle both described luxury negatively as that which leads to softness and undermines courage and endurance. Indeed, the word for courage in classical Greek (*andreia*) held a close relationship to the word for man (*anêr/andra*): to be courageous and brave was to act like a man. In weakening man, luxury undermined manliness.[13]

To protect men from the threat of enslavement and degeneration, Milton's writings decades before *Paradise Lost* frequently urged his fellow men to recognise and to pursue the conditions and activities necessary to become realised fully as rational, free, and upright men of virtue. He adopted an ethical outlook which promoted godliness, reason, and temperance as those virtues which equipped men to live rightly, and castigated idolatry, ignorance, intemperance, and extravagant luxury as emasculating men and enslaving them to brutish appetites.[14] This ethical structure was a broadly Scriptural and classicised one, and Milton was especially indebted to Platonic moral philosophy, understanding the soul through the tripartite division of reason, will, and appetite, and applying this doctrine to understand the relationship between the individual and political society: justice as the harmony of the soul and the city, tyranny as the disordered rule of appetite over reason.[15] From these classical sources Milton often focused on the virtues which aided men in temperate living, in the use of reason, and in the governance of self and others – those which, in short, prepared men for the roles of orator and father – rather than the virtues associated with classical warriors. In a letter to Richard Jones from 21 September 1656, Milton made this distinction explicit by admonishing his former pupil to be weary of power built upon force rather than virtue: 'The victories of princes, which you praise, and similar matters in which force prevails I would not have you admire too much, now that

---

Loeb Classical Library 249 (Cambridge, MA: Harvard University Press, 1931) esp. 602–9. See also Livy, *History of Rome, Volume I: Books 1–2*, trans. B. O. Foster, Loeb Classical Library 114 (Cambridge, MA: Harvard University Press, 1919), 4–7; Sallust, *The War with Catiline. The War with Jugurtha*, ed. John T. Ramsey, trans. J. C. Rolfe, Loeb Classical Library 116 (Cambridge, MA: Harvard University Press, 2013), 35–39.

[13] Plato, *Republic*, 410d, 411a, 590b; Aristotle, *Nicomachean Ethics*, 1150b; Aristotle, *Politics*, 1312a. 58–60. Christopher J. Berry, *The Idea of Luxury: A Conceptual and Historical Investigation* (Cambridge: Cambridge University Press, 1994), 58–60.

[14] In *De Doctrina Christiana* (1825), for example, which Milton composed throughout his career, he outlined this catalogue of 'special virtues' including temperance, sobriety, chastity, frugality, and high-mindedness, as regulating 'our appetite for external advantages'. See *CPW*, VI.117–21, 724–37.

[15] Herbert Agar, *Milton and Plato* (Princeton: Princeton University Press, 1928), 12–18; Irene Samuel, *Plato and Milton* (Ithaca, NY: Cornell University Press, 1965), 159. For example, see *CPW*, I.293. Samuel Taylor Coleridge even deemed Plato, 'Milton's darling!' See *The Collected Letters of Samuel Taylor Coleridge*, ed. Earl Leslie Griggs, vol II (Oxford: Clarendon, 1956), 866.

Milton, Marriage, & Realisation of Republican Manhood   237

you are listening to philosophers', Milton maintained. 'For what is so remarkable if strong horns spring forth in the land of mutton-heads which can powerfully butt down cities and towns? Learn now, from early youth, to consider and recognize great examples, not on the basis of force and strength, but of justice and moderation.'[16]

Much of Milton's early reflections on Greek moral philosophy and poetry occurred during his years at university. In his seventh Prolusion, a disputation he delivered at Cambridge probably in the autumn of 1630, Milton passionately argued the Platonic view that human beings are 'insatiably desirous of the highest wisdom', and that contemplation of the Good, 'conjoined with integrity of life and uprightness of character' would lead men to true happiness.[17] A year earlier, in his 'Elegia Sexta' to his friend Charles Diodati (1629), Milton claimed that the serious epic poet, which he desired to become, should 'live sparingly, like the master of Samos [Pythagoras]' and even when young be 'free of crime and chaste', with 'strict morals, and a hand free from stain'.[18] Milton's notions of the strict and virtuous life ran counter to practices of youthful manhood and misrule that he encountered during his time at Cambridge, although it should be noted that Milton himself did engage in breaking numerous university statutes.[19] Studying the male youth culture in Cambridge during this period, Alexandra Shepard has demonstrated how young men often asserted their manhood by performing rituals of excess, bravado, and violence, including nocturnal escapades, binge drinking, brawling, slanderous speech, and sexual exploits.[20] To 'establish himself as a man', as Anthony Fletcher summarised, a boy was expected to engage fully in this libertine and unruly lifestyle, especially demonstrating his sexual prowess.[21] Milton, however, seems to have remained steadfast in his

---

[16] *CPW*, VII.493.   [17] *CPW*, I.291–92.

[18] Milton, 'Elegia Sexta. Ad Carolum Diodatum Ruri Commorantem', in *The Complete Poetry and Essential Prose of John Milton*, ed. William Kerrigan, John Rumrich, and Stephen M. Fallon (New York: Modern Library Edition, Random House, 2007), 192. With the publication of his 1645 Poems, Milton in a similar vein boasted that he was impervious to becoming frenzied by Cupid's arrows, for the 'shady Academia offered its Socratic streams, and made me unlearn the burden which I had taken up'. Milton, *Haec Ego Mente* (a postscript to his elegies), in *Complete Poetry of Milton*, 198.

[19] Milton grew his hair to what would have been an 'unsuitable length' according to the university statutes, and spent significant time apart from the university cloistered life through visits and stays in London. See Quentin Skinner, 'The Generation of John Milton at Cambridge', in *From Humanism to Hobbes: Studies in Rhetoric and Politics* (Cambridge: Cambridge University Press, 2018), 118–38, esp. 127–29.

[20] Alexandra Shepard, 'Youthful Excess and Fraternal Bonding', in *Meanings of Manhood in Early Modern England* (Oxford: Oxford University Press, 2003), 93–126.

[21] Anthony Fletcher, *Gender, Sex and Subordination in England, 1500–1800* (New Haven: Yale University Press, 1999), 92–93.

238 The Masculine Republic

opposing views of masculinity and what it required. He confided to his friend Alexander Gil that he had 'almost no intellectual companions' during his early student years at Cambridge in the 1620s, and he was generally unpopular for his 'honest haughtiness'.[22] Although his fair complexion may have contributed to taunting, it may have been his rejection of particular aspects of the rowdy culture that earned him the mocking and emasculating nickname, 'The Lady of Christ's College'.[23]

In July 1628, Milton refuted this nickname, and the culture of masculinity supporting it, through serving as the 'Father' over the 'salting' ceremony at his college. The 'salting' was an annual ritual that marked the passage of underclassmen to upperclassmen status, during which upperclassmen comically satirised members of the college community.[24] 'Sportive Exercises on occasion are not inconsistent with philosophical Studies' was Milton's stated theme for this rhetorical exercise, and to answer this prompt, Milton's speech adopted a two-part structure, consisting of an *Oratio*, or more formal oration on a given theme, and a *Prolusio*, a comic speech fulfilling the requirements of the 'salting' ritual. Within the *Oratio*, Milton, perhaps with some playfulness, presented himself as a very earnest student forcibly dragged away from his devoted studies to oversee this ceremony of foolery; comparing himself to Junius Brutus, however, Milton claimed he would be willing to fulfil his duty and 'play the wise fool for a while'.[25] After flattering his audience and reminding them that they had just months before approved of another public speech he delivered, Milton expressed his desire to be received as a grand orator by his audience: 'For I only wish that such a stream of honeyed, or rather nectared, eloquence might be granted me, if but for this once, as of old ever steeped and as it were celestially bedewed the great minds of Athens and of Rome; would that I could suck out all the innermost marrow of persuasion, pilfer the notebooks of Mercury himself, and empty

---

[22] *CPW*, I.314.

[23] *CPW*, III.304; Aubrey claimed that Milton was called the 'Lady' because of his 'exceeding faire' complexion, and Anthony à Wood repeated the information. See *CPW*, I.283n.

[24] The final portion of the ceremony required the new initiates to perform their own comic speeches, usually in Latin. If they failed to drum up sufficient laughter in their audience, they received salted beer to drink to make up for the lack of 'salt', or wit (Latin: *sal*), in their performance. See Jessica Tvordi, 'The Comic Personas of Milton's *Prolusion VI*: Negotiating Masculine Identity Through Self-Directed Humor', in *Laughter in the Middle Ages and Early Modern Times: Epistemology of a Fundamental Human Behavior, Its Meaning, and Consequences*, ed. Albrecht Classen (Berlin: Walter de Gruyter, 2010), 715–16; Roslyn Richek, 'Thomas Randolph's Salting (1628), Its Text and John Milton's Sixth Prolusion as Another Salting', *English Literary Renaissance* 12.1 (Winter 1982): 107–8.

[25] *CPW*, I.266–67.

Milton, Marriage, & Realisation of Republican Manhood   239

all the coffers of wit, that I might produce something worthy of such great expectations ... .'[26]

Milton's willingness to participate with wit and humour in the salting ritual afforded him the opportunity to provide a defence of oratory, intellect, and temperance as truly masculine, and the labelling of opposing behaviours, such as violence, excess, and sexual bravado, as foolish displays of false masculinity. The circumstances of the 'salting' provided a fitting platform for this distinction, as Milton had only been chosen to deliver the speech after a more popular student had been expulsed for leading a group of students to vandalise the city's water supply. Milton referenced this situation in satirical tones, describing the rival student as a 'seasoned warrior', the 'commander of all the Sophisters', who led his comrades 'armed with short staves' to lay siege to the town's water 'in the approved military style'.[27] Remarkably, however, it was he, the so-called Lady, that had received the title 'Father' as the master of ceremonies instead of this brave 'soldier'. Milton capitalised upon this distinction to defend himself and to reject explicitly the masculine codes of behaviour admired by his fellow students:

> Some of late called me 'the Lady.' But why do I seem to them too little of a man? Have they no regard for Priscian? Do these bungling grammarians attribute to the feminine gender what is proper to the masculine, like this? It is, I suppose, because I have never brought myself to toss off great bumpers like a prize-fighter, or because my hand has never grown horny with driving the plough, or because I was never a farm hand at seven or laid myself down full length in the midday sun; or perhaps because I never showed my virility in the way these brothellers do. But I wish they could leave playing the ass as readily as I the woman.[28]

Here Milton explicitly rejected masculine identity as founded in violence, physical labour, a ruddy complexion, or sexual bravado. Virility could be found in virtuous activity, rational speech, and the developed intellect.

5.2   Criticising Catholics and the Court

We find this distinction between false virility and true manliness, and a continued interest in the classical world, in Milton's other youthful writings of the 1620s and 1630s, which often took as their aim institutions, including the Catholic Church, Laudian Church, and Caroline court, that seemingly promoted excessive and un-masculine behaviours,

---

[26] *CPW*, I.269–70.   [27] *CPW*, I.277.   [28] *CPW*, I.284.

240   The Masculine Republic

and which seemed to threaten the native liberty and rationality of men. Milton's writings in this period align in many ways with the imaginative writings considered in earlier chapters, which adopted and appropriated classical stories of tyrants and statesmen to present veiled and significant criticisms of the Stuart monarchs and to contrast the behaviours of these kings and their courts with the conduct of Roman men and their English imitators. Scholars have long debated whether Milton 'at every stage ... took up a reformist and oppositional stance', as Barbara Lewalski has argued, or whether his political radicalisation and animosity towards royalism and the King developed fully only later in his career.[29] Due partially to the complex spectrum of English political associations during this period, and Milton's fusion of both royalist and poetic forms and topics in his early poetry, several scholars have cautioned against arguing that Milton consistently opposed Caroline court culture before his production of *Lycidas* in 1637.[30] However, scholars have often failed to attend closely enough to the centrality of gendered political arguments in Caroline England, and to Milton's employment of gendered language within this context. Like authors discussed in previous chapters, Milton's youthful writings including *In Quintum Novembris* (1626) and *Comus* (1634) maligned false religion and Stuart court culture as effeminate, tyrannical, and dangerous for England and as corrupting for England's men who could become lured by false religion and effeminate vices. Milton's 'oppositional stance' should be understood in this context.

Milton produced *In Quintum Novembris* (1626) at a significant political moment, with England's Protestant allies having just suffered several major

---

[29] Barbara Lewalski, 'How Radical Was the Young Milton?' in *Milton and Heresy*, ed. Stephen B. Dobranski and John P. Rumrich (Cambridge and New York: Cambridge University Press, 1998), 49–72, esp. 50; George F. Sensabaugh, *That Grand Whig Milton* (Stanford: Stanford University Press, 1952); Christopher Hill, *Milton and the English Revolution* (London: Faber & Faber, 1977); Andrew Milner, *John Milton and the English Revolution: A Study in the Sociology of Literature* (Totowa, NJ: Barnes & Noble, 1981); Annabel Patterson, '"Forc'd Fingers": Milton's Early Poems and Ideological Constraint', in *'The Muses Common-weale': Poetry and Politics in the Seventeenth Century*, ed. Claude J. Summers and Ted-Larry Pebworth (Columbia: University of Missouri Press, 1988), 9–22; David Aers and Gunther Kress, 'Historical Process, Individual and Communities in Milton's Early Prose', in *1642: Literature and Power in the Seventeenth Century* (*Proceedings of the Essex Conference on the Sociology of Literature, July 1980*), ed. Francis Baker, et al. (Colchester: University of Essex, 1981), 283–300.

[30] Nicholas McDowell, 'The Caroline Court', in *Milton in Context*, ed. Stephen B. Dobranski (Cambridge: Cambridge University Press, 2010), 237–47, esp. 246; Thomas N. Corns, 'Milton before "Lycidas"', in *Milton and the Terms of Liberty*, ed. Graham Parry and Joad Raymond (Suffolk and Rochester: D. S. Brewer, 2002), 23–36, esp. 23–24. See also David Lowenstein, '"Fair Offspring Nurs't in Princely Lore": On the Question of Milton's Early Radicalism', *Milton Studies* 28 (1992): 37–48.

Milton, Marriage, & Realisation of Republican Manhood 241

blows in the Thirty Years War, and England's new monarch marrying a French Catholic princess. In 1625 and 1626, the Commons had questioned and denounced the royal chaplain Richard Montague for his anti-Calvinism, his leniency towards Rome, and his support of prayers to the saints; meanwhile, with the death of Bishop Lancelot Andrewes, William Laud filled the post of dean of the Chapel Royal and received the promise of the archbishopric of Canterbury. On 15 June 1626, after the House of Commons drew up a Remonstrance of the commonwealth's ills and lampooned the royal favourite, Buckingham, King Charles dissolved parliament and forfeited the military subsidies he needed to support the European war.[31] Much like George Chapman's writings of the 1620s, Milton's poems from 1625–27 celebrated the noble deeds of Protestants fighting on the Continent while characterising Catholics as enforcing idolatrous worship not through open warfare but through trickery befitting of Satan. In 1626, for example, Milton composed his '*Elegia Tertia*' for Lancelot Andrewes, whose death had prompted Laud's promotion. In the poem, Milton supported the Protestant military effort on the Continent and lamented the death of those captains who had suffered defeat in open war: 'And I remembered the heroes whom all Belgia saw snatched up into the skies and mourned as lost leaders.'[32]

Milton's *In Quintum Novembris*, written in commemoration of the Gunpowder Plot of 1605, warned that the English nation must be defended from that 'fierce tyrant' Satan and the treacherously wicked Pope, whose alliance might again result in a plot against England.[33] The miniature epic maligned popery as idolatrous, extravagant, and hypocritical by presenting the ceremonial procession for St. Peter's Eve in mocking terms, with genuflecting Princes and beggarly monks roaring Bacchanalian hymns and 'singing orgiastic songs', bearing with them 'gods made of bread'.[34] In this scene, Milton signified the lost masculinity of these popish practitioners, who in the darkness crouch, wail, and howl like beasts in submission. This scene is followed by a description of the Pope as a thoroughly intemperate man, a 'secret adulterer' who 'does not spend

---

[31] See Chapter 3 and Chapter 4.
[32] Milton, '*Elegia Tertia, In Obitum Præsulis Wintoniensis*', in *Complete Poetry of Milton*, 177; Lewalski, 'How Radical was the Young Milton?', 52. For May and Chapman, see Chapter 4. See also Jamie Gianoutsos, 'Criticizing Kings: Gender, Classical History, and Subversive Writing in Seventeenth-Century England', *Renaissance Quarterly* 70.4 (Winter 2017): 1366–96.
[33] Stella P. Revard, *Milton and the Tangles of Neaera's Hair: The Making of the 1645 Poems* (Columbia: University of Missouri Press, 1997), 56.
[34] Milton, *In Quintum Novembris*, in *Complete Poetry of Milton*, 207.

242   The Masculine Republic

fruitless nights without a soft whore'. In this setting of vicious darkness
and deceit, Satan enters the Pope's chamber in the self-effacing costume of
Saint Francis and bids the Pope to arise from his soft bed and attack those
'sacrilegious' sinners, the English nation. By the end of his speech, Milton's Satan successfully coaxes the Pope to avenge the scattered Spanish
Armada and re-establish Catholicism in England by organising conspirators to blow up the parliamentary meeting house by gunpowder. By the
end of the miniature epic, God saves the English from this wicked plot by
sending Rumour to reveal the Pope's hidden treachery.[35] The 'devout'
James appears in the daylight, summoning lords, noblemen, and aged
councillors to suppress the plot – an image which draws a sharp distinction
with the Roman pope, who meets in the night secretly with a disguised
Satan to enact cowardly plots and conspiracies. Perhaps because of Charles's marriage to a French Catholic the year prior, Milton's epic reminded
his audience that the French and Spanish had planned to invade England
and re-establish Marian rule had the Gunpowder Plot succeeded.[36]

Shortly after leaving Cambridge in 1632, Milton even more forcefully
articulated his staunch opposition to idolatry, extravagance, and intemperance, and those in civil or religious power who displayed their corrupted
characteristics. His lengthiest exploration of the emblematic struggle
between temperate virtue and intemperate vice can be found in *A Mask
Presented at Ludlow-Castle, or Comus* (1634), which he composed for the
Earl of Bridgewater and his family just after the Earl's appointment as Lord
President of Wales and the Marches.[37] Featuring three of the Earl's own
children in its performance at Bridgewater's estate in Wales, Milton's
masque located virtue within the Earl's family and household, while
simultaneously decrying the court revelry found in London and Whitehall.

A Mask Presented at Ludlow-Castle, or Comus celebrated the triumph of
chastity over wanton gluttony and sexual indulgence by telling the tale of a
pure Lady, who becomes lost in a wood and is taken prisoner by the
corrupt and deceitful magician Comus. Comus ensnares the Lady at his
lecherous banqueting hall, but through her steadfast and chaste resolution,
she repels his advances until saved by her brothers, an Attendant Spirit,
and Sabrina the river goddess. Milton's *Mask* provided an extensive

---

[35] Ibid., 211–13.   [36] Ibid., 209.
[37] For a description of the political circumstances of this masque, see Leah Sinanoglou Marcus, 'The
    Milieu of Milton's *Comus*: Judicial Reform at Ludlow and the Problem of Sexual Assault', *Criticism*
    25 (1983): 293–327; see also Marcus, 'Milton's Anti-Laudian Masque', in *The Politics of Mirth:
    Jonson, Herrick, Milton, Marvell, and the Defense of Old Holiday Pastimes* (Chicago: Chicago
    University Press, 1986), 169–212.

Milton, Marriage, & Realisation of Republican Manhood   243

portrait of luxury and sexual perversion through the character of Comus. The offspring of Bacchus and Circe, Comus roams the dark woods searching for a new foolish human to enslave. He is a master necromancer, using his 'orient liquor in a Crystal Glasse' and wand to transform wayward travelers into 'som brutish form' of wild animal, and thus cause their outward appearance to mirror their brutish inner appetites.[38] The stage directions note that these revellers were 'headed like sundry sorts of wilde Beasts, but otherwise like Men and Women'.[39] This mixture of beastly head and human body in the masque's costumes emphasised their condition as corrupted human beings, simultaneously enslaved and bestial, with their appetites ruling as reason should. '[S]o perfect is their misery', the *Mask* explained, that they "Not once perceive their foul disfigurement, / But boast themselves more comely then before'.[40]

Echoing anti-Catholic rhetoric that associated idolatry and moral corruption with the household rebellion of popish mothers and wives, Milton further portrayed Comus and his deceptive activities as effeminate, having been corrupted by his lewd and rebellious mother who named him and brought him up in her 'witcheries'.[41] He seeks power and revelry through treacherous secret plots, much like Satan and the Pope from *In Quintum Novembris*, and he similarly betrays idolatrous tendencies, being so 'awstrook' by the beauty of the Lady's noble brothers that he 'worshipt' them.[42] Intemperate, extravagant, deceptive, effeminate, and idolatrous, Comus embodied Milton's conception of excessive vice.

This ribald spectacle of Comus and his 'rout of Monsters' dancing in a disorderly fashion echoed the anti-masques of the royal court entertainments which the King and Queen had performed in the years just preceding Milton's *Mask*. *Tempe Restor'd* (1632), for example, opened with Circe having enamored a young Gentleman by giving him 'to drinke of an inchanted Cup, and touching him with her golden wand transformed him into a *Lyon*'.[43] *Loues triumph through Callipolis* (1631) also opened with 'certain Sectaries, or deprau'd Louers' dancing 'with anticke

---

[38] Milton, 'A MASK Presented at LUDLOW-Castle, 1634', in *John Milton Complete Shorter Poems*, ed. Stella P. Revard (Chichester: Wiley-Blackwell, 2009), lines 60–70 and 522, pp. 90 and 104.
[39] Ibid., 91.   [40] Ibid., lines 73–75, p. 90.
[41] Ibid., lines 56–58 and 522, pp. 90 and 104. See Peter Lake with Michael Questier, *Anti-Christ's Lewd Hat: Protestants, Papists and Players in Post-Reformation England* (New Haven & London: Yale University Press, 2002), 54–99; Frances E. Dolan, *Whores of Babylon: Catholicism, Gender, and Seventeenth-Century Print Culture* (Ithaca and London: Cornell University Press, 1999), 49–54.
[42] Milton, *Mask*, lines 302–3, p. 98.
[43] Aurelian Townshend, *Tempe Restor'd. A Masque presented by the Queene, and fourteene ladies, to the Kings Maiestie at Whitehall on Shrove-Tuesday. 1631* (London, 1632), 1.

244 The Masculine Republic

gesticulation ... expressing their confus'd affections'.[44] In these royal masques, the Queen and King, through their virtuous splendor and wedded harmony, cleanse the city before transcending into an exquisite garden where '*Beauty* and *Love*' may flourish in their household and kingdom. Milton's masque, however, directly challenged this image of the regal court purifying the disordered and sinful city. In what would have been a shocking departure from generic expectations, Milton's Comus is not overcome or purified by courtiers, but himself transforms into a court masquer, leading the Lady out of the woods into a 'stately Palace, set out with all manner of deliciousness', including 'soft Musick, Tables spread with all dainties'.[45] By bringing the Lady to his 'stately Palace', Comus tempts his aristocratic audience with the extravagant luxury and riotous idolatry that Milton and others associated with Caroline court culture. As Barabara Lewalski and Cedric Brown have demonstrated, the striking political criticism of this scene would not have been missed, especially as Comus's speeches echoed the *Carpe Diem* and *Carpe Floream* poems popular amongst Cavalier poets in the period.[46]

Significantly, Comus's words similarly insulted the ideal conception of beauty which the Queen herself had personified in royal entertainments. *Tempe Restor'd*, for example, had stated that 'Corporeall *Beauty*, consisting in simetry, colour, and certain vnexpressable Graces, shining in the Queenes Maiestie, may draw vs to the contemplation of the *Beauty* of the soule, vnto which it hath Analogy.' Similarly, the lusty Comus in Milton's *Mask* contended that the Lady should 'be not coy', for 'Beauty is natures brag, and must be shown / In courts, at feasts, and high solemnities / Where most may wonder at the workmanship'.[47] The Lady's response to Comus does not defend beauty as the Queen might have – arguing that her outward beauty was a reflection of inner virtue and could, thereby, transfix the observer to contemplating divine beauty. Rather, the Lady described a sobering devotion to chastity, which Comus fails to comprehend due to his depravity:

> Thou hast nor Eare, nor Soul to apprehend
> The sublime notion, and high mystery

---

[44] Ibid., 2.   [45] Milton, *Mask*, 108.

[46] Barbara Lewalski, 'Milton's Comus and the Politics of Masquing', in *The Politics of the Stuart Court Masque*, ed. David Bevington and Peter Holbrook (Cambridge: Cambridge University Press, 1998), 296–320, esp. 309; Cedric Clive Brown, *John Milton's Aristocratic Entertainments* (Cambridge: Cambridge University Press, 1985), 57–77; see also David Norbrook, *Poetry and Politics in the English Renaissance* (Oxford and New York: Oxford University Press, 2002), 238.

[47] Townshend, *Tempe Restor'd*, 19; Milton, *Mask*, lines 739–47, p. 111.

Milton, Marriage, & Realisation of Republican Manhood 245

That must be utter'd to unfold the sage
And serious doctrine of Virginity.[48]

Such virginity opposes intemperate waste, lust, and idolatry of all kinds, according to the Lady. Whereas Comus's speech beckoned the Lady to revel in and worship the 'waste fertility' of nature's bounty, the Lady lives according to the 'sober laws/. . . of spare Temperance', and explains that if 'every just man that now pines with want' had a moderate share in 'that which lewdly-pamper'd Luxury / Now heaps upon som few with vast excess', all would be blessed with plenty.[49]

Royal masques particularly glorified the wedded harmony of the royal couple, with *Albion's Triumph* (1632), for example, proclaiming that Charles and Henrietta's 'happy Vnion . . . was preordeyned by the greatest of the Gods'.[50] Adopting the fashionable Neoplatonism of the Caroline court, the masques styled Henrietta and Charles as complementary lovers – Divine Beauty and Heroic Lover, Intellectual Light and Reason, Will and Understanding – whose union would help them and their kingdom transcend the lower sensual and appetitive desires to achieve rational and psychic harmony. Milton's *Mask*, however, warned of the vicious enslavement of a bad union. Comus becomes enamoured with the Lady after spying her in the woods and hearing her song. Exclaiming that 'such a sacred, and home-felt delight, / Such sober certainty of waking bliss / I never heard till now', he vows that 'she shall be my Queen'.[51]

The brutish Comus and the virtuous Lady would make a disastrous alliance, of course, one comprising only lurid physical sexuality, and the language Milton adopted throughout the *Mask* fittingly emphasized procreation in grotesque and corrupted forms: Comus and his monstrous rout celebrate the 'Dragon woom / Of Stygian darknes' which 'spets her thickest gloom, / And makes one blot of all the ayr'; the Attendant Spirit portrays Comus as hidden 'Within the navil of this hideous Wood'; Comus describes his court as containing 'all the pleasures / That fancy can beget on youthfull thoughts', and Nature as being 'strangl'd with her waste fertility'.[52] This emphasis on sordid reproduction finds its fullest articulation in the elder brother's speech, when he contends that lustful

---

[48] Milton, *Mask*, lines 784–87, p. 112.   [49] Ibid., lines 764–75, pp. 111–12.
[50] Aurelian Townshend, *Albions Triumph, Personated in a maske at court. By the Kings Maiestie and his lords. The Sunday after Twelfe Night. 1631* (London, 1631), 2.
[51] Milton, *Mask*, lines 262–65, p. 97.
[52] Ibid., lines 130–31, 266, 520, 668–69, 729, pp. 92, 97, 104, 109–10.

246 The Masculine Republic

corruption swells up within the body and impregnates one with monstrous
spawn:

> but when lust
> By unchaste looks, loose gestures, and foul talk,
> But most by leud and lavish act of sin,
> Lets in defilement to the inward parts,
> The soul grows clotted by contagion,
> Imbodies, and imbrutes, till she quite loose [lose]
> The divine property of her first being.[53]

Milton stressed that Comus himself has been thus polluted, being born
and bred through Circe's lustful womb, revelling in the swollen woods as
he imbibes intemperate vice. His marriage plans would enact the ravish-
ment of the Lady, impregnating her with metaphorical and actual defilement. Milton's language in the *Mask* emphasised the metaphorical
defilement of lustful procreation, but he would continue to worry about
the actual political ramifications of it. Possibly as early as 1639, Milton
noted in his commonplace book that lecherous or unfit unions would
harm the commonwealth by producing children lacking in virtue and
character: 'Boniface says ... that a people born of lechery and unalwful
union will be sluggish and very destructive of the fatherland.'[54]

In the 1637 expanded edition of the *Mask*, the Lady's story concluded
with a tribute to pure marriage, and perhaps a gesture to the future
marriage of Bridgewater's daughter, Lady Alice, who played the part. In
this speech presented by the Attendant Spirit, the sensual relationship of
Adonis and Venus, who sits 'sadly' by as Adonis heals from his deep
wound, is contrasted with the legitimate and consensual union of 'Celestial
Cupid' who 'farr above in spangled sheen ... Holds his dear *Psyche* sweet
intranc't'.[55] Here the *Mask* followed the tradition of Christian allegorists
who understood Apeleius's fable in *The Golden Ass* of Psyche labouring to
marry Cupid as representing the soul's quest for union with Christ. Psyche
has won her place as Cupid's 'eternal Bride' through 'wandring labours
long', just as Revelation 19:7 described, 'the marriage of the Lamb is come,
and his wife hath made herself ready'.[56] Their offspring are not the messy

---

[53] Ibid., lines 463–69, pp. 102–3.   [54] *CPW*, I.369.

[55] Milton, *Comus*, in *The Riverside Milton*, ed. Roy Flannagan (Boston and New York: Houghton Mifflin, 1998), lines 1003–5, p. 170.

[56] King James Version. See William Shullenberger, *Lady in the Labyrinth: Milton's Comus as Initiation* (Madison, NJ: Fairleigh Dickinson University Press, 2008), 270.

Milton, Marriage, & Realisation of Republican Manhood   247

products of sensual desire, but rather 'Two blissful twins ... / Youth and Joy'.

In these ways, Milton's *Mask* located temperate virtue within the persons and households of the countryside, rather than stately royal palaces. Indeed, the Lady states that 'courtesie, / ... oft is sooner found in lowly sheds / With smoaky rafters, then in tapstry Halls / And Courts of Princes, where it../ is most pretended'.[57] His earlier *In Quintum Novembris* demonstrated the wicked and dangerous plots which could result from vicious, effeminate, and popish belief and practice. By characterising and castigating vice and tyranny through these highly personal and gendered attacks, Milton's early writings reflected and furthered the gendered criticisms which his contemporaries levelled against King Charles through classicised portrayals of tyranny.

5.3   Marriage, Masculinity, and the Commonwealth

Thus far, this chapter has provided a brief analysis of Milton's characterisations of true manhood and its opposition in failed masculinities, emphasising the author's frequent association of manliness with reason, temperance, and freedom, and grounded broadly in an ethical system indebted to classical philosophy and Scripture. As we have seen, Milton's views on manliness and upright living led him to criticise what he considered to be cultures or institutions of excess and effeminate behaviour, including the student culture at Cambridge, 'Popish' institutions, and the Caroline court. These final sections will explore how related conceptions of classical and Scriptural masculinity played a primary role in shaping Milton's views of republican governance. This section considers particularly Milton's defence of the freedom of divorce, through which he articulated the significance of good marriage for inculcating masculine virtue and bringing the commonwealth to a state of liberty and participatory government. As we will see, Milton's important reflections upon the private household and public commonwealth similarly shaped his defence of the regicide, which included portrayals of the late monarch as uxoriously enslaved by his popish wife and as perverting the fabric of family, virtue, liberty, and religion in English society.

Milton's prose writings of the 1640s focused primarily on political, familial, and religious institutions which could greatly aid or hinder man's liberty and the preservation of his virtue. In the later autobiographical

---

[57] Milton, *Mask*, lines 323–26, p. 98.

section of *Defensio Secunda* (1654), Milton described his writings in this period as seeking to advance the 'cause of true and substantial liberty', which existed within society in 'three varieties': 'ecclesiastical liberty, domestic or personal liberty, and civil liberty'. For all three, Milton understood liberty as that 'which must be sought, not without, but within, and which is best achieved not by the sword, but by a life rightly undertaken and rightly conducted'.[58] This definition aligned with views of masculine virtue expressed in Milton's earlier writings, where the writer eschewed violence and excess while touting ethical conduct as protecting freedom and manliness. Within his divorce tracts of the 1640s, in which he provided arguments for domestic or personal liberty, Milton expressed the conviction that 'mariage and the family' were the very foundation of a free commonwealth and that which must be 'set right first' before the commonwealth could be reformed.[59] Furthermore, Milton underscored the household and political society as having a parallel and fundamental relationship, with the aims of these institutions and the means of establishing and protecting these aims as being significantly intertwined. As he explained in the revised introduction to the *Doctrine and Discipline of Divorce; Restor'd to the good of both Sexes* (1644):

> He who marries, intends as little to conspire his own ruine, as he that swears Allegiance: and as a whole people is in proportion to an ill Government, so is one man to an ill mariage ... For no effect of tyranny can sit more heavy on the Common-wealth, then this houshold unhappines on the family. And farewell all hope of true Reformation in the state, while such an evill as this lies undiscern'd or unregarded in the house. On the redresse whereof depends, not only the spiritfull and orderly life of our grown men, but the willing, and carefull education of our children.[60]

In this passage, Milton likened the unhappy household to the tyrannical state, and described how the reformation of the state and the creation of manly citizens now and in future depended upon the reformation of the household. No man entered a marriage seeking his own destruction, Milton argued, but when finding himself suffering from the tyranny of a bad marriage, he had the liberty, and perhaps even the duty, to dissolve the bonds of matrimony. Through his divorce pamphlets, Milton argued for the dissolution of contract, while simultaneously comparing the relationship between the marriage oath and the oath of allegiance, and addressing his treatise '*To The* Parliament of England, with the Assembly' as they

---

[58] *CPW*, IV.624.   [59] *The Ivdgement of Martin Bucer, concerning Divorce* (1644), *CPW*, II.431.
[60] *CPW*, II.229–30.

Milton, Marriage, & Realisation of Republican Manhood 249

waged war against the King. As Sharon Achinstein has demonstrated, the simultaneous context of the Westminster Assembly, which sought to hammer out doctrinal and ecclesiastical reform in the English church, further underscores the relationship between marriage and the state; marriage was viewed more broadly in Milton's England as 'important to matters of democracy, church government, magistracy, the nature of secular institutions, and freedom of debate'.[61] Moreover, the association of marriage with mature manhood, and of household governance with commonwealth governance, had been commonplace for some time.[62] *A Godlie Forme of Household Government* (1598), as one example, argued that it was 'impossible for a man to vnderstand to gouerne the common wealth, that doth not know to rule his owne house, or order his owne person, so that he that knoweth not to gouerne, deserueth not to raigne'.[63]

It has been maintained since Milton's anonymous 'earliest' biographer that although Milton already held strong convictions regarding divorce, these convictions became urgent after his new wife, Mary Powell, abandoned him in 1642.[64] Due largely to this biographical point, Milton's divorce pamphlets have frequently been combed for their personal and autobiographical significance; more work remains to be done, however, on these important tracts for understanding the development of Milton's views on liberty, politics, and the household.[65]

---

[61] Achinstein, "'A Law in this Matter to Himself'", 181.   [62] Shepard, *Meanings of Manhood*, 23.

[63] Robert Cleaver, *A godlie forme of householde gouernment for the ordering of priuate families, according to the direction of Gods word* (London, 1598), 16.

[64] 'He ... could ill bear the disappointment hee mett with by her obstinate absenting: And therefore thought upon a Divorce, that hee might bee free to marry another; concerning which hee also was in treaty. The lawfulness and expedience of this ... had upon full consideration & reading good Authors bin formerly his Opinion: And the necessity of justifying himselfe now concurring with the opportunity, acceptable to him, of instructing others in point of so great concern ... hee ... writt The Doctrine and Discipline of Divorce'. Qtd in Ernest Sirluck, 'Introduction', *CPW*, II.138.

[65] For prior work elucidating the tracts' political significance, see Achinstein, "'A Law in this Matter to Himself'"; Achinstein, 'Saints or Citizens? Ideas of Marriage in Seventeenth-Century English Republicanism', *Seventeenth Century* 25.2 (Autumn 2010): 240–64; Cox, 'Milton, Marriage, and the Politics of Gender'; Hausknecht, 'The Gender of Civic Virtue', in *Milton and Gender*; Cedric Brown, 'Milton and the Idolatrous Consort', *Criticism* 35.3 (Summer 1993): 419–39. Apart from autobiographical concern, scholars have studied the pamphlets in connection to Milton's views on metaphysics, theology, ecclesiastical reformation, and Biblical hermeneutics. See, for example, Arthur Barker, 'Christian Liberty in Milton's Divorce Pamphlets', *The Modern Language Review* 35.2 (Apr. 1940): 153–61; Stephen M. Fallon, 'The Metaphysics of Milton's Divorce Tracts', in *Politics, Poetics, and Hermeneutics in Milton's Prose*, ed. David Lowenstein and J. G. Turner (New York: Cambridge University Press, 1990), 69–83; Kenneth R. Kirby, 'Milton's Biblical Hermeneutics in *The Doctrine and Discipline of Divorce*', *Milton Quarterly* 18 (1984): 116–25; Claude A. Thompson, 'The *Doctrine and Discipline of Divorce*, 1643–45: A Biographical Study', *Transactions of the Cambridge Bibliographical Society* 7.1 (1977): 74–93.

250 The Masculine Republic

Milton developed his account of marriage and domestic liberty in the divorce tracts not only at a moment when his wife abandoned him but also at a moment in which he and other Englishmen had entered civil war with a king they regarded as badly married, being enthralled by the Catholic 'idolatrous heretick', Henrietta Maria. As we will see, in Milton's later works these attacks upon the royal marriage would become coupled with celebrations of entirely masculine representative bodies as the true source of reason and liberty for the commonwealth; in this view, the public household of the king should be traded for public senators who ruled private households. Fittingly, in the *Doctrine and Discipline of Divorce* and other divorce writings concerned with masculine controlled households, Milton argued for good marriage as necessary for men and their common- wealth to attain and maintain liberty and rational self-rule, while warning that the bonds of bad marriage threatened liberty, rationality, and godli- ness individually and corporately. This view of marriage was essential for Milton's conceptualisations of masculinity and his later republican writings.

Milton's divorce tracts outlined an extensive argument for the recogni- tion of divorce as a private liberty, separate from legal policy and religious mandate. Whereas English law deemed divorce a legal and religious violation except in cases of adultery, impotence, or failure to consummate, and at most allowed for separation *a mensa et thoro* without hope of remarriage, Milton pursued a liberalisation of divorce to include mental and temperamental incompatibility as reasonable grounds for separation, and for that separation to include the right of remarriage for both parties.

In *The Doctrine and Discipline of Divorce*, Milton defined marriage and its importance by maintaining that men have a 'pure' and 'inbred desire' not to be left alone, a desire to be joined together in 'conjugall fellowship' with a 'fit conversing soul'. This desire, which 'is properly call'd love', could only be satisfied in marriage by uniting two minds 'fitly dispos'd, and enabl'd to maintain a cherful conversation, to the solace and love of each other, according as God intended and promis'd in the very first foundation of matrimony'.[66] Milton modelled this relationship between husband and wife on the Biblical description of Adam and Eve in Genesis, in which God declared that it was '*not good that man should be alone*', and thereby made a '*help meet for him*' by creating woman.[67] In *Paradise Lost*, Milton later dramatised Adam's recognition of this deep desire for unifi- cation when Adam names the animals in the garden:

---

[66] *CPW*, II.251 and 328.   [67] Ibid., II.245–46.

I named them, as they passed, and understood
Their nature, with such knowledge God endued
My sudden apprehension: but in these
I found not what methought I wanted still.[68]

In this scene, Adam understands and knows the animals, but their company cannot fulfil his rational longing for a 'fit soule' with whom to converse. A wife, in Milton's view, accomplishes her role as a 'help meet' through providing companionship for her husband. Although contemporary interpretations of the Genesis story often limited Eve's role of helping Adam with procreation, Milton treated procreation as a 'secondary end in dignity, though not in necessity' of marriage.[69]

Echoing the distinction between Comus's desire for marriage and the marriage of Cupid and Psyche in his *Mask*, Milton's definition of marriage emphasised the union of minds rather than bodies, signified by his description of the desire for union as a 'rationall burning'. Throughout the pamphlets he vehemently argued that the satisfaction of that 'other burning, which is but as it were the venom of a lusty and over-abounding concoction' and the related procreation of children were not God's primary intended purpose in creating marriage.[70] To make this point palpable to his readers, Milton characterised physical sexuality which lacked 'the souls union and commixture of intellectual delight' as vile and disgusting: 'rather a soiling then a fulfilling of mariage-rites'; the 'disappointing of an impetuous nerve' in the 'channell of concupiscence'; the flowing 'quintessence of an excrement'; and the 'Promiscuous draining of a carnal rage'.[71] In contrast, Milton privileged the 'solace and satisfaction of the mind . . . before the sensitive pleasing of the body'.[72] As Stephen Fallon has argued, Milton chiefly employed dualistic language concerning the mind and body to vilify his contemporaries who affirmed 'the bed to be the highest [end] of mariage'.[73] Milton contended that the tradition of Canon lawyers and the laws of England privileged the body because they limited divorce to bodily justifications, including adultery, non-consummation, and impotence. By defining marriage as a fellowship of souls, Milton could argue for divorce on the grounds of dispositional, mental, and spiritual

---

[68] Milton, *Paradise Lost*, in *Complete Poetry of Milton*, VIII.352–5, p. 507.
[69] *CPW*, II.235. For contemporary views, see Turner, 'The State of Eve: Female ontogeny and the politics of marriage', *One Flesh*, 96–123.
[70] *CPW*, II.251.   [71] Ibid., II.248–49 and II.355.   [72] Ibid., II.246.
[73] Ibid., II.269; Fallon, 'The Metaphysics of Milton's Divorce Tracts', 69. See also Turner, *One Flesh*, 199–210.

252   The Masculine Republic

incompatibility, and could define wedded harmony as bedded upon compatibility and concord of mind, interest, and intellect.[74]

To describe the ideal marriage, Milton instead adopted a monist perspective, which understood souls and bodies as manifestations of the same substance.[75] Through this view, Milton could argue that a marriage which united minds through conversation would not eradicate the union of bodies, but transform it. That which 'flows' in a good marriage would be a 'far more precious mixture' of 'acts of peace and love'; the sexual act would be transformed to 'the pure influence of peace and love, whereof the souls lawfull contentment is the onely fountain'.[76] In such a marriage, the spiritual and sexual are combined, logos and eros made companions.

Good marriages, and the corresponding liberty of divorce to eradicate bad marriages, would make males truly men, Milton maintained, and thus greatly benefit the commonwealth as a whole. In his later *Tretrachordon* (1644/5), Milton argued that 'nothing now adayes is more degenerately forgott'n, then the true dignity of man, almost in every respect, but especially in this prime institution of Matrimony, wherein his native pre-eminence ought most to shine'.[77] In the preface to parliament in the revised second edition of *The Doctrine and Discipline of Divorce*, Milton argued that good marriage and its protection by the allowance of divorce would

> restore this his lost heritage into the household state; wherwith be sure that peace and love, the best subsistence of a Christian family will return home from whence they are now banisht; places of prostitution will be less haunted, the neighbours bed lesse attempted, the yoke of prudent and manly discipline will be generally submitted to, sober and well order'd living will soon spring up in the Common-wealth.[78]

In this passage, Milton argued that good marriages would make good men by endowing them with their 'heritage' of exercising authority and exhibiting prudence as the head of households. As Rosanna Cox has shown, in these passages Milton sought to balance companionate marriage with

---

[74] Cox, 'Milton, Marriage, and the Politics of Gender', 32. However, as Fallon has shown, Milton's monism collapses the strong distinction between body and soul, and thereby renders humoral physiology as partly determining compatibility. See Fallon, 'The Metaphysics of Milton's Divorce Tracts', 78–79.

[75] As Fallon has argued, Milton's mature rationalisation of monism would not be revealed until *De Doctrina Chrstiana* and *Paradise Lost*. See 'The Metaphysics of Milton's Divorce Tracts'; see also 'Material Life: Milton's Animist Materialism', in *Milton Among the Philosophers: Poetry and Materialism in Seventeenth-Century England* (Ithaca and London: Cornell University Press, 1991), 79–110, esp. 89–98.

[76] *CPW*, II.248–49   [77] Ibid., II.587.   [78] Ibid., II.230.

Milton, Marriage, & Realisation of Republican Manhood   253

conceptions of patriarchalism derived from the Apostle Paul. While Milton acknowledged that there may be exceptions to the rule, he argued that men generally proved superior to women in prudence and dexterity, and thereby became natural rulers over their wives – although good wives should not be understood and treated as servants but as virtuous companions.[79] The household thereby became an education and breeding ground (literally and metaphorically) in manliness and civic activity.

Moreover, against opponents who deemed him libertine for supporting divorce and remarriage, Milton argued that the 'liberty' of divorce would support true manliness and guard against sexual 'licence', prostitution, or adultery, not lead to it: 'the agrieved person shall doe more manly, to be extraordinary and singular in claiming the due right [of divorce] whereof he is frustrated, then to piece up his lost contentment by visiting the Stews, or stepping to his neighbours bed, which is the common shift in this misfortune'.[80] And those men whose 'rationall burning' had been fulfilled through good marriage could resist the lower burnings of brutish sexual desire.[81] Because the happily married man, in Milton's account, is physically, intellectually, and spiritually fulfilled, he can live virtuously and in control of his own and his household's affairs. Good marriage thereby made self-mastery possible, which for Milton was the bedrock of both masculinity and of governance. Male authority became founded upon virtuous manhood within the household; outside of the household, husbands would form a community of manly citizens fit for liberty and civic activity.[82]

In further support of this view, we find Milton's divorce pamphlets supplying frequent, vigorous warnings about the harmful effects of bad marriage on individual men and the commonwealth. Whereas good marriage would allow men to perform virtuous acts of peace and love, Milton argued that unfit marriage caused men to 'dispair in vertue', and throughout the pamphlets he described how these men would become enslaved to lust, loneliness, intemperance, inconstancy, wrath, melancholy, and sloth. Whereas good marriage refines the soul to rational and transcendent

---

[79] Cox, 'Milton, Marriage, and the Politics of Gender', 136–37.   [80] *CPW*, II.247.

[81] This is not to claim that Milton supported the commonplace Pauline argument that a purpose of marriage was to satisfy lust. Milton boldly denies this claim. See 'not properly the remedy of lust, but the fulfilling of conjugall love and helpfulness', *CPW*, IV.252–53; II.339; IV.326–27; IV.246–47.

[82] Cox, 'Milton, Marriage, and the Politics of Gender', 140–41. Ng, *Literature and the Politics of the Family*, 55 and 59.

254   The Masculine Republic

existence, bad marriage pulls men down to bestial and corrupt subservience:

> That the ordinance [of marriage] which God gave to our comfort, may not be pinn'd upon us to our undeserved thraldom; to be coop't up as it were in mockery of wedlock, to a perpetual betrothed lonelines and discontent, if nothing wors ensue. There beeing nought els of mariage left between such, but a displeasing and forc't remedy against the sting of a brute desire; which fleshly accustoming without the souls union and commixture of intellectual delight, as it is rather a soiling then a fulfilling of marriage-rites, so it is anough to imbase the mettle of a generous spirit, and sinks him to a low and vulgar pitch of endeavour in all his actions, or, which is wors, leavs him in a dispairing plight of abject & hard'n'd thoughts.[83]

Throughout the divorce pamphlets, Milton's portrait of the man enslaved in bad marriage is rich and evocative. To escape desperation and loneliness, this man loses his 'manly discipline' and seeks brutish sexual pleasure, only to find himself further debased and dissatisfied. Discontentment leads to 'vexation and violence' and 'hatred'; the children produced become '*children of wrath* and anguish'.[84]

At the same time, Milton argued that the man badly married also suffered through 'slavery to an inferior', his wife.[85] Although his view of marriage elevated women from a mere partner of physical procreation to an intellectual 'help meet', Milton decisively supported that 'wholsom Law', as he called it, '*that every man should beare rule in his own house*'.[86] Employing a number of Biblical examples, Milton contended that God created men and women with different *teloi*, the woman being 'created for man, and not man for woman'. For this reason, Milton deemed the unhappily married man without the liberty of divorce 'overthrown' in his authority as 'head of the other sex which was made for him'.[87] His 'honour and pre-eminence' in the household thus overruled, his rationality and virtue overridden, the unhappily married man would become emasculated and enslaved.

According to Milton, the consequences of this unhappy state of marriage are public as well as private, political as well as domestic, extending far beyond the enslaved man to his wife, household, friendships, and wider society. As he later described in *Tetrachordon*, a bad marriage 'degenerates

---

[83] *CPW*, II.339. See also II.254.   [84] Ibid., II.258–60.

[85] For an explanation of this slavery in Aristotelian terms, see David Hawkes, 'The Politics of Character in John Milton's Divorce Tracts', *Journal of the History of Ideas* 62.1 (Jan. 2001): 141–60, esp. 146–47.

[86] *CPW*, II.325; on procreation and marriage, see Turner, *One Flesh*, 120–23.   [87] *CPW*, II.347.

Milton, Marriage, & Realisation of Republican Manhood   255

and disorders the best spirits, leavs them to unsettl'd imaginations, and degraded hopes, careles of themselvs, their houshold and their friends, unactive to all public service, dead to the Common-wealth'.[88] Thraldom to bad marriage causes the 'endles aggravation of evil' by making men incapable of virtue, and thereby incapable of friendship, good household governance, and political activity. These men become fit only for tyranny, within the household and the commonwealth.

5.4   The Tyrannical Marriage of Charles and Henrietta Maria

The political ramifications of Milton's views concerning marriage were significant not only due to the context of civil war and the Westminster Assembly but also due to vocal parliamentary criticisms of the Catholic Henrietta Maria and her influence upon (or supposed power over) England's king, who was deemed a man enthralled in bad marriage. Milton's divorce tracts considered explicitly whether those 'mis-yoked' in religion, such as Charles and Henrietta Maria, could achieve the true fellowship of spouses. His description of Catholic wives as 'Idolatresses' reveals his unyielding conviction that truly Christian men would never find spiritual compatibility being thus 'mis-yoked':

> Where there is no hope of converting, there alwayes ought to be a certain religious aversation and abhorring, which can no way sort with Mariage: Therefore saith S. *Paul, What fellowship hath righteousnesse with unrighteousnesse? what communion hath light with darknesse? what concord hath Christ with Beliall? what part hath he that beleeveth with an Infidell?*[89]

Sacrificing the wedded harmony achieved in good marriage, the man married to a heretic would 'despair in vertue' like all unhappily married men, Milton maintained. Even more worryingly, marriage with a committed Idolatress would 'alienate [a husband's] heart from the true worship of God'.[90] She would 'pervert' her husband 'to superstition by her enticing sorcery' or 'disinable him in the whole service of God through the disturbance of her unhelpful and unfit society'. As they 'shall perpetually at our elbow seduce us from the true worship of God, or defile and daily scandalize our conscience by their hopeles continuance in misbelief', Milton contended, idolatrous wives would weaken their husband's 'Christian fortitude with worldly perswasions', and unsettle their 'constancie

---

[88] *CPW*, II.632. See also II.347.   [89] *CPW*, II.262.

[90] Milton further emphasised the danger of such a match between 'heretick with faithful' and 'godly with ungodly' in *Tetrachordon*. See *CPW*.II.592.

256 The Masculine Republic

with timorous and softning suggestions'.[91] At last, 'through murmuring and despair', the Christian husband would be driven even to 'Atheism'.[92] So ruled by their idolatrous wives, and abject in idolatrous worship, these husbands endure the worst form of slavery, losing simultaneously their manliness, their household governance, and their salvation. Milton thereby urged the Christian man to consider a 'totall and finall separation' from a heretical partner, lest he suffer defilement and be reduced to emasculation, bondage, and irreligion.[93]

Although Milton did not directly label or reference Henrietta Maria as an idolatress in his divorce pamphlets, it is clear he detested her religious practice as idolatrous and feared its influence upon his king and commonwealth. The year after Charles married Henrietta, Milton had crafted *In Quintum Novembris*, and in the years following he consistently identified popery as inherently idolatrous and enslaving. The continuance of this view in the 1640s can be ascertained through the strident criticisms he levelled in five anti-prelatical pamphlets against the ceremonial worship and episcopacy of the Laudian Church, which he likened to the sensual 'Idolatry' of Catholic worship and the placing of a 'Pope in every Parish'.[94] Between May 1641 and April 1642, Milton argued in these pamphlets that ritualistic worship corrupted the soul, pulling her 'wing apace downeward' from heaven by 'over-bodying her . . . in performance of *Religious duties*'.[95] Such practice enslaves the worshipper's soul and prevents him from the true religion and knowledge of God, Milton argued in *Of Reformation* (1641), for with 'her pineons now broken' and her 'heavenly flight' forgotten, the soul is 'left the dull, and droyling carcas to plod on in the old rode, and drudging Trade of outward conformity'.[96] Perverted religion further enslaved the soul in carnal or fleshly pursuits. Exchanging 'cheerefull boldness' for 'Servile, and thral-like feare', Milton contended, the people become subservient to internal fear and external tyranny, both religious and political.[97] Thus, in *An Apology Against a Pamphlet* (1642),

[91] Ibid., II.263.   [92] Ibid., II.260.   [93] Ibid., II.263.

[94] Ibid., I.522 and 570. The ritualistic worship and Arminianism of Laud was most associated with Catholicism. See Marshall, *John Locke, Toleration, and Early Enlightenment Culture: Religious Intolerance and Arguments for Religious Toleration in Early Modern and 'Early Enlightenment' Europe* (Cambridge: Cambridge University Press, 2006), 282–87; Achash Guibbory, 'John Milton: Carnal Idolatry and Reconfiguration of Worship, Part 1, 1634–1660', in *Ceremony and Community from Herbert to Milton: Literature, Religion, and Cultural Conflict in Seventeenth-Century England* (Cambridge: Cambridge University Press, 1998), 147–86; Neil Forsyth, 'The English Church', in *Milton in Context*, 292–302.

[95] *CPW*, I.522.   [96] Ibid.

[97] Ibid. and I.853. See also Blair Worden, 'Milton's Republicanism and the Tyranny of Heaven', in *Machiavelli and Republicanism*, ed. Gisela Bock, Quentin Skinner, and Maurizio Viroli (Cambridge: Cambridge University Press, 1991), 225–46, 236.

Milton, Marriage, & Realisation of Republican Manhood   257

Milton argued that 'God hath inseparably knit together' religion and 'native liberty', and 'hath disclos'd to us that they who seek to corrupt our religion are the same that would inthrall our civill liberty'.[98] He identified 'popery', ritualistic worship, and prelacy as drawing individuals from the true worship of God and the commonwealth from just laws. As he later summarised in his first *Defensio*, 'We cannot bear popery, for we know that it is less a religion than a priestly despotism under the cloak of religion, arrayed in the spoils of temporal power which it has violently appropriated in defiance of the clear teaching of Christ.'[99]

At the same time that Milton prepared these statements for his anti-prelatical pamphlets in the early 1640s, he concluded that marriage 'with one of a different religion [is] dangerous' through a study of the history of Charles's courtship to the Spanish Infanta and his marriage to Henrietta Maria.[100] Drawing upon André Du Chesne's *Histoire D'Angleterre, D'Escosse, et D'Irlande* (1614), Milton noted in his commonplace book the personal and political dangers of a Catholic match for a commonwealth, as it would subject Charles individually and England collectively to the thraldom of the Catholic religion. He recorded that Pope Gregory XV had sent a letter to Charles in 1623 calling him 'a favourer of the Catholick cause ... and of the Roman prælacie, because he sought in marriage a daughter of Spain'. Of special interest to Milton, and to more radical Protestants in this period, were the details of Charles's approval of the terms of his marriage and his permission for English Catholics to practise their religion.[101]

Milton was not alone in flagging Pope Gregory's letter as suspicious. In 1642, perhaps at the same time that Milton wrote his commonplace book entry, an anonymous pamphleteer translated this letter and Charles's cordial reply to the Pope into English, and thereby brought it to the attention of the English public. A year later, William Prynne reprinted the English translation of these letters in *The Popish Royall Favourite* (1643), claiming that the letters and articles of the Spanish Match 'layd the foundation stone of all his Maiesties ensuing favours to Romish Recusants, Priests, Iesuites ... and his good affection and inclination to the Roman Party, if not to that Religion, even since manifested towards

---

[98] *CPW*, I.923–24.   [99] *Defensio pro Populo Anglicano* (1651), *CPW*, IV.2.321–22.
[100] *CPW*, I.399.
[101] This is clear because of the page numbers Milton listed in his commonplace book. See *CPW*, I.399. See also Dolan, *Whores of Babylon*, 98–99.

258   The Masculine Republic

them'.[102] Charles's letter to the Pope could have been interpreted as merely complimentary. According to John Rushworth's translation printed in 1659, Charles expressed only his 'Moderation, as to abstain from such actions which may testifie our hatred against the *Roman* Catholick Religion'.[103] The anonymous pamphlet of 1642 and Prynne's pamphlet in 1643, however, fashioned Charles's reply as a dubious concession to Catholicism, and led Englishmen such as Edward Hyde, earl of Clarendon to assert that 'the letter to the Pope by [Charles's] favour is more than compliment'.[104] Milton himself cited this letter several times as proof of Charles's Catholicism. Arguing in his first *Defensio* that Charles's beheading was not enacted by Protestants against a Protestant king, Milton contended, 'Can he really be called Protestant who in writing to the pope hailed him as "Most Holy Father", and who was always more kindly disposed toward Papists than toward the Orthodox?'[105] And in *Eikonoklastes* (1649), Milton cited the letter a number of times as proof that Charles had 'ingag'd himself to hazard life and estate for the Roman Religion'.[106]

---

[102] *Behold! Two Letters, the one, Written by the Pope to the (then) Prince of Wales, now King of England: the other, An Answere to the said Letter, by the said Prince, now his Maiesty of England. Being an Extract out of the History of England, Scotland, and Ireland; Written in French by Andrew du Chesne, Geographer to the K. of France (lib. 22. fol. 1162. Printed at Paris cum privilegio) and now Translated into English* (London?, 'Printed in the yeare of Discoveries' 1642). Reprinted in 1648. William Prynne, *The Popish royall favourite or, a full discovery of His Majesties extraordinary favours to, and protections of notorious papists, priestes, Jesuites, against all prosecutions and penalties of the laws enacted against them* (London, 1643), 36.

[103] John Rushworth, *Historical collections of private passages of state Weighty matters in law. Remarkable proceedings in five Parliaments. Beginning the sixteenth year of King James, anno 1618. And ending the fifth year of King Charls, anno 1629* (London, 1659), 82–83.

[104] Clarendon letter to Secretary Nicholas, Jersey, 12 Feb. 1646–47, in *Calendar of the Clarendon State Papers*, vol. II, ed. Rev. W. Dunn Macray (Oxford: Clarendon Press, 1869), 337. Compare, for example, the following two translations of the same sentence: 'Therefore your Holiness may be assured, That we are, and always will be of that [A] Moderation, as to abstain from such actions which may testifie our hatred against the *Roman* Catholick Religion; we will rather embrace all occasions whereby through a gentle and fair procedure all sinister suspitions may be taken away; That as we all confess one Individual Trinity, and one [B] Christ Crucified, we may unanimously grow up into one Faith.' Rushworth, *Historical collections*, 82–83. Anonymous Pamphlet: 'Therefore I intreate your Holynesse to believe, that I have been alwaies very far from incouraging Novelties, or to be a part of any Faction against the Catholike, Apostolike Roman Religion: But on the contrary, I have sought all occasions to take away the supicion that might rest upon me, and that I will imploy my selfe for the time to come, to have but one Religion and one faith, seeing that we all beleeve in one Jesus Christ.' *Behold! Two Letters*, 6.

[105] *CPW*, IV.327–28.

[106] Ibid., III.537. Milton here showed his awareness that people debated whether the letter was 'in complement . . . or in earnest'. He contended that either way, 'God, who stood neerer then he for complementing minded, writ down those words; that according to his resolution, so it should come to pass.' See also *CPW*, III.421 and 515.

Milton, Marriage, & Realisation of Republican Manhood   259

Milton thereby considered marriage to one of a different religion to be dangerous in myriad ways due to the emasculation of the husband, the threat to his salvation, and the ill political effects that bad marriage and idolatry could have on the commonwealth as a whole; the consequences of an English king marrying a Catholic who desired to evangelise him and his people would be especially disastrous to the salvation, liberty, and manliness of *all* England's subjects. In another commonplace book entry on Paolo Sarpi's *History of the Council of Trent*, Milton again confirmed this worry by recording the speech of a divine at the Council of Trent who claimed that Philip II of Spain had 'married Mary of England for no other end than to reduce that Island to that religion'.[107] Charles's eventual marriage to the French Henrietta troubled Milton and other Protestants for it threatened evangelisation by contaminating the monarch, royal household, and heir to the throne. Prynne, for example, warned that Englishmen 'have great cause to feare (if *Adams, Solomons,* or *Ahabs* seducements by their wives be duly pondered) that his Majesty (now wholly alienated from his Parliament, and best Protestant Subjects, by the Queen and popish Counsellors . . .) may ere long be seduced to their Religion'.[108] In his commonplace book, Milton recorded that Charles's marriage to the French Henrietta 'was no lesse dangerous if the conditions obtained by the Marquesse D'Effiat, and Richelieu be true'. From the list of these concessions, including Henrietta's 'libre exercice de la Religion Catholique. Apostolique & Romaine' and the placement of private chapels in all of her palaces, Milton noted in particular 'that the children should be bred in the papists religion till 13 years old'.[109]

For Milton, who understood Catholic thought and practice as enslaving the intellect and soul of its practitioners and simultaneously threatening the civil liberty of a commonwealth, this concession would have seemed dangerous indeed. The royal children would be 'bred in the papists religion' in three senses, being formed and birthed through the womb of the Catholic Henrietta, raised in ceremonial practices of the faith, and educated in its doctrine.[110] As medical views in this period generally held that mothers had the ability to shape and alter the disposition and attributes of their foetuses in the womb, Henrietta Maria's Catholic

---

[107] This entry was under the label, 'Mariage with Papists dangerous to England', *CPW*, I.402.

[108] Prynne, *Popish Royall Favourite*, 59.

[109] In his commonplace book, Milton listed the page numbers of where Du Chesne listed these conditions. See André Du Chesne, *Histoire D'Angleterre, D'Escosse, et D'Irlande . . .* 3rd edition rev. et augm (Paris, 1641), 1182–84.

[110] See *OED*, 'breed, v'. definition 1a and 10b and (b).

260 The Masculine Republic

disposition, which would be imprinted upon the future king, posed a substantial threat to the future of English liberty. This marriage concession further reinforced Protestant associations of Catholicism with unruly women, especially the view that Catholic women corrupted the foundations of household and society through their marriages and their rearing of children in the Catholic faith. Catholic households were often characterised as schools of lawlessness and godlessness, so much so that parliament proposed legislation for 'the taking of Papists' children from them' to be educated in Protestant households or schools nine times between 1605 and 1649.[111] After forming the royal children in her womb, the Queen and her Catholic advisors would have 13 years to ensure that the seeds of the Catholic faith would take root and thrive in the minds and hearts of the royal children.[112] Milton's fears were shared by Parliament, which in November 1641 ordered that the Queen relinquish custody of her son to a governor named by Parliament to protect the Prince of Wales from popish, and thereby tyrannical, influence; simultaneously, the publicly printed *Grand Remonstrance* (1641) associated the Irish rising with a Papist faction at court and the Queen's Catholicism, threatening to impeach her.[113] For Milton in the early 1640s, Charles's marriage to Henrietta Maria exemplified the 'danger' of marrying outside one's religion: It would corrupt the monarch, his children and household, and England as a whole. And Charles's contractual terms of marriage ensured that there would be no hope of converting his wife to the 'true religion'.

That Charles did not forsake Henrietta Maria, but indeed appeared to adopt her ritualistic practices and popery for the English Church and state through the Laudian reforms, became a significant contention in Milton's later prose works. His observations that Charles and his household had adopted intemperate practices that went hand-in-hand with idolatry, including debauchery, extravagance, and secret plots, deepened this conviction. In *Eikonoklastes* (1649) and the first *Defensio pro Populo Anglicano* (1651), Milton passionately argued that Charles's tyranny and his failure to rule England for the sake of liberty and right religion had resulted, in part, from his intemperate moral character and from a bad

---

[111] Dolan, *Whores of Babylon*, 137. See also 55–57, 124–27, 136–56.

[112] For similar fears concerning James's formation through the womb of Mary Stuart, see Chapter 3.

[113] Michelle Anne White, *Henrietta Maria and the English Civil Wars* (Burlington, VT: Ashgate, 2006), 49–59; C. V. Wedgwood, *The King's War, 1641–47* (London: Collins, 1959), 47. See *A Remonstrance of the State of the Kingdom*, Die Mercurii 15 Decemb. 1641, *It is this day Resolv'd upon the Question, By the House of Commons, That Order shall be now given for the Printing of this Remonstrance, of the State of the Kingdom* (London, 1641), esp. 5, 13–14, 21, 23–24.

Milton, Marriage, & Realisation of Republican Manhood 261

marriage which had corrupted him and his household. Simultaneously, Milton's attacks upon Charles's household rule took aim at patriarchal conceptions of kingship.

Milton's *Eikonoklastes* (1649) was commissioned to respond to *Eikon Basilike* (1649), a highly popular and sympathetic 'Portrature of his sacred Majesty in his *Solitudes and Sufferings*' which sought to legitimise Charles's rule and presented him as a persecuted king and royal martyr. Central to the imagery of Charles as just king and worthy martyr in this work was the patriarchal image of kingship, with an emphasis upon generation as uniting fatherhood and kingship: As the 'loving father of [His] people', the king begets heirs to the throne and begets laws which ensure the continuance and order of the body politic.[114] Milton intended to shatter Charles's royal portrait as martyr and his patriarchal claims to authority by demonstrating Charles's failures as an actual husband and father within the royal household and as a metaphorical father of the nation. To do so, he developed the theme of uxoriousness throughout *Eikonoklastes*, arguing that Henrietta Maria had greater sway upon Charles than Charles upon her, with the result that the royal household and kingdom became ruled by a female idolatress. Milton found support for this view by frequently referencing the royal letters seized at Naseby and printed in *The Kings Cabinet Opened* (1645).[115] In his chapter upon the '*Letters tak'n and divulg'd*', Milton summarised Charles's many crimes seemingly laid open by the letters, such as 'his good affection to Papists and Irish Rebels, . . . his endeavours to bring in forren Forces', and 'his suttleties and mysterious arts in treating'. [T]o summ up all', Milton explained, 'they shewd him govern'd by a Woman'.[116] Foreign-born, Catholic, and a queen, Henrietta Maria's seeming dominance within the royal marriage and household would result in Charles's pursuance of characteristically effeminate, irrational, and even tyrannical courses of action. The letters, moreover, uncovered Charles's significant lack of the virtues of 'true Religion, Piety, Justice, Prudence, Temperance, Fortitude', upon which the 'happiness and welfare' of men and the governance of household and commonwealth

---

[114] Bruce Boehrer, 'Elementary Structures of Kingship: Milton, Regicide, and the Family', *Milton Studies XXIII*, ed. James D. Simmonds (Pittsburgh: University of Pittsburgh Press, 1987), 97–117, esp. 107; *Eikon Basilike, with selections from Eikonoklastes*, ed. Jim Daems and Holly Faith Nelson (Toronto: Broadview, 2006), 35.

[115] E.g. *CPW*, III.525, 526, 537–43. For more on *The Kings Cabinet Opened*, see Laura Lunger Knoppers, '"Deare heart": Framing the Royal Couple in *The Kings Cabinet Opened*, in *Politicizing Domesticity from Henrietta Maria to Milton's Eve* (Cambridge: Cambridge University Press, 2011), 42–67.

[116] *CPW*, III.537–38.

262   The Masculine Republic

depended. Lacking virtue and control of his wife, the King's own household 'was the most licentious and ill-govern'd in the whole Land'.[117] Significantly, within these passages condemning Charles as uxorious husband, Milton urged his readers to abandon their support of the institution of kingship altogether: 'They in whomsoever these vertues dwell eminently, need not Kings to make them happy, but are the architects of thir own happiness; and whether to themselves or others are not less then Kings.'[118]

Considering the royal marriage in particular, Milton argued that the King had not only failed to convert Henrietta Maria to the 'true religion' but had even hindered her conversion through his own moral and political failings. These failings warranted another long list in *Eikonoklastes*, including the 'dissoluteness of his Court, the scandals of his Clergy, the unsoundness of his own judgement, the lukewarmness of his life, his Letter of compliance to the Pope, his permitting Agents at *Rome*, the Popes *Nuntio*, [and her Jesuited Mother] here'.[119] Notably, in this list and the one above, Milton harped particularly on domestic scandals and on foreign popish threats. While these failures were labelled as Charles's, the origins of these specific faults clearly rested upon Charles's corruption through marriage to a foreign-born and Catholic queen, a woman who not only symbolised but also helped realise these failures in the royal household through her supposedly seductive hold upon her husband. Rather than being drawn to conversion, the Queen 'had bin averse from the Religion of her Husband ... every yeare more and more', Milton claimed.[120] Charles's particular lack of constancy in religion, and his general failure to live a temperate and virtuous life and to rule his household, hindered him from converting his wife, and at the same time made him particularly susceptible to her enchantments. It was 'her Religion', Milton explained, that 'wrought more upon him, then his Religion upon her, and his op'n favouring of Papists, and his hatred of them call'd Puritants ... made most men suspect she had quite perverted him'.[121]

Private uxoriousness and false religion carried dire public consequences, Milton maintained in *Eikonoklastes*, for the charms of Henrietta Maria not only corrupted his own manliness but bewitched Charles from hearing the rational, manly counsel of others:

---

[117] Ibid., III.542.   [118] Ibid., III.542.
[119] Ibid., III.421–22. For the letter to the Pope, see p. 255–56.   [120] Ibid., III.420.   [121] Ibid.

Milton, Marriage, & Realisation of Republican Manhood   263

[Charles] ascribes *Rudeness and barbarity worse then Indians* to the English Parlament, and *all vertue* to his Wife, in straines that come almost to Sonnetting: How fitt to govern men, undervaluing and aspersing the great Counsel of his Kingdom, in comparison of one Woman. Examples are not farr to seek, how great mischeif and dishonour hath befall'n to Nations under the Government of effeminate and Uxorious Magistrates. Who being themselves govern'd and oversward at home under a Feminine usurpation, cannot but be farr short of spirit and autority without dores, to govern a whole Nation.[122]

In this striking passage, Milton sought to emphasise both the irony and the danger of Charles ascribing barbarity to parliament while being himself ruled by a Catholic woman. For decades, Catholics especially in locations such as Ireland had been deemed barbarous due to their supposedly pagan, superstitious, and cruel practices, a view only hardened with news campaigns of atrocities committed against Protestants in the 1641 Irish Uprising.[123] English 'civilitie' and 'good lawes' were often contrasted with the 'barbarous savageness' and rebellion of foreign Catholics.[124] These views concerning the Irish were discursively transferred upon the 'Indians' of the Americas and other colonised groups deemed barbarous.[125] Accounts such as Girolamo Benzoni's *Historia del Mundo Nuovo* (1578, Latin translation) emphasised both the seeming brutishness of Indians, such as the Cumana woman who 'appeared like a monster . . . rather than a human being', and the cruelty of Spanish Catholic conquistadors who raped, tortured, murdered, and enslaved these populations with avarice and cruelty.[126] For

---

[122] *CPW*, III.421.

[123] In his *Observations upon the Articles of Peace with the Irish Rebels* (1649), Milton decried Charles for granting an act of oblivion to Irish rebels who shed the 'bloud of more than 200000. of his Subjects, . . . assassinated and cut in pieces by those *Irish* Barbarians'. See *CPW*, III.308. For the news campaigns, see, for example, Thomas Morley, *Remonstrance of the Barbarous Cruelties and Bloudy Murders Committed By the Irish Rebels Against the Protestants in Ireland . . . Presented to the whole kingdome of England, that thereby they may see the Rebels inhumane dealing, prevent their pernicious practises, relieve thier poore brethrens necessities, and fight for their Religions, Laws, and Liberties* (London, 1644).

[124] 'The inhabitants of the English pale have been in old time so much addicted to their civilitie, and so farre sequestered from barbarous savageness, as their onelie mother toong was English. And trulie, so long as these impaled dwellers did sunder themselves as well in land as in language from the Irish: rudeness was daie by daie in the countrie supplanted, civilitie ingraffed, good lawes established, loyalty observed, rebellion suppressed, and in fine the coine of a yoong England was like to shoot in Ireland.' Raphael Holinshed (ed.), *Chronicles of England, Scotland and Ireland*, vol. 6 (London: Johnson, 1807–8), 4. Qtd in Andrew Hadfield and Wiley Maley, eds., *Representing Ireland: Literature and the Origins of Conflict, 1534–1660* (Cambridge: Cambridge University Press, 1993), 8.

[125] J. Burton and A. Loomba, 'Introduction', in *Race in Early Modern England: A Documentary Companion* (New York: Palgrave Macmillan, 2007), 20–21.

[126] Ibid., 92–93.

264   The Masculine Republic

Milton, Charles's comparison of parliament, a collective of virtuous and Protestant men who speak rational counsel, to uncivilised savages itself appeared to prove the depth of his irrational and uxorious enchantment to Henrietta Maria. The King's near 'Sonnetting' speeches concerning his Catholic wife only further betrayed this emasculated state of mind.[127]

This offence to parliament appears only trumped by a later passage of *Eikonoklastes*, in which Milton accused King Charles of infantilising parliament and the kingdom as a 'great baby'. This statement echoed the *Tenure of Kings and Magistrates* (1649), in which Milton argued that those nations who lack the power of removing their government possess merely a 'ridiculous and painted freedom, fit to coz'n babies', for they lack the power 'to dispose and *oeconomize* in the Land which God hath giv'n them, as Maisters of Family in thir own house and free inheritance'.[128] The *Tenure* extended the image of infantilisation to entail the lack of household governance; in *Eikonoklastes*, Milton similarly coupled infantilisation with the related argument that Charles had reduced parliament to a 'Female' requiring Charles's '*influence*' for '*all natures productions*' concerning law and authority.[129] In this metaphor, parliament became a wife meant to submit and serve as help-meet to her husband, the King. Whereas Charles deemed his 'procreative reason' necessary to the production of laws, Milton argued that parliament, if not male, should at least be considered the mother of Charles and of the office of kingship in England, having 'created both him, and the Royalty he wore'.[130] Echoing Jacobean and Caroline texts which focused upon maternal incest as a mark of Roman tyranny and repulsive household disorder, Milton extended his metaphor of the parliament as mother to declare Charles a tyrant with incestuous dreams: 'And if it hath bin anciently interpreted the presaging signe of a future Tyrant, but to dream of copulation with his Mother, what can it be less then actual Tyranny to affirme waking, that the Parliament, which is his Mother, can neither conceive or bring forth *any autoritative Act* without his Masculine coition ... .'[131] Milton in these ways denounced Charles's conceptions of generative patriarchal authority as both delusional

---

[127] For a further contextualisation of this passage, see Michelle A. White, '"She is the man, and Raignes": Popular Representations of Henrietta Maria during the English Civil Wars', in *Queens & Power in Medieval and Early Modern England*, ed. Carole Levin and Robert Bucholz (Lincoln, NE: University of Nebraska Press, 2009), 205–223.

[128] The passage accusing infantilisation is as follows: 'But *he must chew such Morsels as Propositions ere he let them down*. So let him; but if the Kingdom shall tast nothing but after his chewing, what does he make of the Kingdom, but a great baby', *CPW*, III.467. For the *Tenure*, see *CPW*, III.236–37.

[129] *CPW*, III.468–469.   [130] Ibid., III.467.   [131] Ibid.

Milton, Marriage, & Realisation of Republican Manhood 265

and tyrannical, fitting the pattern of egregious household disorder found in the stories of Roman tyrants.[132] *Eikonoklastes* emphasised that Charles had viewed parliament as barbarous, female, and puerile; the King had sought to emasculate England's ruling men as he himself had been emasculated.

Milton's *Defensio pro Populo Anglicano* (1651) continued these themes of uxoriousness by similarly attacking patriarchal theories of kingship and by further linking Charles's household to corruption, idolatry, and effeminacy, even through direct comparison of Charles with Roman tyrants such as Nero. For the former, Milton argued that those 'failing to distinguish the rights of a father from those of a king' are 'wholly in the dark':

> Fathers and kings are very different things: Our fathers begot us, but our kings did not, and it is we, rather, who created the king. It is nature which gave the people fathers, and the people who gave themselves a king; the people therefore do not exist for the king, but the king for the people. We endure a father though he be harsh and strict, and we endure such a king too; but we do not endure even a father who is tyrannical. If a father kill his son he shall pay with his life: shall not then a king too be subject to this same most just of laws if he has destroyed the people who are his sons? This is the more true since a father cannot abjure his position as father, while a king can easily make himself neither a father nor a king.[133]

Whereas fathers fall under the law of nature, having generated sons, kings have been established by the people; despite this distinction of nature, both kings and fathers are subject to established laws. Milton in these passages adopted a two-pronged argument against Charles, denying that kings are natural and generative fathers of kingdoms in the first place, and denying secondarily that Charles's particular behaviour made him a suitable 'father' of his private household or public kingdom.

Written as a vituperative condemnation of Claudius Salmasius's *Defensio Regia pro Carolo I* (1649), Milton's *Defensio* intermixed fierce argumentation of political principles from classical and Scriptural authorities with attacks upon the personal character of Charles and of his defender. Indeed, with great frequency, Milton employed *ad hominem* attacks to undermine Salmasius's credibility as a man who had lost control of his own wife and household.[134] Like Edmund Bolton in his *Nero Caesar* (1624) and other

---

[132] For incest as a trope of Roman tyranny, see Section 3.4.   [133] *CPW*, IV.326–27.

[134] Amongst the many examples, Milton exclaimed, 'For you are yourself a Gallic cock and said to be rather cocky, but instead of commanding your mate, she commands and hen-pecks you; and if the cock is king of many hens while you are the slave of yours, you must be no cock of the roost but a mere dung-hill Frenchman! As far as books go, certainly no one has heaped up more dung than you, whose crowing over your heap deafens everyone; this is the one characteristic of the cock

266 The Masculine Republic

royalists before him who had sought to separate the public rule from the 'priuate lives of Princes', Salmasius had argued that a king's private character and domestic activities would not dictate his ability to govern well. Even a king *'vinosus est & libidinosus & luxuriousus & prodigus & avarus'*, Salmasius argued, will nonetheless not stand in the way of good governance, for personal vices, including murder and adultery, which may be committed by magistrates as well as private citizens, have nothing in common with those crimes committed in ruling and administering the empire.[135] In the case of King Charles, however, Salmasius claimed that the English had been blessed with a 'good, pious, chaste, and religious prince', whose matchless purity of character brought to perfection the Christian virtues.[136]

Milton countered these arguments directly in his *Defensio* both by arguing for an essential relationship between a monarch's character and his ability to govern for the people's welfare and liberty, and by contending that Charles had been far from saintly in his private life. His immoral example 'did enormous harm to his people', Milton maintained, and the 'time [the King] spent on his lusts and pleasures, which was a great deal, was all stolen from the state'; moreover, King Charles's 'domestic extravagance wasted huge sums of money, countless wealth that was not his own but belonged to the state'. Milton summed up the problem succinctly: 'It was then within his own household that [Charles] began to be a bad king.'[137]

Milton argued that, by placing his own lusts and interests ahead of those of the people, Charles fit the classical definition of tyranny provided by Aristotle.[138] To support his 'life of luxury', the King had 'imposed very heavy taxes on the people' and abolished Parliament; he also forcibly

---

which you possess.' *CPW*, IV.428. See Erin Murphy, *Familial Forms: Politics and Genealogy in Seventeenth-Century English Literature* (Plymouth: University of Delaware, 2011), 84–85.

[135] 'Regum quoque vita, ut & magistratuum interior, & domestica, civium vitiis laborat, quæ nihil habent cum iis criminibus commune, quem in regnando & administrando imperio committuntur ... cui tamen hi mores à bene regendo no obstant ... Non tamen idem semper qui bene vixit, etiam optimè rexit.' Salmasius continued by claiming that the reverse is true: The king who is righteous in his private life may not be a good ruler, citing Emperor Trajan as an example. He named King David as an example of one who lived a vicious private life of homicide and adultery but ruled well. Claudius Salmasius, *Defensio Regia pro Caroli I ad Serenissimum Magnæ Brittaniæ Regem Carolum II. Filium natu majorem, Heredem & Successorem legitimum. Sumptibus Regiis* (n.p.: 1649), 626–28.

[136] 'Si querimus quomodo vixerit Carolus, ne inimici quidem ejus, ac rebelles subjecti, qui caput illi scelerato judicio, quasi homini facinoroso securi carnificis amputarunt, aliter possunt dicere, quin bonus, pius, castus & religiosus princeps fuerit ....' Ibid., 629–30.

[137] *CPW*, IV.520–21.   [138] Ibid., IV.521.

restrained the English people by stationing troops in their towns. At the same time, Charles 'did great violence to the conscience of godly men, and forced on all certain rituals and superstitious practices which he had brought back into the church from the depths of popery'.[139] Himself being 'lured to idolatry' and then enslaved by a popish wife, Charles not only 'lured others by the richest rewards of a corrupt church', Milton further contended, 'but also compelled them by edicts and ecclesiastical regulations to erect those altars which are abhorred by all Protestants, and to worship crucifixes painted on the walls and hanging over these altars'.[140] The King's own subjugation to a woman and her idolatry thereby resulted in the physical and spiritual subjugation of the English people.

5.5 Republicanism and the Restoration of Manhood

'I did but prompt the age to quit their cloggs
By the known rules of ancient liberty.'[141]

This chapter has traced a number of intertwining threads across Milton's thought and early political activities, and developed multiple themes concerning gender, religion, marriage, and monarchy. At core we find a Miltonic ideal of virtuous, rational, and fully grown man, who lives unfettered by besetting vices, false beliefs, or corrupted institutions and contracts, who is fit to live into his native birth right. Milton built his conceptualisations of liberty and of the free commonwealth upon the realisation of manhood thus described. His republican writings, and indeed much of the classical republicanism developed by Milton's contemporaries within this period, must be read through this gendered lens to be understood, for the achievement of masculine citizenship in a commonwealth long emasculated by monarchy became of utmost concern in the 1650s.

Milton outlined three types of liberty as necessary for 'civilized life': ecclesiastical liberty, domestic or personal liberty, and civil liberty.[142] Passages abound within Milton's writings describing these liberties as intertwined and co-dependent, as grounded in a conception of masculinity, and as threatened by un-masculine corruption. In his description in the *Defensio Secunda* (1654) of his writings on domestic or personal liberty,

---

[139] *CPW*, IV.520–22.   [140] Ibid., IV.372–73.
[141] Sonnet XII (1646?) from John Milton, *The Complete Poems and Major Prose*, ed. Merritt Y. Hughes (Indianapolis: Hackett, 1957), 143–44.
[142] *CPW*, IV.624.

268 The Masculine Republic

Milton emphasised that 'in vain does he prattle about liberty in assembly and market-place who at home endures the slavery most unworthy of a man, slavery to an inferior'.[143] When men become 'slaves within doors', ruled by the 'double tyrannie, of Custom from without, and blind affections within', Milton contended in *The Tenure of Kings and Magistrates* (1649), it is 'no wonder that they strive so much to have the public State conformably govern'd to the inward vitious rule, by which they govern themselves'.[144] Moreover, in reference to *Of Education*, he maintained that 'nothing can be more efficacious than education in moulding the minds of men to virtue (whence arises true and internal liberty), in governing the state effectively, and preserving it for the longest possible space of time'.[145] The earlier *Of Reformation* (1641) similarly emphasised that 'Liberty consists in manly and honest labours, in sobriety and rigorous honour to the Marriage Bed, which in both Sexes should be bred up from chast hopes to loyall Enjoyments; and when the people slacken and fall to loosenes, and riot, then doe they as much as if they laid downe their necks for some wily Tyrant to get up and ride.'[146] And in Sonnet XII (1646?) when castigating those who 'bawl for Freedom in their senseless mood', and mean 'Licence ... when they cry Libertie', Milton reminded his readers: 'For who loves [liberty] must first be Wise and Good.'[147]

The restoration of liberty and of manliness thereby would and must occur simultaneously, and Milton emphasised that seeking revolution for a corrupted and un-manly people would lead only to destruction and ruin. As he described in his *Digression* of the *History of Britain* (1648?), concerning particularly the story of Marcus Brutus:

> For stories teach us, that Liberty sought out of season, in a corrupt and degenerate Age, brought *Rome* itself into a farther Slavery: For Liberty hath a sharp and double edge, fit only to be handled by Just and Vertuous Men; to bad and dissolute, it becomes a mischief unweildy in their own hands: neither is it compleatly given, but by them who have the happy skill to know what is grievance, and unjust to a People, and how to remove it wisely; what good Laws are wanting, and how to frame them substantially, that good Men may enjoy the freedom which they merit, and the bad the Curb which they need.[148]

For the English in the 1650s, who had endured decades of religious and political tyranny under an idolatrous royal household, the activity of

---

[143] Ibid., IV.625. [144] Ibid., III.190. [145] Ibid., IV.625. [146] Ibid., I.588.
[147] Milton, *The Complete Poems*, 143–44.
[148] *CPW*, V.1, 448. See also *CPW*, V.1. 402–3, and its explication by Martin Dzelzainis, 'Conquest and Slavery in Milton's *History of Britain*', in *Oxford Handbook of Milton*, 407–23.

Milton, Marriage, & Realisation of Republican Manhood   269

becoming realised as full men would entail not only constitutional solutions but significant moral activity and cleansing. About this prospect, Milton often betrayed significant pessimism, reflecting in the *Defensio Secunda* that 'men who are unworthy of liberty most often prove ungrateful to their very liberators . . . It is not fitting, it is not meet, for such men to be free. However loudly they shout and boast about liberty, slaves they are at home and abroad, although they know it not.' These men, according to Milton, become driven not by the 'love of true liberty' but by 'pride and base desires'. They may perceive their chains, and buck as wild horses against the yoke, but 'they will accomplish naught. They can perhaps change their servitude; they cannot cast it off'.[149]

The primary motivation of Milton's political programme was therefore the renovation of masculinity, for masculinity entailed the full enjoyment of human liberty, and without manly virtue, republican political institutions would be erected in vain and doomed to failure. 'For, my fellow countrymen, your own character is a mighty factor in the acquisition or retention of liberty', Milton argued:

> Unless your liberty is such as can neither be won nor lost by arms, but is of that kind alone which, sprung from piety, justice, temperance, in short, true virtue, has put down the deepest and most far-reaching roots in your souls, there will not be lacking one who will shortly wrench from you, even without weapons, that liberty which you boast of having sought by force of arms.[150]

These statements recognised the fragility of liberty, built upon a foundation of manliness prone to corruption in the postlapsarian state. Milton's republican programme thereby was a moral one, bent upon reforming the nation from vicious degeneration and corruption.[151]

Constitutional forms mattered to Milton insofar as they accomplished the conditions necessary for restoring and protecting virtuous manhood. While Milton early in the 1650s more often castigated tyranny than kingship, and had not yet proposed the constitutional form of the *Readie and Easie Way* (1659), his discussions of virtuous monarchy signified that he envisioned such a type as indeed rare and as only tolerable when

---

[149] Ibid., IV.1, 683.   [150] *CPW*, IV.1.680.

[151] This statement aligns well with Dzelzainis's contention that, much more often than slavery leading to slavishness, Milton understood slavishness as leading to slavery. See Dzelzainis, 'Milton's *History of Britain*', 423.

270 The Masculine Republic

preserving and expanding liberty and masculine virtue.[152] This is on display when Milton, in the *Defensio Secunda*, offered conditional praise for Oliver Cromwell. The Lord Protector's initial martial victories arose from his being a 'victor over himself', Milton argued; his military camp became a 'foremost school, not just of military science, but of religion and piety', and the men he attracted to fight were 'already good and brave' or became so 'chiefly by his own example'.[153] With the later demise of the Long Parliament, Cromwell alone, the man of 'unexcelled virtue', could save the state – 'there is nothing in human society more pleasing to God, or more agreeable to reason, nothing in the state more just, nothing more expedient, than the rule of the man most fit to rule'. Milton contended that Cromwell fit this bill, as 'the greatest and most illustrious citizen', not only due to his coterie of magnanimous and exercised virtues but from his spurning of the idolatrous name of king – a line containing praise, surely, as much as suggestion.[154]

Milton charged Cromwell to honour the brave men who fought to birth the republic, and to honour the resulting liberty that they achieved through sacrifice, and he warned that Cromwell must bear the heaviest burden in protecting the people's liberty from violation, else he would be 'the first of all to become a slave' with its loss.[155] To ensure the protection of this liberty hard won, Milton ascribed the tasks of refusing pleasure, wealth, and pomp, and of leading the people 'from base customs to a better standard of morality and discipline than before', tasks so arduous that war would appear 'a mere game'.[156] In these ways, Milton's *Defensio Secunda* illustrated his primary concern that the English commonwealth be grounded in morality and discipline, which were hallmarks of his definition of masculinity. He ended this section by urging Cromwell to rule by admitting to his counsels fellow virtuous men – those 'eminently modest, upright and brave', who learned through the wars 'justice, the fear of God, and compassion for the lot of mankind'. At the same time, Milton warned

---

[152] For Milton on virtuous monarchy, I am following David Norbrook's reading of the *Defensio Secunda* in *Writing the English Republic: Poetry, Rhetoric and Politics, 1627–1660* (Cambridge: Cambridge University Press, 1999), 332–33. For more on Milton and constitutional forms, see Thomas N. Corns, 'Milton and the Characteristics of a Free Commonwealth', in *Milton and Republicanism*, ed. Armitage, Armand Himy, and Quentin Skinner (Cambridge: Cambridge University Press, 1995), 25–42, esp. 41; Blair Worden, 'Marchamont Nedham and the Beginnings of English Republicanism, 1649–1656', in *Republicanism, Liberty, and Commercial Society*, ed. David Wootton (Stanford: Stanford University Press, 1994), 45–81, esp. 56–58; Worden, 'Milton and the Civil Wars', in *Literature and Politics in Cromwellian England* (Oxford: Oxford University Press, 2007), 154–79.
[153] *CPW*, IV.1, 668. [154] Ibid., IV.1, 671–72. [155] Ibid., IV.1, 673. [156] Ibid., IV.1, 674.

Milton, Marriage, & Realisation of Republican Manhood 271

the English public that they would remain at liberty only by conquering the tyrants within themselves through expelling 'avarice, ambition, and luxury from your minds, yes, and extravagance from your families as well'.[157]

It appears that Milton began composing his fullest republican treatise, *The Readie and Easie Way* (1659), just before the secluded members of Parliament had been re-admitted by General Monck in February 1659; he hurriedly added the work's prefatory paragraph and transmitted the manuscript to printer just before the newly full House resolved to hold elections on 25 April.[158] On this timeline, Milton's *Readie and Easie Way* was a race against the clock of restored monarchy, or restored bondage, as Milton and other republicans from the 'Good Old Cause' argued. Rhetorically urgent and sincere, focused on contrasting the benefits and advantages of a free commonwealth against the significant harm of kingship, the pamphlet provides a final example of the fundamentally gendered concerns of Milton's classical republicanism.

To run 'headlong again with full steam wilfully and obstinately in the same bondage' of monarchy, was to make vain the 'blood of so many thousand faithfull and valiant Englishman, who left us in this libertie, bought with thir lives'.[159] Milton embedded his rhetoric concerning 'a free Commonwealth', 'so dearly purchased', within a heroic reminder of the English men who had sacrificed private interest for public gain, and thus opposed a particular tyrant as well as the inner tyranny that all men must conquer in choice and deed to become free. Milton's *Readie and Easie Way* extolled the 'free Commonwealth', thereby, as that which ennobled men, and afforded them avenues for acts of manly virtue. Such a commonwealth was 'not only held by wisest men in all ages [as] the noblest, the manliest, the equallest, the justest government, the most agreeable to all due libertie and proportiond equalitie, but humane, civil and Christian, most cherishing to vertue and true religion', Milton argued, 'but also ... planely commended or rather enjoind by our Saviour himself, to all Christians ... '; for, as Milton maintained, Christ called his disciples not to imitate Roman rulers who seek lordship and dominion in the enslaving of others, but to dedicate themselves to moral lives and selfless service.[160] As England's soldiers had exemplified in their sacrifice, so too the 'greatest' in a free Commonwealth become 'perpetual servants and drudges to the

---

[157] Ibid., IV.1, 674–75, 680–81.
[158] Robert W. Ayers, 'Preface' to *The Readie & Easie Way to Establish a Free Commonwealth, CPW*, VII.343–45.
[159] *CPW*, VII.358–59. [160] Ibid., VII.359–60.

272 The Masculine Republic

publick at thir own cost and charges, neglect thir own affairs', Milton contended. His description of republican men emphasised that they seek not the 'perpetual bowings and cringings of an abject people' to worship them, but 'live soberly in thir families, walk the streets as other men, may be spoken to freely, familiarly, friendly, without adoration'.[161] In short, these statesmen exhibited the temperate masculinity Milton had commended even since his days as a youthful rhetorician at Cambridge. Simultaneously, they demonstrated that to be truly manly was to be truly English.[162]

In contrast to the state of kingship, within the free Commonwealth men fully realise their manliness:

> The happiness of a nation must needs be firmest and certaintest in a full and free Councel of their own electing, where no single person, but reason only swayes. And what madness is it, for them who might manage nobly their own affairs themselves, sluggishly and weakly to devolve all on a single person; and more like boyes under age then men, to committ all to his patronage and disposal, who neither can perform what he undertakes, and yet for undertaking it, though royally paid, will not be thir servant, but thir lord? how unmanly must it needs be, to count such a one the breath of our nostrils, to hang all our felicitie on him, all our safety, our well-being, for which if we were aught els but sluggards or babies, we need depend on none but God and our own counsels, our own active vertue and industrie.[163]

In language similar to the first *Defensio* and *Tenure*, Milton maligned the state of monarchy as infantilising men and degrading them to a state of dependency and weakness. Men in seventeenth-century England were frequently distinguished from boys in their self-sufficiency and household management; Milton in this significant passage articulated the same for republican government, a commonwealth being managed – much like virtuous households – by rational, industrious, and virtuous men.

As the pamphlet continued, Milton enjoined these languages of rational and mature manhood with warnings that monarchy would enslave, prostrate, degenerate, and make men bestial – imagery which calls to mind the monstrous rout roaming the woods with Comus.[164] Whereas monarchy creates men to be the 'softest, basest, vitiousest, servilest, easiest to be kept under; and not only in fleece, but in minde also sheepishest', a free Commonwealth amongst all governments 'aims most to make the people flourishing, vertuous, noble, and high spirited'.[165] In the second edition of

---

[161] Ibid., VII.360–61.
[162] See Hilary Larkin, *The Making of Englishmen: Debates on National Identity, 1550–1650* (Leiden: Brill, 2014), esp. 280–86.
[163] Ibid., VII.362.   [164] See *CPW*, VI.363, 382–84, 387.   [165] Ibid., VI.384.

The Readie and Easie Way, amended, enlarged, and printed a month before the new elections, Milton further emphasised this dichotomy between masculine free government and emasculated monarchy, in part by increasing the visceral language used to describe monarchical commonwealths as defiled: The desire to return to bondage is here labelled a 'noxious humor' and a 'strange degenerate contagion suddenly spread among us fitted and prepar'd for new slaverie'.[166] Moreover, within this second edition Milton turned with greater industry to the examples of classical history to underscore why his proposal for a perpetual Senate of the ablest and virtuous men would better maintain liberty than popular assemblies like those of ancient Athens, Sparta, or Rome. He advocated that his fellow Englishmen 'grow old anough to be wise to make seasonable use of gravest authorities, experiences, examples', rather than continue 'to wear a yoke', or to seek joy in wearing 'shackles' and being 'knockt on by illegal injurie and violence'.[167]

---

[166] *CPW*, VI.407 and 422.   [167] *CPW*, VII.448.

CHAPTER 6

'Begin now to know themselves men, & to breath after liberty'
Marchamont Nedham and the Republican Empire

In April 1655, after months of expensive preparation, the *Naseby* launched from Woolwich bearing 1,000 tons of burden. The largest warship of the Commonwealth navy, the 80-gun *Naseby* signalled the significant optimism and ambitions of the Cromwellian Protectorate, and its designs to bring further kingdoms and dominions under the new state's authority. The ship itself reflected the imperial moment of its creation through impressive carvings and a gilded figurehead which portrayed Oliver Cromwell upright on horseback, 'trampling six nations under foot, a Scot, Irishman, Dutchman, Frenchman, Spaniard, and English, as was easily made out by their several habits'. The figure of Fame held a laurel over Cromwell's head, with the inscription 'God with us'.[1] These themes were continued on the warship's stern and sides, the carvings of which included a mixture of classical and nationalist motifs displaying the cross of St. George alongside mythological representations of Fame, War, and Wisdom. Cherub-like figures appeared riding on the backs of lions, perhaps heralding Britannia's taming of the royal line. On the stern, the prominent cartouche of St. George bore the commonwealth motto *Pax quæritur bello*: peace is sought by war.[2]

By the launching of the *Naseby* in 1655, the Commonwealth had much 'peace' to boast of from its pursuance of war. Parliamentary armies had defeated the King's armies in the second civil war and beheaded the King, Cromwell had brutally subdued the Irish and Scots, and the Protectorate government had negotiated peace with the Dutch under terms that

---

[1] Recorded 9 Apr. 1655 in *The Diary of John* Evelyn, ed. William Bray, vol. I (London: M. Walter Dunn, 1901), 304. For its launch, see National Archives, SP 18/107 f.144. *Calendar of State Papers, Domestic Series, [Commonwealth] 1649–1660, preserved in the State Paper Department of Her Majesty's Public Record Office*. Ed. Mary Anne Everett Green. Vol. 8: Jan.–Oct. 1655 (London: Longman & Co., 1881), 462.
[2] Andrew Peters, *Ship Decoration: 1630–1780* (Barnsley: Seaforth, 2013), 99–101.

274

'Begin now to know themselves men ...' 275

humiliated these rivals.[3] With the Western Design to confront the Spanish in the Americas, the English commonwealth under Cromwell sought to champion the Protestant cause against foreign Catholic tyranny. The launch of ships from Portsmouth to the Caribbean in 1654 marked the first time that the English state actively engaged in overseas expansion.[4]

News of Cromwellian conquest, its successes and defeat, received ambivalent reception amongst republicans such as John Milton and Marchamont Nedham, both of whom penned public defences of the Protectorate for John Thurloe's office of the Council of State while privately questioning Cromwell's singular title.[5] Nedham's works of the 1650s betrayed great hopes for the imperial expansion of a truly free commonwealth of England, even while intimating doubts that, under a lord protector, the English commonwealth was not truly free. Like Milton's works studied in chapter five, Nedham's republican thought demonstrated his central aim of creating a free-state in which males could become fully realised as men. Nedham's conceptualisation of republican masculinity, however, focused more particularly on the exercise of manliness through warfare, and further promoted the creation of an expanded English empire as desirable and even as a necessary characteristic of a republican and free commonwealth.[6] Whereas Milton's writings had

---

[3] Although critics of the Treaty of Westminster believed it to be too lenient with an enemy who was 'on his knees', the Treaty obliged Dutch ships to salute the Commonwealth flag in territorial waters and to pay compensation for loss of trade sustained during the war, and to accept the Navigation Act. The Dutch would have faced complete economic ruin had Cromwell not ended the war against this fellow Protestant state. See J. D. Davies, 'A Permanent National Maritime Fighting Force, 1642–1689', in *The Oxford Illustrated History of the Royal Navy*, ed. J. R. Hill (Oxford: Oxford University Press, 1995), 69.

[4] Carla Gardina Pestana, *The English Conquest of Jamaica: Oliver Cromwell's Bid for Empire* (Cambridge, MA and London: Belknap Press, 2017), 11.

[5] Milton's nephew described the poet and Nedham as becoming enduring and 'particular' friends in these years. See Helen Darbishire, ed., *The Early Lives of Milton* (London, 1965), 44–45, 74.

[6] Like Nedham, Milton appears to have been influenced in significant ways by conquest discourses – Biblical, colonial, and classical. Disagreement remains in the scholarly community concerning Milton's own imperial views, however. Many view Milton as anti-imperialist or at least ambivalent. David Armitage has argued that Milton was a 'poet against empire', for the poet had been influenced by his reading of Sallust and Machiavelli concerning the difficulty of reconciling liberty and empire. J. Martin Evans has sought to demonstrate how deeply the discourse of New World discovery and the foundation of empire shaped *Paradise Lost*, but he understood the poet's view of European expansion as ambivalent, a position disagreeing with David Quint who understood *Paradise Lost* as an indictment of European colonialism. Martin Dzelzainis has argued, 'If Milton was not an exponent of conquest theory this is not to say that he lacked a theory of conquest.' This theory allowed Milton to make sense of the historical conquest of Britain. Although Milton does repeat the scriptural view that God's blessings upon a people could include the conquest of neighbours, he does not appear to have advocated actively for imperial conquest. Thomas Corns, however, has shown how Milton's *Observation upon the Articles of Peace* served as a preemptive justification for Cromwell's ruthless slaughters in Drogheda and Wexford, and how it voiced a new

276 The Masculine Republic

emphasised masculinity through the models of father and of orator, Nedham's republicanism championed these images alongside that of the classical warrior. His arguments for republican conquest reflected his own hopes for a thoroughly masculine commonwealth capable of subduing or liberating those under the servile yoke of tyranny.

Nedham's credentials as a serious and significant English republican author have been bolstered in recent years. That his reputation required defence can be seen in the seventeenth-century and modern-day scholars who dismissed Nedham as a man lacking principle, conscience, or sincerity due to his propensity to make enemies through his mocking and witty political newswriting and to switch sides through the course of the English civil wars, Interregnum, and Restoration.[7] From 1643–46, Nedham wrote for the parliamentary cause; after a brief stint in jail and heavy fine, he penned invective for the Royalists; thereafter, his open conversion to republican principles in 1650 earned him a decent wage from the new Council of State, as he composed protectorate pamphlets, newsbooks, and translations.[8] Contemporaries insulted him as 'the politick Shittle-cock', a 'Changeling Prophet', a 'Centaure made of Man and Asse'.[9] Restoration writers poured out numerous attacks against Nedham which were exceptionally vicious even by contemporary standards.[10] By the late-eighteenth

---

republican ethos. Jim Daems has further sought to demonstrate how, in the *Observations Upon the Articles of Peace*, Milton 'reasserts an English right, by conquest, in Ireland'. Joad Raymond has questioned these interpretations of the *Observations*, arguing that Milton's real concern in the pamphlet rested with Scottish influence on English politics. See David Armitage, 'John Milton: Poet against Empire', in *Milton and Republicanism*, ed. Armitage, Armand Himy, and Quentin Skinner (Cambridge: Cambridge University Press, 1995), 206–25; J. Martin Evans, *Milton's Imperial Epic: Paradise Lost and the Discourses of Colonialism* (Ithaca and London: Cornell University Press, 1996); David Quint, *Epic and Empire: Politics and Generic Form from Virgil to Milton* (Princeton: Princeton University Press, 1993), 265; Thomas Corns, 'Milton's *Observations upon the Articles of Peace*: Ireland under English Eyes', in *Politics, Poetics, and Hermeneutics in Milton's Prose*, ed. David Lowenstein and J. G. Turner (New York: Cambridge University Press, 1990), 123–34; Jim Daems, 'Dividing Conjunctions: Milton's *Observations upon the Articles of Peace*', *Milton Quarterly* 33.2 (May 1999): 51–55, esp. 54; Joad Raymond, 'Complications of Interest: Milton, Scotland, Ireland, and National Identity in 1649', *The Review of English Studies* 55.220 (Jun., 2004): 315–45.
[7] See, e.g., Vickie B. Sullivan, *Machiavelli, Hobbes, and the Formation of a Liberal Republicanism in England* (Cambridge: Cambridge University Press, 2006), 113; Zera S. Fink, *The Classical Republicans: An Essay on the Recovery of a Pattern of Thought in Seventeenth-Century England* (Evanston, IL: Northwestern University Press, 1945), 85; J. G. A. Pocock, *The Machiavellian Moment: Florentine Political Thought and the Atlantic Republican Tradition* (Princeton, 1975), 381.
[8] Joad Raymond, 'Nedham, Marchamont (*bap.* 1620, *d.* 1678)', *Oxford Dictionary of National Biography*, Oxford University Press, 2004; online ed., Sept. 2015 [www.oxforddnb.com/view/article/19847, accessed 28 Oct. 2016].
[9] Anon., *The Character of Mercurius Politicus* ([London], 1650), 1–3, 8.
[10] Raymond, 'Nedham, Marchamont'.

century, however, Nedham's republican writings won him attention from American revolutionaries, such as John Adams, a tribute from the marquis de Condorcet in *Esquisse d'un tableau historique des progrès de l'esprit humain* (1794), and admiration from French revolutionaries in the Cordeliers Club.[11] Recent defences of Nedham as a serious political thinker and brilliant newsman have placed the writer squarely alongside Milton, Algernon Sidney, and James Harrington as a republican of consequence in the history of ideas.[12]

Nedham's most important and thorough contribution to the English republican tradition was *The Excellencie of a Free-State, Or, the Right Constitution of a Commonwealth* (1656). Printed anonymously by Thomas Brewster (James Harrington's printer), *The Excellencie* was an edited republication of most of the editorials that Nedham had written for the government-sponsored newspaper *Mercurius Politicus* from 1651–52. Whereas the original editorials had taken aim at the Rump Parliament, *The Excellencie* claimed to target a series of 'high and ranting Discourses of personal Prerogative and unbounded Monarchy', most particularly James Howell's royalist treatise, *Som Sober Inspections . . . of the Late-long Parliament* (1655), which had proposed that Charles II be restored to the throne upon Cromwell's death. Like Howell, Nedham argued that England stood at a crossroads between 'unbounded Monarchy' and parliamentary rule; unlike Howell, he reasoned that only the latter – placing the 'Supreme

---

[11] Nedham's work was reprinted in 1767 and 1774, with the earlier version finding wider readership in America; the work was translated into French by the chevalier d'Eon de Beamount in 1774 and by Théophile Mandar in 1790. See Caroline Robbins, *The Eighteenth-Century Commonwealthman* (New York: Antheneum, 1968), 48–50; Perez Zagorin, *A History of Political Thought in the English Revolution* (London: Routledge & Kegan Paul, 1954), 123–25; Rachel Hammersley, *French Revolutionaries and English Republicans: The Cordeliers Club, 1790–1794* (Suffolk: Boydell, 2005), 56–60; Hammersley, 'An Eighteenth-Century French Commonwealthman? Exploring the Contest of the Chevalier d'Eon's Translation of Marchamont Nedham's *The Excellencie of a Free State*', in *The Chevalier D'Eon and His Worlds: Gender, Espionage and Politics in the Eighteenth Century*, ed. Simon Burrows, Jonathan Conlin, Russell Goulbourne, and Valerie Mainz (London and New York: Continuum, 2010), 215–28; A. Clark, 'The Chevalier d'Eon and Wilkes: Masculinity and Politics in the Eighteenth Century', in *Eighteenth Century Studies* xxxii (1998): 19–48.

[12] See, e.g., Blair Worden's treatment of Nedham in multiple works, including *Literature and Politics in Cromwellian England* (Oxford: Oxford University Press, 2008) and in *Republicanism, Liberty, and Commercial Society, 1649–1776*, ed. David Wootton (Stanford: Stanford University Press, 1994); Jonathan Scott's treatment of Nedham alongside other republican authors in *Commonwealth Principles: Republican Writing of the English Revolution* (Cambridge: Cambridge University Press, 2004); Quentin Skinner, *Liberty Before Liberalism* (Cambridge: Cambridge University Press, 1998); and Joad Raymond's numerous articles on Nedham, including 'An Inky Wretch: The Outrageous Genius of Marchamont Nedham', in *The National Interest* 70 (Winter 2002/03): 55–64 and '"A mercury with a winged conscience": Marchamont Nedham, Monopoly, and Censorship', in *Media History* 4:1 (2009): 7–18.

278 The Masculine Republic

Authority in the hands of the Peoples Representatives' – would 'best secure the Liberties and Freedoms of the People from the Incroachments and Usurpations of Tyranny, and answer the true Ends of the late Wars'.[13] Recognising no middle ground between monarchical and parliamentary rule was a significant political position in 1656, a position which raised the question as to whether Cromwell, the Lord Protector, should be crowned king or overthrown for the sake of true parliamentary governance. *The Excellencie* answered this question not only by laying out numerous arguments for a free parliamentary state but also by condemning tyranny in both the Stuart and Cromwellian form, denouncing actual kings as well as 'Kings *de facto*'.[14]

Scholars have noted a number of sources for Nedham's republicanism in *The Excellencie*, including Machiavelli's *Discourses on Livy*, classical writings, and possibly even Leveller tracts.[15] Like other republican writers of the 1650s, Nedham's classicism has often been assessed according to his discussions of ancient constitutions as models of liberty, or for the ways he 'roamed history for illustrations to support his thesis'.[16] Although he drew upon Greek philosophers such as Aristotle, and in the early 1650s seems to have admired the Athenian Assembly for its popular control, Nedham's writings of the mid-1650s had a particularly Roman character, born of a heavy reliance upon Roman historical examples drawn from Livy. Skinner has recognised Nedham as adopting the neo-Roman conception of liberty; other scholars have contrasted Nedham's republicanism with Milton's by

---

[13] Marchamont Nedham, *The Excellencie of a Free-State Or, The Right Constitution of a Commonwealth*, ed. Blair Worden (Indianapolis: Liberty Fund, 2011), 5.

[14] Nedham, *The Excellencie*, 18. See Worden, 'Introduction', in *The Excellencie*, xlix–l. See also Worden, *Literature and Politics in Cromwellian England*, 314–17; Worden, 'Marchamont Nedham and the Beginnings of English Republicanism, 1649–1656', in *Republicanism, Liberty, and Commercial Society*, 78–79. This position marked a change for Nedham. Two years earlier, he had anonymously published a defence for Cromwell's protectorate, and its basis in the Instrument of Government, as a balanced constitutional form which made 'due and full provision for the Peoples Liberties' and 'just Rights'. See *A True state of the case of the Commonvvealth of England, Scotland, and Ireland, and the dominions thereto belonging* (London, 1654).

[15] See Pocock, *The Machiavellian Moment*, 379–83; Sullivan, *Machiavelli, Hobbes, and the Formation of a Liberal Republicanism*, 114–43; Worden, 'Marchamont Nedham and the Beginnings of English Republicanism', 45–81; Scott, *Commonwealth Principles*, 84, 137–39, 177–78; Nigel Smith, *Literature and Revolution in England, 1640–1660* (New Haven and London: Yale, 1994), 184–86. Worden argues that Nedham in *Mercurius Politicus* 'not only extended Leveller ideas but, innovating again, gave them a classical and Machiavellian framework', but Rachel Foxley's study of the Levellers and their influence concludes that John Streater, rather than Nedham, provided a more probable marriage of Levelling and classical republicanism. Worden, 'Introduction', xxxi; Foxley, *The Levellers: Radical Political Thought in the English Revolution* (Manchester: Manchester University Press, 2013), 194–229.

[16] Worden, 'Introduction', xxix.

'*Begin now to know themselves men ...*' 279

emphasising the Roman character of the former as opposed to the Greek or mixed Greek and Roman classicism of the latter.[17] What should be noted, however, is that Nedham's attraction to Rome rested not upon senatorial morality nor the consular power established by Junius Brutus, a man he implicitly likened to Cromwell and whom he criticised as driven by ambition and as cheating the Roman people 'with a meer shadow and pretence of liberty'.[18] Rather, Nedham celebrated the popular, if precarious, liberty established by the commons through their Tribunes and Assemblies of the People, 'which were as Bridles to restrain the Power and Ambition of the Senate, or Nobility'.[19] Nedham's frequent examples from Roman history served a central function of demonstrating the desirability of such liberty and of warning about its fragility.

6.1 Nedham and the Interest of Freedom

When Nedham theorised the conditions necessary for a free and virtuous commonwealth, he conceptualised the conditions necessary for English citizens to become realised as men – *viri* – in the fullest sense of the word. Like many of his classical forebears, Nedham understood the state of liberty as the only state in which males could become men, for the free-state made it possible for men to exercise their reason, virtue, and courage in the governing of self and others. Simultaneously, Nedham imagined the free-state not only as providing the social conditions necessary to realise manhood but as itself requiring the protection and governance of men for its preservation.

Adopting the imagery of sexual assault frequently used by Roman authors to discuss tyranny, Nedham characterised 'interest of freedom' as a vulnerable virgin in need of male protection and governance: 'The Truth of it is, the Interest of Freedom is a Virgin that every one seeks to deflower; and like a Virgin, it must be kept from any other Form, or else (so great is the Lust of mankinde after dominion) there follows a rape upon the first opportunity.'[20] Within this striking passage lies an implicit understanding

---

[17] See Skinner, *Liberty before Liberalism*, 1–57; Worden, *Literature and Politics*, 350–51; Scott, *Commonwealth Principles*, 156–58.

[18] Nedham, *The Excellencie*, 11. Nedham's comments here may partly reflect Livy, who noted that liberty in the early republic mainly consisted in election and limited terms for consuls. Other than these differences, consuls were very much like the former kings, insofar as they were as powerful as kings, ruled by the same oaths, and carried kingly insignia. See Livy, *History of Rome, Vol. I: Bks 1–2*, trans. B. O. Foster, Loeb Classical Library 114 (Cambridge, MA: Harvard University Press, 1919), 220–21. For panegyrics praising Cromwell as Junius Brutus, see Section 7.1.

[19] Nedham, *The Excellencie*, 12–15. [20] Ibid., 30.

280   The Masculine Republic

of gender differentiation connected to a conception of masculine power. Nedham characterises freedom as feminine and virginal, being pure and valuable while simultaneously an alluring and desired object of possession and ruination. This image of freedom as a threatened chaste woman is reminiscent of Livy's description of Tarquin's inflamed desire to rape Lucretia (as translated in 1600): '*Sextus Tarquinius* was bewitched and possessed with wicked wanton lust, for to offer violence and villanie unto *Lucretia*: her passing beauty and her approved chastitie set him on fire and provoked him therto.'[21] Tarquin became inflamed with a desire to assault Lucretia only after witnessing her superior chastity. As we saw in the first chapter, his rape of Lucretia became a primary example of *tyrannus ex parte exercitii* (tyrant due to wicked action) and the impetus for republican revolution due less to the sexual act he performed than the person on which he performed it, for Lucretia was a free-born female citizen and the wife of a free-born male citizen.[22] With his heavy reliance upon Roman history and political thought, and his frequent discussion of Tarquin and Appius Claudius, another wicked Roman ruler who sought to rape a free-born virgin, it is not accidental that Nedham drew such an analogy between sexual lust and the lust for dominion.[23] Classical Roman conceptions of sexual practice emphasised that the self-respecting Roman man must always be the 'active' rather than 'passive' partner of the sexual act, for penetration was both an image of subjugation and that which caused it.[24] Thus conceived, the desire to rape could be understood as a lust for dominion over others, expressed through forcible penetration.

While Nedham stated that 'every one seeks to deflower' such a virgin as freedom, however, he made it clear within the context of this passage that the 'Interest of Freedom' is most vulnerable to violation by the 'Power of Great Ones', and the free-state must thereby 'be kept from any other Form' of government. As he states in the prior sentence, 'the onely way to secure [Liberty] from the reach of Great Ones, is, to place it in the Peoples Hands, adorned with all the Prerogatives and Rights of Supremacy'.[25]

---

[21] *The Romane Historie Written by T. Livius of Padva*, trans. Philemon Holland (London, 1600), 40.

[22] By violating the sexual integrity of a married, free-born Roman citizen, Tarquin's action violated the significant political and legal distinction between free and slave, the bloodline of Collatinus and Lucretia's household, and the proprietary claims of Collatinus as the *paterfamilias* of his household. See Craig A. Williams, *Roman Homosexuality: Ideologies of Masculinity in Classical Antiquity* (Oxford: Oxford University Press, 1999), 18–19, 96–97, 104–6.

[23] Within the *Excellencie*, Nedham explicitly discussed the example of Tarquin twelve times and Appius Claudius eleven times. Nedham also frequently called the young Charles II 'young Tarquin' in *Mercurius Politicus*.

[24] Williams, *Roman Homosexuality*, 18.   [25] Nedham, *The Excellencie*, 30.

Later in the treatise, Nedham again confirms that those who most threaten the commonwealth with 'the Rapes of Usurpation' are those who have grown 'over-great in Power' above the people.[26] Within Nedham's analogy of sexual assault, the people assume the role of the *paterfamilias* within the household, vigilantly guarding and policing the sexual purity of a virgin daughter. 'Liberty must needs lie more secure in the Peoples than in any other hands, because they are most concerned in it,' Nedham concluded, 'and the careful eyeing of this Concernment, is that which makes them both jealous and zealous; so that nothing will satisfie, but the keeping of a constant Guard against the Attempts and Incrochments of any powerful or crafty Underminers.'[27]

Nedham's warning that the English People must vigilantly guard their virgin liberty against 'powerful or crafty Underminers' had significant relevance in the 1650s. His editorials in *Mercurius Politicus* frequently referred to Charles II, the banished son of the executed King Charles, as the 'young Tarquin'. *The Excellencie* implicated Cromwell in this parallel as well, for within his discussions of Tarquin and the early consular government established after the tyrant's banishment, Nedham emphasised that 'onely the name King was expelled, but not the thing':

> For, besides the Rape of *Lucrece*, among the other faults objected against *Tarquin*, this was most considerable, That he had acted all things, after his own head, and discontinued Consultations with the Senate, which was the very height of Arbitrary Power. But yet as soon as the Senate was in the saddle, they forgat what was charged by themselves upon *Tarquin*, and ran into the same Errour, by establishing an Aribitrary, Hereditary, unaccountable Power in themselves, and their Postery, not admitting the people (whose interest and liberty they had pleaded,) into any share in Consultation, or Government, as they ought to have done, by a present erecting of their successive Assemblies: so that you see the same Kingly Interest, which was in one before, resided then in the hands of many.[28]

---

[26] Ibid., 42, 44. Nedham described Julius Caesar's dictatorship through such terms: 'And afterwards, when *Augustus* took upon him the Inheritance and Title, of his Uncle *Caesar*, he did it, *lento pede*, very slowly and warily, for fear of conjuring up the same spirit in the people, that had flown into revenge against his Uncle, for his Rape upon their Liberty' (*The Excellencie*, 94). And more generally, of any type of 'Great Ones' that might wrest freedom from the people, such as in his discussion of why the people must be knowledgeable about their liberty: ' . . . it is without all question, most necessary, that they be made acquainted, and thoroughly instructed in the Meanes and Rules of its preservation, against the Adulterous Wiles and Rapes of any projecting Sophisters that may arise hereafter' (*The Excellencie*, 83).

[27] Nedham, *The Excellencie*, 30.   [28] Ibid., 80.

282 The Masculine Republic

Cromwell, like the consuls and senate in the wake of Tarquin's banishment, had threatened and violated rather than guarded the liberty of the people. Through the language of sexual assault, Nedham warned that the 'Interest to Freedom' lay vulnerable to assult by 'Great Ones', whether monarchical or protectorial.

Moreover, attending to the gendered discourse at play in Nedham's text affords us a deeper understanding of his use of the word 'interest' in these passages. As scholars have documented, 'interest' carried a specific meaning for Nedham and his contemporaries, tied to a political maxim which maintained that people rationally sought their own political interests, and that these interests might be successfully observed and predicted by an outside observer.[29] When Nedham maintained that the 'main Interest and Concernment [of the People] consists in Liberty', and that the 'Interest of Freedom' is at threat for being deflowered, he was arguing both that freedom, much like sexual virginity, is indeed highly vulnerable to usurpation, and that the People have a true and rational interest in its protection, just as a father or husband has an interest in preserving the virginity or chastity of a daughter or wife. As the honour, integrity, and continuation of the household was thought to rest upon the enforcement of sexual chastity by the *paterfamilias*, so Nedham envisioned the virtuous and free commonwealth as dependent upon the vigilant preservation of the interest of freedom by the People. Such a fusion of interest theory and classical conceptions of masculinity help us understand how Nedham could balance notions of interest as a 'social force' and the republican language of virtue.[30]

[29] Nedham developed his views of interest theory when refuting William Prynne in *Interest Will Not Lie, or a View of England's True Interest* (London, 1659). This tract began with the statement: 'It is a Maxim among Politicians, That *Interest will not lie:* Which prudential saying hath a twofold sense, the improving whereof is very useful to a man, either in the conduct of his own Affairs, or in discerning the conduct and end of the Affairs and enterprises of other men' (sig. A2ʳ). Nedham, however, had already been adopting such a vocabulary more than a decade before, such as in his work, *The Case of the Kingdom Stated According to the Proper Interests of Severall Parties Ingaged . . .* (London, 1647). In that year, he was already receiving criticism as one of the chief 'interest-mongers' of England. Englishmen drew the concept from Henri duc de Rohan's *L'interesse des princes* of 1634, which was translated in 1640. See A. W. Gunn, "Interest Will Not Lie': A Seventeenth-Century Political Maxim', *Journal of the History of Ideas* 29.4 (Oct.–Dec., 1968): 551–64, esp. 555–57, 563.

[30] Rachel Foxley has noted that Nedham's interest theory does not seem to 'sit easily' with his republican ideals. Unlike Foxley, this chapter sees the pairing of these concepts as less problematic, in part because it understands Nedham as arguing that the judgement and moral character of the people did matter a great deal for the preservation of the liberty of state. See Foxley, *The Levellers*, 214–15. For the connection between the language of interest and the development of the concept of the 'public' and of popular representation, see Geoff Baldwin, 'The "Public" as a Rhetorical Community', in *Communities in Early Modern England: Networks, Place, Rhetoric*, ed.

'Begin now to know themselves men ...' 283

Throughout *The Excellencie*, Nedham fused this political vocabulary of interest and the free-state with a classical understanding of idealised and realised manhood. *The Excellencie* argued that assemblies in free-states govern through rational legislation to protect the shared interest of freedom; at the same time, such freedom and rational political action provide for the flourishing of manliness within the commonwealth, not least because they require and make possible the exercise of two virtues considered essential to manhood by both classical and early modern writers: reason and courage.[31] The following sections will argue that conceptions of idealised republican masculinity, based particularly upon the model of the Roman empire, lay at the heart of Nedham's arguments for the free-state. These sections will attend to three discourses of manhood within Nedham's *Excellencie*: first, his conceptualisation of manhood in the free-state as fully rational and autonomous; second, his promotion of the free-state as that which enables men to demonstrate their martial prowess; and third, Nedham's defence of political force, conquest, and empire, attending especially to his celebration of republican masculinity as the subdual of rival and weaker peoples and the 'propagation' of liberty.

6.2   Manhood and Rationality in the Free-State

Throughout *The Excellencie of a Free State*, Nedham maintained that the state of liberty provided for the flourishing of masculinity because it required and encouraged reason, a capacity fundamental to manhood. In Roman as well as Greek thought, philosophers theorised that it was the ability to reason and the use of reason that set men apart from other animals. Furthermore, reason allowed men to make judgements concerning their own and others' wellbeing, and thus gave them the ability (and duty) to govern slaves, women, and children, all of whom were viewed as less capable or incapable of the rational judgement necessary for self-governance.[32] In *The Excellencie*, Nedham condemned hereditary

---

Alexandra Shepard and Phil Withington (Manchester: Manchester University Press, 2000), 199–215, esp. 204–5.

[31] For the significance of these traits to manhood in the classical world, see Section 1.2; for the early Stuart emphasis on reason and courage, see Elizabeth Foyster, *Manhood in Early Modern England: Honour, Sex, and Marriage* (London and New York: Longman, 1999), 28–48; Alexandra Shepard, *Meanings of Manhood in Early Modern England* (Oxford: Oxford University Press, 2003), 21–46; and Mark Breitenberg, *Anxious Masculinity in Early Modern England* (Cambridge: Cambridge University Press, 1996), 69–96.

[32] In the simplest formulation, the distinction between man and animal is a distinction of kind, while the distinction between man and slave, woman, or child is a distinction of degree. However,

284 The Masculine Republic

government for depriving men of the use of reason. Men are reduced to a bestial state, Nedham maintained, forced to receive their rulers blindly:

> which course being so destructive to the Reason, common Interest, and Majesty of that Noble Creature, called Man, that he should not in a matter of so high consequence as Government, (wherein the good and safety of all is concerned), have a Freedom of Choice and Judgement, must needs be the most irrational and brutish Principle in the World, and fit onely to be hissed out of the World, together with all Forms of standing Power (whether in Kings, or others) which have served for no other end, but transform Men into Beasts, and mortified mankinde with misery through all Generations.[33]

Here hereditary government was figured as antithetical to the masculinity and even humanity of citizens; not only did it deny citizens their liberty – conceived here as 'neo-Roman' conceptions of non-domination – but even more fundamentally, it denied them their manhood.[34] Denying males the right of election denied them manhood, Nedham contended, for rational judgement and self-determination were what made men 'noble creatures' and not beasts. At the same time, hereditary government failed to serve the 'common Interest' of liberty possessed by these men. Once political power became erected without consent, the people would sink even further into a bestial and vassalised state, Nedham argued, being reduced to the level of the 'Horse and Mule; that they might be Bridled and Sadled, & Ridden, under the wise pretences of being Governed and kept in Order'. This was because monarchical or aristocratic governors exercise power towards their own interests, 'onely to serve the Ends and Interests of Avarice, Pride, and Ambition of a few', as opposed to the interest of freedom shared by the people.[35] In the earlier *The Case of the Common-wealth of England Stated* (1650), Nedham had similarly combined languages of ignorance, bestial

---

classical writings that deemed slaves and women as incapable of exercising the rational judgement necessary to rule themselves do raise the question about the humanity of slaves and women. As we will see later, in the *Politics* Aristotle even likened the anatomy and role of natural slaves to beasts. These distinctions likewise shaped English discourses of male governance over their more irrational, female counterparts. See, e.g., Foyster, *Manhood in Early Modern England*, 29–30.

[33] Nedham, *The Excellencie*, 40.

[34] This theme of monarchy as slavery can be found in numerous editions of *Mercurius Politicus*. See, for example, the end of the epitaph upon the Prince of Orange that Nedham shared: 'But this, hath sav'd the same from Royall Tyranny, /From secret deep conspired slavery, / By th'onely means of his *Most Timely Death*'. *Mercurius Politicus*, no. 33, 16 January to 23 January 1651 (London, 1651), 542.

[35] Nedham, *The Excellencie*, 39 and 113. In *Mercurius Politics*, Nedham had likewise described countries such as France where kings, nobles, and landlords have reduced their countrymen to 'Beasts' by lording over them and preying upon their livelihoods. *Mercurius Politicus*, no. 85, 15 January–22 January 1652.

'*Begin now to know themselves men ...*' 285

subjection, and vassalage, comparing 'such as have been educated under a *Monarchy* or *Tyranny*, to those Beasts which have been caged or coop't up all their lives in a Den, where they seem to live in as much pleasure, as other Beasts that are abroad; and if they be let loose, yet they will returne in againe, because they know not how to value or use their *Liberty*'.[36] Within these passages, Nedham reflected upon what Quentin Skinner has identified as the 'neo-Roman' theory of liberty as non-domination, which was a significant 'third' theory of liberty and one shaping anti-monarchical and republican discourse in the 1640s and 1650s.[37]

Nedham's description of domination within the unfree-state merged languages of beastly irrationality and of slavery. This elision of concepts reflected both Greek and Roman discourses, which frequently characterised the 'natural slave' as a kind of 'thing' (κτῆμα) to be owned like a beast of burden.[38] Aristotle most famously argued that 'the usefulness of slaves diverges little from that of animals; bodily service for the necessities of life is forthcoming from both, from slaves and from domestic animals alike'. For this reason, the 'intention of nature' was to make the very bodies of slaves humble and crouched like a beast of burden, Aristotle maintained.[39] Roman legal statutes departed from Aristotle's argument of natural slavery by delineating slavery as an institution in the law of nations (*ius gentium*) by which one person's subjection to another was contrary to nature (*contra naturam*);[40] however, Roman as well as Greek art, historical writings, and speeches very often type-casted slaves as

---

[36] Nedham, *The case of the Common-wealth of England stated, or, The equity, utility, and necessity of a submission to the present government* . . . (London, 1650), 88.

[37] For 'neo-Roman' conceptions of liberty as 'non-domination', see Skinner, *Liberty before Liberalism*; Skinner, 'Classical Liberty, Renaissance Translation, and the English Civil War', in *Visions of Politics*, vol. II (Cambridge: Cambridge University Press, 2002), 308–43; Skinner, 'Rethinking Political Liberty', *History Workshop Journal* 61 (2006): 156–70.

[38] J. Albert Harrill, 'Invective against Paul (2 Cor. 10:10), the Physiognomics of the Ancient Slave Body, and the Greco-Roman Rhetoric of Manhood', in *Antiquity and Humanity: Essays on Ancient Religion and Philosophy* (Tübingen: Mohr Siebeck, 2001): 189–213, esp. 193.

[39] Aristotle *Politics* 1.2.1–15 [1254b25–35], qtd in Harrill, 'Invective against Paul', 192–93.

[40] *The Digest of Justinian*, ed. Theodor Mommsen and Paul Krueger, trans. Alan Watson. 4 vols. Philadelphia: PA, 1985, I.V.4.35, vol. I, p. 15. See also *The Institutes* I.V 'De Libertinis': '*Quæ res a jure gentium originem sumpsit, utpote cum jure naturali omnes liberi nascerentur, nec esset nota manumissio, cum servitus esset incognita: sed posteaquam jure gentium servitus invasit, secutum est beneficium manumissionis. Et cum uno naturali nomine homines appellaremur, jure gentium tria genera hominum esse cœperunt, liberi et his contrarium servi et tertium genus libertini, qui desierant esse servi*'. *The Institutes of Justinian*, ed. and trans. Thomas Collett Sandars, 13th edition (London: Longmans, Green, 1910), 17. It should be noted, however, that the Roman practice of selling slaves could often reduce them to the level of beasts of burden, and such practices took place at the Forum, the heart of the city of Rome. See Keith Bradley, *Slavery and Society at Rome* (Cambridge: Cambridge University Press, 1994), 52–55.

286   The Masculine Republic

downcast and bestial in appearance and comportment, and as lacking the
reason and courage exhibited by free men. Such a distinction became
visible on Attic vase paintings as early as the mid-sixth century, with free
bodies displayed as upright in carriage, strong, well-proportioned, robust,
and seemly, while slave bodies appeared stunted and crouched in humiliating positions.[41] The appearance of slaves as downcast and bestial was
carried into Greek and Roman drama, and became a regular feature of
invective in Roman oratory.[42] The enslaved male appeared to lose not only
his liberty but his fundamental humanity.

Throughout his writings, Nedham ascribed the bestial state both to
unfree people and to tyrants themselves who ruled by inheritance and not
election, by vicious passions and not reason, by force and not law. He
observed from Roman history 'that all those *Emperors* which ruled by right
of *Inheritance,* proved most of them no better than savage Beasts, and all of
Them wicked, except *Titus;* but such as were advanced by *Election*
approved Themselves noble and vertuous'.[43] This historical description
of hereditary rule took aim at royalist writers who argued that monarchy
better protected the public interest than elective assemblies. In 1642, for
example, the royalist Dudley Digges had argued that Parliament 'must
evidently have more private ends then the King' for 'they must struggle
with solid temptations, desire of riches, desire of honours, there being an
emptinesse in them, whereas He is full and satisfied'.[44] Digges concluded
by arguing from history that wise legislators had always granted the 'greatest power of government' to the monarchy, 'because their private interests
were the same with the publique'.[45] Nedham, alongside Henry Parker and
others arguing for the public interest of parliament, contended that rulers
who held power from inheritance often sought to fulfil their own private
and vicious passions by force: 'If the Right of laws be the way of men, and
force of beasts', Nedham maintained, 'and great ones, not onely advised,
but inclined to the latter, then it concernes any Nation or people to secure
themselves, and keep Great men from degenerating into beasts, by holding
up of law, liberty, priviledge, birthright, elective power, against the ignoble

---

[41] Harrill, 'Invective against Paul', 192.
[42] See, e.g., Cicero, *Orationes Phlippicae,* 8.9; 10.22. Harill, 'Invective against Paul', 192–209.
[43] Nedham, *The case of the Common-wealth of England,* 46–47.
[44] Dudley Digges, *An Answer to a Printed Book, Intituled, Observations upon some of His Maiesties Late
    Answers and Expresses. Printed by His Maiesties Command* (Oxford, 1642), 61. For more on Digges,
    see Baldwin, 'The 'Public' as a Rhetorical Community', 206; Richard Tuck, *Natural Rights Theories:
    Their Origin and Development* (Cambridge: Cambridge University Press, 1979), 101–18.
[45] Digges, *An Answer,* 117.

'Begin now to know themselves men . . .'

beastly way of powerfull domination.'[46] Fittingly, then, Nedham frequently used the adjectives 'brutish' and 'beastly' to describe countries ruled by monarchs as well as monarchs themselves.[47]

Nedham paired this negative language of bestial enslavement with the positive argument that a truly free-state was necessary for males to become men through the exercise of reason, for the free-state allowed men to determine their own governors. In *The Excellencie of a Free-State*, Nedham celebrated that 'men have Liberty [in the Peoples Form of government] to make use of that Reason and Understanding God hath given them, in chusing of Governours, and providing for their own safety in Government'.[48] Indeed, the very process of popular election required an exercise of rationality whereby those seeking power must be 'judged fit' for the service and for the benefit of all members of the commonwealth.[49] Because citizenship entailed the right to self-determination and governance, the deciding factor concerning which men would participate in governance depended not upon wealth, status, or lineage, but upon the question of who was capable of actualising virtuous manhood. This helps explain why Nedham concluded his section on the relationship between free elections, consent, and reason by arguing that certain men – the 'confused promiscuous Body of the people' and men guilty of treason, neutrality towards the revolutionary cause, or apostasy – be excluded from participating in these political processes.[50] In the free-state, then, Nedham explained that 'the door of Dignity stands open to all (without exception) that ascend thither by the steps of Worth and Vertue', not by wealth or bloodline. This had been proven by the high number of 'brave Patriots and Conquerors' in Rome, such as Cincinnatus, who came from the 'meanest fortune' and yet fought valiantly and governed the Roman state virtuously.[51]

In 1656, Nedham's call to manly self-governance was a timely one. He printed *The Excellencie* one month after the decision to call the Parliament of 1656, and 2 days before the council's order of the issuing of electoral writs. The work has thus been described as an 'election manifesto', advising Englishmen to elect 'true' commonwealthsmen against the Cromwellian Protectorate.[52] Participating in these elections, whether through voting or running for office, provided a clear first step for restoring the masculinity of English men.

---

[46] Nedham, *The Excellencie*, 123.   [47] See, for example, *The Excellencie*, 31, 40, 47, 75, and 123.
[48] Ibid., 40.   [49] Ibid., 39.   [50] Ibid., 42.   [51] Ibid., 27–28.
[52] Worden, 'Introduction', l–li.

288   The Masculine Republic

6.3   Courage, Manliness, and the Free-State

Alongside discourses of reason and self-determination, Nedham followed
Roman conceptions of manhood and republicanism by frequently equat-
ing *virtus*, or manliness, with the exercise of martial prowess and by
praising republican government as manly due to the regular exercise of
arms and conquest. Early Latin texts defined *virtus* as martial prowess or
(usually physical) courage, demonstrated on the battlefield. Only with the
writings of Cicero and later Latin texts did discussions of *virtus* begin to
include a wider ethical ideal influenced by the Greek conception of ἀρετή
[*aretê*];[53] however, even these texts continued to praise the Romans as
manly and exemplary particularly due to their martial courage. In *De
Officiis*, Cicero maintained that amongst those things which are counted
honourable, that which is done courageously and with a 'great spirit'
receives the most fulsome praise. 'The very fact that the statues we look
upon are usually in military dress bears witness to our devotion to military
glory', Cicero contended, while insults such as 'You, young men, show a
womanly spirit . . . ' are readily available for those failing in martial spirit.[54]
Roman writers frequently emphasised the significance of martial prowess
for manhood not only due to the state's imperial ambitions but because
the very structure of Roman society required military service for a young
male's entrance into political citizenship and manhood. A Roman son
could only become a *paterfamilias* upon the death of his father, so the
Republic's institutions allowed young Roman men to transition from
being sons under bondage in the private sphere of the *familia* to being
viri of equal status to the *paterfamilias* in the public sphere through
military service.[55]

---

[53] For a discussion of the gradual expansion of *virtus* to include human excellence, the cardinal virtues,
and political virtue in particular, see Myles McDonnell, *Roman Manliness: Virtus and the Roman
Republic* (Cambridge: Cambridge University Press, 2006), 107–41.

[54] Cicero, *De Officiis*, ed. M. T. Griffin and E. M. Atkins (Cambridge: Cambridge University Press,
2003), I.61, 25. See also Cicero, *Tusculan Disputations*, trans. J. E. King, Loeb Classical Library 141
(Cambridge, MA: Harvard University Press, 1927), III.36–37, 269–71.

[55] McDonnell, *Roman Manliness*, 180. Roman youth were thought to move from their childhood
(*pueritia*) to adulthood (*inventa*) at the age of seventeen, which corresponds to the age at which
young men normally began military service. The right of passage marking this transition included
the removal of childhood garments (the *toga praetexta* and the *bulla*) to don the garment of
manhood, *toga virilis*. McDonnell explains that during the republican period, 'this rite of passage
occurred when the *paterfamilias* deemed the youth mature enough to fight in the army' (*Roman
Manliness*, 177). In historiographical writings, the term *vir* could enjoy more flexibility, however.
See Santoro F. L'Hoir, *The Rhetoric of Gender Terms. 'Man', 'Woman', and the Portrayal of Character
in Latin Prose* (1992), 63–76. Moreover, the term *vir* became more problematic in its application to
career soldiers in the last centuries of the Republic due to their decline in social status. By the first

'Begin now to know themselves men ...'

In Rome as well as Stuart England, evaluation of an individual's masculinity rested very much upon his performance of martial exploits as well as his bodily integrity and appearance. Bodily endurance, strength, discipline, bravery, and a 'hardness' of body became traditional marks of masculinity, whereas weakness, malleability, cowardice, and 'softness' signified effeminacy. Softness (*mollita*) in particular often designated the opposite of masculinity.[56] Physiognomics, the practice of reading an individual's body to reveal his inner character, status, or destiny, greatly influenced Greco-Roman perceptions of gender, and classical evaluations of male behaviour were infused with languages analysing the body, from historical accounts of military engagement to drama, works concerning rhetoric, and even classical philosophy.[57] Examples are numerous across the Greco-Roman writings that seventeenth-century Englishmen encountered frequently. Livy, for one, frequently measured the manliness of soldiers through descriptions of their bodily fortitude, contrasting the manliness associated with hard and tenacious bodies and the effeminacy associated with softness and idleness.[58] For example, he bemoaned the state of Hannibal's soldiers who, early in their campaign, had 'endured long, and held out against all travailes and hardnesse that can possibly happen to the body of man', but eventually lost their manliness by becoming 'spoiled' and 'undone' through feasting and sleeping on soft beds and pursuing leisure. As Philemon Holland translated this passage in 1600, these pleasures 'had in such sort weakened their bodies, and made their harts so effeminate, that from that time forward, the reputation and name only of their victories past, defended them more, than any present strength & vigour they had'.[59] As this brief example highlights, Livy's analysis not only assumed that their bodies reflected the inner character of

century, several writers penned hostile commentary against soldiers, deeming them non-*viri* whose power threatened society. See Richard Alston, 'Arms and the Man: Soldiers, Masculinity and Power in Republican and Imperial Rome', in *When Men Were Men: Masculinity, Power, and Identity in Classical Antiquity*, ed. Lin Foxhall and John Salmon (London and New York: Routledge, 1998), 205–24, esp. 211

[56] Williams, *Roman Homosexuality*, 127–28.

[57] See, e.g., Erik Gunderson, 'Discovering the Body in Roman Oratory', in *Parchments of Gender: Deciphering the Bodies of Antiquity*, ed. Maria Wyke (Oxford: Oxford University Press, 1998), 169–90; Williams, *Roman Homosexuality*, esp. 125–59; Elizabeth C. Evans, 'Physiognomics in the Ancient World', *Transactions of the American Philosophical Society* 59.5 (1969): 1–101; Harrill, 'Invective against Paul'.

[58] Williams, *Roman Homosexuality*, 138–39. These pages also provide more examples of the phenomenon across Roman writings.

[59] *The Romane historie vvritten by T. Livius of Padua. Also, the Breviaries of L. Florus: with a chronologie to the whole historie: and the Topographie of Rome in old time. Translated out of Latine into English, by Philemon Holland* (London, 1600), 486.

290 The Masculine Republic

these men – weakened bodies signifying effeminate hearts – but that the treatment of their bodies could actually produce this inner state.

Much like their Roman forebears, Englishmen often espoused a conception of manhood which required men to exhibit 'sheer physical courage' and a 'willingness to engage in violence with other men'. It was argued that men must demonstrate this ability actively, lest they be understood as feminine in mind as well as body.[60] As we have seen, oppositional rhetoric against King James's policies of peace in the early seventeenth century revolved around such a conception of manhood. Nedham's republican writings of the 1650s not only reflected these earlier views but further contended that the ability of males to realise their manhood through hard bodies performing physical courage depended very much upon the constitutional form of one's government. Throughout his earlier newsbook, *Mercurius Politicus*, from which *The Excellencie* was crafted, Nedham emphasised that tyrannical and unfree-states greatly undermine the manliness of their male populations by corrupting and weakening bodies and spirits. A significant example of this was France, Nedham contended, where the people have lost their liberty and now serve as 'only Spunges to the King, the Nobility, and their Landlords, having nothing of their own, but onely for the use of them, and are scarce allowed (as Beasts) enough to keep them able to do service'.[61] The French cannot maintain an infantry not only due to financial constraints, Nedham argued, but because 'the greatest part of the people being miserably opprest, are becom [*sic*] heartless, weak and feeble, & consequently unfit for Military uses . . .'.[62]

---

[60] Laura Levine, *Men in Women's Clothing: Anti-theatricality and Effeminization 1579–1642* (Cambridge: Cambridge University Press, 1994), 8–9; Foyster, *Manhood in Early Modern England*, 28–30; Shepard, *Meanings of Manhood*, 127–51; Anthony Fletcher, *Gender, Sex & Subordination in England 1500-1800* (New Haven: Yale University Press, 1995), 129; Stephen Orgel, 'Nobody's Perfect: Or Why Did the English Stage Take Boys for Women?', in Ronald R. Butters and others, eds., *Displacing Homophobia: Gay Male Perspectives in Literature and Culture* (Durham NC: Duke University Press, 1989), 7–30, esp. 14–15.

[61] Nedham, *Mercurius Politicus*, no. 153, 12–19 May 1653, in *The Excellencie*, ed. Worden, 145.

[62] Ibid. In an earlier pamphlet, Nedham described those in the United Provinces as 'inclined to Luxury, being (to speak mildly) of a more soft and delicate demeanour than is usuall in a state that is really free'. *Mecurius Politicus*, no. 133, 16–23 Dec. 1652, in *The Excellencie*, ed. Worden, 144. In *The case of the Common-wealth of England*, Nedham characterised 'Northern' people as 'more manly' and 'endued with a greater courage and Sence of Liberty' because they 'have no Acquaintance with luxurious Diets and Apparrell, nor care much to obtain Them, nor to taste of those melting Enchantments of more wanton Nations', which has led the 'delicate parts of the world' into 'effeminacy' and 'miserable Slavery, at the will of imperious Tyrants'. Nedham, *The case of the Common-wealth of England*, 42.

'Begin now to know themselves men ...' 291

Fittingly, then, Nedham argued that the 'excellency of a Free-State or Government by the People' is 'above any other Form of Government' because in the free-state 'the People are ever indued with a more magnanimous, active, and noble temper of Spirit, than under the Grandeur of any standing power whatsoever'.[63] It is clear throughout Nedham's description of the 'active spirit' of men in the free-state, which he described through terms such as 'courage', 'magnanimity', and 'valour', that he sought to tie the definition of masculine citizenship to martial acts of bravery exhibited on the battlefield. In *The Case of the Common-wealth*, he also focused upon masculine action as the conduct of war, describing the free-state as that which advanced 'Honor, Profit, and Dominion', for it had 'ever produced many more excellent *Heroes,* than any other *Form,* upon the Stage of Action'.[64] This emphasis on *virtus* as physical courage or martial prowess echoed early Roman understandings of *virtus* in particular.

Within *The Excellencie*, Nedham provided several arguments as to why the Free-State increased the manliness, or *virtus,* of its citizenry. He maintained that one significant reason that republican states such as Rome increased the *virtus* of their citizenry was because every man would have a share in the 'Dominion, Wealth, or Honour' accrued through martial conquest, and all rewards would be bestowed upon 'Valiant, Vertuous, or Learned Persons'.[65] This system of merit-based rewards was thought to stand in contrast to states ruled by hereditary nobility or a monarch, namely because rewards in this latter system would be based upon birth or flattery rather than manly action and because tyrants often become jealous or hostile towards the seeming threat of bravery within their subjects.[66] Moreover, Nedham contended that allowing all citizens to participate in the practice of arms and reap the benefits of martial glory would link the interests of public and private together, and ennoble both. In Rome, 'there was no difference, in order, between the Citizen, the Husbandman, and the Souldier:' he explained, 'for, he that was a Citizen, or Villager yesterday, became a Souldier the next, if the *Publick Liberty* required it'. These men, whom he described as mostly 'men of Estate, Masters of Families', took up arms not principally for pay but *'pro Aris & Focis,* for their Wives, their Children, and their Countrey', thus serving household and commonwealth jointly.[67]

---

[63] Nedham, *The Excellencie*, 34.   [64] Ibid., 93.   [65] Ibid.

[66] See Nedham, *The Excellencie*, 27–28; *The case of the Common-wealth of England*, 96.

[67] Nedham, *The Excellencie*, 90. For a further explanation of the public and private linking of interests, see Baldwin, 'The 'Public' as Rhetorical Community', 208.

292   The Masculine Republic

The Excellencie further contended that promoting martial activity for the sake of glory not only increased the number of fully realised male citizens (*viri*) within a commonwealth but it also was necessary for the continued liberty and preservation of the free-state. In a later passage presenting the 'Rules' whereby free-states historically have been preserved, Nedham explained the rule 'that the people be continually trained up in the Exercise of Arms, and the *Militia* lodged onely in the Peoples hands; or that part of them, which are most firm to the Interest of Liberty . . . '. The 'Exercise of Arms' must only rest 'in the people', he continued, because the 'Sword, and Soveraignty, ever walk hand in hand together'.[68]

Although Nedham by 1657 would write a series of letters mocking James Harrington's utopianism and warning of the dangers of political modelling, his arguments in the *Excellencie* found many similarities with Harrington's concerning the militia as a school of civic virtue as well as a sufficient and desirable defence force.[69] Harrington's *Oceana* (1656) argued for the bearing of arms based upon the possession of property, whereby a freeholder's sword became his own possession and that of the commonwealth's, rather than the possession of an overlord, thus making the freeholder's sword an expression of free public action and civic virtue.[70] Nedham's conception of military service importantly aligned with Harrington's argument that the bearing of arms for citizens within a militia became necessary for the development of manliness and courage within the commonwealth. Harrington contended in *Oceana* that the commonwealth 'being constituted more especially of two elements, arms and councils, driveth by a natural instinct at courage and wisdom, which he who hath atained is arrived at the perfection of human nature'.[71] The 'empire of the world' achieved by Rome, Harrington further maintained, 'was not any miraculous, but a natural (nay, I may safely say necessary) consequence' due to Rome's domestic 'discipline' and the exercise of this military discipline 'in her provinces or conquests'.[72]

Nedham, however, significantly departed from Harrington concerning the relationship between the owning of land and the bearing of arms. As seen previously, Nedham argued that all citizens, regardless of noble status,

---

[68] Nedham, *The Excellencie*, 89–90.
[69] Rosanna Cox, '"*Atlantick* and *Eutopian* Polities": Utopianism, Republicanism and Constitutional Design in the Interregnum', in *New Worlds Reflected: Travel and Utopia in the Early Modern Period*, ed. C. Houston (London: Ashgate, 2010), 179–202.
[70] Pocock, *The Machiavellian Moment*, 386; James Harrington, *The Commonwealth of Oceana* and *A System of Politics*, ed. J. G. A. Pocock (Cambridge: Cambridge University Press, 1992), 205–14.
[71] Harrington, *The Commonwealth of Oceana*, 205.   [72] Ibid., 207; see also 10.

'*Begin now to know themselves men ...*' 293

within a free commonwealth should be invited to participate in the practice of arms and thereby reap its individual and communal benefits, spoils, and glory. Such military action, Nedham maintained, only became destructive if the constitutional form of government was not, in fact, free, and if military activity became divorced from the People. In Rome, for example, Caesar's crossing of the Rubicon marked the moment when Rome lost possession not only of its armies but also of its liberty: 'the Common-wealth, having lost its Arms, lost it self too, the Power being reduced both effectually and formally into the hands of a single Person, and his Dependants, who, ever after, kept the Armes out of the hands of the People'.[73] The practice of arms thereby afforded true manliness and liberty to citizens and stability to the republic, while its loss led to thraldom and emasculating subjection.

Nedham's writings similarly echoed contemporary arguments concerning the control of the militia in the early 1640s and rebukes made against the Lord Protector for assuming power over the militia in the 1650s. As *The Humble Petition of Several Colonels of the Army* contended in 1654, a 'standing Army under a single person' must be mercenary, and the 'commander of the Militia, will at his pleasure be Master of all Parliaments, Freedomes, and resolutions, and of all our Birth-Rights'. The pamphlet equated Cromwell's control of a standing army with the former king's control of the militia.[74] Nedham's descriptions in *The Excellencie* of the threat to liberty posed by 'Great Ones' assuming power and the sword aligned with the concerns of this pamphlet; his earlier *Case of the Commonwealth* provided a much longer and more sustained defence of the basic principle '*That the Power of the Sword is, and ever hath been the Foundation of all Titles to Government*'.[75] This principle, that the 'Sword, and Soveraignty, ever walk hand in hand together', underscores a central reason why Nedham understood courage and martial discipline as necessary for the foundation and preservation of a republic.

---

[73] Nedham, *The Excellencie*, 91–92. In *The Case of the Common-wealth*, Nedham described Caesar's triumph as the following, '[The Romans] made a Title to those also of other Nations, so far, that in the end they entituled themselves *Lords of the whole Earth*, and so continued, till *Cæsar* wresting the *sword* out of their hands, became Master both of it and them' (7).

[74] Colonel Thomas Saunders, *To his Highness the Lord Protector, &c. and our general. The humble petition of several colonels of the army* (London, 1654). See also 'Introduction', *The Political Works of James Harrington, Part One*, ed. J. G. A Pocock (Cambridge: Cambridge University Press, 1977), 8–9; Lois F. Schwoerer, *'No Standing Armies!' The Antiarmy Ideology in Seventeenth-Century England* (Baltimore: Johns Hopkins University Press, 1974).

[75] Nedham, *The Case of the Common-wealth*, 6. For the significance of military virtue in the longer republican tradition, see M. M. Goldsmith, 'Republican Liberty Considered', in *History of Political Thought* 21.3 (200): 543–60, esp. 552–54.

294 The Masculine Republic

In these passages, Nedham's reasoning about the relationship between *virtus* and liberty in many ways closely followed Sallust's *Bellum Catilinae*. A history dating from the death of Julius Caesar, Sallust's work was a staple of both grammar school and university education in England, universally taught in Latin as well as English translation and printed frequently between 1569 and 1629.[76] Although principally a history of Catiline's conspiracy, *Bellum Catilinae* devoted attention to a moral analysis of Rome's historical rise and decline, with a particular emphasis upon the relationship between *virtus* and the glory of empire. Sallust argued that, following the banishment of Tarquin and establishment of the free-state in Rome, young men pursued glory on the battlefield with vigour:

> Now at that time every man began to lift his head higher and to have his talents more in readiness. For kings hold the good in greater suspicion than the wicked, and to them the merit of others is always fraught with danger; still the free state, once liberty was won, waxed incredibly strong and great in a remarkably short time, such was the thirst for glory that had filled men's minds. To begin with, as soon as the young men could endure the hardships of war, they were taught a soldier's duties in camp under a vigorous discipline, and they took more pleasure in handsome arms and war horses than in harlots and revelry. To such men consequently no labour was unfamiliar, no region too rough or too steep, no armed foeman was terrible; valour was all in all.[77]

Sallust here celebrated the manliness of martial prowess – *virtus* – that flourished as a result of the early republican free-state. He went on to praise the feats of Romans on the battlefield who successfully routed great armies time and again with just a handful of men. Sallust's history stressed that the aim of manhood was glory on the battlefield, for which men must develop hard, disciplined bodies and minds. For this reason, he opened his *Bellum Catilinae* by encouraging men to pursue glory with the utmost effort, by means of intellect as well as '*virtus*', and admonished them not to become like those obscure men who are little better than beasts grovelling in the field.[78] As we have seen, Nedham's texts similarly placed a dual emphasis upon the growth of manly intellect and physical courage for the

[76] See Freya Cox Jensen, *Reading the Roman Republic in Early Modern England* (Leiden: Brill, 2012), 27–28, 34–37, 59. Latin editions of *Bellum Catilinae* were printed in 1569, 1573, 1601, and 1615; English translations appeared in print in 1609 and 1629, the first translated by Thomas Heywood.

[77] Sallust, *The War with Catiline. The War with Jugurtha*, ed. John T. Ramsey, trans. J. C. Rolfe, Loeb Classical Library 116 (Cambridge, MA: Harvard University Press, 2013), VII.1–4, 12–15.

[78] '*Omnis homines qui sese student praestare ceteris animalibus summa ope niti decet ne vitam silentio transeant veluti pecora, quae natura prona atque ventri oboedientia finxit*'. Sallust, *The War with Catiline*, I.1, 20.

'Begin now to know themselves men ...'

sake of the free-state, and similarly contrasted such masculine activity with the slavishness of beasts.

6.4 War and Empire

Nedham conceptualised the significance of arms and courage for the republican free-state through a Roman as well as contemporary lens. Like the *Naseby* warship, his thought intermixed classical emblems of martial glory and fame with commentary upon, and support for, the contemporary activities of the English state in the discipline and glory of warfare. Nedham played an active role as a journalist and propagandist for the Commonwealth and Protectorate governments. His original weekly editorials in *Mercurius Politicus*, from which he compiled and created *The Excellencie*, ran alongside significant reporting and commentary on foreign and domestic news. His classical examples in the editorials were contextualised by contemporary wars and politics. In *Mercurius Politicus* from 15–22 January 1652, for example, Nedham's editorial, arguing that the people within the free-state 'are ever endued with a more Magnanimous, active, & noble Temper of spirit', was followed directly by news from Dundee, where English regiments were continuing the work of subduing and organising the Scots under English military rule following victory by Cromwell's forces.[79] Two weeks later, when Nedham drew upon Cicero to argue that the free-state 'is most sutable to the Nature and Reason of Mankinde', whereas monarchical governments deprive men of their reason, the newspaper continued with a discussion of Prince Charles's party in France seeking in vain to accommodate itself to a life deprived of regal trappings. This news was followed with an update from Scotland, wherein a parliamentary declaration required Scotsmen 'to meet in some convenient place within your Borough, and there to nominate and elect one Person of integrety and good affection' to represent their concerns and serve for 'the welfare and Peace of this Island'.[80] In these passages, Nedham signalled the work of the English in Scotland as moving the Scottish people from subdual to liberation. His editorials had provided a framework to distill this news, while the news itself simultaneously seemed to offer further proof of his argument: that free-states encouraged reason, self-determination, and service to the public interest, while monarchies enacted subjugation for the private gain of 'Great Ones'.

---

[79] *Mercurius Politicus*, No. 85, 15–22 Jan. 1652, 1352.
[80] *Mercurius Politicus*, No. 87, 29 Jan.–5 Feb. 1652, 1386–88.

296 The Masculine Republic

Due to this role as newswriter and propagandist, working within the the office of John Thurloe, head of British Intelligence, Nedham witnessed and encouraged the conquest of the Irish and Scots, and also the imperial aspirations of the English republic beyond the confines of the three kingdoms. In the early editions of *Mercurius Politicus*, we find Nedham reporting often on the potential thralldom of Scotland by the 'yong *Tarquin*', Prince Charles, and the continued 'slavery' imposed by Scottish '*Grandees*, who ride their poor *Peasants* and *Clients* a-la-mode after the *French* Fashion, and make them bow like *Asses* under every burthen'.[81] In these accounts, Nedham adopted imagery of bestial subjection and the loss of manhood associated with un-free forms of government consistent with his more theoretical writings.

Nedham's work for the Commonwealth Parliament afforded him opportunities to encourage a bellicose agenda in his newspapers and other publications. In 1652, Parliament called upon Nedham to translate John Selden's *Mare clausum* (1618), which defended British sovereignty over the North Sea and the North Atlantic against Dutch claims. His epistle dedicatory to parliament, written to replace the original dedication to Charles, boasted that the work had 'now faln under a more noble Patronage, in the tuition of such heroïck Patriots, who, observing the errors and defects of former Rulers, are resolved to see our Sea-Territorie as bravely mainteined by the Sword, as it is by his Learned Pen'.[82] Within this dedicatory epistle, Nedham professed confidence in the masculine *virtus* of the English Commonwealth, newly freed by 'wisdom and courage', and in God's support of the English cause.[83] He lauded the members of Parliament as those 'happie Instruments' who had established the 'State of Freedom' through 'the highest Act of Justice'; now, he claimed with certainty, the 'same Spirit of Justice' would 'carrie you on (as you have begun) with the like zeal and magnanimitie, to vindicate those Rights by Sea, against all Forein violations and invasions' – to defend those 'Rights against all that shall dare to ravish them', as he phrased it in a later passage.[84] The English, having won a state of freedom, could now look to defend itself from violent domination by other unfree powers. While this dedication emphasised the maintainence of English dominion, the poem on the frontispiece argued for English expansion: 'For Sea-

---

[81] *Mercurius Politicus*, No. 2, 13–22 Jun. 1650, 21–22, 32.
[82] John Selden, *Of the Dominion, or, Ownership of the Sea*, trans. Marchamont Nedham (London, 1652), B1r–v
[83] Ibid., D2v.   [84] Ibid., B1v and D2r.

'Begin now to know themselves men ...'

Dominion may as well bee gain'd / By new acquests, as by descent maintain'd'.[85]

Moreover, Nedham's rhetoric of conquest harmonised with the policies of the Commonwealth government and the continued activities of the Protectorate upon Cromwell's rise in 1653. The Commonwealth, through trade policies such as the Navigation Act of 1651, sought to integrate the former Stuart kingdoms and the loose conglomeration of colonies in the Atlantic into a centrally governed and commercially integrated empire, one that would encourage trade as well as Protestant expansionism against Catholic and Spanish foes. Justifications for these activities included the claim of the Commonwealth's right by conquest to these colonies – the claim that *imperium* followed *dominium* – and that the English colonies had been planted by the people of England, of whom the Parliament acted as representatives.[86]

Cromwell, who continued and strengthened the Commonwealth's policies in the Atlantic, himself portrayed English expansion in the New World as an act of liberation, especially against the 'Miserable Thraldome and Bondage, both Spirituall and Civill, which the natives and others in the Dominions of the said [Spanish] King in America are subjected to and lye under by meanes of the Popish and cruell Inquisition ... '.[87] In 1654, the Protectorate launched an unprecedented attack on the Spanish West Indies in an attempt to begin the conquest of Spain's Atlantic empire. The 'Western Design' carried the stated aims of 'securing and increasing the interest of this comonwealth in those parts, and for opposing, weakening, and destroying that of the Spaniards'.[88] Its motivation was both imperial and eschatological. Capturing the great wealth of Spanish colonies would enrich the English state, weaken their imperial rivals, augment the

---

[85] Ibid., unsigned page opposite frontispiece. See David Armitage, 'The Cromwellian Protectorate and the Languages of Empire', in *The Historical Journal* 35.3 (1992): 531–55, esp. 534.

[86] Carla Gardina Pestana, *The Atlantic in an Age of Revolution, 1640–1661* (Cambridge, MA: Harvard University Press, 2004), 157–58, 162–63; Armitage, *Ideological Origins of the British Empire* (Cambridge: Cambridge University Press, 2000), 63, 138.

[87] 'The Commission of the Commissioners for the West Indian Expedition', in Wilbur Cortez Abbott, ed., *The Writings and Speeches of Oliver Cromwell*, vol. III (Oxford: Oxford University Press, 1989), 538.

[88] 'Commission to General Venables', in *Writings and Speeches of Oliver Cromwell*, vol. III, 532–33. Such hostility against the Spanish was justified, according to the military commissions, because they rule 'under a pretence of the pope's donation' and have 'not only exercised inhuman cruelties upon the natives, and prohibited all other nations to have any trade, commerce, or correspondence with those parts' but also, 'contrary to the laws of all nations, by force of arms, expelled the people of these islands ... whereof they were the right possessors, destroying and murdering many of their men, and leading others into captivity'.

298 The Masculine Republic

reputation of the English Commonwealth, and create valuable and courageous work for the extensive British navy.

Simultaneously, the Western Design sought to achieve what was viewed as a divine mission to defeat Spanish tyranny and liberate hearts and minds to the 'true religion': 'bringing in the light of the Gospell and power of true Religion and Godliness into those parts'.[89] Images of Spanish Catholicism as an enslaving and cruel force across Europe and the Caribbean were widespread in the early to mid-seventeenth century. Protestant propaganda often focused on the brutality of the Spanish Inquisition, the St. Bartholomew's Day Massacre in France, and the ruthless treatment of New World natives by Spanish colonisers. News of the fate of the Waldensians further fuelled this imagery in the early 1650s.[90] *Mercurius Politicus* of August 1652 cited as further proof of the darkness, cruelty, and tyranny of the 'Pope and Antichrist', the many sects 'deliver'd up to fire and destruction' by Catholics, including the Waldensians, Hussites, Wicklevists, Lutherans, and German and English Protestants.[91]

Due to the newly gained freedom as a commonwealth, and the eschatological vision of this mission to deliver the oppressed from forces of Spanish Catholic tyranny, proponents of the Western Design fully expected the successful conquest of Hispaniola. This expectation of defeating Spanish tyranny within the Caribbean, however, would soon be dashed. The amphibious force that landed on Hispaniola in the second week of April 1655 failed through two attempts to take the capital, San Domingo. At least a thousand British soldiers died from disease, poor supplies, and enemy attack. Nedham's account of this debacle in *Mercurius Politicus* emphasised the 'heat of the weather, and want of water' that plagued the troops in their long jungle march to San Domingo, leading to 'weakness and distemper'.[92] After crawling back out of Hispaniola, the officers changed their sights to Jamaica, planning for the first time to seize an island actively held by European colonists. A month later, and after observing a day of fasting and humiliation, the British successfully took

---

[89] 'The Commission of the Commissioners for the West Indian Expedition', in *Writings and Speeches of Oliver Cromwell*, vol. III, 538; Pestana, *The Atlantic in an Age of Revolution*, 177–78; Armitage, 'Cromwell Languages of Empire', 537–38; Karen Ordahl Kupperman, 'Errand to the Indies: Puritan Colonization from Providence Island through the Western Design', *William and Mary Quarterly*, 3d series, 45.1 (Jan. 1988): 72.

[90] John Marshall, *John Locke, Toleration and Early Enlightenment Culture* (Cambridge: Cambridge University Press, 2006), 62–63.

[91] *Mercurius Politicus*, no. 114, 5–12 Aug. 1652, in *The Excellencie*, ed. Worden, 183.

[92] *Mercurius Politicus*, no. 269, 2–9 Aug. 1655, 5531.

'*Begin now to know themselves men . . .*'   299

control of Jamaica, as the Spanish forces on the island agreed to a treaty without bloodshed.[93]

Government officials and officers involved with the Design sought to manage the public presentation of Hispaniola by boasting of Jamaica as a great prize of conquest. '[O]ur Generals, having relinquished *Hispaniola*, were landed at *Jamaica*, and become Masters of the Island', Nedham explained. He continued by describing Jamaica, in long detail, as a 'pleasant and fruitful island, most happy in the fertility of the soil' and fit for colonisation.[94] The failure of an English fleet of 9,000 to capture Hispaniola from a small band of Spanish troops proved a significant blow to Cromwell and his advisors, however. Although the British forces had successfully captured Jamaica as a kind of consolation prize, Cromwell never recovered from the initial defeat.[95] In a letter to Major-General Fortescue stationed in Jamaica, Cromwell described the disaster of Hispaniola as a humbling 'reproof' from God 'upon the account of our own sins as well as others' and upon the sinful behaviour 'common practised' in the Army, including 'extreme avarice, pride and confidence, disorders and debauchedness, profaneness and wickedness'.[96] As Blair Worden has explained, God's providence served as the 'rock' and 'sure refuge' of Cromwell's life; no other trial in Cromwell's career could parallel the disaster of Hispaniola.[97] If the English had been sent on a providential mission from God, the sins of the English must be the cause of their defeat. Spanish commentators of the defeat at Hispaniola meanwhile touted its seemingly clear verdict as God's protection of the 'Holy Mother Church' from the English – on 'our side we have God's true religion'.[98] For the English, there were many ready to cast stones, although it was unclear whether it was the sins of the nation, of the generals, of the army, or of the Protector himself that had most offended God.[99]

---

[93] Pestana, *The English Conquest of Jamaica*, 117, 122–25; Armitage, 'Cromwellian Languages of Empire', 539–40.

[94] *Mercurius Politicus*, no. 269, 2–9 Aug. 1655, 5530–31. See Nicole Greenspan, 'News and the Politics of Information in the Mid Seventeenth Century: the Western Design and the Conquest of Jamaica', in *History Workshop Journal* 69 (Spring 2010): 1–26, esp. 9.

[95] Kupperman, 'Errand to the Indies', 98; Pestana, *The Atlantic in an Age of Revolution*, 180; Armitage, 'Cromwellian Languages of Empire', 541.

[96] 'To Major-General Fortescue, [at Jamaica]', *Writings and Speeches of Oliver Cromwell*, vol. III, 858.

[97] Worden, 'Oliver Cromwell and the Sin of Achan', in *History, Society, and the Churches*, ed. Derek Beales and Geoffrey Best (Cambridge: Cambridge University Press, 1985), 127 and 135.

[98] Pestana, *The English Conquest of Jamaica*, 110.

[99] Several commentators sought to understand God's seeming punishment by turning to the Old Testament story of the sin of Achan. See Worden, 'Oliver Cromwell and the Sin of Achan'; Armitage, 'Cromwellian Languages of Empire', 543.

300   The Masculine Republic

Nedham wrote his original editorials concerning the free-state prior to the Western Design, predominantly during the period of Scottish conquest; he collected and printed them in *The Excellencie*, however, in 1656 at the end of this 'imperial moment' of the English republic and the defeat of Hispaniola. Significantly, while his peers focused upon explanations of divine providence and retribution for England's imperial failures, Nedham's reflections on conquest in *The Excellencie* pursued a mainly classical rather than Biblical justification, focusing especially on the questions posed by earlier writers such as Machiavelli and classical writers before him. Like the Florentine, Nedham questioned whether the free-state should seek preservation as its primary aim, like the Venetian republic, or seek the glory of expansion and empire, such as Rome.[100] Classical historians such as Livy and Sallust had presented a moralised tale of rise and decline annexed to the *virtus*, law, and liberty of the citizenry. As Sallust described, after the foundation of the republic, the practices of *virtus* and justice – 'boldness in warfare and justice when peace came' – allowed Rome to grow into a glorious empire, even defeating the rival Carthage.[101] Nedham's recounting of Roman history followed these ancient writers closely in their understanding of the relationship between *virtus*, liberty, and empire, arguing that during the 'Vassalage' of the Romans under their kings, they lacked any 'notable Exploits' and were oppressed at home and abroad; however, 'when the State was made free indeed, and the People admitted into a share and interest in the Government, as well as the Great Ones; then it was, and never till then, that their thoughts and power began to exceed the bounds of *Italy*, and aspire towards that prodigious Empire'.[102] Indeed, Nedham quoted Sallust directly in *The Excellencie* to prove that the 'love of Freedom' was 'the most commodious and profitable way of Government, conducing every way to the enlarging a people in Wealth and Dominion'.[103]

---

[100] Machiavelli, *Discorsi*, I.6.

[101] '*Duabus his artibus, audacia in bello, ubi pax evenerat aequitate seque remque publicam curabant*'. Sallust, *The War with Catiline*, IX.3, 33–35.

[102] Nedham, *The Excellencie*, 27–28. In *The Case of the Common-wealth*, Nedham likewise described ' ... when Rome was in its pure estate, vertue begat a desire of Liberty, and this desire begat in them an extraordinary Courage and Resolution to defend it; which three walked a long time hand in hand together, and were the Causes, that the first Founders of their Freedome had so little difficulty, in maintaining themselves, against those Invasions which hapned afterward, by the Tarquins and their Royall Confederates' (89).

[103] Nedham, *The Excellencie*, 16.

'Begin now to know themselves men ...' 301

What is most striking about the imperial language in *The Excellencie*, however, is Nedham's eagerness to promote martial glory and the acquisition of empire, even when challenging rival free-states:

> But at length, when the [Roman] People began to know, claim, and possess their Liberties in being govern'd by a succession of their Supreme Officers and Assemblies; then it was, and never till then, that they laid the Foundation, and built the Structure of that wondrous Empire that overshadowed the whole World. And truely the founding of it must needs be more wonderful, and a great Argument of an extraordinary Courage and Magnanimity, wherewith the People was indued in Recovery of Liberty; *because their first Conquests were laid in the ruine of mighty Nations, and such as were every jot as free as themselves*: which made the difficulties so much the more, by how much the more free (and consequently, the more couragious) they were, against whom they made opposition: for as in those dayes the World abounded with Free-States ... [my emphasis].[104]

Within this passage Nedham especially emphasised the 'extraordinary Courage and Magnanimity' of Rome due to their ability to conquer other free-states – other states where men also possessed *virtus*. The fact that Rome's wars with states such as Carthage were difficult and protracted, Nedham argued, was a testament to how very 'magnanimous' the 'State of Freedom' is, and how very courageous Rome's rivals had become due to their freedom. Indeed, Nedham was at such pains to underscore the great martial spirit of Rome's rivals that he even boasted of Rome's momentary defeats at the hands of enemies: 'This magnanimous State of Freedom ... brought ... the *Gauls* within the Walls of the City, to a besieging of the Capitol; to shew, that their Freedom had given them the courage to rob her of her Maiden-head, who afterwards became Mistriss of the whole World.' Although the state of freedom afforded these enemies great courage, Nedham continued, '*Rome* her self also was beholden to this State of Freedom, for those Sons of Courage ... brought the Necks of her Sister-States and Nations under her Girdle.'[105]

Within this extended passage, Nedham returned to classical, gendered languages of sexual domination to describe imperial domination; this time, however, he did so for a laudatory rather than cautionary purpose. Earlier, Nedham envisioned the threat to the 'Interest of Freedom' as a 'Virgin that every one seeks to deflower', whose protection lay in keeping her from other forms of government, 'or else (so great is the Lust of mankinde after dominion) there follows a rape upon the first opportunity'.[106] In this later

---

[104] Ibid., 35.   [105] Ibid.   [106] Ibid., 30.

302 The Masculine Republic

passage, where Nedham sought to demonstrate that 'In a Free-State, the People are ever more magnanimous and valiant', he reframed these languages of sexual violation to describe an order of domination, and eventual partnership, between free peoples and those they conquered. The Gauls may have robbed Rome of her 'Maiden-head' to prove their great courage born of freedom, but due to their even greater magnanimity and courage, the Romans 'brought the Necks of her Sister-States and Nations under her Girdle'. The metaphorical languages of sexual domination that Nedham adopted in these passages echoed contemporary justifications of the conquest and subdual of Ireland. In the 1620s, Luke Gernon, an English administrator in Ireland, had described 'this Nymph of Ireland' as 'at all points like a young wenche that hath green sickness for want of occupying'.[107] Green sickness, a 'disease of virgins', was thought to cause virginal women, often between the ages of 17 and 21, to suffer menstrual blockages, lack of menstruation, and even violent sexual desire; as the cause for such sickness in the seventeenth century was declared to be virginity, the cure for such sickness was marriage and copulation.[108] Gernon continued this metaphor by arguing that Ireland had been 'drawne out of the wombe of rebellion about sixteen years, by'rly nineteen, and yet she wants a husband, she is not embraced ... '. The island would be 'cured' by England acting as a husband.[109]

Even in comparison to classical Roman and earlier English discourses of domination, however, Nedham's exuberance for imperial dominion – for Carthage stealing Rome's maidenhead, for Rome bringing her sister-states under her girdle – seems to be a departure from Sallust and other late republican writers, for it lacked a cautionary warning that *fortuna* and the luxury found in empire would lead to corruption and decline. Sallust had famously reported that when Rome had 'grown great through toil and the practice of justice [*labore atque iustitia*], when great kings had been vanquished in war, savage tribes and mighty people subdued by force of arms', when Rome's great rival Carthage had been defeated, and 'all seas and lands were open [*cuncta maria terraeque patebant*], then Fortune began

---

[107] Luke Gernon, 'A Discourse of Ireland', in *Illustrations of Irish History and Topography, Mainly of the Seventeenth Century*, ed. C. Litton Falkiner (New York: Longmans, 1904), 349. Qtd in John H. Ball, *Popular Violence in the Irish Uprising of 1641: The 1641 Depositions, Irish Resistance to English Colonialism, and its Representation in English Sources*. PhD Dissertation at the Johns Hopkins University, Baltimore, Oct. 2006, 130.

[108] Helen King, *The Disease of Virgins: Green Sickness, Chlorosis, and the Problems of Puberty* (London and New York: Routledge, 2004), 24–25, 29.

[109] Gernon, 'A Discourse of Ireland', 350; Qtd in Ball, *Popular Violence in the Irish Uprising*, 131.

'Begin now to know themselves men ...'

to grow cruel and to bring confusion into all our affairs'. The Romans fell into decline due to two principal vices, *avaritia* and *ambitio*; avarice destroyed 'honour, integrity, and all other noble qualities' while ambition 'drove many men to become false', deceptive, and driven by self-interest.[110] Avarice in particular, 'steeped as it were with noxious poison, renders the most manly body and soul effeminate', he warned.[111] Through translations of Sallust's narrative and reappraisals of his paradigm in seventeenth-century England, 'luxury' frequently became a 'byword for ill rule and the politically dangerous softening of patriarchal power in extended peacetime'. Especially in imaginative literature examining Roman imperial conquest and its failures, Renaissance writers often portrayed luxury and avarice as a social and political evil and as a feminising force.[112]

Sallust's depiction of this emasculating decline in Rome, especially after the leadership of Lucius Sulla, included corrupt motivations in war and vicious activities by soldiers against conquered peoples: 'all men began to rob and pillage ... the victors showed neither moderation nor restraint, but shamefully and cruelly wronged their fellow citizens'.[113] Similarly, in a later passage of the *Bellum Catilinae*, Julius Caesar denounced the behaviour of Catiline's troops by describing the horror of such activities, 'the rape of maidens and boys, children torn from their parents' arms, matrons subjected to the will of the victors, temples and homes pillaged, bloodshed and fire; in short, arms and corpses everywhere, gore and grief'.[114] Sallust's disgust at the corrupt licence of Sulla and Catiline's soldiers joined a chorus of Roman writers and rhetoricians expressing horror at acts of rape and violence against freeborn peoples conquered in time of war, including the rape of freeborn people who were not Roman.[115] Noticeable also

[110] Sallust, *The War with Catiline*, X.1–6, 35.

[111] ' ... *ea quasi venenis malis imbuta corpus animumque virilem effeminat*'. Sallust, *The War with Catiline*, XI.3, 37.

[112] Alison V. Scott, *Literature and the Idea of Luxury in Early Modern England* (London and New York: Routledge, 2016), 14 and 53–82.

[113] '*Sed postquam L. Sulla armis recepta re publica bonis initiis malos eventus habuit, rapere omnes, trahere, domum alius alius agros cupere, neque modum neque modestiam victores habere, foeda crudeliaque in civis facinora facere*'. Sallust, *The War with Catiline*, XI.4, 37.

[114] '*Plerique eorum qui ante me sententias dixerunt composite atque magnifice casum rei publicae miserati sunt. Quae belli saevitia esset, quae victis acciderent, enumeravere; rapi virgines, pueros, divelli liberos a parentum complexu, matres familiarum pati quae victoribus collubuissent, fana atque domos spoliari, caedem, incendia fieri, postremo armis, cadaveribus, cruore atque luctus omnia compleri*'. Sallust, *The War with Catiline*, LI.9, 110–11.

[115] Within classical Rome a significant distinction was drawn between the rape of slaves and the rape of the freeborn. The slave, in the position of subordination and dependence, could not rightfully resist the master's sexual advances or violence, while the freeborn possessed not only autonomy but

304 The Masculine Republic

within these accounts is revulsion at the avaricious motivations of soldiers who plunder temples and homes for personal profit. Although economic interests were always significant in pre-modern empires such as Rome, they were secondary to political and military interests.[116]

When compared to classical Roman conceptions of decline due to Asiatic luxury and corruption, as well as to Roman sentiments against the rape of the freeborn and avaricious plunder in war, Nedham's language becomes especially significant. Nedham adopted languages of sexual domination to underscore how very magnanimous in spirit and courageous citizens of the free-state become. Moreover, while he did include warnings of Asiatic luxury and corruption within *The Excellencie*, he did so in a narrower and more limited way than classical writers before him, who had argued that the consequences of pursuing *grandezza* (glory in external affairs) would inevitably lead to the loss of liberty and manhood through corruption. In contrast, Nedham's emphasis in *The Excellencie* highlighted the threat of internal rather than external corruption; he focused not upon the corruption which results from conquest and the acquisition of foreign and luxurious wealth by citizens and soldiers but upon the *avaritia* and *ambitio* of 'Kings or Great Ones' who alter the form of government of the free-state.[117] Thus Nedham was at pains throughout *The Excellencie* to articulate how citizens within the free-state could in fact prevent the rise and corruption of 'Great Ones' through a number of means: by only showing preferment based on merit, by passing good laws and following 'Rules of Frugality, Plainness, and Moderation', by having 'very few Offices of Dignity or Profit allowed' within the state, by holding governors accountable for their actions under the law, and by instructing and encouraging citizens in 'zeal against Tyrants and Tyranny'.[118]

Within these passages discussing corruption and luxury, we find a very important departure by Nedham from Machiavelli, a departure that scholars have generally overlooked. Machiavelli had understood empire and liberty as the great 'republican dilemma', as David Armitage has

---

pudicitia, the ideal of physical inviolability which extended both to rape and other forms of physical violence. Cicero, for one, wrote of the corrupt military command of Mark Antony's brother by describing his drunkenness, plundering of fields and estates, and the carrying off of married ladies, maidens, and freeborn boys by the soldiers. Craig Williams provides five more examples of expressed horror for the rape of the freeborn and other atrocities committed during wartime. See *Roman Homosexuality*, 99–102, 105.

[116] J. S. Richardson, 'Imperium Romanum: Empire and the Language of Power', in *The Journal of Roman Studies* 81 (1991): 1–9, esp. 4.

[117] Nedham, *The Excellencie*, 32.   [118] Ibid., 28, 31–33, 37, 44–45.

'Begin now to know themselves men . . .' 305

called it.[119] Rome achieved *grandezza* through *virtus* and extensive military conquests, yet this growth in manliness led inevitably to servitude and emasculation for the Romans due to luxury and corruption. Nedham deviated from this view that liberty, *virtus*, and empire necessarily would lead to corruption, decline, and emasculation, for he contended that the constitutional structures and principles of a free-state would both grow the state and successfully prohibit its corruption, thereby preserving the masculinity and *grandezza* of the commonwealth over time. Should the free-state follow the rules he outlined, practising the regular transfer of power between men through free elections and the consistent subjection of all men to the law, then tyranny and corruption would be ever abolished: 'Such a course as this, cuts the very throat of all Tyranny; and doth not onely root it up when at full growth, but crusheth the Cockatrice in the Egg, destroys it in the Seed, in the principal, and in the very possibilities of its being for ever after.'[120] Nedham believed that an English free-state could both retain internal stability and external mastery by keeping its citizens truly masculine and virtuous.

Nedham elaborated his view of empire in much greater detail in *Mercurius Politicus* from 19–26 February 1652, in which he drew a sharp distcintion between conquest enacted under 'Monarchs and Grandees' and conquest made by a free-state. In this passage, he argued that monarchs 'arrogate all unto themselves, and take Advantage by every new Conquest, for the inslaving of all the rest that are under their Power'. They refuse 'Terms of Indulgence to their Subjects', and further deny those they have conquered naturalisation, incorporation, or the 'Enjoyment of the same Privileges with their Natives, but rather use the one as Instruments to oppress the other, and in the end to deprive them all of their Immunities'. Thus conquest by unfree-states is an instrument of spreading enslavement, motivated by the 'Covetousness and Luxury of particular persons'.[121]

'States governed by the People', however, acquire empires through spreading liberty, Nedham maintained. Free-states treat their neighbours 'nobly', 'admiting them into a participation of the same Liberties and Privileges with themselves, by which means they hold them the more Fast in the bonds of affection and obedience'.[122] Whereas tyrannical conquest

[119] Armitage, 'Empire and Liberty: A Republican Dilemma', in *Republicanism: A Shared European Heritage*, vol. II, ed. Armitage, Martin van Gelderen and Quentin Skinner (Cambridge: Cambridge University Press, 2002), 29–46, esp. 31. See also Armitage, *Ideological Origins of the British Empire*, 127–28.

[120] Nedham, *The Excellencie*, 44.

[121] *Mercurius Politicus*, no. 90, 19–26 Feb. 1652, in *The Excellencie*, ed. Worden, 179–81.

[122] Ibid., 179.

306   The Masculine Republic

abroad leads 'to an increase of Tyranny both there & at home' for 'inslaving of the world', such as in the ancient case of King Philip the Macedonian or the more contemporary example of Caesar Borgia or the Medici, in places such as classical Rome, 'as long as Liberty was in fashion, it was their constant custom to admit such as they conquer'd into the Priviledges of their City, making them free Denisens'. In this way, the free-state conquers not simply for its own glory, but to 'propagate the Interest of Liberty' – liberty becoming the child birthed of conquest.[123] England's failure to conquer Hispaniola betrayed the commonwealth's continued thralldom to a 'Great One' and its urgent need to become truly free.

In contrast, from his discussions of Scotland throughout *Mercurius Politicus*, Nedham appears to have understood Cromwell's conquest of England's northern neighbors as a campaign which indeed had propagated liberty. Cromwell's advances had been intended 'for the freedom of the People of *Scotland*', he argued, a people who, despite the oppression of '*Lords* and *Masters*', 'begin now to know themselves men, & to breath after *Liberty*'. Nedham concluded that 'if the *Scots* be not henceforth as free as the *English*, it must be for want of hearts to receive their own happiness, at the hands of the *English Nation*'. In this account and others, Nedham portrayed the early English commonwealth not as '*Invaders*' but as liber-ators, freeing foreign peoples from the enslavement of tyrannical govern-ments and overlords and the tyrannical religion of popery.[124] Nedham's later reporting on the proposed incorporation of Scotland into the English commonwealth continued to emphasise these activities as the spreading of liberty. '*A Declaration of the Parliament of the Comonwealth of England, about setling Scotland*', which Nedham printed in *Mercurius Politicus* in February 1652, described the settlement of Scotland as the 'advancement of the glory of God, and the welfare of the whole Island', which included the establishment and 'enjoyment' of the same government as the 'free-State and Commonwealth of *England*, as now setled without King or house of Lords'. While reparations would be demanded for the previous wars and rebellions, those '*Vassals or Tenants to, and had dependency upon the Noblemen and Gentry*', who had been drawn into such wars, could not only receive pardon 'but be set free from their former dependencies and bondage services'; they could become freeholders and, 'like a free people', be 'delivered (through Gods goodness) from their former slaveries, vassal-age and oppression'.[125]

---

[123] Ibid., 180–81.   [124] *Mercurius Politicus*, no. 4, 27 Jun.–4 Jul. 1650, 55.
[125] *Mercurius Politicus*, no. 90, 19–26 Feb. 1652, 1439.

'Begin now to know themselves men ...'

Importantly, within this grand narrative of the propagation of liberty through conquest, Nedham did present a significant exception. Whereas the Romans had received into the share of privileges those neighbors 'willing to embrace them', 'they utterly opprest or destroyed' those which 'refused, or scorned the Favor, and by an implacability of spirit rendred themselves incapable of it'.[126] The ancient examples Nedham presented were Carthage and Numantia; in the particular issue of *Mercurius Politicus* in which Nedham presented this view, he did not offer a contemporary example, but he did end with a notable silence. Wales had been incorporated with England following conquest, Nedham maintained, and since 'being brought under the same Laws, and made partakers of the same Liberties and immunities with the English Nation', had 'ever been quiet'.[127] Scotland had not been incorporated after defeat by Edward I, and afterwards made trouble through 'continual Insurrections', yet his other periodicals emphasised the success of Scottish liberty following the invasion of English armies. For Ireland, however, Nedham in this edition of *Mercurius Politicus* remained silent.

Nedham's other editions, however, in their frequent reporting on the subdual of Ireland, betrayed his view that the Irish, unlike the English or eventually the Scottish, would likely not be willing or able to embrace the principles of liberty due to an 'implacability of spirit'. Nedham's discussions of Ireland relied upon Biblical images to portray the Irish as incapable of the principles of liberty and of 'true religion' due to their corruption through popery and due to being stained with blood guilt. Like many of his Engish contemporaries, Nedham understood the Irish as having shed innocent blood, to a catastrophic degree, in their rebellion; with such people, the Lord would have no peace but vengeance.[128] In a letter from

---

[126] Ibid., in *The Excellencie*, ed. Worden, 180.   [127] Ibid., 182.

[128] For the concept of blood guilt and its usage in the English civil wars, see Patricia Crawford, 'Charles Stuart, That Man of Blood', in *Journal of British Studies* 16.2 (Spring, 1977): 41–61.

Nedham's description of Irish rebellion and treachery mirrored that of other published accounts by Protestants. For example, in *Mercurius Politicus* we find the following account: 'A Gentleman sent some Irish wretches to murder the family of an Englishman: The Irish came in to the house pul'd the man out of the bed from his wife and murdered him; then tooke all the rest of the houshold, led them to the seaside, and threw them off the rocks; one of the Children hung about one of the murderers legs, yet was pull'd off and thrown after the rest.' *Mercurius Politicus*, no. 135, 30 Dec. 1652–6 Jan. 1653, 2129. Compare this account with the stories in Daniel Harcourt, *A new remonstrance from Ireland, containing an exact declaration of the cruelties, insolencies, outrages, and murders exercised by the bloudthirsty, Popish rebells in that kingdome upon many hundred Protestants in the province of Vlster, and especially of the ministers there ...* (1643); Henry Jones, *A remonstrance of divers remarkeable passages concerning the church and kingdome of Ireland ...* (London, 1642).

308 The Masculine Republic

Kilkenny, which Nedham printed in an October 1650 issue of *Mercurius*, the writer recounts the horrific conditions of the 'poore Inhabitants' of Ireland, who 'are oft times ruined & destroyed in their substance and dwellings' by both Irish and English armies. The Irish 'seeme to be a people mark'd out to destruction (by the Lord) for their cruelty and bloudinesse', the writer continued, 'there being no way left for them to escape ruine and destruction' even by 'their very sonnes, brothers, and kinsmen'.[129] The author of the letter then cited Isaiah 33:1, a passage delineating the vengeance which will be wreaked upon those who spoil and deal treacherously.[130] In subsequent editions, Nedham portrayed the Irish as continuing to rise in bloody rebellion, adopting Biblical language employed in Exodus to describe the tyranny of Pharoah: 'Thus it hath pleased God to harden the hearts of these bloody treacherous men in their mischiefe, I hope, to their own punishment and ruine.'[131] Years later, on the front page of a 1653 edition, Nedham recounted that '2000 *Tories*', or Irish outlaws, continued to hide in Kerry, Carbery, and the North, 'but we are hunting of them, and giving them little rest, that by degrees, if it please the Lord to bless our endeavours this Summer, it is possible to rid our selves of such Vermin as infest us, and the peaceable *Irish* that live in protection under us'.[132]

Throughout these issues, it seems clear that Nedham considered the Irish, even the 'peaceable Irish', incapable of true liberty and manliness due both to their supposed natural proclivities for treachery, cowardice, and destruction and due to their deserving punishment by God as a wicked people. Nedham's discussion of the battle of Scarriffhollis in Ulster, for example, emphasised the natural proclivities of the free English for valour as compared to the enslaved Irish. Although Sir Charles Coot and Colonel Venebals had been greatly outnumbered, they prevailed for 'it was naturall for *Irish men* to run, and for *English* to conquer'.[133] For Nedham, it appears the greatest corruption of the Irish resulted from their practice of the Catholic religion. In reporting a letter on 23 January 1651 which detailed how all '*Papists* there [in Dublin] are commanded to depart', Nedham argued that 'It were well if all of that *Sect* there, were shipt away

---

[129] *Mercurius Politicus*, no. 19, 10–17 Oct. 1650, 313.
[130] 'Woe to thee that spoilest, and thou *wast* not spoiled; and dealest treacherously, and they dealt not treacherously with thee! when thou shalt cease to spoil, thou shalt be spoiled; *and* when thou shalt make an end to deal treacherously, they shall deal treacherously with thee.' Isaiah 33:1, King James Bible.
[131] *Mercurius Politicus*, no. 33, 16–23 Jan. 1651, 545. This is a frequent theme in Exodus. See Exodus 4:21, 8:15, 8:32, 9:34, 10:1, 11:10, etc.
[132] *Mercurius Politicus*, no. 154, 19–26 May 1653, 2455.
[133] *Mercurius Politicus*, no. 5, 4–11 Jul. 1650, 78.

'Begin now to know themselves men ...'   309

for some other Climat, they being disposed by the principles of their Religion, and a kinde of natural Antipathie, not to keep any Faith or Peace, with the *English* Nation.'[134] Following the Act of Settlement, Nedham described the condemnation and sentencing of Irish rebels, and the transplantation of members of the Irish population, as an act of divine vengeance; the High Court of Justice proceeded in the 'just execution of the hand and Judgement of God, the Avenger of blood and Murder'.[135] England's neighbors in Wales or Scotland could be rendered inheritors of liberty through conquest; the 'bloodie *Irish*' appeared a people requiring vengeance and subjugation, incapable of 'know[ing] themselves men, & ... breath[ing] after *Liberty*' and incapable of being thoroughly purged of popish rebellion.[136]

In Nedham's accounts, English liberty, born of and protected by masculine rationality, independence, and courage, proved both attainable and fragile. The English republic could be established; its greatest threat was not the corruption born of empire but the corruption of the free-state by a 'Great One' – Oliver Cromwell – whose power had become a threat to the masculine freedom and imperial glory of England. The failure of the Western Design cast light not only upon the sins of the English nation but upon the internal corruption of the English free-state by the Protectorate. If ancient free-states could swell so greatly in magnanimous spirit and courage that they could defeat and incorporate rival free peoples, how very much England must have fallen to not defeat rival powers enslaved to Catholic religion and monarchy. Nedham's republican thought relied upon a vision of restoring masculinity to the English people through the restoration and jealous guarding of a free constitution, and through the eventual expansion and propagation of liberty through the practice of arms and conquest. Should the English fail, they would be sacrificing not only their liberty but their fundamental manhood.

---

[134] *Mercurius Politicus*, no. 33, 16–23 Jan. 1651, 550.
[135] *Mercurius Politicus*, no. 128, 11–18 Nov. 1652, 2009.
[136] *Mercurius Politicus*, no. 26, 18 Nov.–5 Dec. 1650, 433; *Mercurius Politicus*, no. 4, 27 Jun.–4 Jul. 1650, 55.

CHAPTER 7

'So much power and piety in one'
Oliver Cromwell and the Masculine Republic

In the devastating armed conflicts of the English civil wars, Cavaliers and Roundheads routinely justified their cause and denounced their rivals through competing conceptions and languages of gender and masculinity. Royalists condemned parliamentary soldiers as cuckolds, their rebellious posture to the King's government mirrored by households in disorder. As one Cavalier summarised, Roundheads and their families rebel against all ten commandments, the laws of nature and society: 'Incests, Adulteries, Rapes, deflowrings, Fornications and other venereal postures & actions . . . daily passe and escape uncontrolled & unpunish'd, and, as it may be conjectur'd tolerated'.[1] Excessive and uncontrolled, lacking masculine temperance and godly virtue, Roundheads engaged in 'all manner of prophane and filthy language of whores and drinke, mixt with a thousand oaths and lyes, to make themselves merry like fooles who make a sport of sinne', another royalist pamphlet argued.[2] In return, the satirical Parliamentary pamphlet *The Picture of an English Antick, with a List of his ridiculous Habits, and apish Gestures* (1646) portrayed a royalist draped in bows and frills, 'His breeches unhooked, ready to drop off . . . His codpeece open, tied at the top with a great bunch of riband'.[3] According to Roundheads, those fighting in the King's army reflected the corrupted and foreign manners of the English royal court, and failed to possess the strength or moral seriousness to restore order or reform religion in England.

---

[1] John Taylor, *The Conversion, Confession, Contrition, Comming to himselfe, & Advice, of a Mis-led, Ill-bred, Rebellious Roundhead. Which is very fitting to be Read as such as weare short Haire, and long Eares, or desire Eares Long* (1643): 8.

[2] Anon. *The soundheads description of the roundhead. Or The roundhead exactly anatomized in his integralls and excrementalls, by the untwistling a threefold knott . . .* (1642), 10.

[3] *The Picture of an English Antick, with a List of his ridiculous Habits, and apish Gestures* (London? 1646?).

'So much power and piety in one'   311

The world 'turned-upside-down' of the 1640s witnessed an unprecedented level of 'gender trouble' in rhetoric as well as action.[4] Female
activity and speech encouraged gender anxieties, with record numbers of
women preaching and protesting about religion and politics. As one
1646 pamphlet described, 'Women-Preachers' had become a 'brazen-
faced, strange, new *Feminine Brood*, '... presuming to advance themselves
before, and over men, transgressing the rules of *Nature, Modestie, Divini-
tie, Discretion, Civilitie, &c.* in triumphing against Authoritie ... '.[5] The
House of Lords and Commons witnessed the delivery of joint petitions by
hundreds of women demanding the reformation of church government
against bishops, and prophetesses such as Mary Cary challenged the social
order through cheap print.[6] While men condemned their rivals through
charges of cuckoldry and sexual licence, salacious pamphlets satirised
female activism as sexual transgression.[7] Examples abound in this period
of the sexualising of dissent, whether by telling tales of Catholic female
'confessors' who met privately with men to 'stuffe their purses with gold,
and their bellies with children' or describing parliamentary women as
cuckold-makers, scolding their husbands to war so that wives might more
easily engage in adultery.[8]

In discourses of the 1640s and 1650s, reflections on the most basic
relationship of power – that of man over woman – and on the perceived
duties of men in positions of authority over household and state, swelled
with anxious strains and perceived urgency. Languages of effeminised and
vicious tyranny expressed against the Stuart regime prior to 1640 expanded
significantly through the breakdown of censorship and through the application of such discourse to political leaders, royalist and parliamentarian
alike. This anxiety would reach its summit as the anointed head of the
English state and royal household, Charles I, marched to the scaffold in

---

[4] As a description of the 1640s, the phrase 'gender trouble' is drawn from Mary Fissell's excellent
work, *Vernacular Bodies: The Politics of Reproduction in Early Modern England* (Oxford: Oxford
University Press, 2004), 90.
[5] *A Spirit Moving in The Women-Preachers: or, Certaine Quæres, Vented and put forth unto this affronted,
brazen-faced, strange, new Feminine Brood* (London, 1646), 2.
[6] *A True Copie of the Petition of the Gentlewomen, and Tradesmens-wives, in and about the City of
London ... February 1641* (London, 1641/2). David Lowenstein, 'Scriptural Exegesis, Female
Prophecy, and Radical Politics in Mary Cary', *Studies in English Literature* 46.1 (Winter 2006):
133–53.
[7] As Fissell helpfully summarised, 'This translation of one kind of transgression into another points us
back to the triad chaste, silent, and obedient – if a woman was outspoken, surely she was unchaste
and disobedient too'. Fissell, *Vernacular Bodies*, 102.
[8] John Stockden, *The Seven Women Confessors* (London, [1641]); *The Resolution of the Women of
London to the Parliament* (London, 1642).

312   The Masculine Republic

1649. *Eikon Basilike* (1649), the purported spiritual biography of Charles I, sought to re-envision the newly beheaded king as a Christ-like father, husband, and ruler, victoriously clasping the bitter crown of martyrdom while trampling down the crown of England as '*vanitas*': 'I slight vain things, and do embrace / Glorie, the just reward of Grace'.[9] Defences of the regicide, however, frequently included images of Charles as failed ruler and emasculated husband.

This complex cultural and political landscape set the stage for the rise of England's most visible political actor, Oliver Cromwell. Those who supported Cromwell's activities as military general and eventually lord protector had to establish his credentials not only as a religious reformer and virtuous statesman but simultaneously as a man capable of re-establishing and ordering British society according to a gendered hierarchy of patriarchal households and restrained sexuality. Legitimising the new government entailed defending regicide to a horrified English and European audience while simultaneously denouncing more radical unorthodox groups bent on erasing distinctions between ruler and ruled, elite and non-elite, male and female. In this moment of rupture, statesmen turned to scripture and to the lessons of history to understand their momentous political moment, to guide and advise their actions, and to justify and legitimise themselves in a country divided and war torn. Following the regicide, political languages drawn from classical stories became one important currency for debating, contesting, and defending the Cromwellian regime. Studies of print culture of the 1640s and even 1650s have emphasised the inventiveness and power of print in this period for crafting political participation, including opposition and subversion as well as legitimisation of government.[10] This chapter will explore the wide range of cheap print, imagery, and imaginative literature in this period in which writers deemed Cromwell Junius Brutus or Julius Caesar, Augustus or Nero, Romulus or Cataline. It will argue that the battle over these exempla provided significant gendered and political judgements about the Lord Protector's legitimacy, authority, and character, while shaping the wider republican discourse of the 1650s.

---

[9] Εἰκὼν Βασιλική, *The Pourtracture of His Sacred Majestie, in his Solitudes and Sufferings* (London, 1649), 'The Explanation of the Embleme'. The devotional cult of Charles grew rapidly in 1649 with forty English-language impressions and issues and twenty more in Latin, Dutch, French, German, and Danish, all hailing an image of sacrificial masculinity by the sovereign.

[10] Jason Peacey, *Print and Public Politics in the English Revolution* (Cambridge: Cambridge University Press, 2013); Nigel Smith, *Literature and Revolution in England, 1640–1660*; Laura Lunger Knoppers, *Constructing Cromwell: Ceremony, Portrait, and Print, 1645–1661* (Cambridge: Cambridge University Press, 2000).

'So much power and piety in one'   313

Stories of Roman heroes and tyrants were a natural place for British writers in the 1640s and 1650s to turn, for few examples of successful republican revolution existed. Within contemporary Europe, war with the Netherlands and the Dutch support of Charles I precluded a positive Dutch model. The contemporary Venetian model may have held more appeal, but its citizens had not displayed the hopes of conquest character-istic of English republicans, and its lessons as a small republic did not map easily onto the more expansive kingdom of England, Wales, Scotland, and Ireland.[11] As we will see, when adopting historical imagery defenders of the regicide and of Cromwell returned particularly to the stories which stood at the bookends of the Roman republican period: the creation of the republic by Lucius Junius Brutus after King Tarquin's son raped Lucretia and the establishment of the Principate under Julius Caesar and Caesar Augustus, against which Brutus's successor, Marcus Junius Brutus, had battled unsuccessfully. These stories helped Englishmen envision them-selves as engaged in an act of restoration, especially of renewing that primitive virtue which had allowed their historical forbears in ancient Rome to live as free men. At the same time, these classical themes could be presented alongside Biblical narratives of the redemption of God's people, the Israelites, from captivity or exile, a narrative that fundamentally shaped Cromwell's self-understanding and revolutionary ideology grounded in providentialism.[12]

Historians who have studied gender and the English Revolution, espe-cially Mary Fissell and Ann Hughes, have convincingly established the social significance of gender construction in this period and the complex ways that gendered discourse, often found in cheap print, shaped political thought and action. Laura Lunger Knoppers's study of Cromwellian imagery has demonstrated significantly how Cromwell and his supporters adopted the republican aesthetic of the early commonwealth and impor-tantly rejected most monarchical forms of representation.[13] Most studies

[11] Jonathan Scott, 'Empire', in *Commonwealth Principles: Republican Writing of the English Revolution* (Cambridge: Cambridge University Press, 2004), 210–32; Idem., 'Classical Republicanism in Seventeenth-Century England and the Netherlands', in *Republicanism: A Shared European Heritage, Volume I*, ed. Martin van Gelderen and Skinner (Cambridge: Cambridge University Press, 2002), 61–84, esp. 70–71; David Armitage, 'John Milton: Poet Against Empire', in *Milton and Republicanism* (Cambridge: Cambridge University Press, 1995), 206–25.
[12] See Colin Davis, 'Cromwell's Religion', in *Oliver Cromwell and the English Revolution*, ed. John Morrill (London: Longman, 1990), 181–208; John Morrill, *The Nature of the English Revolution* (New York: Routledge, 2013), 27–29.
[13] See Knoppers, *Constructing Cromwell*. Her book addresses the important work of Sean Kelsey in *Inventing a Republic: The Political Culture of the English Commonwealth, 1649 to 1653* (Manchester and Stanford: Stanford University Press, 1997). Alongside Kelsey, Knoppers persuasively argues

of Cromwell's constructed image and gendered representation, however, have focused unevenly on the numerous, often vulgar, attacks levelled against Cromwell in print rather than his positive representation.[14] By attending specifically to excessive phallic representations of Cromwell, for example, Diane Purkiss concluded that devastating criticisms against the Lord Protector prevented his regime from establishing a successful iconography of the republic grounded in masculinity.[15]

While these accounts of Cromwell's contested masculinity have argued for the significance of gendered political rhetoric in the English Revolution and Protectorate, the focus on representations of gendered excess has led historians to neglect the significant language of masculine republicanism, grounded upon ideals of classical Roman masculinity and empire, which proponents wielded to support Cromwell's authority. Simultaneously, scholars have overlooked how the historical stories that proponents used to defend Cromwell often provided significant moral arguments for refuting the bombastic cheap print that castigated Cromwell's moral character. More broadly, studies of political representation across the 1650s have argued that the Commonwealth and Protectorate governments failed to establish an authoritative republican culture due to a 'problem of language' which prevented the eradication of conceptions of monarchy from perceptions of power. Kevin Sharpe's argument concerning this problem of language rested upon a fundamental assumption that, for republican culture to establish itself, it had to instil the 'language and image of a republic' while also completely erasing and suppressing 'the language and image of monarchy'.[16] This argument fails to consider the number of republicans who espoused theories of mixed constitutional possibilities which included monarchical elements but nevertheless rejected hereditary

---

against Kevin Sharpe's thesis that Interregnum 'culture was so inscribed and colored with monarchism' that republicans failed to forge a republican culture 'that erased or suppressed the images of kingship'. In this way, Sharpe argued, 'a commonwealth was never established as the government of seventeenth-century Englishmen'. See Sharpe, '"An Image Doting Rabble": The Failure of Republican Culture in Seventeenth-Century England', in *Refiguring Revolutions: Aesthetics and Politics from the English Revolution to the Romantic Revolution*, ed. Sharpe and Steven N. Zwicker (Berkeley: University of California Press, 1998), 25–56.

[14] Diane Purkiss, *Literature, Gender and Politics during the English Civil War* (Cambridge: Cambridge University Press, 2010); Su Fang Ng, *Literature and the Politics of Family in Seventeenth-Century England* (Cambridge: Cambridge University Press, 2007), esp. chapter 4, 'Cromwellian fatherhood and its discontents'; Sharpe, '"An Image Doting Rabble"'; For a more balanced representation of Cromwellian imagery, see Knoppers, *Constructing Cromwell*.

[15] Purkiss, *Literature, Gender and Politics*, 132.

[16] Sharpe, 'An Image Doting Rabble', 26 and 29–30.

'So much power and piety in one'

monarchy as the best and God-given form of government.[17] More fundamentally, English republicans did not need to erase the image of monarchy, but prove their own ability to solve the ills of monarchy and to reclaim a mantle of manly citizenship hampered through decades of perceived corruption.

Through studying how gendered and historical discourses contested and legitimised Cromwell's authority in the 1650s, this final chapter investigates one of the ways that classical republican thought in England became constructed as a solution to the perceived problem of emasculating tyranny experienced under the Stuart kings. The chapter illustrates how classical and gendered languages of tyranny became translated and appropriated in the context of the Interregnum, as Royalists and Presbyterians levelled significant attacks against Cromwell as a usurping tyrant. In response to these attacks, and in response to fears that the English public had been emasculated and disordered through years of Stuart rule, a number of writers sought to defend Cromwell as the best answer to Stuart tyranny and the most virtuous, republican citizen. Whereas scholars of republicanism have generally overlooked gendered political discourses of the 1650s and have focused on republican dismissals of Cromwell, this chapter seeks to underscore how public debates concerning Cromwell provided a significant context for the development of English republican thought, and, specifically, how this context helped to create a classical republicanism motivated by the restoration of manhood in the face of perceived masculine degeneration and tyranny.

7.1 Cromwell as Republican Hero

Oliver Cromwell rose to power through remarkable and divisive military and political performances. His political career commenced in the early 1640s through his position as a godly MP vocally opposing episcopacy and serving on eighteen prominent committees. By 1643, he became a soldier, captain, and colonel of the parliamentary armies in the heartland counties

---

[17] Marchamont Nedham, for example, espoused such a distinction between hereditary monarchy and the position of lord protector in *The True State of the Case of the Commonwealth*: 'Then, who is to administer or govern according to those Laws, and see them put in execution? Not a person claiming an hereditary Right of Soveraignty, or power over the Lives and Liberties of the Nation by birth, allowing the People neither Right nor Liberty, but what depends upon Royal grant and pleasure, according to the tenor of that Prerogative challenged heretofore by the Kings of *England*;... But the Government now is to be managed by a Person that is *elective*, and that Election must take its rise originally and virtually from the People ... '. *True State of the Case of the Commonwealth* (London, 1653), 28.

316 The Masculine Republic

of East Anglia, and it was his bold military performances in the years following which would gain him initial fame and notoriety. Cromwell received high accolades in the London news circuit for his final, decisive charge in the Battle of Marston Moor in 1644, the most significant battle of the first civil war, and by 1646 he had played a pivotal role at Naseby and Langport commanding soldiers as lieutenant-general of the New Model Army.[18] In the second civil war and subsequent campaigns against the Irish and Scots, Cromwell's daring and often brutal tactics earned him further notoriety as a general. In 1648, his armies levelled the Scottish engagers, leaving 2,000 killed and 9,000 captured; in forty weeks in Ireland from 1649–50, his armies occupied twenty-five fortified towns and castles, most infamously slaughtering thousands of soldiers and towns-people at Drogheda and Wexford; and in his final campaign against the Scots from 1650–51, Cromwell claimed to have killed 3,000 Scots and to have captured 10,000.[19] Cromwell's military career was widely advertised in cheap print, with about 90 per cent of print commentators providing broadly sympathetic accounts of his career often complemented by engraved imagery of Cromwell in the armour of a cavalry commander.[20] In 1646 we find Cromwell publicly portrayed in miniature alongside several notable military generals obtaining victories for parliamentary forces; by January 1651, broadsides such as *A perfect List of all the Victories obtained by the Lord General Cromwel* (1651) celebrated Cromwell alone for 334 successful military actions, engagements, or other 'eminent actions' since 1650.[21]

Throughout the 1640s Cromwell played a vital political role as a member of parliament, working to prevent a formal rupture between the army and parliament, acting as chairman at the Putney Debates of 1647,

---

[18] English reports unfairly praised Cromwell and his troops over the efforts of the Scots, under the command of David Leslie. John Morrill, 'Cromwell, Oliver (1599–1658)', in *Oxford Dictionary of National Biography* (Oxford University Press, 2004), online ed., May 2008.

[19] Ibid.; Peter Gaunt, *Oliver Cromwell* (New York: New York University Press, 2004), 84–85 and 89.

[20] Morrill, 'Cromwell, Oliver', *ODNB*.

[21] *A perfect List of all the Victories obtained (through the blessing of God) by the Parliaments Forces under the Command of his Excellency Robert Earl of Essex and Ewe . . . : His Excellency Alexander Lesley, Earle of Leven, . . . : And the right honourable his Excellency Edvvard Lord Mountague, Earle of Manchester, . . . : With his Excellency Sir Thomas Fairfax . . . With the names of the Cities, Townes, Castles, and Forts taken from the enemy since the beginning of these unnatural VVarres, to this present moneth of August 1646* (London, 1646); See also *The Parliament's Kalendar of Black Saints* (London, 1644); *A perfect List of all the Victories obtained by the Lord General Cromwel, from the time that his Excellency was made Cap. Gen. and Commander in Cheif* [sic] *of the Parliament Forces in England, Ireland, and Scotland, (against Charles Stuart King of the Scots, and his Forces in the three Nations,) to this present time; with other eminent Actions* (London, 1651).

'So much power and piety in one'   317

and seeking to negotiate a settlement with Charles before the King's flight to the Isle of Wight. After Pride's Purge, it seems that Cromwell initially sought the King's abdication rather than execution due to concerns over internal and international unrest, but once a trial became inevitable, Cromwell supported the regicide and was the third to sign the death warrant. Even before Thomas Fairfax's resignation as lord general, Cromwell became the most powerful man in England. Although the campaigns in Ireland and Scotland removed Cromwell's imediate personal influence from the Rump Parliament and council of state for the two years following the regicide, upon his triumphant return Cromwell forcefully agitated for the dissolution of the Rump with new elections and the reformation of the laws of religion, including a godly program of moral evangelism and of sanctions against the sins of the flesh.[22] His efforts to obtain these objectives would result in fundamental frustrations and disappointments both for himself and for the army, leading to Cromwell's most controversial and dramatic political manoeuvre: the violent dissolution of parliament in April 1653. In December, Cromwell was sworn in as Lord Protector of England, Wales, Scotland, and Ireland, acting chiefly through the majority will of the council of state. In this role he most passionately pursued a 'reformation of manners' for England, for which he established the rule of major-generals to encourage upright living in the counties while collecting taxes and providing local security. This scheme was widely criticised for being unconstitutional, and while Cromwell definitively rejected the title of king when the 'Instrument of government' was replaced by the 'Humble petition' in 1657, contemporaries fiercely debated whether Cromwell had indeed become a king in all but name.[23] Cromwell's unexpected death in September 1658 provoked a flood of competing representations of his life and rule.

Those who supported Cromwell's military and political efforts and publicly celebrated his accomplishments argued that the Lord Protector displayed ideal masculine qualities which would serve to rejuvenate England from decades of Stuart effeminacy and misrule. To them, the Stuart kings had refused to engage in battle for the Protestant Cause, or failed on the battlefield, while Cromwell and his New Model Army fought victoriously in the name of Christ. The Stuart kings had dressed in luxurious and seemingly effeminate styles, delighted in pleasurable pursuits, danced and acted upon the stage, and in the case of Charles, even

[22] Morrill, 'Cromwell, Oliver', *ODNB*.
[23] See Knoppers's discussion in *Constructing Cromwell*, 107–31.

318   The Masculine Republic

allowed women to do so; Cromwell, however, had pursued an abstemious lifestyle, dressed simply and seemed to pursue the serious activities of arms and letters. To critics, the Stuarts had seemed to blur the lines of gender distinction and corrupted the natural, social order; James appeared to engage in sodomitical activity with his favourites, while Charles appeared to fawn uxoriously over the Catholic Henrietta Maria, succumbing to her charms and popish seductions. Cromwell, however, appeared to direct a godly family, exercising proper authority in his household, advancing morality and the true Protestant religion. In short, for critics who had identified wasteful extravagance, popery, persecution, absolutism, disorder, excess, and effeminacy in Charles, Cromwell seemed to embody simplicity, true religion, reformation, consensual government, order, modesty, and masculinity. As Thomas l'Wright declared upon Cromwell's death in 1658: 'for we find Him not subject to passion, lordlinesse, statelinesse, or presumption, (the common and inseparable flawes and faults of greatnesse) but of an even, grave, stayed, patient and affable comportment towards all men'.[24]

Cromwell was often celebrated or commemorated for these particular qualities as a father, soldier, and public servant during the civil wars and Interregnum in the deluge of pamphlets and cheap print which circulated widely and beyond London to an engaged reading public.[25] Positive constructions of Cromwell's masculinity presented him as the solution to Stuart tyranny and to the English world-turned-upside-down which required an authoritative man to reorder the gendered and social hierarchy. In this moment, rather than needing to reinvent a language of authority as Sharpe contended, statesmen sought to legitimise the new regime by envisioning Cromwell and other central leaders of parliament and the council as truly embodying expectations of virtuous rule and fulfilling what the Stuart kings in particular, and the office of hereditary monarchy in general, could not accomplish.

To identify Cromwell as such a solution, writers drew upon conceptual grammars of masculinity, Christian piety, and classical history to endorse Cromwell's power. Throughout the 1650s and closely following Cromwell's death, these writers portrayed the military general and eventual lord protector as possessing such sound control over his passions and appetites

---

[24] Thomas l'Wright, *An exact character or, narrative of the late right noble, and magnificent lord, Oliver Cromvvell, the Lord Protector of England, Scotland, and Ireland* (London, 1658), 6.

[25] Jason Peacey, 'Accessibility of Print', in *Print and Public Politics in the English Revolution* (Cambridge: Cambridge University Press, 2013), 56–91.

'So much power and piety in one' 319

that he resisted the luring seductions of women and false religion and ruled a godly household, unlike King Charles who had supposedly been wooed by a Catholic wife and 'popish' forms of worship and governance. Edmund Waller's *Panegyrick to My Lord Protector* (1655), for one, touted that before Cromwell ruled England, he had practised 'first over [him] self to Reign', and thereby became an exemplary model for family conduct and governance: 'Your private life did a just Pattern give / How Fathers, Husbands, Pious Sons should live'.[26] l'Wright's *An exact character or, narrative of the late right noble, and magnificent lord, Oliver Cromvvell* (1658) described the late Protector as a loving and devoted husband and father, whose household received God's blessing:

> He was always exceeding loving towards Her, that had the Honour of His bed: and a most Tender and Indulgent Father, towards all those which God had sent Him, by the only dear Consort both of his youth, and old age: a happiness and blessing seldome seen to accompany old and young to their graves: and to see their Issues honourably disposed of in his life time; which is a visible signe and argument, that God had bestowed this great blessing upon Him, and His.[27]

And the English translation of Payne Fisher's *Irenodia Gratulatoria* (1652) emphasised that Cromwell had not only overthrown his enemies but also conquered himself, his appetites and passions.[28] In complete self-possession, he resisted the seducing allure of feminine beauty: 'For *you* a charging horse, and sword embrace / Before the witch-crafts of a womans face'.[29] Throughout this passage, Fisher compared Cromwell to Scipio Africanus, a Roman general often admired for his continence; as the poem described, Scipio was a commander 'whose name no blot / Ever receiv'd, whose vertue ne're had spot'.[30] According to Livy, after capturing the city of New Carthage in the Second Punic War, Scipio's soldiers brought him an extremely attractive woman as part of the spoils of war. Although Scipio was astonished by her beauty, after he learned of her engagement he returned her to her fiancé 'unspotted and

---

[26] Edmund Waller, *A Panegyrick to My Lord Protector, or The present Greatness and joynt Interst of His Highness, and this Nation* (London, 1655), 8. For a fuller discussion of Waller, see Section 7.2.

[27] l'Wright, *An exact character . . . Oliver Cromvvell*, 6. See also 5.

[28] Thomas Manley, *Veni; Vidi; Vici. The Triumphs of the Most Excellent & Illustrious, Oliver Cromwell, &c. Set forth in a Panegyricke. Written Originally in Latine, and faithfully done into English Heroicall Verse, by T[homas] M[anley]* (London, 1652), 11.

[29] Ibid., 72.   [30] Ibid., 73.

320 The Masculine Republic

untouched' and refused to accept her family's ransom payment.[31] Scipio's self-control aided the Roman cause, as this fiancé and his city swore allegiance to Rome as a result.

Andrew Marvell's 'A Poem upon the Death of his Late Highness the Lord Protector' (1659) similarly emphasised Cromwell's private virtues and godly fatherhood, balancing the image of Cromwell as grand military leader with the 'wondrous softness of his heart'. Marvell, a learned and talented friend of Milton and James Harrington, came to know Cromwell's family intimately by serving as governor of Cromwell's nephew and ward, William Dutton, from 1653–57, and by acting as Latin secretary to the council of state and to the head of the government's intelligence service until the Restoration. Cromwell's deep love for his second daughter, Elizabeth, who had died one month before him, became Marvell's central image of Cromwell's family devotion and piety:

> Her when an infant, taken with her charms,
> He oft would flourish in his mighty arms;
> And, lest their force the tender burden wrong,
> Slacken the vigour of his muscles strong (31–34)[32]

Although capable of great force and strength, Cromwell cradled his daughter gently in his 'mighty arms', Marvell imagined; he 'softly' moved his daughter to her mother's breast, 'Which while she drained of milk, she filled with love'. From this tender parenting, Elizabeth 'as with riper years her virtue grew', as well as her beauty and mind. Marvell explained that her and her father's affections became so intimately intertwined that her death led to her father's passing due to his deep love and grief: 'And in himself so oft immortal tried, / Yet in compassion of another died'.[33] These images provided a significant response to pamphlets portraying Cromwell as a bloodthirsty and ruthless Tamburlaine scourging England's own children for his personal gain.

Marvell celebrated that Cromwell had 'Twice ... in open field him victor crowned'; had 'first put arms into Religion's hand, / And tim'rous Conscience unto Courage manned'; had taught soldiers the 'inward mail to wear, / And fearing God how they should nothing fear'; had stormed strong cities 'by his prayer'; had kept contrary minds in agreement through his 'prudence more than human'.[34] Yet, in Marvell's estimation, it was his

---

[31] Livy, *The Romane historie vvritten by T. Livius of Padua. Also, the Breviaries of L. Florus: with a chronologie to the whole historie: and the Topographie of Rome in old time. Translated out of Latine into English, by Philemon Holland* (London, 1600), 623–24.

[32] Andrew Marvell, 'A Poem upon the Death of his Late Highness the Lord Protector', ed. Nigel Smith, in *The Poems of Andrew Marvell*, revised edition (Harlow: Pearson, 2007), 305.

[33] Marvell, 'A Poem upon the Death of his Late Highness', 305–6.   [34] Ibid., 307–9.

'So much power and piety in one' 321

faithful and unfailing fatherly love which demonstrated how very much he cared for the commonwealth:

> Friendship, that sacred virtue, long does claim
> The first foundation of his house and name:
> But within one its narrow limits fall;
> His tenderness extended unto all ...
> If he Eliza loved to that degree,
> (Though who more worthy to be loved than she?)
> If so indulgent to his own, how dear
> To him the children of the highest were?
> For her he once did Nature's tribute pay:
> For these his life adventured ev'ry day.
> And 'twould be found, could we his thoughts have cast,
> Their griefs struck deepest, if Eliza's last (lines 201–4, 209–16).[35]

With his household founded upon virtuous friendship, Cromwell could rightly love his subjects, those 'highest' elect of God, for whom he sacrificed himself daily. Marvell thus portrayed Cromwell as a sacrificial, loving, and complete father of household and commonwealth. His private virtues and familial devotion extended into virtuous ruling – the very opposite of characterisations of Nero, whose personal impiety and viciousness had led to the ruination of family and realm.

The historical stories that writers often adopted during the Stuart period to diagnose tyranny and its effects similarly became significant for defining masculine virtue positively. For every Tarquin, Englishmen sought a Junius Brutus, or for every Appius a Virginius. What has been underappreciated is just how very significant these historical images were in the polemical culture of England in the 1640s and 1650s, especially in defence of Cromwell as a self-controlled and virtuous ruler. After the coaching accident in Hyde Park in May 1654, for example, when Cromwell almost died from his musket exploding after being flung to the ground and dragged behind bolting horses, George Wither defended Cromwell by adopting the classical exemplum of Hippolytus. Wither was a prolific and successful 'country' and prophetic poet, who had been an early and active supporter of parliament in the civil wars both through his sword and pen.[36] He received patronage from Cromwell for his prophetic writings, as well as a number of appointments to political posts by the Commonwealth

---

[35] Ibid., 309.
[36] Wither's significance for the republican literary tradition has been defended by David Norbrook. See *Writing the English Republic: Poetry, Rhetoric and Politics, 1627–1660* (Cambridge: Cambridge University Press, 1999), 86–88, 140–58. Christopher Hill helped pave the way for this reassessment

322 The Masculine Republic

government and Protectorate, and from this platform levelled an important and early defence of popular political representation and participation in government. The exemplum Wither adopted, Hippolytus, served as a model of male chastity and stoic self-control, and, indeed, the very opposite of a Roman tyrant. According to Greek mythology, Theseus's son, Hippolytus, made a vow of chastity and scorned the company of women. Unlike Nero, who according to legend had submitted to his mother's incestuous advances, Hippolytus rejected his stepmother Phaedra's seduction, and as a result, Phaedra falsely accused him of rape. Theseus believed his wife in her accusation and cursed his son, causing Poseidon to send a sea-monster to terrorise Hippolytus' horses and smash their rider underfoot. Although his beautiful body was mangled, broken, crushed under the horses' hooves – an image often depicted in tragic detail by writers and artists – Ovid claimed in his *Metamorphoses* that Hippolytus was healed by Apollo's son, Asclepius, given the name Virbius, and transported to the Grove of Aricia in Italy where he resided as a companion to the goddess Diana.[37]

In *Vaticinium Causuale* (1654), Wither compared Cromwell's accident to Hippolytus's, for it 'was not want of skill, to use the *Raine*' that caused the 'stout, and chast' Hippolytus to fall. Though 'asunder dragd, his *Members* were, / It magnifide his *Wisdome, Love,* and *Care*'. Wither further explained that Hippolytus's fall 'made him sound, more then it harmed him': he was '*Regenerated,* or *New-borne*' into Virbius.[38] Wither argued that Cromwell had similarly fallen to rise, 'And to Arise with an improvement, too', being thankful for escaping from harm and also receiving 'that *Mark,* upon him set, / Of being GOD's especial *Favourite*'. Wither thereby hoped that 'when we have sum'd up all / Which, to his *Highnesse* hapned, by his *Fall,* / His *gaines,* will be much greater than his *cost*'.[39]

In the same year, the tragedy of *Appius and Virginia* (1654), which we have already studied in detail,[40] promoted rule and even revolution by a just, virtuous, military commander over a lustful tyrant who forfeited the preservation of the commonwealth for private passion. Within the dual portraits of Appius and Virginius on display, and the many contemporary

---

in his essay, 'George Wither and John Milton', in *The Collected Essays of Christopher Hill, Vol. I: Writing and Revolution in Seventeenth-Century England* (Brighton: Harvester, 1985), 135–56.

[37] Ovid, *Metamorphoses*, Bk XV. Other classical treatments include Euripides' *Hippolytus* and Seneca the Younger's *Phaedra*.

[38] George Wither, *Vaticinivm Cavsvale. A Rapture Occasioned by the late Miraculous Deliverance of his Highnesse the Lord Protector, From a Desperate Danger* (London, 1654), 4.

[39] Ibid., 4–5.   [40] See Section 2.3.

'So much power and piety in one'   323

references embedded within the play, contemporary audiences would have recognised significant parallels between these Roman figures and Cromwell and Charles. Appius not only adopts the language of Stuart monarchy throughout – employing the 'royal we', describing himself as possessing 'princely' virtues, being flattered by Clodius as creating 'divine policy', and remarking that 'judges are term'd / the Gods on earth'[41] – he is several times compared to an oak tree, identifying him with royalist images of Charles as a felled tree and with his son's escape from the Battle of Worcester in 1651 by hiding in an oak tree.[42] A comparison between Charles and Appius would have charged the late King with injustice, portraying his private yet raging passions as undermining the due process of law, liberty of subjects, and the gendered order of society.

As we have seen, the Jacobean tragedy further provided a significant portrait of the republican commander, Virginius, as an honest and courageous father and military leader defending the needs of his army and the security of Rome as a whole. In an important scene, Virginius rebukes his hungry and mutinous soldiers, and through his virtuous conduct and governance successfully transforms them into a courageous and pious force.[43] Such a scene mirrored the several poems and pamphlets of the early 1650s which celebrated Cromwell for his military valour and governance. Milton, for one, had argued in the *Defensio Secunda* (1654) that Cromwell's camp had proven to be 'the foremost school, not just of military science, but of religion and piety'; even through periods of peace and war, shifts of opinion, varied circumstances, and opposition, Cromwell kept his soldiers 'at their duty, and does so still, not by bribes and the licentiousness typical of the military, but by his authority and their wages alone'.[44] By displaying his prudent governance of the military camp as well as his household, the tragedy further emphasised that Virginius possessed the qualities of a virtuous ruler, including liberality and clemency. We find his household governed by order and chastity, his daughter Virginia vowing to follow his guidance in all affairs. In the end, after reforming the state through revolution, Virginius succeeds as consul, continuing the tradition 'which bold *Iunius Brutus* first / begun in *Tarquins* fall'.[45] The

---

[41] See John Webster [and Thomas Heywood], *Appius and Virginia. A Tragedy* (London, 1654), 7, 8, 22, and 37. Here I am following the spelling of 'Claudius' found in the 1654 printed edition.
[42] See Section 2.3.   [43] Webster [and Heywood], *Appius and Virginia*, 15–19.
[44] *Complete Prose Works of John Milton*, 10 volumes, gen. ed. Don M. Wolfe (New Haven: Yale University Press, 1953–82), IV.668.
[45] Webster [and Heywood], *Appius and Virginia*, 61.

324 The Masculine Republic

revolution presented in this play was not conducted by a headless mob but a well-ordered and disciplined military that is presented as bringing true justice to Rome and thereby restoring Rome's freedom.

Beyond these examples, defenders of the new republic and of Cromwell most often returned to the Roman histories which stood at the bookends of the republican period: the creation of the republic by Lucius Junius Brutus after King Tarquin's son raped Lucretia and the establishment of the Principate under Julius Caesar and Caesar Augustus, against which Brutus's successor, Marcus Junius Brutus, had battled unsuccessfully. The story of Lucretia studied in Chapter 1 uncovered the insatiable lust and cruelty of tyrants, with King Tarquinius Superbus usurping the throne and reigning unjustly by fear, while his son Sextus, who had become 'bewitched and possessed with wicked wanton lust' for the chaste Lucretia, ruthlessly violated her.[46] The actions by both father and son emphasised the enslavement of Rome: the Roman people had been subjected to the whims of a family, a family made tyrannical by its own enslavement to ruthless and insatiable appetites. In avenging Lucretia's honour after the violent rape, Brutus became the 'redeemer of the Citie' by casting out the race of kings and establishing a new constitution by consuls which prized the rule of law. Whereas Tarquin had ruled absolutely above the law and advice of counsel, Machiavelli and other commentators on Livy trumpeted Brutus's extraordinary commitment to justice, law, and the stable establishment of the republic, as seen in his willingness to sentence even his own sons to death for treasonous conspiracy against the republic.[47] Brutus's history so powerfully shaped the conceptions of English statesmen in the aftermath of the regicide in 1649 that the Commonwealth government sought to initiate an oath of loyalty to the new government as Brutus had done upon banishing the Tarquins.[48] For them, Brutus's story legitimised the regicide as necessary to restore the English constitution upon law and liberty.

---

[46] Livy, *Romane Historie*, 34–35 and 40–41.

[47] Livy, *Romane Historie*, 46–47; *Machiavels discourses. upon the first decade of T. Livius*, trans. E [dward] D[acres] (London, 1636), 444–46.

[48] Livy reported that 'whilest the people were yet greedie of this new freedome, for feare least they might any time after he won by entreatie or moved by gifts on the kings part, [Brutus] caused them to swear that they would never suffer any to be king at Rome'. Livy, *Romane historie*, 44. See also Plutarch, *The lives of the noble Grecians and Romanes compared together by that graue learned philosopher and historiographer, Plutarke of Chaeronea*, trans. Thomas North (London, 1579), 107–8. For discussions of the English oath, see Norbrook, *Writing the English Republic*, 192–93; Sarah Barber, 'The Engagement for the Council of State and the Establishment of the Commonwealth Government', *Historical Research* 63 (1990): 44–57.

'So much power and piety in one' 325

In the early 1650s, following the regicide and Cromwell's successful military campaigns in Ireland and Scotland, a number of poets and panegyrists exalted Cromwell specifically as the new Brutus who would establish a prosperous and lawful republic in the wake of tyranny. In his single leaf, emphatic broadsheet, *Radius Heliconicus or, the Resolution of a Free State* (1651), for example, R. Fletcher urged Englishmen to realise their liberty by throwing off the enslavement of monarchical custom and domination.[49] Throughout his poem, in strains similar to Marchamont Nedham's news and political writings as studied in Chapter 6, Fletcher contrasted the cowardice and slavish dependency of failed men subjected to monarchy with the independence, fame, and military valour which free men practised. Fletcher envisioned masculinity as flourishing in a free state, defining true manliness as both a 'life of action', where 'lives & swords' would be the 'seals and labels of [a man's] words', and as a state of independence, where men would be self-determined and serve in positions of authority. In this way, Fletcher legitimised Cromwell's military campaigns in Ireland and Scotland as the battle to wrest a free republic from the hands of enslaving tyrants: 'The pride and will / Of most extortious Tyrannies, are still / The sinew of our quarrels, which alone / Compell'd us to a Reformation'.[50] At this moment of transition for the English state from the 'base yoke of bondage' to manly liberty, Fletcher commanded his fellow citizens to model the Romans of old who had cast off kingship under the leadership of Junius Brutus:

> Let grov'ling Animals submit for feare,
> And bow their necks: we cannot center there.
> Our Resolutions strike a higher string
> Then *Tarquin's* Base, Tenor, or Minikin.
> Which time shall ripen, and successe befriend:
> The glory of a war is in the end.[51]

Fletcher concluded the poem by declaring Britain a new Rome, ripe for triumphant liberty and brave conquest under Cromwell's leadership. 'Though not Roman bands', Fletcher proclaimed, 'Yet we have Roman hearts, and Roman hands.'

Andrew Marvell's 'Horatian Ode upon Cromwell's return from Ireland' (1650) similarly heralded Cromwell's military victories as casting 'the Kingdome old / Into another Mold', as Junius Brutus had done.[52] The

---

[49] R. Fletcher, *Radius heliconicus or, the resolution of a free state* (London, 1650), 1.   [50] Ibid.
[51] Ibid.
[52] Marvell, 'An Horatian Ode upon Cromwell's Return from Ireland', ed. Smith, in *The Poems of Andrew Marvell*, 275 (lines 35–36).

The Masculine Republic

tyrant Tarquin had commanded that a temple to Jupiter be erected, which, according to Livy, 'moved the gods to declare the future mightinesse of so great an Empire' as Rome.[53] The Augurs divined tokens and signs testifying to the perpetuity and greatness of the empire, and the builders discovered as they dug the temple's foundation 'a mans head, face and all, whole & sound'.[54] While Tarquin interpreted this omen as bolstering his own kingdom, republicans who knew the ending of the story understood this omen as prophesying the future grandeur of the Roman republic which Brutus would establish. In Marvell's 'Ode', this bleeding head became a symbol marking the transition between the sacrifice of King Charles and the new foundation laid by Cromwell:

> So when they did design
> The *Capitols* first Line,
> A bleeding Head where they begun,
> Did fright the Architects to run;
> And yet in that the *State*
> Foresaw it's happy Fate.[55]

The bloody sacrifice of Charles may have given England's parliamentary architects pause, but they had broken the line of kings and laid the foundation for a free state.[56]

Although siding with the Royalists in the first civil war, being subsequently imprisoned after defeat at Marston Moor, and opposing the regicide, Payne or Fitzpayne Fisher[57] became Cromwell's most significant panegyrist, producing *Irenodia Gratulatoria* (1652) to celebrate the commonwealth's victories and a series of poems lauding the Lord Protector, including *Inauguratio Olivariana* (1654).[58] With his work published by official printers, with official sponsorship, and decorated with dedicatory verses by other significant Cromwellian authors, Fisher served as 'poet laureate' to the new regime and by 1655 styled himself '*Historiis et Satellitio Domini Protectoris*'.[59] The earliest panegyric, *Irenodia*

---

[53] Livy, *Romane historie*, 38.   [54] Ibid.   [55] Marvell, 'Horatian Ode', 276–77 (lines 67–72).

[56] Norbrook, *Writing the English Republic*, 266–68. Some commentators have interpreted Interregnum poems about Brutus as ambiguous and even ironic. This surely seems true for exile literature written by Royalists, such as Abraham Cowley, but not for pro-Cromwellian panegyrics. See Christopher D'Addario, 'Abraham Cowley and the Ends of Poetry', in *Literatures of Exile in the English Revolution and Its Aftermath, 1640–1690*, ed. Philip Major (Farnham, Surrey: Ashgate, 2010), 119–32, esp. 130–32.

[57] His Latin works also appeared under the name Pagani or Fitzpaganus Piscatoris.

[58] *Panegyrici Cromwello* (1654); *Oratio anniversaria* (1655); *Oratio secunda anniversaria* (1657); and *Paean triumphalis in secundam inaugurationem* (1657).

[59] J. T. Peacey, 'Fisher, Payne (1615/16–1693)', in *Oxford Dictionary of National Biography* (Oxford University Press: 2004), online ed., Jan. 2008 [www.oxforddnb.com/view/article/9506].

'So much power and piety in one'　　327

Gratulatoria (1652), which we have already briefly discussed, hailed Cromwell as a military general dedicated to the public good whose virtues and conquests had brought peace and plenty, true religion and justice again to the realm.[60] The poem circulated not only in Latin but also in an English translation produced by Thomas Manley and entitled, *Veni; Vidi; Vici. The Triumphs of the Most Excellent & Illustrious, Oliver Cromwell* (1652), and as David Norbrook has argued, both Fisher and Manley were keen to encourage Cromwell on a republican path.[61] Manley's translation underscored Fisher's exempla-rich rhetoric, but what scholars have overlooked is how his poem further emphasised the connection between Cromwell and Brutus. In a passage of *Irenodia* in which Fisher described the renewal of the empire under Cromwell's leadership, Manley added a reference to tyrannical rape not found in Fisher's poem; the reference argued that Cromwell, like Brutus before him, had liberated the commonwealth from the (sexual) violence of tyranny:

> Nec minus interea positis moderatior Armis,
> Adventu Rediviva *Tuo Respublica* surgens,
> Lætius Imperii mutatas sensit habenas,
> Relligio *Tecum* rediit, clementia *Tecum*
> Creverit & Pietas (Fisher, *Irenodia Gratulatoria*)

> [no less doth the State,
> Arms being laid aside, grown moderate,
> Revive and rise again even from her urne
> At thy so wished, they so joy'd returne,
> Feeling her changed reines she doth implore,
> *That Tyrants never her may ravish more.*
> Religion saw thee come and hasted hither,
> Mercy and Piety met thee together,
> And here began to settle] (Manley, *Veni; Vidi; Vici,* [my emphasis])[62]

By adding this reference, Manley invited his readers to view Cromwell as a Junius Brutus, freeing a feminised England from vicious tyrants who threatened her liberty and virtue, as Brutus had freed the Romans from Tarquin after the violent rape of Lucretia.

Fisher's employment of exempla throughout his poems most often argued that Cromwell had superseded the great heroes of the past:

---

[60] Payne Fisher, *Irenodia gratulatoria, sive Illustrissimi amplissimiq[ue] viri Oliveri Cromwelli, &c. epinicion* (London, 1652), sigs. A1r and B1r–2r. Knoppers, *Constructing Cromwell,* 58–61; Norbrook, *Writing the English Republic,* 234–35.

[61] Norbrook, *Writing the English Republic,* 236–38.

[62] Fisher, *Irenodia gratulatoria,* sig. B2r; Manley, *Veni; Vidi; Vici,* 4–5.

328   The Masculine Republic

Cromwell reached new heights by possessing their virtues while overcoming their vices. In the later *Inauguratio Olivariana* (1654), Fisher argued that Junius Brutus, the glorious founder of Italy's liberty who restored law and political offices, would have rejoiced to live under such a leader as Cromwell.[63] For Cromwell, it was contended, established a sober commonwealth, avoiding the vices of gluttony and luxury while upholding the (sexual) order of civil and moral society:[64]

> Non ibi deformis *Lucretia* damna rapinæ
> Lugebit, castae nec solvet vincula *zonæ*
> *Virgo* Pudicitiæ compos; *Te vindice* servat
> Jura *Thorus* Thalamúsque; *fidem*: non fędus Adulter
>
> [There Lucretia will not mourn the injury of dishonourable rape,
> nor will the virgin, in full control of her chastity, loosen her
> girdle's bonds; with you as avenger, the marriage bed and bedroom
> preserve the laws and fidelity]

The fidelity of the marriage bed indeed had been supported through the Adultery Act of 1650, passed by the Commonwealth Parliament but enforced under the Protectorate.[65] This unique act in English history recast sexual relations as a concern of the state rather than the church, placing 'the full machinery of the state behind the enforcement of sexual morality' by imposing the death penalty for violators of incest, female adulterers, and their male partners; imprisonment for fornicators; whipping, branding, the pillory, and three years imprisonment for brothel-keepers.[66] The Act arose in the wake of arguments in the 1640s that popish and inefficient church government through bishops had led to the moral degradation of society, especially the 'great increase and frequency of whoredoms and adulteries', as one Root and Branch petition argued.[67] The Act's injunctions against the sins of the flesh aligned with Cromwell's dedication to the godly reformation of England, and with his rise as lord protector, Cromwell pursued the enforcement of sexual and social

---

[63] 'Vivere sub tali gauderet Principe, *Brutus*; / *Brutus* grande decus, Libertatisq; repertor / *Ausoniæ*, qui Jura suis *fascesque* reduxit'. Fisher, *Inauguratio Olivariana, sive Pro Præfectura Serenissimi Principis Angliæ, Scotiæ, & Hiberniæ, Dom. Protectoris Olivari: Carmen Votivum* (London, 1654), 43–44.

[64] 'ubi sobria quisque / Adspersis salibus, nulla formidine, miscet. / Ebrietas ubi non, Gula vel circumflua luxu / Fędatam, norunt vitiis temerare, salutem'. Ibid., 44.

[65] All but five of the thirty-six trials occurred under Cromwell's government.

[66] Keith Thomas, 'The Puritans and Adultery: The Act of 1650 Reconsidered', in *Puritans and Revolutionaries: Essays in Seventeenth-Century History Presented to Christopher Hill*, ed. Donald Pennington and Thomas (Oxford: Oxford University Press, 1978), 257–81, esp. 257; Fissell, *Vernacular Bodies*, 169–76.

[67] Qtd in Thomas, 'Puritans and Adultery', 264.

'So much power and piety in one' 329

morality. His Proclamation of 1655 commanded 'a speedy and due Execution of the Lavvs made against the abominable sins of Drunkenness, profane Swearing and Cursing, Adultery, Fornication, and other acts of uncleanness', as well as setting the 'Poor on Work', 'punishing Rogues and Vagabonds' and those who 'prophane the Lords Day'.[68]

While historians have debated if the Adultery Act formed an effective part of the criminal code, its symbolic importance for ministers and statesmen seeking the godly reformation of the state should not be neglected.[69] Whereas James and Charles had been charged with undermining the gendered order of household and society by promoting luxurious and lascivious behaviour in their own households and the royal court and by failing in their masculine authority, the Commonwealth Parliament and Cromwell sought to establish legislatively an ordered society under the governance of good men and moral householders. The Protectorate tried to ensure that daughters and wives stood protected from violent violation; maidens remained pure; and wives obeyed the authority of their husbands. In connection to these sacred and secular concerns, the story of Junius Brutus provided a positive historical republican image for Cromwell, emphasising his role as liberator from the violent threat and disorder of tyranny. It also aligned with the republican aesthetic of the early Commonwealth government.[70] As we will see, the exemplum also directly challenged criticisms of Cromwell that presented his body as lusty, swollen, and grotesque, his actions and motives as those of Nero, Tamburlaine, or Cataline, as well as former criticisms that had been levelled against James and Charles. These poems displayed the manly Cromwell as republican hero and father, in control of his passions and thus reforming society with law, justice, and true religion.

---

[68] *By the Protector. A Proclamation Commanding a speedy and due Execution of the Lavvs made against the abominable sins of Drunkenness, profane Swearing and Cursing, Adultery, Fornication, and other acts of uncleannesse ... Published by His Highness special Command* (London, 1655). These policies were applied, although often unsuccessfully, on the local level by major-generals overseeing the twelve military districts established in 1655. *Mercurius Politicus*, for example, published an order by Charles Worsley, the Major General of Chester, Lancaster, and Stafford counties, to turn in all persons participating in horse-races, bear-baiting, stage-plays, selling ale or beer, sabbath-breaking, drunkards, swearers, 'reputed Fathers of Bastard-children', frequenters of bawdy houses, and 'Delinquents, Scandalous, or Ignorant Preachers or School-masters'. *Mercurius Politicus, Comprising The sum of Foreine Intelligence, with the Affairs now on Foot in the three Nations of England, Scotland, & Ireland*, no. 294, 24 Jan. to 31 Jan. 1655 (London, 1655), 5928–30.

[69] For a description and more recent assessment of this debate, see Bernard Capp, 'Republican Reformation: Family, Community and the State in Interregnum Middlesex, 1649–60', in *The Family in Early Modern England*, ed. Helen Berry and Elizabeth Foyster (Cambridge: Cambridge University Press, 2007), 40–66, esp. 41.

[70] See Knoppers, *Constructing Cromwell*, 66.

330   The Masculine Republic

7.2   Constructing Cromwell as Caesar

Thus far we have considered the importance of historical exempla for debating the figure of Cromwell in the 1640s and 1650s, examining how supporters of the eventual lord protector publicly constructed Cromwell's masculinity and virtue simultaneously as the solution to tyranny and gender disorder and as the significant foundation for a new republic. Whereas writers employed numerous historical exempla throughout the late 1640s and 1650s to denigrate or celebrate Cromwell, in the early 1650s the exemplum of Junius Brutus became especially significant for justifying Cromwell and the new regime, evoking the powerful themes of violence, justice, and sexual order. These particular ideas mapped onto the gendered and classical vocabularies of tyranny already traced in this book.

Another significant historical exemplum which played a prominent role in understanding Cromwell's achievements and which publicly constructed his positive image, however, potentially undermined republican representations of Cromwell as Junius Brutus. At the other bookend of Roman republican history was Julius Caesar, the renowned military general whose uncontrolled ambition transformed Rome from Republic to Principate. In the republican literary tradition, the three figures most celebrated in these final years were Pompey, Cato, and Marcus Brutus; all three staunchly opposed Caesar's rise to power. A central republican poem, Lucan's *Pharsalia*, which circulated widely in Latin and in English through Thomas May's celebrated translation, bolstered the heroism of these republicans while maligning Caesar for his devastating ambition. Originally, May had dedicated his *Pharsalia* translation to statesmen opposing King Charles's Forced Loan in 1627, aligning their efforts with the heroism of Cato and Pompey, who was 'the true servant of the publike State' in May's estimation. Throughout Lucan's poem, Caesar was represented as subordinating public good to private interest and ambition, extinguishing Rome's liberty through brutal civil war and forcing its citizens to choose between bloodshed and tyrannical peace.[71]

Despite this significant republican heritage, Julius Caesar became a preferred exemplum for panegyrists of Cromwell, especially following his rise to lord protector in 1653. Whereas Pompey, Cato, and Marcus Brutus had shown a resolute constancy and courage in the name of liberty and the

---

[71] Norbrook, *Writing the English Republic*, 34–62.

'So much power and piety in one'

331

public good, Pompey and Brutus failed as military commanders, and Cato chose the passive resistance of suicide to remain free. To contemporaries, Cromwell's extraordinary, decisive, and swift military victories evoked Caesar's triumphal victories rather than these Stoic defeats. Cromwell had been victorious in the civil wars, much as Caesar had, and contemporaries believed that such decisive military engagement was necessary for the future success of the republic. As Jonathan Scott has shown, English republicans, influenced by Machiavelli, sought to build a republic in the model of Rome rather than Venice: building empire and seeking glory, choosing expansion over preservation.[72] We see this in news pamphlets such as *A Modest Narrative of Intelligence Fitted for the Republique of England & Ireland* (16–23 Jun. 1649) which advocated that the republican general 'must wrastle with all difficulties, rather then quit the enterprise; but being once embarqued, on he must, whether win or lose, with a *Cæsarian* Confidence at the *Rubicon* and a *Spartan* Resolution to go on with the Sword'.[73] *The Perfect Politician* (1660) celebrated the comparison between Cromwell and Caesar by boasting that '*Caesar's Veni, Vidi, Vici,* may well be attributed to him, who no sooner came neer an Enemy and beheld him, but he overcame him'. It made the further grand claim that should Caesar have lived until the seventeenth century, he 'might have turned Scholar, and learnt the Rudiments of Modern Discipline, by the Example of this excellent Commander'.[74] I'Wright similarly argued that 'without flattery, it may be said of him, as it is of *Cæsar,* that *Venit, Vidit, & Vicit*'.[75] R. Fletcher's confident tribute to Cromwell further linked his Caesarean might with England's imperial ambitions:

> Let envy swell and burst; Malignancie
> Curse its hard fate, grow sullen, sick, and die:
> Whiles our triumphant palms spread & increase;
> Like the preservers of a common peace.
> *Caesar,* and *Cromwell*: why, 'tis all but *C.*
> And why not *England* now, as *Italie?*
> *Rome's* Basis was as small, as this whereon
> We hope to raise our Fame's encomion:
> Nay, our encouragements are rather more.

[72] Scott, *Commonwealth Principles*, 10–11, 210–32; Scott, 'Classical Republicanism', 70–71.
[73] James Moxon, publisher, *A Modest Narrative of Intelligence Fitted for the Republique of England & Ireland, from Saturday, June 16. to Saturday, June 23, 1649* (London, 1649), 89.
[74] Henry Fletcher, *The perfect politician, or, A full view of the life and action (military and civil) of O. Cromwel whereunto is added his character, and a compleat catalogue of all the honours conferr'd by him on several persons* (London, 1660), 176.
[75] I'Wright, *An exact character ... Oliver Cromvvell,* 5.

332 The Masculine Republic

Smile gentle Fortune, as thou didst before.
Then *Thames* as *Tybur* shall rejoice to be
Crown'd with the spoiles of the worlds royaltie.[76]

Through Cromwell's leadership, England could hope for imperial victory as that acquired by the mighty Caesar. And indeed, for those (particularly Protestant) statesmen who had lived through years of pacific policies under James and then Charles, English military boldness may have seemed especially welcome. As seen in previous chapters, much of the frustration with James from 1618 onwards focused on his seemingly tepid support of Protestants in the Bohemian Crisis and ensuing Thirty Years War. Although Charles sought to reform and restore the honour system and adopted chivalric rhetoric and tropes throughout the 1630s, the Personal Rule required the pursuance of peace for England even as continental religious war ensued. Cromwell's military prowess and swift domination over Ireland and Scotland fulfilled hopeful expectations of strong, authoritative, masculine rule and imperial glory for England.

The exemplum of Julius Caesar highlighted the grand hopes which rested in Cromwell by his supporters, but it simultaneously played into the significant anxieties his leadership produced, especially during the parliamentary elections of 1654 and 1656 in which opponents understood the commonwealth as in danger 'of the utter subversion of Religion, Law, Liberty, Right, and Property'. A 1656 petition, which may have been written by the army officer and politician Sir Arthur Hesilrige, second baronet, warned that the Lord Protector acted from 'lawless ambition': he has 'pretend[ed] that the people have consented to become his slaves' and 'hath assumed an absolute arbitrary soveraignty (as if he came down from the throne of God)', declaring that his proclamations 'shall be binding laws to Parliaments themselves' and judging 'by no other rule or law then his pleasure, as if he were their absolute Lord'.[77] Just as Marcus Brutus and the conspirators had feared that Julius Caesar meant to become king, so Englishmen – many of them republicans – feared that Cromwell sought

---

[76] Fletcher, *Radius Heliconicus*.

[77] Hesilrige was one of the five members whom King Charles accused of treason and attempted to arrest in the Commons' chamber in December 1641. He staunchly supported the constitutional authority of Parliament, and opposed both Charles and Cromwell because of their seemingly unrepresentative rule. Anon., *To all the worthy gentlemen who are duely chosen for the Parliament, which intended to meet at Westminster the 17 of September 1656. And to all the good people of the Common-wealth of England. The humble remonstrance, protection, and appeale of severall knights and gentlemen duly chosen to serve their countrey in Parliament; who attended at Westminster for that purpose, but were violently kept out of the Parliament-house by armed men hired by the Lord Protector* (London, 1656), n. p. [1–3].

'So much power and piety in one'   333

the crown, and at the price of English liberty. In the same year, Nedham's *The Excellencie of a Free-State* (1656), studied in Chapter 6, promoted an imperial vision for England while warning of the dangers of internal corruption from a seemingly power-hungry military general or 'Great One'. Nedham's discussions of Caesar as 'Grandee Usurper', one who had 'continued in power too long' and even committed treason in his crossing of the Rubicon, included veiled references to Cromwell as England's new Grandee.[78] In retrospect, John Toland in his preface to James Harrington's reprinted *Oceana* (1700) would further trumpet this highly critical comparison between Caesar and Cromwell:

> LYCURGUS and ANDREW DORIA, who, when it was in their power to continue Princes, chose rather to be the founders of their Countrys Liberty, will be celebrated for their Virtue thro the course of all Ages, and their very Names convey the highest Ideas of Godlike Generosity; while JULIUS CAESAR, OLIVER CROMWEL, and such others as at any time inslav'd their fellow Citizens, will be for ever remember'd with detestation, and cited as the most execrable Examples of the vilest Treachery and Ingratitude. It is only a refin'd and excellent Genius, a noble Soul ambitious of solid Praise, a sincere lover of Virtue and the good of all Mankind, that is capable of executing so glorious an Undertaking as making a People free.[79]

With Cromwell's violent dissolution of the Rump Parliament in 1653, and his creation as lord protector through the 'Instrument of government', republicans especially employed Caesar's exemplum to criticise bitterly Cromwell's rise to power and to warn about the danger of ambition. Importantly, George Chapman's *Caesar and Pompey: a Roman Tragedy, declaring their warres* was reprinted at this moment in 1653, with the moral declaring, 'Onely a iust man is a free man'. As we have seen, Chapman composed the play around 1604, while crafting a number of plays which offered veiled criticisms of the new monarch.[80] In its original printing of 1631, the play had encouraged statesmen to emulate Cato by remaining

---

[78] See Marchamont Nedham, *The Excellencie of a Free-State Or, The Right Constitution of a Commonwealth*, ed. Blair Worden (Indianapolis: Liberty Fund, 2011), 20–23, 91, 98. Worden discusses this in his 'Introduction', xxxix–xl.

[79] John Toland, ed. *The Oceana of James Harrington and his other works, som [sic] wherof are now first publish'd from his own manuscripts: the whole collected, methodiz'd, and review'd, with an exact account of his life prefix'd* (London, 1700), xx–xxi.

[80] Especially the anti-Scottish satire in *Eastward Ho* (1605), which landed Chapman and his fellow co-authors briefly in prison. See Bertheau, 'Jacques I au miroir de la Tragedie Chapmanienne', *Bulletin de la Société d'Etudes Anglo-Americaines des XVII et XVIII Siècles* 62 (2006): 193–207. See also Bertheau, 'George Chapman's French Tragedies, or, Machiavelli beyond the Mirror', in *Representing France and the French in Early Modern English Drama*, ed. Jean-Christophe Mayer (Newark: University of Delaware Press, 2008), 110–24.

334 The Masculine Republic

constant, virtuous, and honourable even in corrupt times, and promoted a
passive resistance to tyranny.[81] In this new context, with Cromwell gaining
power after a brutal decade of civil wars, the play's bitter censure of Caesar
defeating Pompey reached a heightened significance. The 'Argument' of
the tragedy contrasted Caesar and Pompey, the former commanding his
forces 'vnduly and ambitiously', with the latter fighting 'more for feare of
Cæsars violence to the State, then mou'd with any affectation of his own
greatnesse'.[82] In the opening scene, Cato labelled Caesar 'tyranous' and a
threat to Rome, surrounded by 'such a flocke of Puttocks' drawn to his 'ill-
disposed Purse' as well as 'Impostors, Flatterers, Fauorites, and Bawdes, /
Buffons, Intelligencers, select wits; / Close Murtherers, Montibanckes, and
decaied Theeues'.[83] Cato's suicide near the end of the play is described as a
'thing manly, / and merely heauenly' for the sake of 'iust mens liberties';
his final speeches include praise for his son-in-law Marcus Brutus, whom
the audience knows will later defend Rome's liberty by assassinating
Caesar.[84] Caesar, meanwhile, concludes the play miserably even though
victorious in war. As Cato's severed head is displayed before him in the
final scene, Caesar exclaims that the 'instant rapture' and 'blisse' captured
upon Cato's face is 'the bitterest curse' to Caesar's 'vext and tyrannisde
nature'.[85]

Less than a year after Cromwell assumed the Protectorship, the republican writer John Streater, a close associate of Marchamont Nedham, the
printer of James Harrington's *Oceana* (1656), and a radical articulator of
popular classical republicanism, levelled a sustained charge against Cromwell by providing a detailed historical analysis of Julius Caesar's life drawn
from Suetonius, interlaced with his own political commentary.[86] The work
was entitled *A Politick Commentary on the Life of Caius Julius Caesar* (1654)
and woven throughout his serial news pamphlet, *Perfect and Impartial
Intelligence*. In a small note at the end of a pamphlet from early 1654,
Streater addressed the reader's potential wonderment that he should record
Suetonius's history of Caesar and thereby 'undertake to prove *Cæsar* a
Tyrant and a Usurper' – perhaps especially in a context in which the new

---

[81] See Chapter 4.
[82] George Chapman, *Caesar and Pompey: a Roman tragedy, declaring their vvwares. Out of whose events
is evicted this proposition. Only a iust man is a freeman. As it was acted at the Black-Fryers* (London,
1653), sig. A4v.
[83] Ibid., sig. B1r–v.   [84] Ibid., sig. I2r and I4r.   [85] Ibid., sig. K1v.
[86] For more on Streater's republicanism, see Section 7.3. Smith, 'Popular Republicanism in the
1650s', 138–44; Blair Worden, *Literature and Politics in Cromwellian England* (Oxford: Oxford
University Press, 2007), 313–17.

'So much power and piety in one'   335

Lord Protector Cromwell was very often compared to Caesar. Streater defended his position by explaining that Caesar had 'assumed the Supream authority and altered the Laws of his Country; the Gods as a just reward due for his so doing, permitted him to be slain in that sort he was', and in a provocative comment added that surely, 'I shal not comit treason against him in my undertaking, I am told he is dead long since'.[87] That anyone should want to be called a Caesar seemed preposterous to Streater, he added, for 'to be like *Cæsar* is in effect to say they deserve to be killed by a *Brutus* as he was'.[88] In the ensuing serials, Streater articulated Caesar's history, drawing very evident parallels in his historical glosses between what he understood to be the tyranny of Caesar and Cromwell – parallels evident enough that his work provoked repeated arrests and counter-newsbooks.[89] After describing how Caesar amassed armies to keep the empire in check, for example, Streater explained:

> *Cesar* had no Commission for what he did, but because he had sucess and the Commonwealth the benefit by having its enemies vanquished: *Cesar* is not called to account, in this he usurpt absolute authority in raising forces and attempting to make war without authority of the Senate; by which it appeareth the Senate did decline in their policy as well as the Common-wealth in vertue: the Senate should have taken his head of[f] for that Act, and so have ridded the Commonwealth of a Usurper, the Commonweal of *Rome* turned to a Monarchy because the Senate did not keep the arms of the Commonwealth in their hands: the Senate after the disposing of the absolute power of Arms, signified no more then a Cipher, those Councel and Senates that will be powerfull and just, must be free, not over awed with Arms, those that are, are not free.[90]

The message to Parliament was clear: Cromwell would turn England again into a monarchy because of Parliament's failure to keep control of Crom-well and his army. In this way, Streater passionately argued that Crom-well's great military success had provided him with absolute authority, leading to the decline of law, liberty, and virtue. Caesar's history provided a timely and poignant vehicle through which to understand the activities of the Lord Protector and through which to promote his demise.

Both through their own historical study and through witnessing pam-phlets such as Streater's, Cromwell's supporters recognised the risks of

---

[87] *Perfect and Impartial Intelligence, Of the Affairs, in England, Scotland, and Ireland, And other Parts beyond the Seas, From Tuesday May 16 to Tuesday May 23, 1654* (London, 1654), 8.
[88] Ibid.   [89] Norbrook, *Writing the English Republic*, 320.
[90] *Perfect and Impartial Intelligence . . . , From Tuesday May 23 to Fryday May 26, 1654* (London, 1654), 13–14.

The Masculine Republic

deeming Cromwell a Caesar. As one biography of Cromwell directly questioned: 'Nothing could satisfie *Caesars* Ambition, but a perpetual Dictatorship . . . ; why then should our *Cromwel,* having the same aspiration, (and inspiration above them) be satisfied with less then a perpetual Protectorship?'[91] Fisher's *Irenodia Gratulatoria* (1652), amongst other works, sought to allay this fear by arguing that Cromwell's virtues and religious piety made him *greater* than Caesar, and thereby capable of overcoming the vices of ambition and greed which had plagued the Roman dictator.[92] Cromwell was a better man than Caesar. The significance of Caesar's exemplum within Fisher's poem is highlighted by Manley's English translation, which bore the title, *Veni; Vidi; Vici,* and included an original dedicatory epistle to Cromwell describing how Julius Caesar 'never rejoyced more then when he heard his valiant exploits were spoken of in simple Cottages, alledging this, that a bright Sun shines in every corner, which makes not the beames worse, but the place better'.[93]

After describing Cromwell's victories at Marston Moor, Ireland, and Scotland, Fisher questioned with what military heroes Cromwell should be compared, for the English commander had blameless conduct, while for the famous commanders of old, 'Some crimes their Vertue oftentimes did blot, / Their milky colour oft receiv'd a spot'. In Fisher's poem, the most prominent example of a 'spotted hero' was Caesar, for although 'conquests did his honor raise, / And crown his temples with Imperiall bayes', Caesar's 'treacherous dealing' merited dishonour, shame, and infamy: 'For gold the very temples did he break, / And stayn'd his sword with country mens dear blood, / If His unlawfull pleasures they withstood'.[94] As Lucan's *Pharsalia* had so powerfully described, Caesar's vicious excess led him to desecrate temples and shed innocent blood for ambition and avarice. Fisher countered this negative exemplum by proclaiming that Cromwell, 'Great Sir, Greater then *Caesar* are':

> The Empire of your Vertues reacheth far,
> And keeping Passion under, dost restrain
> Its insolencies with the strongest rain.

---

[91] Fletcher, *The perfect politician,* 252–53.

[92] For another example, see an exposition of Marchamont Nedham's Latin poems on the city of London in Edward Holberton, *Poetry and the Cromwellian Protectorate: Culture, Politics, and Institutions* (Oxford: Oxford University Press, 2008), 44–46.

[93] Manley, *Veni; Vidi; Vici,* epistle dedicatory. Manley's translation will be used for subsequent quotations of Fisher in this section.

[94] Ibid., 70–71.

'So much power and piety in one'   337

> No Avarice with it's [*sic*] destroying hooks
> Inrolles thy Name in Fames infamous books;
> At hopes of Lucre *you* unmoved stand,
> No wretched gold thy spirit can command.[95]

Fisher compared Cromwell's virtues to his empire, having vast dominion over his passions as well as peoples. Through this description, he heeded Livy's warning that the Roman Empire after the rise of Caesar and Augustus faced decline as 'wealth hath brought in avarice, abundant pleasures haue kindled a desire by riot, lust, and loose life, to perish and bring all to naught'.[96] It was this passage amongst others in Livy that convinced Machiavelli in the *Discourses* that the path of empire like Rome would bring greater glory to the republic but also greater risk of corruption and ruin.[97] For Fisher and other supporters, Cromwell ushered in a glorious republican empire while remaining unmoved by Asiatic luxury, free of avarice and faulty passions. Moderation, sobriety, prudence, and clemency ruled the English leader, Fisher argued; forsaking the '*Carthaginian*' pleasures which make one 'grow unfit for *Mars,* effeminate', Cromwell became the true icon of masculinity and imperial grandeur.[98]

Edmund Waller, whom Fisher and Dawbeny praised as the English Vergil, similarly produced *A Panegyrick to My Lord Protector* (1655) to celebrate the Protector as Imperial Roman conqueror.[99] Although Waller was Cromwell's kinsman, his championing of the Cromwellian regime in the 1650s garnered great public notice and significant criticism from republicans and royalists. Part of Waller's notoriety arose from his previous banishment by Parliament in the 1640s for a plot to allow King Charles's armies to enter London during the first civil war.[100] His *Panegyrick* sought to persuade Cromwell's detractors that they should submit to the Protectorate, for Cromwell ruled England justly and amplified the commonwealth's greatness. The importance of this poem can be measured by the large number of satiric poems and anti-panegyrics the work prompted.[101] Waller's *Panegyrick* intertwined imagery of Cromwell's personal virtue and England's Imperial glory, arguing that Cromwell had ushered England into a golden age not only equal to Rome's but surpassing it; for English virtue, restored by Cromwell, would prevent the corruption of Asiatic luxury and greed. Attending to the significant Machiavellian discourse of

---

[95] Ibid., 72.   [96] Livy, *Romane Historie*, 2–3.   [97] Scott, *Commonwealth Principles*, 210–32.
[98] Manley, *Veni; Vidi; Vici*, 72–73.   [99] Norbrook, *Writing the English Republic*, 307 and 311.
[100] Warren Chernaik, 'Waller, Edmund (1606–1687)', *Oxford Dictionary of National Biography* (Oxford: Oxford University Press, 2004), online ed. [www.oxforddnb.com/view/article/28556].
[101] See Norbrook, *Writing the English Republic*, 311–16.

338   The Masculine Republic

the poem, Timothy Raylor has interpreted Waller's poem as one promoting Machiavellian concepts of empire and *grandezza* in its understanding of the rise and fall of states connected to *virtù* and in the policies of imperial expansion it promoted. Within the poem, Cromwell becomes hailed as an Augustus but also as a Machiavellian prince possessing *virtù* in his swiftness of action and thirst for glory.[102]

The opening stanza celebrated Cromwell's own constancy and self-possession as bringing harmony to the souls of his subjects and peace amongst political factions:

> Whilst with a strong, and yet a gentle hand
> You bridle faction, and our hearts command,
> Protect us from our selves, and from the Foe,
> Make us unite, and make us conquer too.[103]

Resurrecting this 'drooping Countrey torn with Civil Hate', Cromwell had remade England into a 'Glorious State' and 'seat of Empire'. He had subdued the Irish and Scotsmen and further established himself not only as England's just ruler but the 'Worlds Protector' by invading 'The Bad' and aiding 'the Good'.[104] This imagery of empire, along with subsequent stanzas describing tributes being paid, Arabic spices, Persian silks, 'drink of ev'ry Vine', and gold pouring into England, graphically recalled the luxurious Roman Empire established by Julius Caesar. In these stanzas, Waller's *Panegyrick* seems to have taken the images of Andrea Mantegna's powerful nine-painting series, *The Triumphs of Caesar*, and translated them into poetry. Although purchased by King Charles, Mantegna's work continued to influence the imagination of Cromwell, who had them hung in his Hampton Court apartments.[105] On each 8 ½ × 9 ft (2.66m × 2.78m) painting in the series, Mantegna had detailed the exotic riches of empire – gold, slaves, armour, trophies, elephants, vases, cloth – paraded before a triumphant Julius Caesar who held the symbols of victory and sovereignty: palm leaf and sceptre. Waller similarly concluded his poem by describing such a triumph for Cromwell:

> Here in low streyns your milder deeds we sing,
> But there (My Lord) we'l Bayes and Olive bring:
>
> To Crown your head while you in Triumph ride
> O'er vanquish'd Nations, and the Sea beside,

---

[102] Timothy Raylor, 'Waller's Machiavellian Cromwell: The Imperial Argument of *A Panegyrick to My Lord Protector*', *Review of English Studies*, 56 (2005): 386–411.
[103] Waller, *A Panegyrick to My Lord Protector*, 1.   [104] Ibid., 2–3.
[105] Paul Kristeller, *Andrea Mantegna* (London: Longmans, Green, 1901), 282.

'So much power and piety in one'

> While all your neighbour-Princes unto you
> Like *Josephs* sheaves pay reverence, and bow.[106]

Waller suggested that whereas English kings before had flattered themselves as a Julius Caesar, Cromwell had accomplished the military triumph over England's enemies.

Waller's *Panegyrick* further praised Cromwell through the historical tradition of Roman Empire by celebrating the Protector's clemency. In a passage echoing Seneca's *De Clementia*, Waller argued that 'Tygres have courage, and the rugged Bear, / But Man alone can whom he Conquers, spare'.[107] Through his mixture of 'power and piety in one', Cromwell ruled with the arts of peace and war, exercising clemency and self-constraint alongside courage and military might. Fisher had resolved the difficulties of comparing Cromwell to Julius Caesar in *Irenodia Gratulatorio* by describing Cromwell's virtues as superior to Caesar's. While also emphasising Cromwell's distinctive virtues, Waller overcame some of the limitations of this comparison between Cromwell and Julius Caesar by introducing a second historical exemplum: Cromwell had become Caesar Augustus, superseding Julius Caesar by ending civil war and ushering in the stability and Imperial riches of the *Pax Romana*:

> As the vext world to finde repose at last
> It self into *Augustus* Arms did cast:
> So *England* now, doth with like toyle opprest,
> Her weary head upon your bosome rest.[108]

According to Waller, Cromwell resembled Julius Caesar for his military might and conquest, but Augustus for his Imperial peace and his ability to unify his empire.[109] Edward Holberton has contextualised Waller's Augustan imagery by emphasising that the poem, at heart, sought to bring about greater political and cultural unity at a moment when the Lord Protector's power came under fire from previously supportive radicals and republicans.

---

[106] Waller, *A Panegyrick to My Lord Protector*, 10.

[107] Ibid., 7. Compare to the contemporary, rhyming English translation of *Lucius Annaeus Seneca, his first book of clemency written to Nero Caesar* (London, 1653), 10: 'Tis womanish, in passion to run on: / And tis the property of beasts, that are / Not generous, with cruelty to tear / Such as lie on the ground. Whereas the rage / Of Elephants, and Lions will asswage, / When once they conquer. But th' ignoble race / Of Bears, and VVolves will dwell upon the place. / Feirce and unbounded anger ill befits / A King:../ But if to men obnoxious he gives life, / Or restores honour, then he does a thing, / That appertaines to none but to a King'.

[108] Waller, *A Panegyrick to My Lord Protector*, 10.

[109] For a description of the wide variety of historical accounts available on Julius Ceasar and Augustus and their multivalent appropriations before the Interregnum, see Freyja Cox Jensen, *Reading the Roman Republic in Early Modern England* (Leiden: Brill, 2012), chapters 6 and 7.

340   The Masculine Republic

This required Waller to emphasise Cromwell as the only centre of power within the *Panegyrick*, and to 'locate the fulcrum of its argument and its *imperium* in the personal qualities of the Protectorate'. As Holberton has underscored, Waller's Augustan imagery comes almost as a warning that the peace, union, and prosperity of Britain was indeed dependent upon Cromwell's control of the state.[110]

In myriad ways, the exemplum of Roman leaders such as Julius Caesar allowed Englishmen to celebrate Cromwell's military victories and express ambitious hopes of empire and conquest. Following 1657, writers found a further parallel between Caesar and Cromwell: both men publicly refused a crown. In February of 1657, Sir Christopher Packe proposed that Cromwell assume the title of king under a contract that modified the terms of the 'Instrument'. Two months later, Cromwell definitively refused the crown, insisting in a speech at Whitehall that the Protectorship had already received 'almost universal obedience ... by all ranks and sorts of men' through that title, that his rule as Protector had witnessed an unprecedented peace under the rule of law with freedom and justice, and that 'God hath seemed Providential ... not only in striking at the Family but at the Name' of king.[111] Significantly, Cromwell further defended his own political aspirations following the regicide as lacking political ambition: 'I say, we were running headlong into confusion and disorder, and would necessarily have run into blood; and I was passive to those that desired me to undertake the Place which I now have ... I profess I had not that apprehension, when I undertook the Place, that I could so much do good; but I did think I might prevent imminent evil.'[112] Interestingly, both Caesar's and Cromwell's public refusals of the crown led to speculation concerning their potential private motivations to power. Cromwell's contemporaries (as well as modern scholars) often deemed Cromwell a king in all but name; similarly, according to Plutarch's account, many believed that Caesar acted as king, and that he had refused the crown publicly only to grow more loved of the people and to be crowned by the senate at a later date.[113] These themes were addressed explicitly in Richard Flecknoe's celebration of the Lord Protector in 1659, in which the poet maintained that Cromwell 'had refus'd the *Crown,* and acquird more glory by't then ever any did by accepting it; in which, as in all his other Actions,

---

[110] Holberton, *Poetry and the Cromwellian Protectorate*, esp. 89–101.
[111] *Oliver Cromwell's Letters and Speeches: With Elucidations by Thomas Carlyle*, vol. 3 (London: Chapman and Hall, 1846), 302–3, 312.
[112] Ibid., 305.   [113] See Knoppers, *Constructing Cromwell*, 118–22.

'So much power and piety in one' 341

he might well be compar'd to *Caesar*, both alike fortunate and victorious in war; both prudent alike in ordering the Civil Government ... '. Similarly to writers before him, however, Flecknoe argued that Cromwell's life had exceeded Caesars, with the Lord Protector dying naturally and prudently leaving England to his son rather than leaving the commonwealth 'imbroyl'd in Civil wars through multiplicity of Competitors ... '.[114]

Cromwell's transition in representation from the Roman republic to the Roman Principate, from being heralded as Junius Brutus to Julius Caesar and Caesar Augustus, unveils how Cromwell's position as lord protector risked alienating republicans and further infuriating royalists. Yet those defending Cromwell as Caesar did so with significant alterations, for they argued that Cromwell possessed greater *virtus* than these former giants. Even more, they claimed that Cromwell restored manliness to Englishmen through encouraging virtuous and pious living and courage displayed in arms. These themes would be importantly developed by English republican writers, although Cromwell's place within the tradition would remain contentious.

7.3   Cromwell as Classical Usurper

While public supporters of Cromwell, including Edmund Waller in his poem *Upon the Late Storme and Death of his Highnesse* (1659), lamented the Lord Protector's death as the demise of a Romulus or Hercules, whose wisdom and valour had tamed the 'Civill Broyls' of Britain to give 'us *Peace*, and *Empire* too',[115] critical responses widely castigated Cromwell's legacy and character. In one such reply, which circulated in manuscript as 'An Answer to *the* Storm', the anonymous author proclaimed 'Tis' well he's gone (O had hee never been)'. England desired no thief such as Romulus, nor could Cromwell be considered a Hercules:

> In Battel Hercules wore *the* Lyons skin
> but our feirce Nero wore *the* beast within
> Whose Heart was brutish more *th*an feet or Eyes
> and in *th*e shape of Man was in disguise[116]

---

[114] Richard Flecknoe, *The idea of His Highness Oliver, late Lord Protector, &c. with certain brief reflexions on his life* (London, 1659), 62.

[115] *Three Poems Upon the Death of his late Highnesse Oliver Lord Protector of England, Scotland, and Ireland. Written by Mr. Edm. Waller, Mr. Jo. Dryden, Mr. Sprat, of Oxford* (London, 1659), 31.

[116] British Library Add. MS 28758 fols. 108r–v.

342 The Masculine Republic

The poem deemed Cromwell a ferocious Nero acting by savagery rather than by reason; what was more, he had practised dissimulation, disguising the 'beast within' his brutish heart to rule the commonwealth lawlessly and with cruelty.

Although celebrated in print for his military valour, beginning in 1647 Cromwell also became the target of sustained personal attack, as Royalists and Presbyterians charged Cromwell as a crafty, untrustworthy, violent, and ambitious machiavel. Echoing the language of tyranny wielded against Charles and even James in England prior to the 1640s, opponents of Cromwell frequently drew upon classical history to characterise misgovernance in highly gendered terms, castigating Cromwell as a tyrant and failed man. Their critical representations of Cromwell at times drew upon the very same classical stories and figures adopted in earlier decades against the Stuart monarchs, yet the overall portrayal of tyranny and failed manhood within Cromwellian accounts included striking differences depending upon the particular activities and characteristics of each man.

As we have seen, most frequently Charles had been castigated as suffering from uxoriousness, effeminacy, and cowardice, and thereby, as lacking manly attributes; opponents had envisioned Charles's lack of masculinity as causing him to be ruled by his passions rather than reason, resulting in subservience especially to his Catholic wife and to Archbishop Laud. Opponents of Cromwell similarly charged him with a failure of masculinity, but in the opposite register, claiming that Cromwell exemplified excessive rather than deficient masculinity. Whereas Charles had supposedly lacked courage, critics charged that Cromwell's lust for blood led him into the rash and vicious slaughters of the English, Irish, and Scottish people. Moreover, because Cromwell had no hereditary claim to power, characterisations of his rage very often castigated him as rebellious usurper. In classical terminology, Charles had been labelled *tyrannus ex parte exercitii*, one rightly in power who committed tyrannical or unjust actions; Cromwell's classification, in contrast, was as *tyrannus ex defectu tituli*, one who rose to power, without title, through force or the use of terror. Censorious characterisations of Cromwell also included significant discussions of his perceived moral and masculine failures beyond the usurpation of power, however, for it was argued that Cromwell's intemperance and over-lustiness for power extended to adulterous exploits. His rise to power entailed a dual violation of state and household. Despite this oppositional relationship in representation, criticisms of Charles and of Cromwell shared a conceptual grammar due to their focus on the

'*So much power and piety in one*' 343

uncontrolled and dangerous appetites that it was believed both failed men exhibited. Seventeenth-century Englishmen discussed failures in masculinity, whether from possessing excessive or deficient masculine qualities (whether from striking above or below the 'mean' or virtue of masculinity), as resulting in the loss of reason and true strength necessary for autonomy and for ruling others.

Beginning in 1647, criticisms of Cromwell detailed his seeming lack of control over himself and others and his excessive passions by focusing on his body, his family, or his military and political exploits. In criticising his body, royalist satire envisioned Cromwell as hypermasculine, his body as enormous, monstrous, and grotesque. The Dutch satire, *The Coronation of Oliver Cromwell* (1649), for example, portrayed Cromwell with a monstrous and absurd codpiece, dominating his otherwise beastly body which included paw-like feet and an ermine cloak forming a serpentine tail. His figure eclipsed the scaffold upon which Charles's decapitated and yet well-formed body spews blood, thereby linking Cromwell's hypermasculine sexual rapaciousness with bloodlust, violence, and ambition. The image emphasised that Cromwell's usurpation of masculine power, expressed in Charles's gruesome beheading, exposed Cromwell's own loss of masculine self-control and the unleashing of the 'beast within'.

An especially popular target for criticising Cromwell's body was his supposedly large nose, which critics used to represent a seemingly unwieldy phallus as well as a dangerous, rebellious, and excessive masculine appetite: 'If any Man, Angell or Devill can tell where the bodies of Oliver Cromwell and Tom Fairfax are now resident', one satire explained, 'you may know the one by his refulgent copper nose, which he euer kept well burnisht, that so he might not be constrained to trouble the devill to light him, or grope out his way to hell'.[117] The cultural imagination of early Stuart England drew a significant connection between noses and genitalia, believing that through the nose (as well as ears) one could understand, mock, and discipline the hidden body through the socially revealed body.[118] These sexual connections underscore why the public

[117] Anon., *A Case for Nol Cromwells Nose, and the Cure of Tom Farifax's Gout. Both which Rebells are dead, and their deaths kept close, by the policy of our new States* ([London], 1648), 1. See also John Cleveland, *The character of a London-diurnall with several select poems* ([London], 1647), 4–5; *Mercurius Elencticus* (15–22 Mar.), *Communicating the unparallell'd proceedings at Westminster, the head-quarters, and other places; discovering their designes, reproving their crimes, and advising the kingdome* (London, 1648), 131; Anon., *The Famous Tragedie of King Charles I* ([London], 1649), 2.

[118] The connection between noses and genitalia became encouraged due to the ways that diseases such as syphilis could ravage the nose. Moreover, on the English stage, noses were often portrayed as

344   The Masculine Republic

mutilation and amputation of noses and ears were punishments enacted upon those condemned for having unworthily assumed authority, such as William Prynne, Henry Burton, and John Bastwick.[119] Moreover, Englishmen often articulated not only a correlation between sexual misbehaviour and the usurpation of authority but also causation between sexual licence and political or religious licence.[120] Cromwell's seemingly large nose, and by extension his unwieldy phallus, appeared to represent his rebellious lust for power, his excessive and dangerous masculinity. As another satire, *The Disease of the House* (1649), exclaimed:

> Cromwel, how soon will thy *Nose* be consumed, when the fire is in't already? and how just will it be, that it should burn thee downwards, as far as thy rotten dissembling heart; when thou hast unheaded thy King, and destroyed that Scepter held in the hand of God: prithee, who shall answer for all the Treasons, Murders, Rapines, Burnings, Spoyles, Desolations, Dammage and mischief of this Nation then? CHARLS STUART, or *Noll Crumwell* and his Agents; the *Evill counsellors,* or the *treacherous Estates?*[121]

According to the tragicomedy *Craftie Cromwell* (1648) by the prolific pamphleteer and bookseller John Crouch, members of parliament had themselves become 'foolish Cuckolds, that will suffer thus their noses to be bored!' for bending their will to Cromwell's rebellious machinations, just as a husband might fail to control his wife's errant sexuality.[122]

In criticisms of his family, writers castigated Cromwell for his seeming failure to act as a responsible subject and head of household. Pamphlets such as *Cromwell's Bloody Slaughter-house* (1660) envisioned the regicide as a bloody and vile patricide, with Cromwell so driven by lust and covetousness that he murdered his father, the King, raped the Church, and left

---

     orifices vulnerable to sexual stimulation through perfume and other odours. See Holly Dugan, *The Ephemeral History of Perfume: Scent and Sense in Early Modern England* (Baltimore: The Johns Hopkins University Press, 2011), 12–14, 120.

[119] See Section 4.6.

[120] For sexuality and usurpation, see Garthine Walker, *Crime Gender and Social Order in Early Modern England* (Cambridge: Cambridge University Press, 2008), 91–93; Laura Gowing, *Domestic Dangers: Women, Words, and Sex in Early Modern London* (Oxford: Oxford University Press, 1999), 80–81 and 103–4; Elizabeth A. Foyster, *Manhood in Early Modern England: Honour, Sex and Marriage* (London and New York: Longman, 1999), 81; John Marshall, *John Locke, Toleration and Early Enlightenment Culture* (Cambridge: Cambridge University Press, 2006), esp. 218–19, and also 130–31, 264, 270, 304–7, 318.

[121] Presumably a 'fire in the nose' indicated both a burning, lustful passion as well as venereal disease. Anon., *The disease of the House: or, the State Mountebanck: Administring Physick to a Sick Parliament* ([London], 1649), 7.

[122] Mercurius Melancholicus, *Craftie Cromwell: or, Oliver ordering our New State. A Tragi-comedie. Wherein is discovered the Trayterous undertakings and proceedings of the said Nol, and his Levelling Crew* (London, 1648), 5.

'So much power and piety in one' 345

the State widowed: 'You are like cursed *Cams*, not mockers only, but murtherers of the Father of your Countrey, impudent Ravishers both of Church and State, to satisfie your most abominable lusts of Tyranny, Covetousnesse, and all licentious profanenesse.'[123] With Cromwell's rise to the position of lord protector, opponents extended and adapted the family-state analogy to ridicule Cromwell as an unnatural or failed father and husband, both literally and metaphorically. Cromwell was frequently accused of adulterous exploits with 'Young Nell', the wife of John Lambert. Some pamphlets described Cromwell's wife, Elizabeth, as an adulterous scold and his household as a hive of sexual licence and anarchy, all of which he could not control nor tame; analogously, they envisioned the English state as overtaken by a tyrannical father who threatened peace, order, and godliness.[124] As one pamphlet remarked, upon his death 'Old Oliver' was well equipped to be 'house-keeper in Hell'.[125]

Pamphlets further maligned Cromwell for his military exploits, portraying him as horrifyingly bloodthirsty and violent for the sake of private gain. Violence, as Alexandra Shepard has demonstrated, was a 'very powerful patriarchal resource', but early Stuart Englishmen condemned and frequently punished excessive violence as hypermasculine and a threat to the social order.[126] As we will see in greater detail later, royalists and other detractors denounced Cromwell's military victories as merciless bloodbaths, motivated by excessive anger, bloodlust, and ambition; according to these accounts, Cromwell gloried in the suffering and slaughter of his fellow countrymen. Simultaneously, they characterised Cromwell's political policies as violent towards the constitution and liberties of England. It is within these charges of political and military violence particularly that we find Cromwell frequently associated with tyrants and tropes drawn from classical history.

With the dissolution of the Rump Parliament in 1653, for example, Fifth Monarchy Men, republicans who had supported the Commonwealth government, and royalists all extensively employed the exemplum of Nero to castigate Cromwell's government, beyond what we have already seen in

---

[123] *Cromwell's Bloody Slaughter-House* (London, 1660), 7. See also 16–17 for widowhood.

[124] The satirical dialogue between Cromwell and his wife, entitled *The Case Is Altered. Or, Dreadful News from Hell* (1660), for example, painted Cromwell's wife as a scold, as 'part of [her husband's] venom, lighted upon [her] tongue, and twas never wipt of yet.'..; when Cromwell questions his wife where she located her den of sedition, she replied that she 'was at home at my own joynture at the Cock-pit'. *The Case is Altered* ... (London, 1660), 7.

[125] Ibid., 16.

[126] Alexandra Shepard, *Meanings of Manhood in Early Modern England* (Oxford: Oxford University Press, 2003), 127–51.

346 The Masculine Republic

'An Answer to the Storm'. For example, the apologetical epistle, *The Faithfull Narrative of the Late Testimony and demand made to Oliver Cromwel, and his powers, on the behalf of the Lords prisoners, in the name of the Lord Jehovah* (1654), which was signed by twelve Fifth Monarchy Men and addressed to the 'Faithful Remnant of the Lamb ... ingaged against the BEAST and his GOVERNMENT', offered a report on the petitions made to Cromwell on behalf of the imprisoned Fifth Monarchists John Rogers, John Simpson, and Christopher Feake. The account argued that Cromwell's government continued the history of 'State-policy' and the 'practise of *proud Tyrants*, Pedagogues, and *persecutors*' by '*creating lyes against the Saints, and then bringing them into sufferings*'. This principle and practice is revived again under this *Government Nero like*', the account claimed, 'to inrobe the *faithfullest* of the *assertors* of the truth and *testimony* of *Jesus* with *Bear-skins*, then to bait them with their *Mastiffs* or *Blood hounds; like men that will report their *dogs mad*, when they have a mind to hang them?'[127] Charging Cromwell's government with deceitful and violent tyranny, the Fifth Monarchists adopted the image of Christian persecution so powerfully wielded by Prynne, Burton, and Bastwick against King Charles in the 1630s.

John Streater, a prolific political pamphleteer, similarly chastised Cromwell by deeming his actions Neronian. Streater began vocally opposing Cromwell with the dissolution of the Rump Parliament in 1653. Through his reading of classical philosophy and history, Streater came to believe that England required a republican settlement through a commonwealth government comprising the most virtuous and duty-bound citizens who would rule by law in the protection of liberties. One-year term limits, freedom from censorship, free speech and public assembly, and the sharing of political wisdom amongst the populace all characterised Streater's republican vision.[128] Beyond comparing Cromwell to Julius Caesar, as

---

[127] *The Faithfull narrative of the late testimony and demand made to Oliver Cromwel, and his powers, on the behalf of the Lords prisoners, in the name of the Lord Jehovah (Jesus Christ,) king of saints and nations. Published by faithful hands, members of churches (out of the original copies) to prevent mistakes, and misreports thereupon. To the faithful remnant of the Lamb, who are in this day of great rebuke and blasphemy, ingaged against the beast and his government, especially, to the new nonconforming churches, and saints in city and country, commonly called by the name of fifth monarchy men* ([London], 1654), sig. A2b. It was printed no later than 21 Mar. 1655.

[128] Streater believed these principles would support the public good over private corruption. Nigel Smith, 'Popular Republicanism in the 1650s: John Streater's "Heroick Mechanicks"', in *Milton and Republicanism*, ed. David Armitage, Armand Himy, and Quentin Skinner (Cambridge: Cambridge University Press, 1995), 137–55, esp. 137–44; Adrian Johns, 'Streater, John (c.1620–1677)', in *Oxford Dictionary of National Biography* (Oxford: Oxford University Press, 2004), online ed., Jan. 2008 [www.oxforddnb.com/view/article/26656].

'So much power and piety in one'

we have already seen, Streater employed Nero's history to charge Cromwell with destroying the city of London and persecuting its religious citizens. After blaming Cromwell for a tumult which erupted in St. Paul's Churchyard in October 1653, Streater reminded his readers that: 'Nero set on, fired Rome, and laid it on the Christians; he thereby did punish Rome, and took an occasion to persecute the Christians.'[129]

At the other end of the political spectrum, the Church of England clergyman and chaplain to the royalist commander Lord Hopton, Richard Watson, argued that those flatterers extolling Cromwell were gravely mistaken: 'Thus highly you extol the worst of men; / Whilst Nero is by you, as Trajan, show'n, / And you, by praysing, make his crimes your owne'.[130] Abraham Cowley similarly directly condemned Cromwell as Nero in *A vision, concerning his late pretended highnesse Cromwell, the Wicked* (1661). Cowley's earlier poetic and satirical writings in the 1640s had vigorously supported the royalist cause; his couplet satire *The puritan and the papist* (1643) roundly criticised both religious extremes, although Cowley admitted, were he forced to choose, he would himself become a papist.[131] In *A vision*, which he published in the early Restoration after his return from exile, Cowley questioned Cromwell's rebellious motivations by comparing the late Protector to Nero: 'But did Cromwell think, like Nero, to set the City on fire, onely that he might have the honour of being founder of a new and more beautiful one?' Cowley then dismissed Cromwell's motives in destroying the monarchical house and family, deeming them less virtuous than Nero's in burning down the city of Rome for the sake of founding a more beautiful city: '[Cromwell] could not have such a shadow of Virtue in his wickednesse; he meant onely to rob more securely and more richly in midst of the combustion'.[132] In Cowley's view, Cromwell lacked a 'shadow of Virtue', which even Nero possessed; the Protector's motives were more corrupt than the famed tyrant's, as Cromwell was driven by an insatiable desire for other men's wealth.[133]

---

[129] *A Further Continuance of the Grand Politick Informer*, 31 Oct. 1653 (London, 1653), 43.

[130] Richard Watson, *The panegyrike and the storme two poetike libells by Ed. Waller, vassa'll to the usuper answered by more faythfull subjects to His Sacred Ma'ty King Charles ye Second* (Bruges?, 1659), sig. A4v.

[131] Alexander Lindsay, 'Cowley, Abraham (1618–1667)', in *Oxford Dictionary of National Biography* (Oxford: Oxford University Press, 2004), online ed. [www.oxforddnb.com/view/article/6499].

[132] Abraham Cowley, *A vision, concerning his late pretended highnesse, Cromwell, the Wicked containing a discourse in vindication of him by a pretended angel, and the confutation thereof, by the Author* (London, 1661), 39–40.

[133] Ibid.

348 The Masculine Republic

As Cromwell, unlike James and Charles, had no hereditary claim to power, Englishmen also deployed a range of new historical exempla to characterise him as lusty tyrant while emphasising his role as rebellious usurper. One commonly cited and significant exemplum was Damocles, whose story Cicero related in his *Tusculan Disputations*. Damocles was a regular flatterer of the tyrant Dionysius, and after reckoning up the tyrant's 'power, myght, maiestie, and rule: his greate aboundaunce of all thinges, and his magnificence in building', he declared to Dionysius that there must be no man who had ever been happier.[134] Dionysius responded that since Damocles was so delighted by the king's fortune, he himself might try his pleasure at it. When Damocles heartily accepted, Dionysius commanded him to be robed in cloths of gold, precious ointments, and perfumes, seated on his throne, surrounded by costly goods and tables spread with delectable treats, and young, beautiful boys attending to his every whim. 'Then, seemed Damocles to be happy', Cicero reported. However, in the midst of this auspicious luxury, Dionysius also 'commaunded a glisterynge sword, to be hanged ouer [Damocles's] head, by a horse heare. So that it might well nye touche his necke'. Completely robbed of his happiness and filled with fear, the 'crownes fell downe from [Damocles's] head' and he abandoned the throne.[135]

At heart, Cicero's story warned that what may look like the happiest and most enviable life, filled with luxury, power, and fame, was in reality fraught with terror and subject to fortune – a mere hair away from disaster. As *Craftie Cromwell* described it, 'the winding-paths that *Fortune* treads . . . can make even Kings to know her power'.[136] Cromwell's opponents argued that, as a Damocles, Cromwell had envied King Charles's throne, and like the flatterer of old, he was a mere usurper incapable of assuming the terrifying weight of regal power. *The Second Part of Crafty Crvmwell* (1648), by the prolific pamphleteer Crouch, beckoned Cromwell enthroned to 'look how ore thy head doth / A sharp and threatning sword / Denouncing terror to thy gang / And thee their perjurd Lord'.[137] This image was even extended to the commonwealth as a whole in *The English*

---

[134] Marcus Tullius Cicero, *Those fyue questions, which Marke Tullye Cicero, disputed in his manor of Tusculanum: written afterwardes by him, in as manye bookes, to his frende, and familiar Brutus, in the Latine tounge*, trans. John Dolman (London, 1561), 277 (my pagination).

[135] Ibid., 277–78 (my pagination).   [136] Melancholicus, *Craftie Cromwell*, 4.

[137] Mercurius Melancholicus, *The second part of Crafty Crvmwell, or, Oliver in his glory as king a trage commedie wherein is presented, the late treasonable undertakings, and proceedings, of the rebells, their murthering of Capt. Burley, with their underhand workings to betray their King* (London, 1648), 32. See Knoppers, *Constructing Cromwell*, 17–18.

'So much power and piety in one' 349

Devil (1660), which claimed that due to Cromwell's tyranny, 'Ruine hung over the Heads of the People, by as slender a Thrid, as the Sword did over the Head of *Damocles* at the Banquet.'[138]

The exemplum had great power in the early Stuart imagination, but it was also fraught with problems for royalists, for by emphasising that even kings were subject to the whims of fortune, King Charles's defeat might seem less extraordinary or offensive to human and divine law. The tragicomedy *Craftie Cromwell* resolved this difficulty by emphasising the divine protection of rightful kings: After one interlocutor described the moral of Damocles as '[Fortune] can make even Kings to know her power', his friend replied, 'But yet the Heavens strong armes do compasse Kings; an host of *Angels* guards the Royall Throne'.[139] Divine protection could stay even fortune's blade.

In addition to the exemplum of Damocles, Cromwell was often compared to other usurping tyrants famous especially for their cruelty. One such exemplum was Tamburlaine, the despotic central Asian conqueror who ruled with an insatiable hunger for power and bloodlust in the fourteenth century, and who had been made infamous in the English imagination through Christopher Marlowe's play of that name. Through the history of Tamburlaine, royalists and other detractors portrayed Cromwell's military victories as merciless bloodbaths, with Cromwell glorying in the suffering and slaughter of his fellow countrymen. As *On the Death of that Grand Imposter Oliver Cromwell* (1661) explained:

> E're he had perfected that black Design,
> Which to this day brands the first *Cataline*,
> And stopt those lowder cries of bloud that call
> For Curses, to attend his Funeral.
> The tracing of those sanguine paths he trod
> *Made* Atila *be styl'd*, The Scourge of God.
> Well made this *Scarlet Hypocrite* his boast,
> Not in the Prince of Peace, but Lord of Hoast
> Though to rejoice in numbers of Men slaine
> Suits not with *David*, but with *Tamberlain*.[140]

Cromwell's 'black Design' in shedding blood was motivated by excessive anger and obsessive, dominating violence, and this depiction hearkened

---

[138] Anon., *The English devil: or, Cromwel and his monstrous witch discover'd at White-Hall* (London, 1660), 4.

[139] Melancholicus, *Craftie Cromwell*, 4.

[140] Anon., *On the death of that grand imposter Oliver Cromwell, who died September the 3. 1658* (London, 1661).

350 The Masculine Republic

back to the slew of Interregnum pamphlets characterising Cromwell as hypermasculine. Whereas male disciplinary violence was a central instrument of state and household correction for the regulation of social relations in England, and violence was further considered a vital tool for men's maintenance of reputation, an excess of rage or madness by a grown man undermined his masculinity by proving him overruled by unbridled passions rather than reason. Men were understood as more prone to the vice of choleric, malicious violence due to the dry and hot composition of their bodies, and the heat of battle which called upon men to display anger, courage, and martial prowess simultaneously threatened to undermine their moderation and rational self-control.[141] Here Cromwell's pleasure in the number of men slain emphasised his dangerous failure to order his passions.

Other descriptions of Cromwell as Tamburlaine included the playlet *The Famous Tragedie of King Charles I Basely Butchered* (1649): 'like great *Tamberlaine* with his *Bajazet*, canst render him within an Iron-Cage a spectacle of mirth, when e're thou pleasest'.[142] After defeating the Turkish King Bajazeth, Tamburlaine had placed the King in a cage, only allowing his release in order for him to serve as Tamburlaine's footstool. Alongside these portrayals of scornful pride and violence, Cromwell's enemies emphasised his rebelliousness by deeming him Cataline, the famous Roman conspirator whom Cicero railed against for leading a rebellion. Asking 'What Traytor ere like *NOl*, that mischief sought, / So-often, and so valliantly hath fought', *A Case for Nol Cromwells Nose* (1648) answered that Cromwell 'acted *Cataline* in every limme: / He hated God, and Charles, with all his heart, / And to unking him us'd his utmost art'.[143]

This passage from *On the Death of that Grand Imposter Oliver Cromwell* further characterised Cromwell's rise to power and subsequent rule as bathed and stained in pools of scarlet-red blood. Blood, 'a most pure Sweet *Homogeneous, Balsamick, Vital Juice* ... ordained to be the seat of Life, the principal matter for Sense, Motion, Nutrition, Accretion, and Generation', as one seventeenth-century physician described it, held great

---

[141] Ann Hughes, *Gender and the English Revolution* (New York: Routledge 2012), 13–14, 90–93; Anthony Fletcher, *Gender, Sex and Subordination in England, 1500–1800* (New Haven: Yale University Press, 1999), 44–47 and 108; Shepard, *Meanings of Manhood*, 127–51; Walker, *Crime, Gender and the Social Order*, 73.

[142] Anon., *The famous tragedie of King Charles I basely butchered by those who are, omne nesas proni patare pudoris inanes crudeles, violenti, importunique tyranni mendaces, falsi, perversi, perfidiosi, faedifragi, falsis verbis infunda loquentes in which is included, the several combinations and machinations that brought that incomparable Prince to the block* (London?, 1649), 2.

[143] *Case for Nol Cromwells Nose*, 4.

'So much power and piety in one'

symbolic weight and power in seventeenth-century England.[144] The description of blood in this passage, as bleeding wounds violated by Cromwell's sword cry out and condemn him, portrayed Cromwell as a 'man of blood', a man defiled by blood guilt. In the 1640s, accusations of Charles as a 'man of blood', especially by the Army, had been instrumental in bringing the King to the scaffold; it was argued that a 'king polluted by blood could be a king no more', and numerous Biblical passages made clear that God required vengeance for the shedding of innocent blood.[145] Many Englishmen, parliamentarian and royalist, interpreted the bloodshed of the English civil wars as divine retribution for the corporate sins of England; their deliverance rested upon penitence as well as atonement, and vengeance upon those particularly guilty of the innocent shedding of blood.

Throughout the 1650s and early 1660s, Royalists further interpreted the King's death as a terrible act which made parliamentarians in particular guilty of blood and which required expiation. In this vein, *On the Death of that Grand Imposter Oliver Cromwell* graphically portrayed Cromwell as the *true* man of blood who had been allowed to scourge England, Ireland, and Scotland for their sins, but who ultimately deserved vengeance. During the Irish campaign, Cromwell's armies killed over 3,000 in Drogheda alone, including several hundred townspeople; in Wexford he had claimed the lives of over 2,000; and at Dunbar in Scotland, Cromwell boasted that his army killed 3,000 and imprisoned 10,000.[146] For these slaughters the pamphlet deemed Cromwell Attila the Hun, whose merciless cruelty and bloodshed had been interpreted as God's divine punishment against a sinful fifth-century Europe, thereby earning him the name 'scourge of God (*flagellum Dei*)'. In a sermon calling the citizens of London to make supplication for their own sins against God and thereby be delivered, the Church of England clergyman Thomas Reeve presented Attila the Hun as an exemplum of one who defended his vices with 'impudence' rather than repent of them, for 'when he was reprehended for his extream cruelty, he was not ashamed to say, I am Atila, King of the Hunnes, the scourge of God'.[147] Oliver Cromwell, too, had

---

[144] Qtd from Gail Kern Paster, *The Body Embarrassed: Drama and the Disciplines of Shame in Early Modern England* (Ithaca: Cornell University Press, 1993), 65.

[145] Patricia Crawford, 'Charles Stuart, That Man of Blood', *Journal of British Studies* 16.2 (Spring 1977): 41–61.

[146] Gaunt, *Oliver Cromwell*, 84–85 and 89.

[147] Thomas Reeve, *God's plea for Nineveh: or, London's Precedent for Mercy. Delivered in certain sermons, within the City of London* (London, 1657), 138.

352 The Masculine Republic

proven himself an unrepentant and merciless man of blood, Royalists argued, and a man so overruled by vicious passions that he might never rule England justly.

In the rhetorical battles of the 1650s, classical exempla of revolutionaries and of tyrants helped formed the contours and content of political debate. As this book has demonstrated, these classical and gendered discourses of tyranny had developed in England decades before civil war and revolution and had afforded Englishmen rich and multivalent languages through which to criticise the moral and political failings of rulers, the activities of kings in the bedroom as well as the throne room. Classical conceptualisations of tyranny helped to erode images of sacred monarchy in the early Stuart period, and applied significant standards through which King James and King Charles, and thereafter Cromwell, could be justified or condemned. It is within this context that classical republican thought developed in England. Writers such as Milton and Nedham envisioned the English republic as restoring true manhood to citizens long stripped of their *virtus* through emasculated and emasculating tyrants. Cromwell and the Protectorate government, however, failed to erect a commonwealth in which such hopes could be realised.

Conclusion

> Onely the persons and Actors of the Historie
> doe succeede new every age; and the names
> being changed, the stories are now told as it
> were of our selves. [1]

Early modern Englishmen, steeped in the reading of classical history, saw extensive connections between the distant past and their political present. History unveiled repeating patterns of constitutional change – from monarchy to tyranny, aristocracy to oligarchy, democracy to ochlocracy and back again – as humanists inspired by Polybius regularly described. By attending to these patterns, and by frequently drawing upon the moralising tales of good governance and tyranny found in these histories, seventeenth-century writers and readers conceptualised and articulated their duties and the duties of others in the political arenas of battlefield, household, senate house, and palace. As we have seen, this early modern grammar of historical discourse placed gender at the heart of political thinking. It forged debate and conflict through affording Englishmen a language to counsel, to warn, and to criticise those who ruled over them. It provided significant images of tyranny which eroded support for the Stuart monarchs and thereafter also for Oliver Cromwell. And relatedly, it offered an historical account of England grounded not in the island's dynastic history since William the Conqueror but in the more expansive rise and fall of classical empires, revolutions, and heroes. Simultaneously, this gendered and historical discourse provided the urgency for, and the central foundation of, English republican thought both before and during the English Revolution, as Englishmen sought to repair the emasculating effects of tyranny through republican solutions.

The potency of this discursive legacy across the period in question can be glimpsed in the militaristic Cromwellian 1656 broadsheet, *A Brief*

---

[1] [I. R.], *Organon reipvblicae* (London 1605), sig. c4r. Qtd and trans. in Markku Peltonen, *Classical Humanism and Republicanism in English Political Thought, 1570–1640* (Cambridge: Cambridge University Press, 1995), 168–69.

Figure 1 Anon., A Brief Cronology of Great Britain (London, 1656).
© The British Library Board Thomason/ 669.f.20.[39.]; Wing (2nd ed., 1994) / B4553.
Used with permission.

Cronology of GREAT BRITAIN, which advertised its recounting of Britain's imperial history through a series of five images representing the male conquerors who had ruled the island since its foundation: 'A BRITAINE. A ROMAN. A SAXON. A DANE. A NORMAN' (see Figure 1).[2] The

---

[2] Anon., *A Brief Cronology of Great Britain* (London, 1656).

Conclusion

355

performance of national identity in these images is highly masculine and martial, with each successive figure suited in military armour and weaponry. Probably drawn from adaptations of John White and Theodor de Bry's depictions of ancient Britons and Picts, the half-clothed body of the 'Britaine' in the *Cronology* appears decorated with the image of a lion on the upper shoulder and painted patterns across his legs and arms. The choice of the 'Britaine's' weaponry followed Herodian's account in his *Roman History*: 'Now they are a most warlike nation, and very greedy of slaughter, content to bee armed onely with a narrow shield and a speare, with a sword besides hanging downe by their naked bodies.'[3] Immediately to the right of the Britaine, the Roman figure wears the recognisable tunic, breastplate, sash, and plumed helmet of a centurion, and each subsequent warrior stands bedecked in his national version of the same. Rather than a female and allegorical figuration of Britain, here one finds male representatives of the British people over time – nationhood conceptualised through a linear progression of manhood and conquest.[4]

These figures were not unique to *A Brief Cronology*. The artist recreated them from the well-known frontispiece of John Speed's *The History of Great Britaine under the conquests of ye Romans, Saxons, Danes and Normans* and its accompanying atlas volume, *The Theatre of the empire of Great Britaine* (see Figure 2), which were printed together initially in 1611–12. The title of the Jacobean work is framed by stately columns and arches displaying the 'Britaine' prominently at top and centre, with the Roman, Saxon, Dane, and Norman occupying smaller alcoves around the four corners of the structure; all bear their ceremonial armour and weaponry. The postures and figures in Speed's frontispiece display greater anatomical precision and grace than that achieved by the artist of *A Brief Cronology*.

---

[3] Herodian's account as translated by Philemon Holland for William Camden's *Britainnia* (1610). The Herodian account of their body art and clothing likewise fits the image: 'They knowe no use at all of garments, but about their belly onely and necke, they weare yron; supposing that to be a goodly ornament, and a proofe of their wealth, like as all other Barbarians esteeme of gold. For why? their very bare bodies they marke with sundry pictures, representing all maner of liuing creatures; and therefore it is verily, that they will not be clad, for hiding (forsooth) that painting of their bodies.' William Camden, *Britain, or A chorograhicall description of the most flourishing kingdomes, England, Scotland, and Ireland, and the ilands adioyning, out of the depth of antiquitie*. Trans. Philemon Holland (London, 1610), 30. See Sam Smiles, 'John White and British Antiquity: Savage Origins in the Context of Tudor Historiography', in *European Visions, American Voices*, ed. Kim Sloane (London: British Museum Research Publication, 2009), 106–12.

[4] For the conceptual shift from the 'female country to the male nation' in English drama and imagery, see Ralf Hertel, *Staging England in the Elizabethan History Play: Performing National Identity* (London and New York: Routledge, 2016), 201. See also Jodi Makalachki, *The Legacy of Boadicea: Gender and Nation in Early Modern England* (London and New York: Routledge, 1998), 33–35.

356　　　　　　　　　　　Conclusion

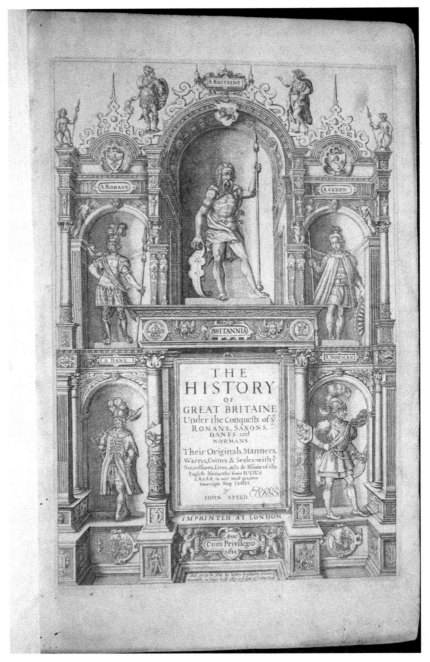

Figure 2　Titlepage, John Speed, *The history of Great Britaine under the conquests of ye Romans, Saxons, Danes and Normans* (London, 1611).
Rare Book and Special Collections Division of the Library of Congress, Washington, DC.

Conclusion 357

This borrowing of imagery, and its differences in precision, likewise mirrored the borrowing of textual content. The writer of *A Brief Cronology* drew most of his single-page description of Britain's history directly from Speed, while selecting and arranging passages to suit a strikingly different political agenda.[5] A brief comparison of Speed's *The History of Great Britaine* and the anonymous *A Brief Cronology of Great Britain* reveals the enduring significance of historical thinking for English political thought in this period and, simultaneously, the important malleability of such a discourse, as discussed in the preceding book.

The History of Great Britaine has been characterised as the 'last of the great early modern chronicles', comprehensive in its scope, patriotic in its tone, and supportive of its king through the narration of the island of Britain as a royal *res gestae* from Julius Caesar to King James. Crafted during the height of debates concerning the union of England and Scotland, and published with royal privilege, Speed created a dynastic and nationalist narrative of the entire island, with a chorography of the physical monuments, towns, and landscapes which testified materially to this history.[6] 'Britain' or 'Great Britain' was itself a mythical name of great significance to King James, who coined the term to denote his composite dominion through the Union of the Crowns in 1603 over the three kingdoms of England, Scotland, and Ireland, and the principality of Wales. Speed's adoption of the phrase, 'the Empire of Great Britaine', reflected his king's desire for union between English and Scottish subjects under and through the crown.[7] This connection would be drawn even more forcefully on the cover of John Stow and Edmund Howes's *The Annales or Generall Chronicle of England begun first by maister Iohn Stow* (1615), which borrowed Speed's frontispiece of the five warriors, but

---

[5] For example, compare the opening line of the *Cronology* ('The Isle of Great Britain is Bounded . . . ') with John Speed, *The history of Great Britaine under the conquests of ye Romans, Saxons, Danes and Normans* (London, 1611), 156.

[6] Igor Djordjevic, *King John (Mis)Remembered: The Dunmow Chronicle, the Lord Admiral's Men, and the Formation of Cultural Memory* (Farnham: Ashgate, 2015), 117; Michael Neill, *Putting History to the Question: Power, Politics, and Society in English Renaissance Drama* (New York: Columbia University Press, 2000), 378–85. It should be noted, however, that Speed himself called his work a history instead of a chronicle, although his research techniques as a literal 'scissors-and-paste' historian reveal close affinities to Holinshed. Daniel Woolf describes Speed as occupying the 'borderland' between history and chronicle in Renaissance England. See D. R. Woolf, 'Genre into Artifact: The Decline of the English Chronicle in the Sixteenth Century', *The Sixteenth Century Journal* 19.3 (Autumn 1988): 321–54, esp. 328–29.

[7] Nicholas Canny, 'The Origins of Empire: An Introduction', in *The Oxford History of the British Empire: Volume I: The Origins of Empire*, ed. Canny (Oxford: Oxford University Press, 2001), 1–33, esp. 1–2.

358   Conclusion

replaced the 'Britaine' in the top centre with a royal portrait of King James himself holding orb and sceptre. Queen Anne and Prince Charles flank the monarch, and the royal coat of arms is displayed prominently below (see Figure 3).[8]

Speed completed his 900-page historical and chorographical folio following nearly a decade of printing and designing royal representations of King James that celebrated the monarch ruling not by conquest but by inheritance. With James's accession to the English throne in 1603, engraved or wood-blocked portraits became a highly popular and fashionable form of royal representation; especially popular in the early years were engraved representations of genealogical tables displaying the lineage of James and Anne of Denmark, underlying their rightful claim to the throne and the marriage of the northern and southern kingdoms.[9] As Speed compiled materials for *The History of Great Britain*, he received payments from the King for creating maps and printing royal genealogies. One such genealogy, *The most happy vnions contracted betwixt the princes of the blood royall of theis towe famovs kingdomes of England & Scotland, contynewed from the Normans conquest to our most gracious Soueraigne Iames the I* (1603?), engraved by Renold Elstrak and printed by Speed, displayed portraits of James and Anne beside their royal arms, the English lion, and the Scottish unicorn, at the top of an elaborate genealogical tree. Speed flanked the engraving with two side columns of text celebrating the matrimonial union of the island, which had ceased the shedding of noble and royal blood in civil wars:

> Through all which, as the intent of man semed to be frustrat. yet hath God himselfe at last confirmed our peace in a full periode, by placing the trew, and only next heire of both, vpon the imperiall seat of both their dominions; wherby to all our happines, in his most Royall persone is confirmed the successiue inheritance and iust title of both theise Realmes: and the

---

[8] Notably, Howes's use of this frontispiece image began in 1615, following John Speed's publication. Howes's earlier abridgements of Stow's *English Chronicle* employed a much less elaborate frontispiece. Compare John Stow and Edmund Howes, *The Annales, or, a generall chronicle of England begun first by maister Iohn Stow, and after him continued and augmented with matters forreyne and domestique, auncient and moderne, vnto the ende of this present yeere 1614* (London, 1615); and Edmund Howes, *The abridgement or summarie of the English chronicle, first collected by master Iohn Stow, and after him augmented with sundry memorable antiquities, and continued with maters forrein and domesticall, vnto this present yeare 1607* (London, 1607). These men likely exchanged materials through the Society of Antiquaries and other informal associations.

[9] Kevin Sharpe, *Image Wars: Promoting Kings and Commonwealths in England, 1603–1660* (New Haven and London: Yale University Press, 2010), 70–71. See also Linda Levy Peck, *The Mental World of the Jacobean Court* (Cambridge: Cambridge University Press, 1991), 6.

Conclusion

Figure 3 Titlepage, John Stow and Edmund Howes, *The Annales, or, a generall chronicle of England* ... (London, 1615).
Rare Book and Special Collections Division of the Library of Congress, Washington, DC.

360   Conclusion

whole Iland of Britanie (so long deuided in gouernment, and infested with troubles) brought into a most quiet peace, and one intire Monarchie.[10]

Similar to these genealogies, Speed's maps portrayed not only James's material kingdoms but also the political ideologies and social structures which were thought to unify these lands.[11] *The History of Great Britain* represented a continuation of these themes, articulating the 'Successions, Lines, Acts and Isues of the English Monarches, from Ivlivs Cæsar, to ovr most, gratious Soueraigne King Iames', as the frontispiece explained, with James's reign described in a final chapter of the lengthy history as a natural and providential inheritance reuniting and bringing peace to the isle of Britain.[12] In 1611–12, the work served as a monument to monarchy.

In light of this inheritance, *A Brief Cronology of Great Britain*, printed anonymously in 1656, is striking in its careful re-telling of Britain's history despite its nearly verbatim copying of passages from Speed. The title advertises a chronology of conquest rather than of monarchical inheritance: '*From the first discoveries of this Isle, through the severall Conquests of the Romans, Saxons, Danes, and Normans*'. Following a sentence describing Britain's geography (drawn from Speed's first chapter), *A Brief Cronology* opened with the declaration:

> The ancient Government of Great Britain was at first rather after the manner of an *Aristocratie*, that is by certain great Nobles and potent men, or Petty Kings, so *Cæsar* himselfe found the state of Britain. The Glorious Romans that were become Lords of the world, were the first that set foot with displayed Ensign for the Conquest of Britain, and the first that Assayed this was *Iulius Cæsar* from the coasts of *Gallia*.[13]

Although clearly drawn from the fifth chapter of *The History of Great Britaine*, these lines differed significantly from their original. Speed's *History* began with a description of 'the succession of *Great Britains* Monarchs, at the entrance and person of *Iulius Caesar*'; *A Brief Cronology* recast Caesar principally as military conqueror rather than first monarch.[14] The broadsheet continued by noting the successive conquests of Britain by the Saxons and Danes and bloody wars with the Scots and Picts, these

---

[10] Renold Elstrak and John Speed, *The most happy vnions contracted betwixt the princes of the blood royall of theis towe famous kingdomes of England & Scotland contynewed from the Normans conquest to our most gracious soueraigne Iames the I. King of England, Scotland, France, & Ireland. Defender of the Fayth* (London? 1603?).

[11] See J. B. Hartley, 'Meaning and Ambiguity in Tudor Cartography', in *English Map-Making, 1500–1650*, ed. Sarah Tyacke (London: The British Library, 1983), esp. 35–39.

[12] See Speed, *The History of Great Britaine*, title page and 883.   [13] Anon., *A Brief Cronology*, 1.

[14] Speed, *The History of Great Britain*, 170.

Conclusion 361

parts being lifted from Speed's 'A summary Conclusion of the vvhole' at the end of his 900-page work. This emphasis on battle and conquest engulfed the description of '*William* the Bastard' (i.e. the Norman Conqueror), who 'won the English Crown from King *Harold*, that held it in a bloody field at battail in *Sussex*'. Inherited monarchy only 'bud forth' in Britain, according to the broadsheet, through the line of the Tudors, from the 'richest and wisest King of this Western World', Henry VII, until 'Britain returned again to the old Britains, and to her old name, *viz.* King James'.

This narration of British history as one of military conquest, and the description of Julius Caesar as conqueror rather than as prince, had great importance in 1656. As seen in the final chapter of this book, panegyrists in the 1650s frequently compared Oliver Cromwell to Julius Caesar, especially following Cromwell's Scottish and Irish military campaigns and rise to lord protector in 1653. R. Fletcher celebrated, '*Caesar*, and *Cromwell*: why, 'tis all but *C. / *And why not *England* now, as *Italie?*'; Payne Fisher's *Irenodia Gratulatoria* (1652) lauded Cromwell as a Caesar with far greater virtue.[15] The year before the publishing of *A Brief Cronology*, Cromwell's military conquests included expansion through the Western Design, with English naval forces eventually capturing Jamaica after failure in Hispaniola. Moreover, emphasis upon conquest by sword reflected the political writings and propaganda pieces of the 1650s which urged English subjects to swear allegiance to the Commonwealth and Protectorate in the wake of civil war and regicide. Marchamont Nedham's *The Case of the Common-wealth of England Stated* (1650) argued '*That the Power of the* Sword *is, and ever hath been the Foundation of all Titles to Government.*' The history of kingdoms and empires demonstrated over and again cycles of violence and usurpation; by the *jus gentium*, all such conquerors were entitled to secure their 'right of dominion', and the people owed obedience to such *de facto* powers.[16] In the same year as *A Brief Cronology*, Nedham's newly printed *The Excellencie of a Free State* reiterated that 'The Sword, and Soveraignty, ever walk hand in hand together.'[17] The successive figures of warriors bedecked in armour and weaponry displayed at the top of *A Brief Cronology* well represented the

---

[15] See Section 7.2.

[16] Marchamont Nedham, *The case of the Common-wealth of England stated, or, The equity, utility, and necessity of a submission to the present government* ... (London, 1650), 6, 28–30.

[17] Nedham, *The Excellencie of a Free-State Or, The Right Constitution of a Commonwealth*, ed. Blair Worden (Indianapolis: Liberty Fund, 2011), 90.

362   Conclusion

successive rule of Britain by masculine conquest. Cromwell, a new Julius Caesar, had continued this historic pattern.

As we saw in earlier chapters, between the year Speed published his history in 1611 and the anonymous pamphleteer printed his chronology in 1656, interest in the history of Roman tyrants, and particularly in Nero, peaked in numerous plays, poems, libels, histories, and treatises. Especially in the 1620s and 1630s, Nero's history became the site of debates concerning monarchical absolutism and fertile ground for imagining tyranny as failed manhood. Speed's history included lengthy descriptions of the Roman emperors interwoven with the activities and revolts of Boudica and other Britons against the Roman yoke. *A Brief Cronology* wielded this grammar to significant effect by including a paragraph entitled, '*Brief observations upon the untimely ends of the Roman Emperours*', just following the salute to King James as the recent unifier of Britain. Through fourteen lines of text, *A Brief Cronology* listed the horrific deaths of twenty-nine emperors: first Nero and Otho who 'slew themselves', followed by Tiberius who was 'smothered to death', Claudus and Commodus who were 'poysoned by their Wives', and so on. The list ended by mentioning that 'some few (and them favouring Christians) died in their beds'.[18]

Following this recitation of the early and gruesome deaths of tyrants, a final section fulfilled the title of the broadsheet by providing a 'cronology', or computation of time, of the world's significant empires or kingdoms.[19] This section appears not to follow Speed, but Edmund Howes's extension of *The annales, or a generall chronicle of England, begun first by maister Ion Stow* (1615).[20] Through a brief list, the broadsheet concluded by observing that most kingdoms – the Roman monarchy, the 'state of Gods own peculiar people' from Abraham through Moses and Moses through Solomon, the kingdom of Athens, the Saxons through King Egbert, etc. – flourished for approximately 500 years. But from the Norman Conquest through the entrance of King James, Great Britain enjoyed 536 years, 'which so continued until the 25. year of the Reign of *Charles* where that

---

[18] The source of this particular list could, perhaps, be Richard Brathwaite's *History surveyed in a brief epitomy, or, A nursery for gentry comprised in an intermixt discourse upon historicall and poeticall relations* (London, 1651), 359–60.

[19] See 'chronology, n.' OED 1a 'The science of computing and adjusting time or periods of time, and of recording and arranging events in the order of time; computation of time, assignation of events to their correct dates.'

[20] See Howes, 'An Historicall Preface to this Booke', *The Annales, or, a generall chronicle of England*, unpaginated. Howes, however, principally described the 500-year revolutions of Britain without mentioning the ancient examples, which means another source may have been used as well (or used instead).

Conclusion 363

line is extinct'. On this abrupt note, the broadsheet ended. Like the Roman Emperors listed above, and unlike those 'favouring Christians' who had died in their beds, Charles had met an untimely end. The Isle of Great Britain was then conquered by Cromwell, figured as a new Julius Caesar.

***

These two examples from 1611 and 1656 briefly illustrate the vibrancy and malleability of historical discourse across the early seventeenth century and some of the ways that the republic created in 1649 both continued and broke with preceding modes of thought. Scholarship on the history of history has demonstrated the significance of historical thinking in early modern England in the humanist grammar school and university curricula; in the political and cultural imagination of English statesmen; and in English legal structures and political customs drawn from the ancient constitution, common law, and the Roman legal tradition.[21] This book has sought to deepen still further our understanding of the extent and character of historical thinking in England by attending to the significant ways that ancient historical exempla shaped early modern conceptualisations of tyranny and of good governance, and especially of the ways that Roman history emphasised idealised visions of masculinity and made distinctions between those who could possess *virtus*, or manliness, and those who could not. Seventeenth-century writers explicitly recognised and discussed the distinctions made in the classical period between *vir* and *homo*. Unlike a *homo*, the generic or sometimes hostile word used for a person in ancient Rome, the word *vir* usually entailed a mature man of the

[21] See Mordechai Feingold, 'The Humanities', in N. Tyacke, ed. *The History of the University of Oxford, Volume IV: Seventeenth Century Oxford* (Oxford: Oxford University Press, 1997), 211–357, esp. 257–60; Jensen, *Reading the Roman Republic*, 25–37; Daniel Woolf, *The Idea of History in Early Stuart England: Erudition, Ideology, and the 'Light of Truth' from the Accession of James I to the Civil War* (Toronto: University of Toronto, 1990); R. Malcolm Smuts, 'Court-Centred Politics and the Uses of Roman Historians, c. 1590–1630', in *Culture and Politics in Early Stuart England*, ed. Kevin Sharpe and Peter Lake (Basingstoke: Palgrave Macmillan, 1994), 21–43; Paulina Kewes, ed., *The Uses of History in Early Modern England* (San Marino, CA: Huntington Library Press, 2006); David Norbrook, *Writing the English Republic: Poetry, Rhetoric and Politics, 1627–1660* (Cambridge: Cambridge University Press, 1999); Lisa Jardine and Anthony Grafton, '"Studied for Action": How Gabriel Harvey Read his Livy', *Past and Present* 129 (Nov. 1990): 30–78; J. G. A. Pocock, *The Ancient Constitution and the Feudal Law: A Study of English Historical Thought in the Seventeenth Century* (Cambridge: Cambridge University Press, 1957 and 1987); Andrew Lewis, '"What Marcellus says is against you": Roman Law and Common Law', in *The Roman Law Tradition*, ed. A. D. E. Lewis and D. J. Ibbetson (Cambridge: Cambridge University Press, 1994), 199–208; D. J. Seipp, 'Roman Legal Categories in the Early Common Law', in *Legal Records and Historical Reality*, ed. T. G. Watkin (London and Ronceverte: Hambledon, 1989), 9–36.

364   Conclusion

upper class who wielded legitimate power as a *paterfamilias*, the oldest living male of a *familia*.[22] The opposition between *vir* and non-*vir* – between 'real man' and woman, child, slave, effeminate, or beast – revolved largely around the issue of whether one was a free man exercising power and authority over oneself and others, or whether one was subject to vicious habits which prevented self-governance, or was subject to the power and authority of another.[23] The possession of *virtus* involved the public practice of the virtues in numerous arenas within and beyond the household, providing both an ideological and real connection between the exercise of governance as male householder and as political actor. This pattern of thought significantly shaped the reading of classical history and the rehearsing of classical exempla in Stuart and then Cromwellian England.

As we have seen, thinking with classical history led the seventeenth-century reader to contemplate the contours of political power and subjection, the duties of monarchs and statesmen, and the limitations of citizenship and political legitimacy. In the thought of ancient philosophers such as Cicero and Aristotle, and in the sweeping histories of Livy, Sallust, Tacitus, and other highly important classical authors read in the grammar school classroom, moral goodness and governance were persistently coded through multivalent languages of masculinity which described masculine achievement and diagnosed masculine failure as occurring in the political forum, on the battlefield, and also in the bedroom. Stories of Tarquin, Appius Claudius, Nero, and other vicious rulers made it clear that the lustful tyrant in the bedroom would also be the lustful tyrant in the throne room. These portrayals of tyranny provided significant languages of counsel and of criticism in Stuart England, as debates and scandals erupted over the Chancery Court and the Overbury Affair, as King James and King Charles hampered military intervention in continental religious conflicts, as statesmen defended and disputed the grandeur and cost of a lavish court

---

[22] Although a Roman son could only become a *paterfamilias* upon the death of his father, the Republic's institutions allowed young Roman men to transition from being sons under bondage in the private sphere of the *familia* to being *viri* of equal status to the *paterfamilias* in the public sphere through military service. Myles McDonnell explains that during the republican period, 'this rite of passage occurred when the *paterfamilias* deemed the youth mature enough to fight in the army', which was usually around the age of seventeen. See McDonnell, *Roman Manliness: Virtus and the Roman Republic* (Cambridge: Cambridge University Press, 2006), 177–80.

[23] Erik Gunderson, 'Discovering the Body in Roman Oratory', in *Parchments of Gender: Deciphering the Bodies of Antiquity*, ed. Maria Wyke (Oxford: Oxford University Press, 1998), 169–90, esp. 170; Jennifer Larson, 'Paul's Masculinity', *Journal of Biblical Literature* 123.1 (Spring 2004): 85–97, esp. 93.

Conclusion

culture, and as Laudian religious persecution and Charles's marriage to Henrietta Maria appeared to threaten the practice of 'true religion' in England.

Even as this book is titled *The Rule of Manhood*, it has sought to examine ways in which 'manhood' was a crucially important while not a singular phenomenon. Across the seventeenth century, Englishmen desired rule of their society by men who realised their potential as males, but the image and cultural representations of what such manhood comprised – how a man performed, what he did, how others should speak about him – was, in reality, contested and debated, the source of considerable disagreement and anxiety. Those who articulated visions of masculine governance or emasculate failure spoke frequently as if they described the only proper, dominant, or agreed-upon vision of manhood; in fact, their articulations betray a plurality of competing views and, at very least, the frequent inability of rulers at the household or national level to recognise or to meet a diversity of standards.

Especially in Part I, this book has sought to expand 'post-revisionist' studies which have explored a number of ruptures within the political culture of early Stuart England through attending to the ways that court scandal, political satire, and numerous forms of manuscripts, cheap print, and news writings shaped public perceptions of politics and forged early ideological divisions in this period.[24] This book has argued that the availability of histories, stories, poems, and ideas concerning classical tyranny mattered very greatly in seventeenth-century England, especially as the Stuart kings welcomed comparison with ancient rulers by frequently representing themselves as Roman emperors and the natural and rightful inheritors of a classical and dynastic past, such as that presented by Speed's *The History of Great Britaine*. Through their study of history, Englishmen were skilled readers of these monarchical representations and also formed significant expectations of how their political leaders should behave in

---

[24] See, e.g., Alastair Bellany and Thomas Cogswell, *The Murder of King James I* (New Haven: Yale University Press, 2015); Bellany, *The Politics of Court Scandal in Early Modern England: News Culture and the Overbury Affair, 1603–1660* (Cambridge: Cambridge University Press, 2002); Cogswell, *The Blessed Revolution: English Politics and the Coming of War, 1621–1624* (Cambridge: Cambridge University Press, 1989); Andrew McRae, *Literature, Satire, and the Early Stuart State* (Cambridge: Cambridge University Press, 2004); Curtis Perry, *Literature and Favoritism in Early Modern England* (Cambridge: Cambridge University Press, 2006); Anne Hughes, *The Causes of the English Civil War* (London: Macmillan, 1991); Johann Sommerville, *Politics and Ideology in England, 1603–1640* (London: Longmans, 1986); L. J. Reeve, *Charles I and the Road to Personal Rule* (New York and Cambridge: Cambridge University Press, 1989); Richard Cust, *The Forced Loan and English Politics, 1626–1628* (Oxford: Oxford University Press, 1987).

366 Conclusion

public and in private. Who the ruler married, how he conducted himself with his family, at court, at church, on his horse, on the stage and in spectacles – all of these activities welcomed examination and could create alarm for Englishmen when they judged their ruler as failing in *virtus*. The historical study of tyranny and of masculinity could animate Englishmen to rid themselves of tyrants, Stuart and Cromwellian, and to articulate republican forms of rule intended to restore the *virtus* of Englishmen through their activities as fathers, warriors, and law-givers. This study has suggested that these discourses need to be understood as part of the cultural and intellectual origins of the English Revolution – as part of what made revolution possible because conceivable.

English discussions of Roman revolution and republican forms of governance at times sought to extend the political franchise to men well beyond the contours of king and court; indeed, we have seen that stories about tyrants and republican revolutions recurrently stress that true masculine virtue and valour would more often be found in the cottages of swains than in the palaces of princes. Republican writers such as Marchamont Nedham promoted the free state in which 'the People are ever indued with a more magnanimous, active, and noble temper of Spirit' through the exercise of their reason in determining their own political governors, proving their valour on the battlefield, and expanding liberty through empire. The free state would expand political participation and, relatedly, the *virtus* of English citizens, for 'the door of Dignity stands open to all (without exception) that ascend thither by the steps of Worth and Vertue'.[25] John Milton understood the virtuous character of men – piety, justice, temperance – as 'a mighty factory in the acquisition or retention of liberty'.[26] Eschewing the rule of hereditary princes, who enthralled and infantilised their subjects and who themselves were enthralled by their own vicious character and vicious spouse (in the case of Charles I and Henrietta Maria, for example), Milton called for the rule of a full and free elected council of virtuous men, who would 'live soberly in thir families, walk the streets as other men, may be spoken to freely, familiarly, friendly, without adoration'.[27] The ability to hold one's leaders responsible for their character for their character, to promote the common good over personal desire or vice, to root out corruption through elections and just laws – these

---

[25] Nedham, *The Excellencie*, 34 and 27–28.
[26] John Milton, *Defensio Secunda, in The Complete Prose Works of John Milton*, 10 volumes, gen. ed. Don M. Wolfe (New Haven: Yale University Press, 1953–82), IV.I.680.
[27] *Readie and Easie Way, CPW* VII.360

Conclusion

significant goods were justified and legitimised in English classical republican thought of the 1650s.

At the same time, however, that republicans called for the expansion of political participation, demanded autonomy for the English commonwealth and citizenry, and provided the languages needed for the challenge to absolutist and hereditary monarchy, republican thought articulated or assumed great restrictions on citizenship that were tied to gender, age, freed status, and property. Conceptions of the good life in ancient political texts rested upon a notion of elite, patriarchal, and militaristic masculinity; these languages and restrictions remained a central part of the fabric of English Revolutionary republican thought. Classical republicanism encouraged Englishmen to consider themselves citizens rather than subjects and promoted the exercise of reason, courage, and justice in multiple realms of political participation from the household to the halls of justice. As we have seen, understood through the lens of patriarchy, injustice by tyrants was often conceived through the threat of sexual violence and disorder in the household – an image that could motivate political revolution and also reinforce patriarchal submission. As part of his promotion of the 'propagation' of liberty at home and abroad, for example, Nedham warned about the threat of rape to maiden liberty made by tyrants and overweening 'Great Ones'; he celebrated the conquest of the Scots and argued that English rule allowed Scotsmen to 'begin now to know themselves men, & to breath after *Liberty*'.[28] Simultaneously, he lauded the conquest of Jamaica and promoted the bloody subduing of the Irish, citing their alleged inability to live as freemen. These languages, forged from highly masculinist and patriarchal narratives of human 'excellence', justified patriarchal rule by a 'band of fathers' and promoted the regulation of all non-*viri*, at home and abroad, by true *viri*.

Although fundamental to Greek and Roman texts and recognised as such by seventeenth-century writers, scholars of English classical republicanism have significantly neglected *virtus*, or manliness, as a primary motivator of republican thought.[29] Most accounts of seventeenth-century classical republican thought have only discussed gender briefly, if at all; more broadly, feminist scholarship on the development of modern political

---

[28] See Section 6.4.
[29] However, there has been profitable work more generally on the importance of gender for understanding and producing a coherent account of social and political history in the early to mid-seventeenth century. For a review of these studies, see Susan Amussen, 'The Irrelevance of Revisionism: Gender, Politics, and Society in Early Modern England', *Huntington Library Quarterly* 78.4 (Winter 2015): 683–701.

368 Conclusion

theory has emphasised the significance of gender in later republican modes of thought, most frequently through the model of a 'band of brothers' overthrowing the monarchical father figure. This description was ascribed to the republicans of the French Revolution in the work of Lynn Hunt, and afterward shaped numerous studies which examined how the French Revolution and American Revolution excluded women from politics and mandated their 'private' roles through the enforcement of 'domesticity' and idealisations of 'republican motherhood'.[30] These analyses have often aligned with Carole Pateman's account of the contractual foundations of modern politics as shifting political legitimacy away from natural and divine modes of rule and espousing men's freedom and the exclusion of women through instituting both a public, often fraternal social order, and a 'sexual contract' in the private sphere. 'Men governed women', promising that all in the contract enjoyed freedom while obscuring the fact of female subordination, Pateman argued.[31] The significance of *The Sexual Contract* for feminist thought cannot be overstated as it uncovered and challenged the patriarchal dimensions of political contract theory. We must exercise caution, however, in attaching these models to the early and mid-seventeenth century. English republicans in the 1650s did not desire to banish father for brother nor did they develop political theories which obscured patriarchy; they sought instead to secure the proper ordering of their commonwealth through virtuous fathers who would rule the great commonwealth of state and the smaller commonwealths of the household after first commanding themselves in virtue. As glimpsed in Nedham, even discourses of conquest and the 'propagation of liberty' abroad found their grounding in languages of masculine self-command and the command of household.

---

[30] Lynn Hunt, *The Family Romance of the French Revolution* (Berkeley: University of California Press, 1992). See, for example, Sarah Maza, *Private Lives and Public Affairs: The Causes Célèbres in Pre-Revolution France* (Berkeley: University of California Press, 1993); Joan B. Landes, *Women and the Public Sphere in the Age of the French Revolution* (Ithaca and London: Cornell University Press, 1988); Lynn Hunt, 'Male Virtue and Republican Motherhood', in *The French Revolution and the Creation of Modern Political Culture*, ed. Keith Michael Baker (Bingley: Emerald, 1994), 195–208; Linda K. Kerber, *Women of the Republic: Intellect & Ideology in Revolutionary America* (Chapel Hill, University of North Carolina Press, 1980). For the American Revolution, see Jay Fliegelman, *Prodigals & Pilgrims: The American Revolution against Patriarchal Authority, 1750–1800* (Cambridge: Cambridge University Press, 1982).

[31] Carole Pateman, *The Sexual Contract* (Oxford: Polity Press, 1988). For recent discussions of the significance of this work, see Sharon Thompson, Lydia Hayes, Daniel Newman, and Pateman, '*The Sexual Contract* 30 Years on: A Conversation with Carole Pateman', in *Feminist Legal Studies* 26.1 (Apr. 2018): 93–104.

Conclusion 369

In these ways, this book has argued that the history of classical republican thought cannot be understood properly without attending to gender, for not only did *virtus* – its inherent instability and restoration – motivate the development of republican discourses but within the grammar of republicanism drawn from the classical tradition, *virtus* was the primary concept and fundamental *telos* from which conceptualisations of virtue and liberty arose. To exercise reason, justice, courage, and temperance through political participation and to guard one's autonomy and freedom from domination in the republic was to seek the realisation of one's full potential as *vir*. The power of this discourse lay in its ability to motivate and to justify, in its ability to encourage and to allow Englishmen to question not only the actions of particular monarchs but also monarchy itself. Did the institution of monarchy lead to rule by the most virtuous? Did the institution of monarchy promote or hamper male subjects from becoming themselves fully realised men? These questions would encourage revolutionary discourses and classical solutions.

Bibliography

PRIMARY SOURCES (PRINTED)

Anon *To all the worthy gentlemen who are duely chosen for the Parliament, which intended to meet at Westminster the 17 of September 1656. And to all the good people of the Common-wealth of England. The humble remonstrance, protection, and appeale of severall knights and gentlemen duly chosen to serve their countrey in Parliament; who attended at Westminster for that purpose, but were violently kept out of the Parliament-house by armed men hired by the Lord Protector.* London, 1656.

Behold! Two Letters, the one, Written by the Pope to the (then) Prince of Wales, now King of England: the other, An Answere to the said Letter, by the said Prince, now his Maiesty of England. Being an Extract out of the History of England, Scotland, and Ireland; Written in French by Andrew du Chesne, Geographer to the K. of France Printed at Paris cum privilegio and now Translated into English. London?, 1642.

A Brief Cronology of Great Britain. London, 1656.

A Brief relation of certain speciall and most materiall passages, and speeches in the Starre-Chamber, occasioned and delivered Iune the 14th 1637. Amsterdam, 1637.

The Case is Altered. Or, Dreadful News from Hell. London, 1660.

A Case for Nol Cromwells Nose, and the Cure of Tom Farifax's Gout. Both which Rebells are dead, and their deaths kept close, by the policy of our new States. London, 1648.

The Character of Mercurius Politicus. London, 1650.

The Christen rule or state of all the worlde from the hyghest to the lowest: and how euery man shulde lyue to please God in hys callynge. Item, the Christian state of matrimony and how man and wife shuld kepe house together with loue. Item, the maner oe [sic] saynge grace after the holy scrypture. London?, 1548?.

Cromwell's Bloody Slaughter-House. London, 1660.

On the death of that grand imposter Oliver Cromwell, who died September the 3. 1658. London, 1661.

The disease of the House: or, the State Mountebanck: Administring Physick To a Sick Parliament. London, 1649.

Εἰκὼν Βασιλική, *The Pourtracture of His Sacred Majestie, in his Solitudes and Sufferings.* London, 1649.

370

Bibliography 371

The English devil: or, Cromwel and his monstrous witch discover'd at White-Hall. London, 1660.

The Faithfull narrative of the late testimony and demand made to Oliver Cromwel, and his powers, on the behalf of the Lords prisoners, in the name of the Lord Jehovah (Jesus Christ,) king of saints and nations. London, 1654.

The famous tragedie of King Charles I basely butchered by those who are, omne nesas proni patare pudoris inanes crudeles, violenti, importunique tyranni mendaces, falsi, perversi, perfidiosi, faedifragi, falsis verbis infunda loquentes in which is included, the several combinations and machinations that brought that incomparable Prince to the block. London?, 1649.

A Further Continuance of the Grand Politick Informer (31 Oct. 1653). London, 1653.

A godly and profitable treatise, intituled Absolom his fall, or the ruin of Roysters, Wherein euery Christian may in a Mirrour behold the vile and abominable abuse of curled long hair. London, 1590.

The great eclipse of the sun, or, Charles his waine over-clouded, by the evill influences of the moon, the malignancie of ill-aspected planets, and the constellations of retrograde and irregular starres. [London], 1644.

Hæc-vir; or The womanish-man: being an answere to a late booke intituled Hic-mulier. Exprest in a briefe dialogue betweene Hæc-vir the womanish-man, and Hic-mulier the man-woman. London, 1620.

The Invincible Weapon, or Truths triumph over Errors. London? 1647.

A Modest Narrative of Intelligence Fitted for the Republique of England & Ireland, from Saturday, June 16. to Saturday, June 23 1649. Published by James Moxon. London, 1649.

The Parliament's Kalendar of Black Saints. London, 1644.

A perfect List of all the Victories obtained by the Lord General Cromwel, from the time that his Excellency was made Cap. Gen. and Commander in Cheif [sic] of the Parliament Forces in England, Ireland, and Scotland, (against Charles Stuart King of the Scots, and his Forces in the three Nations,) to this present time; with other eminent Actions. London, 1651.

A perfect List of all the Victories obtained (through the blessing of God) by the Parliaments Forces under the Command of his Excellency Robert Earl of Essex and Ewe...: His Excellency Alexander Lesley, Earle of Leven, ... : And the right honourable his Excellency Edvvard Lord Mountague, Earle of Manchester, ... : With his Excellency Sir Thomas Fairfax ... With the names of the Cities, Townes, Castles, and Forts taken from the enemy since the beginning of these unnatural VVwares, to this present moneth of August 1646. London, 1646.

Perfect and Impartial Intelligence, Of the Affairs, in England, Scotland, and Ireland, And other Parts beyond the Seas, From Tuesday May 16 to Tuesday May 23, 1654. London, 1654.

Perfect and Impartial Intelligence, of the Affairs, in England, Scotland, and Ireland, And other Parts beyond the Seas. Together with the Continuation of the History of Caius Julius Caesar, From Tuesday May 23. to Fryday May 26, 1654. London, 1654.

372   *Bibliography*

The Picture of an English Antick, with a List of his ridiculous Habits, and apish Gestures. London?, 1646?.

A Remonstrance of the State of the Kingdom, Die Mercurii 15 Decemb. 1641, It is this day Resolv'd upon the Question, By the House of Commons, That Order shall be now given for the Printing of this Remonstrance, *of the State of the Kingdom.* London, 1641.

The Resolution of the Women of London to the Parliament. London, 1642.

The Seconde Tome of Homilies, of such matters as were promysed and intituled in the former part of homilies, set out by the authoritie of the Queenes Maiestie. And to be read in euery paryshe Church agreablye. London, 1563.

The Seven Women Confessors. London, [1641].

The soundheads description of the roundhead. Or The roundhead exactly anatomized in his integralls and excrementalls, by the untwistling a threefold knott. London, 1642.

A Spirit Moving in The Women-Preachers: or, Certaine Quæres, Vented and put forth unto this affronted, brazen-faced, strange, new Feminine Brood. London, 1646.

Three Poems Upon the Death of his late Highnesse Oliver Lord Protector of England, Scotland, and Ireland. Written by Mr. Edm. Waller, Mr. Jo. Dryden, Mr. Sprat, of Oxford. London, 1659.

Tom Tell Troath or A free discourse touching the manners of the tyme. Directed to his Majestie by way of humble advertisement. Holland?, 1630.

The Tragedy of Nero. London, 1624.

A True Copie of the Petition of the Gentlewomen, and Tradesmens-wives, in and about the City of London ... *February 1641.* London, 1641/2.

Alexander, William. *A Paraenesis to the Prince.* London, 1604.

Augustine. *St. Augustine, Of the citie of God vvith the learned comments of Io. Lod. Viues.* Englished by I. H. London, 1610.

Bandello, Matteo. *Certaine tragicall discourses written out of Frenche and Latin, by Geffraie Fenton.* London, 1567.

Barckley, Sir Richard. *The felicitie of man, or, his summum bonum.* London, 1631.

Barston, John. *The safegarde of societie: describing the institution of lavves and policies, to preserue euery felowship of people by degrees of ciuill gouernements.* London, 1576.

Bastwick, John. *The answer of John Bastvvick, Doctor of Phisicke, to the information of Sir Iohn Bancks Knight, Atturney universall.* Leiden, 1637.

Independency not Gods ordinance: or A treatise concerning church-government, occasioned by the distractions of these times. London, 1645.

Praxeis ton episkopon sive apologeticus ad praesules Anglicanos criminum ecclesiasticorum in curia celsae commissionis. Leiden?, 1636.

Bernard, Richard. *Dauids musick: or Psalmes of that royall prophet, once the sweete singer of that Israel vnfolded logically, expounded paraphrastically, and then followeth a more particular explanation of the words, with manifold doctrines and vses briefly obserued out of the same.* London, 1616.

Bibliography

373

Bolton, Edmund. *Nero Caesar, or Monarchie Depraved.* London, 1624.

Nero Cæsar, or Monarchie depraued. An Historicall worke. Dedicated, with leaue, to the Dvke of Bvckingham, Lord Admirall, by the translator of Lvcivs Florvs. London, 1627.

Brabourne, Theophilus. *A Discourse vpon the Sabbath.* London?, 1628.

Brathwaite, Richard. *History surveyed in a brief epitomy, or, A nursery for gentry comprised in an intermixt discourse upon historicall and poeticall relations.* London, 1651.

A survey of history: or, a nursery for gentry Contrived and comprised in an intermixt discourse upon historicall and poeticall relations. London, 1638.

Burton, Henry. *An apology of an appeale.* 1636.

A Narration of the Life of Henry Burton. London, 1634.

Calvert, George, Lord Baltimore. *The answer to Tom-Tell-Troth the practise of princes and the lamentations of the kirke.* London, 1642.

Camden, William. *Britain, or A chorograhicall description of the most flourishing kingdomes, England, Scotland, and Ireland, and the ilands adioyning, out of the depth of antiquitie.* Translated by Philemon Holland. London, 1610.

The historie of the life and death of Mary Stuart Queene of Scotland. London, 1624.

Casaubon, Isaac. *Auli Persi Flacci Satirarum Liber. Isaacus Casaubonus recensuit, & Commentario Libro illustravit.* London, 1647.

Chapman, George. *Caesar and Pompey: a Roman tragedy, declaring their vvares. Out of whose events is evicted this proposition. Only a iust man is a freeman. As it was acted at the Black-Fryers.* London, 1653.

The conspiracie, and tragedie of Charles Duke of Byron, Marshall of France. Acted lately in two playes, at the Black-Friers. London, 1608.

Euthymiæ Raptus; or The Teares of Peace: With Interlocutions. London, 1609.

Homer prince of poets: translated according to the Greeke, in twelue bookes of his Iliads. London, 1609.

A iustification of a strange action of Nero; in burying with a solemne funerall, one of the cast hayres of his mistresse Poppaea. Also a iust reproofe of a Romane smell-feast, being the fifth satyre of Iuuenall. Translated by George Chapman. London, 1629.

Ovid's banqvet of sence. A coronet for his mistresse philosophy; and his amorous zodiack. London, 1595.

Pro Vere, Avtvmni Lachrymæ. Inscribed to the Immortal Memorie of the most Pious and Incomparable Souldier, Sir Horatio Vere, Knight: Besieged, and distrest in Mainhem. London, 1622.

The Revenge of Bussy D'Ambois. A Tragedie. London, 1613.

The Warre of Pompey and Caesar, Out of whose euents is euicted this Poposition. Only a iust man is a freeman. London, 1631.

Charles I. *His Maiesties dclaration [sic] to all his louing Subiects, of the causes which moued him to dissolue the last Parliament.* London, 1628.

374   *Bibliography*

The Kings Maiesties Declaration to His Subiects, Concerning lawfull Sports to bee used. London, 1633.

Du Chesne, André. *Histoire D'Angleterre, D'Escosse, et D'Irlande* 3rd ed. Paris, 1641.

Cicero, Marcus Tullius. *Those fyue questions, which Marke Tullye Cicero, disputed in his manor of Tusculanum: written afterwardes by him, in as manye bookes, to his frende, and familiar Brutus, in the Latine tounge.* Translated by John Dolman. London, 1561.

Cleaver, Robert. *A godlie forme of householde gouernment for the ordering of priuate families, according to the direction of Gods word.* London, 1598.

Cleland, James. *Propaideia, or the Institution of a Young Noble Man.* Oxford, 1607.

Cleveland, John. *The character of a London-diurnall with several select poems.* [London], 1647.

Cowley, Abraham. *A vision, concerning his late pretended highnesse, Cromwell, the Wicked containing a discourse in vindication of him by a pretended angel, and the confutation thereof, by the Author.* London, 1661.

Cromwell, Oliver. *By the Protector. A Proclamation Commanding a speedy and due Execution of the Lavvs made against the abominable sins of Drunkenness, profane Swearing and Cursing, Adultery, Fornication, and other acts of uncleannesse.* London, 1655.

D[awbeny], H[enry]. *Historie & Policie Re-viewed, in the heroick transactions of His Most Serene Highnesse, Oliver, late Lord Protector. From his cradle, to his tomb: Declaring his steps to Princely Perfection; as they are drawn in lively Parallels to the Ascents of the Great Patriarch Moses, in thirty Degrees, to the Height of Honour.* London, 1659.

D. P. *Severall politique and militarie observations: upon the civill, and militarie governments; the birth, increase, and decay of monarchies, the carriage of princes, magistrates, commanders, and favourites.* London, 1648.

Digby, Sir Kenelm. *A Late Discourse Made in a Solemne Assembly of Nobles and Learned Men at Montpellier in France, Touching the Cure of Wounds by the Powder of Sympathy, with Instructions how to make the said Powder; whereby many other Secrets of Nature are unfolded.* Translated by R. White. London, 1658.

Digges, Dudley. *An Answer to a Printed Book, Intituled, Observations upon some of His Maiesties Late Answers and Expresses. Printed by His Maiesties Command.* Oxford, 1642.

Dryden, John, trans. and ed. *The satires of Decimus Junius Juvenalis. Translated into English verse. By Mr. Dryden and several other eminent hands. Together with the satires of Aulus Persius Flaccus. Made English by Mr. Dryden.* London, 1693.

Elstrak, Renold and John Speed. *The most happy vnions contracted betwixt the princes of the blood royall of theis towe famous kingdomes of England & Scotland contynewed from the Normans conquest to our most gracious soueraigne Iames the I. King of England, Scotland, France, & Ireland. Defender of the Fayth.* London? 1603?

Bibliography 375

Elyot, Sir Thomas. *The boke named the Governour.* London, 1531.

Fisher, Payne. *Inauguratio Olivariana, sive Pro Præfectura Serenissimi Principis Angliæ, Scotiæ, & Hiberniæ, Dom. Protectoris Olivari: Carmen Votivum.* London, 1654.

Irenodia gratulatoria, sive Illustrissimi amplissimiq[ue] viri Oliveri Cromwelli, &c. epinicion. London, 1652.

Oratio anniversaria in diem inaugurationis serenissimi nostri principis Olivari, D.G. Ang. Scot. & Hybern. London, 1655.

Oratio secunda anniversaria in honorem serenissimi pientissimi ac potentissimi nostri principis Olivari, prout nuper habita est Westmonast. in aedibus ancrumianis unà cum ode quae per dom. London, 1657.

Paean triumphalis in secundum inaugurationem serenissimi nostri principis Olivari ubi celebriores terra marique victoriae brevissimè perstringuntur: dedecatus Cardinali Mazarino. London, 1657.

Flecknoe, Richard. *The idea of His Highness Oliver, late Lord Protector, &c. with certain brief reflexions on his life.* London, 1659.

Fletcher, Henry. *The perfect politician, or, A full view of the life and action (military and civil) of O. Cromwel whereunto is added his character, and a compleat catalogue of all the honours conferr'd by him on several persons.* London, 1660.

Fletcher, R. *Radius heliconicus or, the resolution of a free state.* London, 1650.

Fulbecke, William. *An abridgement, or rather, A bridge of Roman histories to passe the neerest way from Titvs Livivs to Cornelivs Tacitvs.* London, 1608.

An historicall collection of the continuall factions, tumults, and massacres of the Romans and Italians during the space of one hundred and twentie yeares next before the peaceable empire of Augustus Caesar. London, 1601.

Garey, Samuel. *Great Brittans little calendar: or, Triple diarie, in remembrances of three daies Diuided into three treatises.* London, 1618.

Gerbier, Sir Balthazar. *The None-Such Charles his Character: Extracted, Out of divers Originall Transactions, Dispatches and the Notes of severall Publick Ministers, and Councellours of State as wel at home as abroad.* London, 1650.

Gouge, William. *The dignitie of chivalry; Set forth in a Sermon preached before the Artillery Company of London, 13. Iune 1626.* London, 1626.

Of Domesticall Duties. Eight Treatises. London, 1622.

H. G. *The Mirrour of Maiestie: or, the Badges of Honour Conceitedly Emblazoned: with Emblems Annexed, Poetically Unfolded.* London, 1618.

Hall, Joseph. *Two Guides to a good Life. The Genealogy of Vertue and The Anathomy of Sinne. Liuely displaying the worth of the one, and the vanity of the other.* London, 1604.

Harcourt, Daniel. *A new remonstrance from Ireland.* 1643.

Hayward, Sir John. *A treatise of vnion of the two realmes of England and Scotland.* London, 1604.

Herrick, Robert. *Hesperides, or, The works both humane & divine of Robert Herrick, Esq.* London, 1648.

376 *Bibliography*

Heywood, Thomas. *A curtaine lecture as it is read by a countrey farmers wife to her good man.* London, 1637.

The Rape of Lucrece a true Roman tragedie. London, 1608.

Higgins, John. *The falles of unfortunate princes.* London, 1619.

Holdsworth, Richard. *The Valley of Vision, or A clear sight of sundry sacred Truths. Delivered in Twenty-one Sermons.* London, 1651.

Howes, Edmund. *The abridgement or summarie of the English chronicle, first collected by master Iohn Stow, and after him augmented with sundry memorable antiquities, and continued with maters forrein and domesticall, vnto this present yeere 1607.* London, 1607.

The Annales, or, a generall chronicle of England begun first by maister Iohn Stow, and after him continued and augmented with matters forreyne and domestique, auncient and moderne, vnto the ende of this present yeere 1614. London, 1615.

Hume, David. *The History of Great Britain, Under the House of Stuart.* London: Millar, 1759.

I. R. *Organon reipvblicae.* London, 1605.

James VI and I. *The Essayes of a Prentise, in the Divine Art of Poesie.* Edinburgh, 1584.

The Kings Maiesties Declaration to His Subiects, Concerning lawfull Sports to be vsed. London, 1618.

A Meditation Vpon the 27. 28. 29. Verses of the XXVIII. Chapter of Saint Matthew. Or A Paterne for a Kings Inavgvration. Written by the Kings Maiestie. London, 1619.

Jewel, J, ed. *The Seconde Tome of Homilies, of such matters as were promysed and intituled in the former part of homilies, set out by the authoritie of the Queenes Maiestie. And to be read in euery paryshe Church agreablye.* London, 1563.

Jones, Henry. *A remonstrance of divers remarkeable passages concerning the church and kingdome of Ireland.* London, 1642.

Jonson, Ben. *His Part of King James his Royall and Magnificent Entertainment through his Honorable Cittie of London, Thurseday the 15. of March 1603.* London, 1604.

Laud, William. *A Speech develiered in the Starr-Chamber.* London, 1637.

Leighton, Sir William. *Vertve Trivmphant, or A Lively Description of the Fovre Vertves Cardinall: Dedicated to the Kings Maiestie.* London, 1603.

Lemnie, Levine. *The Tovchstone of Complexions: Expedient and profitable for all such as bee desirous and carefull of their bodily health.* London, 1633.

Lilburne, John and Richard Overton. *The out-cryes of oppressed Commons.* London, 1647.

Littleton, Adam. *Linguae Latinae Liber Didionarius Quadripartitus.* London, 1678.

Livius, Titus. *The Romane historie vvritten by T. Livius of Padua. Also, the Breviaries of L. Florus: with a chronologie to the whole historie: and the Topographie of Rome in old time.* Translated by Philemon Holland. London, 1600.

Bibliography

Lloyd, Daniel. *Memoires of the Lives, Actions, Sufferings and Deaths of those Personages, that suffered by Death, Sequestration, Decimation: or otherwise for the Protestant Religion and the great Principle thereof, Allegiance to their Soveraigne,* in *our late intestine Wars from the Year 1637 to 1660: With the Life and Martyrdom of King Charles I.* London, 1668.

Lloyd, Lodowick. *The Consent of time disciphering the errors of the Grecians in their Olympiads...and of the vanities of the Gentiles in fables of antiquities...Wherein is also set downe the beginning, continuance, succession and ouerthrowes of kings, kingdomes, states, and gouernments.* London, 1590.

The pilgrimage of princes. London, 1573?.

Machiavels Discovrses. *upon the first Decade of T. Livius.* Translated by E[dward] D[acres]. London, 1636.

Manley, Thomas, trans. *Veni; Vidi; Vici. The Triumphs of the Most Excellent & Illustrious, Oliver Cromwell, &c. Set forth in a Panegyricke.* London, 1652.

Markham, Francis. *The Booke of Honour; or, Five Decads of Epistles of Honour.* London, 1625.

May, Thomas. *The Tragedy of Julia Agrippina, Empresse of Rome.* London, 1639.

trans. *Lvcan's Pharsalia: or The Civill Warres of Rome, between Pompey the great, and Ivlivs Cæsar. The whole ten Bookes.* London, 1627.

Mercurius Elencticus [pseud.]. *Communicating the unparallell'd proceedings at Westminster, the head-quarters, and other places; discovering their designes, reproving their crimes, and advising the kingdome* (15–22 Mar.). London, 1648.

Mercurius Melancholicus [pseud.] *Craftie Cromwell: or, Oliver ordering our New State. A Tragi-comedie. Wherein is discovered the Trayterous undertakings and proceedings of the said Nol, and his Levelling Crew.* London, 1648.

The second part of Crafty Crvmwell, or, Oliver in his glory as king a trage commedie wherein is presented, the late treasonable undertakings, and proceedings, of the rebells, their murthering of Capt. Burley, with their underhand workings to betray their King. London,1648.

Mercurius Politicus, Comprising The sum of Foreine Intelligence, with the Affairs now on Foot in the three Nations of England, Scotland, & Ireland. London, Jun. 1650–Dec. 1660.

Mexía, Pedro. *The imperiall historie: or The liues of the emperours, from Iulius Caesar, the first founder of the Roman monarchy, vnto this present yeere containing their liues and actions, with the rising and declining of that empire; the originall, and successe, of all those barbarous nations that haue inuaded it, and ruined it by peece-meele.* Translated by W. T. Corrected, amplified and continued to these times by Edvvard Grimeston Sergeant at Armes. London, 1623.

Morley, Thomas. *Remonstrance of the Barbarous Cruelties and Bloudy Murders Committed By the Irish Rebels Against the Protestants in Ireland.* London, 1644.

Bibliography

Morton, Thomas. *A sermon preached before the Kings most excellent Majestie, in the cathedrall church of Durham Upon Sunday, being the fifth day of May. 1639. By the Right Reverend Father in God, Thomas Lord Bishop of Duresme*. London, 1639.

Nash, Thomas. *Quaternio or A fourefold vvay to a happie life set forth in a dialogue between a countryman and a citizen, a divine and a lawyer*. London, 1633.

Nedham, Marchamont. *The Case of the Common-Wealth of England, Stated: or The Equity, Utility, and Necessity, of a Submission to the present Government*. 2nd ed. London, 1650.

The Case of the Kingdom Stated according to the Proper Interests of Severall Parties Ingaged. London, 1647.

Interest Will Not Lie, or a View of England's True Interest. London, 1659.

A True state of the case of the Commonvvealth of England, Scotland, and Ireland, and the dominions thereto belonging. London, 1654.

Painter, William. *The Palace of Pleasure beautified, adorned, and well furnished, with pleasaunt histories and excellent nouelles, selected out of diuers good and commendable authors*. London, 1566.

Petowe, Henry. *Englands Caesar*. London, 1603.

Phillips, Edward. *The new world of English words, or, A general dictionary containing the interpretations of such hard words as are derived from other languages*. London, 1658.

Pliny the Elder, *The historie of the vvorld Commonly called, the naturall historie of C. Plinius Secundus*. Translated by Philemon Holland. London, 1601.

Plutarch, *The lives of the noble Grecians and Romanes compared together by that graue learned philosopher and historiographer, Plutarke of Chaeronea*. Translated by Thomas North. London, 1579.

Polybius, *The History of Polybivs the Megalopolitan. The fiue first bookes entire*. Translated by Edward Grimeston. London, 1633.

Pricket, Robert. *A souldiers vvish vnto His Soveraigne Lord King Iames*. London, 1603.

La Primaudaye, Pierre. *The French academie Fully discoursed and finished in foure bookes*. London, 1618.

Prynne, William. *Certaine quaeres propounded to the bowers at the name of Iesvs and to the patrons thereof. Wherein the authorities, and reasons alleadged by Bishop Andrewes and his followers, in defence of this ceremony, are briefly examined and refuted*. Amsterdam, 1636.

Histrio-mastix, the Players Scovrge, or, Actors Tragædie. London, 1633.

A looking-glasse for all lordly prelates?, 1636.

Mr William Prynn his defence of stage-plays, or A retractation of a former book of his called Histrio-mastix. London, 1649.

A new discovery of the prelates tyranny, in their late prosecutions of Mr William Pryn, an eminent Lawyer; Dr. Iohn Bastwick, a learned physitian; and Mr. Henry Burton, a reverent divine. London, 1641.

Bibliography 379

Newes from Ipswich. Discovering certaine late detestable practises of some domineering Lordly Prelates, to undermine the established doctrine and discipline of our Church, extirpate all Orthodox sincere Preachers and preaching of Gods Word, usher in Popery, Superstition and Idolatry. Amsterdam? or Edinburgh?, 1636.

The Popish royall favourite or, a full discovery of His Majesties extraordinary favours to, and protections of notorious papists, priestes, Jesuites, against all prosecutions and penalties of the laws enacted against them. London, 1643.

The unbishoping of Timothy and Titus. Or A briefe elaborate discourse, prooving Timothy to be no bishop (much lesse any sole, or diocaesan bishop) of Ephesus, nor Titus of Crete and that the power of ordination, or imposition of hands, belongs jure divino to presbyters, as well as to bishops, and not to bishops onely. Amsterdam, 1636.

The Vnlouelinesse, of Love-Lockes. or, A Svmmarie Discovrse proouing: The wearing, and nourishing of a Locke, or Loue-Locke, to be altogether vnseemely, and vnlawfull vnto Christians. London, 1628.

R. B. *A new Tragicall Comedie of Apius and Virginia, Wherein is liuely expressed a rare example of the vertue of Chastitie, by Virginias constancy, in wishing rather to be slayne in her own fathers handes, then to be deflowred of the wicked Iudge Apius.* London, 1575.

R. B. *The Lives of all the Roman Emperors, being exactly Collected, from Iulius Cæsar, unto the now reigning Ferdinand the second. With their Births, Governments, remarkable Actions, & Deaths.* London, 1636.

Reeve, Thomas. *God's plea for Nineveh: or, London's Precedent for Mercy. Delivered in certain sermons, within the City of London.* London, 1657.

Reynolds, John. *Votivae Angliae: Or the Desires and VVishes of England. Contayned in a Patheticall Discourse, presented to the King on New-yeares Day last.* Utrecht, 1624.

Rogers, Timothy. *The Roman-Catharist: or the Papist is a Puritane. A declaration, shewing that they of the religion and Church of Rome, are notorious Puritans.* London?, 1621.

Le Roy, Loys. *Aristotles Politiqves, or Discovrses of Government. Translated ovt of Greeke to French, with Expositions taken out of the best Authours . . . , Concerning the beginning, proceeding, and excellencie of Ciuile Gouernment.* London, 1598.

Rushworth, John. *Historical collections of private passages of state Weighty matters in law. Remarkable proceedings in five Parliaments. Beginning the sixteenth year of King James, anno 1618. And ending the fifth year of King Charls, anno 1629.* London, 1659.

Sallust, *The true patriot's speech to the people of Rome.* London, 1656.

The tvvo most vvorthy and notable histories which remaine vnmained to posterity (viz:) the conspiracie of Cateline, vndertaken against the gouernment of the Senate of Rome, and the vvarre which Iugurth for many yeares maintained against the same state. London, 1609.

380   *Bibliography*

Salmasius, Claudius. *Defensio Regia pro Caroli I ad Serenissimum Magnæ Brittaniæ Regem Carolum II. Filium natu majorem, Heredem & Successorem legitimum. Sumptibus Regiis.* 1649.

Saunders, Thomas. *To his Highness the Lord Protector, &c. and our general. The humble petition of several colonels of the army.* London, 1654.

Scot, Thomas. *Philomythie or Philomythologie, wherin Outlandish Birds, Beasts, and Fishes are taught to Speake true English plainely.* London, 1616.

The second part of Vox populi, or Gondomar appearing in the likenes of Machiauell in a Spanish parliament. Goricum, 1624.

Vox Populi, or Newes from Spayne, translated according to the Spanish coppie. Which may serve to forwarn both England and the Vnited Provinces how farre to trust to Spanish pretences. London, 1620.

Segar, William. *Honor Military, and Civill.* London, 1602.

Selden, John. *Of the Dominion, or, Ownership of the Sea.* Translated by Marchamont Nedham. London, 1652.

Seneca, Lucius Annaeus. *L. & M. Annaei Senecae tragoediae: post omnes omnium editiones recensionesque editae denuò & notis Tho. Farnabii illustratae.* London, 1624.

Annaeus Seneca, his first book of clemency written to Nero Caesar. London, 1653.

Shakespeare, William. *Lucrece.* London, 1594.

Sibbes, Richard. *A glance of Heaven, or, A precious taste of a glorious feast.* London, 1638.

Sidney, Sir Philip. *The Defence of Poesie.* London, 1595.

Siluayn, Alexander. *The orator handling a hundred seueral discourses, in forme of declamations.* Translated by L. P. London, 1596.

Speed, John. *The history of Great Britaine under the conquests of ye Romans, Saxons, Danes and Normans.* London, 1611.

Stockden, John. *The Seven Women Confessors.* London, 1641.

Tacitus, Cornelius. *The Annales of Corenlivs Tacitvs. The Description of Germanie.* Translated by Richard Grenewey. London, 1598.

Taylor, John. *All the vvorkes of Iohn Taylor the water-poet Beeing sixty and three in number.* London, 1630.

The Conversion, Confession, Contrition, Comming to himselfe, & Advice, of a Misled, Ill-bred, Rebellious Roundhead. Which is very fitting to be Read as such as weare short Haire, and long Eares, or desire Eares Long. 1643.

Toland, John, ed. *The Oceana of James Harrington and his other works, som [sic] wherof are now first publish'd from his own manuscripts : the whole collected, methodiz'd, and review'd, with an exact account of his life prefix'd.* London, 1700.

Townshend, Aurelian. *Albions Triumph, Personated in a maske at court. By the Kings Maiestie and his lords. The Sunday after Twelfe Night. 1631.* London, 1631.

Tempe Restor'd. A Masque presented by the Queene, and fourteene ladies, to the Kings Maiestie at Whitehall on Shrove-Tuesday. 1631. London, 1632.

Bibliography

Tuke, Thomas. *A Discourse against painting and tincturing of women*. London, 1616.

W. B., *That Which Seemes Best is Worst. Exprest in a Paraphrastical Transcript of Ivvenals tenth Satyre. Together with the Tragicall Narration of Virginias death inserted*. London, 1617.

Waller, Edmund. *A Panegyrick to My Lord Protector, or The present Greatness and joynt Interst of His Highness, and this Nation*. London, 1655.

Watson, Richard. *The panegyrike and the storme two poetike libells by Ed. Waller, vassa'll to the usuper answered by more faythfull subjects to His Sacred Ma'ty King Charles ye Second*. Bruges?, 1659.

Webster, John [and Thomas Heywood]. *Appius and Virginia. A Tragedy*. London, 1654.

Weldon, Sir Anthony. *The Court and Character of King James*. London, 1650.

Willymat, William. *A loyal subiects looking-glasse, or a good subiects direction*. London, 1604.

Wilson, Arthur *The history of Great Britain being the life and reign of King James the First, relating to what passed from his first access to the crown, till his death*. London, 1653.

Winstanley, William. *England's Worthies. Seclect Lives of the most Eminent Persons from Constantine the Great, to the death of Oliver Cromwel late Protector*. London, 1660.

Wither, George. *Respublica Anglicana, or The Historie of the Parliament in their late Proceedings*. London, 1650.

Vaticinivm Cavsvale. A Rapture Occasioned by the late Miraculous Deliverance of his Highnesse the Lord Protector, From a Desperate Danger. London, 1654.

l'Wright, Thomas. *An exact character or, narrative of the late right noble, and magnificent lord, Oliver Cromvvell, the Lord Protector of England, Scotland, and Ireland*. London, 1658.

PRIMARY SOURCES, MODERN EDITIONS

Aristotle, *Athenian Constitution. Eudemian Ethics. Virtues and Vices*. Translated by H. Rackham. Loeb Classical Library 285. Cambridge, MA: Harvard University Press, 1935.

Nicomachean Ethics. Translated by H. Rackham. Loeb Classical Library 73. Cambridge, MA: Harvard University Press, 1926.

Politics. Translated by H. Rackham. Loeb Classical Library 264. Cambridge, MA: Harvard University Press, 1932.

Aubrey, John. *Brief Lives*. Edited by Andrew Clark. London: Oxford, 1898.

Bacon, Francis. *Bacon's Essays*. Edited by F. G. Selby. London and New York: Macmillan, 1892.

Bellany, Alastair and Andrew McRae, eds. 'Early Stuart Libels: An Edition of Poetry from Manuscript Sources'. *Early Modern Literary Studies Text Series* I, 2005. http://purl.oclc.org/emls/texts/libels/.

382 *Bibliography*

Calendar of the Clarendon State Papers. Edited by Rev. W. Dunn Macray. Oxford: Clarendon Press, 1869.

Chapman, George, Ben Jonson, and John Marston. *Eastward Ho*. Edited by R. W. Van Fossen. Manchester: Manchester University Press, 1999.

Cicero, Marcus Tullius. *De Officiis*. Edited by M. T. Griffin and E. M. Atkins. Cambridge: Cambridge University Press, 2003.

On Duties. Translated by Walter Miller. Loeb Classical Library 30. Cambridge, MA: Harvard University Press, 1913.

On the Republic. On the Laws. Translated by Clinton W. Keyes. Loeb Classical Library 213. Cambridge, MA: Harvard University Press, 1928.

Tusculan Disputations. Translated by J. E. King. Loeb Classical Library 141. Cambridge, MA: Harvard University Press, 1927.

Coleridge, Samuel Taylor. *The Collected Letters of Samuel Taylor Coleridge*. Edited by Earl Leslie Griggs. Oxford: Clarendon Press, 1956.

Commons Debates 1628: Volume II: 17 March – 19 April 1628. Edited by Robert C. Johnson and Maija Jansson Cole. New Haven and London: Yale University Press, 1977.

Cromwell, Oliver. *Oliver Cromwell's letters and speeches: with Elucidations by Thomas Carlyle*, vol. 3. London: Chapman and Hall, 1846.

The Writings and Speeches of Oliver Cromwell. Edited by Wilbur Cortez Abbott. Oxford: Oxford University Press, 1989.

Dio, Cassius, *Roman History, Volume I: Books 1–11*. Translated by Earnest Cary and Herbert B. Foster. Loeb Classical Library 32. Cambridge, MA: Harvard University Press, 1914.

Dionysius of Halicarnassus. *Roman Antiquities, Volume VII: Books 11–20*. Translated by Earnest Cary. Loeb Classical Library 388. Cambridge, MA: Harvard University Press, 1950.

Dodsley, Robert and John Payne Collier, eds. *A Select Collection of Old Plays in Twelve Volumes*. London: Septimus Prowett, 1827.

An Edition of R. B.'s Appius and Virginia. Edited by Judith Hedley. New York and London: Garland, 1988.

Eikon Basilike, with selections from Eikonoklastes. Edited by Jim Daems and Holly Faith Nelson. Toronto: Broadview, 2006.

The Emperor's Favourite. Edited by Siobhan Keenan. Manchester: Manchester University Press, 2010.

Erasmus, Desiderius. *Education of a Christian Prince*. Edited by Lisa Jardine. Cambridge: Cambridge University Press, 1997.

Eusebius. *The History of the Church from Christ to Constantine*. Translated by G. A. Williamson. New York: New York University Press, 1966.

Foxe, John. *The Unabridged Acts and Monuments Online or TAMO*. HRI Online Publications, Sheffield, 2011. www.johnfoxe.org

Gardiner, Samuel Rawson, ed. *Documents Relating to the Proceedings against William Prynne, in 1634 and 1637*. London: Camden Society, 1877.

Bibliography

Guicciardini, Francesco. *Dialogue on the Government of Florence*. Edited by Alison Brown. Cambridge: Cambridge University Press, 1994.

Harington, Henry, ed. *Nugæ Antiquæ*, vol. I. London: Vernor and Hood, 1804.

Harrington, James. *The Commonwealth of Oceana and a System of Politics*. Edited by J. G. A. Pocock. Cambridge: Cambridge University Press, 1992.

Hobbes, Thomas. *Leviathan*. Edited by Richard Tuck. Cambridge: Cambridge University Press, 1996.

Holinshed, Raphael. *Chronicles of England, Scotland and Ireland*. London: Johnson, 1807–8.

Holles, Sir John. *Historical Manuscripts Commission, Manuscripts of His Grace the Duke of Rutland*. London: HM Stationery Office, 1888.

Journal of the House of Commons: volume 2: 1640–1643. British History Online. University of London & History of Parliament Trust. Nov. 2013 version. www.british-history.ac.uk/report.aspx?compid=9825&strquery=star chamber.

Justinian. *The Digest of Justinian*. Edited by Theodor Mommsen and Paul Krueger. Translated by Alan Watson. 4 vols. Philadelphia: Penn, 1985.

The Institutes of Justinian. Edited and translated by Thomas Collett Sandars. 13th edition. London: Longmans, Green, 1910.

Juvenal. *The Satires*. Translated by Niall Rudd. Oxford: Clarendon Press, 1991.

Juvenal and Persius. Edited and translated by Susanna Morton Braund. Loeb Classical Library Edition. Ann Arbor, MI: Edwards, 2004.

King James VI and I: Political Writings. Edited by Johann P. Sommerville. Cambridge: Cambridge University Press, 1994.

Livy. *History of Rome, Volume I: Books 1–2*. Translated by B. O. Foster. Loeb Classical Library 114. Cambridge, MA: Harvard University Press, 1919.

Marvell, Andrew. *The Poems of Andrew Marvell*. Edited by Nigel Smith. Harlow: Pearson, 2007.

May, Thomas. *Julia Agrippina*. Edited by F. Ernst Schmid. Louvain: Uystpruyst, 1914.

McClure, N. E., ed. *The Letters of John Chamberlain*, 2 vols. Philadelphia, 1939.

Milton, John. *The Complete Poems and Major Prose*. Edited by Merritt Y. Hughes. Indianapolis: Hackett, 1957.

The Complete Poetry and Essential Prose of John Milton. Edited by William Kerrigan, John Rumrich, and Stephen M. Fallon. New York: Modern Library Edition, Random House, 2007.

Complete Prose Works of John Milton. 10 vols. General editor Don M. Wolfe. New Haven: Yale University Press, 1953–1982.

John Milton Complete Shorter Poems. Edited by Stella P. Revard. Chichester: Wiley-Blackwell, 2009.

The Riverside Milton. Edited by Roy Flannagan. Boston and New York: Houghton Mifflin, 1998.

Nedham, Marchamont. *The Excellencie of a Free-State Or, The Right Constitution of a Commonwealth*. Edited by Blair Worden. Indianapolis: Liberty Fund, 2011.

384 *Bibliography*

Plato: Complete Works. Edited by John M. Cooper. Translated by G. M. A. Grube. Revised by C. D. C. Reeve. Indianapolis and Cambridge: Hackett, 1997.

Plutarch. *Moralia, Volume I.* Translated by Frank Cole Babbitt. Loeb Classical Library 197. Cambridge, MA: Harvard University Press, 1927.

Proceedings in Parliament, 1614 (House of Commons). Edited by Maija Jansson. Philadelphia: American Philosophical Society, 1988.

Proceedings in Parliament 1625. Edited by William B. Bidwell and Maija Jansson. Rochester: University of Rochester Press, 1987.

Sallust. *The War with Catiline. The War with Jugurtha.* Edited by John T. Ramsey. Translated by J. C. Rolfe. Loeb Classical Library 116. Cambridge, MA: Harvard University Press, 2013.

Seneca. *Moral Essays, Volume I: De Providentia. De Constantia. De Ira. De Clementia.* Translated by John W. Basore. Loeb Classical Library 214. Cambridge, MA: Harvard University Press, 1928.

Shakespeare, William. *The Oxford Shakespeare: The Complete Works.* Edited by Stanley Wells, Gary Taylor, John Jowett, and William Montgomery, 2nd ed. Oxford: Clarendon, 2005.

Shakespeare's Poems (Arden). Edited by Katherine Duncan-Jones and H. R. Woudhuysen. London: Thomson Learning, 2007

Sidney, Algernon. *Court Maxims.* Edited by Hans W. Blom, Eco Haitsma Mulier, and Ronald Janse. Cambridge: Cambridge University Press, 1996.

Stuart Royal Proclamations, Volume I: Royal Proclamations of James I, 1603–1625. Edited by James F. Larkin and Paul L. Hughes. Oxford: Clarendon Press, 1973.

Tacitus, Publius Cornelius. *Annals: Books 4–6, 11–12.* Translated by John Jackson. Loeb Classical Library 312. Cambridge, MA: Harvard University Press, 1937.

The Complete Works of Tacitus. Edited by Moses Hadas. Translated by Alfred John Church and William Jackson Brodribb. New York: Modern Library, 1942.

Histories: Books 4–5. Annals: Books 1–3. Translated by Clifford H. Moore and John Jackson. Loeb Classical Library 249. Cambridge, MA: Harvard University Press, 1931.

Tranquillus, Gaius Suetonius. *Lives of the Caesars, Volume II.* Translated by J. C. Rolfe. Loeb Classical Library 38. Cambridge, MA: Harvard University Press, 1914.

The Twelve Caesars. Translated by Robert Graves. Aylesbury: Penguin, 1979.

Webster, John. *The Complete Works of John Webster.* Edited by F. L. Lucas. London: Chatto & Windus, 1928.

Works of John Webster. Edited by D. Gunby, et al. Cambridge: Cambridge University Press, 2003.

Xenophon. *Memorabilia. Oeconomicus. Symposium. Apology.* Translated by E. C. Marchant and O. J. Todd. Revised by Jeffrey Henderson. Loeb Classical Library 168. Cambridge, MA: Harvard University Press, 2013.

SECONDARY SOURCES

A. B. G. 'Barksted, William (fl. 1611)'. In *The Oxford Dictionary of National Biography*. 3rd volume. Edited by Sir Leslie Stephen. London: Smith, Elder, 1885.

Achinstein, Sharon. "'A Law in this matter to himself': Contextualizing Milton's Divorce Tracts'. In *The Oxford Handbook of Milton*, edited by Nicholas McDowell and Nigel Smith, 174–85. Oxford: Oxford University Press, 2011.

'Saints or Citizens? Ideas of Marriage in Seventeenth-Century English Republicanism'. *The Seventeenth Century* 25.2 (2010): 240–64.

Adams, Joseph Quincy, ed. *The Dramatic Records of Sir Henry Herbert: Master of the Revels, 1623–1673*. New Haven: Yale University Press, 1917.

Adams, Simon. 'Foreign Policy and the Parliaments of 1621 and 1624'. In *Faction and Parliament: Essays on Early Stuart History*, edited by Kevin Sharpe, 139–71. Oxford: Oxford University Press, 1978.

'Spain or the Netherlands? The Dilemmas of Early Stuart Foreign Policy'. In *Before the Civil War: Essays on Early Stuart Politics and Government*, edited by Howard Tomlinson, 79–101. London: Macmillan, 1983.

Adamson, J. S. A. 'Chivalry and Political Culture'. In *Culture and Politics in Early Stuart England*, edited by Kevin Sharpe and Peter Lake, 161–98. Stanford: Stanford University Press, 1993.

Aers, David and Gunther Kress. 'Historical Process, Individual and Communities in Milton's Early Prose'. In *1642: Literature and Power in the Seventeenth Century* (Proceedings of the Essex Conference on the Sociology of Literature, Jul. 1980), edited by Francis Baker et al., 283–300. Colchester: University of Essex, 1981.

Agar, Herbert. *Milton and Plato*. Princeton: Princeton University Press, 1928.

Alston, Richard. 'Arms and the Man: Soldiers, Masculinity and Power in Republican and Imperial Rome'. In *When Men Were Men: Masculinity, Power, and Identity in Classical Antiquity*, edited by Lin Foxhall and John Salmon, 205–24. London and New York: Routledge, 1998.

Amussen, Susan Dwyer. *An Ordered Society: Gender and Class in Early Modern England*. Oxford: Basil Blackwell, 1988.

'The Irrelevance of Revisionism: Gender, Politics, and Society in Early Modern England,' *Huntington Library Quarterly* 78.4 (Winter 2015): 683–701.

and David Underdown. *Gender, Culture, and Politics in England, 1560–1640: Turning the World Upside Down*. London: Bloomsbury, 2017.

Anglo, Sydney. 'Machiavelli as a Military Authority. Some Early Sources'. In *Florence and Italy: Renaissance Studies in Honour of Nicolai Rubinstein*, edited by Peter Denley and Caroline Elam, 321–34. London: Committee for Medieval Studies, 1988.

Arendt, Hannah. *Between Past and Future: Eight Exercises in Political Thought*. New York: Penguin (reprint), 2006.

386   *Bibliography*

Armitage, David. 'The Cromwellian Protectorate and the Languages of Empire'. *The Historical Journal* 35.3 (1992): 531–55.

'Empire and Liberty: A Republican Dilemma'. In *Republicanism: A Shared European Heritage, volume 2: The Values of Republicanism in Early Modern Europe*, edited by Martin van Gelderen and Quentin Skinner, 29–46. Cambridge: Cambridge University Press, 2002.

Ideological Origins of the British Empire. Cambridge: Cambridge University Press, 2000.

'John Milton: Poet against Empire'. In *Milton and Republicanism*, edited by Armitage, Armand Himy, and Quentin Skinner, 206–25. Cambridge: Cambridge University Press, 1995.

Atherton, Ian and Julie Sanders, eds. *1630s: Interdisciplinary essays on culture and politics in the Caroline era*. Manchester and New York: Manchester University Press, 2006.

Badenhausen, Richard. 'Disarming the Infant Warrior: Prince Henry, King James, and the Chivalric Revival'. *Papers on Language and Literature* 31 (1995): 20–37.

Baker, John Hamilton. *The Legal Profession and the Common Law: Historical Essays*. London: Hambledon, 1986.

Baker, Keith Michael. *Inventing the French Revolution: Essays on French Political Culture in the Eighteenth Century*. Cambridge: Cambridge University Press, 1990.

Baldwin, Geoff. 'The 'Public' as a Rhetorical Community'. In *Communities in Early Modern England: Networks, Place, Rhetoric*, edited by Alexandra Shepard and Phil Withington, 199–215. Manchester: Manchester University Press, 2000.

Ball, John H. *Popular Violence in the Irish Uprising of 1641: The 1641 Depositions, Irish Resistance to English Colonialism, and its Representation in English Sources*. PhD Dissertation at the Johns Hopkins University, Baltimore, Oct. 2006.

Bamford, Karen. *Sexual Violence on the Jacobean Stage*. New York: St. Martin's Press, 2000.

Barber, Sarah, 'The Engagement for the Council of State and the Establishment of the Commonwealth Government'. *Historical Research* 63 (1990): 44–57.

Barker, Arthur. 'Christian Liberty in Milton's Divorce Pamphlets'. *The Modern Language Review* 35.2 (Apr. 1940): 153–61.

Barnes, Susan J., Nora De Poorter, Oliver Millar, and Horst Vey. *Van Dyck: A Complete Catalogue of the Paintings*. New Haven and London: Yale University Press, 2004.

Bartlett, Phyllis Brooks, ed. *The Poems of George Chapman*. New York: MLA, 1941.

Bassi, Karen. 'The Semantics of Manliness in Ancient Greece'. In *Andreia: Studies in Manliness and Courage in Classical Antiquity*, edited by Ralph M. Rosen and Ineke Sluiter, 25–58. Leiden: Brill, 2003.

Bibliography 387

Bellany, Alastair. 'The Embarrassment of Libels: Perceptions and Representations of Verse Libelling in Early Stuart England'. In *The Politics of the Public Sphere in Early Modern England*, 144–67. Manchester: Manchester University Press, 2012.

'Libels in Action: Ritual, Subversion, and the English Literary Underground, 1603-42'. In *The Politics of the Excluded, c. 1500–1850*, edited by Tim Harris, 99–124. Basingstoke: Palgrave Macmillan, 2001.

'Railing Rhymes Revisited: Libels, Scandals, and Early Stuart Politics'. *History Compass* 5.4 (2007): 1136–79.

The Politics of Court Scandal in Early Modern England: News Culture and the Overbury Affair, 1603–1660. Cambridge: Cambridge University Press, 2002.

Bellany, Alastair and Thomas Cogswell. *The Murder of King James I*. New Haven: Yale University Press, 2015.

Belsey, Catherine. 'Tarquin Dispossessed: Expropriation and Consent in *The Rape of Lucrece*'. *Shakespeare Quarterly* 52.3 (2001): 315–35.

Bentley, Gerald Eades. *The Jacobean and Caroline Stage: Plays and Playwrights*. Oxford: Clarendon Press, 1956.

Bergeron, David M. *English Civic Pageantry, 1558–1642*. Tempe: Arizona Center for Medieval and Renaissance Studies, 2003.

King James and Letters of Homoerotic Desire. Iowa City: University of Iowa Press, 2002.

Berry, Christopher J. *The Idea of Luxury: A Conceptual and Historical Investigation*. Cambridge: Cambridge University Press, 1994.

Bertheau, Gilles. 'George Chapman's French Tragedies, or, Machiavelli beyond the Mirror'. In *Representing France and the French in Early Modern English Drama*, edited by Jean-Christophe Mayer, 110–24. Newark: University of Delaware Press, 2008.

'Jacques I au miroir de la Tragedie Chapmanienne'. *Bulletin de la Société d'Etudes Anglo-Americaines des XVII et XVIII Siècles* 62 (2006): 193–207.

'Prince Henry as Chapman's "Absolute Man"'. In *Prince Henry Revived: Image and Exemplarity in Early Modern England*, edited by Timothy Wilks, 134–45. London: Paul Holberton, 2007.

Blackburn, Thomas. *Edmund Bolton, Critic, Antiquary, and Historian: A Biographical and Critical Study with an Edition of Hypercritica*. PhD diss., Stanford University, 1963.

Blits, Jan H. 'Redeeming Lost Honor: Shakespeare's Rape of Lucrece'. *Review of Politics* 71.3 (Summer 2009): 411–27.

Boehrer, Bruce. 'Elementary Structures of Kingship: Milton, Regicide, and the Family'. In *Milton Studies XXIII*, edited by James D. Simmonds, 97–117. Pittsburgh: University of Pittsburgh Press, 1987.

Bowers, Fredson, ed. *Dictionary of Literary Biography*, 62. Detroit: Gale Research, 1987.

Braddick, Michael and John Walter. *Negotiating Power in Early Modern England*. Cambridge: Cambridge University Press, 2001.

388 *Bibliography*

Braden, Gordon. 'George Chapman'. In *Elizabethan Dramatists*, edited by Fredson Bowers. *Dictionary of Literary Biography* 62. Detroit: Gale Research, 1987.

Bradford, Alan T. 'Stuart Absolutism and the 'Utility' of Tacitus'. *Huntington Library Quarterly* 46.2 (Spring 1983): 127–55.

Bradley, Keith. *Slavery and Society at Rome*. Cambridge: Cambridge University Press, 1994.

Bradstock, Andrew. *Radical Religion in Cromwell's England*. London: IB Tauris, 2011.

Brautigam, Dwight D. 'The Court and the Country Revisited'. In *Court, Country, and Culture: Essays on Early Modern British History in Honor of Perez Zagorin*, edited by Bonnelyn Young Kunze and Brautigam, 55–64. Rochester: University of Rochester Press, 1992.

Bray, Alan. 'Homosexuality and the Signs of Male Friendship in Elizabethan England'. *History Workshop* 29 (Spring 1990): 1–19.

Homosexuality in Renaissance England. London: Gay Men's Press, 1982.

Breitenberg, Mark. *Anxious Masculinity in Early Modern England*. Cambridge: Cambridge University Press, 1996.

Bromley, Laura G. 'Lucrece's Re-Creation'. *Shakespeare Quarterly* 34.2 (Summer 1983): 200–11.

Brooke, Rupert. 'The Authorship of the later *Appius and Virginia*'. *Modern Language Review* 8, no. 4 (1913): 433–53.

John Webster and the Elizabethan Drama. New York: John Lane, 1916.

Brown, Cedric Clive. *John Milton's Aristocratic Entertainments*. Cambridge: Cambridge University Press, 1985.

'Milton and the Idolatrous Consort'. *Criticism* 35.3 (Summer 1993): 419–39.

Bryson, Anna. *From Courtesy to Civility: Changing Codes of Conduct in Early Modern England*. Oxford: Clarendon Press, 1998.

Bullen, A. H., ed. 'Introduction to the *Tragedy of Nero*'. In *A Collection of Old English Plays*, I.3–10. London: Wyman & Sons, 1882.

Burgess, Glenn. *Absolute Monarchy and the Stuart Constitution*. New Haven and London: Yale University Press, 1996.

Burke, Peter. 'A Survey of the Popularity of Ancient Historians, 1450–1700'. *History and Theory* 2 (1966): 135–52.

'Tacitism, Scepticism, and Reason of State'. In *The Cambridge History of Political Thought 1450–1750*, edited by. J. H. Burns and Mark Goldie, 479–98. Cambridge: Cambridge University Press, 1991.

Burnett, Mark Thornton. 'Chapman, George (1559/60–1634)'. In *Oxford Dictionary of National Biography*. Oxford: Oxford University Press, 2004, online ed., May 2006, www.oxforddnb.com/view/article/5118.

Burton, J. and A. Loomba. *Race in Early Modern England: A Documentary Companion*. New York: Palgrave Macmillan, 2007.

Bushnell, Rebecca. *Tragedies of Tyrants: Political Thought and Theater in the English Renaissance*. Ithaca, NY: Cornell University Press, 1990.

Bibliography

Butler, Martin. *The Stuart Court Masque and Political Culture*. Cambridge: Cambridge University Press, 2008.

Butler, Todd Wayne. *Imagination and Politics in Seventeenth-Century England*. Burlington, VT: Ashgate, 2008.

Camino, Mercedes Maroto. *The Stage Am I? Raping Lucrece in Early Modern England*. New York: E. Mellen, 1995.

Campbell, Gordon. 'Gil, Alexander, the younger (1596/7–1642?)'. In *The Oxford Dictionary of National Biography*. Oxford: Oxford University Press, 2004, online ed., Jan. 2008, www.oxforddnb.com/view/article/10730.

Canny, Nicholas. 'The Origins of Empire: An Introduction'. In *The Oxford History of the British Empire: Volume I: The Origins of Empire*, edited by Canny, 1–33. Oxford: Oxford University Press, 2001.

Capp, Bernard. 'Republican Reformation: Family, Community and the State in Interregnum Middlesex, 1649–60'. In *The Family in Early Modern England*, edited by Helen Berry and Elizabeth Foyster, 40–66. Cambridge: Cambridge University Press, 2007.

Carter, C. H. 'Gondomar: Ambassador to James I'. *The Historical Journal* 7.2 (1964): 189–208.

Chartier, Roger. *The Cultural Origins of the French Revolution*. Translated by Lydia G. Cochrane. Durham, NC: Duke University Press, 1991.

Chernaik, Warren. *The Myth of Rome in Shakespeare and his Contemporaries*. Cambridge: Cambridge University Press 2011.

'Waller, Edmund (1606–1687)'. In *The Oxford Dictionary of National Biography*. Oxford: Oxford University Press, 2004, online ed., www.oxforddnb .com/view/article/28556.

Christianson, Paul. 'Royal and Parliamentary Voices on the Ancient Constitution, c. 1604–1621'. In *The Mental World of the Jacobean Court*, edited by Linda Levy Peck, 71–95. Cambridge: Cambridge University Press, 1991.

Clark, A. 'The Chevalier d'Eon and Wilkes: Masculinity and Politics in the Eighteenth Century'. *Eighteenth Century Studies* xxxii (1998): 19–48.

Clarke, Elizabeth. *Politics, Religion, and the Song of Songs in Seventeenth Century England*. Basingstoke: Palgrave Macmillan, 2011.

Clegg, Cyndia Susan. *Press Censorship in Caroline England*. Cambridge: Cambridge University Press, 2008.

Press Censorship in Jacobean England. New York: Cambridge University Press, 2001.

Cogswell, Thomas. *The Blessed Revolution: English Politics and the Coming of War, 1621–1624*. Cambridge: Cambridge University Press, 1989.

'England and the Spanish Match'. In *Conflict in Early Stuart England: Studies in Religion and Politics 1603–1642*, edited by Richard Cust and Ann Hughes, 107–33. London: Routledge, 2014.

'Phaeton's Chariot: The Parliament-Men and the Continental Crisis of 1621'. In *The Political World of Thomas Wentworth, Earl of Strafford, 1621–1641*, edited by J. F. Merritt, 24–46. Cambridge: Cambridge University Press, 1996.

'Underground Verse and the Transformation of Early Stuart Political Culture'. In *Political Culture and Cultural Politics in Early Modern England*, edited by David Underdown, Mark Kishlansky, and Susan D. Amussen, 277–300. Manchester: Manchester University Press, 1995.

Colclough, David. *Freedom of Speech in Early Stuart England*. Cambridge: Cambridge University Press, 2005.

Collinson, Patrick. *Elizabethans*. London: Bloomsbury, 2003.

Combe, Kirk. 'Clandestine Protest against William III in Dryden's Translations of Juvenal and Persius'. *Modern Philology* 87 (1989): 36–50.

Condren, Conal. *The Language of Politics in Seventeenth-Century England*. New York: St. Martin's Press, 1994.

Cooper, Tim. 'Reassessing the Radicals'. *The Historical Journal* 50.1 (Mar. 2007): 241–52.

Corns, Thomas N. 'Milton before "Lycidas."' In *Milton and the Terms of Liberty*, edited by Graham Parry and Joad Raymond, 23–36. Suffolk and Rochester: D. S. Brewer, 2002.

'Milton's *Observations Upon the Articles of Peace*: Ireland under English Eyes'. In *Politics, Poetics, and Hermeneutics in Milton's Prose*, edited by David Lowenstein and J. G. Turner, 123–34. New York: Cambridge University Press, 1990.

Uncloistered Virtue: English Political Literature, 1640–1660. Oxford: Clarendon Press, 1992.

Cox, Rosanna. '"Atlantick and Eutopian Polities": Utopianism, Republicanism and Constitutional Design in the Interregnum'. In *New Worlds Reflected: Travel and Utopia in the Early Modern Period*, edited by C. Houston, 179–202. London: Ashgate, 2010).

'Milton, Marriage, and the Politics of Gender'. In *John Milton: Life, Writing, and Reputation*, edited by Paul Hammond and Blair Worden, 125–45. Oxford: Oxford University Press, 2010.

Crawford, Patricia. 'Charles Stuart, That Man of Blood'. *Journal of British Studies* 16.2 (Spring 1977): 41–61.

Cressy, David. *Charles I & the People of England*. Oxford: Oxford University Press, 2015.

Dangerous Talk: Scandalous, Seditious, and Treasonable Speech in Pre-Modern England. Oxford: Oxford University Press, 2010.

'Puritan Martyrs in Island Prisons', *Journal of British Studies* 57 (2018): 736–54.

Travesties and Transgression in Tudor and Stuart England. New York: Oxford University Press, 2000.

Culhane, Peter. 'The Date of Heywood and Webster's *Appius and Virginia*'. *Notes & Queries* 51.3 (Sept. 2004): 300–1.

Cust, Richard. *Charles I: A Political Life*. New York: Routledge, 2007.

Charles I and the Aristocracy, 1625–1642. Cambridge: Cambridge University Press, 2013.

Bibliography

'Charles I, the Privy Council, and the Forced Loan'. *Journal of British Studies* 24 (Apr. 1985): 208-35.

The Forced Loan and English Politics 1626–1628. Oxford: Oxford, 1987.

'The 'Public Man' in Late Tudor and Early Stuart England'. In *The Politics of the Public Sphere in Early Modern England*, 116–43. Manchester: Manchester University Press, 2012.

Cust, Richard and Anne Hughes, eds., *The English Civil War*. New York and London: Arnold, 1997.

Cust and Hughes, eds. *Conflict in Early Stuart England*. New York: Longman, 1989.

Cuttica, Cesare. 'The English Regicide and Patriarchalism: Representing Commonwealth Ideology and Practice in the Early 1650s'. *Renaissance and Reformation* 36.2 (Spring 2013): 131–64.

Sir Robert Filmer, (1588–1653) and the Patriotic Monarch: Patriarchalism in Seventeenth-Century Political Thought. Manchester: Manchester University Press, 2012.

D'Addario, Christopher. 'Abraham Cowley and the Ends of Poetry'. In *Literatures of Exile in the English Revolution and Its Aftermath, 1640–1690.* Edited by Philip Major, 119–32. Farnham, Surrey: Ashgate, 2010.

Daems, Jim. 'Dividing Conjunctions: Milton's *Observations upon the Articles of Peace*'. *Milton Quarterly* 33.2 (May 1999): 51–55.

Darbishire, Helen, ed. *The Early Lives of Milton*. London, 1965.

Darnton, Robert. *The Literary Underground of the Old Regime*. Cambridge, MA: Harvard University Press, 1982.

Daston, Lorraine and Katharine Park. *Wonders and the Order of Nature: 1150–1750.* New York: Zone Books, 2001.

Davies, J. D. 'A Permanent National Maritime Fighting Force, 1642–1689'. In *The Oxford Illustrated History of the Royal Navy*, edited by J. R. Hill, 56–79. Oxford: Oxford University Press, 1995.

Davies, Kathleen M. 'Continuity and Change in Literary Advice on Marriage'. In *Marriage and Society: Studies in the Social History of Marriage*, edited by R. B. Outwaite, 58–78. London: Europa, 1981.

Davis, Colin. 'Cromwell's Religion'. In *Oliver Cromwell and the English Revolution.* Edited by John Morrill, 181–208. London: Longman, 1990.

Davis, Natalie Zemon. *Society and Culture in Early Modern France: Eight Essays.* Stanford: Stanford University Press, 1975.

Desan, Suzanne. *The Family on Trial in Revolutionary France*. Berkeley: University of California Press, 2006.

Ditchfield, Simon and Helen Smith, eds. *Conversions: Gender and Religious Change in Early Modern Europe*. Manchester: Manchester University Press, 2017.

Djordjevic, Igor. *King John (Mis)Remembered: The Dunmow Chronicle, the Lord Admiral's Men, and the Formation of Cultural Memory*. Farnham: Ashgate, 2015.

Bibliography

Dolan, Francis E. 'Taking the Pencil out of God's Hand: Art, Nature, and the Face-Painting Debate in Early Modern England'. *Publications of the Modern Language Association of America* 108.2 (Mar., 1993): 224–39.

Whores of Babylon: Catholicism, Gender, and Seventeenth-Century Print Culture. Ithaca and London: Cornell University Press, 1999.

Donagan, Barbara. 'The York House Conference Revisited: Laymen, Calvinists and Arminians', *Historical Research* 64:155 (1991), 312–330.

Dugan, Holly. *The Ephemeral History of Perfume: Scent and Sense in Early Modern England*. Baltimore: The Johns Hopkins University Press, 2011.

Duncan, Sarah L. 'The Two Virgin Queens'. In *Elizabeth I and the 'Sovereign Arts': Essays in Literature, History and Culture*, edited by Donald Stump, Linda Shenk, and Carole Levin. Tempe: Arizona Center for Medieval and Renaissance Studies, 2011.

Dunnigan, Sarah M. 'Discovering Desire in the *Amatoria*'. In *Royal Subjects: Essays on the Writings of James VI and I*, edited by Daniel Fischlin and Mark Fortier, 149–81. Detroit: Wayne State University Press, 2002.

Dzelzainis, Martin. 'Milton's Classical Republicanism'. In *Milton and Republicanism*, edited by David Armitage, Armand Himy, and Quentin Skinner, 3–24. Cambridge: Cambridge University Press, 1995.

'Republicanism'. In *A Companion to Milton*, edited by Thomas Corns, 294–308. Oxford: Blackwell, 2001.

Enterline, Lynn. *The Rhetoric of the Body from Ovid to Shakespeare*. Cambridge: Cambridge University Press, 2000.

Evans, Elizabeth C. 'Physiognomics in the Ancient World'. *Transactions of the American Philosophical Society* 59.5 (1969): 1–101.

Evans, J. Martin. *Milton's Imperial Epic:* Paradise Lost *and the Discourses of Colonialism*. Ithaca and London: Cornell University Press, 1996.

Fallon, Stephen M. 'The Metaphysics of Milton's Divorce Tracts'. In *Politics, Poetics, and Hermeneutics in Milton's Prose*, edited by David Lowenstein and J. G. Turner, 69–83. New York: Cambridge University Press, 1990.

Milton Among the Philosophers: Poetry and Materialism in Seventeenth-Century England. Ithaca and London: Cornell University Press, 1991.

Fauré, Christine. 'Rights or Virtues: Women and the Republic'. In *Republicanism: A Shared European Heritage, Volume 2: The Values of Republicanism in Early Modern Europe*, edited by Martin van Gelderen and Quentin Skinner, 125–38. Cambridge: Cambridge University Press, 2002.

Feingold, Mordechai. 'The Humanities'. In *The History of the University of Oxford, Volume IV: Seventeenth Century Oxford*, edited by N. Tyacke, 211–357. Oxford: Oxford University Press, 1997.

Ferguson, William. *Scotland's Relations with England: A Survey to 1707*. Edinburgh: Saltire Society, 1994.

Feroli, Teresa. *Political Speaking Justified: Women Prophets and the English Revolution*. Newark: University of Delaware Press, 2006.

Fink, Zera S. *The Classical Republicans: An Essay on the Recovery of a Pattern of Thought in Seventeenth-Century England*. Evanston, IL: Northwestern University Press, 1945.

Bibliography
393

Fisher, Will. *Materializing Gender in Early Modern English Literature and Culture.* Cambridge: Cambridge University Press, 2006.

Fissell, Mary. *Vernacular Bodies: The Politics of Reproduction in Early Modern England.* Oxford: Oxford University Press, 2004.

Fleay, F. G. *Biographical Chronicle of English Drama, 1559–1642.* London: Reeves and Turner, 1891.

Fletcher, Anthony. *A County Community in Peace and War: Sussex, 1600–1660.* London: Longman, 1975.

Gender, Sex and Subordination in England, 1500–1800. New Haven: Yale University Press, 1999.

Fliegelman, Jay. *Prodigals & Pilgrims: The American Revolution against Patriarchal Authority, 1750–1800.* Cambridge: Cambridge University Press, 1982.

Forsyth, Neil. 'The English Church'. In *Milton in Context*, edited by Stephen B. Dobranski, 292–302. Cambridge: Cambridge 2010.

Foyster, Elizabeth A. *Manhood in Early Modern England: Honour, Sex and Marriage.* London and New York: Longman, 1999.

Fox, Adam. 'Ballads, Libels, and Popular Ridicule in Jacobean England'. *Past and Present* 145 (1994): 47–83.

Foxhall, Lin. *Studying Gender in Classical Antiquity.* Cambridge: Cambridge University Press, 2013.

Foxley, Rachel. *The Levellers: Radical Political Thought in the English Revolution.* Manchester: Manchester University Press, 2013.

Franssen, Paul. 'George Chapman's Learned Drama'. In *The Cambridge Companion to Shakespeare and Contemporary Dramatists*, edited by Tom Hoenselaars, 134–48. Cambridge: Cambridge University Press, 2012.

Gadd, Ian. 'Stationers'. In *The Milton Encyclopedia*, edited by Thomas M. Corns, 348–52. New Haven: Yale University Press, 2012.

Gardiner, Samuel Rawson. *History of England from the Accession of James I to the Outbreak of the Civil War, 1603–1642*, 10 vols. London: Longmans, Green, & Co., 1884.

Garside-Allen, Christine. 'Can a Woman be Good in the Same Way as a Man?' *Dialogue* 10 (1971), 534–44.

Gaunt, Peter. *Oliver Cromwell.* New York: New York University Press, 2004.

Gernon, Luke. 'A Discourse of Ireland'. In *Illustrations of Irish History and Topography, Mainly of the Seventeenth Century*, edited by C. Litton Falkiner, 345–62. New York: Longmans, 1904.

Gianoutsos, Jamie. 'Criticizing Kings: Gender, Classical History, and Subversive Writing in Seventeenth-Century England'. *Renaissance Quarterly* 70.4 (Winter 2017): 1366–96.

'Loyalty to a Nero? Publicising Puritan Persecution in the 1630s'. In *Loyalty to the Monarchs of Late Medieval and Early Modern Britain, c. 1400–1688*, edited by Matthew Ward and Matthew Hefferan, 174–99. London: Palgrave Macmillan, 2020.

Goldberg, Jonathan. *James I and the Politics of Literature: Jonson, Shakespeare, Donne, and their Contemporaries.* Stanford: Stanford University Press, 1989.

Bibliography

Goldsmith, Maurice. 'Republican Liberty Considered'. *History of Political Thought* 21.3 (Mar. 2000): 543–59.

Gowing, Laura. *Common Bodies: Women, Touch and Power in Seventeenth Century England*. New Haven: Yale University Press, 2003.

Domestic Dangers: Women, Words, and Sex in Early Modern London. Oxford: Clarendon Press, 1996.

Grafton, Anthony and Lisa Jardine. '"Studied for Action": How Gabriel Harvey Read his Livy'. *Past and Present* 129 (Nov. 1990): 30–78.

Greenspan, Nicole. 'News and the Politics of Information in the Mid Seventeenth Century: The Western Design and the Conquest of Jamaica'. *History Workshop Journal* 69 (Spring 2010): 1–26.

Guibbory, Achash. 'John Milton: Carnal Idolatry and Reconfiguration of Worship, Part 1, 1634–1660'. In *Ceremony and Community from Herbert to Milton: Literature, Religion, and Cultural Conflict in Seventeenth-Century England*, 147–86. Cambridge: Cambridge University Press, 1998.

Guillory, John. 'Milton, Narcissism, Gender: On the Genealogy of Male Self-Esteem'. In *Critical Essays on John Milton*, edited by Christopher Kendrick, 165–93. New York: GK Hall, 1995.

Gunby, D. and H. Lees-Jeffries, 'George Villiers, Duke of Buckingham and the Dating of Webster and Heywood's *Appius and Virginia*'. *Notes & Queries* 49.3 (2002): 324–27.

Gunderson, Erik. 'Discovering the Body in Roman Oratory'. In *Parchments of Gender: Deciphering the Bodies of Antiquity*, edited by Maria Wyke, 169–90. Oxford: Oxford University Press, 1998.

Gunn, A. W. '"Interest Will Not Lie": A Seventeenth-Century Political Maxim'. *Journal of the History of Ideas* 29.4 (Oct.–Dec. 1968): 551–64.

Guy, John. 'The Rhetoric of Counsel in Early Modern England'. In *Tudor Political Culture*, edited by Dale Hoak, 292–310. Cambridge: Cambridge University Press, 1995.

Hadfield, Andrew. 'Republicanism in Sixteenth- and Seventeenth-Century Britain'. In *British Political Thought in History, Literature, and Theory, 1500–1800*, edited by David Armitage, 111–28. Cambridge: Cambridge University Press, 2006.

Shakespeare and Republicanism. Cambridge: Cambridge University Press, 2005.

Hadfield, Andrew and Wiley Maley, eds. *Representing Ireland: Literature and the Origins of Conflict, 1534–1660*. Cambridge: Cambridge University Press, 1993.

Hammer, Dean. *Roman Political Thought: From Cicero to Augustine*. Cambridge: Cambridge University Press, 2014.

Hammersley, Rachel. *French Revolutionaries and English Republicans: The Cordeliers Club, 1790–1794*. Suffolk: Boydell, 2005.

'An Eighteenth-Century French Commonwealthman? Exploring the Contest of the Chevalier d'Eon's Translation of Marchamont Nedham's *The Excellencie of a Free State*'. In *The Chevalier D'Eon and His Worlds: Gender, Espionage and Politics in the Eighteenth Century*, edited by Simon Burrows,

Bibliography

Jonathan Conlin, Russell Goulbourne, and Valerie Mainz, 215–28. London and New York: Continuum, 2010.

Harrill, J. Albert 'Invective against Paul (2 Cor. 10:10), the Physiognomics of the Ancient Slave Body, and the Greco-Roman Rhetoric of Manhood'. In *Antiquity and Humanity: Essays on Ancient Religion and Philosophy*, edited by A. Yarbro Collins, and M. M. Mitchell, 189–213. Tübingen: Mohr Siebeck, 2001.

Harris, C. R. 'The Court and Character of James I'. *Notes & Queries*, 3rd series, vol. V, (Jan.–Jun. 1864): 451–53.

Hart, W. H. *Index Expurgatorius Anglicanus: Or, a Descriptive Catalogue of the Principal Books Printed or Published in England, Which Have Been Suppressed, or Burnt by the Common Hangman, or Censured, or for Which the Authors, Printers, or Publishers Have Been Prosecuted*. London: John Russell Smith, 1872.

Hartley, J. B. 'Meaning and Ambiguity in Tudor Cartography'. In *English Map-Making, 1500–1650*, edited by Sarah Tyacke. London: The British Library, 1983.

Hausknecht, Gina. 'The Gender of Civic Virtue'. In *Milton and Gender*, edited by Catherine Gimelli, Martin, 19–33. Cambridge: Cambridge University Press, 2004.

Hawkes, David. 'The Politics of Character in John Milton's Divorce Tracts'. *Journal of the History of Ideas* 62.1 (Jan. 2001): 141–60.

Hearn, Karen, ed. *Van Dyck & Britain*. London: Tate, 2009.

Helmholz, R. H. 'The Roman Law of Guardianship in England, 1300–1600'. *Tulane Law Review* 52.2 (1978): 223–57.

Hertel, Ralf. *Staging England in the Elizabethan History Play: Performing National Identity*. London and New York: Routledge, 2016.

Hibbard, Caroline 'Henrietta Maria in the 1630s: Perspectives on the Role of Consort Queens in *Ancien Régime* Courts'. In *The 1630s: Interdisciplinary Essays on Culture and Politics in the Caroline Era*, edited by Ian Atherton and Julie Sanders, 92–110. Manchester: Manchester University Press, 2006.

Hill, Christopher. *Antichrist in Seventeenth-Century England*. London: Oxford University Press, 1971.

'George Wither and John Milton'. In *The Collected Essays of Christopher Hill, Vol. I: Writing and Revolution in Seventeenth-Century England*, 135–56. Brighton: Harvester, 1985.

'The Many-Headed Monster in Late Tudor and Early Stuart Political Thinking'. In *From the Renaissance to the Counter-Reformation, Essays in Honour of Garrett Mattingly*, edited by C. H. Carter, 296–324. New York: Random House, 1966.

Milton and the English Revolution. London: Faber & Faber, 1977.

Holberton, Edward. *Poetry and the Cromwellian Protectorate: Culture, Politics, and Institutions*. Oxford: Oxford University Press, 2008.

Houston, S. J. *James I*. 2nd ed. London and New York: Longman, 1995.

Hoyt, Robert S. 'The Coronation Oath of 1308'. *English Historical Review* 71.280 (Jul. 1956): 353–83.

Bibliography

Huet, Marie-Hélène. *Monstrous Imagination*. London and Cambridge, MA: Harvard University Press, 1993.

Hufton, Olwen. *Women and the Limits of Citizenship*. Toronto: Toronto University Press, 1992.

Hughes, Anne. *The Causes of the English Civil War*. London: Macmillan, 1991.

Gender and the English Revolution. New York: Routledge, 2012.

'Militancy and Localism: Warwickshire Politics and Westminster Politics, 1643–1647'. *Transactions of the Royal Historical Society*, 5th ser., 31 (1981): 51–68.

Hume, David. *The History of Great Britain, Under the House of Stuart*. London: Millar, 1759.

Hunt, Lynn. *The Family Romance of the French Revolution*. Berkeley: University of California Press, 1992.

'Male Virtue and Republican Motherhood'. In *The French Revolution and the Creation of Modern Political Culture*, edited by Keith Michael Baker, 195–210. Bingley: Emerald, 1994.

'The Many Bodies of Marie Antoinette'. In *The French Revolution: Recent Debates*, 201–18. London: Routledge 2006.

Hunt, William. 'Civic Chivalry and the English Civil War'. In *The Transmission of Culture in Early Modern Europe*, edited by Anthony Grafton and Ann Blair, 204–37. Philadelphia: University of Pennsylvania Press, 1990.

Ingram, Martin. 'Scolding Women Cucked or Washed'. In *Women, Crime and the Courts in Early Modern England*, edited by Jennifer Kermode and Garthine Walker, 47–80. London: University College London Press, 1994.

Jacquot, Jean. *George Chapman (1559–1634), sa vie, sa poésie, son théâtre, sa pensée*. Paris, Société D'éditions 'Les Belles Lettres', 1951.

James, Mervyn. *Society, Politics and Culture: Studies in Early Modern England*. Cambridge: Cambridge University Press, 1986.

Jensen, Freyja Cox. *Reading the Roman Republic in Early Modern England*. Leiden: Brill, 2012.

Johns, Adrian 'Streater, John (c.1620–1677)'. In *The Oxford Dictionary of National Biography*. Oxford: Oxford University Press, 2004, online ed., Jan. 2008, www.oxforddnb.com/view/article/26656.

Kahn, Coppélia. 'The Rape in Shakespeare's Lucrece'. *Shakespeare Studies* 9 (1976): 45–72.

Kane, Brendan. *The Politics and Culture of Honour in Britain and Ireland, 1541–1641*. Cambridge: Cambridge University Press, 2010.

Kanemura, Rei. *The Idea of Sovereignty in English Historical Writing, 1599–1627*. PhD Diss., University of Cambridge, 2012.

Keblusek, Maria and Badeloch Vera Noldus, eds. *Double Agents: Cultural and Political Brokerage in Early Modern Europe*. Leiden: Koninklijke Brill NV, 2011.

Keenan, Siobhan. 'Staging Roman History, Stuart Politics, and the Duke of Buckingham: The Example of *The Emperor's Favourite*'. *Early Theatre* 14 (2002): 63–103.

Bibliography

Kelley, Donald R. 'Philosophy and Humanistic Disciplines: The Theory of History'. In *The Cambridge History of Renaissance Philosophy*, edited by C. B. Schmitt, Quentin Skinner, Eckhard Kessler, and Jill Kraye, 746–62. Cambridge: Cambridge University Press, 1988.

Kelsey, Sean. *Inventing a Republic: The Political Culture of the English Commonwealth, 1649 to 1653*. Manchester and Stanford: Stanford University Press, 1997.

Kenyon, J. P. *The Stuart Constitution*. Cambridge: Cambridge University Press, 1966.

Kerber, Linda K. *Women of the Republic: Intellect & Ideology in Revolutionary America*. Chapel Hill: University of North Carolina Press, 1980.

Kerly, Sir Duncan Mackenzie. *An Historical Sketch of the Equitable Jurisdiction of the Court of Chancery*. Cambridge: Cambridge University Press, 1890.

Kewes, Paulina. 'Julius Caesar in Jacobean England'. *The Seventeenth Century* 17 (2002): 155–86.

ed. *The Uses of History in Early Modern England*. San Marino, CA: Huntington Library, 2006.

King, Helen. *The Disease of Virgins: Green Sickness, Chlorosis, and the Problems of Puberty*. London and New York: Routledge, 2004.

Kirby, Ethyn Williams. *William Prynne: A Study in Puritanism*. Cambridge, MA: Harvard University Press, 1931.

Kirby, Kenneth R. 'Milton's Biblical Hermeneutics in *The Doctrine and Discipline of Divorce*'. *Milton Quarterly* 18 (1984): 116–25.

Kishlansky, Mark A. *A Monarchy Transformed: Britain 1603–1714*. London: Allen Lane, Penguin Press, 1996.

'A Whipper Whipped: The Sedition of William Prynne'. *The Historical Journal* 56.3 (2013): 603–27.

Kishlansky, Mark A. and John Morrill. 'Charles I (1600–1649)'. In *The Oxford Dictionary of National Biography*. Oxford: Oxford University Press, 2004, online ed., Oct. 2008, www.oxforddnb.com/view/article/5143.

Kitch, Aaron W. 'Printing Bastards: Monstrous Birth Broadsides in Early Modern England'. In *Printing and Parenting in Early Modern England*, edited by Douglas A. Brooks, 221–36. London: Ashgate, 2005.

Knoppers, Laura Lunger. *Constructing Cromwell: Ceremony, Portrait, and Print, 1645–1661*. Cambridge: Cambridge University Press, 2000.

Politicizing Domesticity from Henrietta Maria to Milton's Eve. Cambridge: Cambridge University Press, 2011.

Kraye, Jill. 'Philologists and Philosophers'. In *The Cambridge Companion to Renaissance Humanism*, 142–60. Cambridge: Cambridge University Press, 1996.

Kristeller, Paul. *Andrea Mantegna*. London, New York, and Bombay: Longmans, Green, 1901.

Kristeller, Paul Oskar. 'Humanism'. In *The Cambridge History of Renaissance Philosophy*, edited by C. B. Schmitt, Quentin Skinner, Eckhard Kessler, and Jill Kraye, 111–38. Cambridge: Cambridge University Press, 1988.

Bibliography

'Humanism and Moral Philosophy'. In *Renaissance Humanism: Foundations, Forms and Legacy*, vol. 3, edited by Albert Rabil, Jr., 271–309. Philadelphia: University of Pennsylvania Press, 1988.

Kupperman, Karen Ordahl. 'Errand to the Indies: Puritan Colonization from Providence Island through the Western Design'. *William and Mary Quarterly*, 3d series, 45.1 (Jan. 1988): 70–99.

Lake, Peter with Michael Questier. *Anti-Christ's Lewd Hat: Protestants, Papists and Players in Post-Reformation England*. New Haven and London: Yale University Press, 2002.

Lake. 'Anti-Popery: The Structure of a Prejudice'. In *Conflict in Early Stuart England*, edited by Richard Cust and Anne Hughes, 72–106. New York: Longman, 1989.

'Constitutional Consensus and Puritan Opposition in the 1620s: Thomas Scott and the Spanish Match', *Historical Journal* 25.4 (1982): 805–25.

'The King (the Queen) and the Jesuit: James Stuart's *True Law of Free Monarchies* in context/s'. In *Transactions of the Royal Historical Society*, vol. 14, 243–61. Cambridge: Cambridge University Press, 2004.

and Steven Pincus eds.. *The Politics of the Public Sphere in Early Modern England*. Manchester: Manchester University Press, 2007.

and Pincus. 'Rethinking the Public Sphere in Early Modern England'. *The Journal of British Studies* 45.2 (Apr. 2006): 270–92.

Lambert, Sheila. 'The Beginning of Printing for the House of Commons, 1640–42'. *The Library* 6, ser III (1981): 43–61.

'The Printers and the Government, 1604–1640.' In *Aspects of Printing from 1600*, eds. Robin Myers and Michael Harris. Oxford: Oxford University Press, 1987.

Lamont, William. *Marginal Prynne*. London: Routledge & Kegan Paul, 1963.

'Prynne, William (1600–1669)'. In *The Oxford Dictionary of National Biography*. Oxford: Oxford University Press, 2004, online ed., May 2011, www.oxforddnb.com/view/article/22854.

Landes, Joan B. *Women and the Public Sphere in the Age of the French Revolution*. Ithaca and London: Cornell University Press, 1988.

Lange, Lynda. 'Woman Is Not a Rational Animal: On Aristotle's Biology of Reproduction'. In *Discovering Reality*, edited by Sandra Harding and Merrill B. Hintikka, 1–15. Dordrecht: Kluwer, 2003.

Larkin, Hilary. *The Making of Englishmen: Debates on National Identity, 1550–1650*. Leiden: Brill, 2014.

Larrére, Catherine. 'Women, Republicanism, and the Growth of Commerce'. In *Republicanism: A Shared European Heritage, volume 2: The Values of Republicanism in Early Modern Europe*, edited by Martin van Gelderen and Quentin Skinner, 139–56. Cambridge: Cambridge University Press, 2002.

Larson, Charles. 'Fairfax's Wood: Marvell and Seventeenth-Century Trees'. *Durham University Journal* 80 (1987): 27–35.

Bibliography

Larson, Jennifer. 'Paul's Masculinity'. *Journal of Biblical Literature* 123.1 (Spring 2004): 85–97.

Lee, Jr., Maurice. *Great Britain's Solomon: James VI and I and His Three Kingdoms.* Urbana: Illinois University Press, 1990.

Legg, Leopold G. Wickham, ed. *English Coronation Records.* Westminster: Archibald Constable, 1901.

Levin, Carole. *Heart and Stomach of a King: Elizabeth I and the Politics of Sex and Power.* 2nd ed. Philadelphia: University of Pennsylvania, 2013.

Levine, Laura. *Men in Women's Clothing: Anti-Theatricality and Effeminization, 1579–1642.* Cambridge: Cambridge Univeraity Press, 1994.

Levy, Leonard Williams. *Origins of the Fifth Amendment: The Right against Self-Incrimination.* New York: Oxford University Press, 1968.

Lewalski, Barbara. 'How Radical was the Young Milton?' In *Milton and Heresy,* edited by Stephen B. Dobranski and John P. Rumrich, 49–72. Cambridge and New York: Cambridge University Press, 1998.

The Life of John Milton: A Critical Biography. Oxford: Blackwell, 2000.

'Milton's Comus and the Politics of Masquing'. In *The Politics of the Stuart Court Masque,* edited by David Bevington and Peter Holbrook, 296–320. Cambridge: Cambridge University Press, 1998.

Lewis, Andrew. '"What Marcellus Says Is against You": Roman law and Common Law'. In *The Roman Law Tradition,* edited by A. D. E. Lewis and D. J. Ibbetson, 199–208. Cambridge: Cambridge University Press, 1994.

Lim, Walter S. H. *The Arts of Empire: The Poetics of Colonialism from Raleigh to Milton.* Newark: University of Delaware Press, 1998.

Lindley, David. *Trials of Frances Howard: Fact and Fiction at the Court of King James.* London: Routledge, 1993.

Lindsay, Alexander. 'Cowley, Abraham (1618–1667)'. In *The Oxford Dictionary of National Biography.* Oxford: Oxford University Press, 2004, online ed., www.oxforddnb.com/view/article/6499.

Lockyer, Roger. *James VI and I.* London and New York: Longman, 1998.

'Villiers, George, First Duke of Buckingham (1592–1628)'. In *The Oxford Dictionary of National Biography.* Oxford: Oxford University Press, 2004, online ed., May 2011, www.oxforddnb.com/view/article/28293.

Longueville, Thomas. *The Life of Sir Kenelm Digby.* London and New York: Longmans, 1896.

Love, Harold. *The Culture and Commerce of Texts: Scribal Publication in Seventeenth-Century England.* Amherst: University of Massachusetts Press, 1993.

Lovett, Frank, 'Republicanism'. In *The Stanford Encyclopedia of Philosophy* (Spring 2017 Edition), edited by Edward N. Zalta. https://plato.stanford.edu/archives/spr2017/entries/republicanism/.

Lowenstein, David. '"Fair Offspring Nurs't in Princely Lore": On the Question of Milton's Early Radicalism'. *Milton Studies* 28 (1992): 37–48.

Milton and the Drama of History: Historical Vision, Iconoclasm, and the Literary Imagination. Cambridge: Cambridge University Press, 1990.

Bibliography

'The Radical Religious Politics of *Paradise Lost*'. In *A New Companion to Milton*, edited by Thomas N. Corns, 376–90. Chichester: Wiley Blackwell, 2016.

'Scriptural Exegesis, Female Prophecy, and Radical Politics in Mary Cary'. *Studies in English Literature* 46.1 (Winter 2006): 133–53.

Lowndes, William Thomas and Henry G. Bohn, *The bibliographer's manual of English literature*. 2nd vol. London: Bell & Daddy, 1871.

Lynch, Michael. 'Queen Mary's Triumph: The Baptismal Celebrations at Stirling in December 1566'. *Scottish Historical Review* 69 (1990): 1–12.

Mack, Peter. *Elizabethan Rhetoric: Theory and Practice*. Cambridge: Cambridge University Press, 2004.

MacKenzie, W. Roy. *The English Moralities from the Point of View of Allegory*. New York: Haskell, 1970.

Mahlberg, Gaby. 'Patriarchalism and Monarchical Republicans'. In *Monarchism and Absolutism in Early Modern Europe*, edited by Cesare Cuttica and Glenn Burgess, 47–60. London: Pickering & Chatto, 2012.

Makalachki, Jodi. *The Legacy of Boadicea: Gender and Nation in Early Modern England*. London and New York: Routledge, 1998.

Manley, Lawrence. 'Scripts for the Pageant: the Ceremonies of London'. In *Literature and Culture in Early Modern London*, 212–93. Cambridge and New York: Cambridge University Press, 1995.

Marcus, Leah Sinanoglou. 'The Milieu of Milton's *Comus*: Judicial Reform at Ludlow and the Problem of Sexual Assault'. *Criticism* 25 (1983): 293–327.

The Politics of Mirth: Jonson, Herrick, Milton, Marvell, and the Defense of Old Holiday Pastimes. Chicago: Chicago University Press, 1986.

Puzzling Shakespeare: Local Reading and Its Discontents. Berkeley: University of California Press, 1988.

Marshall, John. *John Locke, Toleration and Early Enlightenment Culture: Religious Intolerance and Arguments for Religious Toleration in Early Modern and 'Early Enlightenment' Europe*. Cambridge: Cambridge University Press, 2006.

Martin, Catherine Gimelli, ed.. *Milton and Gender*. Cambridge: Cambridge University Press, 2004.

Maza, Sarah. *Private Lives and Public Affairs: The Cause Célèbres of Prerevolutionary France*. Berkeley: University of California Press, 1993.

McConica, James. 'Humanism and Aristotle in Tudor Oxford'. *The English Historical Review* 94.371 (Apr. 1979): 291–317.

McDonnell, Myles. *Roman Manliness: Virtus and the Roman Republic*. Cambridge: Cambridge University Press, 2006.

'Roman Men and Greek Virtue'. In *Andreia: Studies in Manliness and Courage in Classical Antiquity*, edited by Ralph M. Rosen and Ineke Sluiter, 235–61. Leiden: Brill, 2003.

McDowell, Nicholas. 'The Caroline Court'. In *Milton in Context*, edited by Stephen B. Dobranski, 237–47. Cambridge: Cambridge University Press, 2010.

Bibliography 401

McLaren, A. N. *Political Culture in the Reign of Elizabeth I: Queen and Commonwealth, 1558–1585*. Cambridge: Cambridge University Press, 1999.

McRae, Andrew. *Literature, Satire, and the Early Stuart State*. Cambridge: Cambridge University Press, 2004.

Miller, Henry Knight. 'The Paradoxical Encomium with Special Reference to Its Vogue in England, 1600–1800'. *Modern Philology* 53.3 (Feb. 1956): 145–78.

Millstone, Noah. *Manuscript Circulation and the Invention of Politics in Early Stuart England*. Cambridge: Cambridge University Press, 2016.

Milner, Andrew. *John Milton and the English Revolution: A Study in the Sociology of Literature*. Totowa, NJ: Barnes & Noble, 1981.

Milton, Antony. 'Licensing, Censorship, and Religious Orthodoxy in Early Stuart England'. *Historical Journal* 41 (1998): 625–51.

Morrill, John. 'Cromwell, Oliver (1599–1658)'. In *The Oxford Dictionary of National Biography*. Oxford: Oxford University Press, 2004, online ed., May 2008, www.oxforddnb.com/view/article/6765.

The Nature of the English Revolution. New York: Routledge, 2013.

'Revisionism's Wounded Legacies'. *Huntington Library Quarterly* 78.4 (Winter 2015): 577–94.

The Revolt of the Provinces. London: George Allen and Unwin, 1976.

Murphy, Erin. *Familial Forms: Politics and Genealogy in Seventeenth-Century English Literature*. Plymouth: University of Delaware, 2011.

Nadel, George H. 'Philosophy of History before Historicism'. *History and Theory* 3.3 (1964): 291–315.

Neill, Michael. *Putting History to the Question: Power, Politics, and Society in English Renaissance Drama*. New York: Columbia University Press, 2000.

Nelson, Eric. *The Greek Tradition in Republican Thought*. Cambridge: Cambridge University Press, 2004.

The Hebrew Republic: Jewish Sources and the Transformation of European Political Thought. Cambridge, MA: Harvard University Press, 2011.

Newell, Waller R. *Tyranny: A New Interpretation*. Cambridge: Cambridge University Press, 2013.

Ng, Su Fang. *Literature and the Politics of Family in Seventeenth-Century England*. Cambridge: Cambridge University Press, 2007.

Nichols, John. *The Progresses, Processions and Magnificent Festivities of King James the First, His Royal Consort, Family, and Court*, vol. II. London: J. B. Nichols, 1828.

Norbrook, David. 'May, Thomas (b. in or after 1596, d. 1650)'. In *The Oxford Dictionary of National Biography*. Oxford: Oxford University Press, 2004, online ed. Jan. 2008, www.oxforddnb.com/view/article/18423.

Poetry and Politics in the English Renaissance. Oxford and New York: Oxford University Press, 2002.

Writing the English Republic: Poetry, Rhetoric and Politics, 1627–1660. Cambridge: Cambridge University Press, 1999.

Nussbaum, Martha C. 'Duties of Justice, Duties of Material Aid: Cicero's Problematic Legacy'. *Journal of Political Philosophy* 8.2 (Jun. 2000): 10–17.

Nyquist, Mary. *Arbritrary Rule: Slavery, Tyranny, and the Power of Life and Death.* Chicago: University of Chicago Press, 2013.

'The Genesis of Gendered Subjectivity in the Divorce Tracts and *Paradise Lost*'. In *Re-membering Milton: Essays on the Texts and Traditions*, edited by Nyquist and Margaret W. Ferguson, 99–127. New York: Methuen, 1987.

O'Callaghan, Michelle. '"Talking Politics": Tyranny, Parliament, and Christopher Brooke's the Ghost of Richard the Third (1614)'. *The Historical Journal* 41.1 (Mar., 1998): 97–120.

Ollard, Richard. *The Image of the King: Charles I and Charles II.* London: Phoenix Press, 2000.

Orgel, Stephen. *The Illusion of Power: Political Theater in the English Renaissance.* Berkeley and Los Angeles: University of California Press, 1975.

James I and the Politics of Literature: Jonson, Shakespeare, Donne, and their Contemporaries. Baltimore: Johns Hopkins University Press, 1983.

'Nobody's Perfect: Or Why Did the English Stage Take Boys for Women?' In *Displacing Homophobia: Gay Male Perspectives in Literature and Culture*, edited by Ronald R. Butters, 7–30. Durham, NC: Duke University Press, 1989.

Osmond, Patricia J. 'Edmund Bolton's Vindication of Tiberius Caesar: A "Lost" Manuscript Comes to Light'. *International Journal of the Classical Tradition* 11.3 (Winter 2005): 329–43.

Park, Katharine. *Secrets of Women: Gender, Generation, and the Origins of Human Dissection.* New York: Zone Books, 2006.

Parker, Barbara. *Plato's Republic and Shakespeare's Rome: A Political Study of the Roman Works.* Cranbury, NJ: Rosemont, 2004.

Paster, Gail Kern. *The Body Embarrassed: Drama and the Disciplines of Shame in Early Modern England.* Ithaca: Cornell University Press, 1993.

Pateman, Carole. *The Sexual Contract.* Oxford: Polity Press, 1988.

Patrides, C. A. '"The greatest of the kingly race": The Death of Henry Stuart'. *The Historian* 47 (1985): 402–8.

Patterson, Annabel M. *Censorship and Interpretation: The Conditions of Writing and Reading in Early Modern England.* Madison: University of Wisconsin Press, 1984.

'"Forc'd Fingers": Milton's Early Poems and Ideological Constraint'. In *'The Muses Common-weale': Poetry and Politics in the Seventeenth Century*, edited by Claude J. Summers and Ted-Larry Pebworth, 9–22. Columbia: University of Missouri Press, 1988.

'"Roman-Cast Similitude": Ben Jonson and the English Use of Roman History'. In *Rome in the Renaissance: The City and the Myth*, edited by P. A. Ramsey, 381–94. Binghamton, Center for Medieval and Early Renaissance Studies, 1982.

Patterson, W. B. *James VI and I and the Reunion of Christendom.* Cambridge: Cambridge University Press, 1997.

Bibliography

Peacey, Jason. 'Fisher, Payne (1615/16–1693)'. In *The Oxford Dictionary of National Biography*. Oxford: Oxford University Press, 2004, online ed., Jan. 2008, www.oxforddnb.com/view/article/9506.

Print and Public Politics in the English Revolution. Cambridge: Cambridge University Press, 2013.

Peacock, John. 'The Image of Charles I as a Roman emperor'. In *The 1630s: Interdisciplinary Essays on Culture and Politics in the Caroline Era*, edited by Ian Atherton and Julie Sanders, 50–73. Manchester and New York: Manchester University Press, 2006.

Peck, Linda Levy. '"For a King Not To Be Bountiful Were a Fault": Perspectives on Court Patronage in Early Stuart England'. *Journal of British Studies* 25.1 (1986): 31–61.

The Mental World of the Jacobean Court. Cambridge: Cambridge University Press, 1991.

Peltonen, Markku. *Classical Humanism and Republicanism in English Political Thought, 1570–1640*. Cambridge: Cambridge University Press, 1995.

Perry, Curtis. *Literature and Favoritism in Early Modern England*. Cambridge: Cambridge University Press, 2006.

The Making of Jacobean Culture: James I and the Renegotiation of Elizabethan Literary Practice. Cambridge: Cambridge University Press, 1997.

'The Politics of Access and Representations of the Sodomite King in Early Modern England'. *Renaissance Quarterly* 53.4 (2000): 1075–77.

'Royal Authorship and Problems of Manuscript Attribution in the Poems of King James VI & I'. *Notes & Queries* 46.2 (1999): 243–46.

Pestana, Carla Gardina. *The Atlantic in an Age of Revolution, 1640–1661*. Cambridge, MA: Harvard University Press, 2004.

The English Conquest of Jamaica: Oliver Cromwell's Bid for Empire. Cambridge, MA and London: Belknap Press, 2017.

Peters, Andrew. *Ship Decoration: 1630–1780*. Barnsley: Seaforth, 2013.

Peters, Edward. *Inquisition*. Berkeley and Los Angeles: University of California Press, 1989.

Pettit, Philip H. *Equity and the Law of Trusts*. 11th ed. Oxford: Oxford University Press, 2009.

Republicanism: A Theory of Freedom and Government. Oxford: Clarendon Press, 1997.

Picciotto, Joanna. *Labors of Innocence in Early Modern England*. Cambridge, MA: Harvard University Press, 2010.

Pitkin, Hanna. *Fortune is a Woman: Gender & Politics in the Thought of Niccolò Machiavelli*. Chicago: University of Chicago Press, 1984.

Pocock, J. G. A. *The Ancient Constitution and the Feudal Law: A Study of English Historical Thought in the Seventeenth Century*. Cambridge: Cambridge University Press, 1957 and 1987.

'Introduction'. In *Political Works of James Harrington*. Cambridge: Cambridge University Press, 1977.

The Machiavellian Moment: Florentine Political Thought and the Atlantic Republican Tradition. Princeton and London: Princeton University Press, 1975.

404   Bibliography

Political Thought and History: Essays on Theory and Method. Cambridge: Cambridge University Press, 2008.

Politics, Language and Time: Essays on Political Thought and History. Chicago: University of Chicago Press, 1989.

'Thomas May and the Narrative of Civil War'. In *Writing and Political Engagement in Seventeenth-Century England*, edited by Derek Hirst and Richard Strier, 112–44. Cambridge: Cambridge University Press, 1999.

Pollnitz, Aysha. *Princely Education in Early Modern Britain*. Cambridge: Cambridge University Press, 2015.

Portal, Ethel M. 'The Academ Roial of King James I'. *Proceedings of the British Academy* (1915–16): 189–208.

Purkiss, Diane. *Literature, Gender and Politics during the English Civil War*. Cambridge: Cambridge University Press, 2010.

'Whose Liberty? The Rhetoric of Milton's Divorce Tracts'. In *The Oxford Handbook of Milton*, edited by Nicholas McDowell and Nigel Smith, 186–99. Oxford: Oxford University Press, 2011.

Pursell, Brennan C. 'James I, Gondomar, and the Dissolution of the Parliament of 1621'. *History* 85.279 (Jul. 2000): 428–45.

Questier, Michael. *Catholicism and Community in Early Modern England*. Cambridge: Cambridge University Press, 2006.

Quint, David. *Epic and Empire: Politics and Generic Form from Virgil to Milton*. Princeton: Princeton University Press, 1993.

Raab, Felix. *The English Face of Machiavelli*. London: Routledge and Kegan Paul, 1964.

Raffield, Paul. *Images and Cultures of Law in Early Modern England: Justice and Political Power, 1558–1660*. Cambridge: Cambridge University Press, 2004.

Rahe, Paul A. *Against Throne and Altar: Machiavelli and Political Theory under the English Republic*. Cambridge: Cambridge University Press, 2008.

'The Classical Republicanism of John Milton'. *History of Political Thought* 25.2 (Summer 2004): 243–75.

Ramsay, Lee C. 'The Sentence of It Sooth: Chaucer's "Physician's Tale"'. *The Chaucer Review* 6.3 (Winter 1972): 185–97.

Raylor, Timothy. 'Waller's Machiavellian Cromwell: The Imperial Argument of *A Panegyrick to My Lord Protector*'. *Review of English Studies*, 56 (2005): 386–411.

Raymond, Joad. 'Complications of Interest: Milton, Scotland, Ireland, and National Identity in 1649'. *The Review of English Studies* 55.220 (Jun. 2004): 315–45.

'An Inky Wretch: The Outrageous Genius of Marchamont Nedham'. *The National Interest* 70 (Winter 2002/03): 55–64.

The Invention of the Newspaper: English Newsbooks 1641–1649. Oxford: Clarendon, 1996.

'"A Mercury with a Winged Conscience": Marchamont Nedham, Monopoly, and Censorship'. *Media History* 4:1 (2009): 7–18.

Bibliography

'Nedham, Marchamont (*bap.* 1620, *d.* 1678)'. *Oxford Dictionary of National Biography*. Oxford: Oxford University Press, 2004; online ed., Sept. 2015 [www.oxforddnb.com/view/article/19847]

Reese, Christine Noelle. *Controlling Print? Burton, Bastwick and Prynne and the Politics of Memory*. PhD diss., Pennsylvania State University, 2007.

Reeser, Todd W. *Moderating Masculinity in Early Modern Culture*. Chapel Hill: North Caroline studies in the Roman Languages and Literatures, 2006.

Reeve, L. J. *Charles I and the Road to Personal Rule*. New York and Cambridge: Cambridge University Press, 1989.

Revard, Stella P. *Milton and the Tangles of Neaera's Hair: The Making of the 1645 Poems*. Columbia: University of Missouri Press, 1997.

Richardson, J. S. 'Imperium Romanum: Empire and the Language of Power'. *The Journal of Roman Studies* 81 (1991): 1–9.

Richek, Roslyn. 'Thomas Randolph's *Salting* (1628), Its Text and John Milton's *Sixth Prolusion* as Another *Salting*'. *English Literary Renaissance* 12.1 (Winter 1982): 107–8.

Rimbault, Edward F. 'William Basse and His Poems'. *Notes & Queries* 17 (Feb. 23, 1850): 265–66.

Ripley, John. *Julius Caesar on Stage in England and America, 1599–1973*. Cambridge: Cambridge University Press, 1980.

Ristine, Frank Humphrey. *English Tragicomedy: Its Origin and History*. New York: Columbia University Press, 1910.

Robbins, Caroline. *The Eighteenth-Century Commonwealthman*. New York: Antheneum, 1968.

Roberts, Sasha. *Reading Shakespeare's Poems in Early Modern England*. London: Palgrave Macmillan, 2003.

Robinson, Philip. 'Multiple Meanings of Troy in Early Modern London's Mayoral Show'. *Seventeenth Century* 26.2 (Oct. 2011): 221–39.

Rogers, John. *The Matter of Revolution: Science, Poetry, and Politics in the Age of Milton*. Ithaca: Cornell University Press, 1996.

Romack, Katherine. *Women and the Poetics of Dissent in the English Revolution*. London: Taylor & Francis, 2016.

Roper, Lyndal. *The Holy Household: Women and Morals in Reformation Augsburg*. Oxford: Clarendon Press, 1989.

Russell, Conrad. *Crisis of Parliaments: English History 1509–1660*. Oxford: Oxford University Press, 1971.

    ed. *The Origins of the English Civil War*. Basingstoke: Macmillan, 1973.

    'Parliamentary History in Perspective, 1604–1629'. *History* 61 (1976): 1–27.

    Parliaments and English Politics, 1621–1629. Oxford: Oxford University Press, 1979.

Salmon, J. H. M. *Renaissance and Revolt: Essays in the Intellectual and Social History of Early Modern France*. Cambridge: Cambridge University Press, 2003.

406 Bibliography

'Seneca and Tacitus in Jacobean England'. In *The Mental World of the Jacobean Court*, edited by Linda Levy Peck, 169–88. Cambridge: Cambridge University Press, 1991.

'Stoicism and Roman Example: Seneca and Tacitus in Jacobean England'. *Journal of the History of Ideas* 50.2 (Apr.–Jun. 1989): 199–225.

Salmon, Marylynn. 'The Cultural Significance of Breastfeeding and Infant Care in Early Modern England and America'. *Journal of Social History* 28.2 (Winter, 1994): 247–69.

Samuel, Irene. *Plato and Milton*. Ithaca, NY: Cornell University Press, 1965.

Saslow, James M. *Ganymede in the Renaissance*. New Haven: Yale University Press, 1986.

Schama, Simon. *The Embarrassment of Riches: An Interpretation of Dutch Culture in the Golden Age*. Berkeley and Los Angeles: University of California Press, 1988.

Schmitt, Charles B. 'Towards a Reassessment of Renaissance Aristotelianism'. *History of Science* 11 (1973): 159–93.

Schochet, Gordon J. *Patriarchalism in Political Thought: The Authoritarian Family and Political Speculation and Attitudes Especially in Seventeenth-Century England*. New York: Basic Books, 1975.

Schoell, Franck L. *Etudes Sur L'humanisme Continental En Angleterre À La Fin De La Renaissance*. Paris: Honoré Champion, 1926.

Schoenfeldt, Michael Carl. *Bodies and Selves in Early Modern England*. Cambridge: Cambridge University Press, 1999.

Schwoerer, Lois F. *'No Standing Armies!' The Antiarmy Ideology in Seventeenth-Century England*. Baltimore: Johns Hopkins University Press, 1974.

Scott, Alison V. *Literature and the Idea of Luxury in Early Modern England*. London and New York: Routledge, 2016.

Scott, Joan Wallach. *Gender and the Politics of History*. rev. ed. New York: Columbia University Press, 1999.

Scott, Jonathan. 'Classical Republicanism in Seventeenth-Century England and the Netherlands'. In *Republicanism: A Shared European Heritage, Volume 1: Republicanism and Constitutionalism in Early Modern Europe*, edited by Martin van Gelderen and Quentin Skinner, 61–84. Cambridge: Cambridge University Press, 2002.

Commonwealth Principles: Republican Writing of the English Revolution. Cambridge: Cambridge University Press, 2004.

England's Troubles: Seventeenth-Century English Political Instability in European Context. Cambridge: Cambridge University Press, 2000.

Seipp, D. J. 'Roman Legal Categories in the Early Common Law'. In *Legal Records and Historical Reality*, edited by T. G. Watkin, 9–36. London and Ronceverte: Hambledon, 1989.

Selden, Raman. *English Verse Satire, 1590–1765*. London: George Allen & Unwin, 1978.

Sensabaugh, George F. *That Grand Whig Milton*. Stanford: Stanford University Press, 1952.

Bibliography

Sharpe, Kevin. 'A Commonwealth of Meanings: Languages, Analogues, Ideas and Politics'. In *Politics & Ideas in Early Stuart England*, 3–71. London and New York: Pinter, 1989.

Criticism and Compliments: The Politics of Literature in the England of Charles I. Cambridge: Cambridge University Press, 1987.

'"An Image Doting Rabble": The Failure of Republican Culture in Seventeenth-Century England'. In *Refiguring Revolutions: Aesthetics and Politics from the English Revolution to the Romantic Revolution*, edited by Sharpe and Steven N. Zwicker, 25–56. Berkeley: University of California Press, 1998.

Image Wars: Promoting Kings and Commonwealths in England, 1603–1660. New Haven and London: Yale University Press, 2010.

The Personal Rule of Charles I. London and New Haven: Yale University Press, 1992.

Shepard, Alexandra. *Meanings of Manhood in Early Modern England*. Oxford: Oxford University Press, 2003.

Shohet, Lauren. *Reading Masques: The English Masque and Public Culture in the Seventeenth Century*. Oxford: Oxford University Press, 2010.

Shuger, Debora. *Censorship and Cultural Sensibility: The Regulation of Language in Tudor-Stuart England*. Philadelphia: University of Pennsylvania Press, 2006.

Shullenberger, William. *Lady in the Labyrinth: Milton's Comus as Initiation*. Madison, NJ: Fairleigh Dickinson University Press, 2008.

Skinner, Quentin. *The Foundations of Modern Political Thought*, 2 vols. Cambridge: Cambridge University Press, 1978.

From Humanism to Hobbes: Studies in Rhetoric and Politics. Cambridge: Cambridge University Press, 2018.

Liberty before Liberalism. Cambridge: Cambridge University Press, 1998.

Reason and Rhetoric in the Philosophy of Hobbes. Cambridge: Cambridge University Press, 1996.

'Rethinking Political Liberty'. *History Workshop Journal* 61 (2006): 156–70.

'A Third Concept of Liberty'. *Proceedings of the British Academy* 117 (2002): 237–68.

Visions of Politics. 3 vols. Cambridge: Cambridge University Press 2002.

Sloan, LaRue Love. '"I'll Watch Him Tame, and Talk Him Out of Patience": The Curtain Lecture and Shakespeare's *Othello*'. In *Oral Traditions and Gender in Early Modern Literary Texts*, edited by Mary Ellen Lamb and Karen Bamford, 85–100. Burlington, VT: Ashgate Publishing, 2008.

Smiles, Sam. 'John White and British Antiquity: Savage Origins in the Context of Tudor Historiography'. In *European Visions, American Voices*, edited by Kim Sloane, 106–12. London: British Museum Research Publication 2009.

Smith, Bruce R. *Homosexual Desire in Shakespeare's England*. Chicago: Chicago University Press, 1991.

Shakespeare and Masculinity. Oxford: Oxford University Press, 2000.

Smith, Hilda. *All Men and Both Sexes: Gender, Politics, and the False Universal in England, 1640–1832*. Cambridge: Cambridge University Press, 2005.

408 *Bibliography*

Smith, Nigel. *Literature and Revolution in England, 1640–1660*. New Haven and London: Yale University Press, 1994.

'Popular Republicanism in the 1650s: John Streater's 'Heroick Mechanicks'. In *Milton and Republicanism*, edited by David Armitage, Armand Himy, and Quentin Skinner, 137–55. Cambridge: Cambridge University Press, 1995.

Smuts, Malcolm. 'Court-Centred Politics and the Uses of Roman Historians, *c.*1590–1630'. In *Culture and Politics in Early Stuart England*, edited by Kevin Sharpe and Peter Lake, 21–44. Stanford: Stanford University Press, 1993.

Court Culture and the Origins of a Royalist Tradition in Early Stuart England. Philadelphia: University of Pennsylvania Press, 1987.

Culture and Power in England, 1585–1685. Basingstoke: Palgrave Macmillan, 1999.

'The Making of *Rex Pacificus*: James VI and I and the Problem of Peace in an Age of Religious War'. In *Royal Subjects: Essays on the Writings of James VI and I*, edited by Daniel Fischlin and Mark Fortier, 371–88. Detroit: Wayne State University Press, 2002.

Solt, Leo E. *Church and State in Early Modern England, 1509–1640*. Oxford: Oxford University Press, 1990.

Sommerville, J. P. 'Absolutism and Royalism'. In *The Cambridge History of Political Thought, 1450–1700*, edited by J. H. Burns, 347–73. New York and Cambridge: Cambridge University Press, 1991.

Politics and Ideology in England, 1603–1640. London and New York: Longman, 1986.

Sommerville, Margaret R. *Sex & Subjection: Attitudes to Women in Early Modern Society*. London and New York: Arnold, 1995.

Stacey, Peter. *Roman Monarchy and the Renaissance Prince*. Cambridge: Cambridge University Press, 2007.

Stallybrass, Peter. 'Patriarchal Territories: The Body Enclosed'. In *Rewriting the Renaissance: The Discourses of Sexual Difference in Early Modern Europe*, edited by Margaret Ferguson, Maureen Quilligan, and Nancy J. Vickers, 123–42. Chicago: Chicago University Press, 1986.

Steppat, Michael Payne. 'John Webster's *Appius and Virginia*'. *American Notes and Queries* 20, issue 7/8 (1982): 101.

Stone, Lawrence. *The Causes of the English Revolution, 1529–1642*. London: ARK, 1972.

Family, Sex and Marriage in England, 1500–1800. London: Harper & Row, 1977.

Strong, Roy. *Cult of Elizabeth: Elizabethan Portraiture and Pageantry*. Wallop, Hampshire: Thames and Hudson, 1977.

Henry, Prince of Wales, and England's lost Renaissance. New York: Thames and Hudson, 1986.

Van Dyck, Charles I on Horseback. London: Allen Lane, 1972.

Streufert, Paul D. and Jonathan Walker, eds. *Early Modern Academic Drama*. New York: Routledge, 2016.

Bibliography 409

Sullivan, Vickie B. *Machiavelli, Hobbes, and the Formation of a Liberal Republicanism in England.* Cambridge: Cambridge University Press, 2006.

Sutton, James M. 'Henry Frederick, Prince of Wales (1594–1612)'. In *The Oxford Dictionary of National Biography.* Oxford: Oxford University Press, 2004, online ed., Jan. 2008, www.oxforddnb.com/view/article/12961.

Tenney, Mary F. 'Tacitus in the Politics of Early Stuart England'. *The Classical Journal* 37.3 (Dec. 1941): 151–63.

Thomas, Keith. 'The Puritans and Adultery: The Act of 1650 Reconsidered'. In *Puritans and Revolutionaries: Essays in Seventeenth-Century History Presented to Christopher Hill,* edited by Donald Pennington and Keith Thomas, 257–81. Oxford: Oxford University Press, 1978.

Thompson, Claude A. 'The *Doctrine and Discipline of Divorce, 1643–45*: A Biographical Study'. *Transactions of the Cambridge Bibliographical Society* 7.1 (1977): 74–93.

Thompson, Sharon, Lydia Hayes, Daniel Newman, and Carole Pateman. '*The Sexual Contract* 30 Years on: A Conversation with Carole Pateman'. *Feminist Legal Studies* 26.1 (Apr. 2018): 93–104.

Tosh, John. 'What Should Historians Do with Masculinity? Reflections on Nineteenth-Century Britain'. *History Workshop Journal* 38 (1994): 179–202.

Tuck, Richard. 'Humanism and Political Thought'. In *The Impact of Humanism on Western Europe during the Renaissance,* edited by A. Goodman and Angus Mackay, 43–65. London and New York: Routledge, 1990.

Natural Rights Theories: Their Origin and Development. Cambridge: Cambridge University Press, 1979.

Philosophy and Government, 1572–1651. Cambridge: Cambridge University Press, 1993.

Turner, James Grantham. *One Flesh: Paradisal Marriage and Sexual Relations in the Age of Milton.* Oxford: Clarendon Press, 1987.

Tvordi, Jessica. 'The Comic Personas of Milton's *Prolusion VI*: Negotiating Masculine Identity Through Self-Directed Humor'. In *Laughter in the Middle Ages and Early Modern Times,* edited by Albrecht Classen, 715–34. Berlin: Walter de Gruyter, 2010.

Underdown, David. 'The Taming of the Scold: The Enforcement of Patriarchal Authority in Early Modern England'. In *Order and Disorder in Early Modern England,* edited by Anthony Fletcher and John Stevenson, 116–36. Cambridge: Cambridge University Press, 1985.

Vega, Judith A. 'Feminst Republicanism and the Political Perception of Gender'. In *Republicanism: A Shared European Heritage, Volume 2: The Values of Republicanism in Early Modern Europe,* edited by Martin van Gelderen and Quentin Skinner, 157–75. Cambridge: Cambridge University Press, 2002.

Vickers, Brian. 'Rhetoric and Poetics.' In *The Cambridge History of Renaissance Philosophy,* edited by C. B. Schmitt, Quentin Skinner, Eckhard Kessler, and Jill Kraye, 713–45. Cambridge: Cambridge University Press, 1988.

Bibliography

Viroli, Maurizio. *Machiavelli*. Oxford: Oxford University Press, 1998.

From Politics to Reason of State: The Acquisition and Transformation of the Language of Politics, 1250–1600. Cambridge: Cambridge University Press, 1992.

Republicanism. Translated by Antony Shugaar. New York: Hill and Wang, 2002.

Walker, Garthine. *Crime, Gender and the Social Order in Early Modern England*. Cambridge: Cambridge University Press, 2003.

Walker, Julia, ed. *Dissing Elizabeth: Negative Representations of Gloriana*. Durham: Duke University Press, 2004.

ed. *Milton and the Idea of Woman*. Urbana-Champagne: University of Illinois Press, 1988.

Wedgwood, C. V. *The King's War, 1641–47*. London: Collins, 1959.

Weil, Rachel. *Political Passions: Gender, the Family and Political Argument in England, 1680–1714*. Manchester: Manchester University Press, 1999.

Wells, Robin Headlam. *Shakespeare on Masculinity*. Cambridge: Cambridge University Press, 2004.

Spenser's Faerie Queen and the Cult of Elizabeth. Totowa, NJ: Barnes and Noble, 1983.

Weston, Corinne C. 'England: Ancient Constitution and Common Law'. In *The Cambridge History of Political Thought, 1450–1700*, edited by J. H. Burns with the assistance of Mark Goldie, 374–411. Cambridge: Cambridge University Press, 1991.

White, Michelle Anne. *Henrietta Maria and the English Civil Wars*. Burlington: Ashgate, 2006.

'"She is the Man, and Raignes": Popular Representations of Henrietta Maria during the English Civil Wars'. In *Queens & Power in Medieval and Early Modern England*, edited by Carole Levin and Robert Bucholz, 205–23. Lincoln: University of Nebraska Press, 2009.

Whiting, Amanda Jane. *Women and Petitioning in the Seventeenth-century English Revolution: Deference, Difference, and Dissent*. Late Medieval and Early Modern Studies 25. Turnhout: Brepols, 2015.

Wittreich, Joseph. *Feminist Milton*. Ithaca: Cornell University Press, 1988.

Williams, Craig A. *Roman Homosexuality: Ideologies of Masculinity in Classical Antiquity*. Oxford: Oxford University Press, 1999.

Williams, Gordon, ed. *A Dictionary of Sexual Language and Imagery in Shakespearean and Stuart Literature*. London: Athlone, 1994.

Williamson, Jerry Wayne. *The Myth of the Conqueror: Prince Henry Stuart, a Study in Seventeenth Century Personation*. New York: AMS Press, 1978.

Wilson, Elkin Calhoun. *England's Eliza*. Cambridge, MA: Harvard University Press, 1939.

Wiltenburg, Joy. *Disorderly Women and Female Power in the Street Literature of Early Modern England and Germany*. Charlottesville: University Press of Virginia, 1992.

Bibliography

411

Wood, Jeremy. 'Gerbier, Sir Balthazar (1592–1663/1667)'. In *The Oxford Dictionary of National Biography*. Oxford: Oxford University Press, 2004, online ed., Jan. 2008, www.oxforddnb.com/view/article/10562.

'Van Dyck's 'Cabinet de Titien': The Contents and Dispersal of His Collection'. *The Burlington Magazine* 132.1052 (Oct. 1990): 680–95.

Wood, Neal. *Cicero's Social and Political Thought*. Berkeley: University of California Press, 1991.

Woolf, Daniel. 'Bolton, Edmund Mary (b. 1574/5, d. in or after 1634)'. In *The Oxford Dictionary of National Biography*. Oxford: Oxford University Press, 2004) online ed. Jan. 2008, www.oxforddnb.com/view/article/2800.

'From Hystories to the Historical: Five Transitions in Thinking about the Past, 1500–1700'. In *The Uses of History in Early Modern England*, edited by Paulina Kewes, 31–68. San Marino, CA: Huntington Library, 2006.

'Genre into Artifact: The Decline of the English Chronicle in the Sixteenth Century'. *The Sixteenth Century Journal* 19.3 (Autumn 1988): 321–54.

The Idea of History in Early Stuart England: Erudition, Ideology, and the 'Light of Truth' from the Accession of James I to the Civil War. Toronto: University of Toronto, 1990.

Wootton, David, ed. *Republicanism, Liberty, and Commercial Society, 1649–1776*. Stanford: Stanford University Press, 1994.

Worden, Blair. *God's Instruments: Political Conduct in the England of Oliver Cromwell*. New York and Oxford: Oxford University Press, 2012.

Literature and Politics in Cromwellian England: John Milton, Andrew Marvell, Marchamont Nedham. Oxford: Oxford University Press, 2007.

'Milton's Republicanism and the Tyranny of Heaven'. In *Machiavelli and Republicanism*, edited by Gisela Bock, Quentin Skinner, and Maurizio Viroli, 225–46. Cambridge: Cambridge University Press, 1991.

'Oliver Cromwell and the sin of Achan'. In *History, Society, and the Churches*, edited by Derek Beales and Geoffrey Best, 125–46. Cambridge: Cambridge University Press, 1985.

Republicanism, Liberty, and Commercial Society, 1649–1776, edited by David Wootton. Stanford: Stanford University Press, 1994.

'Republicanism, Regicide and Republic: The English Experience'. In *Republicanism: A Shared European Heritage, volume 1: Republicanism and Constitutionalism in Early Modern Europe*, edited by Martin van Gelderen and Quentin Skinner, 307–27. Cambridge: Cambridge University Press, 2002.

The Sound of Virtue: Philip Sidney's Arcadia *and Elizabethan Politics*. New Haven: Yale University Press, 1996.

Wordsworth, C., ed. *The Manner of the Coronation of King Charles I*. London: Harrison and Sons, 1892.

Yates, Frances. *Astraea: The Imperial Theme in the Sixteenth Century*. London: Routledge and Kegan Paul, 1975.

Young, Michael B. *James VI and I and the History of Homosexuality*. Basingstoke: Macmillan, 2000.

Zagorin, Perez. *A History of Political Thought in the English Revolution*. London: Routledge & Kegan Paul, 1954.

Zaller, Robert. *The Discourse of Legitimacy in Early Modern England*. Stanford: Stanford University Press, 2007.

"'Interest of State": James I and the Palatinate'. *Albion* 6.2 (Summer, 1974): 144–75.

Zaret, David. *Origins of Democratic Culture: Printing, Petitions, and the Public Sphere in Early Modern England*. Princeton, NJ: Princeton University Press, 2000.

Index

Page references in *italics* indicate illustrations. Titles of works have been abbreviated where necessary, following the form used in the text.

Abbot, George, 139–40
absolutism, 37–39, 51, 69, 163, 195
   defence of, 110–12, 144–45
actors, 163, 202–4
adolescence, 150, 237, 288
adulatio (flattery), 44–45, 191
adultery, 126–27, 146, 193, 328
Adultery Act (1650), 328–29
adulthood, 32, 150, 288
age
   maturity, 32, 150, 288
   youth, 150, 237, 288
Agrippina. *See* Julia Agrippina
Albanactus, 161
Alleine, Richard, 111
ambition, 303, 330, 333, 336
andreia [ἀνδρεία] (martial courage), 46, 225
Anne of Denmark, Queen Consort, *359*
'Answer to the Storm, An', 341–42
anti-Catholicism, 132–34, 182–83, 240–43, 255–61
   imperialism, motivation for, 298
   and the Irish, 308–9
   and Spain, 118, 170
Anton, Robert, 79
Appius Claudius. *See* Claudius, Appius
aretê [ἀρετή] (character excellence), 46, 288
Aristotle, 4–5, 24, 46, 97, 236, 285
   Politics, 41, 170–71
armies, 292–93, 315–16
Arminianism, 176
Armitage, David, 101, 304
arms, bearing of, 292–93
assassination, 182, 193
Attila the Hun, 351
Augustus (Caesar Augustus), 21, 122–23, 313, 339–40

authority
   and class, 32–33
   household, 229
   monarchical, 120
   parliamentary, 38
   patriarchal, 52–53
   women, subordinate to, 233
autonomy, 8, 38
avarice, 303, 336

Bacon, Sir Francis, 89
barbarity, 263–64
Barkstead, William, 81
Barston, John, 32
Basse, William, 81
Bastwick, John, 211, 214–18
   The answer of John Bastwick, 214
   Independency not Gods ordinance, 215
   trial of, 208–10, 212–14
beauty, 244
Bellany, Alastair, 39, 132–33, 184
Bernard, Richard, 111
Bertheau, Gilles, 163, 167
bestialisation, 243, 272, 343
   of slaves, 234–35, 284–86
   of tyrants, 41, 43–44, 195
   of women, 284
birth, 147–48, 259
blood, 155, 350–52
blood guilt, 351–52
bloodlust, 343, 345, 349–51
bodies. *See also* hair
   breasts, 155–56
   criticism of, 343–44
   female, 86, 155–56
   genitalia, 343–44
   hearts, 156
   hypermasculine, 343–44

413

414   *Index*

bodies. (cont.)
  masculine, 289–90, 343–44
  and minds, 251–52
  noses, 343–44
  phalluses, 343–44
  violated, 86
  wombs, 147–48, 155, 197–98
Bohemian Crisis, 116–20, 133, 139–40, 142
Bolton, Edmund
  AVERRVNCI, 143
  Hypercritica, 141
  Nero Caesar, 120, 141–57, 190
Bothwell, 4th Earl of (James Hepburn), 136
Bower, Richard, 72
Braden, Gordon, 165
Braithwaite, Richard, 50
breasts, 155–56
Breitenberg, Mark, 59
Bridgewater, 1st Earl of (John Egerton), 242
Brief Cronology of GREAT BRITAIN, A
  (broadsheet), 353–57, *354*, 360–63
Bright, William, 1
Britannicus, 134–35, 146, 151–52, 196
broadsheets, 353–57, *354*, 360–63
Brown, Cedric, 244
Brutus, Lucius Junius, 43, 53–65, 279
Brutus, Marcus Junius, 166, 188, 268, 324, 326
Buckingham, 1st Duke of (George Villiers), 60,
    79, 93, 108, 130, 132, 174
  as Sejanus, 108–9
  assassination, 182
  and Charles I, 159
  death of, 49
  and Edmund Bolton, 141–44
  as Ganymede, 132
  James I, alleged poisoning of, 184
  literary representations, 184–85
  Parliamentary attack on, 176
Burton, Henry, 216–18
  An apology of an appeal, 214
  A Narration of the Life of Mr. Henry Burton,
    215–16
  trial of, 208–10, 214
Butler, Samuel (1613-80), 121

Caesar Augustus, 21, 122–23, 313, 339–40
Caesar, Julius, 165–66, 303, 324, 330–41
Caligula, 190
Carr, Robert (1st Earl of Somerset), 87
Carthage, 301–2
Case for Nol Cromwells Nose, A, 350
Cassius Dio, Lucius, 141, 149, 152, 155
Cataline, 350
Catholicism, 48, 133, *see also* anti-Catholicism
  of Charles I, supposed, 257–58

criticism of, 240–42
and gender disruption, 204
in households, 260
persecution of, 142
Pope, 241–42, 257–58
religione vana, 132
sodomy, association with, 132–33
support for, 118–19
women, associated with, 260
Cato, 165–66, 188, 333–34
Cavaliers, 310
censorship, 28–29, 177, 198–99
Chapman, George, 158, 162–74
  Bussy D'Ambois, 163
  Caesar and Pompey, 165–66, 333–34
  Conspiracie, and tragedie of . . . Byron, 163,
    167–68
  Eastward Ho, 164, 333
  An epicede, 163
  Euthymiæ raptus, 164
  A Iustification, 158, 177–83
  masculinity, concept of, 164–66
  Pro Vere, 168–74
Charles I, 22–23, 111–12, 116, 130, 358, *359*
  and Buckingham, Duke of, 159
  and Catholicism, 257–58
  court of, 201–2, 240, 242–47
  criticism of, 159–60, 198–202, 207
  execution, 311–12, 316–17, 324, 343,
    350–52
  exempla
    Appius Claudius, 92–93, 322–23
    Nero, 204–5
  extravagance, 206
  as father, 265
  and favouritism, 109
  Forced Loan, 176
  hair of, 180
  Henrietta Maria, marriage to, 182–83, 250,
    255–67
  impact of private life on state, 265–66
  as martyr, 261
  and masques/plays, 161–62, 198–201, 207,
    243
  peacemaking, 49
  popularity, 174–75
  portraiture, 160–62
  power, use of, 92, 175–77
  resistance to, 188
  Roman emperor, represented as, 160–61
  uxoriousness, 182–83, 261
  war in Europe, support for, 175
  as warrior, 48–50
Charles II, 260, 281, 296
Chartier, Roger, 11

Index

chastity, 68, 71, 73–74, 126, 244–45, 322
chivalry, 30, 48–49, 163
Christianity, 34–36, *see also* Catholicism; Protestantism
Church of England, 176, 260
Cicero, Marcus Tullius, 5, 24, 46, 192–93
   De Officiis, 31–32, 191–92
   De Re Publica, 42–43, 86–87
   on justice, 31–32
   Tusculan Disputations, 43–44, 75, 347–48
   tyranny, theories of, 42–44
   on *virtus*, 225
citizenship, 226–27, 287
civil disobedience, 176
civil wars, 29, 310, 315–16
civis (free subject), 226
class, social
   aristocratic, 32–33
   elite, 32–33, 280–82, 304
   and moral standards, 182
Claudius (Emperor), 135, 149, 152, 193–94
Claudius, Appius, 66–68, 74–76, 83–85, 280, 322
   as monarch, 93–95
   as exemplum, 92–93
   as judge, 83–85
clemency, 99–102
Clinton, Theophilus (4th Earl of Lincoln), 188
clothing, 62
Cogswell, Thomas, 39, 184
Coke, Sir Edward, 87–90
Collatinus, Lucius Tarquinius, 54, 57
common law, 79–80, 84–85, 87–90
Commonwealth, 271–73, 275–76, 295–97, 324
conquest, 360–62
corruption
   of children, by mothers, 137–38, 149–50, 243
   court, 38–39, 183–84
   of emotion, 132
   of fathers/fatherhood, 104
   by lust, 95
   luxury and, 304–5
   of monarchy, 94–95
   passions, 132
   by plays, 198–99, 205–8
   Roman, 189–90
cosmetics, 201–2
counsel/counsellors, 50–51
courage
   failure of, 63–64
   and the free-state, 294–95
   martial, 45, 47–50, 61–62, 294–95
   physical, 225
Court of Chancery, 87–90

courts
   Caroline, 201–2, 240, 242–47
   corruption in, 38–39
   criticism of, 240, 242–47
   disorder in, 62–63
   entertainments, 49, 124–25, 243–45
   fashions, 201–2
   Jacobean, 62–63, 201
   masques, 243–45
   participation in, 47
cowardice, 123–24, 129, 137–39
Cowley, Abraham, 347
Cox, Rosanna, 252
Crassinus. *See* Claudius, Appius
Cressy, David, 159
Cromwell, Elizabeth, 320
Cromwell, Oliver, 4, 103, 270–71, 312, 315–52
   bloodlust, 349–52
   body, criticism of, 343–44
   as classical usurper, 341–52
   criticism of, 313–14, 332–35, 341–52
   crown, refusal of, 340–41
   exempla
      Augustus, 339–40
      Brutus, Lucius Junius, 55, 324–29
      Cataline, 350
      Damocles, 347–49
      Hippolytus, 321–22
      Julius Caesar, 330–41
      Nero, 341, 345–47
      Tamburlaine, 349–50
      Virginius, 323–24
   as father, 344–45
   household, disordered, 344–45
   imperialism, 297–99, 331–32, 337–38
   as masculine ideal, 317–18
   military prowess, 293, 315–16, 323–26, 331–32
   monarchical ambitions, 332–33, 335–36
   passions, excessive, 342–45, 349–50
   as republican hero, 315–29
   self-control, 337
   as tyrant, 332–35, 342–43
   violence of, 345–47, 349–50
Cromwell's Bloody Slaughter-house (pamphlet), 344
Crouch, John, 344, 348–49
cuckoldry, 126–27, 194
Cust, Richard, 49

Damocles, 347–49
Darnley, Lord (Henry Stewart), 136
Davenant, Sir William, 186
death, 76, *see also* martyrdom; murder
   assassination, 182, 193

416   *Index*

death (cont.)
  regicide, 9, 311–12, 316–17, 324, 343,
    350–52
  suicide, 54, 58, 129, 166, 189
deception, 152–53, 201–2
deference, 39
democracy, 279–81, 291
Devereux, Robert (2nd Earl of Essex), 163, 168
Devereux, Robert (3rd Earl of Essex), 188
Digges, Sir Dudley, 109, 286
Dio Cassius, Lucius, 141, 149, 152, 155
Diodati, Charles, 237
Dionysius of Halicarnassus, 67–68
disobedience
  civil, 176
  of wives, 126–27
disorder
  at court, 62–63
  family, 134–35
  gender, 117, 168
  household, 60, 74, 126–27, 181–82, 344–45
  social, 83–84, 86, 103–4, 170–71, 181–82,
    205–6, 208
divorce, 248–50, 252–55
Domitius Ænobarbus, Gnaeus, 149
drama, 128–29
  actors, 163, 202–4
  of classical history, 27–28
  as corrupting force, 198–99, 205–8
  as criticism, 184–85
  criticism of, 198–99
  masques, 161–62, 183
    Comus, 121, 242–47
    at court, 243–45
Du Chesne, André, 257
Dutton, William, 320
Dyck, Anthony Van, 160–62
  Charles I on Horseback, 161
  Charles with Monsieur de St Antoine, 22, 160

education, 268
  ethical value of, 164–65
  failures of, 149–50
  grammar schools, 24
  humanist, 24–29
effeminacy, 4, 43–44, 243
  avarice, due to, 303
  of Cavaliers, 310
  and hairstyles, 179–80
  and liberty, 8
  peacemaking as, 117, 123–24, 170–72
  and plays, 207
  through sexual appetite, 83–84
  and softness, 289
  of Stuart Kings, 317–18

Egerton, John (1st Earl of Bridgewater), 242
Eikon Basilike (biography), 261, 312
Eliot, Sir John, 108–9, 175
elites, 32–33, 280–82, 304
Elizabeth (Queen of Bohemia), 116
Elizabeth I, 136–37, 163, 167–68, 172
Ellesmere, Thomas Egerton, 88, 97
emasculation, 4, 117, 263–65
  and imperialism, 304–5
  of monarchy, 272–73
  through tyranny, 60
emotion, 155, *see also* lust
  corrupted, 132
  and effeminacy, 83–84
  excessive, 181, 194–98, 342–45, 349–50
  fear, 37, 137–39
Emperor's Favourite, The (play), 184–85
emperors. *See* monarchy
encomia, paradoxical, 177–78
enslavement, 182, 284–86
  bestialisation of slaves, 234–35, 284–86
  through corrupt liberty, 268
  in marriage, 254–56, 268
  monarchy as, 186–88, 295–96
  and rape, 303
  Roman, 103–4, 235, 285–86, 324
  of tyrants, 195
Erasmus, Desiderius, 177
Essex, 2nd Earl of (Robert Devereux), 163, 168
Essex, 3rd Earl of (Robert Devereux), 188
exempla, historical, 2–3, 11–12, 25, 27, 217–18
  of bloodlust, 349–51
  of Charles I
    Appius Claudius, 92–93, 322–23
    Nero, 204–5
  of chastity, 321–22
  of conquest, 361–63
  of conspiracy, 350
  of Cromwell
    Attila the Hun, 351
    Augustus, 339–40
    Brutus, Lucius Junius, 55, 324–29
    Cataline, 350
    Damocles, 347–49
    Hippolytus, 321–22
    Julius Caesar, 330–41, 361–63
    Nero, 342, 345–47
    Tamburlaine, 349–50
    Virginius, 323–24
  denigratory, 204–5
  of fortune, 347–49
  of James I
    Augustus, 123
    Nero, 122–23
    Tarquin the Proud, 62–65

Index

417

of justice, 56–57, 324–29
masculine, 102–3
and monarchical authority, 120
power of, 108–9
republican, 100–1
rex pacificus, 123
of tyranny, 92–93
for women, 66–67, 71
extravagance, 124–25
of Charles I, 206
of James I, 123–25, 170, 174, 206
of Nero, 206

Faithfull Narrative of the Late Testimony, The
(epistle), 345–46
Fallon, Stephen, 251
family. *See also* fathers/fatherhood; mothers/
motherhood
disordered, 134–35
inversion of, 181–82
patriarchal, 59
Famous Tragedie of King Charles I Basely
Butchered, The (play), 350
fashion, 62, 179–80, 201–2
fathers/fatherhood, 30, 51–53, 57, 102–3,
320–21
corruption of, 104
and kingship, 113–15, 265
paterfamilias, 33, 52, 364
favouritism, 62, 108–9, 131–33, 184–85
fear, 37, 137–39
femininity, 71, 197–98, 232–34, 319, *see also*
effeminacy
feminisation, 264–65, 303
Ferdinand II (Holy Roman Emperor), 116
Fifth Monarchy Men, 345–46
Fisher, Payne
Inauguratio Olivariana, 327–28
Irenodia Gratulatoria, 319–20, 326–28,
336–37, 361
Fissell, Mary, 313
flattery (*adulatio*), 44–45, 191
Fletcher, John, *Little French Lawyer*, 121
Fletcher, R., 325, 331, 361
Florus, 141
force
armed, 169
rule by, 39–40, 86, 286–87, 342
Forced Loan, 176, 187–88
foreignness, 179, 183
'Fortunes wheele. or Rota fortunæ in gyro' (libel),
122
Foxe, John, *Actes and Monuments*, 211–12
Frederick V (Elector Palatine), 116, 119,
139–40, 175

freedom. *See* liberty
free-state, 100, 277–78, 283, 305–9
and imperialism, 299–301, 305–6
and manhood, realisation of, 279, 325
and martial courage, 294–95
and rationality, 287–94
Roman, 100, 104
Fulbecke, William, 57
funeral, for strand of Poppaea's hair, 158,
178–79

Gainsford, Thomas, 38–39
Ganymede, 131–32
gender, 3–7, *see also* effeminacy; femininity;
masculinity
and Catholicism, 204
construction, 313
disorder, 117, 168
disruption, 73–74, 193–94, 202–4
hierarchy, 232–33, 250–51
in historical analysis, 5–8
inversion, 197–98
and republicanism, 228–29
genealogies, royal, 358–60
genitalia, 343–44
Gerbier, Sir Balthazar, 130, 132
Gernon, Luke, 302
God/Gods, 299
kings as, 64–65, 94
Gouge, William, 34
grammar schools, 24
Greco-Roman syncretism, 227
Greece
in grammar school curriculum, 24
masculinity, concepts of, 45–46
republican heritage of, 227
slavery, 285–86
tyranny, theories of, 40–41
Greek language, 24
Gregory XV, Pope, 257–58
Greneway, Richard, 24–25
Grosvenor, Sir Richard, 97
Guicciardini, Francesco, 26
Gunpowder Plot, 241–42

Habsburg, House of, 116, 118
Hæc vir: or The womanish-man (pamphlet), 117,
168
hair, 158, 178–82, 203–4
lovelocks, 179–80, 201
men's, 179–80, 201, 203–4, 237
women's, 201, 203–4
hardness, 289
Harington, Sir John, 63
Harrington, James, 320

418 — Index

Harrington, James (cont.)
  Oceana, 292, 333
Haward, Sir William, 135
Hayward, John, 57
hearts, 156
Henrietta Maria (Queen Consort), 49, 159, 162, 182–83
  criticism of, 202–4, 250, 255–57
  masques, performance in, 202–4, 243–44
Henry Frederick (Prince of Wales), 48, 60, 135, 163
  as masculine ideal, 166–67
Hepburn, James (4th Earl of Bothwell), 136
Herbert, Philip (4th Earl of Pembroke), 188
heredity, 140
  of masculinity, 172
  and monarchy, 140, 146, 284–87, 315
  tainted, 134–35, 137–38, 149
Herrick, Robert, 'All Things Decay and Die', 94–95
Hesilrige, Sir Arthur, 332
Heywood, Thomas
  Appius and Virginia, 79, 92–107, 322–24
  Curtaine Lecture, 66–67
  The Rape of Lucrece, 55, 59–62, 79
Hic mvlier: or, The man-woman (pamphlet), 117, 168
hierarchy
  class, 32–33, 182, 280–82, 304
  of gender, 232–33, 250–51
Hippolytus, 321–22
Hispaniola, 298–99
historiography, 141–42, 145–46, 353–63
history, 185–86, *see also* exempla, historical
  as a guide, 24–25
  publication of, 222–23
  republican thought, foundation for, 353
  revisionist, 9–11
  study of, 1–3, 2, 24–29
Hobbes, Thomas, 8
Holdsworth, Richard, 34–36
Holles, Sir John, 82
Homer, 24
homo (person), 33
homosexuality, 131–34, 151
honour, 30–31, 57, 76
honours system, 49
Horace, 24, 81
House of Commons, 92, 176–77, 241, 322
household, 229
  Catholic, 260
  criminality within, 113
  disordered, 60, 74, 126–27, 181–82, 344–45
  female rule of, 261
  ordered, 73–74, 329

patriarchal governance of, 52, 59, 68, 73–74, 156, 252–53, 318–21
  state, equated with, 248–49
Howes, Edmund, *The Annales*, 357, 359, 362
Hughes, Ann, 313
humanism
  civic, 225
  continental, 2
  education, 2, 26
  new, 91, 192
  political models of, 191–92
humanity, loss of, 43
Hunt, Lynn, 11
hypermasculinity, 342–44

idleness, 60
idolatry, 244
immorality, sexual, 109
impartiality, 96–98
imperialism
  and anti-Catholicism, 298
  of Cromwell, 274, 297–309
  and emasculation, 304–5
  and the free-state, 299–301
  Ireland, 302, 307–9, 351
  as liberation, 306–7
  and masculinity, 300–1, 304–5
  and metaphors of sexual violence, 301–2
  Roman, 300–4
  Scotland, 295–96, 306–7, 351
  and *virtus*, 300–1
  West Indies, 297–300
  Western Design, 297–300
incest, 146, 148, 193, 264, 322
infantilisation, 159, 264
injustice, 78, 84–85, 98–100, 212
interest theory, 282–83
interest, private, 97, 271, 286, 330
Ireland, 302, 307–9, 351

Jacquot, Jean, 167
Jamaica, 298–99
James I, 21–22, 242, 359
  and absolutism, 37
  alleged poisoning of, 184
  and Bohemian Crisis, 116, 133
  and Catholicism, 133
  and common law, 79–80
  coronation, 78, 123
  court of, 62–63, 201
  cowardice of, 137–39
  criticism of, 62–65, 116–18, 130–31, 169–70

Index

419

and divine-right monarchy, 64–65,
  114
and Edmund Bolton, 143–44
effeminacy of, 171–72
exempla
  Augustus, 123
  Nero, 122–23
  Tarquin the Proud, 62–65
extravagance of, 123–25, 170, 174, 206
favouritism, 62, 131–33
fearfulness of, 137–39
historical representations of, 356–60
and history, study of, 26
homosexuality, accusations of, 131–34
as judge, 96
and judicial process, 87–90
and kings as fathers, 113–15
masculinity, lack of, 117, 171–72
peacemaking, 118–20, 138–39
portraiture, 358
ridicule of, 164
Spanish Match crisis, 133
as warrior, 48
works
  Basilicon Doron, 52, 64, 96, 99–100,
    113–14
  His Maiesties Declaration, 38, 119
  Meditation, 123
  Trew Law of Free Monarchies, 37, 51,
    113–14, 139, 145, 154
Jones, Inigo, 161, 206
Jonson, Ben, 21, 206
  Eastward Ho, 164, 333
Josephus, Titus Flavius, 141, 151
judges, 89–90, 96–98
Julia Agrippina, 113, 127, 134, 136, 146–49
  Britannicus, blamed for murder of, 151–52
  incestuous, 193
  murder of, 127, 148, 152–56, 196–98
  power, usurpation of, 190–94
Julius Caesar, 165–66, 303, 324, 330–41,
    360–63
justice, 31–32, 97–98
  exempla, historical, 56–57, 324–29
  failures of, 43
  injustice in, 68
  kingly, 96, 99–100
  murder as, 153–56
Justus Lipsius, 192
Juvenal, 'Tenth Satire', 80–83, 91

Kings Cabinet Opened, The (letters), 261
kings/kingship. *See* monarchy
Kishlansky, Mark, 200
Knoppers, Laura Lunger, 313

La Primaudaye, Pierre, 34
Latin language, 24
Laud, Archbishop William, 208–9, 241
law
  common, 79–80, 84–85, 87–90
  rule of, 40, 86, 286
law-giver role, 30, 45
Leighton, Sir William, *Vertve Trivmphant*, 56
Lewalski, Barabara, 244
libel, 117, 122, 130–40, 209
liberality, 101–2
liberty, 7–8, 103–6, 267–69, 279–83, *see also*
    free-state
  as non-domination, 7–8, 226–27
  through conquest, 306–7
  democratic, 279
  through ethical conduct, 247–48
  Petition of Right, defined in, 176
  political, 225–29
  private, 250
  rationality, dependent on, 234
  of subjects, 132–33, 226
  threats to, 132–33
  virginity, as metaphor of, 279–82
  of women, 105–6
Lincoln, 4th Earl of (Theophilus Clinton), 188
Littleton, Adam, 33
Livy, 24–25, 100, 280, 289–90
  Ab Urbe Condita, 54–55
  Virginia, story of, 67–68, 104
Loues triumph through Callipolis (masque), 243
lovelocks, 179–80, 201
loyalty, 49, 324
Lucan, 188–89
  Pharsalia, 186–89, 330
Lucretia, 53–65, 70, 280, 324
  and Virginia, 70–71
lust, 1, 53–65, 67–68, 70, 74–76, 246, 253
  for blood, 343, 345, 349–51
  corruption by, 95
  and enslavement, 84–85
  for power, 151, 202–4, 344
  as tyranny, 194
  of women, 73, 156
luxury, 60, 235–36, 244, 303–5

Machiavelli, Niccolò, 26, 68, 101, 324–29, 338
manhood, 3, 5, 288, *see also* effeminacy;
    emasculation; fathers/fatherhood;
    masculinity
  absolute man, 167–68
  adulthood, 32, 150, 288
  arms, bearing of, 292
  classical, 4
  concepts of

420 · Index

manhood (cont.)
  English, 30–39, 46–53
  Greek, 45–46
  Roman, 8, 30–36, 45
  contested, 45–53
  denial of, 284–86
  and Englishness, 272
  failed, 4, 39–45, 63–64, 193–94, 207–8,
    234–36
  ideals of, 8, 30–32, 236–39, 267, 271–72,
    317–18
  and liberty, 8, 267–69
  and marriage, 248–50, 252–53
  as martial courage, 45, 47–50, 61–64
  as moral goodness, 45
  through moral reform, 268–69
  and rationality, 234, 287–94
  realised, 272, 287
  and republicanism, 4, 224–25, 228–29
  and social order, 166
  and violence, 290
  warrior role, 34, 45, 47–50, 172–73, 225
  youth, 150, 237, 288
Manley, Thomas, *Veni; Vidi; Vici.*, 319–20, 327,
  336–37
Mantegna, Andrea, *Triumphs of Caesar*, 160, 338
Marcus, Leah, 63
Maria Ana of Spain, 116
marriage, 32, 162, 245–47, 328–29
  adultery, 126–27, 146, 193, 328
  alliances, 63, 116, 133, 144, 175
  bad, 253–55, 258–59
  cuckoldry, 126–27, 194
  divorce, 248–50, 252–55
  ideal, 250–52
  and manhood, 248–50, 252–53
  mixed, 255–57
martial prowess, 45, 47–50, 206, 225
  courage, 46, 61–62, 225, 294–95
  of Cromwell, 315–16
  failure of, 63–64
  warrior role, 34, 45, 47–50, 172–73, 225
martyrdom, 76–77, 111, 209–11
  of Charles I, 261
  of Paul the Apostle, 211–12, 216
Marvell, Andrew
  'Horatian Ode upon Cromwell's return from
    Ireland', 325–26
  'A Poem upon the Death of his Late Highness
    the Lord Protector', 320–21
Mary Queen of Scots, 135–39
masculinity, 9, *see also* effeminacy; emasculation;
  manhood
  autonomy, 38
  and the body, 289–90

and Christianity, 34–36
and excellence, 35–36
excessive, 342–44
failed, 4, 39–45, 63–64, 193–94, 207–8,
  234–36
false, 239
and hairstyles, 179–80
honour, 30–31
ideals of, 8, 30–32, 236–39, 267, 271–72,
  317–18
and imperialism, 304–5
justice, 31–32
and liberty, 8, 267–69
of women, 197–98
performative, 167
and power, 33
and rationality, 234, 287–94
and Stoicism, 164–66
Massinger, Philip, *Little French Lawyer*, 121
Mathewes, Augustine, 121
matricide, 127, 134, 148, 152–56, 196–98
maturity, 32, 150, 288
May, Thomas, 121–22, 186
  *Discourse Concerning the Success of Former
    Parliaments*, 186
  History of the Parliament of England, 186
  Pharsalia, 186–89
  Tragedy of Julia Agrippina, 186, 189–98
McDonnell, Myles, 45
McRae, Andrew, 82, 132, 184
Mercurius Politicus (news-journal), 298, 305–8
metaphors
  for imperialism, 301–2
  of monarchy, 94–95
  of liberty, 279–82
  for tyranny, 324, 327
  for uncolonised land, 302
militias, 292–93
Milton, John, 237–39, 249–50, 320
  anti-Catholicism, 240–42, 255–61
  Areopagitica, 234
  Comus, 121, 242–47
  Defensio pro Populo Anglicano, 265
  Defensio Secunda, 247–48, 267, 269–71, 323
  Doctrine and Discipline of Divorce, 248–53
  Eikonoklastes, 258, 260–65
  Elegia Sexta, 237
  History of Britain, 268
  and imperialism, 275
  In Quintum Novembris, 240–42
  Lycidas, 240
  manhood, concepts of, 232–39
  Of Education, 268
  Of Reformation, 235, 256, 268
  Paradise Lost, 232–34

Index

421

Readie and Easie Way, 269, 271–73
republicanism, 269–73
Samson Agonistes, 231–32
Tenure of Kings and Magistrates, 264, 268
Tretrachordon, 252
mind/body relationship, 251–52
Modest Narrative of Intelligence, A (pamphlet), 331
monarchy. *See also* Charles I; Charles II; Elizabeth I; James I
absolutist, 37–39, 51, 69
criticism of, 163
defence of, 110–12, 144–45
arguments against, 271
corrupted, 94–95
criticism of, 93–95, 128–30, 163
divine-right, 51, 64–65, 114
elected, 116, 139–40
emasculated, 272–73
in English historiography, 354–60
as enslavement, 186–88, 295–96
hereditary, 140, 146, 284–87, 315
impact of private life on state, 145, 151, 156, 205–6, 208, 265–66
and justice, 96, 99–100
kings
as fathers, 113–15
history, importance of study of, 26
and honour, 30
as judges, 89–90
masculinity, failed, 62
as ministers of God, 111
Roman emperors, portrayed as, 21–23
kingship
models of, 99–100
mysteries of, 38
refusal of, 340–41
versus fatherhood, 265
metaphors of, 94–95
paternal models of, 51–53
prerogative, 38, 87–90
resistance to, 11, 112, 114, 129–30, 188
succession, 146
support for, 143–45
tyranny, as perversion of, 40–41
Montagu, Richard, 176, 241
Montague, Sir Henry, 97
Montague, Walter, 202
morality, 46, 288
and class, 182
failures of, 83–84, 109
masculinity as, 4, 45
sexual, 109
and social disorder, 83–84
Morton, Thomas, 111–12

mothers/motherhood, 155, 197
as corrupters of children, 137–38, 149–50, 243, 259
matricide, 127, 134, 148, 152–56, 196–98
Parliament as, 264–65
vicious, 146–49
murder, 127–28, 135, 146
assassination, 182, 193
as justice, 153–56
matricide, 127, 134, 148, 152–56, 196–98
parricide, 151–52, 190, 196
treasonous, 194
mutilation, 344
Mytens, Daniel, 120, 162

Naseby (ship), 274
Nedham, Marchamont, 101, 275–309
The Case of the Common-wealth, 291, 315, 361
The Excellencie of a Free-State, 277–95, 300–2, 333, 361
and interest of freedom, 279–83
and martial courage, 294–95
Mercurius Politicus, 295–96, 298, 305–6
and rationality, 287–94
republicanism, 276–77
and warfare, 295
neostoicism, 91
Nero, 110–15, 135, 145–46
Britannicus, murder of, 151–52
Cromwell, Oliver, compared to, 341, 345–47
effeminacy, 123–24, 207
extravagance, 206
as failed patriarch, 126–27, 181–82
and favouritism, 184–85
hedonism, 149–50
as historical exemplum, 122–23, 204–5, 217–18, 341, 345–47
impact of private life on state, 145, 151, 156
James I, equated with, 122–23
Julia Agrippina, influence of, 146–49
and martyrdom of Paul the Apostle, 211–12
matricide, 127, 134, 148, 152–56, 196–98
parricide, 151–52, 190, 196
passions of, 181, 194–98
paternal line of, 149
Pisonian conspiracy, 188
and Poppaea, 152–53, 158, 178–79
sexual depravity, 150–51
in *Tragedy of Nero*, 122, 126–29
triviality of, 178–79
non-domination, 8, 226–27, 284
None-Such Charles, The (pamphlet), 130, 132
non-*vir* (lesser/non-male), 8, 33, 289
Norbrook, David, 187, 223

422   *Index*

Norton, John, 121
noses, 343–44
Noy, William, 198, 204–5

oaths, 78, 214
obedience, 37–38, 67–68
  unlimited, 110–11, 114–15
  of women, 73–74, 126–27
On the Death of that Grand Imposter Oliver
    Cromwell (verses), 349–51
oratory, 50, 238–39
Osmond, Patricia, 143
Overbury Murder Trials, 87
Overbury, Thomas, 87
Ovid, 24
Oxinden, Henry, 25

pacificism. *See* peacemaking
pageants, 178
pamphlets, 117–18, 168, 192
  against Charles I, 257–58
  Cromwell's Bloody Slaughter-house, 344
  Cromwellian, 331, 344–45
  Hæc vir: or The womanish-man, 117, 168
  Hic mvlier: or, The man-woman, 117, 168
  A Modest Narrative of Intelligence, 331
  The None-Such Charles, 130, 132
  The Perfect Politician, 331
  Perfect and Impartial Intelligence, 334–35
  Protestant, 170
  Tom Tell Troath, 168
  Votivæ Angliæ, 117–18, 170
paradox
  of absolutism, 195
  in encomia, 177–78
Parliament
  authority, denial of, 38
  barbarity, 263–64
  Charles I, interactions with, 175–77, 241,
    263–65
  Commonwealth, 296–97
  debates, 82–83
  feminisation of, 264–65
  House of Commons, 92, 176–77, 241, 332
  infantilisation, 264
  Privy Council, 209
  Rump Parliament, 317, 333, 345
  Star Chamber, 121, 209
parricide, 151–52, 190, 196
passions. *See also* lust
  corrupted, 132
  and effeminacy, 83–84
  excessive, 181, 194–98, 342–45,
    349–50
Pateman, Carole, 368

paterfamilias (family head), 33, 52, 364
patriarchy, 109–15, 252–53
  and authority, 52–53
  failures of, 126–27, 181–82
  household, 52, 59, 68, 73–74, 156, 252–53,
    318–21
  submission to, 67, 71
Patterson, Annabel, 199
Paul the Apostle, 110–11, 211–12, 216
Paulinae Lollia, 193
peacemaking, 48–49, 63–64, 118–20
  as effeminacy, 49, 117, 124, 170–72
Peck, Linda Levy, 183
Peltonen, Markku, 36
Pembroke, 4th Earl of (Philip Herbert), 188
penetration, 280
Perfect and Impartial Intelligence (pamphlet),
  334–35
Perfect Politician, The (pamphlet), 331
Perry, Curtis, 132, 184
persecution, religious, 211, 217–18, 346
Persius, 173–74
perversity, 60
Petition of Right, 176–77
phalluses, 343–44
Phelips, Sir Robert, 92
pilgrimages, 183
Piso, Gaius Calpurnius, 188
Plato, *Republic*, 40–41, 75, 195, 236
plays, 128–29
  of classical history, 27–28
  as corrupting force, 198–99, 205–8
  as criticism, 184–85
  masques, 161–62, 183
    Comus, 121, 242–47
    at court, 243–45
Pliny the Elder, 193
  Natural History, 147–48, 181
Plutarch, 45
Pocock, J. G. A., 225, 227
poisoning, 151–52, 196
politics. *See also* free-state; Parliament;
  republicanism
  democracy, 279–81, 291
  humanist, 191–92
  liberty in, 225–29
  new humanist, 192
  participation, 225–27, 311
  'reason of state', 167, 191–93
  vita activa (active political life), 26, 31, 36–37,
    39, 50
  women's activism, 311
Polybius, 25
Pompey, 165–66, 188, 333–34
Pope (Catholic Church), 241–42, 257–58

Index

Poppaea, 123–24, 126, 151–54, 195
  strand of hair, Nero's funeral for, 158, 178–81
Porter, Endymion, 142, 144
Porter, Margaret, 142
portraiture, 160–62, 358
power, 4
  democratic, 280–81
  of historical exempla, 108–9
  lust for, 151, 202–4, 342
  masculine, 33
  monarchical, 92
  of women, 136–37, 190–94, 261
print culture, 353–63, *see also* pamphlets
  broadsheets, 353–57, *354*, 360–63
  medals, 23
  tracts, 170
printing, 121, 177
private life, versus public, 145, 151, 156, 265–66
Privy Council, 209
procreation, 246
Procter, Thomas, 101
propaganda, 295–96
Protectorate, 295, 297
Protestantism, 48
  Arminianism, 176
  and Bohemian Crisis, 116
  Church of England, 176, 260
  Henry Frederick, champion of, 135
  persecution of, 128, 298
  tracts, 170
Prynne, William, 165, 200, 202, 204, 216–18, 259
  Histrio-mastix, 198–208
  Newes from Ipswich, 209
  The Popish Royall Favourite, 257–58
  The Vnloueliness of Loue-Locks, 179–80, 204
  trial of, 198–99, 208–10, 213
public life, 39, 145–46, 156, 229, 265–66
public service, 26, 31, 36–37, 39, 50, 226, 271
punishment, 199, 209–10, 214
  execution, 311–12, 316–17, 324, 343, 350–52
  exile, 209, 214–15
  imprisonment, 214–15
  mutilation, 209–10, 216
Pyne, Hugh, 159

R. B. (author), *Apius and Virginia*, 72–78, 84
Raleigh, Sir Walter, 163
Rand, William, 29
rape, 54, 75, 154–56, 279–82, 303–4, 322
ratio (reason), 5, 59
rationality, 231, 234, 236–37
  and the free-state, 287–94
  and liberty, 234

and marriage, 250
  masculinity, foundation for, 287–94
Raylor, Timothy, 338
reason (*ratio*), 5, 59
'reason of state' politics, 167, 191–93
Reeve, Thomas, 351
regicide, 9, 311–12, 316–17, 324, 350–52
religion, 179, *see also* Catholicism; Protestantism
  persecution, 211, 217–18, 346
  pilgrimages, 183
religione vana (Catholicism), 132
republicanism, 4, 9, 186–88
  classical, 100–1, 106, 227, 278–79
  exempla, historical, 100–1
  and gender, 228–29
  historical thought, foundation for, 353
  and manhood, 4, 224–25, 228–29
  of Milton, 269–73
  of Nedham, 276–77
  and patriarchal authority, 52–53
  restrictiveness, 227
  Roman, 106, 278–79
  as solution to tyranny, 223–24
  virtues, 225
resistance, against monarchy, 11, 112, 114, 129–30, 188
retribution, 54–55, 153–54
revolution
  military, 93
  Roman, 57–58, 106
rhetoric, 27, 37, 238–39
Rich, Robert (2nd Earl of Warwick), 188
Roman de la Rose, 67–68
Rome
  corruption, 189–90
  Decemvirate, 67–68, 86–87
  democracy of, 292–93
  destruction of, 127–28
  in English historiography, 353–55, 360, 362
  enslavement, 103–4, 235, 285–86, 324
  in grammar school curriculum, 24
  imperialism, 300–4
  laws of, 84–85
  liberty, 103–6
    of women, 105–6
  liberty, definition of, 7–8
  merit-based rewards, 291
  Principate, 109, 112, 324, 330
  Republic, 55, 57–58, 106, 186–88, 324
  republicanism, influence on, 227, 278–79
  revolution, 57–58, 106
  tyranny, theories of, 41–45

424   *Index*

Roundheads, 310
royalism, 143–45
rulers. *See* monarchy
Rump Parliament, 317, 333, 345

Sabbath observance, 202, 208
Sackville, Thomas (Lord Buckhurst, 1st earl of
    Dorset), 125
Sallust, 24, 100–1, 300, 302–4
    Bellum Catilinae, 293–95, 303–4
Salmasius, Claudius, *Defensio Regia pro Carolo I*,
    265–66
Sandys, Sir Edwin, 82–83
Satan, 241–42
satire, 81–83
scepticism, 192
Scipio Africanus, 319–20
Scotland, 295–96, 306–7, 351
Scott, Joan Wallach, 6
Scott, Thomas, 36
    'Regalis Iustitia Iacobi', 90
    Vox Populi, 168, 170
sedition, 198–200
seduction, 193
Segar, William, 31
Sejanus, Lucius Aelius, 108–9
Selden, John, *Mare clausum*, 296
self-control, 43, 166–68, 319–20, 322, 337,
    349–50
Seneca, 141, 149, 152, 155, 178, 188, 193
    and Julia Agrippina, 192
    kingship model, 99–100
    new humanism, 192
servants, 74
service, public, 26, 31, 36–37, 39, 50, 226, 271
servility, 7–8
Sextus Tarquinius, 54, 280–82, 296, 324
sexual relations, 251–52
    adultery, 146, 193, 328
    and immorality, 109
    impropriety, 125–27
    punishment of, 328–29
sexual violence, 110, 154–56, 193, 303
    as metaphor, 279–82, 301–2, 324, 327
    rape, 54, 75, 154–56, 279–82, 303–4, 322
    in warfare, 303–4
sexuality, 245–46
    homosexuality, 131–34, 151
    and political conduct, 195–96
Shakespeare, William
    Julius Caesar, 28
    Lucrece, 55, 58–59, 86
Sharpe, Kevin, 314
Shepard, Alexandra, 345
Sidney, Algernon, 101

Sidney, Sir Philip, 129, 163
sin, 131, 214, 299, 351
Skinner, Quentin, 7, 226–27, 278
slavery. *See* enslavement
slavishness, 43
social class
    aristocratic, 32–33
    elite, 32–33, 280–82, 304
    and moral standards, 182
society
    disorder, 83–84, 86, 103–4, 170–71, 181–82,
        205–6, 208
    order, 105–6, 329
sodomy, 131–34, 151
softness, 289
Somerset, 1st Earl of (Robert Carr), 87
Spain, 63, 116–20, 170, 297–300
Spanish Inquisition, 128
Spanish Match crisis, 116, 133, 144, 175
Sparkes, Michael, 121
spectacle, 174, 178
Speed, John, *The History of Great Britaine*,
    354–60, *356*, 358
Star Chamber, 121, 209
statesmen, 51
    counsel/counsellors, 50–51, 61, 65, 191,
        262–64
    emasculation of, 60
    failed manhood of, 44–45
    history, study of, 26–27
    law-giver role, 30, 45
    under tyranny, 44–45
    virtues of, 101–2
    withdrawal of, 192
Stewart, Henry (Lord Darnley), 136
stoicism, 91, 164–66, 192
Stow, John, *The Annales*, 357, *359*, 362
Streater, John, 334–36, 346–47
submission
    male, 193–94
    to patriarchy, 67, 71
succession, 146
Suetonius (Gaius Suetonius Tranquillus), 109,
    141, 149, 151, 155, 193, 334
suicide, 54, 58, 129, 166, 189

Tacitus, Publius Cornelius, 38, 192–93
    Annals, 24, 44–45, 143
    on Nero, 141, 149, 151, 155
    on Sejanus, 108–9
Tamburlaine, 349–50
Tarquin the Proud (Lucius Tarquinius
    Superbus), 43, 53–65, 324
taxation, 1, 176, 187–88
Tempe Restor'd (masque), 243

Index

temperance, 31, 231, 234, 236–37, 239
 lack of, 63
Terence, 24
theatre, 128–29
 actors, 163, 202–4
 of classical history, 27–28
 as corrupting force, 198–99, 205–8
 as criticism, 184–85
 masques, 161–62, 183
  Comus, 121, 242–47
  at court, 243–45
Thirty Years' War, 116, 175, 177, 187–88, 241
Thurloe, John, 296
Tiberius, 44–45, 108–9, 143
Titian
 The Emperor, Charles V at Mühlberg,
  161
 Twelve Caesars, 160–61
Toland, John, 333
Tom Tell Troath (pamphlet), 168
torture, 128
tracts, 170
Tragedy of Nero (play), 120–30
treason, 137
trials, 209–14
Troy, 127–28
Tuke, Sir Samuel, 134–35, 137–38
Tuke, Thomas, 153, 201
Tullia Minor, 60, 62, 64–65
tyranny, 3–4, 11–12
 and bestialisation, 41, 43–44, 195
 elites, 280–82, 304
 female, 156–57, 190–94
 as gender disruption, 193–94
 judicial, 83–92, 209–14
 and lust, 194–98
 male, 156–57, 194–98
 and moral failings, 40
 as perversion of monarchy, 40–41, 68
 as pseudo-state, 42
 and the soul, 40–41
 by unjust/wicked practice, 39–40,
  74–76, 98
 by usurpation, 39–40

usurpation, 151–52, 341–52
 tyranny by, 39–40
 by women, 190–94
uxoriousness, 182–83, 193–94, 261

Van Dyck, Anthony, 160–62
 Charles I on Horseback, 161
 Charles with Monsieur de St Antoine, 22, 160
vanity, 153, 171, 181
Venus, 171–72

Vere, Horace, 168–69, 172–73, 188
Vergil, 21, 24
Villiers, George. *See* Buckingham, 1st Duke of
violence, 110, 345–47, 349–50
 force, 39–40, 86, 286–87, 342
violence, sexual, 110, 154–56, 193, 303
 as metaphor, 279–82, 301–2, 324, 327
 rape, 54, 75, 154–56, 279–82, 303–4, 322
 in warfare, 303–4
vir (man, aristocratic), 8, 32–36, 288
 non-*vir* (lesser/non-male), 8, 33, 289
 Virginius, exemplum of, 102–3
Virginia, 66–69
 in *Apius and Virginia* (R. B.), 71–78
 in *Appius and Virginia* (Webster and
  Heywood), 105–6
 and Lucretia, 70–71
 in *That Which Seems Best* (W. B.), 85–86
virginity, 67–68, 71
 as metaphor, 279–82, 302
Virginius, 66–67, 76–77, 91, 100–1
virtues. *See also* courage; justice; temperance
 aretê [ἀρετή] (character excellence), 46, 288
 cardinal, 97–98
 chastity, 68, 71, 73–74, 126, 244–45, 322
 chivalry, 30, 48–49, 163
 civic, 227, 231
 clemency, 99–102
 justice as, 97–98
 liberality, 101–2
 republican, 225
 virginity, 71
 of women, 61, 70–71, 105–6
virtus (manliness/virtue), 5, 8, 33–34, 236–39
 definitions of, 46
 imperialism, 300–1
 as martial courage, 45, 294–95
 and Roman democracy, 291
 Roman definitions of, 225
vita activa (active political life), 26, 31, 36–37,
  39, 50, 226
vivere civile (civic way of life), 225
Votivæ Angliæ (pamphlet), 118, 170

W. B. (author), *That Which Seemes Best is Worst*,
  79–87, 90–92
Waller, Edmund, 319
 Panegyrick, 337–40
 Upon the Late Storme, 341
war/warfare, 293–95, *see also* martial prowess
 arguments for, 117–18
 imperial, 274
 sexual violence in, 303–4
warrior role, 30–31, 34, 45, 47–50, 172–73,
  225

426 *Index*

Warwick, 2nd Earl of (Robert Rich), 188
Watson, Richard, 347
Webster, John, *Appius and Virginia*, 79, 92–107, 322–24
Western Design (imperial policy), 297–300
widows, 147
Willymat, William, 37
Wither, George, 321–22
wives, 54, 60, 254
wombs, 147–48, 155, 197–98
women. *See also* mothers/motherhood
  actors, 202–4
  bestialisation of, 284
  bodies, 86, 155–56
  Catholicism, associated with, 260
  and cosmetics, 201–2
  dissimulation of, 152–53
  hair, 201, 203–4
  historical exempla for, 66–67, 71
  household, rule of, 60, 261
  liberty of, 105–6
  masculine, 117, 191, 197–98
  as metaphor for liberty, 279–82

  obedience, 73–74, 126–27
  political activism of, 311
  and power, 136–37, 190–94, 261
  preachers, 311
  restraint of, 170–71
  sexuality of, 73, 126–27, 136, 146–49, 156, 193–94
  and social disorder, 170–71
  subordinate status of, 71, 136, 233, 254
  tyrants, 156–57, 190–94
  vanity of, 153
  virtues, 61, 70–71, 105–6
  widows, 147
  wives, 54, 60, 254
Worden, Blair, 9, 223, 299
Wraxall, William, 160
Wren, Matthew, 208
l'Wright, Thomas, 319, 331

Xenophon, 40, 86

youth, 150, 237, 288

Lightning Source UK Ltd.
Milton Keynes UK
UKHW020042031220
374536UK00004B/41